Ethical and Social Perspectives on Global Business Interaction in Emerging Markets

Minwir Al-Shammari
University of Bahrain, Bahrain

Hatem Masri
University of Bahrain, Bahrain

A volume in the Advances in Business Strategy and Competitive Advantage (ABSCA) Book Series

BUSINESS SCIENCE Reference
An Imprint of IGI Global

Published in the United States of America by
Business Science Reference (an imprint of IGI Global)
701 E. Chocolate Avenue
Hershey PA, USA 17033
Tel: 717-533-8845
Fax: 717-533-8661
E-mail: cust@igi-global.com
Web site: http://www.igi-global.com

Library of Congress Cataloging-in-Publication Data

Names: Al-Shammari, Minwir, 1962- editor. | Masri, Hatem, 1964- editor.
Title: Ethical and social perspectives on global business interaction in emerging markets / Minwir Al-Shammari and Hatem Masri, editors.
Description: Hershey, PA : Business Science Reference, [2016] | Includes bibliographical references and index.
Identifiers: LCCN 2015046852| ISBN 9781466698642 (hardcover : alk. paper) | ISBN 9781466698659 (ebook : alk. paper)
Subjects: LCSH: Business ethics--Developing countries. | Social responsibility of business--Developing countries. | Developing countries--Commerce--Moral and ethical aspects.
Classification: LCC HF5387.5.D44 E84 2016 | DDC 174/.4--dc23 LC record available at http://lccn.loc.gov/2015046852

This book is published in the IGI Global book series Advances in Business Strategy and Competitive Advantage (ABSCA) (ISSN: 2327-3429; eISSN: 2327-3437)

British Cataloguing in Publication Data
A Cataloguing in Publication record for this book is available from the British Library.

For electronic access to this publication, please contact: eresources@igi-global.com.

Advances in Business Strategy and Competitive Advantage (ABSCA) Book Series

Patricia Ordóñez de Pablos
Universidad de Oviedo, Spain

ISSN: 2327-3429
EISSN: 2327-3437

MISSION

Business entities are constantly seeking new ways through which to gain advantage over their competitors and strengthen their position within the business environment. With competition at an all-time high due to technological advancements allowing for competition on a global scale, firms continue to seek new ways through which to improve and strengthen their business processes, procedures, and profitability.

The **Advances in Business Strategy and Competitive Advantage (ABSCA) Book Series** is a timely series responding to the high demand for state-of-the-art research on how business strategies are created, implemented and re-designed to meet the demands of globalized competitive markets. With a focus on local and global challenges, business opportunities and the needs of society, the **ABSCA** encourages scientific discourse on doing business and managing information technologies for the creation of sustainable competitive advantage.

COVERAGE

- Entrepreneurship & Innovation
- Ethics and Business Strategy
- Balanced Scorecard
- Economies of Scale
- Foreign Investment Decision Process
- Outsourcing
- Joint Ventures
- Small and Medium Enterprises
- Value Creation
- Tacit Knowledge

IGI Global is currently accepting manuscripts for publication within this series. To submit a proposal for a volume in this series, please contact our Acquisition Editors at Acquisitions@igi-global.com or visit: http://www.igi-global.com/publish/.

The Advances in Business Strategy and Competitive Advantage (ABSCA) Book Series (ISSN 2327-3429) is published by IGI Global, 701 E. Chocolate Avenue, Hershey, PA 17033-1240, USA, www.igi-global.com. This series is composed of titles available for purchase individually; each title is edited to be contextually exclusive from any other title within the series. For pricing and ordering information please visit http://www.igi-global.com/book-series/advances-business-strategy-competitive-advantage/73672. Postmaster: Send all address changes to above address.

Titles in this Series

For a list of additional titles in this series, please visit: www.igi-global.com

Strategic Approaches to Successful Crowdfunding
Djamchid Assadi (Burgundy School of Business, France)
Business Science Reference • copyright 2016 • 378pp • H/C (ISBN: 9781466696044) • US $205.00 (our price)

Handbook of Research on Entrepreneurship in the Contemporary Knowledge-Based Global Economy
Neeta Baporikar (University of Pune, India)
Business Science Reference • copyright 2016 • 607pp • H/C (ISBN: 9781466687981) • US $345.00 (our price)

Competitive Strategies for Academic Entrepreneurship Commercialization of Research-Based Products
Anna Szopa (Jagiellonian University, Poland) Waldemar Karwowski (University of Central Florida, USA) and David Barbe (University of Maryland, College Park, USA)
Business Science Reference • copyright 2015 • 317pp • H/C (ISBN: 9781466684874) • US $195.00 (our price)

Incorporating Business Models and Strategies into Social Entrepreneurship
Ziska Fields (University of KwaZulu-Natal, South Africa)
Business Science Reference • copyright 2016 • 362pp • H/C (ISBN: 9781466687486) • US $190.00 (our price)

Technological Solutions for Sustainable Business Practice in Asia
Patricia Ordóñez de Pablos (Universidad de Oviedo, Spain)
Business Science Reference • copyright 2015 • 375pp • H/C (ISBN: 9781466684621) • US $200.00 (our price)

Handbook of Research on Global Competitive Advantage through Innovation and Entrepreneurship
Luís M. Carmo Farinha (Polytechnic Institute of Castelo Branco & NECE – Research Unit, Portugal) João J. M. Ferreira (University of Beira Interior & NECE – Research Unit, Portugal) Helen Lawton Smith (Birkbeck, University of London & Oxfordshire Economic Observatory, Oxford University, UK) and Sharmistha Bagchi-Sen (State University of New York – Buffalo, Buffalo, NY, USA)
Business Science Reference • copyright 2015 • 780pp • H/C (ISBN: 9781466683488) • US $375.00 (our price)

Strategic Infrastructure Development for Economic Growth and Social Change
Nilanjan Ray (Royal Thimphu College, Bhutan) Dillip Kumar Das (Sikkim Central University, India) Somnath Chaudhuri (Royal Thimphu College, Bhutan) and Arindam Ghosh (Royal Thimphu College, Bhutan)
Business Science Reference • copyright 2015 • 404pp • H/C (ISBN: 9781466674707) • US $210.00 (our price)

Handbook of Research on Business Ethics and Corporate Responsibilities
Daniel E. Palmer (Kent State University, USA)
Business Science Reference • copyright 2015 • 508pp • H/C (ISBN: 9781466674769) • US $265.00 (our price)

List of Reviewers

Ebtihaj Al-Aali, *University of Bahrain, Bahrain*
Amin Al Agha, *University of Bahrain, Bahrain*
Lamya Al-Arrayed, *University of Bahrain, Bahrain*
Mohamed Al-Mosawi, *University of Bahrain, Bahrain*
Fouad Ben Abdelaziz, *NEOMA Business School, France*
Shahira Abdel-Hameid, *Emirates College of Technology, UAE*
Samir Abuznaid, *Hebron University, Palestine*
Asma Ayari, *University of LILLE 1, France*
Elinda Esa, *Malaysia National Energy University, Malaysia*
Naglaa El Dessouky, *University of Bahrain, Bahrain*
Nabil El Kadhi, *University of Buraimi, Sultanate of Oman*
Mehdi Garrab, *University of Sousse, Tunisia*
Shaju George, *University of Bahrain, Bahrain*
Ahmed Nawaz Hakro, *SCPD-UNDP, Kuwait*
Khamoussi Halioui, *Al-Imam Muhammad Ibn Saud Islamic University, Saudi Arabia*
John D Haynes, *University of Nizwa, Oman*
Jaber Jemai, *AMA International University Bahrain, Bahrain*
Anis Khayati, *University of Bahrain, Bahrain*
Hichem Khelif, *University of Sfax, Tunisia*
Lassaad Ben Mahjoub, *Al-Imam Muhammad Ibn Saud Islamic University, KSA*
Amir Manzoor, *Bahria University, Pakistan*
Meryem Masmoudi, *University of Bahrain, Bahrain*
Sélim Mekdessi, *Lebanese University, Lebanon*
Mehdi Mili, *University of Bahrain, Bahrain*
Khali Mofuoa, *Charles Sturt University, South Africa*
Mohammad Shahriari, *Konya Necmettin Erbakan University, Sweden*
Paul Van Seters, *Tilburg University, The Netherlands*
Shefali Virkar, *University of Oxford, UK*
Sami Zaguia, *Ministry of Education, Bahrain*

Table of Contents

Detailed Table of Contents

gains from, for example, efforts that lead to a consistently good reputation. Thematic Management (TM) is based on the premise: "As Outside so Inside". TM occurs where senior management consistently experiments with creating an internal environment of trust between employees and management. TM allows for staff members to be organized into special teams, which are mentored, to emulate, inside the business, the ethical and socially responsible behavioral theme of engagement in the market outside the business. TM provides for staff taking (monitored) risks; having senior team leaders engage in debates with senior management, among other practices, all with a view to an improvement in staff creativity, innovation, and finally intuition and wisdom for core knowledge retention and strategic sustainability.

The purpose of this study is to give a description of ethical business cultures in Bahraini construction companies. Construction companies in the Middle East are facing charges in terms of exploitation of workers and poor working conditions. The construction sector is one of the most dynamic in Bahrain, and its participation in national GDP is increasing. It is also the most important sector in the creation of jobs. Bahrain, as in the Gulf countries, employs a workforce from India and Asia, one of the lowest in the international labor market. This study analyzes the reality of the CSR in the construction sector and proposes some guidelines for the role of Bahraini stakeholders in the implementation of the social responsibility.

Corporate Social Responsibility (CSR) has become a significant field of studies to stress the importance of the new role of organizations towards the society for sustainable development. Nowadays, an enormous number of authors have been participating in this field to highlight the responsibility of organizations towards the community, society and the natural environment where they are operating. Despite the growing number of researches related to CSR in the developed countries little empirical studies have been devoted to examine CSR concept and practice in the African countries, the MENA region (Middle-East and North Africa), as well as in the Golf countries. This chapter seeks to study CSR concept and practice in the emerging market economies (EMEs). It will mainly focus on the implementations of CSR by the public banking sector. We will investigate the role of the public banking sector existing in an Arab country in comparison to an Asian country to explain and analyze the similarities and differences of CSR activities in both experiences. In this comparative study we will primarily examine Banque Misr, as one of the oldest and largest public bank in Egypt and the Malayan Banking Berhad (trading as Maybank) as the largest public bank in Malaysia. After a meticulous review of literature, we propose a systemic framework to study CSR practices and policy implementations. We illustrated the CSR as a constant process where all variables are interrelated and are affecting each other in a mutual approach. In this systemic framework we advocated to study all significant variables related to CSR practice

This study advocates that universities are prominent driving force behind corporate social responsibility. It highlights the commitment of universities in social responsibility (SR) and civic engagement with special reference to the experience of Ahfad University for Women (AUW) as a model for CSR. The main objective of this study is to develop a better understanding of the roles of universities in social responsibility (SR) and civic engagement (CE) to reveal best practices that can be useful for other universities. The unique evolution of AUW exemplified in its philosophy has created a solid foundation for SR. The study found that university social responsibility (USR) was embedded at the student, faculty and community members level supported by the values and commitment of top management.

Ethical consumerism is the outcome of an ethical decision-making process. This research examines situational factors exemplified in context-related issues affecting decision-making as perceived by business students at the University of Bahrain. Reward systems, authority, bureaucracy, work role, organizational culture and national and cultural context are investigated. Qualitative research employing open-ended questions in questionnaire form is used. Two hundred and forty students participated in this research. Five questions were asked in the research. Themes involved are illustrations of reward systems, bureaucracy, organizational culture, national and cultural context and work roles. This research suggests that work roles require to be thoroughly investigated in future research. The research also shows that students are unaware of ethical consumerism. This explains reasons for not translating views of students to behavior as a reflection of ethical consumerism.

Following the Asian economic tumult 1997, most of the researchers in Malaysian have been focusing on the issues of disclosure, transparency and boardroom failures. The crisis had led to statements about corporate governance in times of financial crisis and the lessons that can be learnt. A lot of prior literature examined the factors influencing the aspects of disclosure without giving reference to the educational and occupational background of the board of directors and the ownership structure, which influence

Preface

Nowadays, one of the most important questions is how an ethical business is conducted in emerging markets. Governments were involved in the judgment of businesses according to certain imposed requirements and thus labeling them as ethical or unethical, legal or illegal. In this book, we focus on business ethics and social responsibility in emerging market's business decision making. We aim to show how companies have dealt ethically with decisions related to investment, corporate governance, consumer behavior understanding, and leadership, etc. The important role of teaching business ethics in schools and companies and the impact of regulations on business ethics are reported. In emerging markets, social responsibility, culture, and religion do exercise a huge influence in defining business ethics. This book is regarded as an up-to-date overview of business ethics, practices, and social responsibilities in emerging markets.

This book contains 15 selected chapters from 41 proposals that were submitted by researchers from 23 different countries. It is also part of the book series "The Advances in Business Strategy and Competitive Advantage (ABSCA)" which is a timely series responding to the high demand for state-of-the-art research on how business strategies are created, implemented and re-designed to meet the demands of the globalized competitive markets. With a focus on the local and global challenges, business opportunities and the needs of the society, the ABSCA encourages scientific discourse on doing business and managing information technologies for the creation of sustainable competitive advantage.

We tried to produce an easy-reading book that can be used by researchers and practitioners to better understand challenges related to business ethics and social responsibility emerging markets. This book includes theoretical and real case studies with a short, precise, and concise up-to-date information about business ethics and social responsibility in emerging markets.

The topics included are the following:

- Business ethics in emerging markets
- Social responsibility of business and sustainability in emerging markets
- Decision making in emerging markets — moral and ethical aspects
- Investments in emerging markets –moral and ethical aspects
- Corporate governance in emerging markets
- Business ethics and consumers' behavior in emerging markets
- Ethical leadership in emerging markets
- Education of business ethics in schools and companies
- Emerging markets regulation, rule of law, and business ethics
- Cross-cultural comparison of business ethics between emerging markets

- Social culture, religion, and economic crimes in an emerging markets business
- Case studies in business ethics from emerging markets

In the first chapter, authors describe some corporate social responsibility strategies in Emerging Markets focusing on the decision-making processes and business practices for sustainability in a global economy.

The second chapter provides ten reasons on how Emerging Markets offer Businesses and E- Business great opportunities to increase productivity, growth and innovation. Authors conclude that social responsibility and ethical approaches are the right way for the sustainability of a new entrant Business within Emerging Markets.

The third chapter is a case study on how corporate social responsibility is understood in Bahraini construction companies. From this exploratory study, the author highlights guidelines for companies and recruitment agencies on the social responsibility implementation.

In chapter 4, the authors provide a comparison between corporate social responsibility of the public banking sector in two emerging markets, Egypt and Malaysia. The study offered a room for improvement for both countries to insure sustainable development requirements.

Chapter 5 discusses ethics and corporate social responsibility in Palestine Telecommunication Company (PalTel Group) and its impact on Palestine's emerging market in the West Bank and Gaza.

Another case study from one of the promising markets in the world, Sub-Saharan Africa. The author introduces the Setho ethics that refer to the moral beliefs and practices of the largely Bantu-speaking people of Africa.

Universities can be considered as a driver or a model for corporate social responsibility. The authors in chapter 7 report how "Ahfad University for Women" helped in improving social responsibility and good corporate citizenship within the Sudan.

Chapter 8 presents another exploratory research from the College of Business Administration at University of Bahrain where authors address the issue of Ethical Consumerism and how ethical practices may affect the decision-making processes inside a college of higher education.

A statistical study on directors' remuneration disclosure in Malaysia's 100 largest listed companies, is reported in chapter 9. The authors concluded that company's size, government's ownership and family's ownership have significant influences on directors' remuneration disclosure in annual reports.

Chapter 10 aims to define business ethics and the cost related to unethical decision making through analyzing the case of Shell Brent Spar. Results show that neglecting ethical principles may cause unwanted losses.

Financial performance of Islamic Banks in emerging markets is the topic discussed in chapter 11. The authors focus on ethical values that are embedded within the Islamic corporate governance in the Malaysian Banks.

Social and ethical perspectives in corporate governance is the subject of Chapter 12. The author affirms that corporate social responsibility can be of a direct economic value to any company and that the relationship between a firm and its stakeholders is of a great importance.

Chapter 13 discusses the impact of trust and ethics on Foreign Direct Investment decisions in the emerging economies. Some markets, like the Tunisian stocks lost a lot of value because of perceived risk by investors.

Chapter 14 discusses the risk-reducing strategies in the Tunisian stock market and presents a risk-behavior model. It also explores the use of experiential marketing as a business model and marketing communication channels to achieve Emerging Markets objectives.

We hope this book would serve as a useful source for the readers who are interested in research and practice in Ethics and Social responsibility, in general, and in Emerging Markets, in particular.

Minwir Al Shammari
University of Bahrain, Bahrain

Hatem Masri
University of Bahrain, Bahrain

Chapter 1
CSR Strategies in Emerging Markets:
Socially Responsible Decision Making Processes and Business Practices for Sustainability

Claudia Ogrean
"Lucian Blaga" University of Sibiu, Romania

Mihaela Herciu
"Lucian Blaga" University of Sibiu, Romania

ABSTRACT

The purpose of the chapter is to emphasize on the roles of businesses – as an effective (sustainable) development agent in emerging markets, on one hand, and of their CSR strategies – as an efficient sustainable development tool, on the other hand, in order to identify valuable business practices able to lead the emerging markets towards sustainability – through socially responsible decision making processes at business level. Having in the fore-ground the ideas of sustainability (which basically is a macro-economic concern) and responsibility (and especially its micro-economic correspondent that usually embraces the form of CSR), it will try to discover the general and specific features of the business models that capitalize the best the synergy between the social responsibility of business and the ensuring of sustainability in emerging markets.

INTRODUCTION

Generally speaking, businesses do not exist per se. They exist and operate in order to fulfill social needs (by delivering goods and services), and this is happening as long as they properly meet these needs. Basically, this kind of (socially responsible) behavior would be necessary and sufficient to ensure the sustainable development in emerging markets. But the reality of business is far from being so simple:

DOI: 10.4018/978-1-4666-9864-2.ch001

shareholder value is still overrated, and the practice of CSR (as concern towards sustainability) is still in the shadow of profits (on the expense of sustainability itself). Ultimately, this kind of a zero-sum game is prejudicial not 'only' for sustainability, but also, on the long run, for businesses themselves – in terms of losing their legitimacy and, eventually, diminishing of their profits (Werther Jr, & Chandler, 2010).

Nevertheless, some encouraging good news have to be considered in order to draw the entire picture of the relationships between businesses and society as they are nowadays: research directions such as stakeholder relations management (Steurer, Langer, Konrad, & Martinuzzi, 2005); theories such as the bottom of the pyramid (Prahalad, 2006) and the business case for CSR (Carroll, & Shabana, 2010); concepts such as shared value (Porter, & Kramer, 2011); or even new business models that have emerged from these concepts and theories (Michelini, & Fiorentino, 2012). All (and each one) of these breakthroughs, if considered, will enable businesses to take the lead on breaking the vicious circle of unsustainability – by reinforcing their relationships with the society while gaining competitive advantage (Porter, & Kramer, 2006).

These shifts are particularly significant and worthy to be considered in the case of emerging markets and their businesses – forasmuch as they do not consider sustainability concerns and practices in terms of additional costs for businesses (which are rather difficult to be found and hardly to be justified in terms of effectiveness and efficiency), but as essential endeavors and tools leading to a never ending virtuous circle of sustainable competitiveness and development for both businesses and the society.

Having this broad approaching perspective in mind when arguing about both the reasons (to exist) and the purposes (to succeed) of businesses, there are some comforting premises which allow and favor an eventually bet on both businesses as an effective sustainable development agent and strategic CSR as an efficient sustainable development tool in emerging markets:

- Needs (in general) have the vocation of being synchronically unlimited and diachronically evolving (as the human kind is developing itself), forcing businesses to accordingly adjust their actions and behaviors in order to successfully survive;
- Each business is (more or less consciously) a network of internal and external networks, which is defined and governed by all the features and principles of complexity, including: co-evolution with the environment, linkages, contagions, self-organization, and the butterfly effect (Ramalingam, et al., 2008);
- The assumption (resulted from the extrapolation of the recent dynamics and trends registered by the emerging markets so far) that *over the next two decades, most of the world's growth is expected to occur in today's emerging markets* (Cavusgil, Ghauri, & Akcal, 2012);
- The real, significant and specific sustainability related problems, challenges and dilemmas that the emerging markets confront and try to deal with (Khanna, & Palepu, 2013);
- The relatively recent, but increasingly powerful concerns regarding the sustainable development, coming from academia, as well as from national and international bodies, and asking for sustaining nature, life support and community while developing people, economy and society (UN, 2013);
- The strong connections between sustainable development – as (national and) global desiderate – and CSR – as business practice that brings together, into a unique and contextually different framework, the economic, legal, ethical and philanthropic responsibilities of business (Johnson, 2012);

- The growing pressure towards CSR reporting (of the economic, social and environmental impacts of business), transparency and accountability – coming from a variety of global actors and stakeholders: consumer groups, NGOs, formal and informal supranational structures and so on;
- The efforts, actions and concrete steps that both academia (Urip, 2010) and businesses (Pfitzer, Bockstette, & Stamp, 2013) have made towards integrating CSR into the business core in emerging markets.

All of the aforementioned dynamics and shifts are happening because *we live in a small world, where everything is linked to everything else* (Barabasi, & Frangos, 2002), and each agent is *competing with everyone from everywhere for everything* (Sirkin, Hemerling, & Bhattacharya, 2008). This kind of 'small world' could represent either the biggest opportunity or the highest risk for the emerging markets and their businesses (SMEs and MNEs as well) – which are all looking for sustainable development and competitiveness. On the other hand, it is well known that emerging markets have, all and each one of them, idiosyncratic features and development patterns, which are, in the same time, cause and effect of/for specific problems, dilemmas and constraints, and ask for particular approaches, strategies and solutions at business level (Kearney, 2012).

However, no matter the particular situation of each emerging market and/or business within it, the challenges of sustainable development – within the complex and networked global economy of nowadays – are forcing businesses to reconsider their strategies and business models in order to successfully survive. In this light, a systemic CSR approach could be the best solution businesses can come with. It will enable businesses to reveal themselves as effective (sustainable) development agent, by leveraging their potential through CSR strategies – acting, at their turn, as an efficient sustainable development tool.

Therefore, the chapter will argue the case for CSR strategies as socially responsible decision making processes and business practices for sustainability in emerging markets; accordingly, the chapter discusses the following main objectives:

- To outline the overall context of businesses in emerging markets – defined by the urge for sustainable development, and to place businesses – and their specific needs for CSR-related strategies – within it;
- To argue that the complex and networked global economy of nowadays defines the most appropriate framework for businesses in emerging markets in order to integrate CSR into their core strategy – while emphasizing the need for a co-evolutionary approach;
- To identify the particular challenges and opportunities of CSR and their vocation to determine strengths and/or weaknesses for businesses and their decision making processes in emerging markets;
- To develop a SWOT analysis, followed by possible solutions and strategies (resulted from the analysis of good practices in the field) – able to determine a critical mass of businesses toward integrating CSR into the business core and eventually to give direction to such a generalized behavior.

The new realities, dynamics and trends that characterize the global system in its search for sustainability, on one hand, and the (particular) challenges that emerging markets and their businesses have to confront with, as increasingly significant actors on the ever-changing global arena, on the other hand, highlight the importance of the topic this chapter covers. By taking an integrative and interdisciplinary approach (which is not exhaustive, but comprehensive), the chapter will try to fill a gap in the literature by enlarging the perspective – up to the complex and networked global economy, and the role of businesses in emerging markets, while offering significant insights – on the SWOT analysis, possible solutions and CSR strategies in emerging markets.

BACKGROUND

Since the Bruntland Report (1987) – arguing for development which *meets the needs of the present without compromising the ability of future generations to meet their own needs* (UN, 1987), sustainability has undeniable become a common presence on the global agenda. Although basically everyone (academics, politicians, non-governmental organizations, national states and international bodies) admits that the concept of sustainable development *strongly links environmental and socio-economic issues* (Hopwood, Mellor, & O'Brien, 2005), it is also true that *the expression 'sustainable development' has been used in a variety of ways, depending on whether it is employed in an academic context or that of planning, business or environmental policy* (Redclift, 2005).

But one thing is for sure now: the challenges of sustainability, as global concern towards a desirable 'end' of all humankind endeavors, have transformed all the global actors and each one of them into (consciously or not) global stakeholders, with different (and most often contradictory) needs and expectations, on one hand, pressures and influences towards satisfying these claims, on another hand (Carroll, 2004). In this context, responsibility seems to be the best answer businesses could give to these challenges (Waddock, Bodwell, & Graves, 2002), while local, specific practices are the most suitable 'means' in order to meet them (Oliveira, 2012). This kind of *think globally, and act locally* approach – integrating the concept of responsibility into the practice of business strategy – would be both a contribution to the broad sustainability imperative, and a solution for particular sustainability related issues, emphasizing on the role of responsible business.

However, during the last few decades, the relationships between responsibility and business have raised a lot of questions and controversies about what businesses are responsible for, and to whom, leading academia to different answers and arguments. Thus, Davis (1973) discussed about *the case for and against business assumption of social responsibilities*; Langtry (1994) analyzed *stakeholders and the moral responsibilities of business*; Utting (2000) argued about *business responsibility for sustainable development*; Whetten, Rands, & Godfrey (2002) questioned on *what are the responsibilities of business to society*; and Friedman (2007) argued that *the social responsibility of business is to increase its profits*. In the same time, different theories and (recommendations for) business practices have been developed, in order to achieve the responsible business desideratum: *stakeholder theory* (Donaldson, & Preston, 1995) and *stakeholder management* (Hillman, & Keim, 2001), the *triple bottom line* (Elkington, 1998), *the sustainable/holistic firm* (Knez-Riedl, & Mulej, 2008), the *social business* (Yunus, 2007), or the *ethical and socially responsible management* (Davidson, Wood, & Griffin, 2009), and so on.

Within this framework, corporate social responsibility (CSR) is the most common concept and practice which translate sustainable development at business level – because *CSR refers broadly to actions that business and corporations voluntarily undertake both to promote social and environmental goals and to minimize any potential social and environmental costs associated with their business activities* (Clapp, & Rowlands, 2014, p. 42). The strategic dimension of CSR is increasingly embraced and promoted by academia (Orlitzky, Siegel, & Waldman, 2011) – as it stands for *the incorporation of a holistic CSR perspective within a firm strategic planning and core operations so that the firm is managed in the interests of a broad set of stakeholders to achieve maximum economic and social value over the medium to long term* (Werther Jr, & Chandler, 2010, p. xiii). Accordingly, CSR (related) strategies could be conceptualized as (genuine and/or questionable – in terms of their motives) socially responsible decision making processes and business practices for sustainability.

Therefore, an abundant literature has been developed in the field of CSR, trying: to define the concept and its internal components (Garriga, & Melé, 2004; Dahlsrud, 2008); to argue for and/or against CSR (Campbell, 2007; Argandoña, 2012); to guide the business behavior towards CSR (Carroll, 1991; Young, & Makhija, 2014); to measure the impact CSR has – on the business itself and on different stakeholders (Peloza, & Shang, 2011; Epstein, & Buhovac, 2014); and to predict the future of CSR (Robins, 2005; Lee, 2008).

The abovementioned breakthroughs were both cause and result of/for new developments as regards the relationships between business and society, allowing for new business models to emerge and grow. For instance, Stubbs, & Cocklin (2008) have researched on *conceptualizing a "sustainability business model"*, while Birkin, Polesie, & Lewis (2009) argued for *a new business model for sustainable development*, and Varey, & Storbacka (2011) have sketched a *business model design for sustainable society*. But, unfortunately, they failed to entirely transform the business landscape. Therefore, besides the responsible business, the 'dark side' of the 'irresponsible' business still exists – some call it *corporate social irresponsibility* (Clark, & Grantham, 2012), while others argue about *irresponsible management practices* (Tyagi, & Vasiljeviene, 2013) or emphasize on *grey areas: irresponsible corporations and reputational dynamics* (Jackson et al., 2014) – and asks for more (theoretical) exploration, in order to properly (and practically) address to it, through consistent and articulated responsible strategies at business level.

The picture becomes more complicated when referring to the case of CSR strategies in emerging markets. Although a growing body of relevant and valuable studies has appeared (mainly) in the last decade (Baskin, 2006; Li, et al., 2010; Su, Peng, Tan, & Cheung, 2014), both the literature and the practice in the field of CSR strategies in emerging markets are younger, on one hand, while the solutions seem to be more diversified and less cohesive, on the other hand. This situation is due to a variety of reasons, such as: different approaching angles (authors and/or practitioners coming from different cultural backgrounds, valorizing their own knowledge and expertise and emphasizing on a specific theory when doing that), and different contexts (with specific needs and concerns, regulations, access to resources, perceptions on and behaviors towards CSR). That is why a closer and deeper look, in order to eventually identify both the proximate genus and the specific difference in terms of CSR strategies in emerging markets is more than necessary.

Accordingly, the study will progressively address the following problems and research questions: (1). the changing global (economic) environment – more and more characterized by complexity and interdependencies – which asks for new approaches as concern the relationships between businesses and society, based on co-evolution and symbiosis; (2). the impact that the complex and global economy has on the emerging market economies, and especially on the role of businesses in emerging markets – considering their search for both development and sustainability; (3). a SWOT analysis, followed by possible solutions and CSR related strategies in emerging market economies – in order to identify best practices, able to serve as behavioral guidance.

The Complex and Networked Global Economy

Both sustainability (as continuous and never-ending desired outcome of all humankind endeavors) and responsibility (as permanent and context-related feature that has to define each agent's behavior) need to be placed and considered, in order to be properly achieved, within the general evolution framework that conditions them. As the process of (economic) globalization – which defined (with its cohorts of goods and bads, pros and cons) the last half of the twentieth century – has offered the fertile ground for the sustainability issue to sprout and become a global concern, the complex and networked global economy of nowadays sets new coordinates – in terms of opportunities and threats as well – for responsibility to occur.

Undoubtedly, *globalization is one of the most used, but also one of the most* misused *and one of the most* confu*sed, words around today* (Dicken, 2007, p. 3). Beyond all the theories and controversies that surround it (Held, & McGrew, 2007; Jones, 2010), and generally speaking, *globalization is a process that encompasses the causes, course, and consequences of transnational and transcultural integration of human and non-human activities* (Al-Rodhan, & Stoudmann, 2006). Very generous in their nature and expression, *the transformative powers of globalization reach deeply into all dimensions of contemporary social life* (Steger, 2013, p. xii): economic, political, cultural and ecological. As defining feature and major dimension of the globalization process, the *economic globalization refers to the increasing interdependence of world economies as a result of the growing scale of cross-border trade of commodities and services, flow of international capital and wide and rapid spread of technologies* (Shangquan, 2000); it also is the fuel which powers the engine of today's complex and networked global economy.

According to Maznevski, Steger, & Amann (2007) there are *four major sources of complexity that interact together to create today's environment: diversity, interdependence, ambiguity* and *flux*. In other words, myriads of different actors (individuals, on one hand, and all types of structures, on the other hand: companies, states, international bodies, interest groups) are playing their roles on the global arena, by continuously interacting with each other while constantly looking for information that is both abundant (generally) and rare (if talking in terms of relevance) in order to successfully survive; and all these premises change permanently – adding more complexity to the environment.

Therefore, *our economy, especially the global economy, is a complex system* (Homer-Dixon, 2011), proving all the properties Homer-Dixon (2011) claims to characterize such an entity: (a). *many components* – considering all the small-to-global companies that operate around the world; (b). *a high degree of connectivity between components* – the even existence of each company depends on a lot of connections with its stakeholders (suppliers, clients, employees, to name just a few of them); (c). *thermodynamically open* – each company evolves as a network of networks with variable architecture, never knowing exactly where it starts and where it ends in terms of its boundaries; (d). *information, matter and energy* – which are continuously flowing and fueling the system, in order to keep it vivid; (e). *nonlinear behavior* – as opposed to mechanical systems, the global economy as a complex system develops 'irrational behaviors', demonstrating that the butterfly effect not only works for meteorology; (f). *emergence* – the existence and evolution of the global economic system is more / different than its parts, developing a trajectory of its own – as 'nonlinear' and/or unpredictable result of all the above-mentioned features.

Both the global environment – placed under the auspices of complexity, which characterizes *the behavior of macroscopic collections of such units that are endowed with the potential to evolve in time*

(Coveney, & Highfield, 1995, p. 7) – and the global economy – which can be seen as a *complex network, whose nodes are companies and whose links represent the various economic and financial ties connecting them* (Barabasi, & Frangos, 2002) – are now defined by the presence and behavior of businesses as complex adaptive systems. They *are composed by a diversity of agents that interact with each other, mutually affect each other, and in so doing generate novel, emergent behavior for the system as a whole. The system is constantly adapting to the conditions around it, and over time it evolves* (Lewin, 2000, p. 198). In conclusion, the idea of symbiosis and co-evolution with the environment is crucial for businesses to survive because, *in today's fast-changing business environment, companies will survive only if they are able constantly to adapt and evolve through operating optimally as a complex adaptive system* (Lewin, 2000, p. 198).

The Overall Context and the Role of Businesses in Emerging Markets

In addition to the emphasizing on a new, *evolutionary* (economic) *perspective* (Boschma, & Martin, 2007), the *new economic geography* (Krugman, 2011) of globalization literarily *reshapes economic geography* (Rigg, et al., 2009), if considering the dynamics that the global economy has registered during the last few decades and the current trends it develops. *Today we increasingly recognize that nothing happens in isolation. Most events and phenomena are connected, caused by, and interacting with a huge number of other pieces of a complex universal puzzle* (Barabasi and Frangos, 2002, p. 7); then, *we look forward and see a new era emerging. (…) a different kind of environment, in which business flows in every direction. (…) Western business orthodoxy entwines with eastern business philosophy and creates a whole new mind-set that embraces profit and competition as well as sustainability and collaboration* (Sirkin, Hemerling, & Bhattacharya, 2008, pp. 1-2).

Under these circumstances, and because *sustainable development itself is a global vision* (Schmidheiny, 1992, p. xxi), the global challenges to sustainable development – which *have been driven by a broad set of "megatrends", such as changing demographic profiles, changing economic and social dynamics, advancements in technology and trends towards environmental deterioration* (United Nations, 2013) – ask for unanimous concern and concerted actions, able to integrate its economic, social and environmental dimensions. On the other hand, corporate responsibility – which *fundamentally (…) has to do with corporations fulfilling their obligations to society in ways that reflect a social contract between business and society* (Smith, Bhattacharya, Vogel, & Levine, 2010, p. 6) – *has gone global* (Smith, Bhattacharya, Vogel, & Levine, 2010, p. 1), while being *one of the ways that companies and others have used to navigate the new terrain associated with globalization that is not necessarily good or bad, but simply different from preceding eras* (Blowfield, Murray, 2011, pp. 110-111). Therefore, as the world is neither flat (Friedman, 2003) nor curved (Smick, 2008), but rather complex (Porter, & Derry, 2012), CSR strategies – as socially responsible decision making processes and business practices for sustainability – should be characterized by the same logic (in terms of determinants, features, behaviors and impacts) of complexity.

Within this framework, academia generally acknowledges and proclaims that *the rise of emerging markets – their emergence after more than 200 years of being relatively minor players in the global economy – is causing one of the most significant shifts in the global economic and geopolitical structure since the beginning of the industrial revolution* (Ciravegna, Fitzgerald, & Kundu, 2013, p. 1). Having *firms and states* as *major shapers*, this global shift has led to *a multi-polar, kaleidoscopic global economy* (Dicken, 2003) – defined and dominated by:

- The multiplying of the global centers of power and of their determinants, both diachronically (from states to firms – and especially multinational companies) and synchronically (from 'center' – the old Triad, to 'periphery' – the new emerging markets), within a business environment characterized by multi-polarity (Falk, 2009; Layne, 2012);
- The emergence and development of multinationals from emerging markets (Goldstein, 2009; and the rise of new global giants from emerging markets (Ghemawat, & Hout, 2008);
- New approaches and strategies at firm level (domestic and multinational companies as well, originated and/or hosted in/by emerging markets) – aiming for (global) competitiveness by valorizing the new – internal and external – dynamics and trends (Hoskisson, Eden, Lau, & Wright, 2000; Pillania, 2009).

Although the definition and the content of the term are still subjects to debates – for both researchers (Ciravegna, Fitzgerald, & Kundu, 2013) and international institutions (The World Bank, The International Monetary Fund) – it is generally recognized that the emerging markets possess some *core characteristics* that distinguish them from other countries – *(1). they are dynamic economies; (2). their institutional environments were buffeted in the 1990s by a contagious tidal wave of policy shocks (liberalization, privatization, deregulation); and (3). they suffer from missing or weak market-based institutions, particularly in terms of property rights and legal infrastructure* (Mendoza, & Irmak, 2008, pp. 333-334). By taking a dynamic and evolutionary perspective, Kvint (2010) goes even further, and identifies 45 *major characteristics that all EMCs* (emerging-market countries) *have, had, or will have at some stage during their process of economic maturation and development* (Kvint, 2010, p. 82).

It is also true that the emerging markets category is far from being homogenous, as the literature emphasizes on the fact that they *differ in many manners: size; political, regulatory, and legal regimes; the role of governments; economic reforms and industry structure transformation* (Luo, 2002, pp. 7-8), which leaded to the reality that *the overall improvement in the fundamentals of EMEs masks a great dispersion regarding most of the benchmark indicators (notably GDP growth, inflation, balance of payments, foreign currency reserves and public* finances) (Odonnat, & Rahmouni, 2006).

Given the emerging markets common characteristics, on one hand, and their idiosyncratic features and development paths, on the other hand, academia recommends that *businesses still need to distinguish emerging markets – collectively from developed markets and individually from each other* (Khanna, & Palepu, 2013, p. 3). Therefore, as relatively new – but very vigorous – entrants on the global arena as players that count and decisively contribute to the reshaping of the global economic architecture (Dicken, 2003; Ravenhill, 2014), the emerging market economies are confronted with the transformative realities of nowadays, on one hand, while struggling with particular challenges of their own (common and / or different), on the other hand. As recent studies and reports have revealed, although *after decades of stalled and even regressed convergence, emerging markets* (EMs) *started closing the income gap with advanced economies in the last decade* (Cubeddu, et al., 2014), they also *face growing domestic vulnerabilities along with a heightened sensitivity to global conditions* (International Monetary Fund, 2014).

SWOT ANALYSIS, POSSIBLE SOLUTIONS AND CSR STRATEGIES IN EMERGING MARKETS

The increasing pressures towards sustainability and responsibility – coming from myriads of global stakeholders concerned about the impact of the (rather irresponsible as concern CSR) business models and business practices dominating in emerging markets (Rettab, Brik, & Mellahi, 2009; Reimann, Ehrgott, Kaufmann, & Carter, 2012) – force the companies (both domestic or multinational, originated from or hosted by an emerging market) to take the issue of CSR (and especially the CSR strategies) in emerging markets more and more seriously. Therefore, the (generic) SWOT analysis – undertaken prior to proposing and developing a CSR strategy at firm level – might serve as a valuable instrument able to offer significant insights on the internal and external determinants of CSR strategies in emerging markets, as well as possible guidance regarding effective and efficient behaviors.

Although both the emerging markets and their firms are quite different, some general aspects have to be taken into account when considering (both the idea and the formulation of) a CSR strategy:

- It is based on the internal and external audits of the firm – developed in accordance with: the strategic management approach (David, 2011), a combined strategic management approach with a stakeholder approach (Freeman, 2010) and/or a stakeholder approach of CSR (Jamali, 2008);
- These combined internal and external audits lead to specific lists of:
  - Strengths and weaknesses – coming from within the firm (either domestic or multinational – originated from / or hosted by an emerging market) and determining CSR strategies in emerging markets as socially responsible business practices;
  - Opportunities and threats – raised by the external environment (at global level and at national – emerging market – level) – and determining CSR strategies in emerging markets as business practices for sustainability.

Therefore, performing such a SWOT analysis will imply for each company a unique interpretation of the internal and external forces shaping its riverbed of evolution, and will generate a unique integration – looking for the best suited CSR strategy, able to deliver a symbiosis of the stakeholders needs, expectations and interests while maintaining the company on the competitiveness map – of the following:

- The impact of *globalization on different* (internal and external) *stakeholder groups*: *shareholders; consumers; suppliers and competitors; civil society; government and regulation* (Crane, & Matten, 2010, p. 25);
- The *characteristics of emerging markets and the opportunities they create: markets and culture are demanding; there are high rates of emigration to the developed world; markets are fragmented; populations are youthful and growing; there is limited income and space; infrastructure is weak; technology is underdeveloped; distribution channels are weak; markets are changing rapidly* (Mahajan, & Banga, 2005);
- The *business challenges* – emphasizing on *the importance of good corporate governance and CSR* – determined by *globalization: more demanding consumers, competitive differentiation, emergence of NGOs, complexity of market and environment, government policy and regulation, tightening margins, converge and consolidation, the importance of developing human resources, competition in capability* (Urip, 2010, p. 4);

- The new insights that firm related approaches bring to support the (internal and external) environmental assessment:
    - The resource-based view of the firm – looking for the capitalizing of: *resources, dynamic capabilities and knowledge; corporate governance; management buy-outs and venture capital financing; institutional environment; entrepreneurship*, and, particularly, *a uniquely ethical culture* (Barney, Wright, & Ketchen, 2001), in order to reach a *sustained competitive advantage* (Barney, & Clark, 2007);
    - The value-chain analysis – bringing together *key elements* such as *barriers to entry and rent; governance; and systemic efficiency* – within a process *which includes the whole cycle of the organization, production and delivery of products from inception to use and recycling* in a manner consistent with the idea that *it is not so much a matter of whether to participate in global processes, but how to do so in a way which provides sustainable income growth for poor people and for poor countries* (Kaplinsky, 2000);
    - The CSR view of the firm – which, starting from the hypothesis that *a firm's level of CSR will depend on its size, level of diversification, research and development, advertising, government sales, consumer income, labor market conditions, and stage in the industry life cycle*, emphasizes on the idea that *there is an "ideal" level of CSR, which managers can determine via cost-benefit analysis* (McWilliams, & Siegel, 2001).

The solutions that academia brings to the problem of CSR strategies – aiming to transform the company into a sustainable development agent while operating on the basis of CSR as a sustainable development tool – are quite diverse (some of them more realistic, as opposed to quite idealistic others), and may be divided into general and specific (emerging markets based) ones.

Within the first category, the *sustainable business*, based on the concept and practice of the *triple bottom line* (profit, people, and planet) is one of the most known and referred to. As Elkington (2004) argued, *in the simplest terms, the TBL agenda focuses corporations not just on the economic value that they add, but also on the environmental and social value that they add – or destroy*. Considering their different stages *along the evolutionary path to a chrysalis economy*, the author insists on the fact that *the key to developing environmental policies that facilitate the transition to sustainability is to understand that the roles of government need to be different in relation to the four different types of corporation* (Elkington, 2004).

More than that, Porter and Kramer (2011) claim that *companies must take the lead in bringing business and society back together* (…and …) *the solution lies in the principle of shared value, which involves creating economic value in a way that also creates value for society by addressing its needs and challenges*. This would be possible through: *reconceiving products and markets, redefining productivity in the value chain* (in terms of *energy use and logistics, resource use, procurement, distribution, employee productivity, location*), *and building supportive industry clusters at the company's locations* (Porter, & Kramer, 2011), and by being aware and valorizing the fact that each one of these actions has a leverage effect on the others, and on the entire company.

Yunus (2007), on the other hand, makes a distinction between two types of businesses – based on the CSR approach they embrace: (a). companies promoting a "*weak CSR*" *credo*: *do not harm to people or the planet (unless that means sacrificing profit)* – category which refers to businesses which *avoid selling defective goods, dumping factory wastes into rivers or landfills, or bribing government officials*; (b). companies promoting a *"strong CSR" credo*: *do good for people and the planet (as long as you can do so without sacrificing profit)* – category which refers to businesses which *may work to develop green products and practices, provide educational opportunities and health plans for their employees, and support initiatives to bring transparency and fairness to government regulation of business* (Yunus, 2007, pp. 15-16). But, rather pessimistic about the transformative power of CSR on the entire business landscape, he comes with the solution of *social business* – which is developed *to pursue specific social goals,* as opposed to the *profit-maximizing businesses* (Yunus, 2007).

Taking a broader view, Young (2003) advocates for *reconciling private interest with the public good* – based on the fact that *the enterprise is not self-contained and self-sufficient but, rather, is importantly dependent on inputs controlled by others. It must please others in order to prosper. That service is a moral activity, subordinating self to what is beyond the self* (Young, 2003, p. 3). Therefore, the solution he comes with is the *moral capitalism*, considered to be *the most appropriate means by which our modern, global human civilization can empower people and enrich their lives materially and spiritually* (Young, 2003, p. 1).

When specifically addressing the case of CSR in emerging markets, academia generally insists on: (a). aspects such as *context and consequences dependency* (Halme, Roome, & Dobers, 2009) – arguing that *CSR should be seen as a local, not a universal, concept. The historical and national context of communities, especially their corporate and societal governance frameworks and business-society relations, impact on how CSR may be practiced in these areas.* (Zhang, 2008); (b). the main particular concern such an endeavor should pursue – considering that *a real contribution to the society will happen only when this is enabled to have its own sustainable development. The empowerment of people through providing them the capability of developing their own instruments of income should be the ultimate objective of a responsible corporate* (Pelle, 2007, p. 172).

Regarding the particular case of those positioned at *the bottom of the pyramid* – category that encompasses more than four billion people living on less than two American dollars per day (Prahalad, 2006) – theory insists on a perspective shift, leading to a symbiotic development. Thus, *if we stop thinking of the poor as victims or as a burden and start recognizing them as resilient and creative entrepreneurs and value-conscious consumers, a whole new world of opportunity will open up*, based on *an approach that involves partnering with them to innovate and achieve sustainable win-win scenarios where the poor are actively engaged and, at the same time, the companies providing products and services to them are profitable* (Prahalad, 2006, pp. 1-3).

Given this discussion framework, the CSR strategies that companies embrace in emerging markets are, at theirs turn, quite different. However, some general *aspects related to the formulation of corporate social strategy* could be mentioned: *(a). market opportunities; (b) resources; (c) corporate values; (d) structure of industry; (e) stakeholders; (f) CSR alignment to core business; and (g) the social impact of corporation competitiveness* (Sousa Filho, Wanderley, Gómez, & Farache, 2010); in the same time, some particular business models integrating CSR strategies could be noticed in the case of both multinationals – hosted by / or originated in an emerging market – and local companies.

Thus, as concerns the MNEs hosted by emerging markets and their CSR strategy, studies generally revealed that:

- *Global MNEs face a clear choice. They can (...) manage local and global CSR issues on a case-by-case analysis of the pressures for integration and responsiveness surrounding each issue: in short, they can become 'transnational' in their CSR strategy. Alternatively, they can ignore local subtleties and nuances in their CSR agenda, with the attendant risks* (Husted, & Allen, 2006);

- More attention should be paid to the *politics, corruption, and corporate social responsibility lenses on the multinational enterprise* and *the potential linkages across* them – because MNEs *operate in multiple countries and institutional environments throughout the world. As local residents, they must respond to local rules and institutions, adapt to diverse socio-economic conditions, and respond to multiple stakeholders* (Rodriguez, Siegel, Hillman, & Eden, 2006);
- *A comprehensive CSR strategic framework must include key components for MNEs (...): (1). to define a CSR mission reflecting corporate values and objectives; (2). to assess existing programs, codes of conducts, guidelines, standards (...) and reflect how they can be included into policy and decision-making; (3). to develop a CSR strategy based on the above; (4). to gather a team of international leaders, reflecting the diversity of the organization in charge of implementing and monitoring the process; (5). to get feedback from employees, governmental and non-governmental institutions about the positive impacts and/or limitations of implemented policies; (6). to review compliance mechanisms and performance requirements.* (Lévy, 2007).

On the other hand, as regards the MNEs originated in emerging markets, they develop particular business models and CSR strategy – by specifically addressing the opportunities and challenges they face in their home countries, while leveraging their idiosyncratic strengths. Regardless of their country of origin, the development paths they pursue, and/or the generic umbrella that covers them – *southern multinationals* (Battat, & Aykut, 2005), *emerging economies' multinationals* (Salehizadeh, 2007), *global latinas* (Casanova, 2009), *global players from India* (Taylor, & Nölke, 2010), *non-triad multinationals* (Nölke, & Taylor, 2010), *Chinese multinationals* (Hobdari, Sinani, Papanastassiou, & Pearce, 2010), *emerging Russian multinational companies* (Filippov, 2012) and so on – the emerging market multinationals are not only sensitive to CSR concerns, but they sometimes take over leadership regarding CSR development within their countries of origin (Torres-Baumgarten, & Yucetepe, 2009).

As Deutsche Gesellschaft für Internationale Zusammenarbeit (2011) argues, *these companies do more than just provide good jobs to many thousands of people in emerging and developing economies. They also: (a). nurture a professional class that commands higher wages and can spur further development in the public, cultural and educational arenas; (b). provide business opportunities for the vendors, small businesses and entrepreneurs from which they source; (c). create innovations that boost productivity and drive sustainable national economic growth; (d). bring profits home and contribute to the tax base so that governments can sponsor development across the socioeconomic spectrum.*

More than that, the emerging market multinationals have the vocation of spreading their beneficial influence beyond economic development, towards human development, through: *(a). discovering and serving new markets, potentially growing revenue and profits – and at the same time address unsatisfied needs; (b). creating disruptive innovations in products, processes and business models that are well received not only in their home countries, but also in host markets; (c). improving the business environment so they can operate more effectively – and at the same time addressing development goals such as building infrastructure, combating disease, and educating local populations; (d). engaging in a policy dialogue, and at the same time bolstering their reputation with civic leaders nationally and globally; (e). building their brands in the minds of consumers concerned about social responsibility* (GIZ, 2011).

The analysis of the CSR strategies in the case of domestic (emerging market) companies also indicates practices which respond, through particular actions, to local contexts and expectations, by reconciling businesses and society. But, as the emerging markets are quite different between them, so are their approaches towards CSR – in terms of motivators, actions/behaviors, impacts and reporting/communicating

(Vives, 2006; Rivera, 2010; Katamba, Katamba, Zipfel, Haag, & Tushabomwe-Kazooba, 2012; Chahal, Mishra, Raina, & Soni, 2014).

SOLUTIONS AND RECOMMENDATIONS

Due to a variety of reasons – such as solely pursuit of (quick) profits and a myopic interpretation of the CSR paradigm (exclusively in terms of additional costs for business) – and against the background of no serious scrutiny (which favored the lack of businesses' accountability and transparency) – CSR strategies have been rather a peripheral concern for businesses in emerging markets until recently. But, under the auspices that define the new dynamics of both the global (economic) system and the understandings of the CSR paradigm, a series of quite influential determinants – coming from academia, regulatory bodies and different (formal/informal, as well as national/international) pressure groups – has brought the issue into the spotlight of the businesses' core strategy.

Thus, a growing body of (increasingly refined) proofs and evidences has emerged in order to build the case for CSR strategies in emerging markets, emphasizing on both business and country-related effects and positive impacts. So, the arguments on favor of *how corporate social responsibility pays off* in terms of *strategic benefits* for companies (Burke, & Logsdon, 1996), were complimented by those referring to how CSR is *supporting the business case* in terms of *the long-run benefits for companies* – through: *cost savings, enhanced staff loyalty, improved government relations, innovation and learning, enhanced reputation, consumer response* (Luetkenhorst, 2004); and all of the above-mentioned arguments were circumscribed by those related to how *collective corporate social responsibility (CSR) activities amongst various corporations and its stakeholders could contribute to the microeconomic development of a developing country through sustainable benefit to all* (Urip, 2010, p. xiii).

Consequently, despite the fact that, *unfortunately, the majority of companies still see such concepts as sustainability and social responsibility as pursuits that only the rich can afford* (Handy, 2002), the reality reveals that *today, a growing number of creative new business models (..) demonstrate that social and environmental purposes do not have to be sacrificed for profits, and that profits do not have to be sacrificed for social and environmental purposes. Rather than conflicting, the two purposes can mutually reinforce each other. Even better, these innovative, purpose-driven business models can become a source of competitive advantage* (Osterwalder, & Pigneur, 2011). This kind of 'open minded' search for (sustainable) competitive advantage – that only a strategic approach of CSR can provide – would be able to break the vicious circle of unsustainability that surrounds the emerging markets and their businesses, by unleashing the latent potential of contingent creativity and capitalizing on it, for the mutual benefit of all the stakeholders.

The concept of *strategic corporate social responsibility* should be transposed into business models which reveal a *business strategy that is integrated with core business objectives and core competencies to create business value and positive social/environmental value, and is embedded in day-to-day business culture and operations* (McElhaney, 2007). This kind of simultaneously short and long-term perspective, which equally encompasses daily routines and overall goals, while contributing to the sustainability of both the emerging markets and their businesses, can only be achieved if (long-term) socially responsible decision making processes are operationalized through (short-term) business practices for sustainability.

In this way, strategic corporate social responsibility could serve *as a tool for managing the current situation and helping firms overcome the consequences of the crisis* that was partially caused by *the lack of CSR* itself (Fernández-Feijóo Souto, 2009); more than that, it could help moving businesses forward, towards: (1). higher competitiveness – if considering that *firms who better understand their social responsibilities and who begin to more adequately explore how they can build CSR into strategy are likely to reap the rewards of improved competitive positions in the future, to the benefit of their shareholders, but also to the benefit of society at large* (Galbreath, 2009); (2). expanding and deepening the *CSR boundaries* – if considering that in the case of *emerging or transitional societies, transnational corporations (TNCs) can find themselves the catalyst for legal or conceptual reform* (Mullerat, 2010, p.4). By playing such a role, businesses can contribute to the overall development of the emerging markets, while helping them to climb on the ladder of responsibility and sustainability.

Certainly, such an approach will not be an easy way for businesses in emerging markets, especially if taking into account: (a). the institutional and regulatory voids that still define emerging markets – allowing businesses to act irresponsible without being scrutinized and/or punished for their behaviors; (b). the discretionary dimension that usually characterizes CSR – which makes other than economic values and 'bottom lines' to be easily overlooked and/or ignored; (c). the urge for economic development on the basis of 'no matter' how – which justifies, against the background of no penalties, almost any kind of profit; (d). the lack, until now, of an indubitable proof of a direct causal link between CSR and financial performance – even though different empirical studies have directly, as well as indirectly demonstrated the correlations between those two; (e) the knowledge gap that characterizes both the theory and the practice in the field of strategic CSR – encapsulating all the above.

But it could be the only way for the emerging markets (and their businesses) in order to overcome the sustainability (economic-social-environmental) gaps and to meet the challenges of the complex and networked economy of nowadays. And this is especially true if considering the new age – *of responsibility* – and stage of business responsibility – *systemic CSR* – which is about to emerge, according to Visser (2011). Following *the ages of: greed, philanthropy, marketing and management – characterized by: defensive CSR, charitable CSR, promotional CSR, and strategic CSR* respectively – *systemic CSR* represents a step forward for business (thinking and action) and could become a benchmark for the companies from emerging markets, because it *focuses its activities on identifying and tackling the root causes of our present unsustainability and irresponsibility, typically through innovating business models, revolutionizing their processes, products and services and lobbying for progressive national and international polices* (Visser, 2011).

Therefore, the ideas of co-evolution (with the environment) and symbiosis (between stakeholders' needs and expectations) – considered in terms of both premises and consequences – should accompany any strategic endeavor. They would help businesses to properly asses their (internal and external) environment and to define their most appropriate systemic CSR approach accordingly. As a growing number of businesses will embrace this approach, the interdependencies (between the global stakeholders) will multiply and strengthen, while the overall 'sustainability outcome' will (exponentially) be rising. The 'best fitted' businesses will be able to take the lead in terms of competitiveness, while the others will be left behind. Therefore, due to sustainability related reasons will be essential that a critical mass of businesses to make the move towards integrating systemic CSR into their core business. Thus, the challenges of development and sustainability (as moving targets for the emerging markets and their businesses) will get their best answers, enabling emerging markets to catch-up – on one hand, and businesses to be competitive – on the other hand. And the virtuous circle will be continued…

FUTURE RESEARCH DIRECTIONS

The topic of the chapter is at the same time broad and deep, as well as uneven and controversial, therefore it could not be entirely covered. Moreover, it opens new perspectives and research directions in relationship with the generic topic of the book – which deserve to get a closer look and to be thoroughly explored. In this light, some of the future research directions might envisage: firstly, practical case studies for particular contexts – countries and companies – in order to emphasize on the models for good practice in the field of CSR in emerging markets and to extract similarities and differences that define such behaviors; secondly, developing of a flexible strategic model – integrating various inputs and able to generate different CSR strategies, based on particular situations and scenarios and integrating the results of a relevant number of case studies; thirdly, determining of an 'flexible' equilibrium point – in terms of costs versus benefits of different CSR strategies – as result of a comprehensive analysis and serving as decision criterion when developing a CSR strategy; and fourthly, designing, implementing, and evaluating a CSR strategy into an emerging market (Romania) – in accordance with all the above-mentioned, and taking into account the challenges of responsibility and sustainability, on one hand, and of the complex and networked global economy, on the other hand.

CONCLUSION

The chapter brings new insights on the thorny and controversial issue of CSR strategies in emerging markets, insisting on the need for responsibility at firm level, which, in turn, will have the vocation of leading towards sustainability at broader levels (from national to global). Such a view on the relationship between business and society will enable firms in emerging markets to operate as sustainable development agents, while their CSR strategies will act as sustainable development tools, contributing in the same time to a systemic (and long-term) reconciliation of interests between business and society.

The multilevel (firm - country - global), multidisciplinary (management - strategic management - international business) and multifaceted (internal and external global stakeholders) approach of the chapter has revealed the main characteristics that define the challenging (and continuously changing) context of business in emerging markets: the complex and networked global economy of nowadays, the increasing role of the emerging markets on the global arena, the specific internal and external challenges emerging markets and their companies (local and/or multinationals) face, and the growing pressures toward corporate social responsibility coming from different stakeholders. All and each one of the above represent genuine and valuable cues that need to be properly considered and optimally valorized by companies in emerging markets when designing and implementing their best suited CSR strategy.

Both theory and practice offer recommendations and/or solutions for good practices in the field, but this is not enough – given the great diversity of particular situations. Each business in emerging market has to identify and pursue its own development path while defining and building its own relationships with the society through its CSR strategy. More than that, in search for (global) sustainable competitiveness, it should synergistically integrate the new concepts and practices that have recently emerged – such as *shared value* and *systemic CSR* – into its business core; but this would be a long and difficult process, which asks for a paradigm shift as regards the idea of business itself.

In conclusion, the study has developed a general discussion framework – placed under the auspices of the complex, networked global economy, where each business is a complex adaptive system which has to operate in co-evolution with the environment – on the issue of CSR strategies in emerging markets – by covering from both sides (and through multiple lens) the relationships between (responsible) business and (sustainable) society, while opening new lines of debates and new directions for future research.

REFERENCES

Al-Rodhan, N. R., & Stoudmann, G. (2006). Definitions of globalization: A comprehensive overview and a proposed definition. *Geneva Centre for Security Policy*. Retrieved from http://s3.amazonaws.com/academia.edu.documents/30929642/

Argandoña, A. (2012). The "Management Case" for Corporate Social Responsibility. In R. J. E. Costa, & J. M. R. Marti (Eds.), *Towards a New Theory of the Firm*. Bilbao: Fundacion BBVA.

Barabasi, A. L., & Frangos, J. (2002). *Linked: The New Science of Networks*. Perseus Publishing.

Barney, J., Wright, M., & Ketchen, D. J. (2001). The resource-based view of the firm: Ten years after 1991. *Journal of Management, 27*(6), 625–641. doi:10.1177/014920630102700601

Barney, J. B., & Clark, D. N. (2007). *Resource-based theory: Creating and sustaining competitive advantage*. Oxford: Oxford University Press.

Baskin, J. (2006). Corporate responsibility in emerging markets. *Journal of Corporate Citizenship, 2006*(24), 29–47. doi:10.9774/GLEAF.4700.2006.wi.00006

Battat, J., & Aykut, D. (2005). Southern Multinationals–A Growing Phenomenon. *Note prepared for the conference Southern Multinationals: A Rising Force in the World Economy* (Vol. 9).

Birkin, F., Polesie, T., & Lewis, L. (2009). A new business model for sustainable development: An exploratory study using the theory of constraints in Nordic organizations. *Business Strategy and the Environment, 18*(5), 277–290. doi:10.1002/bse.581

Blowfield, M., & Murray, A. (2011). *Corporate Responsibility*. Oxford University Press.

Boschma, R., & Martin, R. (2007). Editorial: Constructing an evolutionary economic geography. *Journal of Economic Geography*, (June): 18.

Burke, L., & Logsdon, J. M. (1996). How corporate social responsibility pays off. *Long Range Planning, 29*(4), 495–502. doi:10.1016/0024-6301(96)00041-6

Campbell, J. L. (2007). Why would corporations behave in socially responsible ways? An institutional theory of corporate social responsibility. *Academy of Management Review, 32*(3), 946–967. doi:10.5465/AMR.2007.25275684

Carroll, A. B. (1991). The pyramid of corporate social responsibility: Toward the moral management of organizational stakeholders. *Business Horizons, 34*(4), 39–48. doi:10.1016/0007-6813(91)90005-G

Carroll, A. B. (2004). Managing ethically with global stakeholders: A present and future challenge. *The Academy of Management Executive, 18*(2), 114–120. doi:10.5465/AME.2004.13836269

Carroll, A. B., & Shabana, K. M. (2010). The business case for corporate social responsibility: A review of concepts, research and practice. *International Journal of Management Reviews*, *12*(1), 85–105. doi:10.1111/j.1468-2370.2009.00275.x

Casanova, L. (2009). *Global Latinas: Latin America's Emerging Multinationals*. Palgrave Macmillan. doi:10.1057/9780230235021

Cavusgil, S. T., Ghauri, P. N., & Akcal, A. A. (2012). Doing business in emerging markets. *Sage (Atlanta, Ga.)*.

Chahal, H., Mishra, S., Raina, S., & Soni, T. (2014). A comprehensive model of business social responsibility (BSR) for small scale enterprises in Indian context. *Journal of Small Business and Enterprise Development*, *21*(4), 716–739. doi:10.1108/JSBED-05-2014-0091

Ciravegna, L., Fitzgerald, R., & Kundu, S. (2013). *Operating in emerging markets: a guide to management and strategy in the new international economy*. FT Press.

Clapp, J., & Rowlands, I. H. (2014). Corporate Social Responsibility. In J. F. Morin & A. Orsini (Eds.), *The Essential Guide to Global Environmental Governance*. Routledge.

Clark, T. S., & Grantham, K. N. (2012). What CSR is not: Corporate social irresponsibility. *Critical Studies on Corporate Responsibility. Governance and Sustainability*, *4*, 23–41.

Coveney, P., & Highfield, R. (1995). *Frontiers of complexity: The search for order in a chaotic world*. New York: Ballantine.

Crane, A., & Matten, D. (2010). *Business ethics: Managing corporate citizenship and sustainability in the age of globalization*. Oxford University Press.

Cubeddu, M. L. M., Culiuc, M. A., Fayad, M. G., Gao, Y., Kochhar, M. K., Kyobe, A., . . . Zhang, Z. (2014). Emerging Markets in Transition: Growth Prospects and Challenges (No. 14-16). International Monetary Fund.

Dahlsrud, A. (2008). How corporate social responsibility is defined: An analysis of 37 definitions. *Corporate Social Responsibility and Environmental Management*, *15*(1), 1–13. doi:10.1002/csr.132

David, F. R. (2011). *Strategic management: Concepts and cases*. Pearson Education, Inc.

Davidson, P., Wood, S., & Griffin, R. W. (2009). *Management*. John Wiley and Sons Australia.

Davis, K. (1973). The case for and against business assumption of social responsibilities. *Academy of Management Journal*, *16*(2), 312–322. doi:10.2307/255331

Deutsche Gesellschaft für Internationale Zusammenarbeit (GIZ) GmbH. (2011). *Fast Growth and Big Impacts: How Emerging Market Multinationals are Advancing Sustainable Development*. Retrieved from http://www.giz.de/Wirtschaft/de/downloads/giz2011-de-fastgrowth-incl-impacts.pdf

Dicken, P. (2003). Global shift: Reshaping the global economic map in the 21st century. *Sage (Atlanta, Ga.)*.

Dicken, P. (2007). *Global shift: Mapping the changing contours of the world economy*. Sage Publications Ltd.

Donaldson, T., & Preston, L. E. (1995). The stakeholder theory of the corporation: Concepts, evidence, and implications. *Academy of Management Review*, *20*(1), 65–91.

Elkington, J. (1998). Partnership from cannibals with forks: The triple bottom line of 21st century business. *Environmental Quality Management*, *8*(1), 37–51. doi:10.1002/tqem.3310080106

Elkington, J. (2004). Enter the triple bottom line. *The triple bottom line: Does it all add up*, 1-16.

Epstein, M. J., & Buhovac, A. R. (2014). *Making sustainability work: Best practices in managing and measuring corporate social, environmental, and economic impacts*. Berrett-Koehler Publishers.

Falk, S. (2009). "Shift of power" or multipolarity? *Zeitschrift für Politikberatung*, *2*(4), 577–589. doi:10.1007/s12392-010-0223-2

Fernández-Feijóo Souto, B. (2009). Crisis and corporate social responsibility: threat or opportunity? *International Journal of Economic Sciences and Applied Research*, 2(1), 36-50.

Filippov, S. (2012). Emerging Russian Multinational Companies: Managerial and corporate challenges. *European Journal of International Management*, *6*(3), 323–341. doi:10.1504/EJIM.2012.047027

Freeman, R. E. (2010). *Strategic management: A stakeholder approach*. Cambridge University Press. doi:10.1017/CBO9781139192675

Friedman, M. (2007). *The social responsibility of business is to increase its profits* (pp. 173–178). Springer Berlin Heidelberg. doi:10.1007/978-3-540-70818-6_14

Friedman, T. L. (2003). *The world is flat*. New York: Farrar, Straus and Giroux.

Galbreath, J. (2009). Building corporate social responsibility into strategy. *European Business Review*, *21*(2), 109–127. doi:10.1108/09555340910940123

Garriga, E., & Melé, D. (2004). Corporate social responsibility theories: Mapping the territory. *Journal of Business Ethics*, *53*(1-2), 51–71. doi:10.1023/B:BUSI.0000039399.90587.34

Ghemawat, P., & Hout, T. (2008). Tomorrow's Global Giants. Not the usual suspects. *Harvard Business Review*, *86*(11), 80–88.

Goldstein, A. (2009). Multinational Companies from Emerging Economies Composition, Conceptualization & Direction in the Global Economy. *Indian Journal of Industrial Relations*, 45(1), 137–147.

Halme, M., Roome, N., & Dobers, P. (2009). Corporate responsibility: Reflections on context and consequences. *Scandinavian Journal of Management*, *25*(1), 1–9. doi:10.1016/j.scaman.2008.12.001

Handy, C. (2002). What is a Business for? *Harvard Business Review*, 80(12), 49–55. PMID:12510537

Held, D., & McGrew, A. G. (Eds.). (2007). *Globalization theory: Approaches and controversies* (Vol. 4). Cambridge: Polity.

Hillman, A. J., & Keim, G. D. (2001). Shareholder value, stakeholder management, and social issues: What's the bottom line? *Strategic Management Journal*, *22*(2), 125–139. doi:10.1002/1097-0266(200101)22:2<125::AID-SMJ150>3.0.CO;2-H

Hobdari, B., Sinani, E., Papanastassiou, M., & Pearce, R. (2010). The determinants of global integration strategies of Chinese multinationals - Some empirical evidence. *Review of Market Integration*, *2*(1), 61–86. doi:10.1177/097492921000200105

Homer-Dixon, T. (2011) Complexity Science. Oxford Leadership Journal, 2(1).

Hopwood, B., Mellor, M., & O'Brien, G. (2005). Sustainable development: Mapping different approaches. *Sustainable Development*, *13*(1), 38–52. doi:10.1002/sd.244

Hoskisson, R. E., Eden, L., Lau, C. M., & Wright, M. (2000). Strategy in emerging economies. *Academy of Management Journal*, *43*(3), 249–267. doi:10.2307/1556394

Husted, B. W., & Allen, D. B. (2006). Corporate social responsibility in the multinational enterprise: Strategic and institutional approaches. *Journal of International Business Studies*, *37*(6), 838–849. doi:10.1057/palgrave.jibs.8400227

International Monetary Fund. (2014, April). *Global Financial Stability Report. Moving from Liquidity-to Growth-Driven Markets*. Retrieved from http://www.imf.org/

Jackson, G., Brammer, S., Karpoff, J. M., Lange, D., Zavyalova, A., Harrington, B., & Deephouse, D. L. et al. (2014). Grey areas: Irresponsible corporations and reputational dynamics. *Socio-economic Review*, *12*(1), 153–218. doi:10.1093/ser/mwt021

Jamali, D. (2008). A stakeholder approach to corporate social responsibility: A fresh perspective into theory and practice. *Journal of Business Ethics*, *82*(1), 213–231. doi:10.1007/s10551-007-9572-4

Johnson, C. (2012). *Organizational Ethics. A Practical Approach*. SAGE Publications.

Jones, A. (2010). *Globalization: key thinkers* (Vol. 1). Polity.

Kaplinsky, R. (2000). Globalisation and unequalisation: What can be learned from value chain analysis? *The Journal of Development Studies*, *37*(2), 117–146. doi:10.1080/713600071

Katamba, D., Katamba, D., Zipfel, C., Haag, D., & Tushabomwe-Kazooba, C. (2012). *Principles of Corporate Social Responsibility (Csr): A Companion for Students and Practicing Managers in Developing and Emerging Markets*. Strategic Book Publishing.

Kearney, C. (2012). Emerging markets research: Trends, issues and future directions. *Emerging Markets Review*, *13*(2), 159–183. doi:10.1016/j.ememar.2012.01.003

Khanna, T., & Palepu, K. (2013). *Winning in emerging markets: A road map for strategy and execution*. Harvard Business Press.

Knez-Riedl, J., & Mulej, M. (2008). Developing a sustainable/holistic firm. In E. A. Stuhler & S. Misra (Eds.), *Across disciplinary boundaries towards a sustainable life: psychodynamic reflection on human behaviour; dedicated with eternal gratitude and in high esteem to Prof. Dr. Rainer Fuchs* (pp. 217–226). Munchen: Hampp.

Krugman, P. (2011). The new economic geography, now middle-aged. *Regional Studies*, *45*(1), 1–7. doi:10.1080/00343404.2011.537127

Kvint, V. (2010). *The global emerging market: strategic management and economics*. Routledge.

Langtry, B. (1994). Stakeholders and the moral responsibilities of business. *Business Ethics Quarterly*, *4*(4), 431–443. doi:10.2307/3857342

Layne, C. (2012). This time it's real: The end of unipolarity and the Pax Americana. *International Studies Quarterly*, *56*(1), 203–213. doi:10.1111/j.1468-2478.2011.00704.x

Lee, M. D. P. (2008). A review of the theories of corporate social responsibility: Its evolutionary path and the road ahead. *International Journal of Management Reviews*, *10*(1), 53–73. doi:10.1111/j.1468-2370.2007.00226.x

Lévy, B. (2007). The interface between globalization, trade and development: Theoretical issues for international business studies. *International Business Review*, *16*(5), 594–612. doi:10.1016/j.ibusrev.2007.06.004

Lewin, R. (2000). *Complexity*. University of Chicago Press Economics Books.

Li, S., Fetscherin, M., Alon, I., Lattemann, C., & Yeh, K. (2010). Corporate social responsibility in emerging markets. *Management International Review*, *50*(5), 635–654. doi:10.1007/s11575-010-0049-9

Luetkenhorst, W. (2004). Corporate social responsibility and the development agenda. *Inter Economics*, *39*(3), 157–166. doi:10.1007/BF02933583

Luo, Y. (2002). *Multinational enterprises in emerging markets*. Copenhagen Business School Press DK.

Mahajan, V., & Banga, K. (2005). *The 86 percent solution: How to succeed in the biggest market opportunity of the next 50 years*. Pearson Education.

Maznevski, M., Steger, U., & Amann, W. (2007) *Managing complexity in global organizations*. IMD. No. 141, February.

McElhaney, K. (2007). Strategic CSR. *Sustainable Enterprise Quarterly*, *4*(1), 1–7.

McWilliams, A., & Siegel, D. (2001). Corporate social responsibility: A theory of the firm perspective. *Academy of Management Review*, *26*(1), 117–127.

Mendoza, K., & Irmak, I. (2008). K. P. Sauvant (Ed.), *The rise of transnational corporations from emerging markets: threat or opportunity?* Edward Elgar Publishing.

Michelini, L., & Fiorentino, D. (2012). New business models for creating shared value. *Social Responsibility Journal*, *8*(4), 561–577. doi:10.1108/17471111211272129

Mullerat, R. (2010). *International corporate social responsibility: The role of corporations in the economic order of the 21st century*. Kluwer Law International.

Nölke, A., & Taylor, H. (2010). Non-triad multinationals and global governance. In M. Ougaard, & A. Leander (Eds.), *Business and Global Governance* (pp. 156–178). Oxon: Routledge.

Odonnat, I., & Rahmouni, I. (2006). Do emerging market economies still constitute a homogenous asset class? *Banque de France, Financial Stability Review*, (9), 39-48.

Oliveira, J. A. (2012). Rio+ 20: what we can learn from the process and what is missing. *Cadernos EBAPE. BR, 10*(3), 492-507.

Orlitzky, M., Siegel, D. S., & Waldman, D. A. (2011). Strategic corporate social responsibility and environmental sustainability. *Business & Society, 50*(1), 6–27. doi:10.1177/0007650310394323

Osterwalder, A., & Pigneur, Y. (2011). Aligning profit and purpose through business model innovation. *Responsible management practices for the 21st century. Pearson International*, 61-75.

Pelle, S. (2007). Understanding emerging markets: Building business BRIC by brick. *Sage (Atlanta, Ga.)*.

Peloza, J., & Shang, J. (2011). How can corporate social responsibility activities create value for stakeholders? A systematic review. *Journal of the Academy of Marketing Science, 39*(1), 117–135. doi:10.1007/s11747-010-0213-6

Pfitzer, M., Bockstette, V., & Stamp, M. (2013). Innovating for shared value. *Harvard Business Review, September*, 100–107.

Pillania, R. K. (2009). Multinationals and emerging markets. *Business Strategy Series, 10*(2), 100–103. doi:10.1108/17515630910942232

Porter, M. E., & Kramer, M. R. (2006). The link between competitive advantage and corporate social responsibility. *Harvard Business Review, 84*(12), 78–92. PMID:17183795

Porter, M. E., & Kramer, M. R. (2011). Creating shared value. *Harvard Business Review, 89*(1/2), 62–77.

Porter, T., & Derry, R. (2012). Sustainability and business in a complex world. *Business and Society Review, 117*(1), 33–53. doi:10.1111/j.1467-8594.2012.00398.x

Prahalad, C. K. (2006). *The Fortune at the Bottom of the Pyramid*. Pearson Education India.

Ramalingam, B., Jones, H., Reba, T., & Young, J. (2008). *Exploring the science of complexity: Ideas and implications for development and humanitarian efforts* (Vol. 285). London: Overseas Development Institute.

Ravenhill, J. (Ed.). (2014). *Global political economy*. Oxford University Press.

Redclift, M. (2005). Sustainable development (1987–2005): An oxymoron comes of age. *Sustainable Development, 13*(4), 212–227. doi:10.1002/sd.281

Reimann, F., Ehrgott, M., Kaufmann, L., & Carter, C. R. (2012). Local stakeholders and local legitimacy: MNEs' social strategies in emerging economies. *Journal of International Management, 18*(1), 1–17. doi:10.1016/j.intman.2011.06.002

Rettab, B., Brik, A. B., & Mellahi, K. (2009). A study of management perceptions of the impact of corporate social responsibility on organisational performance in emerging economies: The case of Dubai. *Journal of Business Ethics, 89*(3), 371–390. doi:10.1007/s10551-008-0005-9

Rigg, J., Bebbington, A., Gough, K. V., Bryceson, D. F., Agergaard, J., Fold, N., & Tacoli, C. (2009). The World Development Report 2009 'reshapes economic geography': Geographical reflections. *Transactions of the Institute of British Geographers*, *34*(2), 128–136. doi:10.1111/j.1475-5661.2009.00340.x

Rivera, I. M. (2010). What drives indigenous corporations in the developing world to engage in CSR as a management strategy? Case study of the sugarcane and ethanol industry in the Cauca Valley, Colombia. Retrieved from http://www.banrepcultural.org/sites/default/files/Isabella-Marino-rivera-Dissertation-280810-what-drives-indigenous-corporations.pdf

Robins, F. (2005). The future of corporate social responsibility. *Asian Business & Management*, *4*(2), 95–115. doi:10.1057/palgrave.abm.9200125

Rodriguez, P., Siegel, D. S., Hillman, A., & Eden, L. (2006). Three lenses on the multinational enterprise: Politics, corruption, and corporate social responsibility. *Journal of International Business Studies*, *37*(6), 733–746. doi:10.1057/palgrave.jibs.8400229

Salehizadeh, M. (2007). Emerging economies' multinationals: Current status and future prospects. *Third World Quarterly*, *28*(6), 1151–1166. doi:10.1080/01436590701507586

Schmidheiny, S. (1992). *Changing course: A global business perspective on development and the environment* (Vol. 1). MIT Press.

Shangquan, G. (2000). Economic globalization: Trends, risks and risk prevention. *Economic & Social Affairs, CDP Backround Paper* 1.

Sirkin, H., Hemerling, J., & Bhattacharya, A. (2008). *Globality: Competing with everyone from everywhere for everything*. Hachette Digital, Inc.

Smick, D. M. (2008). *The world is curved: Hidden dangers to the global economy*. Penguin.

Smith, N. C., Bhattacharya, C. B., Vogel, D., & Levine, D. I. (Eds.). (2010). *Global challenges in responsible business*. Cambridge University Press. doi:10.1017/CBO9780511777660

Sousa Filho, J. M. D., Wanderley, L. S. O., Gómez, C. P., & Farache, F. (2010). Strategic corporate social responsibility management for competitive advantage. *BAR-Brazilian Administration Review*, *7*(3), 294–309. doi:10.1590/S1807-76922010000300006

Steger, M. (2013). *Globalization: A Very Short Introduction*. Oxford University Press. doi:10.1093/actrade/9780199662661.001.0001

Steurer, R., Langer, M. E., Konrad, A., & Martinuzzi, A. (2005). Corporations, stakeholders and sustainable development I: A theoretical exploration of business–society relations. *Journal of Business Ethics*, *61*(3), 263–281. doi:10.1007/s10551-005-7054-0

Stubbs, W., & Cocklin, C. (2008). Conceptualizing a "sustainability business model". *Organization & Environment*, *21*(2), 103–127. doi:10.1177/1086026608318042

Su, W., Peng, M. W., Tan, W., & Cheung, Y. L. (2014). The Signaling Effect of Corporate Social Responsibility in Emerging Economies. *Journal of Business Ethics*.

Taylor, H., & Nölke, A. (2010). Global Players from India: A Political Economy Perspective. In K. P. Sauvant, G. McAllister, & W. A. Maschek (Eds.), *Foreign Direct Investments from Emerging Markets: The Challenges Ahead* (pp. 145–172). New York: Palgrave MacMillan.

Torres-Baumgarten, G., & Yucetepe, V. (2009). Multinational firms' leadership role in corporate social responsibility in Latin America. *Journal of Business Ethics*, *85*(1), 217–224. doi:10.1007/s10551-008-9940-8

Tyagi, R. K., & Vasiljeviene, N. (2013). The case of CSR and irresponsible management practices. *Competitiveness Review: An International Business Journal incorporating Journal of Global Competitiveness, 23*(4/5), 372-383.

United Nations. (1987). *Report of the World Commission on Environment and Development: Our Common Future*. Retrieved from http://www.un-documents.net/our-common-future.pdf

United Nations. (2013). *Global Sustainable Development Report – Executive Summary: Building the Common Future We Want*. New York: United Nations Department of Economic and Social Affairs, Division for Sustainable Development. Retrieved from http://sustainabledevelopment.un.org/

United Nations. (2013). *World Economic and Social Survey 2013. Sustainable Development Challenges*. Retrieved from http://sustainabledevelopment.un.org/content/documents/2843WESS2013.pdf

Urip, S. (2010). *CSR strategies: corporate social responsibility for a competitive edge in emerging markets*. John Wiley & Sons.

Utting, P. (2000). Business responsibility for sustainable development (Vol. 2). Geneva: United Nations Research Institute for Social Development. Retrieved from http://www.unrisd.org/

Varey, R. J., & Storbacka, K. (2011). *Business model design for sustainable society: Therapy for the consumerist mindset*. ANZMAC.

Visser, W. (2011). *The age of responsibility: CSR 2.0 and the new DNA of business*. John Wiley & Sons.

Vives, A. (2006). Social and environmental responsibility in small and medium enterprises in Latin America. *Journal of Corporate Citizenship*, *2006*(21), 39–50. doi:10.9774/GLEAF.4700.2006.sp.00006

Waddock, S. A., Bodwell, C., & Graves, S. B. (2002). Responsibility: The new business imperative. *The Academy of Management Executive*, *16*(2), 132–148. doi:10.5465/AME.2002.7173581

Werther, W. B. Jr, & Chandler, D. (2010). *Strategic corporate social responsibility: Stakeholders in a global environment*. Sage Publications.

Whetten, D. A., Rands, G., & Godfrey, P. (2002). What are the responsibilities of business to society. Handbook of Strategy and Management, 373-408.

Young, S. (2003). *Moral capitalism: reconciling private interest with the public good*. Berrett-Koehler Publishers.

Young, S. L., & Makhija, M. V. (2014). Firms' corporate social responsibility behavior: An integration of institutional and profit maximization approaches. *Journal of International Business Studies*, *45*(6), 670–698. doi:10.1057/jibs.2014.29

Yunus, M. (2007). *Creating a world without poverty: Social business and the future of capitalism*. Public Affairs.

Zhang, F. (2008). Corporate Social Responsibility in Emerging Markets: The Role of Multinational Corporations. *The Foreign Policy Centre*. Retrieved from http://fpc.org.uk/fsblob/920.pdf

KEY TERMS AND DEFINITIONS

Business Core: The (unique) identity of a company, defined by its most important value / feature.

Business Model: Particular pattern of evolution that is followed by a company in order to succeed.

Business Practice for Sustainability: Activity undertaken by a company in order to have a positive (economic, social and environmental) impact over the long run.

Complex Adaptive System: View on the company, emphasizing on the idea of a multi-component structure, with multiple internal and external links, designed to be able to co-evolve with its environment.

Complex and Networked Global Economy: The world economy as it is today, a global network of networks which permanently evolves according to its own, non-deterministic and subtle rules.

Corporate Social Responsibility: Part of a business model that translate the concept of sustainable (economic, social and environmental) development into a business practice.

Socially Responsible Decision Making Process: Set of activities – part of the business model – pursued by a company in consideration of its (social and environmental) impact.

Stakeholder: Any individual and/or group which have a particular interest into a company or which might be affected by a company's decisions and/or behaviors.

Systemic Corporate Social Responsibility: A new approach on corporate social responsibility aiming at bringing together business and society by considering all the connections between them and their consequences.

Chapter 2

Business and E Business Strategies for Coopetition and Thematic Management as a Sustained Basis for Ethics and Social Responsibility in Emerging Markets

John D Haynes
University of Nizwa, Oman

Mohammad Al Rashdi
University of Nizwa, Oman

S. Arockiasamy
University of Nizwa, Oman

Said Al Rashdi
University of Nizwa, Oman

ABSTRACT

This chapter firstly explains why Emerging Markets offer Businesses tremendous opportunities for long term growth. As a sustained basis to that growth, specifically for Emerging Markets (EMs), this chapter then presents working details for a business management model, Thematic Management, which is aimed at providing the necessary enabling circumstances for trust through the introduction and importance of the gradual fulfillment of ethics and social responsibility within an EM. These enabling circumstances provide the foundation for the importance of Thematic Management as a strategic basis for successful and sustained engagement in Coopetition within Emerging Markets. Coopetition is defined as a combination of cooperation and competition. Cooperation relates to an alliance with another similar or complimentary business where the joint venture provides for mutually beneficial gains. We believe that an ethical and socially responsible approach to competition also has benefits for the engaging business in terms of unexpected gains from, for example, efforts that lead to a consistently good reputation. Thematic Management (TM) is based on the premise: "As Outside so Inside". TM occurs where senior management consistently experiments with creating an internal environment of trust between employees and management. TM allows for staff members to be organized into special teams, which are mentored, to emulate, inside the business, the ethical and socially responsible behavioral theme of engagement in the market outside the business. TM provides for staff taking (monitored) risks; having senior team leaders engage in debates with senior management, among other practices, all with a view to an improvement in staff creativity, innovation, and finally intuition and wisdom for core knowledge retention and strategic sustainability.

DOI: 10.4018/978-1-4666-9864-2.ch002

INTRODUCTION

In this chapter firstly we consider the notion of Emerging Markets in terms of a definition. Secondly, we determine why Emerging Markets offer external businesses great opportunities for setting up new branches in an Emerging Market. Thirdly, we consider a way of sustaining that growth with a management technique that entails Coopetition, which we have entitled Thematic Management.

In Section 2, Rapoza (2011) gives us several definitions for Emerging Markets in a developing country that is categorized as having been "third world" and is now "emerging" financially in terms of annual increments in GDP. The question then arises how could Emerging Markets represent an excellent investment and offer excellent growth for Businesses that wish to create a branch of their company in such an Emerging Market? Section 2 expands on the following ten main reasons why Emerging that markets represent excellent potential for growth. First, there is the fact that in an Emerging Market there is clearly demonstrated annual growth in GDP, which offers an immediate opportunity for the growth of an expanding expat business. Second, Emerging Markets provide great potential for diversification and for innovation. Third, 70% of world growth will come from Emerging Markets in the next 10 years. Fourth, there are often lower rates of taxation in the Emerging Market. Fifth, during the major USA credit crash of 2008, the world was saved from a major financial collapse by the growth of Emerging Markets thus signaling a new world order in terms of market growth and financial and product investment. Sixth, the balance of payments in Emerging Markets which are in surplus, are significantly better that Western countries. Surpluses offer their own incentive for rewarding investments. Seventh, Emerging Markets have large populations of young workers which can provide retirees in their families with financial support. Young populations are more agile, potentially innovative and hardworking. Eight, Emerging Market companies are getting bigger, hence a reason to get in now while the prospects are still good. Ninth, resources can be problematic, but most Emerging Market countries are resource rich or potentially so. China is one exception, and therefore remains a big importer of resources; hence in-country resource suppliers will make more profits than outside suppliers. Tenth, Emerging Markets are technologically savvy, connecting immediately with their Western counterparts who can also establish in-country production.

As we further detail in Section 2, for each of the above reasons, we show the connection to socially responsible Coopetition between commencing and existing expat Emerging Market Businesses together with an ethical approach to working within the Emerging Market.

Next, the nature of Coopetition (Kraut, 2001, p. 6), is explicated in Section 3. Coopetition is a combination of business engagement in both cooperation and competition. Originally the idea derived from Value Net Theory, which in turn derived from Game Theory (see Figure 1). Coopetition is thought of 'cooperating to make a pie and competing to carve it up into pieces'. But cooperation (within Coopetition) must have transparency of goals, motivations and agendas in order for the cooperator to have trust in the cooperating business. As we see this is best achieved with the e business component of the business providing for accessible intranet usage and access. Transparency means being socially responsible. To be socially responsible means maintaining an ethical behavior. Next we examine who are the complementors, since a way of engaging with a cooperator alliance is to connect at the level of complementarity of product or service. In terms of an excellent example of complementarity, we examine, just to mention one, GM's Ralph Szygenda's On-Star.

Figure 1. Value Net Framework - Co-opetition Framework Source Brandenburger, & Nalebuff, (1997)

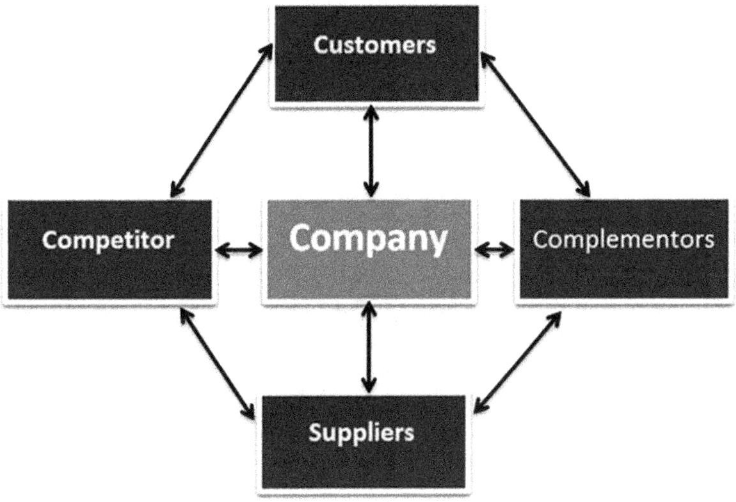

In Section 4 we consider the relationship between ethics, intuition, innovation and social responsibility. In so doing we examine the nature (or definition) of ethics; how intuition and innovation is related to coopetition, and draw all the threads together in Figure 2.

Next we consider the importance of core knowledge management and its relationship to a socially responsible (and wise) approach to maintaining it. For example, sack all your key staff and you will lose your core knowledge and to the great detriment of the business, and moreover, you will discover it will take a long time to recover it (unless, of course, you have gone broke in the meantime, and then it won't matter).

In Section 5, we consider the details underlying an ethical approach to business practice together with examples from Jack Welch, former CEO of General Electrics and former President of the USA,

Figure 2. The Relationship of Ethics, Intuition, Innovation to Coopetition

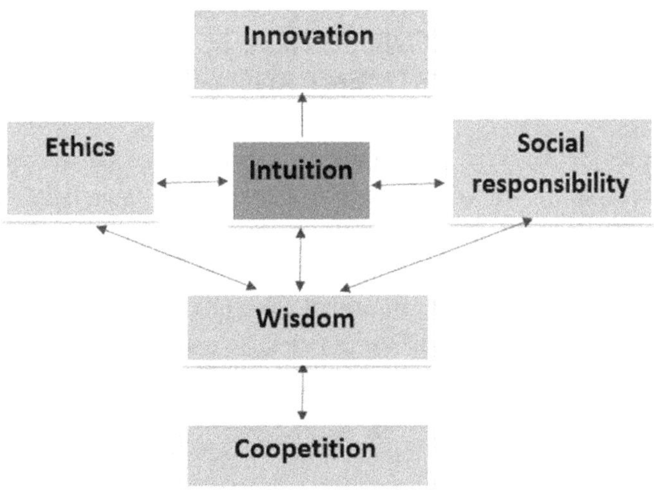

Figure 3. Ethical and Socially Responsible Business Preservation Factors

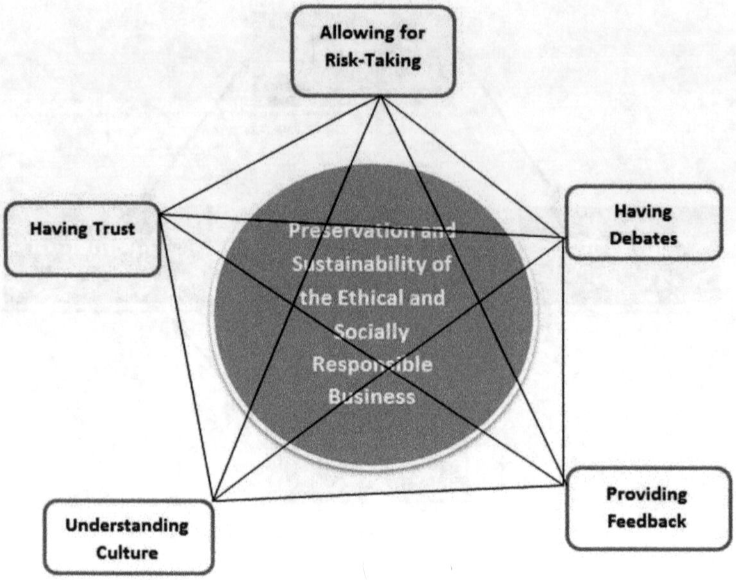

Jimmy Carter. Next we revisit the goals for this chapter in point form, followed by a consideration of their enabling circumstances, and then consider ways of achieving those enabling circumstances. This is followed by an explication of why coopetition is the best solution for a business and e business in an emerging market (also see Figure 3 in terms of preservation factors).

In Section 6, we introduce the ethical and innovative environment of Thematic Management with Figure 4 representing the 'As Outside, so Inside' motto of Thematic Management, as it is expanded in this chapter, from its original roots in (Haynes, 2003). Then we outline and explicate all five of the component teams, ways of mentoring, senior management fostering and IT and Internet specialist supporting elements. We end, before the conclusion, with what makes cooperation and competition successful.

REASONS FOR, AND THE COOPERATION, SOCIALLY RESPONSIBLE, AND ETHICAL CONNECTION TO, EMERGING MARKETS FOR BUSINESS INVESTMENT AND GROWTH

Firstly let us define Emerging Markets. We define Emerging Markets as a developing country that is categorized as having been "third world" and are now "emerging" financially in terms of annual increments in GDP. These increments in GDP, seemingly ironically, in some cases show higher GDP growth than some existing non Emerging Markets that have "run out of steam", such as Germany in 2011 whose annualized GDP at 6% could be their top limit, Repoza (op cit).

In the remainder of this section we indicate ten clear reasons (ibid) why Emerging Markets offer excellent opportunities for the introduction of a new Expat Business in terms of growth and in terms of the sustainability of that growth and success in the initial business implementation. For each of the

Figure 4. The 'As Outside so Inside' Thematic Management Model

reasons we will discuss why coopetition, and social responsibility, engendered in an ethical way, is the preferred approach for that Emerging Market Business introduction.

First, within an Emerging Market, there is demonstrated annual growth in GDP, which is, in itself, a sufficient reason to invest in an Emerging Market and a perfect opportunity to "hop on the bandwagon" for a new branch of a Business. The idea of hopping on the bandwagon already suggests a cooperative approach will succeed best.

Second, Emerging Markets provide great potential for diversification and for innovation which means there is a greater need for working with other companies that offer complementary products. To diversify and to innovate successfully in growing markets, trust (for the complementor and by the diversifier), is a key ingredient with demonstrated actions of social responsibility and ethics sustaining that element of trust.

Third, 70% of world growth will come from Emerging Markets in the next 10 years (ibid). Which means, that it is crucial for an ex-pat Business establishing itself in an Emerging Market to create business practices that are trustworthy and thereby sustainable.

Fourth, there are often lower rates of taxation in the Emerging Market, or at least, or in addition to, tax benefits offered by the ex-pat business home country (ibid). One way that an establishing ex-pat business can honor those lower rates of taxation is by being socially responsible and clearly demonstrating from the beginning of their establishment that they are offering opportunities to the workforce of the Emerging Market, such as increasing education and technical expertise, promotion pathways, leadership, etc.

Fifth, during the major USA credit crash of 2008, the world was saved from a major financial collapse by the growth of Emerging Markets thus signaling a new world order in terms of market growth and financial and product investment. If a western Business intending to expand into an Emerging Market were sufficiently wise they would investigate why the USA credit crash occurred and realize that high on the priority for new possibilities for re-ordering is sustainability, and that sustainability is directly connected with trust and the growth and preservation of customers is directly connected with social responsibility.

Sixth, the balance of payments in Emerging Markets which are in surplus (ibid), are significantly better that in Western countries. To maintain the momentum for that Emerging Market surplus it is the long-term that needs to be carefully planned for. An excellent strategy for the long term is innovation, and working with other existing Emerging Market competitors in a cooperative way offers great opportunities for that innovation.

Seventh, Emerging Markets have large populations of young workers which can provide retirees in their families with financial support. Young populations are more agile, potentially innovative and hardworking. This fact offers ex-pat Businesses establishing themselves in Emerging Markets the perfect opportunity to be socially responsible and reap the rewards of that social responsibility in carefully guiding these young, agile and innovative workers.

Eight, now is the time for an expanding business to establish itself in an Emerging Market, because Emerging Market companies are getting bigger (ibid). Therefore to enter an Emerging Market under these circumstances, strategy therefore is all the more important. How does a new market entrant deal with an ever growing competitor? One key strategy is Coopetition, and specifically in the case of an Emerging Market there exists a situation of diversification and innovation which inherently offers greater possibilities for discovering a complementary connection with a large competitor.

Ninth, a resource supplier who is on the ground (within an Emerging Market) has the greatest potential for success because they are closer to the culture. Most Emerging Market countries are resource rich or potentially so, but China is one exception (ibid), and so remains a big importer of resources, hence in-country ex-pat resource suppliers will make more profits than outside suppliers. To succeed within China a deliberate cooperative strategy needs to be implemented.

Tenth, Emerging Markets are technologically savvy (ibid). This very fact offers great strategic possibilities for Businesses wishing to establish themselves in an Emerging Market. One strategy is to connect with those of the best technologically savvy workers by offering them high salaries as the Ex-pat Business establishes itself in the Emerging Market and then enhancing their abilities, in a socially responsible way, by connecting them immediately with their Western counterparts for greater potential in innovation within the Emerging Market.

It should be clear from the above that Emerging Markets are an excellent vehicle for growth and innovation, and given, above, connections to the business strategy of sustainability in each of ten reasons for that growth and innovation, it should also be very clear why there is a connection between sustainability, social responsibility and ethics for a strategy that entails Coopetition in an Emerging Market.

For the remainder of this Chapter we shall focus on the underlying factors that support these necessary strategies for Coopetition, Ethics and Social Responsibility, necessary for a Business to establish and sustain itself within an Emerging Market.

THE NATURE OF COOPETITION

Brandenburger and Nalebuff, (1997) elaborated the concept of coopetition in the following way:

In its purest form, business can be considered as a game in which money represents points won or lost. The person or company who gathers the greatest numbers of points wins. The biggest opportunities in business don't come from playing the game better than everyone else - they come from changing the fundamental nature of the game itself to your advantage. Business strategy, and the concept of co-opetition, is designed to provide a framework by which companies can gain a sustainable competitive advantage by changing the game to their own advantage.

They based the above ideas on a Value Net framework, derived originally from Game Theory.

However, to change the 'fundamental nature of the game', the engaged players need not only to be clever they also need to be intuitive. In this chapter we provide sustained reasons for the view that intuition is necessary for an ethical approach, and that ethics itself is the most beneficial way of playing the game of coopetition. Our notion of intuition fits in with Brandenburger and Nailbuff's (op cit) view of successful coopetition as a means of shaping the future of the industry the way you would like it to be.

We can see from Figure 1 that Coopetition is a blend of co-operating with complementary industries and competing with industry competitors, both of whom need to access suppliers and satisfy customers (Hendy, 2014).

Thus Coopetition is thought of "cooperating to make a pie and competing to carve it up into pieces" (Kraut, R. 2001 p. 6). Furthermore, he says: "in many circumstances forming Coopetition is better than traditional collaborations, because they create transparency about motivation, agendas and goals".

Coopetition Transparency in Motivation, Goals, Agendas

In this chapter we have also included e business because we believe this is the most obvious way to be transparent, in all of motivation, agendas and goals. That transparency is afforded by allowing the complementor business's e business processes to access sufficient areas of the intranet of the business in question.

Who are the Complementors?

It is fairly clear who a business's competitors are, but who are their complementors? We can describe it in the following way. A complementation is an aspect of a business that needs to match up with a complementation in another business. For example, educational organizations extensively require information technology. Information technology businesses benefit from serving educational organizations because the educational organizations are in a position to promote their IT products through their students and research connected clients. Thus educational organizations and information technology businesses are a good match as complementors. Similarly automotive manufacturers, parts manufacturers and insurance companies are all complementors. As are medical organizations and hospitals and health insurance companies; hospitals and information technology industries; drug companies and insurance companies.

Perhaps one of the most powerful and ethically beneficial recent examples of mutually fulfilling interaction between complementary industries, that also saved and protected human lives, was the powerful cooperation aspect of coopetition between the police, the medical industry, the insurance companies and General Motors. The complementary interaction arose from a software application, known as On-Star innovated post 1996 by GM's CIO, Ralph Szygenda (Slywotzky &Wise, 2003).

On-Star was a complex vehicle integrated navigation system, connected to satellite location, installed in GM vehicles that could contact the police, medical authorities, insurance companies and GM in the event of a shutdown of any installed On-Star GM vehicle's motor, in addition to the connected IT detection of an accident. In an internal analysis report to GM Bergh, Lefkovitch, Scotti, & Warner, (2009). The authors recommended a strategic alliance with Apple to further extend the On-star system globally through Google Earth which would then allow cars to be sold with this same On-Star capability in countries such as China, etc. Meaning ethical and socially responsible cooperation works, with big sales following!

Furthermore, from the viewpoint of Coopetition, in an interview with Computer Weekly, Ralph Szygenda, (Saran 2015) made a series of crucial statements, "you can only drive innovation by learning what is happening in other sectors" and he gave the example of "in logistics we may look at how Fed-Ex or Walmart does shipping" (ibid). Further statements in terms of preparing for and activating innovation, he made in the interview are, "in a corporation you have to get stability first"; "you have to engender a culture of risk-taking"; "you must have debates [with your staff]"; "you must understand the business processes that are happening outside your industry"; "you must know your competitors"; "you must measure the business results" (ibid).

From the above we can see that Coopetition offers possibilities for a whole new strategic approach to business practice in which the nature of the business environment itself can be changed. This change is focused in the direction and favor of the engaging participator who demonstrates the best intuition and hence the best vision for their product and/or service. We see intuition (and hence innovation), ethics and social responsibility as the key elements to foster in a business enterprise of any size, because what emerges in the coopetitive dynamic is a situation that has not occurred before. Thus accordingly, previous knowledge is less useful compared to wise guesses, risk-taking, understanding both complementors and competitors, and, the allowance for debate within the business enterprise to choose the wisest strategies. Bosses aren't bosses, always necessarily, because they are bright, or even necessarily that experienced. From a good debate many parties can learn (they just have to leave their egos aside).

In the next sections we shall move towards recommendations for how a Business (and their associated e business) can foster intuition, ethics and social responsibility in their organization for an emerging market. But first we need to understand what is ethics and how is it connected to intuition, innovation and social responsibility and what makes the combination of all four categories a powerful force for innovation and success in any emerging market business.

ETHICS, INTUITION, INNOVATION AND SOCIAL RESPONSIBILITY

A business must first move past its survival phase before it can embrace the full scope of an ethical approach that further engenders intuition and hence innovation. Nor are we implying in its survival phase it should be unethical. The business just needs to get through its survival as best as it can (and ethically). In the following sections we will see that genuine ethics is always based upon human intuition. Yet the fact is that all (at least normal) human beings have intuition, why then is their combined or individual intuition not developed as one of the most valued assets of any organization?

What is Ethics?

According to Aristotle, Ethics "must match its subject matter – good action" (Kraut, 2001), and "practical wisdom", as he conceives it, cannot be acquired solely by learning general rules. We must also acquire, through practice, those deliberative, emotional, and social skills that enable us to put our general understanding of well-being into practice in ways that are suitable to each occasion" (ibid). It follows, as it is used in medicine, (in the term beneficence), that is, "a principle of medical ethics according to which a person should do good to others, especially when one has a professional duty to do so" (Jonas, op cit), that ethics is performing good action for all including the individual. Furthermore, to determine, in advance, what is good action, especially "suitable for each occasion" (Kraut op cit), one cannot rely on rules. If one cannot rely on rules, because for a new situation it would be unwise to apply a general rule, then it is only intuition from one's own wisdom that can create a new 'good' approach and thus assist in that specific situation. Hence innovation is also connected with intuition, because a new course of good action, for a new situation, must be 'innovated' for each new situation.

How is Intuition and Innovation Related to Coopetition?

You cannot have intuition, which literally means inner teaching, without first having wisdom, and wisdom, in turn comes from the lessons life has taught an individual. Nor can you innovate without first having intuition, because innovation is the bringing into being of something new. To create something new you are not drawing on something already known, you have to draw on the inner resource of intuition. We have also seen, above, that ethics also is a product of intuition. It follows then that social responsibility must also be founded by intuition, because social responsibility is an ethical action. To participate in coopetition in a sustained way, that is, to cooperate with complementors and to compete with competitors, wisdom, which draws together the capacity to innovate with the actions of ethics and social responsibility, must be the basis of the sustained interactivity of one complementary business with another. We can see the above-mentioned relationships in Figure 2, as follows.

In the next section we will extend ethics, intuition and innovation to core knowledge management, because without core knowledge management the business cannot be sustainable. Core knowledge management is the basis for the sustainability of the business; it is in essence, the preservation of the knowledge of the culture of ethical and innovative accomplishments. In other words, a business moves forward on what it has achieved, embedded in its reputation, and that reputation is kept intact by core knowledge management.

The Importance of Core Knowledge Management

In an International Conference Key Note address, Haynes (2013) made the following observations:

- Ethics is necessary for genuine Social Responsibility;
- Social Responsibility allows for sustainability;
- Sustainability preserves "core" Knowledge Management;
- Core Knowledge Management allows for Ethics.

Core knowledge maintenance and retention is so important, that if a very senior manager is foolish enough, for whatever reason, to sack, at some point in time, all his/her key staff then core knowledge (the vital history and experience of the business in terms of their specialties), will be virtually lost. The attempt to recover core knowledge management, after such a foolish strategic move, could cost the business its livelihood (or, at least, perhaps, its reputation).

In the next section we take the above relationships further and thereby consider what could constitute an effective management practice that allows for ethics; intuition; innovation; the nurturing of wisdom, and later return to the importance of the preservation of core knowledge and knowledge management.

For the time being we shall say that such a practice is a strategy, not only for the sustainability, and profitability, of the business itself, but for the sustainability of an effective, and growing form of Coopetition especially in emerging markets.

AN ETHICAL APPROACH TO BUSINESS PRACTICE WITH COOPETITION

In our view the effective management practice of ethics and social responsibility is based upon recognizing themes within an organization and developing those as organized management practices as Thematic Management this term is coined and explicated by Haynes (2003). Thematic Management arises, we believe sometimes automatically, when management demonstrates (knowingly or unknowingly), thereby revealing compassion in their management practices, the crucial difference between a thing (German: dinge) and a thing-in-itself (German: dinge-an-sich). While this may sound fanciful, it is based solidly on the philosophical long-standing area of Phenomenology which dates back to Plotinus and Plato and given modern expression by the German philosophers such as Hegel, Heidegger, Nietzsche, and Husserl to name a few as well as Haynes in his book *Perspectival Thinking* (2007). Similarly in Haynes, (2003) and Haynes, (2003 p.p.12-18), are indicated the following.

The body of a person is a thing, but what the person as identity; as his/her worth; as his/her being a human-being, is his/her thingness-in-itself. The fundamental inability to distinguish between things and things-in-themselves is a fundamental lack in our capacity for indirectness; a critical loss of 'inward-forming', Haynes, (2007, ibid). We see many examples of managers who treat people as objects (things), and sometimes we wonder why there is no compassion for their staff that they "manage", who, in many cases, deserve to be treated better. Compassion comes not only from understanding humanity, but also from understanding oneself (one's strengths and weaknesses) together with many years of experience in dealing with many varieties of persons, in a management setting, to obtain their best efforts. All the really great (good) leaders have demonstrated compassion. For example, Jack Welch, former CEO of General Electrics, often indicated similar expressions to 'if I could visit all my staff every day I would and I would cheer them on'. We believe Ex-President Jimmy Carter also demonstrated such compassion in his speech, and subsequent action, to the USA nation, in a broadcast on national television when USA was in a significant crisis. Subsequently, Carter was not afraid to call for national feedback to be openly discussed in a Camp David conference. There are many examples, from many good leaders. But brute force; overly hierarchical structures; lack of genuine participation, and compassion, by the senior management; lack of critical feedback from staff, and so on, just don't work, especially where an environment of ethics and social responsibility for Coopetition is aimed for. The saying "as above so below", translates, in the context of this chapter to, as outside, so inside: what is wished for outside the business is needed to be emulated within the business. We shall see later that Thematic Management is one way of achieving this objective.

To embrace, ethics, social responsibility, and engender innovation and intuition, all in the need for effective coopetition and consequent sustainability of the business and e business enterprise in emerging markets, we believe an effective manager has to regularly involve all his staff, not dictate policy, nor manage them with other sub-managers. How could this be achieved? It is a well-known fact that Jack Welch, who managed tens of thousands of staff members, used to write personal notes to many of them, often apparently daily, by receiving constant feedback on those within the ranks, to the lowest rung, who were performing well. Ralph Szygenda (Saran, op. cit), former CIO of General Motors, despite an extremely busy workload, used to have five hour sessions with all his considerable immediate staff every Thursday of the working week and he wanted full-on criticism and debate about current issues (among which were questions such as: what are we doing wrong? What are we doing right?).

Human-beings have enormous capabilities when they are managed effectively (even when they manage themselves), especially from compassionate managers, who purposely draw out the innovative and intuitive contributions of all their staff members. These innovations and intuitions arise naturally when there is an atmosphere of trust, and consequently a willingness to serve without question arises in those staff because their views are allowed for and listened to (as long as they are making significant contributions).

In the following section we will see, in the light of the foregoing discussion, how the process of Thematic Management provides the foundation for key enabling circumstances for the following goals. But first, let us summarize as follows.

1. Specific Goals for this Chapter:
    a. To sustain a business and e business enterprise in emerging markets, via the recommended solution of:
    b. Maintaining effective Coopetition.
2. Enabling Circumstances for the above Goals:
    a. Compassion from the very top down, to provide for the development of
    b. innovation and intuition;
    c. ethics and social responsibility, leading to
    d. Wisdom in negotiation and enterprise maintenance.
3. Ways of achieving the above Enabling Circumstances:
    a. understanding cultural differences;
    b. providing a culture of trust, leading to
    c. allowance for risk taking, leading to
    d. allowance for critical debate – reflecting pro and con, leading to
    e. effective business and e business feedback, leading to
    f. a preservation of core knowledge management, leading to
    g. The sustainability of the Business and E Business enterprise.

Why is Coopetition the Best Solution for Emerging Market Business and E-Business?

For a business management environment to allow for risk-taking; team leader debates with senior management and promotion of the understanding of culture and for engendering trust, none of the fore-going can evolve unless there is effective feedback. As discovered in Al Amri and Haynes (2014), monitored error making with feedback (in non-administrative tasks) within innovation and research type teams is a necessary human process towards discovery. Moreover the process extends to self-discovery and if guided in a wise manner it can be shown, that, in an environment of trust, errors can make highly important contributions especially under monitored risk-taking. In the specific case of an emerging market, competition can be fierce, not only from suppliers, new entrants, customers switching products, and given that invariably the market will be largely situated on the internet, competition can also arise from firms who have superior IT and knowledge of the internet. Therefore, especially in an emerging market, alliances are crucial. An alliance is the cooperation side of coopetition. To maintain a cooperative alliance, trust is the main ingredient, and trust is best demonstrated by an openness, and transparency of goals, motivations and agendas. As mentioned earlier in the chapter, allowing an alliance business partner access to appropriate areas of the intranet of the connecting business is a wise strategy. If the connecting business already has a culture of trust and is moving forwards in the development of both the enabling circumstances (B-1-1 through B-1-3), and C-1-1 through C-1-7 achievement ways, then there is a basis for continuing the alliance partnership. That basis is grounded in the connecting business's capacity to contribute to the alliance through innovation and by providing wise counsel and strategy. Once there is an effective cooperation alliance then it follows that the combined alliance can more effectively compete even under fierce competition, and thereby satisfies the second competition element of coopetition. Thus effective cooperation also overflows into effective competition. Note that it is not vice versa.

In the next section we will see how a business and e business could be organized to move in a positive direction towards the seven key elements underlying the enabling circumstances for sustaining the business enterprise in relation to coopetition.

THE ETHICAL AND INNOVATIVE ENVIRONMENT OF THEMATIC MANAGEMENT

For Thematic Management to be effective the themes that are apparent outside the business need to be emulated within the business. This is even more crucial in the cases of ethics and socially responsibility within emerging markets in the case of coopetition.

Ultimately if an environment of creativity, that is both ethical and socially responsible, is to be engendered, then staff need to be recruited who already exemplify those qualities to promote those capacities within the existing staff compliment. Management can't just say "OK we are going to be ethical and socially responsible now and we now need to be more creative and innovative". Such qualities must be allowed to grow, in an environment of trust and mutual team respect. Growth will occur more quickly with an infusion of new staff that already has those qualities. Moreover a business that is socially responsible outside their business, needs to be socially responsible within the business as well

From Figure 4, we can see that internal to the business utilizing Thematic Management are processes that emulate, within the organization, ethical and social responsible behaviors outside the organization:

1. Staff Cooperating Teams: Internal staff teams create alliances with other internal teams, so the culture of cooperative alliance is already a feature within the business. These teams work on research, product development and marketing and how to maintain cooperative alliances outside once they have reached a level of productivity with ethical and internally socially responsible goals. At that point, then, they form the various bodies of engagement with the Cooperative alliances outside the business.
2. Staff Competing Teams: Internal Staff teams that compete, which would usually comprise the marketing and sales forces, which then act as the go between for the Competitors outside the business. These teams also maintain ethical and socially responsible behaviors.
3. Staff Team Mentors: Senior specialists or out-sourced specialists that monitor both the cooperative and competitive internal teams. Their duties would include providing support in terms of up to date market knowledge, research, strategic approaches, and new innovations within the markets. Giving advice and encouragement for monitored risk-taking and ensuring a culturally sensitive environ-

ment and approach in both cooperating and competing internal teams. According to Richardson, Courtney and Haynes (2006), mentoring is crucial in the case of medical disease (e.g. bipolar), because it establishes trust and a place to turn for advice, and precisely for these reasons mentoring is also crucial to establish trust and visionary coherence for staff teams. This mentoring and support is especially essential in the early days of an entrance into emerging markets, because senior specialist guidance is required. It is through the staff team mentors that essential feedback is maintained between both internal teams and the market in terms of trends generally and alliances and competitors specifically.

4. Connecting Senior Management: CEO and senior management connecting with the leaders of both the cooperating internal teams and competing internal teams. Such activities would include the allowance for regular team leader debates with senior management, sharing of updates on higher level strategies and new coopetition market horizons. Haynes (2008) developed a sustained argument for the differences between 'relating to' (in this case, the person as a staff member) and 'relating with' (the staff member as a person). We gave two examples, above, of a former CEO and a former President of the USA, who clearly demonstrated the behaviors of 'relating with', respectively, persons in his employ, and persons throughout, potentially, an entire country. A CEO and his/her senior management cannot connect at the level of humanity with the persons in their employ if they do not 'relate with' them. With the combination of the type of CEO and senior management interaction (mentioned above) and team specialist mentors, eventually an environment of trust will emerge into an environment of developing intuition (Haynes, 2003). Once this happens then a new form of management, the Management of Intuition Haynes, (ibid), is necessary (but outside the scope of this chapter).
5. Internal Team IT and Internet support: A section of the IT department is connected with the cooperating and competing teams to technically match up with their technical aspirations and also provide IT and internet advice for research, product development and market strategies. This IT and internet support is essential in the early days of engaging in emerging markets. This IT support further continues in providing an effective intranet that connects to the staff cooperating teams and specialist team mentors with cooperating alliances in the market place. Also part of the job of the IT team support group is to keep the staff team mentors requests for specific information up to date with latest internet market searches.

SUCCESSFUL COOPERATION ALLIANCES WITHIN COOPETITION

The process of creating successful cooperative alliances during the process of entering Emerging Markets requires a delicate touch that is critically assisted by a demonstration on the part of the proposing business that it has something to offer the alliance. An openness of motivation and agenda via an intranet interchange of ideas between the external body and the internal cooperating teams is therefore of paramount importance. Of course it is assumed that the proposing business already has the required level of expertise. We believe the Thematic Management Model, as proposed above, supports this openness both internally and for external communication and provides the necessary flexibility with mentored and senior management connectivity to allow for expansion of expertise as the need arises.

Successful Competition within Coopetition

In emerging markets the goal posts can change quickly as a result of fierce competition. As outlined in the Thematic Management Model, internet specialists within the IT and internet team support group are available to provide all the detail required, as specific searches generated from the staff team mentors. Marketing and sales personnel cannot be expected to be specialists also in internet searching (although they may like to think that they are), hence their reliance, through the mentor, on the IT and internet specialist support group.

CONCLUSION

We have discussed ten clear reasons why Emerging Markets offer Businesses who wish to establish themselves within an Emerging Market great opportunities to ride the wave of productivity, growth and innovation inherent within such an Emerging Market. We have also discussed clear connecting ideas, in each of those ten reasons, for Emerging Market growth, that support Coopetition, social responsibility and an ethical approach as the way forward for the sustainability of the Business within the Emerging Market either as a new entrant or as an existing growing company.

The current state of the development of the internet is now a crucial world arena for both emerging and continuing markets. Businesses need to realize that competitors who have specialist internet IT personnel pose a serious threat, and unless they do likewise, they will soon fall away. Businesses also need to realize that ethics and social responsibility and mechanisms (such as access to each other's intranet) for indicating openness of motivation and agenda are collectively the only wise way to engage successfully in a co-operative alliance. In the case of cooperative alliances, it is also critically important for each alliance business to continue to demonstrate contributions made in terms of creativity and innovation of ideas and product development and/or reduced cost complementarities.

This chapter has provided a management model, Thematic Management, which we believe successfully integrates all of the above requirements into a workable internal management solution for both aspects of effective Coopetition especially in emerging markets. In addition Thematic Management, as it is outlined in this chapter, provides further ingredients for successful Coopetition, especially for the cooperation aspect, namely, through the development and maintenance of ethics and social responsibility.

The Thematic Management Model incorporates ethics and social responsibility, in an encouraged environment of trust, by providing for the interaction of two types of teams. More precisely, the teams are cooperation based and competition based, within the organization. Each team is mentored by senior strategy specialists, supported by IT and internet specialists and given support, and advised by, top management who also allow time for team leaders to engage in debating sessions, with the senior management, and provide encouragement for (monitored) risk-taking.

The motto of Thematic Management, as it is developed in this chapter, is As Outside, So Inside. The continuing theme throughout the chapter is that a business needs to enact ethics and social responsibility in conjunction with creativity and innovation as exemplars outside its organization. In the case of this chapter, such exemplars are in relation to its customers, suppliers, cooperative alliances and to its competitors. How then can customers, suppliers, alliances and competitors take this recommended kind of business seriously if the business (and its e business processes) itself, cannot also provide the same appropriate exemplars within its organization? The question, once raised, should answer itself.

REFERENCES

Al Amri, A., & Haynes, J. (2014). ICT and Organizations: A Model for the Management of Errors in Organizations with Reference to SMEs in Oman. *Proceedings of the 2nd International Conference on Applied Information and Communication Technologies, ICAICT*. Muscat.

Arockiasamy, S., Haynes, J., & Al Rashdi, M. (2012). Strategic Planning to Protect Information Resources in the Event of Disasters and Suggestions for Recovery (with Importance for Oman). *Proceedings of the International Conference on Psychological Sciences and Behaviors ICPSB '12*, Hong Kong, China (Vol. 40, pp. 101-104). IPEDR. Retrieved from http://www.ipedr.com/vol40/021-ICPSB2012-P10012.pdf

Bergh, K., Lefkovitch, J., Scotti, S., & Warner, B. (2009). *General Motors Corporation Case One – Internal Analysis*.

Brandenburger, A., & Nalebuff, B. (1997). *Coopetition*. New York: Doubleday.

Haynes, J. (2003). *Perspectival Thinking: A Phenomenological Approach to Knowledge Management*. Retrieved from http://www.dfki.uni-kl.de/~klein/wm2003-pre-proceedings/pdf/haynes.pdf

Haynes, J. (2003). The Management of Intuition. *AJIS*, *11*(1), 12–18. doi:10.3127/ajis.v11i1.135

Haynes, J. (2007). *Perspectival Thinking: For Inquiring Organizations*. California: Information Science Press.

Haynes, J. (2008). *Technique and Technology: Ethical Guidelines for the Role of Technology for Medical Science in Arab Countries. Journal of the Arab Society For Medical Research, 3(2), 185 – 191.* Retrieved from.

Haynes, J. (2013). Why 'Ethics and Social Responsibility' is Important for Knowledge Management. Muscat: *International Conference on Knowledge and Resource Sharing*.

Hendy, N. (2014). Co-opetition: the new business buzzword. *The Age*. Retrieved from http://www.theage.com.au/small-business/franchising/coopetition-the-new-business-buzzword-20140304-341lc.html

Jonas, W. (2005). *Mosby's dictionary of complementary & alternative medicine*. St. Louis, Mo.: Elsevier Mosby.

Kraut, R. (2001). *Aristotle's Ethics. Plato.stanford.edu*. Retrieved from http://plato.stanford.edu/entries/aristotle-ethics/

Nalebuff, B. (1996). Co-opetition. Presentation. Yale School of Management, New Haven, CT, USA

Rapoza, K. (2011). *Forbes Welcome. Forbes.com*.

Richardson, S., Courtney, J., & Haynes, J. (2006). Theoretical principles for knowledge management system design: Application to pediatric bipolar disorder. *Decision Support Systems*, *42*(3), 1321–1337. doi:10.1016/j.dss.2005.11.001

Saran, C. (2015). *Interview: Ralph Szygenda, group vice-president and CIO at General Motors. ComputerWeekly*.

Slywotzky, A., & Wise, R. (2003). Demand innovation: GM's OnStar case. *Strategy and Leadership*, *31*(4), 17–22. doi:10.1108/10878570310483942

Chapter 3
Corporate Social Responsibility in the Bahraini Construction Companies

Asma Ayari
LILLE 1 University, France

ABSTRACT

The purpose of this study is to give a description of ethical business cultures in Bahraini construction companies. Construction companies in the Middle East are facing charges in terms of exploitation of workers and poor working conditions. The construction sector is one of the most dynamic in Bahrain, and its participation in national GDP is increasing. It is also the most important sector in the creation of jobs. Bahrain, as in the Gulf countries, employs a workforce from India and Asia, one of the lowest in the international labor market. This study analyzes the reality of the CSR in the construction sector and proposes some guidelines for the role of Bahraini stakeholders in the implementation of the social responsibility.

INTRODUCTION

The interest in the concept of corporate social responsibility (CSR) has increased in recent years, both theoretically in order to explain this, and operationally so as to develop performance indicators in the long term. The construction sector, particularly in the Gulf countries, has received attention as a research topic in CSR. Certainly, the growth and development of the economies of the Gulf in general are based on oil revenues, but the non-hydrocarbon activity will continue to be dynamic, in particular the construction and real estate sector has regained ground after being severely affected by the 2009 financial crisis. Growth in construction and real estate has spawned a wave of massive recruitment of Asian labor for labor positions require no qualifications or skills.

In recent years, Gulf countries are under much criticism by the organizations which works on protecting the rights of migrant workers. Although this is an international situation but it takes a special significance in the Gulf countries, especially UAE and Qatar, as they always have large construction

DOI: 10.4018/978-1-4666-9864-2.ch003

projects. These countries are often put on the spot when it comes to denounce the conditions of workers in the construction sector. Workers in the construction sector are often face difficult working conditions. Despite the seriousness of laws and legislations organizing this sector, the conditions are so difficult that they can cause, according to international organizations, worker exploitation and abuse against them1.

In the kingdom of Bahrain, "the economic sector with the highest number of new work permits for regular workers continued (in 2014) to be the Construction sector with a share of 36.8% of total regular work permits issued, followed by Wholesale and retail trade achieving 20.2%, then Manufacturing sector at 11.4%."2

This study will consider, in its first part, the concept of corporate social responsibility (CSR). In the second part, it will explore the government and company's procedures to improve the work condition in the Bahraini construction sector.

1. THEORETICAL FRAMEWORK

Theoretical research on business ethics developed in the 1960s at the request of stakeholders. Many theorists have taken part in this debate, contributed to the identification of the stakeholder's attributes, and determined the reasons for their action (Anderson, 1978; Carroll, 1989; Clarkson, 1991, 1995; Egri & Herman, 2000; Freeman, 1984; Freeman & Reed, 1983; Goodpastor, 1991; Mitchell, Agle, & Wood, 1997; Rowley & Moldoveanu, 2003; Wood, 1994).

The principle of responsibility is an old legal principle and a new moral principle of our time. Formally, the word responsibility is not in contradiction with its etymology; it is always about the actions and decisions and their impact on others. Take responsibility, be responsible implies a willingness called sometimes engagement.

Operating in a globalized environment, companies are expected to adopt a clear and transparent approach of Social Responsibility.

For companies, CSR is, at the same time, a symbolic tool for legitimacy, a political tool to control or influence the very strong relationship between business and society, an economic tool favoring short and long-term results or a strategic tool for better integrating the company into its environment (Paone, 2009). Nevertheless, CSR is a voluntary approach and a free interpretation of the obligations that the company recognizes.

1.1. Emergence and Definition of the Concept

Early research on CSR (1950s) has focused on the assessment of this phenomenon contours. The studies that followed the emergence of the concept sought to determine the responsibilities of the company towards the society.

Over 50 years, academics and practitioners have tried to understand and analyze the CSR. Several researchers have gained recognition for their scientific studies on CSR (Bowen, 1953; Carroll, 1979). Immediately, this concept became popular. The phenomenon has grown in importance over the years and now occupies its place at the heart of corporate strategy (Capron & Quairel-Lanoizelee, 2007).

Bowen insists that companies are vital centers of power and decision-making, and that their actions affect the lives of citizens in many areas. He concludes that companies are accountable for their actions in a much wider sphere than that of the economy. His book aims to educate businesspersons in the values "considered desirable in our society".

The CSR concept is built gradually from one phase to another. It goes through a categorization of responsibilities and a question on how to act. In this sense, if for some, the responsibility is economic, whereas for others, it goes beyond the law.

However, despite all the literature produced on the CSR concept and the important contributions of recent decades, it continues to elude any unanimous or universal definition. The definition and delimitation of the concept of social performance are still controversial. However, we will try to explore in the following some definitions that generate less controversy.

Bowen (1953) defines CSR as "a requirement for businessmen to implement the policies, decisions and follow guidelines that meet the goals and values considered desirable in our society" (p. 6). The author refers to the obligation to follow a certain course of action and policies that reflect the goals and values of the society, which must comply with those of society. This definition does not necessarily mean that the businessperson, as a member of the society, has no right to criticize those values and contribute to their improvement [...] However, they cannot place their own values above those of society.

Given the growing importance of CSR, it is important to recognize that Bowen is one of the first to demonstrate that the debate on CSR has not become only acceptable, but also fashionable in the business sphere.

Bowen analyzed the issue of Social Responsibility on a macro scale. He was able to demonstrate its critical importance to the US economy and establish links between the public interest and private interest. After fifty years of development, following a long history of "stop and go", the concept of CSR has continued to evolve and Bowen's followers have made tremendous progress and helped create a new academic field - "Business in Society".

Carroll (1979) has defined the concept of CSR as a set of obligations to the society: "the social responsibility of business encompasses everything: economic expectations, legal, ethical, and other discretionary expectations of society in relation to a company in a time given"3. Carroll (1979) distinguishes four types of bonds: economic (be profitable, producing products that meet quality standards...), legal compliance (with laws and regulations), ethical (act in accordance with moral principles shared within the company) and philanthropic (charitable act and charity). Carroll's definition is considered to be the foundation of several theoretical approaches to CSR (Attarca & Jacquot, 2005).

The European Commission defines the concept of CSR as the "voluntary integration by companies of social and environmental concerns in their business operations and in their interaction with their stakeholders". In the same vein, the WBCSD (World Business Council for Sustainable Development) (2002) speaks of "business contribution to sustainable economic development, working with employees, their families, the local community and society at large to improve their quality of life" (Low Kim Cheng & Ang Sik, 2012, p 94).

The main idea that emerges from the definitions shown above would be the contingent nature of the content of CSR in terms of the company's business (national or international) or organization. "Most definitions of corporate social responsibility describe it as a concept whereby companies integrate social and environmental concerns in their business operations and in their relationships with their stakeholders. Being socially responsible means not only fulfilling legal expectations, but also going beyond compliance and investing "more" into human capital, the environment and relations with stakeholders" (Commission of The European Communities, 2001, p 8).

These definitions emphasize the importance of the concept of corporate commitment, and state that this commitment must go beyond the legal requirements and expectations. However, these approaches differ in how to approach the CSR structure. Thus, most of the international institutions tend to concentrate on the relations with the local community and employee family (WBCSD), with a focus on more specific issues such as child labor.

Finally, divergences in defining CSR can be explained by differences in the institutional, economic and social history and system values. In the US, for example, CSR has traditionally been defined as a philanthropic model. Businesses spend a portion of their profits to charitable purposes. The European model, meanwhile, is much more focused on applying the criteria related to social interaction at all stages of business activities.

1.2. Stakeholder Theory: The Dominant Approach of Corporate Social Responsibility

According to the neoliberal traditional mannerism, the debate about the role of business in society was mainly centered on the company and its performance, while the broader context in which it operated was marginalized.

In 1970, the economist Milton Friedman, Nobel laureate, quoted his own book: "The company has one and only one social responsibility of business - to use its resources and engage in activities designed to increase its profits, so long as it stays within the rules of the game, which is to say, engages in open and free competition without deception or fraud".

After stating this reflection, Friedman, who by vocation was monetarist, became the leader of the neoliberal doctrine whose credo is "profit is the sole criterion of all values". In the book "Capitalism and Freedom" (1962), Friedman severely criticized the new tendency (Wolf, 2001) that social responsibility is included in the strategy of corporations, while affirming that managers in this way destroy the foundations of a free society. According to him, managers should think "make as much money for their stockholders as possible ".

Why did Friedman embrace this intellectual attitude towards the CSR concept? One possible explanation is that his attitude emanated from his opinion regarding the concepts of CSR and CFP (Corporate Financial Performance). Obviously, these concepts are in an adversarial relationship because their goals are mutually exclusive. Having declared supporter of CSR, Friedman believed that spending money for something that gives questionable results was absolutely not in the interest of companies. It follows that such cases are not fair play towards shareholders. According to him, it is advisable to avoid paying money (wasting part of the profit) for everything and anything in relation with CSR (Wolf, 2001)

In connection with the attitude developed towards money, he also stated a very descriptive statement: "Nobody spends somebody else's money as carefully as he spends his own. Nobody uses somebody else's resources as carefully as he uses his own".

Since his article, which made headlines in the 1970s which was often criticized in the debates on financial ethics, Friedman repeated in 2000 his extreme view: "The only entities who can have responsibilities are individuals" (Marks, 2006). Friedman's statements have generated a debate among leaders and managers in the US and around the world, especially in the major academic and political institutions. Today, the mission of the company is the object of controversy in the United States (Stalk & Lachenauer, 2005).

Figure 1. A convergence of interests

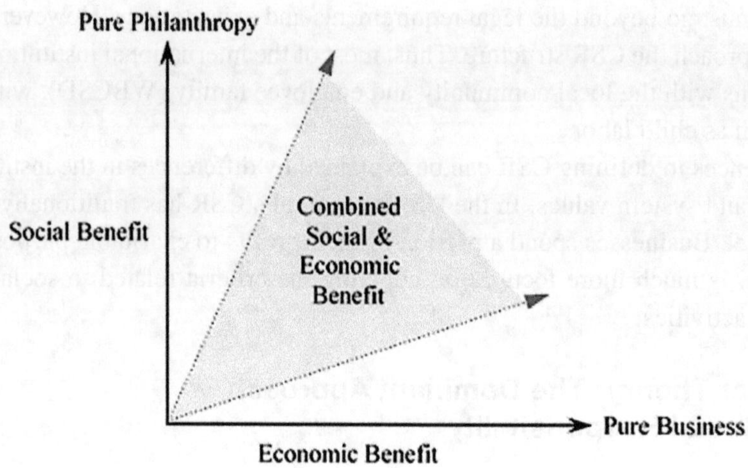

In terms of CSR, it is legitimate to confirm that it is impossible for companies to act individually as the interests and objectives of stakeholders are very different. It is therefore highly recommended to make a balance that would take into account the legitimate interests of all. To do this, consultation is required between the stakeholders to implement CSR.

Regarded as the essence of the Stakeholder Theory, convergence is shown in the figure 1 below.

Freeman and his colleagues (Wicks & Parmar, 2004) refer to the stakeholder management as the issue that needs to be well thought out to successfully create wealth. Economic value is created by people who voluntarily associate and cooperate in improving the living conditions of all. They think that managers must develop relationships, inspire stakeholders and create communities where everyone will try to give one's best to deliver the value promised by the company.

The stakeholder theory is primarily intended for managers; it guides them to develop their shares and motivate leaders to respect the interests of all stakeholders in the decision process, while considering the profit creation as the main objective (Freeman, Wicks & Parmar, 2004).

Advocates of stakeholder theory have also raised the issue of the position and the role of governments. Opinions differ on how governments should encourage the rapid implementation of the concept of CSR. Most theorists defend the idea that the government should provide indirect support and reduce direct intervention in this area. That's why the concept of CSR still maintains its voluntary nature (Andag, 2010). Despite this voluntariness, the CSR concept, whose standards are becoming increasingly high, is experiencing a permanent expansion (Hopkins, 2011).

2. THE CONSTRUCTION SECTOR IN BAHRAIN

2.1. The Economic Context

Rich in hydrocarbons, member countries of the Gulf Cooperation Countries (GCC) are the growing power of the Gulf oil-exporting Countries. They are becoming a major hub for investment given their large trade activity and strategic geographical position.

Bahrain is experiencing a continuous economic development. For nearly half a century, it hosts the most audacious investors and major projects. All came to participate in the construction of a major regional center (Macdonald, 2013).

Investments in the oil sector have created a rush for black gold since the 1940s, but more recently, the country's leaders realized that their dependence on oil and gas makes them vulnerable to price changes of these resources (Hvidt, 2013). Also, hydrocarbons are not evidently eternal resources.

A significant portion of revenues generated by oil has been reinvested in economic diversification projects, especially in areas with high yields and for which domestic demand was high, namely the construction and real estate sector4.

Every year new real estate projects are being launched by the government or private investors. The real estate market in Bahrain is certainly in an evolutionary stage. Oxford Business Group (OBG) (2009) concludes, in its latest report on Bahrain that the construction sector of the Kingdom has proven to be quite resilient despite high inflation, lack of land and rising material costs.

According to the report "Bahrain Building Construction Industry" (2004)5, the construction industry in Bahrain is steadily increasing. It is witnessing a housing bubble similar to what is happening in Qatar and, to a lesser extent, in Dubai. The construction sector is one of the most dynamic in Bahrain, and its participation in national GDP is increasing. It is also the most important sector in the creation of jobs.

In line with the legal frameworks set out in the National Strategic Master Plan for Bahrain, outlook 2030, the Ministry of Works is responsible for carrying out major projects in the construction sector and putting forward the strategy of the country that focuses on infrastructure as a driver of the country's economic growth6.

To accomplish this strategic plan, Bahrain seeks to attract public and private investments to create and maintain the infrastructure and services required7.

The study of the construction sector shows that the competition is very fierce between developers and companies to offer the lowest prices and the most comprehensive services. To achieve these goals, both private and public developers rely on reducing costs, especially those related to labor. For this, Bahrain, as in the Gulf countries, employs a workforce from India and Asia, one of the lowest in the international labor market8.

2.2. Recruitment of Labor

The number of foreigners working in the Gulf countries varies by country. According to United Nations statistics, 7.8 million immigrants (out of a total population of 9.2 million, 2013) work in the UAE. In Bahrain, out of the 647.578 people currently in employment, 499.797 are expatriates (Labour Market Regulatory Authority Stats, LMRA, 013). With immigrants mainly from India, Sri Lanka, Nepal, Pakistan, Bangladesh.., Bahrain, like other Gulf countries, attracts low- and high-skilled expatriates because of its economic attractiveness and motivating infrastructure. The recruitment of labor among these nationalities could be justified by the low cost of labor compared to other nationalities (Shah, 2006).

The construction sector occupies a prominent place among sectors employing foreigners. Workers in this sector are usually recruited by construction companies. Otherwise, in most cases by specialized recruitment agencies. The recruitment of workers in the building sector is carried out exclusively through a local sponsor (Kafeel) who is responsible for their visa and legal residence (Kapiszewski, 2006).

Immigrants should pay a fee for his trip and visa. Often these costs amounted to several months of work on site. Once there, the immigrant is entrusted to his Kafeel, who keeps his passport and agrees to pay his wages and guarantee him decent housing and good working conditions (Shah, 2006).

3. THE REALITY OF CSR IN THE CONSTRUCTION COMPANIES

Most Bahraini construction companies are family businesses. The management of the company is usually held by family members and decision-making power passes from father to son9. The new generation of directors of these family businesses are mostly young graduates coming from different horizons (business, engineering, architecture...). They usually have the required capabilities that allow them to improve and implement approaches to CSR. They are more flexible and perceive CSR as an asset and not as a constraint. They would likely to be more open to implement actions, to improve the loyalty of consumers and customers, to improve the working conditions of the employees and respect the environment. However, the reality seems to be different. Indeed, even the youngest managers justify the absence of CSR into their business by a lack of financial resources and time. They do not seem capable of releasing "time" to fully integrate CSR activities in their vision of development of the company.

4. THE REALITY OF THE WORK CONDITION OF EMPLOYEES IN THE CONSTRUCTION SECTOR

Employees in the construction sector, who emigrate to escape poverty and unemployment in their countries of origin, seem to endure poor working conditions. This is a reality that has been noted several times in international reports on the situation of foreign workers in the Gulf countries; especially those of human rights (such as Human Rights Watch) or work (such as the International Labor Organization). Unlike Bahrain, where working conditions seem to be better, the UAE and Qatar have always been accused of making little effort in terms of workers' rights (e.g. The construction of football stadiums for the 2022 World Football Cup to be held in Qatar[10]).

As reported by Human Rights Watch[11] (2013): "migrant workers reported extensive labor law violations. Common complaints included late or unpaid wages. Some lived in overcrowded and unsanitary labor camps, and lacked access to potable water. Many workers said they received false information about their jobs and salaries before arriving and signed contracts in Qatar under coercive circumstance".

Despite the fact that the working conditions seem to be much better in Bahrain as the new Labour Law for the private sector (2012) ensures proper rights for workers, some shortcomings should be highlighted because they come under the CSR in companies working in the field of construction. It is noteworthy here that 63% of Bahraini SMEs had more than 60 Bahraini Employees[12].

It should be noted that the difficulties encountered by workers begin before arriving in the host country. Indeed, construction companies and recruitment agencies tend to make full use of the inadequacy of the workers by giving empty promises. It generally starts with fairly high amounts that workers must pay for recruitment agencies before their departure for the host country or upon return to the country of origin. According to the report "*Bahrain Building Construction Industry" (2004)*, the cost of work visas is usually between 2000 $ and 3000 $. It goes without saying that it is a high price for the citizens of poor countries. Upon arrival, workers are asked to give their passports to the employer. This way, the employer retains the immigrants and prevents any attempt to escape. Working conditions are often unconventional and uncomfortable (housing, transportation, food.). Generally, basic wages are below international standards and do not exceed in most cases 100 BD (± $ 260). In addition, these salaries are not always paid on time.

As developers are often working under pressure and engaged in contracts with deadlines, they are forced to increase the working hours. Workers are then asked to work overtime. They can spend up to 12 hours on site. Workers feel compelled to accept this situation because they have no other alternatives. They prefer to keep their jobs despite they are hard to bear[13]. Whatever happens, the situation is still better than what they could endure back home. It should also be emphasized that the choice to come to live and work in Bahrain is personal. Gulf countries are often presented as countries offering career opportunities and attractive wages.

The difficult situation and work conditions induce a feeling of dissatisfaction among workers. However, they are completely unable to express this feeling without the legal structures that enable them to assert their rights. They live all the time with the fear of being sent back to their country of origin as companies hold their passports.

4.1. Organizations' Responsibility

Corporate Social Responsibility must be conceptualized through a pyramid in which ethical responsibilities are prioritized after economic and legal responsibilities. Building Construction companies must recognize the importance of construction workers instead of treating them as second degrees workers (Green, 2008).

It is worth mentioning here that the dependence on foreign labor will continue as long as it is still not possible to replace it by a local work force and as the Gulf countries still undertake major projects. To some extent, this workforce is the cornerstone of the building sector (Jones, Confort & Hillier, 2006).

Thus, the Social Responsibility goes mainly through the payment of decent wages in accordance with the terms of the contract and ensuring proper working conditions. Any form of injustice and discrimination in the company should be sanctioned. Companies must undertake serious efforts to improve working conditions. They must comply with the laws and regulations organizing the business and guaranteeing the rights of all. Also, they must have strict safety guidelines to ensure the safety of worker in both the workplace and in its environment.

Thus, the moral obligation of the company is to have an RS strategy that could bring the principles and values -to be taken into account in the company's management- into reality as interventions for the benefit of workers. Companies should seek continually their interest while taking into account the changing regulatory and ethical framework (soft law). Ethical conduct of the companies should be considered as a management tool because the Social business performance is measured in terms of its social sensitivity. (Gond, 2010). Of course, ethical conduct can be costly but its absence is much more expensive.

Also, they should make voluntary commitments beyond regulatory constraints in order to meet the expectations of stakeholders. The initiatives undertaken by companies contribute to a better alignment between the management decisions and the economic and social objectives.

However, companies should not assume alone the responsibility of poor working conditions and workers' disaffection. Recruitment agencies must also take on their responsibility in providing reliable information to workers and avoiding false promises.

4.2. Government Responsibility

The Bahraini government has definitely a major responsibility in the process of improving the working conditions of workers and the integration of CSR in the public and private construction companies. The role of government is to ensure the implementation of laws and regulations by recruitment agencies and companies (Murray & Dainty, 2009).

Several companies defend themselves by arguing that they have no idea of how recruitment agencies are working, in particular with regard to the recruitment of immigrant workers.

The government also has the responsibility to change the laws and regulations related to labor law when they are no longer effective. It is a way to force the companies and recruitment agencies to comply with this legal framework. This effectively ensures decent wages and adequate housing for immigrants. The main reason that some companies are acting irresponsibly towards immigrant workers is the absence/ weaknesses of laws and regulations.

The efforts undertaken to improve the legal framework (The Labour Law, No. 36 of 2012) must be supported by monitoring and controlling units. Also, the initiatives taken by the Municipality of the Capital on mandatory housing conditions for immigrant workers (40 square feet of space per person, adequate ventilation, air conditioning and lighting, as well as a minimum number of toilets. must be implemented and generalized.

It is therefore not fair to simply blame the construction companies for exploiting and abusing immigrant workers since the laws are either poorly enforced or not enforced at all.

CONCLUSION

This chapter offers a preliminary exploration of the reality of the corporate social responsibility (CSR) in the Bahraini construction sector and proposes some guidelines for the role of Bahraini stakeholders in the implementation of the social responsibility.

The study mentioned that Bahraini construction companies have their own specific approach to CSR. Although, corporate social responsibility is widely adopted in the Bahrain construction industry, the law only set minimum standards and not the upper limit of what can be done. Problems of the poor conditions of workers persist. Companies should not assume alone the responsibility of poor working conditions and workers' disaffection. Recruitment agencies and the Bahraini government should also take their responsibility to improve the work conditions.

This study provides an accessible review of issues in the area of CSR in the Bahraini construction industry. It might interest other researchers, professionals and practitioners to explore the issues related to the CSR implementation strategies in this sector.

REFERENCES

Ackerman, R., & Bauer, R. (1976), Corporate Social Responsiveness: The Modern Dilemma, VA, Reston.

Acquier, A., & Gond, J. P. (2007). Aux sources de la responsabilité sociale de l'entreprise: À la (re) découverte d'un ouvrage fondateur, Social Responsabilities of the Businessman d'Howard Bowen. *Finance Contrôle Stratégie*, *10*(2), 5–35.

Andag, R. A. (2010). Corporate social responsibility and the mining industry. Ingraining people's participation in mining communities through CSR (pp. 25–27). Human Rights Forum. Retrieved from http://smallbusiness.chron.com/corporate-social-responsibility-construction-industry-72475.html

Attarca, M., & Jacquot, T. (2005). La représentation de la Responsabilité Sociale des Entreprises: une confrontation entre les approches théoriques et les visions managériales. Paper presented at *Journée Développement Durable de l'Association Internationale de Management Stratégique, Aix en Provence.*

Bakr, A., & Homewood, B. (2013). Alarming exploitation of workers in Qatar. *Reuters*. Retrieved from http://www.reuters.com/article/2013/11/18/us-soccer-world-qatar-amnesty-idUSBRE9AH0HH20131118

Blowfield, M., & Murray, A. (2008). *Corporate Responsibility: A critical introduction*. Oxford: Oxford University press.

Bowen, H.-R. (1953). *Social Responsibilities of the Businessman* (p. 6). Brothers, New York: Harper.

Capron, M., & Quairel-Lanoizelée, F. (2007). La responsabilité sociale d'entreprise. Coll. Repères, éd. La Découverte.

Carroll, A. B. (1979). A Three-Dimensional Conceptual Model of Corporate Performance. *Academy of Management Review*, *4*, 497–505.

Chauveau, A., & Rosé, J.-J. (2003). *L'entreprise responsable: responsabilité sociale-éthique*. Editions d'Organisation.

Commission of the European Communities. (2009). Green Paper, Promoting a European Framework for Corporate Social responsibility.

Crane, A., & Matten, D. (2004). *Business Ethics*. Oxford University Press.

Freeman, R. E., Wicks, A. C., & Parmar, B. (2004). Stakeholder Theory and the "Corporate Objective Revisited". *Organization Science*, *15*(3), 364–369. doi:10.1287/orsc.1040.0066

Green, S. (2008). The evolution of corporate social responsibility in construction: defining the parameters. In A. Murray & M. Dainty (Eds.), *Corporate Social Responsibility in the Construction Industry* (pp. 24–53). Abingdon: Taylor & Francis.

Green, S. (2009). The evolution of corporate social responsibility in construction: defining the parameters. In M. Murray & A. Dainty (Eds.), *Corporate social responsibility in the construction industry* (pp. 24–53). Oxon: Taylor & Francis.

Hopkins, M. (2011). A Planetary Bargain: Corporate Social Responsibility Comes of Age.

Hvidt, M. (2013). *Kuwait programme on development, governance and globalization in the gulf states. Economic diversification in GCC countries: Past record and Future trends*. The London School of Economics and Political Science.

Jones, P., Comfort, D., & Hillier, D. (2006). Corporate social responsibility and the UK construction industry. *Journal of Corporate Real Estate*, *8*(3), 134–150. doi:10.1108/14630010610711757

Jones, R. (2004). Construction sector in Qatar in 3.35% growth. *Arabian Business*. Retrieved from http://www.arabianbusiness.com/construction-sector-in-qatar-in-3-35-growth-134074.html

Low Kim Cheng, P., & Ang Sik, L. (2012). Confucian leadership and corporate social responsibility (CSR), the way forward. *Asian Journal of Business Research*, *2*(1), 92–116.

MacDonald, A. (2015). GCC construction sector may face skills shortage. Retrieved from http://www.gulf-dailynews.com/NewsDetails.aspx?storyid=347321

Mankin, D. (2009). *Human resource development*. Oxford University Press.

Murray, M., & Dainty, A. (2009). Corporate social responsibility: challenging the construction industry. In M. Murray & A. Dainty (Eds.), *Corporate social responsibility in the construction industry* (pp. 3–23). Oxon: Taylor & Francis.

Pedersen, E. R. (2006). Making corporate responsibility (CSR) operable: How companies translate stakeholder dialogue into practice. *Business and Society Review*, *111*(2), 137–163. doi:10.1111/j.1467-8594.2006.00265.x

Porter, M.-E., & Kramer, M.-R. (2006). Strategy and society: The link between competitive advantage and corporate social responsibility. *Harvard Business Review*, *84*(12), 78–92. PMID:17183795

Qatar Admits Deaths in Migrant Workers. (2014, May 14). *The Guardian*. Retrieved from http://www.theguardian.com/world/2014/may/14/qatar-admits-deaths-in-migrant-workers

Report Qatar Construction Industry. (2011, February). Ventures Middle East ID 1574166.

Tchaman, J.-P., & Estay, Ch. (2004). La pratique de la responsabilité sociale et ses implications dans l'entreprise. *Gestion*, *2000*(July-August), 31–47.

ENDNOTES

1 For example, see Amnesty's international report on poor conditions of work and daily life of foreign workers in Qatar, published on November 17th, 2013.

2 Bahrain Labour Market Indicators, 2014, http://blmi.lmra.bh/2014/09/mi_dashboard.xml Study of the key problems and challenges of SMEs in Bahrain, Report commensurate to Phase 1 of the D&B-Tamkeen Engagement October 2008. Available online: http://www.lf.bh/Reports/Study%20of%20Key%20Problems%20%20Challenges%20of%20SMEs%20in%20Bahrain%20-%20Report%20deliverable%20for%20Phase%201.pdf

3 Archie CARROLL, "A Three-Dimensional Conceptual Model of Corporate Performance", *Academy of Management Review*, Vol. 4, no. 4, October 1979, p. 500.

4 Saudi Arabia Power Report Q1 2015, December 2014, Business Monitor International- 70p.

5 Bahrain_building_construction_industry, (2004), Retrieved from: http://www.researchandmarkets.com/reports/2010711/ bahrain_building_construction_industry.

6 http://www.works.gov.bh/English/Pages/home2.aspx.

7 Bahrain_building_construction_industry, (2004), Retrieved from: http://www.researchandmarkets.com/reports/2010711/ bahrain_building_construction_industry

8 Ibid.

9 Bahrain_building_construction_industry, (2004), Retrieved from: http://www.researchandmarkets.com/reports/2010711/ bahrain_building_construction_industry

10 The Guardian

11 http://www.hrw.org/world-report/2013/country-chapters/qatar.

12 Bahrain Labour Market Indicators, 2014, http://blmi.lmra.bh/2014/09/mi_dashboard.xml Study of the key problems and challenges of SMEs in Bahrain, Report commensurate to Phase 1 of the D&B-Tamkeen Engagement October 2008. Available online: http://www.lf.bh/Reports/Study%20of%20Key%20Problems%20%20Challenges%20of%20SMEs%20in%20Bahrain%20-%20Report%20deliverable%20for%20Phase%201.pdf

13 http://www.theguardian.com/world/2014/may/14/qatar-admits-deaths-in-migrant-workers.

Chapter 4
Corporate Social Responsibility of Public Banking Sector for Sustainable Development:
A Comparative Study between Malaysia and Egypt

Naglaa Fathy El Dessouky
Sadat Academy for Management Sciences (SAMS), Egypt & University of Bahrain (UOB), Bahrain

ABSTRACT

Corporate Social Responsibility (CSR) has become a significant field of studies to stress the importance of the new role of organizations towards the society for sustainable development. Nowadays, an enormous number of authors have been participating in this field to highlight the responsibility of organizations towards the community, society and the natural environment where they are operating. Despite the growing number of researches related to CSR in the developed countries little empirical studies have been devoted to examine CSR concept and practice in the African countries, the MENA region (Middle-East and North Africa), as well as in the Golf countries. This chapter seeks to study CSR concept and practice in the emerging market economies (EMEs). It will mainly focus on the implementations of CSR by the public banking sector. We will investigate the role of the public banking sector existing in an Arab country in comparison to an Asian country to explain and analyze the similarities and differences of CSR activities in both experiences. In this comparative study we will primarily examine Banque Misr, as one of the oldest and largest public bank in Egypt and the Malayan Banking Berhad (trading as Maybank) as the largest public bank in Malaysia. After a meticulous review of literature, we propose a systemic framework to study CSR practices and policy implementations. We illustrated the CSR as a constant process where all variables are interrelated and are affecting each other in a mutual approach. In this systemic framework we advocated to study all significant variables related to CSR practice as: the history/philosophy development, core-values, CSR adopted definition, motives, key players, approaches, stakeholders focus, sectors of intervention and mechanisms of policy implementations. The chapter concludes that common CSR policies exist between the Malaysian and the Egyptian experience. Nevertheless the Malaysian model has formulated an elaborated and further sophisticated CSR public banking program. Meanwhile, the Egyptian model needs to adopt more global oriented CSR public banking policies, in particular to assure the sustainable development requirements.

DOI: 10.4018/978-1-4666-9864-2.ch004

INTRODUCTION

Corporate Social Responsibility (CSR) was introduced by authors as a momentous concept to declare the new role of organizations towards the broad society and community. The concept of CSR encourages the organizations, public and private alike, to take a fully considerations of the community, the society and the natural environment where they are operating.

Since then CSR represents a paradigm shift for organizations' activities to be more ethical, social and environment oriented. This movement of CSR aims to create an enabling environment for organizations where ethics and sustainable development are more fostered. A proliferation of definitions and practices related to CSR has been developed however no specific concept or program has been allocated yet.

The chapter will start with a review of literature dealing with the CSR theory and practice, more specific, which parallel the core objective of the research. Afterwards, the chapter will attempt to introduce a systemic framework to study CSR practices and implementations. Through this framework, the chapter will mainly investigate the role of the public banking sector existing in an Arab country in comparison to an Asian country to explain and analyze the similarities and differences of CSR activities in both experiences. In this comparative study we will primarily examine Banque Misr in Egypt and the Malayan Banking Berhad (trading as Maybank) in Malaysia. The conceptual framework will mostly explore: the history/ philosophy development of corporate social responsibility, the core-values of CSR, the adopted definition of CSR, the motives of CSR, key players: external or internal CSR initiatives, the CSR adopted approaches, external or internal stakeholders focus, and finally, multilateral or unilateral sector of intervention and the mechanisms of intervention. At the end, the chapter will present a synthesis comparison between the two models where we will highlight the similarities and discrepancies between both experiences the Malaysian and the Egyptian to allocate areas of improvement and development.

Research Problem

Over the last few years writings about CSR have been dedicated a momentum attention to the theoretical and empirical backgrounds of the concept of Corporate Social Responsibility. The concept fosters organizations to adopt ethical, social and environmental activities towards the society where they are operating. Despite the growing attention dedicated to the concept, no specific description or classification for its activities has been allocated yet.

Recently, greater interests have been devoted to study CSR and business ethics in countries of emerging market economies (EMEs) since these countries are considered nowadays as the new key players participating in the development and the growth of the global economy. Despite the growing number of researches related to CSR in the developed countries little empirical studies have been devoted to examine CSR theory and practice in the countries of emerging market economies (EMEs), more especially, in Africa and the Arab world (for more details see, among others, Fathy El Dessouky, 2011; Lindgreen et al., 2010; Lindgreen et al., 2009; Visser, 2006a, 2006b, 2008; Lockett et al., 2006; Amaeshi et al., 2006; Bio-Tchné and Christensen, 2006; Eweje, 2006; Prahalad, 2004; Welford, 2004).

Moreover, a thorough review of the literature demonstrates that the interest of the researchers towards the study of CSR related to the public sector remains relatively limited in comparison to the studies related to the private sector (Petkoski and Twose (eds), 2003). Through the literature, the private sector has been demonstrated as the key player in the implementations of CSR activities whereas very poor number of writings has been dedicated to examine the role of the public sector to foster the practices of CSR.

Research Objective

This chapter seeks to study the CSR concept and practice in the emerging market economies (EMEs). It will mainly focus on the implementations of CSR by the public banking sector. We will investigate the role of the public banking sector existing in an Arab country in comparison to an Asian country to explain and analyze the similarities and differences of CSR activities in both environments.

In this comparative study we will primarily examine Banque Misr, as one of the oldest and largest public bank in Egypt[1], and Malayan Banking Berhad (trading as Maybank) as the largest public bank in Malaysia. To study Bank Misr we will be particularly guided by our earlier research published in 2011, titled: *corporate social responsibility approaches and practices in developing countries: Lessons to be learned from Egypt.*

After a meticulous review of literature, the chapter aims to propose a systemic framework to study CSR practices and policy implementations. Through this framework, we aspire to illustrate the CSR as a constant process where all variables are interrelated and are affecting each other in a mutual approach.

Research Methodology

This chapter presents a qualitative comparative study which will mainly investigate the practices of CSR in the emerging market economies (EMEs). We will study the role of public banking sector in the implementations of CSR activities.

The research is relying on secondary data analysis by elaborating a thorough literature review for the purpose to introduce a systemic framework to study the CSR practices and policy implementation.

Through a detailed data analysis of specific two case studies, the chapter will mainly explore and analyze the role of Banque Misr in Egypt and Malayan Banking Berhad in Malaysia. For this purpose we will examine the studies related to each bank, the banks website, annual reports, brochures, periodicals, etc.

Yin (2003), in *Case Study Research Design and Methods*, describes case study research as: *"an empirical inquiry that investigates a contemporary phenomenon within its real-life context, especially when the boundaries between phenomenon and context are not clearly evident"* (Yin 2003, p. 13). The importance of case study research methodology is very well highlighted through the writings of Yin (2003). The author stresses this significance in three key roles. The first role is *descriptive/exploratory*, the second role is *evaluation* and the third role is *hypothesis testing*. Despite the importance of case study roles, different authors (see, in specific, Stake, 1995, 2000; Yin, 2003, Feagin *et al.,* 1991; Huberman and Miles, 1991, 1994) questioned the validity and credibility of this research tool and mostly emphasised the question of generalization. A number of pre-qualifications were proposed for this issue as: the delimitation and conceptualization of the case study, the selection of the case study has to be strongly related to the research questions, the patterns of research questions have to participate in the development of the research problem, the triangulation of key data collected, the selection of interpretations to be followed and finally, the development of assertions or generalizations about the case study (see in specific, Stake, 2000).

Nevertheless Yin (2003), believes that case studies are often generalized at the level of the theoretical propositions and not to the population or the universe. Case study research methodology, in his view, does not embody a sample and the purpose of the investigator is to extrapolate and generalize theories (theoretical generalization) and not to enumerate frequencies (statistical generalization) (Yin, 2003, p. 10).

In summary, we may postulate that case study research is an inclusive research methodology which embraces the development of a theoretical background, research conceptual framework, rigorous and implicit data collection and analysis, and consistent results which support theory generalization.

Literature Review

At the beginning of the 21st century, Corporate Social Responsibility (CSR) has become a significant field of studies to stress the importance of the new role of organizations towards the society. An enormous number of authors have been participating in this field to highlight the responsibility of organizations, public and private alike, towards the community, society and the natural environment where they are operating (For more details see, among others, Carroll and Buchholtz, 2014; Sarita, 2013; Fathy El Dessouky, 2011; Carroll & Shabana, 2010; Lindgreen & Swaen, 2010; Crane et al.(eds.), 2008; Matten and Moon, 2008; Paul Lee, 2008; Secchi, 2007; Visser et al.(eds), 2007; Campbell, 2006; McWilliams et al., 2006; Sahlin-Andersson, 2006; De Bakker et al., 2005; Waddock, 2004; Garriga & Melé, 2004; Marrewijk, 2003; Wheeler et al., 2003; Moon, 2002; McWilliams & Siegel, 2001; Madsen & Ulhoi, 2001; Windsor, 2001; Husted, 2000; Swanson, 1995; Roberts, 1992; Wood, 1991; Frederick, 1987, 1994; Carroll, 1979 1983, 1991, 1994, 1998, 1999, 2000, 2004, 2008).

Although the concept has gained contemporary considerations, the researches regarding the theoretical and empirical background of CSR may find its roots in the work of Howard Rothmann Bowen titled "Social Responsibilities of the Businessman" published in 1953.

A thorough review of literature reveals that writings on CSR have been dedicated special attention to the concept and its practices in developed countries while less attention was given to developing countries. However, in some exceptional cases, a number of researches have been elaborated to study "China, India, Malaysia, Pakistan, South Africa and Thailand" (Visser, 2008, p.476). Moreover, a meticulous survey of the literature divulges that the studies regarding the CSR concept and practices in the African countries, the MENA region (Middle-East and North Africa), as well as in the Golf countries remain an embryonic field needs to be elaborated (for more details see, among others, Fathy El Dessouky, 2011; Lindgreen *et al.,* 2009; Visser, 2006a, 2006b, 2008; Bio-Tchné & Christensen, 2006; Eweje, 2006; Lockett et al., 2006; Schmidheiny, 2006; Prahalad, 2004).

Furthermore, a detailed review of the literature demonstrates that the interest of the researchers towards the study of CSR related to the public sector remains relatively limited in comparison to the studies related to the private sector (Petkoski and Twose (eds), 2003). Through the literature, the private sector has been demonstrated as the dominant key player in the implementations of the CSR activities while few researches investigated the role of the public sector in fostering the practices of CSR.

Through the literature most authors agree that corporate social responsibility is a concept which promotes the organizations' ethical activities in diverse areas of intervention regarding community, society and environmental issues. As the concept and its practices show discrepancies, different authors have been participating in this field by providing different perspectives. These authors can be organized into different categories regarding the purposes of their researches as: the evolution of the concept and definition of CSR; the different theories which do support the elaboration of the CSR concept; CSR approaches; CSR practices whether in developed or developing countries and finally, we will present a number of contemporary work elaborated by different authors to demonstrate the direct relationship between CSR and sustainability.

A group of researchers proceeded in their writings and focused on the evolution of the concept of CSR and its different definitions. One of the fundamental authors who participated in this field by providing an exhaustive portrait of the CSR concepts and definitions is Carroll (1999) in his work titled "Corporate Social Responsibility: Evolution of a Definitional Construct". In his study, the author provided the evolution of the concept back to the 1950s in comparison to the years 1960s, 1970s, 1980s and the new developments in the 1990s. Another study of Carroll (2008) presented an overview of the development of the notions of Social Responsibility (SR) and Corporate Social Responsibility (CSR) and how the focus of CSR has shifted to be more global oriented.

Different group of authors put emphasis on the different theories which do support the elaboration of the CSR concept. A good synthesis of these theories was illustrated in the work of Lindgreen and Swaen (2010). The authors overviewed the writings of Carroll (1979), Wartick and Cochran (1985), McWilliams *et al.* (2002), and Windsor (2006). Thus Lindgreen and Swaen reviewed various theories behind the development of CSR, for instance, "the Stakeholder Theory, Agency Theory, Institutional Theory, the Theory of the Firm, the Stewardship Theory and the resource-based view of the firm".

Another group of researchers has highlighted the CSR different approaches. Through the literature, one of the classics and most cited by authors regarding the CSR approaches, is the work of Carroll's CSR pyramid (1991). Carroll proposed four levels of responsibilities arranged from the bottom to the top as "Economic, Legal, Ethical and Philanthropic (Discretionary)". A thorough review of the literature reveals that most of authors in their empirical researches, regarding the developed and developing countries alike, have approved Carroll's CSR approaches, however few authors suggested different priorities for the four responsibilities, especially in the developing countries. Moreover, Carroll and Buchholtz (2003) and Carroll (2004) proposed the notion of "Stakeholders" to be integrated in the writings concerning the CSR. Nevertheless, the researches related to the study of CSR and its impact on different stakeholders remains relatively scarce.

A number of contemporary authors provided a thorough literature review of CSR concept, theories and approaches from academic field and corporations. For instance, Su et al. (2015) presented a study titled: *Literature Review on Corporate Social Responsibility*. Moreover, Wang, S. (2015), introduced a research titled: *Literature Review of Corporate Social Responsibility*. Another study to propose is Pour et al.(2014), titled: *Corporate social responsibility: A literature review*. Furthermore, the Ministry of foreign Affairs of Netherland, Policy and Operations Evaluation Department Study (IOB) (2013), participated with an interesting work titled: *Corporate Social Responsibility: the role of public policy*, where IOB presented a systematic literature review of the effects of government supported interventions on the corporate social responsibility (CSR) behavior of enterprises in developing countries. In the same vein, Rani and Hooda (2013) elaborated a research titled: *Corporate Social Responsibility: Review of Literature*. For this purpose, we may also consult the study of Kraus and Brtitzelmaier, (2012) titled: *A literature review on corporate social responsibility: definitions, theories and recent empirical research.*

Another group of authors proceeded in their writings to focus on the relationship between the concept of corporate social responsibility and the concept of sustainable development. One of the inclusive studies was presented by Montiel (2008) titled: "*Corporate Social Responsibility and Corporate Sustainability: Separate Pasts, Common Futures*". The author presented an interesting literature review about the similarities and differences of the two concepts of CSR and SD. Later, a number of contemporary writings have been investigating the relationship between CSR and organizational process to manage sustainability development. Idowu et al. (2015) proposed a study titled "*Corporate Social Responsibility in Europe:*

United in Sustainable Diversity". In their work the authors study and analyze different experiences of the EU countries which already have taken their way to implement CSR to achieve sustainability development where credibility and trust are presented as inevitable key pillars for organizations to achieve stakeholders' satisfaction. Przychodzeń and Przychodzeń (2014) presented a study titled: "*Corporate Social Responsibility for Sustainability*". The authors introduced the concept of corporate social responsibility for sustainability (CSRS) and investigated how this new concept is participating in the sustainability of organizations' actions to accomplish a competitive advantage through social and environmental gains. Epstein and Buhovac, (2014) in their work "*Making Sustainability Work: Best Practices in Managing and Measuring Corporate Social, Environmental, and Economic Impacts*", have highlighted the benefits of sustainability for corporations and society. The authors proposed an innovative model or framework for corporations to measure and integrate social, environmental and economic impacts in their corporate strategy and decision making for sustainability performance. The work of Eweje (ed.) (2014) "*Corporate Social Responsibility and Sustainability: Emerging Trends in Developing Economies*", is another interesting study to present. In this book, different authors presented different perspectives to examine the trends of CSR and sustainability jointly in emerging and developing economics. The authors support that the concepts of CSR and sustainability are growing in developing countries and many stakeholders including governments, policy makers, business and universities are working towards achieving sustainability through a strict implementation of CSR programs. In their study, "*Corporate social responsibility and sustainable development study of most valuable companies*", Raval and Raval (2014), analysed the CSR and sustainability initiatives of some of the top companies across with multiple variables to improve operational efficiency. Fontaine (2013), in his study "*Corporate Social Responsibility and Sustainability: The New Bottom Line?*" stresses the importance of CSR and demonstrates how companies integrate CSR in their strategies and actions to achieve sustainability development of the environment, consumers, employees, communities, stakeholders and the public sphere. In the same vein, Geetanee (2013) presented the work "*Incorporating CSR and sustainability in business strategy*" where he focused on the significance of organizations to be proactive and to incorporate CSR in their strategies to positively impact on growth and sustainable development in the developing world. In their research, "*An Embedded Corporate Social Responsibility Matrix: A Way Ahead for Sustainable and Equitable Benefit for the Firm and the Society*", Jothi and Mathiraj (2013), proposed an adopted matrix as an innovative tool for organizations to achieve sustainable development for business and society globally. In summary, we may postulate that writings didn't distinguish between the two concepts of corporate social responsibility and sustainable development and no clear definition was provided, but instead, authors have been demonstrated that both are generally focusing on the social, economic and environmental responsibilities regarding organizations' activities.

Conceptual Framework: A Systemic Framework to Study CSR Practice

This chapter presents a first attempt to explore the discrepancies related to the implementations of the CSR activities in the public banking sector in two different countries of emerging market economies (EMEs), mainly Malaysia and Egypt.

A review of literature dealing with the CSR theory and practice reveals that researchers are specific in their lenses of analysis and thus, it is difficult to determine all variables of analysis related to the study of this topic. After a meticulous review of literature, we propose a systemic framework to study CSR

Figure 1. Systemic framework to study CSR practice

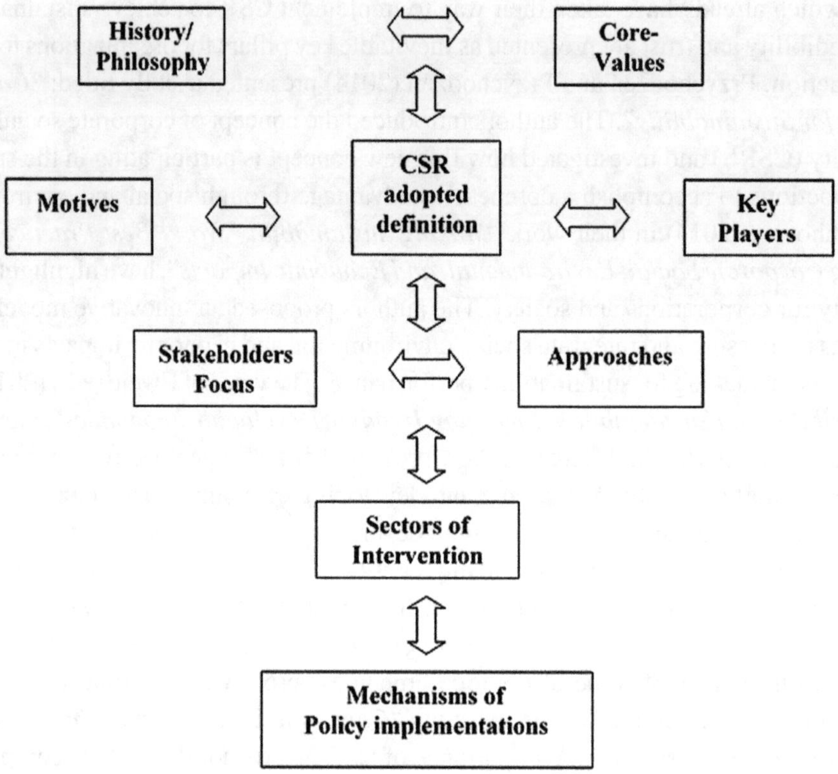

practices and implementations. The following figure illustrates the CSR as a constant process where all variables are interrelated and are affecting each other in a mutual means.

In this systemic framework we advocate to study all related variables regarding CSR practice as: the history/philosophy development, core-values, CSR adopted definition, motives, key players, approaches, stakeholders focus, sectors of intervention and mechanisms of policy implementations.

The History/ Philosophy Development of Corporate Social Responsibility

A thorough analysis of CSR activities related to each bank, reveals that the history and the development of philosophy regarding the practice of these activities in Banque Misr in Egypt goes back as far as the creation of the bank despite the fact that these activities during that time were not identified as CSR. Maybank in Malaysia adopted CSR activities in later time in comparison to Banque Misr, however, Maybank has been formulating an elaborated and more sophisticated CSR programs.

Since it was established in 1920 by the nationalist and economist Mohamed Talaat Pasha Harb, Banque Misr has adopted a national mission to participate in the economic welfare and social development in Egypt (Banque Misr website, *Mohamed Talaat Pasha Harb*). Recently, in 2007, BM decided the creation of "Banque Misr Foundation for Community Development and Welfare (BMFCDW)". The Foundation is a non-profit independent legal entity approved by the Ministry of Social Solidarity under registration number of 7045/2007. The Foundation is managed by a board of trustees to carry out several social

Table 1. The history/ philosophy development of corporate social responsibility

The History/ Philosophy Development of CSR	Malayan Banking Berhad	Banque Misr
	- Corporate responsibly adopted since the creation of the bank in 1960. - The creation of "the Tabung Kebajikan Kumpulan Maybank (TKKM)" in 1990.	- A national mission to participate in the economic welfare and social development in Egypt was adopted since the creation of the bank in 1920. - The creation of "Banque Misr Foundation for Community Development and Welfare (BMFCDW)" in 2007. It was replaced later by Maybank Foundation in 2010.

projects and programs in collaboration with different partners of NGOs and civil society institutions in Egypt adopting the same objectives (Banque Misr).

Maybank was founded in 1960 and there has been a deep believe adopted by the bank to integrate the corporate responsibility in all their activities. In 1990 the bank started to dedicate further attention to the CSR programs by establishing a trust fund known at that time as "the Tabung Kebajikan Kumpulan Maybank (TKKM)". This identity was replaced later in 2010 by Maybank Foundation (Maybank Foundation website, *history*). Maybank Foundation enjoys the support of the board of trustees which includes highly experienced members (Maybank Foundation website, *Corporate Governance*). Moreover, there is a Corporate Responsibility Committee (CSC) who assists the board of trustees especially to accomplish its objectives related to corporate governance (Table 1) (Maybank Foundation).

The Core-Values of Corporate Social Responsibility

An examination of the *vision* and *mission* of each bank regarding its CSR programs equipped us with a good understanding of their core-values related to the concept. For both banks, we may discern that they elaborated the vision and mission of their Foundations to be in parallel with the vision and mission of the bank.

On the first hand, the vision of Maybank Foundation is derived mainly from the vision of the bank itself as "Humanising financial services across Asia" (Maybank Foundation website, *who we are, Mission*). In this regard, we may distinguish two key core-values. The first is highlighting the human-oriented nature of the CSR practices. These orientations appear very obvious as well in the mantras of Maybank Foundation as "A bank with a heart" and "Being at the heart of the community" (Maybank Foundation website, *Home*). The second core-value is the region-oriented activities of the bank. As Maybank is an international bank which is existing in 20 countries, its vision is to start empowering the community first in Kuala Lumpur Malaysia, where the headquarters exists, as well as to spread its CSR activities region wide where the bank is operating.

The mission of Maybank Foundation is "To set a new standard in Corporate Responsibility" (Maybank Foundation website, *who we are, Mission*). For this purpose the Foundation aims to accomplish "high impact, regionwide value-creation programmes that deliver lasting results" [...] "flagship programmes will reinforce the differentiation we are simultaneously achieving in our business operations" (Maybank Foundation website, *who we are, Mission*). Three core-values may be discerned in this regard. The first is the excellence in performance regarding the CSR activities, the second is the high impact and the value-oriented practices of CSR, and the third is the sustainability of CSR activities.

Table 2. The core-values of corporate social responsibility

The core values of CSR		Malayan Banking Berhad	Banque Misr
	Vision	- Human-oriented - Region-oriented	- CSR leadership - Impact-creation - National-oriented
		Mission	**Message**
		- Excellence/ Differentiation in performance - Value-oriented - Sustainability	- Constructive performance - Partnership with NGOs and the civil society

On the other hand, the vision of Banque Misr Foundation for Community Development and Welfare (BMFCDW) is "To achieve a pioneering position in Social Development, as well as putting a positive impact on the Egyptian community within the framework of Banque Misr`s Corporate Social Responsibility platform" (Banque Misr website, *about us, CSR*). We may investigate three core-values adopted by Banque Misr regarding its CSR activities. The first is corporate social responsibility leadership in the Egyptian society, the second is the adoption of an impact-creation perspective, and the third is to be national-oriented through CSR practices.

Banque Misr Foundation for Community Development and Welfare (BMFCDW) didn't employ the word "mission" to describe the reasons for which it is practicing the CSR activities within the Egyptian society. The bank uses instead the word "Message" and it developed its message as "Contributing positively and constructively in social development through specific projects carried out by the Foundation itself or by its partners, including NGO`s and development oriented civil society institutions" (table 2) (Banque Misr).

The Adopted Definition of Corporate Social Responsibility

By examining the concept of CSR according to the Malayan Banking Berhad in Malysia and Banque Misr in Egypt, we may conclude that no particular definition is provided by both banks but instead they provide an interpretation of what they believe CSR represents to their institution. It is interesting to know that both banks consider CSR as core concept embedded in their approaches of caring out all activities.

For the Malayan Banking Berhad, CSR is "integral to the way we do business". "We have believed in and actively practised 'Putting People First'– be it our customers, investors, partners, employee or even the community" (Maybank Foundation website, *history*). According to Banque Misr, CSR is: "an integral part of how we operate, and acts well as a key to our success in maintaining sustainability. Through responsible business we aim to create value for society and strive for economic achievement" (BM website-about us, *CSR*).

It is obvious that Maybank put further emphasis on the human factor of CSR. The bank through its CSR programs attempts to improve the nature of its financial activities by directing them into more humane-oriented actions to be for the benefit of all stakeholders dealing with the Bank. For Banque Misr, it focuses more on the creation of a value-added to the society through its financial activities. CSR for BM can be seen as more value-oriented concept (table 3).

Table 3. The adopted definition of corporate social responsibility

The definition of CSR	Malayan Banking Berhad	Banque Misr
	More Humane-oriented	More Value-oriented

The Motives of Corporate Social Responsibility

In this section of the chapter, it is very crucial to highlight the motives for each bank and the reasons energizing their decisions to adopt CSR activities. As it is beyond the aim of this chapter to analyse the broad cognitive system adopted by each bank, we will systematically examine the mission as well as the objectives and goals of each bank's Foundation. Our analysis will put emphasis on the motives of each bank by structuring these reasons according to two main unit of analysis which is the external and internal environment of the bank. For the external environment we are investigating the indirect external environment of each bank as the social, economic, environmental reasons, etc. and the direct external environment which includes the relationship of the banks with all stakeholders as consumers, suppliers, competitors, governmental institutions, industry institution, NGOs and the civil society, etc.

As general remark, we may conclude that Maybank Foundation devote attention to ameliorate CSR practices in Malaysia but furthermore, the bank gives more attention to the international standards of CSR as its foremost motive is to achieve a high impact regionwide in Asia.

Banque Misr, in contrast, is more dedicated to participate in solving the national problems existing in Egypt as the unemployment, health and environmental problems, youth and women empowerment, education and research inefficiency, etc. This particular role of Banque Misr is obviously driven by an aspiration to support sustainable development currently taking place in Egypt especially after the country's two recent revolutions in 25 January, 2011 and 30 Jun, 2013. (table 4)

Key Players: External or Internal CSR Initiatives

Nowadays, the international standards put CSR at the heart of operations accomplished by public and private organizations alike. Numerous international, regional and national pressures are facing organizations at present and corporate social responsibility grows to be a corner stone in the organizations' philosophy in order to answer the crucial question of why it exists.

Maybank Foundation, despite the fact that its CSR activities are more dedicated to the sustainable development regionwide in Asia, the internal initiatives of the bank represents a cornerstone in the adoption of its CSR programs. Since it was established in 1960, Malayan Banking Berhad along with its financial group has adopted a concrete philosophy to integrate the corporate responsibility concept within all their activities. The CSR internal initiations of the bank support that through the human-oriented nature of its activities and through its CSR believes to elaborate further region-oriented activities, Malayan Banking Berhad may accomplish its main goals to achieve sustainable development regionwide.

On the other hand, since it was established in 1920 by the great Egyptian economist Mohamed Talaat Pasha Harb, Banque Misr has adopted a national mission to participate in the economic and social development in Egypt. The bank believes that through its CSR activities, it may achieve a leadership in sustainable development as well as an effective contribution and positive impact in the Egyptian society (table 5).

Table 4. The motives of corporate social responsibility

<table>
<tr><th></th><th colspan="2"></th><th>Malayan Banking Berhad</th><th>Banque Misr</th></tr>
<tr><td rowspan="3">The motives of CSR</td><td rowspan="2">The external environment</td><td>Indirect External environment</td><td>- Reach a global audience
- Enhancing the lives of communities
- Empowerment of the less fortunate and vulnerable people
- Wildlife, nature and natural heritage conservation by elaborating concrete and measurable ways and by networking with other institutions
- Sustainable development to build a better future both for present and future generations</td><td>- Youth empowerment
- Women empowerment
- Education and Research enhancement
- New job opportunities creation
- Civil society support in carrying out development projects
- Health protection
- Environmental Protection
- Economic development nationwide
- Social development nationwide
- Sustainable developement</td></tr>
<tr><td>Direct External environment</td><td>- Ensure transparency and accountability with stakeholders
- Maintain open communication with stakeholders</td><td>- Product and services competiveness enhancement
- Elaboration of Social Responsibility Policies for good governance
- Supplier Professional and Ethical Code of Conduct</td></tr>
<tr><td colspan="2">The internal environment of the bank</td><td>- Improve employee volunteerism in CSR activities.
- Creating a highly transparent and objective Corporate Governance system.
- Promoting friendly environment activities through its operational work.</td><td>- Better involvement of the Bank`s employees in CSR activities.
-Elaboration of Social Responsibility Policies including Corporate Governance.
-</td></tr>
</table>

Table 5. Key Players: External or internal CSR initiatives

External or internal CSR initiatives	Malayan Banking Berhad	Banque Misr
	Internal initiatives	**Internal initiatives**

The Corporate Social Responsibility Adopted Approaches

Carroll's CSR pyramid proposed in 1991, suggests that CSR activities follow four major approaches arranged according to their importance from bottom to top as "economic, legal, ethical and philanthropic (discretionary) responsibilities" (Carroll, 1991).

A meticulous analysis of CSR approaches adopted by Maybank Foundation may reveal that the Foundation focuses mainly on the ethical and economic approaches which go further than only following philanthropic responsibility. It is obvious that the ethical responsibility for the Foundation is the foremost approach that the bank follows to accomplish its CSR role. By devoting a special focus on "humanizing the financial activities", Maybank is striving not to harm the people and the environment where it is operating. For this reason, the community and the environment were the two fundamental pillars in the bank philosophy for applying its CSR activities. This approach goes in the same vein as the concept of CSR adopted by the Bank as, through its CSR programs, Maybank attempts to develop its financial activities to be more humane-oriented and to be for the benefit of all stakeholders dealing with the Bank in addition to the environmental and heritage protection. Moreover, Maybank Foundation adopts an economic approach through the implementations of its CSR activities. Through this approach, the Foundation seems very enthusiastic to deliver CSR projects and programs which are promoting

Table 6. The corporate social responsibility adopted approaches

CSR adopted approach	Malayan Banking Berhad	Banque Misr
	More ethical and economic responsibility	More philanthropic and economic responsibility

economic and social development in the Asian area where the bank is operating. These CSR projects are mainly funded by the bank's financial group with an initial pledge of 50 million Malaysian Ringgit (RM) (Maybank Foundation website, *Who we are, Mission*).

Nevertheless, Banque Misr appears to put the philanthropic responsibility at the heart of its activities. It is clear that "Charity and Zakat" (Islamic financial contribution principle) are considered as cornerstone in the implementations of CSR activities elaborated by Banque Misr Foundation (Banque Misr website, *About us, CSR*). To accomplish its charity projects, the Foundation gets financial contribution from Banque Misr yearly net profit, from different associations and institutions adopting the same objectives and from individuals' donations (Banque Misr website, *About us, CSR*). Moreover, we may discern that the Foundation favors an economic responsibility approach for the implementations of its CSR projects by devoting attention to the elaboration of projects which support the objectives of the economic and social development at the national level. This adopted approach goes in parallel with the bank's perception about CSR which focuses primarily on the creation of a value-added to the Egyptian society (table 6).

To conclude, we may discern that, Maybank Foundation puts foremost the ethical and economic responsibility in the implementations of its CSR activities. Banque Misr Foundation, on the other hand, devotes more attention to the philanthropic and economic responsibility. While, the legal responsibility is not very well seen in the CSR approaches adopted by Maybank Foundation and Banque Misr Foundation, we may possibly consider its existence in the activities of both Foundations in order to be compliant to the laws and regulations of the countries where both banks are operating.

External or Internal Stakeholders Focus

Carroll and Buchholtz, (2003); Carroll, (2004); Lockett et al., (2006); Visser et al. (eds), (2007); Visser, (2008); Lindgreen et al., (2009); Zu, (2009); Yakovleva and Vazquez-Brust, (2012); introduced the stakeholders as a significant element of CSR. It is important in this section of the chapter to investigate the focus of each Foundation to distinguish whether it is devoted to its external or internal stakeholders.

Noteworthy, Maybank Foundation and Banque Misr Foundation are devoting attention to both external and internal stakeholders. Both banks aim to enhance their impact in the community where they are operating through building an ethical relationship between the bank and its external stakeholders. Furthermore, both banks are targeting a good corporate governance system and a genuine empowerment for their employees in order to achieve their CSR purposes.

Maybank Foundation is putting the people at the heart of its CSR operations. The Foundation through its CSR programs is seeking to develop the quality of its financial activities by strengthening its actions to be more humane-oriented and to be for the benefit of all stakeholders dealing with the Bank either external or internal. For the Foundation, external stakeholders may include, for instance, customers, investors, partners or even the community. Through its open communication with the external stakeholders in addition to its networking and strategic alliances with different institutions regionwide, the Foundation aims to achieve sustainable development for the community in general and the bank's CSR operations in specific (Maybank Foundation website, *history*).

Besides, the Foundation through its CSR programs is targeting the internal stakeholders which may incorporate the bank's employees and stockholders, not only which existing in Malaysia but also in Malayan Banking Berhad financial group. This special attention aims to support transparent and accountable corporate governance in order to maintain efficiency and effectiveness for both the managerial and the supervision system of the Bank (Maybank Foundation website, *Who We Are, Corporate Governance*).

Banque Misr Foundation in order to achieve its CSR targets devotes a special attention to operate ethically with its external stakeholders. The Foundation is elaborating different programs targeting its customers in specific and the Egyptian community in general to achieve an economic and social development at the national level. The Foundation has been elaborated as well the "Supplier Professional and Ethical Code of Conduct" and the "Social Responsibility Policies for good governance" to keep a good and ethical relationship with all its external stakeholders. Likewise, the Foundation is going through an ethical partnership with different NGOs and civil society institutions to accomplish common CSR goals for the general benefit of the Egyptian society.

In addition, the Foundation is targeting the internal stakeholders of Banque Misr. The Foundation is adopting good corporate governance in order to achieve a sustainable improvement of the bank's CSR activities. Moreover, the Foundation is very eager to maintain an ethical relationship with its internal employees in order to achieve the bank's employees' empowerment in CSR activities (table 7).

Multilateral or Unilateral Sector of Intervention and the Mechanisms of Intervention

Both Maybank Foundation and Banque Misr Foundation dedicate significant attention to different sectors of intervention. The CSR programs and activities of both banks can perhaps be more accurately described as multilateral intervention.

Maybank is focusing on two major pillars concerning the CSR activities. The first pillar is related to the community and the second concerns the environment. Maybank philosophy is empowering communities as "helping them develop in ways that are not merely beneficial but sustainable" (Maybank Foundation website, *Programs and Partnership, Community*). For this purpose the bank has been devoted to several sectors of intervention as: Maybank Volunteerism Programme - Cahaya Kasih; Education; Arts and Culture and Health sector (Maybank Foundation website, *Programs and Partnership, Community*). The bank philosophy regarding the environmental protection is "the future will be green, or not at all" (Maybank Foundation website, *Programs and Partnership, Environment*). For this purpose, the bank has been elaborated several activities related to different sectors of intervention as: Wildlife Conservation and Responsible Business programs (Maybank Foundation website, *Programs and Partnership, Environment*). Also, the bank, through its group's operational work, promotes friendly environment activities ((Maybank Foundation website, *Home*).

Table 7. External or Internal stakeholders focus

External or internal stakeholders focus	**Malayan Banking Berhad**	**Banque Misr**
	Both external and internal stakeholders focus	**Both external and internal stakeholders focus**

For the implementations of its CSR activities, Maybank Foundation has been elaborated particular mechanisms and tools for this purpose. The bank selected to follow an incremental approach for the implementations based on regular assessment of measurable results which, according to the bank's beliefs, will enable a good verification and then generalization of results. The Foundation is eager as well in assessing not only its CSR activities but also puts the impacts assessment at the heart of its work to evaluate the consequences of its activities on the development of the community (Maybank Foundation website, *Who We Are, Mission*). Another interesting mechanism adopted by Mayank Foundation is to ensure open communication with all stakeholders for transparency and accountability purposes. The Foundation dedicates its official website to present all its CSR activities, in addition to its annual report called "Maybank's annual Sustainability Report" (Maybank Foundation website, *Who we are, Mission*). The Foundation is also adopting an "employee voluntarism" tool as a key driver regarding CSR activities (Maybank Foundation website, *Who We Are, Mission*). Moreover, the Foundation is networking with different institutions through strategic alliances to reach sustainable development and value creation across the region (Maybank Foundation website, *Who we are, Goals*).

The philosophy of Banque Misr Foundation regarding its CSR activities may be very well distinguished in three major pillars. The first pillar is community development with a special attention to youth and women empowerment as well as the environmental protection. For this purpose the bank has been devoted to support several sectors of intervention as education and research improvement through offering scholarships to outstanding students and supporting research centers, schools, universities and public hospitals. In addition the bank supports activities with a special focus on issues related to better health and better environment. The second pillar is economic welfare in consistency with sustainability development purposes. For this purpose the bank has been devoted to support the civil society in initiating and implementing development project and has been supported existing projects in improving competitiveness of products and services. The third pillar is social solidarity at the national level in Egypt. For this purpose the bank has been devoted to initiating several projects to create new job opportunities at the national level (Banque Misr Foundation website, *About us, CSR*).

For the implementations of its CSR activities, Banque Misr Foundation has been elaborated particular mechanisms and tools for this purpose. The Foundation follows a constructive mechanism to carry out its CSR activities (Banque Misr website, *About us, CSR*). Through this tool of intervention we may consider the Foundation's focus on the sustainable improvement of its work. Moreover, the Foundation is building a partnership with different NGOs and civil society institutions which are adopting the same CSR purposes. The Foundation is also following an empowerment mechanism of all its employees to be vigorously involved in its CSR activities (Banque Misr website, *About us, CSR*). Furthermore, the Foundation is publishing regular "Foundation Bulletin" for the follow-up and presentation of the bank's CSR activities (table 8).

In summary, the chapter attempts to introduce a systemic framework to study CSR practices and implementations. Through this framework, a comparative study is elaborated to primarily examine Banque Misr in Egypt and the Malayan Banking Berhad (trading as Maybank) in Malaysia. We explored: the history/ philosophy development of corporate social responsibility, the core-values of CSR, the adopted definition of CSR, the motives of CSR, key players: external or internal CSR initiatives, the CSR adopted approaches, external or internal stakeholders focus, and finally, multilateral or unilateral sector of intervention and the mechanisms of intervention.

Table 8. Multilateral or unilateral sector of intervention and the mechanisms of intervention

	Malayan Banking Berhad	Banque Misr
Sectors of intervention	**Multilateral**	**Multilateral**
Mechanisms of intervention	- Incremental approach for assessment - Assessment of activities and their impact - Open communication with stakeholders - Transparency and Accountability by publishing "Maybank's annual Sustainability Report" - Employee voluntarism tool - Networking and Strategic Alliances with different institutions	- Constructive mechanism to carry out activities - Partnership with different NGOs and civil society institutions - The bank's employees empowerment in CSR activities - Follow-up and presentation of the bank's CSR activities by publishing the "Foundation Bulletin"

The following table illustrates our comparative study of the two CSR models elaborated by the Malayan Banking in Malaysia and Banque Misr in Egypt (table 9).

CONCLUSION

Corporate Social Responsibility (CSR) has become a salient concept to reveal the new role of organizations, public and private alike, towards the broad society and community where they are operating. A meticulous survey of the literature divulges that the studies regarding CSR concept and practices in the African countries, the MENA region (Middle-East and North Africa), as well as in the Golf countries remain an embryonic field needs to be elaborated. Furthermore, through the literature, the private sector has been highlighted as the dominant actor in the implementations of the CSR concept while very little is known about the role of the public sector to foster the practices of CSR.

The purpose of this chapter was to present an original analysis of CSR approaches and practices in the banking public sector, by carrying out a detailed comparison between Banque Misr, as one of the oldest and largest public bank in Egypt and the Malayan Banking Berhad (trading as Maybank) as the largest public bank in Malaysia.

After a meticulous review of literature, we proposed a systemic framework to study CSR practices and policy implementations. We illustrated the CSR as a constant process where all variables are interrelated and are affecting each other in a mutual approach. In this systemic framework we advocated to study all significant variables related to CSR practice as: the history/philosophy development, core-values, CSR adopted definition, motives, key players, approaches, stakeholders focus, sectors of intervention and mechanisms of policy implementations.

In summary, we may divulge that common CSR policies exist between the Malaysian and the Egyptian experience. Nevertheless the Malaysian model has formulated an elaborated and further sophisticated CSR programs. Moreover, the Egyptian model needs to adopt more global oriented CSR policies, in particular to assure the sustainable development requirements.

Table 9. Comparative study of the two CSR models of the Malayan Banking in Malaysia and Banque Misr in Egypt

The History/ Philosophy Development of CSR		Malayan Banking Berhad	Banque Misr
		- Corporate responsibly adopted since the creation of the bank in 1960. - The creation of "the Tabung Kebajikan Kumpulan Maybank (TKKM)" in 1990.	- A national mission to participate in the economic welfare and social development in Egypt was adopted since the creation of the bank in 1920. - The creation of "Banque Misr Foundation for Community Development and Welfare (BMFCDW)" in 2007. It was replaced later by Maybank Foundation in 2010.
The core values of CSR	Vision	- Human-oriented - Region-oriented	- CSR leadership - Impact-creation - National-oriented
		Mission	Message
		- Excellence/ Differentiation in performance - Value-oriented - Sustainability	- Constructive performance - Partnership with NGOs and the civil society
The definition of CSR		More Humane-oriented	More Value-oriented
The motives of CSR	The external environment: Indirect External environment	- Reach a global audience - Enhancing the lives of communities - Empowerment of the less fortunate and vulnerable people - Wildlife, nature and natural heritage conservation by elaborating concrete and measurable ways and by networking with other institutions - Sustainable development to build a better future both for present and future generations	- Youth empowerment - Women empowerment - Education and Research enhancement - New job opportunities creation - Civil society support in carrying out development projects - Health protection - Environmental Protection - Economic development nationwide - Social development nationwide - Sustainable development
	The external environment: Direct External environment	- Ensure transparency and accountability with stakeholders - Maintain open communication with stakeholders	- Product and services competiveness enhancement - Elaboration of Social Responsibility Policies for good governance - Supplier Professional and Ethical Code of Conduct
	The internal environment of the bank	- Improve employee volunteerism in CSR activities. - Creating a highly transparent and objective Corporate Governance system - Promoting friendly environment activities through its operational work.	- Better involvement of the Bank's employees in CSR activities. -Elaboration of Social Responsibility Policies including Corporate Governance. -
External or internal CSR initiatives		Internal initiatives	Internal initiatives
CSR adopted approach		More ethical and economic responsibility	More philanthropic and economic responsibility
External or internal stakeholders focus		Both external and internal stakeholders focus	Both external and internal stakeholders focus
Sectors of intervention		Multilateral	Multilateral
Mechanisms of intervention		- Incremental approach for assessment - Assessment of activities and their impact - Open communication with stakeholders - Transparency and Accountability by publishing "Maybank's annual Sustainability Report" - Employee voluntarism tool - Networking and Strategic Alliances with different institutions	- Constructive mechanism to carry out activities - Partnership with different NGOs and civil society institutions - The bank's employees empowerment in CSR activities - Follow-up and presentation of the bank's CSR activities by publishing the "Foundation Bulletin"

REFERENCES

Adam, L., Valérie, S., & Johnston, W. J. (2009). Corporate Social Responsibility: An Empirical Investigation of U.S. Organizations. *Journal of Business Ethics*, *85*(2), 303–323.

Amaeshi, K. B., Ogbechie, A. C., & Amao, O. (2006). Corporate Social Responsibility in Nigeria: Western Mimicry or Indigenous Influences. *Journal of Corporate Citizenship*, *24*(Winter), 83–99.

Banque Misr website. (n. d.). Retrieved from http://www.banquemisr.com

Banque Misr website. (n. d.). *About us, CSR*. Retrieved from http://www.banquemisr.com/sites/engbm/Pages/csr1.aspx

Banque Misr website. (n. d.). *Mohamed Talaat Pasha Harb*. Retrieved from http://www.banquemisr.com/sites/engbm/Pages/TalaatHarb.aspx

Bowen, H. R. (1953). *Social Responsibility of the Businessman* (1st ed.). New York: Harper & Brothers.

Bio-Tchné, & Christensen B. (2006). Right Time for Africa. *Finance & Development*, *43*(4), 8–13.

Carroll, A. B. (1979). A Three-Dimensional Model of Corporate Performance. *Academy of Management Review*, *4*(4), 497–505.

Carroll, A. B. (1983). Corporate social responsibility: Will industry respond to cut-backs in social program funding? *Vital Speeches of the Day*, *49*, 604–608.

Carroll, A. B. (1991). The Pyramid of Corporate Social Responsibility: Toward the Moral Management of Organizational Stakeholders. *Business Horizons*, *34*(4), 39–48. doi:10.1016/0007-6813(91)90005-G

Carroll, A. B. (1994). Social issues in management research: Experts' views, analysis and commentary. *Business & Society*, *33*(1), 5–29. doi:10.1177/000765039403300102

Carroll, A. B. (1998). The Four Faces of Corporate Citizenship. *Business and Society Review*, *100*(1), 1–7. doi:10.1111/0045-3609.00008

Carroll, A. B. (2000). Ethical Challenges for Business in the New Millennium: Corporate Social Responsibility and Models of Management Morality. *Business Ethics Quarterly*, *10*(1), 33–42. doi:10.2307/3857692

Carroll, A. B. (2004). Managing Ethically With Global Stakeholders: A Present and Future Challenge. *The Academy of Management Executive*, *18*(2), 114–120. doi:10.5465/AME.2004.13836269

Carroll, A. B. (2008). A History of Corporate Social Responsibility: Concepts and Practices. In A. Crane, D. Matten, A. McWilliams, J. Moon, & D.S. Siegel. (Eds.), Oxford Handbook of Corporate Social Responsibility (pp. 19-46). USA: Oxford University Press.

Carroll, A.B. & Buchholtz, A. (2014). *Business and Society: Ethics, Sustainability, and Stakeholder Management* (9th ed.). USA: Cengage Learning.

Carroll, A. B., & Kareem, M. (2010, March). The Business Case for Corporate Social Responsibility: A Review of Concepts, Research and Practice. *International Journal of Management Reviews*, *12*(1), 85–105. doi:10.1111/j.1468-2370.2009.00275.x

Carroll, A. B., & Buchholtz, A. K. (2003). *Business and Society: Ethics and Stakeholder Management* (5th ed.). Australia: Thomson South-Western.

Carroll, A. B. (1999). Corporate Social Responsibility: Evolution of a Definitional Construct. *Business & Society*, *38*(3), 268–295. doi:10.1177/000765039903800303

Crane, A., & Matten, D., McWilliams, A., Moon, J., & Siegel, D.S. (Eds.), (2008). Oxford Handbook of Corporate Social Responsibility. USA: Oxford University Press.

Crane, A., & Matten, D. (2004). *Business Ethics*. USA: Oxford University Press.

De Bakker, G. A., Groenwegen, P., & Den Hond, F. (2005). A Bibliometric Analysis of 30 years of Research and Theory on Corporate Social Responsibility and Corporate Social Performance. *Business & Society*, *44*(3), 283–317. doi:10.1177/0007650305278086

Epstein, M., & Buhovac, A.R. (2014). Making Sustainability Work: Best Practices in Managing and Measuring Corporate Social, Environmental, and Economic Impacts (2nd revised updated vers.). San Francisco, California: Berrett-Koehler Publishers.

Eweje, G. (2006). Environmental costs and responsibilities resulting from oil exploitation in developing countries: The case of the Niger Delta of Nigeria. *Journal of Business Ethics*, *69*(1), 27–56. doi:10.1007/s10551-006-9067-8

Eweje, G. (Ed.), (2014). Corporate Social Responsibility and Sustainability: Emerging Trends in Developing Economies. Book Series: Critical Studies on Corporate Responsibility, Governance and Sustainability (Vol.8). Emerald Group Publishing Limited.

Fathy, N. (2011). Corporate social responsibility approaches and practices in developing countries: Lessons to be learned from Egypt. *International Journal of Arts and Science*, *4*(7), 123–135.

Feagin, J., Orum, A., & Sjoberg, J. (Eds.). (1991). *A case for the case study*. Chapel Hill, London: The University of North California Press.

Fontaine, M. (2013). Corporate Social Responsibility and Sustainability: The New Bottom Line? *International Journal of Business & Social Science*, *4*(4), 110–119.

Frederick, W. C. (1987). Theories of Corporate Social Performance. In S. Prakash Sethi, & C.M. Falbe (Ed.), Business and Society: Dimensions of Conflict and Cooperation (pp. 142-61). MA: Lexington Books.

Frederick, W. C. (1994). From CSR1 to CSR2: The Maturing of Business-and-Society Thought. *Business & Society*, *33*(2), 150–164. doi:10.1177/000765039403300202

Garriga, E., & Melé, D. (2004). Corporate social responsibility theories: Mapping the territory. *Journal of Business Ethics*, *53*(1/2), 51–71. doi:10.1023/B:BUSI.0000039399.90587.34

Geetanee, N. (2013). Incorporating CSR and sustainability in business strategy. *Proceedings of the Annual International Conference on Enterprise Marketing & Global* (p. 189).

Huberman, M., & Miles, M. (1994). Data management and analysis methods. In N.K Denzin, & Y.S Lincoln (Eds.), Handbook of Qualitative Research (pp. 428-444). London/New Delhi: SAGE Publications.

Huberman, M., & Miles, M. (1991). *Analyse des données qualitatives: recueil de nouvelles méthodes*. Bruxelles: De Boeck Université.

Husted, B. W. (2000). A contingency theory of corporate social performance. *Business & Journal of Corporate Citizenship*, *17*, 33–50.

Idowu, S., Schmidpeter, R., & Fifka, M. S. (Eds.). (2015). *Corporate Social Responsibility in Europe: United in Sustainable Diversity*. Switzerland: Springer International Publishing. doi:10.1007/978-3-319-13566-3

Jothi, M., & Mathiraj, S. P. (2013). An Embedded Corporate Social Responsibility Matrix: A Way Ahead for Sustainable and Equitable Benefit for the Firm and the Society. *International Journal of Research in Computer Application & Management*, *3*(6), 62–68.

Kraus, P., & Bernd, B. (2012). A literature review on corporate social responsibility: definitions, theories and recent empirical research. *International Journal of Management Cases* (Special Issue: *Papers from the 9th International CIRCLE Conference)*, 14(4), 282-296.

Lindgreen, A., & Swaen, V. (2010). Corporate Social Responsibility. *International Journal of Management Reviews*, *12*(1), 1–7. doi:10.1111/j.1468-2370.2009.00277.x

Lindgreen, A., Córdoba, J.-R., Maon, F., & Mendoza, J. M. (2010). Corporate Social Responsibility in Colombia: Making Sense of Social Strategies. *Journal of Business Ethics*, *91*(2), 229–242. doi:10.1007/s10551-010-0616-9

Lindgreen, A., Valérie, S., & Campbell, T. T. (2009). Corporate Social Responsibility Practices in Developing and Transitional Countries: Botswana and Malawi. *Journal of Business Ethics*, *90*(S3), 429–440. doi:10.1007/s10551-010-0415-3

Lockett, A., Moon, J., & Visser, W. (2006). Corporate Social Responsibility in Management Research: Focus, Nature, Salience and Sources of Influences. *Journal of Management Studies*, *43*(1), 115–136. doi:10.1111/j.1467-6486.2006.00585.x

Madsen, H., & Ulhoi, J. P. (2001). Integrating Environmental and Stakeholder Management. *Business Strategy and the Environment*, *10*(2), 77–88. doi:10.1002/bse.279

Malayan Banking Berhad website. (n. d.). Retrieved from http://www.baybank.com

MayBank Foundation website. (n. d.). *Corporate Governance*. Retrieved from http://www.maybank-Foundation.com/corporate_governance.html

Maybank Foundation website. (n. d.). *Corporate Responsibility Committee*. Retrieved from http://www.maybankFoundation.com/corporate_responsibility.html

Maybank Foundation website. (n. d.). *History*. Retrieved from http://www.maybankFoundation.com/history.html

Maybank Foundation website. (n. d.). *Mission*. Retrieved from http://www.maybankFoundation.com/mission.html

Marrewijk, M. V. (2003). Concepts and Definitions of CSR and Corporate Sustainability: Between Agency and Communion. *Journal of Business Ethics*, *44*(2), 95–105. doi:10.1023/A:1023331212247

Matten, D., & Moon, J. (2008). Implicit and Explicit CSR: A Conceptual Framework for a Comparative Understanding of Corporate Social Responsibility. *Academy of Management Review*, *33*(2), 404–424. doi:10.5465/AMR.2008.31193458

McWilliams, A., & Siegel, D. (2001). Corporate social responsibility: A theory of the firm perspective. *Academy of Management Review*, *26*(1), 117–127.

McWilliams, A., Siegel, D. S., & Wright, P. M. (2006). Corporate Social Responsibility: Strategic Implications. *Journal of Management Studies*, *43*(1), 1–18. doi:10.1111/j.1467-6486.2006.00580.x

Ministry of foreign Affairs of Netherland, Policy and Operations Evaluation Department Study (IOB). (2013). *Corporate Social Responsibility: the role of public policy - A systematic literature review of the effects of government supported interventions on the corporate social responsibility (CSR) behavior of enterprises in developing countries.* The Hague: The Netherlands.

Moharana, S. (2013, November-December). Corporate Social Responsibility: A Study of Selected Public Sector Banks in India. *Journal of Business and Management*, *15*(4), 1–9.

Montiel, I. (2008). Corporate Social Responsibility and Corporate Sustainability: Separate Pasts, Common Futures. *Organization & Environment*, *21*(3), 245–269. doi:10.1177/1086026608321329

Moon, J. (2002). Corporate Social Responsibility: An Overview. In C. Hartley (Ed.), The International Directory of Corporate Philanthropy (1st ed., pp. 3-14). London and New York: Europa Publications.

Paul Lee, M. (2008). A review of the theories of corporate social responsibility: Its evolutionary path and the road ahead. *International Journal of Management Reviews*, *10*(1), 53–73. doi:10.1111/j.1468-2370.2007.00226.x

Petkoski, D., & Twose, N. (Eds.), (2003). *Public Policy for Corporate Social Responsibility*. World Bank Institute Series on Corporate Responsibility, Accountability and Sustainable Competitiveness.

Pour, B. S., Kamran, N., & Mostafa, E. (2014). Corporate social responsibility: A literature review. *African Journal of Business Management*, *8*(7), 228–234. doi:10.5897/AJBM12.106

Prahalad, C. K. (2004). *The Fortune at the Bottom of the Pyramid: Eradicating Poverty Through Profits*. London: FT Prentice Hall.

Przychodzeń, W., & Justyna, P. (2014). Corporate Social Responsibility for Sustainability. *Management and Business Administration Central Europe*, *2*(125), 80–97. doi:10.7206/mba.ce.2084-3356.100

Rani, G., & Kalpana, H. (2013). Corporate Social Responsibility: Review of Literature. *International Journal of Social Science & Interdisciplinary Research*, *2*(6), 38–44.

Raval, K., & Himanshu, R. (2014). Corporate social responsibility and sustainable development study of most valuable companies. *Indian Streams Research Journal*, *IV*(II), 1–11.

Roberts, R. W. (1992). Determinants of corporate social responsibility disclosure: An application of stakeholder theory. *Accounting, Organizations and Society*, *17*(6), 595–612. doi:10.1016/0361-3682(92)90015-K

Sahlin-Andersson, K. (2006). Corporate Social Responsibility: A Trend and a Movement, but of What and For What? *Corporate Governance*, *6*(5), 595–608. doi:10.1108/14720700610706081

Schmidheiny, S. (2006). A View of Corporate Citizenships in Latin America. *Journal of Corporate Citizenship*, *21*(Spring), 21–24. doi:10.9774/GLEAF.4700.2006.sp.00004

Secchi, D. (2007). Utilitarian, managerial and relational theories of corporate social responsibility. *International Journal of Management Reviews*, *9*(4), 347–373. doi:10.1111/j.1468-2370.2007.00215.x

Stake, R. (1995). *The Art of Case Study Research*. Thousand Oaks, CA: Sage.

Stake, R. (2000). Case studies. In N.K. Denzin, & Y.S. Lincoln (Eds.). Handbook of qualitative research (2nd ed., pp. 435-454). Thousand Oaks, California: Sage.

Su, R.-J., & Jie, X.-W. (2015). Literature Review on Corporate Social Responsibility. *Proceedings of the International Conference on Management Engineering and Management Innovation.*

Swanson, D. L. (1995). Addressing a Theoretical Problem by Reorienting the Corporate Social Performance Model. *Academy of Management Review*, *20*(1), 43–64.

Visser, W. (2006a). Revising Carroll's CSR Pyramid: An African Perspective. In E.R. Pedersen, & M. Huniche (Eds.), Corporate Citizenship in Developing Countries (pp. 29–56). Copenhagen: Copenhagen Business School Press.

Visser, W. (2006b). Research on Corporate Social Responsibility in Africa: a Ten-Year Review (1995-2005). In W. Visser, M. McIntosh, & C. Middleton (Eds.), Corporate citizenship in Africa: Lessons from the past; paths to the future (pp. 18-28). Sheffield: Greenleaf.

Visser, W. (2008). Corporate social responsibility in developing countries, In A. Crane, A. McWilliams, D. Matten, J. Moon & D. Siegel (Eds.), The Oxford Handbook of Corporate Social Responsibility (pp. 473-479). Oxford: Oxford University Press.

Visser, W., Matten, D., Pohl, M., & Tolhurst, N. (Eds.), (2007). *The A to Z of Corporate Social Responsibility: a Complete Reference Guide to Concepts, Codes and Organizations*. London: Wiley.

Waddock, S. (2004). Parallel universes: Companies, academics and the progress of corporate citizenship. *Business and Society Review*, *109*(1), 5–42. doi:10.1111/j.0045-3609.2004.00002.x

Wang, S. (2015). Literature Review of Corporate Social Responsibility. In S. Wang, (Ed.), Chinese Strategic Decision making on CSR (pp. 7-19). Springer. doi:10.1007/978-3-662-44997-4_2

Welford, R. (2004). Corporate Social Responsibility in Europe and Asia: Critical Elements and Best Practice. *Journal of Corporate Citizenship*, *2004*(13), 31–47. doi:10.9774/GLEAF.4700.2004.sp.00007

Wheeler, D., Colbert, B., & Freeman, R. E. (2003). Focusing on value: Corporate social responsibility, sustainability and a stakeholder approach in a network world. *Journal of General Management*, *28*(3), 1–28.

Windsor, D. (2001). The future of corporate social responsibility. *The International Journal of Organizational Analysis*, *9*(3), 225–256. doi:10.1108/eb028934

Wood, D. (1991). Corporate Social Performance Revisited. *Academy of Management Review*, *16*(4), 691–718.

Yakovleva, N., & Diego, V.-B. (2012). Stakeholder Perspectives on CSR of Mining MNCs in Argentina. *Journal of Business Ethics*, *106*(2), 191–211. doi:10.1007/s10551-011-0989-4

Yin, R. K. (2003). *Case Study Research Design and Methods*. Thousand Oaks, California: Sage Publications.

Zu, L. (2009). *Corporate Social Responsibility, Corporate Restructuring and Firm's Performance: Empirical Evidence from Chinese Enterprises* (1st ed.). Springer.

ENDNOTES

1 My study about Banque Misr was published in a previous research titled: Fathy El Dessouky, Naglaa (2011), corporate social responsibility approaches and practices in developing countries: Lessons to be learned from Egypt, International Journal of Arts and Science, 4(7), 123-135.
The research was first presented in the International Journal of Arts & Sciences (IJAS) conference for academic disciplines held at the University of Washington Rome Center, Rome, Italy, November 22 – 25, 2010.

Chapter 5
Ethics and Corporate Social Responsibility:
The Case of Palestine

Samir Ahmad Abuznaid
Hebron University, Palestine

ABSTRACT

"...Science will continue to surprise us with what it discovers and creates; then it will astound us by devising new methods to surprise us. At the core of science's self-modification is technology. New tools enable new structures of knowledge and new ways of discovery" (Kelly, 2014). How important is it for organizations to be socially responsible and ethical? This chapter will define ethics and corporate social responsibility (CSR), explain the competitive advantage of creating and maintaining an ethical organization, and discuss the role played by organizations and managers in enhancing ethics and corporate social responsibility. The main focus will be on Palestine Telecommunication Company's (PalTel Group) CSR program and its impact on Palestinian people and organizations. The chapter will conclude by shedding light on major opportunities and challenges facing PalTel Group and its CSR program. Background information is provided, as well as a literature review regarding ethics and corporate social responsibility within Palestine and Palestine Telecommunication Group. A brief discussion of a rival of CSRat PalTel's, Wataniya, has been made in order to ensure that the scope of the chapter's content is complete. The chapter, however, does not examine (employee treatment) nor PalTel Group's ethics policies and their impact on employees and their particular work attitudes. Further, the chapter does not explore how PalTel determines where to invest the resources in social and environmental programs to benefit the community and enhance business performance profitability and reputation. Nor does it measure the impact of CSR practices on competitive advantages, reputation and customer satisfaction. Green washing is common phenomenon in Palestine where almost all businesses claim to be scoring high in the social responsibility parameter. Apart from its academic contribution this chapter may also assist managers and senior officers in strategizing for their organizations in this age of social responsibility.

DOI: 10.4018/978-1-4666-9864-2.ch005

LEARNING OBJECTIVES

After reading this chapter, you should be able to

1. Define ethics and corporate social responsibility.
2. Discuss what it means to be socially responsible and ethical.
3. Answer the question, "Why should organizations be ethical and socially responsible?"
4. Describe the ways in which management can influence ethical behavior at work.
5. Discuss PalTel's corporate social responsibility program.
6. Discuss PalTel's role in enhancing ethics and corporate social responsibility.

Businesses aim to generate profits and long term wealth for their owners. However, that does not mean they can do whatever it takes to get the maximum profits. Businesses do, however have other secondary purposes including: providing goods and services, creating employment and gain maximum profits for stakeholders including employees, customers, and the community at large, Elliottet al. (2014). That does not mean businesses can do whatever it takes to get the maximum profits. Effective leaders must not forget the underlying foundation for such behavior-its people, individuals like you and me, which make the important decisions, ethically or not. Leaders must get serious about the moral aspects and social implications of decision making in organizations. They must understand how the success of their organizations is intertwined with ethical and social issues and recognize that sustainable economic growth, a high level of integrity and superior performance is not feasible without full realization of the needs, wants and demands of society. Organizations are increasingly facing questions from the public in regard to sustainable development programs. This illustrates how difficult facing ethical issues can be and symbolizes the growing importance of discussing ethical and social responsibility. For businesses, the balance between profit motivated activities and meeting the needs and expectations of stakeholders has long been debated. To examine this problem this chapter will define ethics and corporate social responsibility, and discuss PalTel Group's corporate social responsibility program. This can't be done however, without giving a better understanding of the socio- political environment in Palestine and analyzing the macro and micro environment. The chapter will examine PalTel Group's CSR program and sustainable marketing, examine their ethical and corporate social responsibility program, and will discuss major opportunities and challenges facing PalTel Group. As for the methodology, the author has conducted interviews with PalTel's CSR and human resource officers, as well as used resources such as PalTel Group's Third Sustainability Report, 2013 which was put at the author disposal by management.

ETHICS AND CORPORATE SOCIAL RESPONSIBILITY

Ethics and social responsibility are hot topics for today. A leader's most important responsibility is to establish the ethical environment and culture of the organization-that is the values that underlie the behavior of all employees, partners and other stakeholders (Collins,2009).The practice of CSR initiatives varies widely from developed countries to developing countries. Robbins and Judge (2015) indicated that organizational culture is not neutral in its ethical orientation, even when an organization is openly pursing ethical goals. Many things influence ethical behavior at work. Dessler (2015) in his work concluded that ethical behavior reflects "Bad Apples, Bad Cases, and Bad Barrels".

The strong effective leader will accept the fact that he or she is vulnerable to the possibility of making mistakes and poor decisions and be prepared to take appropriate swift corrective action (Collins, 2009). They should not be so arrogant to undermine accountability.

Ethics has always been a concern for managers .The practice of ethical behavior is a basic requirement for higher performance and long term competitive sustainability. The failure of ethical leadership in an organization is very destructive. It demoralizes the workforce; creates public distrust and, ultimately organizational decay (Collins, 2009).Wide spread moral lapses and corporate financial scandals have brought the topics of business ethics and corporate social responsibility to the forefront. The topics of ethics and social responsibility are not required courses in most undergraduate business curricula. However, these terms are commonly used in every day almost interchangeably. Business ethics has to do with how an organization behaves. It involves applying general ethical principles and standards to business activities, behavior and decisions, while social responsibility is a subset of ethics in that it deals with social consequences of ethical decisions and the way that these decisions improve or harm the surrounding community.

WHAT IS MANAGERIAL ETHICS?

Ethics is difficult to define. Velasquez (1992) has defined ethics as "the principles of conduct governing an individual or a group; specifically, the standards you use to decide what your conduct should be? In a general sense, ethics is defined as the principles, values, and beliefs that define right and wrong decisions and behavior Davis and Fredrick (1996).It is a branch of philosophy that deals with moral behavior. Morality is complex concept; it can be defined as society's accepted standards of behavior and always involves basic questions of right and wrong such as stealing, murder, and how to treat other people (Dessler, 2015). Morality can be understood in terms of both means and ends. Means is the process which occurs, while ends refers to the consequences (Cherrington and Cherrington, 1995).Ethics may also be defined as:

[…} a systematic inquiry into the beliefs we have had and the management we make about what is morally right or wrong or morally good or evil. It is an inquiry that attempts to answer the following question: what kinds of conduct are morally right or wrong? And what things are good and what things are evil? (Cherrington and Cherrington, 1995).

Our interest in ethical behavior also applies at the level of the organization as a whole. Ethics sets standards as to what is good or bad in conduct and decision making Shea (1988) and Trevino (1986). Ethical behavior is what is accepted as good and right as opposed to "bad" or wrong in the context of governing moral code. Over time, ethical work climate (EWC), or the shared concept of right and wrong behavior in the workplace, develops as part of the organizational climate (Robbins and Judge, 2015). When making decisions managers need to consider the process and take into account those who will be affected by those decisions. Managers need to think about the rights and duties between the company and its employees, suppliers, customers and neighbors. For managers who are working in foreign cultures, they need to consider the socio-cultural, political and legal influence of what is considered acceptable behavior in that international environment. The method of addressing ethical questions has often been criticized by contemporary views. One of the main arguments against this is that moral right or wrong depends on one's own judgment, so what is considered ethical in one culture is regarded as unethical in other cultures. Are ethical standards universal? Although some moral beliefs exist, social and cultural differences between countries are important factors that determine ethical and unethical behavior. For example, say that a manager in a Mexican firm bribes several high ranking government officials in Mexico City to secure a profitable government contract. Although this business practice is unethical (and illegal) in the United Kingdom, it is acceptable in Mexico (Robins and Coulter, 2009).Ethics in business or what is called corporate ethics is so important for businesses. Ethical business can: attract customers to the firm's products, promote employee retention, attract the most talented employees, attract investors, keep company shares high, create a healthy business environment, increase efficiency and performance, and enhance long term sustainability for the business and society.

ETHICAL COMMONALITIES

Our lives are filled with moral issues, almost everything we do has amoral component. Unfortunately, we don't think about the moral component in our daily decisions and practices, and tend to think only about the economic gains and other beneficial transactions that might be of benefit to others. However, regardless of the cultural differences that determine what is ethical and what is not ethical. Cherrington and Cherrington (1995) named 14 prominent moral issues that are common between religions:

1. Stealing: one should not steal and take things that do not belong to him or her.
2. Lying: one should not lie or say things he or she knows are not true.
3. Fraud and deceit: one should not give or allow false impressions.
4. Bribery: one should not buy influence as one engages in conflict of interest (bribes, payoffs, kickbacks).
5. Hiding versus divulging information: one should be responsible for protecting information under his authority.
6. Taking unfair advantage/cheating: one should not use inside information to his own advantage or in making investment decisions.
7. Organizational abuse: abusive practices in business are prohibited and considered unethical.
8. Perpetrating interpersonal abuse such as physical violence: sexual harassment, racism and sexism.
9. Violating rules and regulations: individuals should obey rules whether organizational, social or religious commitment.
10. Balancing ethical dilemmas: one only has to choose between two equally desirable or undesirable options (dilemma).It is the opposite of (lapse) where it is very clear that this is right or wrong.
11. Reporting unethical behavior: once individuals witness an unethical act, they are obliged to report it.
12. Committing to personal excellence: maximizing efforts above standards
13. Serving the poor: those who have the means are obliged to give to those who are poor in order to alleviate their suffering.
14. Compassion and love for others: the golden rule requires us to do unto others as we would have others do unto us.

CORPORATE SOCIAL RESPONSIBILITY (CSR)

The concept of corporate social responsibility is easy to understand. Daft (2006) viewed corporate social responsibility as knowing right from wrong and doing right. To him corporate social responsibility means being a good corporate citizen. Corporate social responsibility is a business intention, beyond its legal and economic obligations, to do the right things and act in ways that are good for society Robbins and Coulter (2009). Social responsibility refers to what the business does, over the above statutory requirement, for the benefit of society. Social responsibility has to do with the goodness and welfare of the public (Robbins et al., 2011).

Corporate social responsibility has been described in different ways. It has been called "profit making only, "going beyond profit making,'' "any discretionary corporate activity intended to further social welfare,'" and "improving social and environmental conditions Barnett (2007).As such, Individual marketers must exercise their social conscience in specific dealings with customers and stakeholders (Kotler and Keller, 2012).

Corporate social responsibility is the process by which businesses negotiate their role in society (Kotler and Armstrong, 2010).It is about how companies manage the business process to produce an overall positive impact on society. Itis an obligation to act in a way that serves both its own interests and the interests of society at large. Social responsibility is going beyond what is required by law. Businesses need to be socially responsible; they should be proactive and promote positive changes.

Although ethics and corporate social responsibility are linked in most firms, CSR activities are no guarantee of ethical behavior and social involvement is not a cause for higher economic performance. It could simply mean that high profits can help companies become more luxurious and socially involved (Seifert et.al., 2004).For example, large global corporations lower their costs by outsourcing to countries where human rights are not a high priority and justify it by saying they are bringing in jobs and helping strengthen the local economies (Robbins and Coulter, 2011).

A socially responsible company gains the reputation of being a good corporate citizen and at the same time builds a good corporate image with consumers and other stakeholders (Berens, 2004; Carroll, 1999). Any firm and in order to succeed, its internal marketing activities must be matched by a strong sense of social responsibility (Wilkie and Moore, 2002).Corporate social responsibility is a strategic investment, that is similar to technology or innovation, and must be pursued and effectively implemented by the firm. It is no longer acceptable to accept the traditional view of social responsibility which argues that the purpose of business is profit maximization or the prime purpose of business is business. Companies need to evaluate whether they are truly practicing ethical and socially responsible marketing. According to the Economist (2002) a company's practice of higher level of corporate governance is driven by rising customer expectations, changing employee expectations, government legislation and pressure, investor's interest in social criteria, and changing business procurement practices. It is widely agreed that the most admired companies in the world abide by a code of serving people interests, not only their own (Kotler and Keller, 2012).There is a growing interest in corporate social responsibility in the Arabworld. In fact many managers in the Arab region are becoming increasingly aware of CSR and its benefits (Robbins et al., 2011).For example, the Kuwait project company (KIOCO)-which won an award in Kuwait's first CSR awards event-has addressed a learning disability called dyslexia, which affects almost 105of people (Robbins et. al., 2011).

PALESTINE: ENVIRONMENTAL ANALYSIS

Political and Historical Background

Palestinian people now number about ten million; five million living in Palestine and five million living abroad as refugees. Palestinians are Arabs and speak Arabic and they are either Muslims or Christians. They are well educated, motivated and driven people who want to advance themselves and their country. According to the Palestinian Human Resource Development Report (2004) the literacy rate is 92%, the life expectancy at birth is 73 years for females and 70 years for males and the adjusted real per capita GDP is about 1203 US dollars .The average family size is about six people.

A careful review has been made of the dynamics over time of Israeli -Palestinian relations, the corresponding policy framework, and the institutional arrangements designed to manage those relations, reveals that policy and regulatory reform to date has not sufficiently addressed the core weakness arising from prolonged and continuing occupation. While the Palestinian authority has acquired the attributes of an interim self-governing authority, the key to successful economic development consistent with independence and statehood, meaning sovereignty, remains on the agenda. Meanwhile the economic policymaking space that is needed to ensure viability of the Palestinian national economic security-has yet to be marshaled. Since the 1970s there has been a parallel effort to find terms upon which peace could be agreed to in both the Arab-Israeli conflict and in the Palestinian–Israeli conflict. Some countries have signed peace treaties, such as Egypt and Israel in1979, Jordan and Israel in 1994, whereas some have not yet to find a mutual basis to do so.

Since 1967 Israel has maintained various economic and political restrictions on the Palestinian peoples' activities and institutions which has had detrimental effects on the Palestinian economy and quality of life. While Israel justifies its acts as security concerns, the Palestinians view these acts as an obstacle to Palestinian statehood.

Since 1996, there have been numerous efforts carried out by Arab states and the international community to achieve peace in the region. The Hebron and Wye River agreements were concluded in 1997 and 1998 respectively to facilitate the implementation of the Oslo Accords signed at the White House in 1993 in presence of President Bill Clinton. These agreements have not produced any result. The 2000 Camp David Peace Summit between the late Palestinian President Yasser Arafat and former Israeli Prime Minister Ehud Barak ended without reaching an agreement. In the month that followed, the Likud Party's Ariel Sharon was elected as the Israeli Prime Minister in February, 2001. In March 2002, the Beirut Arab summit was held to present plans to defuse the Israeli-Palestinian conflict. Arab leaders put forth an initiative at the summit that offered comprehensive peace in the region, based on the internationally accepted formula of "land for peace" (in return to the 4th of 1967 borders, normalization of relations and a final peace treaty). In response former Israeli foreign minister Shimon Peres welcomed the initiative. Unfortunately, this internationally recognized formula was not implemented by Israel because it was not ready to withdraw to the1967 borders and rejected the right of return to Palestinian refugees (Wikipedia.org., 2014).

In July 2002, the "International Quartet" made up of the United States, the European Union, the United Nations, and Russia outlined the principles of a "road map" for peace including an independent Palestinian state.

The Israeli army, however, still regularly carried out and continues to carry out incursions into Palestinian controlled areas. More evidently, Israel launched its destructive attack on Gaza in late 2008

(Fayyad, 2005).Two additional wars happened in 2012 and 2014, respectively. This latest war followed eight years of blockade that crippled the economy in Gaza and denied Palestinians the access to basic goods and commodities. Gaza's economy during this blockade was called a tunnel economy. In the summer of 2014 war, Israel launched its attacks in the Hamas controlled Gaza Strip. During the seven weeks of Israeli bombardment, Israeli rocket attacks and ground fighting resulted in 22,000 Palestinian deaths,(of which 75% were civilians), and 11,100 wounded where you see the destruction of buildings and young Gaza girl showing sign of victory. In contrast, 66 Israeli soldiers and four civilians were killed, and 450 Israeli soldiers and 80 Israeli civilians were wounded. The Israeli bombardment also resulted in 17,000 Palestinian homes, schools and mosques been reduced to rubble. The New York Times noted that damage in the third war was more severe than the two proceeding wars. Gaza's main power plant was destroyed, leaving the strip with only electric generator power for the next year. Two sewage-pumping stations were destroyed, and businesses were targeted and destroyed. As a result, many businesses have been demolished, and a number of tunnels leading to both Israel and Egypt have been destroyed. On the 26th of August, 2014, Egypt brokered a ceasefire agreement between the Palestinians and Israelis. Palestinians and Israeli leaders signed the agreement promising only a limited change to conditions in Gaza and left unresolved the broader issues underpinning the conflict.

Socio-Economic Factors

The International Labor Organization (2009) indicated that in the face of economic and social hardships, Palestinians have developed noble aspirations of living in peace, rearing their children and building their state. These aspirations are constantly being challenged by today's grim prospects which leave little room for hope. Yet hope is vital to counter extreme alternatives that hold no future.

For four decades the Israeli relations with the occupied territory have been prescribed by the Israeli Defense Forces (IDF). In 1967 the Israeli civil administration assumed authority for Palestinian economic, political and institutional affairs, some of which have since been transferred to the Palestinian Authority. Such polices directly affected Palestinian economic affairs such as taxation, customs, banking, money and insurance, agriculture, industry and crafts, land, water, labor and other resources UNCTAD (1986).

Today Palestine is almost 100 percent dependent on Israel for electricity. There is a small generating capacity in Gaza, and almost none in the West Bank. Electricity is produced in Israel and sold to Palestinians through three Palestinian Electricity companies as main distributors of electricity. They sell electricity to Palestinian inhabitants, businesses and institutions. Palestinian companies are responsible for collection and payment to the Israeli electricity company.

Palestinian Business Women's Association (2010) stressed that the occupation, however, not only influences Palestinian values, but also shapes the economic life of the average Palestinian. The Palestinian economy suffers tremendously from Israeli practices and restrictions, which restrict freedom of movement for people and goods, and create transportation problems. Within the West Bank, these restrictions include obstacles or "closures" in the form of checkpoints, road blocks, metal gates, earth mounds, walls, road barriers and trenches. In addition, the Israeli's have built an apartheid wall predominantly east of the Green Line and inside the West Bank, with Gaza effectively been sealed from the rest of the world. The separation wall has turned the West Bank into a fragmented set of social and economic islands or enclaves cut off from one another. It has surrounded Gaza with a perimeter fence with heavily controlled crossings ASALA (2010).Physical barriers are further reinforced by intricate administrative procedures, including a highly restrictive permit requirement system. The total number of checkpoints increased from 558 in December 2007 to 630 by September 2008, not including temporary "flying" checkpoints. Moreover, this number represents a 59% increase over the 396 closures that were in place at the time of signing of the Agreement on Movement and Access in November 2005. United Nations Office for the Coordination of Humanitarian Affairs (2009). Obstacles such as the high cost of transport due to closures, and poor infrastructure have prevented the Palestinian economy from stimulating trade without Israeli participation. The phenomenon of Israeli firms subcontracting work to the Palestinian labor-surplus economy for re-export to Israel and beyond which emerged in the 1980s has since become one of the main features of Israeli-Palestinian trade and economic relations. Such economic relations have minimal spillover effects on the local Palestinian economy and productive capacity, as subcontracting has shifted from one branch to another in line with the changing trade dynamism of a liberalized Israeli economy, while technology transfer was minimal OCHA (2009). The Israeli strategy throughout the 1980s actively supported and funded by the United States –was conducted under the "theme" of improving the quality of life of Palestinians, which aimed at permitting personal prosperity but forcibly restraining communal development OCHA (2009). Ever since, Israeli -Palestinian trade relations has been dominated by much higher levels of Israeli exports to the occupied Palestinian territories, while Palestinian agriculture and manufacturing has remained focused on low value- added, uncompetitive, labor intensive production processes.

It is worth mentioning that Israel has divided the West Bank into three different administrative areas:

Area A: Under Palestinian administrative and security control. This area includes civil gatherings in major cities.

Area B: Under Palestinian and Israeli security control, this area includes the communities around cities and towns.

Area C: Under full Israeli control, this area is a state land outside the inhabited areas. Unfortunately Area C comprises 75% of the Palestinian land under which Palestinian Authority have no control. Having Israel control 75% of Palestinian land under the so called "classification C" denies Palestinian businessmen and entrepreneurs the opportunity to establish industrial parks in this vast land; taking into account that this land can absorb major industries which can't be located in residential areas like in area A or B.

In the West Bank, marketing is usually handled by local agents and representatives. Exhibitions and trade fairs remain the best arena for promoting products, though there are relatively few of them. Telemarketing and the internet are increasingly popular marketing methods; although the shortage of telephone lines limits this option at present (Foreign Commonwealth Office, UK., n.d.).

The West Bank and Gaza have few department stores and supermarkets, with the majority of retail outlets being in Hebron governorate. About 60% of Palestinian industrial products are sold and distributed without any marketing effort, and only 18% of total family firms have exclusive agents to distribute their products.

OVERVIEW OF PALESTINE TELECOMMUNICATION GROUP

Palestine Telecommunications Group (PalTel Group) is the largest private sector company operating in Palestine. The company consists of six companies owned by PalTel called the PalTel Group: Palestine

Telecommunications Company (PalTel), Palestine Cellular Communications Ltd, (Jawwal), Hadara, PalMedia, Reach, and Hulul. The company's headquarters are located in different areas of the West Bank and Gaza Strip and employ 3000 people. PalTel Group is considered the biggest employer after the government. Since its inception, PalTel Group has shown great commitment to disclosure and transparency standards.

As of end 2012, PalTel Group's main achievements included: 396 fixed line subscribers, 185,000 ADSL lines, enhancement of employee working conditions, installation and operation of the internal technology, such as OI(Voice Over Internet). The group also added and developed programs that helped facilitate processes within companies, such as an automatic activation system for the services of ADSL. The Al-Etisalat Academy was established to provide training for all PalTel Group companies as well as related logistics and administrative services to training courses.

Palestine Telecommunications Company (PALTEL)

Palestine Telecommunications Company (PalTel) was established in 1995 and initiated its services in January 1997 as an operator and service provider of the communications services in Palestine. The company is one of the largest companies nationally, and one of the most important players in the national economy. Since its establishment, PalTel has sought to build and distribute an advanced digital telecommunications network in Palestine. PalTel is a public holding company and represents the most actively traded stock in Palestine security exchange. It is the first Palestinian company to register its stock at the standard for the S&P-AFE 40 and Dow Jones –FEAS 50.

Palestine Cellular Communications Ltd. (JAWWAL)

Since its inception, Jawwal has contributed significantly to the growth of mobile communications in Palestine, playing a major role in the progress and growth of the Palestinian economy. By end of 2012, Jawwal had over 2.5 million subscribers, and renewed their ISO 14001 certificate for 2012. Their net enhancement in data and voice domain West Bank and Gaza, launched a "business keys campaign" addressing the needs of local and international investors. Further, they contributed to the community with a focus on the youth sector, provided services through 25 show rooms and 400 suppliers, and provided roaming services in cooperation with364 cellular companies operating in 156 countries worldwide. Aside from Israeli mobile communication competition, Wataniya Mobile Palestine is Jawwal's major and sole competitor in Palestine.

Hadara

Since its establishment in 2005, Hadara contributed to the spread of technological knowledge in Palestine through distinct internet services. Hadara continued developing its services by employing the latest technology, and the most experienced and talented young Palestinian workers. Hadara has provided internet services to all segments of Palestinian society and helped foster a generation which is conscious and aware of the importance of technology. Hadara has kept up to date with the latest technology to maintain high quality and competitive prices.

Hulul

Hulul was introduced in 2010.It specialized in providing technological services internally for PalTel group companies. Technological support includes billing systems for fixed lines, internet, and mobile. In addition, it supports a variety of applications programs for companies, does data base management systems, and customer relations. Hadara runs the companies' technical services and centers, networks and communication systems including their central communication and data protection.

Reach

Reach is the first Palestinian –based contract center to offer high quality performance driven services at competitive costs. Reach aims to fundamentally reshape the dynamics of call center customer relations through strategic solutions that fulfill client needs and help expand the client base. Reach agents file is over 67,000 inbound and outbound calls per day using the Cisco IPCC technology systems, operating around the clock, serving customers around the world with the help of 563 employees. All calls are recorded and screen-captured and customers are allowed to listen to calls to observe how Reach performs its tasks, and provide customers with random sample.

Palmedia

PalMedia has added new dimension to the services of the group. PalMedia offers various essential services in the world of journalism and media. PalMedia offices are used for making television interviews with government officials and the public in cities and towns where Palestine TV, the official media not available or does not have the necessary technology; therefore, saving time that could be up to two hours, for interviewees driving from South or North of West Bank to television headquarter in Ramallah.

PALTEL Group Stakeholders

PalTel Group stakeholders are those who affect and are affected by PalTel Group decisions, activities and services .They include the government, customers, institutions, organizations, the community, employees, and shareholders.

PALTEL Corporate Social Responsibility Program

Do Arab businesses care? In the Middle East the CSR is still in its infancy, it is very much associated with 'giving' through charitable donations (Kotler and Armstrong, 2010).The World Economic Forum (WEF) has worked with businesses and governments in the Middle East to promote corporate social responsibility in the region (Kotler and Armstrong, 2010).Similar calls have been made by Arab leaders. His Majesty King Abdullah of Jordan (2010) pointed out that….

{businesses should make more efforts to welcome young people into the workplace environment by becoming more involved inactive training programs}.Sheikh Mohammad bin Rashid Al Maktoum of Dubai (2010) had made a major announcement at the World Economic Forum in Jordan saying …. {Dubai was investing $10 billion in its attempt to help bridge the perceived gap in education and knowledge in the Middle East compared to the West}(Kotler and Armstrong (2010).Many businesses in

Palestine have their own CSR programs and are carried out under different slogans. They all contribute to the community and well-being of individuals in Palestine. The CSR programs are not limited to the private sector. Almost all banks and microfinance NGOs have their own social responsibility programs and are active in development. Increasingly, people want information about company's record on social and environmental responsibility to help them decide which companies to buy from, invest in, and work for (Hatch and Schultz, 2005).

How does PalTel integrate CSR program within its practices? How do different stakeholders, including different departments in PalTel contribute to implementation of CSR actions?

How socially responsible is PalTel? Since its inception, PalTel group has committed itself to social responsibility. It has assigned a social responsibility officer, Imad Lahham, to administer its social responsibility program. As for the execution of the program, the Group contributed to the establishment of different projects in the West Bank and Gaza. A social Responsibility Fund was established to help achieve the objectives of social responsibility program. The Fund was established to help meet short term and emergency needs, especially in marginalized areas, and to implement long term sustainable development initiatives and programs.

For community development purposes, in 2008 PalTel Group implemented through its PalTel Group Foundation (PGF), an independent, nonprofit organization established to implement projects and programs that have long term impact and sustainable development. The Fund has focused on the important and essential needs of Palestinian society, taking into consideration the specific and immediate needs of the most marginalized and needy groups.

As of 2013 the achievements of PGF are summarized in the following:

- Provision of scholarships to 1,995 students.
- Over 192 community based organizations benefited from PC initiative and have received PCs for their operations
- 23 organizations have benefited from the program by receiving PC labs.
- Provision of families with income generation projects under decent life program scheme. Over 70 families have benefited from such projects.
- Connecting 90 schools to Internet and donating 50 computers donated to schools Pc labs through the Abjad Net Program.
- Kindergartens have benefited from Sharaa Sim Sim partnership. It is reported that 1000 kindergartens have had direct benefit from the program.
- Launching vocational training and establishing training centers in Kalandia refugee camp as part of vocational training contribution. (Kalandia is a Palestinian refugee camp outside Ramallah).
- Construction projects. Over 12 streets were constructed in Gaza
- Providing health care coverage to many people (73% elderly, 17% youth and 10% children).
- Contribution to Higher and Professional Education

Contribution to Scholarship Programs

PalTel group has launched scholarship programs for undergraduate students studying at Palestinian universities using clear criteria that target academically distinguished students from destitute families families (see Figure 1), where you see the Palestinian minister of higher education and PalTel group providing scholarships for Palestinian students.

Figure 1.

PhD Scholarship Program (IFAD)

Under this program scholarships were provided to professors from Birzeit University to help them obtain their PhD degrees from well recognized international universities. Scholarships were targeting specializations like computer science, nursing, geography and media (see Figure 2) where you find PalTel Group advertisement for university scholarships for Palestinian.

In addition to that, this project provided support to Vocational education technology.

In cooperation with UNRWA, PalTel Group has rehabilitated training laboratories in the Kalandia Institute for Vocational Training (QIVT) in the field of land communication network and maintenance of Jawwal phone sets. Under this project youth were trained for the sake of unemployment reduction and help generate self-supporting projects.

Figure 2.

Contribution to Preschool and Basic Education

The Abjadnet program aims at increasing education opportunities and decreasing technology illiteracy through the development of electronic culture at Palestinian schools through the provision of appropriate infrastructure that includes connecting schools to internet services and enabling access to the internet in cooperation with the Ministry of Education. As a result, 90 schools have been connected to internet and 50PCs were provided to four labs in four schools.

University Connectivity

The Group has supported innovation in IT by investing in existing incubators and providing its expertise to businesses. Part of this initiative was the enhancement of technology within universities and provision of universities with computers, printers, photo copy machines, furniture, office equipment, and free internet access and training courses.

Sesame Street Project

The project aims to help children develop skills and abilities in thinking, analyzing and interacting with their environment, and to enhance their sense of responsibility and promote child safety standards when it comes to crossing roads and streets.

Contribution to Technology Sector

Under this scheme, the Group has initiated the PC initiative program in cooperation with NGOs development center to help develop the Palestinian people and spread the culture of internet and computing. The initiative seeks to provide PCs and free internet access to for a period of time to organizations in remote and marginalized areas to help them provide services to women, youth and orphans and promote the principles of volunteering. As a result of this project, 192 institutions were equipped with PCs and internet connectivity and training, 23 institutions were supplied with PCs, while 192 institutions have benefitted from free one year access to internet services.

Mobile Application Development and Innovators Program

This project was implemented in cooperation with Palestine Information and Communications Technology Incubator (PICTI).It aims to provide incentives to Palestinian young entrepreneurs to share their innovative ideas in the area of mobile phone applications, and provides them with the necessary financing.

The Right for Decent Life Program

The decent life program was launched to secure a sustainable source of living for the poorest families in the poorest areas in Palestine (see Figure 3) where you find PalTel staff providing blankets to Gaza in the aftermath of the 1914 war.

Figure 3.

The CSR Emergency and Short-Term Projects

This project aims at providing PCs, free internet access, humanitarian, social, environmental, health, cultural and sport services to all segments of all areas in Gaza (see Figure 4).

The total contribution reached 2 million Jordanian dinars. The targeted sectors under this project are education, health, economy and social services. The activities in these sectors included the sponsoring of events like conferences, festivals, marches for education, contributions to The President Abbas Fund for needy and distinguished students scholarships, equipping clinics and helping the disabled.

- Economy Development and Creating Socio –Economic Opportunity

Figure 4.

This project covers activities like sponsoring industrial and agricultural exhibitions, festivals and supporting Palestinian consumption and promoting national brands like the sponsorships of olive exhibition (see Figure 4).

- Social services

PalTel Group contributed to the Palestinian community through the enhancement of sectors like health, education, technology and humanitarian initiatives.

These are some of the projects implemented by PalTel Group. However, there are other programs like annual scholarships programs, PC initiative programs, Jawwal youth sponsorship, and education and Palestine international awards for excellence and creativity.

GAZA 2014 WAR IMPACT ON THE GROUP

PalTel Group Updated Estimated Damage

As a result of the recent war on Gaza Strip, PalTel Group has suffered from devastating damages from frequent bombings, which affected wide areas in Gaza Strip. The damage was mainly done to networks, assets damage and lost revenues. The preliminary estimated damages cost as of September 2, 2014 was 32.57 Million dollars.

PalTel Ethics

An ethical organization is composed of people in which all employees feel a great sense of organizational commitment, honesty, ownership and accountability. It consists of morally perfect people empowered to operate within a culture of trust and integrity. When organizations hire employees these employees bring their ethics to the organization. They bring to their jobs their own ideas of what is morally right or wrong. Each person must shoulder much of the credit (or blame) for his or her ethical choices (Dessler, 2013).For example researchers surveyed CEOs to study the CEOs' intentions to engage in two questionable practices: soliciting a competitor's technological secrets, and making illegal payments to foreign officials. The researchers concluded that the CEOs' personal predispositions more strongly affected their decisions than did outside pressures or characteristics of their firms (Morris et al., 1995).However; hiring unethical candidates bring unethical practices and behavior to the organization. Ethical organizations have competitive advantage over unethical ones. Companies that are ethical and socially responsible perform as well as –and often better than-those that are not socially responsible (Daft, 2006).Governments and People would rather work with ethical organizations .Ethical organizations have several competitive advantages. They:

- Attract and retain higher quality employees
- Attract and retain higher quality customers
- Attract and retain higher quality suppliers
- Attract and retain higher quality investors
- Earn goodwill with community members and government officials

- Achieve greater efficiency and decision making, based on more reliable information from stakeholders
- Achieve higher product quality
- Need less employee supervision
- Attract more donations to the organization
- Will last longer and become more sustainable
- Will have the community lobby for the organization and stand by the organization during crisis
- Get rewarded (Collins, 2009).

Are ethical standards universal? Although some common oral beliefs exist, social and cultural differences between countries are important factors that determine ethical and unethical behavior (Bailey and Spicer, 2006).Ethical organizations are supported by three pillars: ethical individuals, ethical leadership, and organizational structure and systems. These include codes of ethics, ethics committees, chief ethics officers, training programs, and mechanisms to protect whistle-blowers (Daft, 2006).Managers who are essentially ethical individuals come at the top of the pillars. These individuals possess qualities like honesty and integrity which is reflected in their behavior. Such qualities make people inside and outside the company trust them because they are reliable people. People rely on them because they are fair, treat people right, and are ethical in their dealings with others. Ethical managers encourage the moral development of others (Kaptein, 2003).Ethical leadership is the second pillar needed to provide ethical business practices in an organization. Managers own behavior always sets the tone for organization's ethics. In addition ethical leadership makes a commitment to ethical values and help others throughout the organization embody and reflect those values (Trevin et al.,1999).Employees are actually aware of their bosses' ethical lapses, and the company grapevine quickly communicates situations in which top managers choose an expedient action over an ethical one. The business leader's most important job is to establish the organization's ethical boundaries, convey clear and explicit expectations of leadership team, and teach these principles to all employees, so that ethical thinking becomes part of the organizations genetic code (Barrier,1998).Organizational structures and systems are the third pillar of ethical organizations. They are the set of tools used by managers to shape values and promote ethical behavior throughout the organization. Among the tools are codes of ethics, ethical structures, and mechanisms for supporting whistle blowers. Whistle-blowers are individuals, frequently employees, who use procedural or legal channels to report incidents of unethical behavior to company ethics officers or to legal authorities (Collins, 2009).

Most marketing situations and activities do not involve a simple choice between right and wrong and what is ethical and unethical .Responsible businesses often implement a code of ethics or code of conduct to help govern and guide employees' actions and guide their decisions and behavior. Employees with formalized ethics training have more positive perceptions about their organizations ethics and greater job satisfaction. Empowering the workforce will enhance employee commitment, financial performance, teamwork, superior customer service, and corporate reputation (Robbins et. al., 2011).

Corporations may espouse laudable corporate values, such as quality, integrity, and community, but these all spring from ethics-essentially, knowing the difference between right and wrong Collins (2009).

Employees arrive at the organization with a wide variety of backgrounds. They could come from ethical or unethical environment. How ethical is PalTel as an organization? In an interview conducted with PalTel head of corporate social responsibility program using a questionnaire, it was found that PalTel is always keen to hire ethical employees. The Group has developed a code of ethics document to enhance ethical behavior and a code of conduct to help guide employees behavior. The code of ethics and code of conduct documents are well communicated to all employees. Organizations are increasingly spending money on ethics training programs for employees. It is believed that ethics training programs promote ethical behavior.

It is believed that ethics training initiates dialogue at work around contentious issues and has a great impact on employees' behaviors than the presence of an ethics code or from memos from the boss. Ethics training helps create a culture of trust (Collins,2009).As for PalTel, training is conducted in the form of workshops, seminars, lectures and conferences. PalTel administered an internal reporting system for ethical and unethical issues, yet management did not devote a line to help employees to report and discuss ethical issues with management. PalTel contracted Ernst & Young as a social auditor for its CSR program. The social auditor reports directly to the CEO of PalTel Group.

As shown in the attitudinal survey in Table 1, PalTel scored low on issues like ethics assessment training in which employees annually assess PalTel's ethical performance based on its Code of ethics. Although the company has a CSR officer, it did not assign ethics compliance officer and did not create a separate ombudsman position within the company(see Table 1).It is widely agreed that a failure in ethics internal communication system can result in external whistle-blowing, which can be damaging for both the organization and whistleblowers(Daft,2006). These are areas for improvements that should be taken seriously by the management of PalTel.

Table 1. PalTel Group Ethics Compliance Attitudinal Survey

No.	Items	Response 1-5
1	In the company we always try to hire ethical employees.	5
2.	We developed a code of ethics document to enhance employee's ethical behavior.	5
3.	We developed a code of conduct document for our employees to help guide their behavior.	5
4.	The code of ethics document is well communicated to all employees.	4
5.	The code of conduct document is well communicated to all employees	4
6.	We conduct ethical training for our employees (I.e. workshops, lectures, meetings etc.)	4
7.	We conduct code of ethics assessment training for our employees.	2
8.	We conduct code of conduct training for our employees.	2
9.	We administer internal reporting system for ethical/unethical issue.	4
10.	We assigned an ethics compliance officer within our company.	2
11.	We established an ombudsman position within our company.	2
12.	An ombudsman is appointed to help communicate information about potential ethical and legal violations in the company.	2
13.	We devoted a line to receive employee complaints by telephone or internet.	2
14.	Do you have social auditor? If yes, name the company? Yes (Ernst & Young). Social auditor is one who audits CSR program. To whom does social auditor report to? (Give title not name) .He reports to Global Report Initiative (GRI) plus PalTel Group Board represented by the CEO. Any additional information you would like to add regarding ethics and ethical issues within your company that have not been mentioned (You may use additional sheet) -- Thank you for your kind cooperation.The author	

Questionnaire

Please use the 1-5 scale below to assess how well each of the following statements applies to your company.

Place the number that best describe your response in the space provided:

1=strongly disagree, 2=Disagree, 3=neither agree nor disagree, 4=agree, 5=strongly agree. No. Items Response 1-5

Major Challenges Facing PalTel Group

What are PalTel's key strategic challenges associated with CSR? PalTel Chief Executive Officer, Ammar Aker, has stressed PalTel's management adaptation to challenges, internal reform and transforation and company relationship management. The company has adapted itself to the economic situation in Palestine and the decrease in paying capabilities of customers due to the economic conditions and fiscal crises. As such, the company has gone through an assessment process of the pricing policies, customer care and service provision. The company has gone through management restructuring, better community engagement and has become more responsive to clients and operations. Overall the company has shown deeper commitments, stronger achievements and a better relationship marketing management.

Making investment in Palestine is a challenge due to political instability. The challenges facing PalTel include physical, administrative and security restrictions that continue to hamper development of the public sector. Palestinian access to area C is a major problem; taking into account that area C makes up more than 70% of the west bank. Therefore, reaching customers and making projects in this area is not easy, because it is fully controlled by Israel. Telecommunication companies are denied access to this area, and all work in this area (improving network services, installing networking equipment to carry on coverage for voice, data and mobile services) needs the consent and approval of the occupier.

The communication sector, like other sectors still faces some challenges, such as international perceptions of the local ICT sector, market access, travel impediments, scalability of labor pool, access to equity finance and VC funds, and inadequate legal and regulatory frameworks.

The last challenge is competition. PalTel's major competitors in the area of mobile communication are Alwataniya and Israeli communication companies.

However, opportunities still exist for this sector and they are mainly in web development, mobile apps, various aspects of IP technology and business process outsourcing. Outsourcing is growing in scope and weight and offers more room for expansion globally. The PalTel group continues to meet customers' needs in the best manner. The companies continue to invest in advanced technology, and infrastructure projects are carried out on a partnership basis to enhance sector advocacy.

As for the future, PalTel the Company will: continue leading the market of telecommunication and technology in Palestine, maintain the highest level of efficiency, increase diversity in the value-added services, keep up the latest technological applications, continue to foster local innovations and initiatives in the field of technology, focus on various segment's needs, enhance international relations and strengthen partnership with foreign markets.

Wataniya Mobile: Jawwal's Competitor

Wataniya Mobile Palestine is a member of Oredoo Group, which was launched in November 2009 as a mobile company that aims to be the communications leader of choice. Part of its strategy is to help build an independent and vibrant Palestinian economy. Aside from Israeli competition, Wataniya is considered as Jawwal's major rival. Since its inception in 2009, the company became socially active in the region through the execution of sponsorship programs though on a small scale compared to Jawwal. Alwataniya's corporate social responsibility program is mainly confined to sponsorship of activities and events and does not do strategic or sustainable projects. Some of Wataniya's CSR sponsorship programs have included: a women's football team, a "Filistinashabab" award ceremony, the mobile circus, holy month of Ramadan activities, Santa Claus sponsorship, the smile campaign in cooperation with the ministry of health, educational forums, Palestine week festival, Mohammad Assaf's first album signing, a charity concert for Mohammad Assaf in partnership with Al Quds University, sponsorship for Spanish singer Abdun Alkaraz's to support cancer patients, Gaza libraries in partnership with Friends School, and the construction of multi-purpose halls for chambers of commerce. Although Wataniya Mobile committed itself through its website to give serious considerations to all applications for sponsorship, most of the sponsorship so far has been on a small scale compared to Jawwal (Wataniya, 2015).

CHAPTER SECTION SUMMARIES

1. Ethics and social responsibility are hot topics for today. Ethics is difficult to define. Ethics refers to' the principles of conduct governing an individual or a group; specifically, the standards you use to decide what your conduct should be. It is the code of moral principles and values that govern the behavior of a person or group with respect to what is right or wrong. Corporate social responsibility means distinguishing right from wrong or doing right .It means being a good corporate citizen. It is the business intention, beyond its legal and economic obligations, to do the right thing and act in ways that are good for society. Firms committed to CSR gain advantages in terms of acquiring and exclusively enjoying reputational capital.
2. Employees come to the organization with a wide variety of backgrounds. They could come from ethical or unethical environments. They bring their bad or good behavior. Ethical organizations are supported by three pillars: ethical individuals, ethical leadership, and organization structure and systems. The business leader's most important job is to establish the organization's ethical boundaries, convey clear and explicit expectations of leadership team, and teach these principles to all employees, so that ethical thinking becomes part of the organizations genetic code
3. Managers can use different methods and tools to promote ethics in the work place. For example, selecting and hiring the right people, emphasizing the fairness of the selection process, conducting ethics trainings, conducting fair and just performance appraisals, rewarding ethical behavior, establishing and following a code of ethics, having ethical structures, and developing mechanisms for supporting whistleblowers.
4. Corporate ethics is so important for businesses. Ethical business can attract customers to the firm's products, promote employee retention, attract the most talented employees to the organization, attract investors, keep company shares high, create healthy business environments, increase efficiency and performance, and enhance long term sustainability for the business. Managers need to think about the rights and duties between the company and its employees, suppliers, customers and neighbors. As for managers who are working in foreign cultures, they need to consider the socio-cultural, political and legal influence of what is considered acceptable behavior in that international environment.

5. Despite the complex and unstable political environment in Palestine, PalTel group has committed itself to social responsibility. Its social responsibility program is considered one of the most successful programs in the region. The Group contributed to the establishment of different projects in the West Bank and Gaza. It has helped to meet both the short term and emergency needs of the region, especially in mobilized. It has implemented long term, sustainable development initiatives and programs. PalTel is considered one of the most important players in the Palestine national economy. It is the biggest employer after the government. PalTel management is always keen to hire ethical employees. The Group has developed a code of ethics and code of conduct document to enhance ethical behavior and help guide employees behavior.

LEARNING OUTCOMES

1. Define social responsibility and managerial ethics.
2. Discuss important factors that shape ethical behavior at work.
3. Discuss organizations and management role in enhancing corporate ethics and social responsibility.
4. Discuss PalTel Group corporate social responsibility program and its impact on Palestinians in the West Bank and Gaza.

ACKNOWLEDGMENT

The Author would like to express his deep gratitude and appreciation to PalTel Group management and staff for their support to him while writing this chapter. More specifically, special thanks go to PalTel Group Chief Executive Officer Mr. Ammar Aker, Public Relation Senior Director and Corporate Social Responsibility Officer Mr. Imad Lahham, Ms. Nida Morrar, Director for International Corporate Communications, Abd Majeed Milhim, General Manager of Jawwal and Maan Milhim, General Manager of Palestine Telecommunication Company “PalTel”. Had it not been for their continued support and backing this chapter would have never been completed.

REFERENCES

Bailey, W., & Spicer, A. (2007, December). When Does National Identity Matter? Convergence and Divergence in International Business Ethics. *Academy of Management Journal*, *50*(6), 1462–1480. doi:10.5465/AMJ.2007.28225989

Sims, R. L. (2006). Comparing Ethical Attitudes across Cultures. *Cross Cultural Management: An International Journal*, *13*(2), 101–113. doi:10.1108/13527600610662294

Barnett, M. L. (2007). Stakeholder Influence Capacity and Variability of Financial Return to Corporate Social Responsibility. *Academy of Management Review*, *32*(3), 794–816. doi:10.5465/AMR.2007.25275520

Mackey, A., & Barney, J. B. (2007, July). Corporate Social Responsibility and Firm Performance: Investor Preference s and Corporate Strategies. *Academy of Management Review*, *32*(3), 817–835. doi:10.5465/AMR.2007.25275676

Carroll, A. B. October (1979). A three –Dimensional Conceptual Model of Corporate Performance. Academy of Management Review, 4(4), 497-505.

Barrier, , M et al. (1998). Doing the Right Thing. *Nation's Business*, March, 33–38.

Badaracoo, J.L., Jr., Webb, A.P. (1995). Business Ethics: A view from the Trenches. *California Management Review*, *37*(2), 8–28. doi:10.2307/41165786

Berens, C. (2004). Green Grossers. *Financial Management*, September, 20.

British Consulate. (2015, May 11). *Doing Business with the Palestinian Territories, the Palestinian Economy and Britain.*

Buccholz, R. A. (2009). *Essentials of Public Policy for Management* (2nd ed.). Upper Saddle River, NJ: Prentice Hall.

Robbins, S., & Coulter, M. (1990). *Management* (10th ed.). Pearson Education International.

Business Roundtable Institute for Corporate Ethics. (1988, February).

Carroll, A. B. (1999). Corporate Social Responsibility Evolution of a Definitional Construct. *Business & Society*, *38*(3), 268–295. doi:10.1177/000765039903800303

Cherrington, J. O., & Cherrington, D. J. (1995). *Ethical Decision Making*. Englewood, CO: Micro Mash.

Abuznaid, S. (2009) Business Ethics in Islam: The Glaring Gap in Practice, International *Journal of Islamic and Middle Eastern Finance and Management*, 2(4), 279.

Collins, D. (2009). *Essentials of Business Ethics: Creating an Organization of High Integrity and Superior Performance*. John Wiley & Sons Inc. doi:10.1002/9781118386163

Corporate Social Responsibility Picks up in Kuwait. CSR Middle East, AME Info online. Retrieved from www.ameinfo.com/145699.html

Daft, R. L. (2006). *The New Era of Management* (International ed.). South-Western.

Davis, K., & Fredrick, W. C. (1996). *Business and Society: Corporate Strategy, Public policy, Ethics* (8th ed.). New York: McGraw Hill.

Dessler, G. (2011). *Human Resource Management* (12th ed.). Pearson Education Inco.

Dessler, G. (2013). *Human Resource Management* (13th ed.). Pearson Education Limited.

Dessler, G. (2015). *Human Resource Management* (14th ed.). Pearson.

Elliott, G., Rundle-Thiele, S., & Waller, D. (2014). Marketing (3rd ed.). John Wiley &Sons Australia, Ltd.

Fayyad, S. (2005). *Conference in Support of the Palestinian Economy for the Construction of Gaza*. Egypt: Sharm El Shiekh.

Hatch, M. J., & Schultz, M. (2008). *Taking Brand Initiative: How Companies Can Align Strategy, Culture and Identity Through Corporate Branding*. San Francisco: Jossey–Bass.

International Labor Office. (2009). Geneva: ILO.

Kaptein, S. P., & Kolthof, E. (2003). Six principles for ethical leadership. *PA Times*, *26*(4), 8–9.

Kelly, K. (2014). Speculations On The Future Of Science. Retrieved from http:edge.org/3rd_culture/kelly06/kelly06_index/htm

Kotler, P., & Armstrong, G. (2010). Principles of Marketing (13th ed.). Pearson education Incorporation, New Jersey.

Kotler, P., & Keller, K. L. (2012). *Marketing Management, Global edition* (14th ed.). Pearson.

Kotler, P., & Keller, K. L. (2012). *Marketing Management, 12e* (p. 706). Upper Saddle River, New Jersey: Pearson Education, Inc.

Muel, K. (2003). The Dimond of Managerial Integrity. *European Management Journal*, *21*(1), 99–108. doi:10.1016/S0263-2373(02)00157-3

Morris, S., Rehbein, K. A., Hosselni, J. C., & Armacost, R. L. (1995). A test of Environmental, Situational, and Personal Influences on the Ethical Intentions of CEOs. *Business & Society*, *34*(2), 119–147. doi:10.1177/000765039503400202

Palestinian Business Women's Association. (2010). Women's Economic Empowerment in the West Bank. Palestine.

Palestine Human Resource Development Report (PHRDR). (2004). Birzeit University.

Robbins, S., & Coulter, M. (2009). Management (10th ed.). Pearson Education Incorporation, 118.

Robbins, S., & Judge, T. (2015). *Organizational Behavior* (16th ed.). Pearson.

Robbins, S., Coulter, M., Sidani, Y., & Jamali, D. (2011). *Management (Arab World Edition)*. Pearson Education Limited.

Seifert, B., Morris, S. A., & Bartkus, B. R. (2004). Having, Giving, and Getting: Slack Resources, Corporate Philanthropy, and Firm Financial Resources. Business and Society (pp. 135-161).

McGuire, J. B., Sundgren, A., & Schneeweis, T. (1988). Corporate Social Responsibility and Firm Financial Performance. *Academy of Management Journal*, *31*(4), 854–872. doi:10.2307/256342

Shea, G. F. (1988). Practical Ethics, New York: American Management Association.

Trevino, L. K. (1986). Ethical Decision Making in Organizations: A Person Situation Integrationist Model. *Academy of Management Review*, *11*, 601–617.

Report, S. (2002, December). Corporate Social Responsibility. *The Economist*, 62-63.

Treviño, L. K., Weaver, G. R., Gibson, D. G., & Toffler, B. L. (1999). Managing Ethics and Local Compliance: What Works and What Hurts? *California Management Review*, *41*(2), 131–151. doi:10.2307/41165990

UNCTAD. (1986). Recent Economic Development in the Occupied Territories, UNCTAD/TD/B/1102.

United Nations Office for the Coordination of Humanitarian Affairs (OCHA). (2009). *Humanitarian Overview*. Presentation.

Velasquez, M. (1992). *Business Ethics: Concepts and Cases*. Upper Saddle River, NJ: Prentice Hall.

Ferrell, O. C., Fraedrich, J., & Ferrel, L. (2008). *Business Ethics*. Boston: Houghton Miffin.

Dessler, D. (2013). *Human Resource Management* (13th ed.). Pearson Education Limited.

Wilkie, W. L., & Moore, E. S. (2002). Marketing's Relationship to Society. In B. A. Weitz & R. Wensley (Eds.), *Handbook of Marketing* (pp. 1–38). London: Sage Publications. doi:10.4135/9781848608283.n2

Kelly, K. (2006). Speculations on the Future of Science. *Edge*. Retrieved from www.edge.org/3rd_culture/kelly06/kelly06_index/htmal

Wataniya Report. (n. d.). Retrieved from http://www.wataniya.ps/en/corporate/about

Middle East-peace process. (n. d.). *Wikipedia.* Retrieved from http://en.wikipedia.org/wiki/MiddleEast-peaceprocess

Chapter 6
The Normative Grounding of Social Responsibility in African Emerging Markets:
A Setho Ethics Approach

Khali Mofuoa
Charles Sturt University, Australia

ABSTRACT

In African emerging markets (AEMs), the prevailing notions of social responsibility (SR) are based chiefly on Western ethics. Even discussions of corporate social responsibility (CSR) have, more often than not, been couched in the similar manner. Consequently, the field of CSR in AEMs is largely unaware of Setho ethics that for it are germane as a basis for thinking and talking about SR. In this chapter, the author proposes Setho ethics rooted in Botho, which sees the communal, interdependence and inter-relatedness of beings, as an alternative vision of CSR in AEMs. In fact, people in Sub-Saharan Africa (SSA) see themselves in a symbiotic relationship with society, a point well-articulated by Mbiti (1969, p. 24) thus, "I am because you are, and since we are, therefore I am". This African view through the Setho ethics lenses generates a different notion of an ideal SR of business to society worth illuminating in the CSR discourse today.

INTRODUCTION

In African emerging markets (AEMs), ethical consumerism is a growing phenomenon that underpins ethical trade activities of business (Boluk, 2011; Blowfiled & Dolan, 2008; Darkwa, 2014; Dolan, 2005, 2010; Hughes, et al., 2012; Tallontire et al., 2001; Tustin & De Jongh, 2008). Consumers are increasingly making ethically conscious decisions regarding the consumption of products and services they obtain from business (Busch, 2014; Johnston et al., 2011; Smith, 2008; Tallontire et al., 2001). Therefore, an increasing number of consumers make their consumption decisions on the basis of ethical values (Grauel, 2014; Pecoraro & Uusitalo, 2014; Tallontire et al., 2001). Such values include, but are not limited to environmentally friendly products and production methods; labour standards (wage rates and working conditions); and human rights (Tallontire et al., 2001).

DOI: 10.4018/978-1-4666-9864-2.ch006

Indeed, the demand among customers for ethical products and services is certainly growing, intensifying the ethical and social pressures on business to behave in a socially responsible manner (Connolly & Prothero, 2008). Under these circumstances, business can no longer afford to ignore their social responsibilities or take them for granted. The message is currently clear, "A statement of corporate social responsibility (CSR) is a must-have accessory no large company wants to be without" (Thomas, 2005), at its' own peril. These days, ethically-attuned consumers want business to undertake ethical business actions that benefit them and their immediate communities first and foremost.

From an ethical consumerism perspective, the concept of CSR is based on perceptions or recognition about business that: Firstly, it is part of society. Secondly, it has the potential to make a positive contribution to societal goals and aspirations. It is within this regard that Ponte, Richey and Baab (2009) refer to CSR as the continuing commitment by business to behave ethically and contribute towards societal goals and aspirations. Hence, CSR is seen as a compelling business moral imperative or phenomenon that business cannot afford to ignore any longer (Rossouw & Van Vuuren, 2003), particularly in the AEMs.

Both, the impact of ethical consumerism and the influence of socio-ethical social pressures on CSR practice are increasingly becoming compelling change agents on the relentless calls for business to behave in a socially responsible manner. Indeed, they can be now legitimately taken to be established matters of fact in CSR discourse in AEMs, although the extent to which these developments impact on business practices in these markets remains unclear. What is yet to emerge, however, is an African normative grounding that provides accepted moral basis for the practice of CSR in AEMs, and legitimises the socio-ethical pressures that encourage its development in these markets.

Today, the prevailing analysis and discussions on socio-ethical issues in business in AEMs are based chiefly on Western ethics i.e. moral beliefs and practices of people largely living in North America, Europe and Australasia. Even discussions on CSR have, more often than not, been couched in the similar manner. This has led to a prevailing view of Western ethics as the moral basis of all CSR discourse in these markets. As a consequence, the field of CSR in these markets is largely unaware of *Setho* ethics. It is also not aware of *Setho* ethics principles that for it are germane and attractive as a basis for normative grounding of CSR for business in these markets. In general, *Setho* ethics loosely refers to moral beliefs and practices of the largely Bantu-speaking people of Africa found in Sub-Saharan Africa (SSA) (Futhwa, 2012).

The primary aim of this chapter is to ignite and expand discussions on the normative grounding of CSR phenomenon in AEMs from the African worldview of *Setho* ethics using the *Basotho* of Lesotho as a reference point. In doing so, it intends to focus on the analysis of CSR from a normative-historical perspective and the extent to which the discourse of *Setho* ethics could be successfully be deployed to provide the moral basis for the theory and practice of CSR in AEMs. It should be noted that *Setho* ethics demands moral agents to always "perform their duties in all their affairs with humane purity of thought and unmitigated truthfulness" (Mokhehle, 1976, p.31). Here, the African normative account of CSR based on *Setho* ethics raises important issues that when neglected could threaten the credibility of CSR programmes, and impede the articulation and implementation of CSR policies in AEMs.

Furthermore, the confusion relating to the theoretical orientation of the concept of CSR and its moral basis in literature (Crowther & Aras, 2008; Kashyap et al., 2011) gives credence to twisted discourse of CSR as a morally compelling business practice in AEMs. There is, therefore, a need for more robust and sustained normative discourse on CSR to have the much needed moral legitimacy in these markets as a distinctive factor within business decision-making. Thus, the chapter does not seek to establish an abstract philosophical grounding of CSR based on Setho ethics, but rather a normative one that has the potential to be accepted as a common ground or practice to facilitate CSR discourse in AEMs. This in turn will enable business in these markets to behave in a socially responsible manner.

Based on the aforementioned points, this chapter is divided into seven sections. Here, section 1 makes introductory remarks about the chapter. section 2 provides an overview of the normative-historical orientation of the notion of CSR as a business imperative. Next, section 3 opens the way for normative grounding of CSR discourse in the African context. This is followed by section 4 that presents *Setho* ethics as grounding rationale for fashioning intrinsic CSR in the AEMs. section 5 reflects on *Botho* socio-ethical values influence on CSR practice in AEMs. Next, section 6 discusses some implications of *Setho* ethics for CSR theory and practice in AEMs. Lastly, section 7 concludes the chapter.

NORMATIVE-HISTORICAL ORIENTATION OF THE NOTION OF CSR AS A BUSINESS IMPERATIVE: AN OVERVIEW

Historically, after being unrelentingly attacked and rejected by business leaders and scholars alike for decades, the notion of CSR has become a central facet of the modern-day business. It has been transformed from an irrelevant and often frowned-upon idea to one of the most orthodox and widely accepted concepts in the business world during the last twenty years or so (Lee, 2008, p. 53). Some of the well-known historical leaders in the CSR discourse that viciously attacked CSR were Levitt (1958), Friedman (1970), Drucker (1984) and Jensen (2001). Levitt, in 1958, exhorted businessmen to take heed of the dangers of social responsibility. Likewise, in 1970, Friedman warned about the negative consequences of social responsibility and offered a conservative, economic view of CSR. In a *New York Times* article, Friedman (1970 asserted, "There is one and only one social responsibility of business – to use its resources and engage in activities designed to increase its profits so long as it stays within the rules of the game" (Friedman, p. 230). Also, in 1984, Drucker was even more cynical in his view of the real motives of CSR as a corporate activity. Similarly, in 2000s, Jensen and his colleagues in The Monitor Group argued that, "as far as business organisations are concerned, organisational change efforts towards maximisation of value should be guided by the sole purpose of increasing shareholder value" (Jensen, 2001, p. 298).

In addition, Easterbrook and Fischel (1991), Hetherington (1973), Margolis and Walsh (2003), Sternberg (1997), are other known proponents of the shareholder value dogma as a sole purpose of the business. The reasons given in support of the shareholder value dogma are many and varied. For instance, Hetherington (1973, p. 37) argued that, "There is no reason to think that shareholders are willing to tolerate an amount of corporate non-profit activity which appreciably reduces either dividends or the market performance of the stock." Avi-Yonah (2005, pp. 769-770) summarised them thus: firstly, since management are deploying the shareholders' money, they should not be permitted to do so in ways that do not directly benefit the shareholders; and secondly, permitting more than one measure of managerial success would enhance the agency cost problem and make it impossible to evaluate managers with any reasonable degree of objectivity.

Despite the negative aforementioned CSR discourse, the conviction that, in many cases, business organisations are in a better position to help human development than either governments or not-for-profit organisations persisted and took root in CSR debates. Thanks to the seminal works of Bowen (1953) on *Social Responsibilities of the Businessmen* that set the tone for CSR and that of Freeman (1984) on *Strategic Management: A Stakeholder Approach* in which he argued that managers have a moral obligation to consider and appropriately balance the interests of all stakeholders.

Further published works that supported CSR discourse included Berle and Means (1932); Berle and Dodd (1932); Barnard (1938); Gossett (1957); Johnson (1971); Eberstadt (1973); Carroll (1979; 1999); Jones (1980); Drucker (1984); Goodpaster (1991); Wood (1991); Donald and Preston (1995); Wheeler and Sillanpaa (1997); De Wit and Meyer (2002); Smith (2003); and Jenkins (2005) just to mention a few. In fact, Jenkins argued that, while the current wave of interest in CSR dates from the early 1990s, it is only a new manifestation of "a longstanding debate over the relationship between business and society" (Jenkins, 2005, p. 526). In fact, Eberstadt (1973) argued that concepts analogous to social responsibility have been with us for centuries, even millennia, from classical Greece to medieval period comprising European and American aristocracies. In this regard, Avi-Yonah (2005, p. 768) encapsulates the view of CSR as business organisational corporate activity thus: Firstly, business organisations are seen as typically smaller and more efficient than unwieldy government bureaucracies and, in the developing world, are also less corrupt. Secondly, they are also seen to possess greater resources, both financial and technical, than most not-for-profit non-governmental organisations.

There is no doubt that as the forgoing historical CSR debates raged, various researchers had applied normative ethics overtones as to what ought be the moral obligations of the business organisations. From an applied normative ethics perspective, CSR is a search for a practical litmus test of proper behaviour or conduct of business organisations as metaphysical persons *qua* moral persons (French, 1979). As such, CSR is seen as an ethical approach to business, denoting ethical dimensions in the conduct of business. In this regard, CSR is thus defined as "all the cases of ethics that businessmen can follow effectively in performing their respective social responsibilities" (Velentzas & Broni, 2010, p. 795).

The fundamental idea of CSR is that business has an obligation to work for social betterment (Frederick, 1986). Therefore, one of the business primary goals is their obligation to operate in a socially responsible manner (Carroll, 1979; Colley et al., 2004). Hence, the recognition that the modern business organisations carry vast power (Carroll, 2000; Minzberg, 1983) and the call for them to equally use that power responsibly is seen an important message for managers (French, 1995).

The first comprehensive approach to modern era social responsibility was ushered in 1953 with the publication of Howard R. Bowen's book *Social Responsibility of the Businessman*. Bowen (1953) had the view that public responsibility, social obligations, and business morality were synonyms for social responsibility and described the term social responsibilities of businessmen. For the author, social responsibility of businessmen refers to their obligation to pursue those policies, to make those decisions, or to follow those lines of action which are desirable in terms of objectives and values of their respective societies where their businesses operate (Bowen, 1978). In this regard, the social responsibility of business encompasses the economic, legal, ethical, and discretionary expectations that their respective societies where they operate have of them at a given point in time (Archie, 2000; Kitson - Campbell, 1996).

Indeed, it is now fairly well accepted among scholars that the economic behaviour of business is impacted by its social milieu (Besser et al., 2006; Galaskiewicz, 1997; Granovetter, 1985; Johannisson, et al., 2002; Navarro, 1988; Portes & Sensenbrenner, 1993; Uzzi, 1999). Hence, in the context of cultural relativism from economic or business sense, it can be argued that it is neither appropriate nor useful for business in AEMs to copy Western oriented organisational models for its CSR business theory and practice (Adeleye 2011; Ngugi 2009). In essence, it has become a strategic business imperative for business organisations to theorise their organisational CSR models and practices through *Setho* ethics, which is now much needed for them to re-invent their CSR mandate within the African context (Mbigi 2005; Theimann, et al., 2006).

In this regard, therefore, *Setho* ethics could add value so as to deepen social embeddedness of economic behaviour of business from the CSR perspective. Further, the *Setho* ethics principles of sharing, compassion and respect could better assist business in dealing with issues of greed, competition, intolerance, arrogance and self-claimed superiority, which characterise so much of the modern social life and business practices. The author lacks space in this chapter to do a comparative study of universally accepted principles of CSR with that of *Setho* ethics but he would not be surprised that they might have a striking resemblance despite their contrasting philosophical orientation. In the paragraphs to follow, the author suggests that applying *Setho* ethics to CSR in AEMs can find socio-ethical touchstones that can inform the moral foundation of CSR theories, models and practices in these markets.

NORMATIVE GROUNDING OF CORPORATE SOCIAL RESPONSIBILITY DISCOURSE IN THE AFRICAN CONTEXT: A HISTORICAL SNAPSHOT

It is generally now accepted that cultural beliefs and philosophies are fundamental in shaping a society (Khomba et al., 2013). Similarly it is also now accepted that economic activities of business is influenced by its societal context for its continued performance and sustainability (Amaeshi et al., 2006; Dartey-Baah & Amponsah-Tawiah, 2011; de George, 2008; Owolabi & Olu-Owolabi, 2009; Phillips, 2006; Visser, 2005; Visser et al., 2006; White 2008). In turn, such societal context is shaped by history, mores, beliefs and values of people of a given society at any given point of time. As a business activity, therefore, CSR is equally informed by its societal cultures and traditions (White, 2008). Thus, CSR societal context is nowadays generally perceived as "a function of the different social structures and cultural milieu" (De George, 2008, p. 74).

Sadly, however, the CSR performance of business in AEMs is still based on the monolithic Western moral thought, models and practices. As a consequence, the CSR field is largely unaware of *Setho* ethics that for it are germane to normative grounding or practice of business CSR initiatives in these markets. From *Setho* ethics perspective within the African societal context, CSR means one informed or influenced by salient traditions, customs, beliefs, mores, values and practices of African people, particularly by those residing below the Sahara desert. Within an African context, Amaeshi et al (2006) find that CSR in Nigeria is framed by socio-cultural influences like communalism, ethnic religious beliefs, and charitable traditions. Dartey-Baah and Amponsah-Tawiah (2011) argue that what happens in Nigeria is not different from what pertains in Ghana and/or where else in Africa. In fact, Visser (2006) suggests that the values-based traditional philosophy of African humanism is what underpins most of approaches to CSR in Africa. Speaking of the nature of CSR in Africa, Dartey-Baah and Amponsah-Tawiah (2011, p.130) quote Visser (2005) thus, "The spirit and practice of CSR is often strongly resonant with traditional communitarian values…, for example, African humanism".

Further substantiating Amaeshi et al (2006), Dartey-Baah and Amponsah-Tawiah (2011) and Visser (2006) remarks regarding CSR within an African context, Phillips (2006: 23) states that, "Being socially responsible has been a way of life in Africa, long before the Western world "exported" a much more formalised and corporate approach to corporate social responsibility (CSR) issues". In fact, the author is of the view that "Africa's collective approach to problem-solving and the impact of the extended family system, reinforced by the strong 'village' community mentality and philosophy, all point to an inherently socially responsible race of people" (Phillips, 2006, p 23). Thus, according to Phillips (2006), Africans have long been socially responsible with their own home-grown approach.

In the above regard, Owolabi and Olu-Owolabi (2009) make a very important point in support of Phillips's argument. In the words of Owolabi and Olu-Owolabi (2009, p. 230), "Th[e] idea of social responsibility is not at all strange to Africa". Further, according to Owolabi and Olu-Owolabi (2009, p. 230), "Until colonialism came to shatter the moral fabric of the society, the responsibility of any group in the traditional society was to the community [and], [t]he communalistic spirit in most traditional African society is based on the idea of constant responsibility to the commonwealth." Visser, McIntosh, and Middleton (2006, pp. 10-17) further elaborate on the aforementioned point by relating their experiences of CSR in Africa thus, "The idea that business is part of society, and therefore has community and national responsibilities is established in the culture and economic history of many African countries."

De George (2008, p. 76) agrees that, "corporate social responsibility…reflect[s] the expectations and demands of the societies in which the corporations are found and/or where, they operate". In Africa where lived experiences are based on communalism, Owolabi and Olu-Owolabi (2009, p. 230) are of the view that, "… the foundation of th[e] new project of corporate responsibility [for AEMs can be fashioned]. The challenge… is how to transform those [African] ideas into a systematic moral philosophy of corporate responsibility". In this regard, Cerff (2004, p.1) argues that, "the events of history illustrate that the traditional African way of life has been misunderstood and compromised in humankind's quest for development". He further argues that, "there are significant moral and ethical values that could serve as common ground, as well as admirable values that can be gleaned from traditional African culture (Cerff, 2004, p.2). It is within this view that, in the next section, the author presents *Setho* ethics as the grounding rationale for fashioning intrinsic CSR in the AEMs.

SETHO ETHICS AS A NORMATIVE GROUNDING RATIONALE FOR FASHIONING CORPORATE SOCIAL RESPONSIBILITY IN THE AFRICAN EMERGING MARKETS

The useful introduction to the essence of *Setho* ethics or morality was first ushered in 2011 with the publication of Fezekile Futhwa's book *Setho: Afrikan Thought & Belief System.* This book is probably the most extensive and scholarly account of *Setho*–its customs and constructions currently in print. Using the *Basotho* of Lesotho as a reference point, Futhwa (2011) describes *Setho* as an indigenous belief system of the Bantu speaking people found in different parts of western, central, eastern and southern Africa. For him, *Setho* refers to an African thought and belief system of the Bantu speaking people of Africa about their socio-ethical systems (Futhwa, 2011).

According to Futhwa (2011), individuality is not celebrated in Setho but only accepted within the confines of society as long as it does not compete with the general interests of society. In this regard, individuals are seen as part of society with socio-ethical obligations and responsibilities to promote the general well-being of the society from the *Setho* ethical worldview. More importantly, according to him, *Setho* seeks to equip individuals with the ethical sensitivity and insight needed in order to put their acquired knowledge and resources to use in ways that would benefit not only themselves and their own personal achievement, but the larger society as well (Futhwa, 2011).

Without diminishing Fezekile Futhwa's published contribution towards *Setho*, in actuality Chief Mohlomi (1720 – 1815) is regarded as the first *Mosotho* to preach *Setho* ethics or morality among the *Basotho of* Lesotho in southern Africa (Mokhehle, 1976). He is an astute legendary *Mosotho* credited for playing a special philosophical role in the field of *Setho* ideas that was outside the scope of *Basotho* collective wisdom at the time (Machobane, 1978). For Chief Mohlomi, *Setho* is a philosophy of life and/or a belief system of "humane purity of thought and unmitigated truthfulness" (Mokhehle, 1976, p. 31), whose maxims live on in this modern-day *Lesotho*. His *Setho* aphorisms, like "medicine for a village is a good heart" and "it is better to grow corn than to brandish the spear", which spelled the themes of peace and justice showed his sagacious frame of mind on socio-ethical matters. Notably, most of Chief Mohlomi *Setho* sayings, that have become a part of *Basotho* morality, had to do with social responsibility issues, which were in his opinion absent from the *Basotho* society of his time.

Further, Chief Mohlomi taught that a moral agent ethical sensitivity and insight which is able to respond in the best possible way to any given situation is guided by *Setho,* whose agency is *Botho*. He maintained that only *Botho* as an ethical system of *Setho* can motivate people to achieve their humane excellence and goodwill in every kind of situation for the betterment of the general well-being of the society. In *Setho* ethics, the term *Botho* is used to describe "a person who has a well-rounded character, who is well-mannered, courteous and disciplined, and realises his or her full potential both as an individual and as a part of the community to which he or she belongs (Mapadimeng, 2009). As a concept of *Setho, its* core defining values are respect, solidarity, conformity, compassion, human dignity and humaneness, collective unity and solidarity, sharing, universal brotherhood, communalism, interdependence, and hospitality (Mapadimeng, 2009, p. 76). Furthermore, as a concept of *Setho*, it is most famously affiliated with the maxim that "a person is a person through other persons," or as Mbiti puts it, "I am because we are and since we are therefore I am" (Mbiti, 1988, p.108). Alternatively, Battle (2009) interprets this maxim as "I in You and You in Me".

As an agency of *Setho ethics, Botho* finds its expression in various *Bantu* African languages expressions throughout Sub-Saharan Africa. In Southern Africa, it derives its expression in *Sesotho* saying '*Motho ke motho ka batho'*, or '*Umuntu ngumuntu ngabantu*' in *isiZulu*, which translates into 'a human being is a human being because of other human beings' (Letseka, 2012, p. 55). It can also derive its proverbial expression in *iziXhosa* saying '*Umuntu ngumuntu ngabanye Bantu',* which literally means 'each individual's humanity is ideally expressed in relationship with others and, in turn, individuality is truly expressed or a person depends on other persons to be a person' (Battle, 1996, p. 99). In fact, nowadays, most scholars agree that *Botho* is fundamentally, if not entirely, an ethical discourse, and has the potential to serve as a moral theory for social responsibility for moral agents in their diversities. This claim is enthused by the works of Bessler (2008); Broodryk (2002); Khoza (2005); Letseka (2013; 2012; 2000); Metz (2013; 2007); Metz and Gaie (2010); Mokgoro (1998); Mbiti (1988); Ramose (2002); Sindane and Liebenberg (2000); Sindane (1994); Shutte (1994); Teffo (1994); Tutu (1999) to mention but a few. In fact, Metz and Gaie (2010) see *Botho* as a strong competitor to typical Western approaches to morality, especially in CSR terms.

According to Venter (2004, p. 156) *Botho* is "a concrete manifestation of the interconnectedness of human beings – it is the embodiment of *Setho* African culture and lifestyle." Beets and Le Grange (2005, p.1200) agree that *Botho* is to be aware of one's duties towards one's neighbour in *Setho* moral terms. This theme of human interconnectedness is commonly cited as pivotal throughout recent *Botho* literature. Metz quoted in De Jager (2010, p. 21) amplifies this point by stating that: "[In *Botho*] an action is right just insofar as it produces harmony and reduces discord; where harmony is constituted by shared identity (a 'we' engaged in co-ordination) and solidarity (pro-attitudes towards another's well-being) and discord is a matter of division (an 'us' and them seeking subordination) and ill-will (con attitudes towards another's well-being)". Metz's account thus depicts the *Setho* moral injunction of *Botho* to recognise interconnectedness and harmoniousness. It provides some answer to the moral question "what ought moral agents to do?" by establishing open relationships that could be applied interchangeably to individuals or collectives.

It is therefore not unexpected that *Botho* is now being applied in discussions on socially responsible development (Yirenkyi-Boateng, 2011, p.6). In simple *Setho* ethical terms, *Botho* is believed to be based on the idea of interconnectedness and harmoniousness in business relations with the prospects of adding more value to the CSR discourse in AEMs. The reason for this belief is that *Botho* is based on the *Setho* idea that human progress needs to be rooted on the principles of cooperation, reciprocity and social justice.

It is therefore concluded that *Botho* as a *Setho* ethical system of social interaction and morality in modern day Lesotho was a social construct of Chief Mohlomi aimed at educating *Basotho* to be morally and ethically upright. Chief Mohlomi is further credited to have propounded, canvassed and popularised *Botho* in his *Setho* philosophical teachings in all its manifestations – social, economic, spiritual, environmental and political. It is therefore no coincidence that Chief Mohlomi's teachings were embodied in the *Setho* concept of *Botho*–respect for the sanctity of the human being and a human beings connectedness to other people. In this regard, it is evident that *Botho* as an agency of *Setho* became a national philosophical principle and the practice of being humane, which gave content to life for *Basotho* during Chief Mohlomi's time and modern-day Lesotho.

The influence of *Botho* as in an agency of *Setho* in pre-colonial, colonial and post-colonial *Lesotho* and elsewhere in Africa cannot be over-emphasised. It simply became an ethical system that guided *Basotho*'s philosophy of life as propounded, canvassed, popularised and kept alive by Chief Mohlomi who did not only preach it but lived it. Therefore, today Chief Mohlomi is widely considered as a symbol of *Setho* morality and an impeccable model of *Botho* morals – see figure 1 for Setho ethical worldview. *Basotho* often refer to the 'high *Setho* ethical standards or principles' of Chief Mohlomi, and talk of him as one of the history's great *Setho* ethical or moral leaders of all time in southern Africa. In the next section, the *Botho* socio-ethical values adduced from the crucible of *Setho* heritage that can fashion philosophical reflection of CSR in AEMs are discussed.

Figure 1. Setho Ethical Worldview

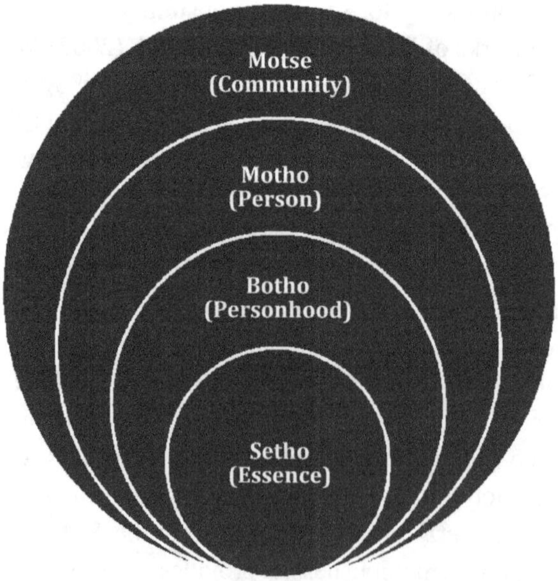

BOTHO SOCIO-ETHICAL VALUES AND SOCIAL CORPORATE RESPONSIBILITY IN AFRICAN EMERGING MARKETS

There is no doubt that the socio-ethical values of *Botho* as an agency of *Setho ethics* can inform, shape and underline CSR philosophical reflection in AEMs. By its nature, CSR is a value-ridden business concept and practice. Further, it is about open and transparent business practices that are based on socio-ethical values that commit business to behave fairly and responsibly and contribute to develop 'sustainable shared value' to all organisational stakeholders. This has led CSR to becoming so important that many business organisations have re-branded their core values to include social responsibility (Khan et al., 2012, p. 41). The notion of social responsibility connotes 'conscious enterprise' by business organisations in support of communal values where they operate. In fact, evidence suggests that CSR in developing countries draws strongly on indigenous cultural traditions of philanthropy, business ethics, and community "embeddedness" (Amaeshi et al., 2006; Dartey-Baah & Amponsah-Tawiah, 2011; Ofori, 2007; Visser, 2005). Below are some of the key *Botho* socio-ethical values as adduced from the crucible of *Setho* ethical tradition of *Basotho* of Lesotho that can inform, shape and underline CSR philosophical reflection in AEMs, and these are illustrated in figure 2.

Figure 2. Botho socio-ethical values and CSR philosophical reflection in AEMs

The Value of Unity

Basotho are historically attached to the socio-cultural and ethical value of unity (*kopano*). The importance of alliance or unity for the common good is evidenced in *Basotho's* history and expressed in the traditional proverb, "*Lets'oele le beta poho*," which translates to, "A crowd can easily overpower a bull" (Mokitimi, 1997, p.18) or "*kopano ke matla*" which means "unity is strength". Therefore, working in harmony or unity with one another is a *Basotho* traditional value considered to be important to the welfare of the society. In fact, unity can be said to be a key *Basotho* value that may inform, shape and underline CSR's philosophical reflection in AEMs.

The Value of Sharing in the Community

Sharing within the community is one of key socio-ethical values of *Basotho*. In fact, sharing which connotes interdependence has always been at the core of *Basotho* livelihood strategies. This has been possible because of the traditional institutions of reciprocity that continue to function today. *Basotho* have always been able to expect economic and social support from their kin and neighbours, and – in ways mediated by their status – have felt obliged to give it. Such support ranged from the traditional *tsimo ea lira* (a communal field belonging to the chief and worked by his subjects) to the widespread livestock-loaning institution of *mafisa* (Ashton, 1967; Mohasi & Turner, 1999; Sheddick, 1954).

Another example of this institution of sharing concerns pooled input to agricultural production - *Letsema*. The *letsema* or work party, where people come together to do a day's farm work in exchange for beer and food, was a standard way of getting the season's tasks in agricultural production done as communal activity. Mohasi and Turner (1999) quote the example of *lijo tsa meelela*, or work in people's fields for payment in grain or other produce as one of the key sharing and support mechanism for *Basotho*. There is no doubt that the interdependence and mutuality emphasised by the value of sharing in community can also inform, shape and underline CSR's philosophical reflection in AEMs.

The Value of Service for the Benefit of Society

The *Basotho* see themselves in terms of "their membership in and servitude to a family and a wider community" (Mpeli & Monnapula-Mapesela, 2009, p. 7). Indeed, in Lesotho "a person's usefulness is measured in terms of [their] contribution to the observable welfare of family and community" (Matsela, 1979, pp. 132-137). Through the value of servitude, King Moshoeshoe who founded *Basotho* nation used the ancient resources of African chieftainship to unite several fragmented tribes into a single people (Sanders, 1975; Thompson, 1975). He united "communities fleeing without livestock by lending them cattle under the *mafisa* system – each man took cattle and became responsible for the care and well-being of the animals, receiving in exchange the right to their milk and some of their offspring" (Mahao, 2006, p.28).

Also under *mafisa*, herds of cattle that were captured in war also became property of the chief, and the subjects gladly became the depositaries and guardians of these new acquisitions for they could use them for farming i.e. oxen as a beast of burden, cattle as source of milk and keep the calves, thus obtaining cattle of their own eventually. There is no doubt that the value of servitude via *mafisa* system can also inform, shape and underline CSR's philosophical reflection in AEMs.

The Value of Shared Humanity

The *Basotho* acknowledges the fundamental moral value of a shared humanity. In Lesotho, the word *Botho* in *Sesotho* (language spoken by the *Basotho*) refers to recognition of shared humanity, as mentioned by Archbishop Tutu (1999, p. 31) that "person with *Botho* is open and available to others, affirming of others, does not feel threatened that others are able and good, for he or she has a proper self-assurance that comes from knowing that he or she belongs in a greater whole…"

The duty of *Botho* thus morally requires *Basotho* to conduct their relations with each other in accordance with ethical principles consistent with the intrinsic value and dignity of a shared humanity. Indeed, the *Basotho* have always attached a great significance on the important contribution that the family and the society as a whole should have in providing social protection to the needy and vulnerable. To every *Mosotho*, this translates into provision of love, care and support to all regardless of their economic and vulnerability status out of sense of shared value of humanity. There is also no doubt that the value of shared humanity can also inform, shape and underline CSR's philosophical approach in AEMs.

The Value of Human Life

All *Basotho* socio-ethical values are based on the precious gift of life. In fact, every social activity – birth, marriage, funerals rituals and other ceremonies – are about celebrating the sacredness of human life and the need to defend, protect and promote it. *Basotho* believe in *Molimo* (God) and *Balimo* (Ancestral Spirits) as well (Futhwa, 2011). The songs of prayer in times of *nala* (plenty) or *thloko* (need) are a witness to *Basotho's* faith in *Molimo* as the ultimate guardian of the value of human life. *Balimo* are used as mediators between people and *Molimo* (Matsela 1979, pp. 132-137) for protection and blessings. For example, in the rite of renewal – the ritual of the first fruits – the first-fruits were ceremonially consumed at the chief's place for thanksgiving to *Molimo* and *Balimo.* The pulp of the leaves was rubbed onto the body and a new fire was kindled. Comarroff quoted in Tlhagale (n.d) writes that "this ritual served to tie the maturation of the crops to the recreation of the social community. The rubbing of parts of the body with pulp from the leaves of the first fruits suggests an intimacy with nature as it renews itself. In their symbolic interaction, human beings participate in the process of revitalization. The kindling of a new fire symbolised the release of new personal and social energy needed for protection, preservation and promotion human life".

These socio-ethical values of *Botho* from the psyche of *Basotho* connote respect for others, helpfulness, community, sharing, caring, trust and unselfishness. They are also seen as a basis for a morality of co-operation, compassion, and communalism which are vital for CSR theory and practice. They capture the spirit in which CSR should be understood and implemented. These properties can provide a supporting basis or frame of reference for CSR theory and practice in AEMs. Indeed, their communal, reciprocal and relational emphasis has a potential to enrich CSR philosophical reflection in AEMs, and provide the ethical basis for its practice. The critical question, however, is: "How the socio-ethical values of *Botho* should be understood and applied to enrich CSR philosophical reflection and practice in the AEMs?" Such is the challenge of *Setho* ethics. This brings us to the next section in which the implications of *Setho* ethics for CSR theory and practice in AEMs are discussed.

SOME IMPLICATIONS OF *SETHO* ETHICS FOR SORPORATE SOCIAL RESPONSIBILITY THEORY AND PRACTICE IN AFRICAM EMERGING MARKETS

It is widely accepted that CSR is the process by which businesses negotiate their role in society. Thus, CSR activities of business seek to integrate business with society for mutual gain. In this regard CSR is perceived as the solution to corporate ethics problems that hinder mutual relations between business and society. According to Mandela (2006) *Botho* as an agency of *Setho* morality can help bridge relational gaps between businesses and the broader society. As a *Setho* ethical system thus *Botho* connotes principles of sharing and caring for one another in social responsibility terms (Broodryk 2002; Ramose 2002). Ramose (2002, p.643) discusses two *Setho* aphorisms connoting *Botho* sharing and caring "to be found in almost all indigenous African languages", namely "*Motho ke motho ka batho*" and "*Ha le fete kgomo le tshware motho*". The first aphorism means that "to be human is to affirm one's humanity by recognising the humanity of others and, on that basis, establish humane respectful relations with them." Accordingly, it is *Botho* which constitutes the core meaning of the aphorism. The second aphorism means that "if and when one is faced with a decisive choice between wealth and the preservation of life of another human being, then one should opt for the preservation of life" (Ramose, 2002, p.644).

Nussbaum (2003) suggests that such connectivity is also portrayed in such indigenous aphorisms and proverbs as: "Your pain is My pain, My wealth is Your wealth. Your salvation is My salvation", or the Sotho saying "It is through others that one attains selfhood", or through the slogan "an injury to one is an injury to all" or through the slogan "an injury to one is an injury to all". The author argues that these metaphorically capture interconnectedness, common humanity, and shared responsibilities of the members of the society.

Following this analysis one can ask: What are the implications of *Setho* morality informed by *Botho* principles and practices for CSR in AEMs? How would the intertwining of CSR with the *Botho* principles of communalism and humanity expressed in Setho aphorisms such as "*Motho ke motho ka batho*" or "*Umunto ungumuntu ngabanye abantu*", which can be translated as "people are people because of other people" mean for CSR in AEMs?

From the *Setho* perspective, CSR thus recognises the importance of communal, interdependent and interrelated relationships between a business and the community. Therefore, business is part of the community and, individuals in the community need to have a sense of belonging to that business as well. Khumalo (2001, p. 59) argues once a business recognises that it is part of the community, helping that society becomes a natural part of the business conduct. Khumalo (2001) continues to argue that the involvement of business in the society through CSR initiatives would be an acknowledgement by business that it exists because of the community. Fundamentally, *Setho* morality emphasise a sense of belonging for members of the society, and this is a challenge for business to redefine itself as part of a community to which individuals in the surrounding society belongs.

This notion of redefining a business as a community where an individual belongs has also been articulated by leading Western management scholars, but *Setho* morality states this point more profoundly. Handy (1997, p. 28) contends that, "a public corporation should now be regarded not as a piece of property but as a community - although not as a community created by common purpose but rather by a common place". Understanding business as a community effectively challenges more traditional ways of thinking about a company as property and in turn, proposes a new thinking about ownership of property. Handy (1997) actually emphasises the viewpoint that viewing business as a community is important; as it recognises that a business is a community to which everyone belongs. This redefinition of business as a community creates a bond between the individual in society and the corporation as well as between the corporation and other stakeholders.

As part of society, business is expected to be involved in solving society's social concerns. *Setho* morality embodies this concept of collective responsibility of solving societal problems, as every person in the society is expected to strive for the well-being of others. Khumalo (2001) argues that dealing with the problems of society should not be the prerogative of government alone nor should it be the sole concern of those affected by them. All of people are part of the society and what affects society affects each of them in one way or another.

This concept of working together to lessen social problems collectively is also found in *Setho* morality, which affirms that socially responsible growth and development derive from the collective wisdom and experiences of all members of the society. *Setho* morality is relevant in today's business environment that is devoid of the voice of humanity. In a world where business conduct is driven by the financial bottom line figures, it is time for business leaders to bring another voice to the table - the voice of *Setho* morality expressed through the ethical system of *Botho*.

By embracing *Setho* morality, CSR in AEMs can naturally become part of business conduct and operations. Business, especially big business, can become more socially responsive by actively channelling resources towards the "social embeddedness of business in society" (Khumalo, 2001). Here, the author argues that, "[business] responsibility to society increases with the power [they] have" (Khumalo, 2001, p.57). In the same spirit of *Setho*, the community likewise should also be supportive of business in its endeavours. Lamberti (2002) praises *Botho*, an agency of *Setho* morality, as an imperative for (South) African business leaders by arguing that, "this sense of unity with broader society means that a commitment solely to shareholders is simply not a sustainable basis for business success". Lamberti (2002) further concedes that with the huge economic disparities in (South) Africa, business leaders cannot be judged on the same criteria as their counterparts in Europe or America.

However, taking the socio-economic context of (South) Africa into account, business leaders need to demonstrate long-term sensitivity to all stakeholders including the local communities in which they operate. This is the essence of CSR in the context of *Setho* morality, where its spirit and practice strongly resonates with African traditional communitarian values. As previously stated by Ole-Owolabi (2009) the idea of CSR is not all strange to Africa. The moral fabric of the African traditional society is such that (i) the responsibility of any group in the society was to the community; and (ii) the communistic spirit was based on the idea of constant responsibility to the commonwealth.

So, the implication of *Setho* ethics to business in relation to society in AEMs is to re-think and re-organise its prevailing CSR theories, models and practices. This implies that current CSR activities in AEMs must be transformed from what Manteaw (2008, p.440) dubbed "'external affairs' necessity into a collaborative learning agenda based on the principle of give and take rather than take and give". This transformation requires businesses to engage in what Manteaw (2008) refers to as the "processes of reversals", described by Chambers (1983) as "Putting the last first and Putting the first last". Such a process, according to Chambers (1997) must begin with the fundamental question: "Whose reality counts?" Indeed, the course for social responsibility (SR) by business to society in terms of CSR tin the context of AEMs is never going to be served by prevailing Western moral relativism and selectivity. On the contrary, it would be truly served by the mark of *Botho*, the creed that has held many Africans to an ideal that affirms one's humanity as being tied up with the humanity of others. This is what the *Setho* ethics approach to CSR proposes and envisions for AEMs.

CONCLUSION

Setho ethics approach to the normative grounding of CSR in AEMs generates a very different notion of ideal SR for business to society. Whether or not one is persuaded by this *Setho* ethics approach to CSR as articulated herein in this chapter, the discussion serves to illuminate the need to broaden the terms of the debate over the appropriate role of business to society, at least within the context of AEMs in Sub-Saharan Africa. The application of *Setho* ethics approach as an alternative vision of CSR in AEMs can go a long way in epitomizing *Botho* organisational setting in CSR terms for businesses in AEMs. Such an organisational setting has the potential to make *Setho* ethics an answer to the impasse of individual consciousness that underpins current CSR theory and practice in AEMs. It is hoped that beyond sentiments and hagiography, this chapter has proven that *Setho* ethics, with its communal, reciprocal and relational emphasis, can provide the required humane normative grounding for CSR theory and practice in AEMs. As a communitarian and humanistic paradigm, *Setho* ethics has the potential to bring about the much-needed philosophical and practical reflection within the field of CSR within the AEMs.

REFERENCES

Amaeshi, K., Adi, B., Ogbechie, C., & Amao, O. (2006). *Corporate Social Responsibility in Nigeria: Western Mimicry or Indigenous Influences?* ICCSR Research Paper Series, The University of Nottingham, Nottingham.

Amaeshi, K. M., Adi, B., Ogbechie, C., & Amao, O. O. (2006). Corporate Social Responsibility in Nigeria: Western Mimicry or Indigenous Influence? *Journal of Corporate Citizenship*, *2006*(24), 83–99. doi:10.9774/GLEAF.4700.2006.wi.00009

Ashton, H. (1967). *The Basuto: A Social Study of Traditional and Modern Lesotho* (2nd ed.). London, UK: Oxford University Press.

Avi-Yonah, R. S. (2005). The Cyclical Transformations of the Corporate Form: A Historical Perspective on Corporate Social Responsibility, *Delaware. The Journal of Corporation Law*, *30*(3), 767–818.

Battle, M. (1996). The Ubuntu Theology of Desmond Tutu. In L. Huley et al. (Eds.), *Archbishop Tutu: Prophetic witness in South Africa*. Cape Town: Human & Rousseau.

Battle, M. (2009). *Ubuntu: I in You and You in Me*. New York: Seabury Books.

Beets, P., & Le Grange, L. (2005). 'Africanising' Assessment Practices: Does the Notion of Ubuntu Hold Any Promise? *SAJHE* (Special Issue), 19, 1197-1207.

Bessler, J. D. (2008). In the Spirit of Ubuntu: Enforcing the Rights of Orphans and Vulnerable Children Affected by HIV/AIDS in South Africa. *Hastings International and Comparative Law Review*, *31*(1), 33–113.

Blowfield, M. E., & Dolan, C. S. (2008). Stewards of Virtue? The Dilemma of CSR in African Agriculture. *Development and Change*, *39*(1), 1–23. doi:10.1111/j.1467-7660.2008.00465.x

Boluk, K. A. (2011). Fair Trade Tourism South Africa: Consumer virtue or moral selving? *Journal of Ecotourism*, *10*(3), 235–249. doi:10.1080/14724049.2011.617451

Bowen, H. R. (1953). *Social Responsibilities of the Businessman*. New York: Harper & Row.

Bowen, H. R. (1978). Social responsibilities of the businessman: Twenty years later. In E. Epstein, & E.D. Votaw (Eds.), Rationality, Legitimacy, Responsibility: Search for New Directions in Business and Society (pp. 116-130). Santa Monica, CA: Goodyear Publishing Co.

Broodryk, J. (2002). *Ubuntu: Life lessons from Africa*. Pretoria: Ubuntu School of Philosophy.

Busch, L. (2014). Individual Choice and Social Values: Choice in the Agrifood Sector. *Journal of Consumer Culture*, *26*(May). doi:10.1177/1469540514536190

Carroll, A. (1979). A Three Dimensional Conceptual Model of Corporate Performance. *Academy of Management Review*, *4*(4), 497–505.

Carroll, A. (2000). A Commentary and Overview of Key Questions on Corporate Social Performance Measurement. *Business & Society*, *39*(4), 466–478. doi:10.1177/000765030003900406

Cerff, K. (2004). *Exploring Ubuntu and the African Renaissance: A Conceptual Study of Servant Leadership from an African Perspective*. Regent University: the School of Leadership Studies.

Chambers, R. (1983). *Rural Development: Putting the Last First*. Harlow, London: Pearson Education.

Chambers, R. (2007). *Whose Really Counts? Putting the First Last*. London: Intermediate Technology.

Colley, J., Doyle, J., Logan, G., & Stettinius, W. (2004). *What is Corporate Governance?* London: McGraw-Hill.

Connolly, J., & Prothero, A. (2008). Green Consumption: Life-politics, risk and contradictions. *Journal of Consumer Culture*, *8*(1), 117–145. doi:10.1177/1469540507086422

Darkwa, S. (2014). Knowledge of nutrition fact on food labels and their impact on food choices on consumers in Koforidua, Ghana: A case study. *South African Journal of Clinical Nutrition*, *27*(1), 13–17.

Dartey-Baah, K., & Amponsah-Tawiah, K. (2011). Exploring the limits of Western Corporate Social Responsibility Theories in Africa. *International Journal of Business and Social Science*, *2*(18), 126–137.

De George, R. T. (2008). An American perspective on corporate social responsibility and the tenuous relevance of Jacques Derrida. *Business Ethics (Oxford, England)*, *17*(1), 74–86. doi:10.1111/j.1467-8608.2008.00522.x

De Jager, P. (2010). *Ubuntu, Zimbabwe and the Ethics of Intervention* [Unpublished masters dissertation]. University of the Witwatersrand, Johannesburg, South Africa.

Dolan, C. S. (2005). Fields of Obligation Rooting ethical sourcing in Kenya horticulture. *Journal of Consumer Culture*, *5*(3), 365–389. doi:10.1177/1469540505056796

Dolan, C. S. (2010). Virtual moralities: The mainstreaming of Fairtrade in Kenya tea fields. *Geoforum*, *41*(1), 33–43. doi:10.1016/j.geoforum.2009.01.002

Drucker, P. F. (1984). The New Meaning of Corporate Social Responsibility. *California Management Review*, *26*(2), 53–63. doi:10.2307/41165066

Frederick, W. C. (1986). Towards CSR3: Why Ethical Analysis is Indispensable and Unavoidable in Corporate Affairs. *California Management Review*, *28*(2), 126–141. doi:10.2307/41165190

French, P. A. (1979). The Corporation as a Moral Person. *American Philosophical Quarterly*, *16*(3), 207–215.

French, P. A. (1995). *Corporate Ethics. Harcourt Brace*. Florida: ICSA Publishing.

Friedman, M. (1970) The Social Responsibility of Business is to Increase its Profits. *New York Times Magazine*, 33, 122-26.

Friedman, M. (2002). The social responsibility of business is to increase its profits. In L. P. Hartman (Ed.), *Perspectives in business ethics* (2nd ed., pp. 260–264). New York: The McGraw-Hill Companies. (Original work published 1970).

Gossett, W. T. (1957). *Corporate Citizenship*. Lexington, VA: Washington and Lee University Press.

Grauel, J. (2014, July 7). Being authentic or being responsible? Food consumption, morality and the presentation of self. *Journal of Consumer Culture, 2014*. doi:10.1177/1469540514541880

Handy, C. (1997). The Citizen Corporation. *Harvard Business Review*, *75*(5), 26–28.

Hughes, A., McEwan, C., & Bek, D. (2013). Retailers, Supply Networks and Changing Articulations of Ethicality: Lessons from Flower Valley in South Africa. *Journal of Economic Geography*, *13*(2), 211–230. doi:10.1093/jeg/lbs049

Jenkins, R. (2005). Globalization, Corporate Social Responsibility and Poverty. *International Affairs*, *81*(3), 525–540. doi:10.1111/j.1468-2346.2005.00467.x

Jensen, M. C. (2001). Value Maximization, Stakeholder Theory, and the Corporate Objective Function. *European Financial Management*, *7*(3), 297–317. doi:10.1111/1468-036X.00158

Jensen, M. C., & Meckling, W. (1976). The Theory of the Firm: Managerial Behavior, Agency Costs, and Ownership Structure. *Journal of Financial Economics*, *3*(4), 305–360. doi:10.1016/0304-405X(76)90026-X

Johnston, J., Szabo, M., & Rodney, A. (2011). Good food, good people: Understanding the cultural repertoire of ethical eating. *Journal of Consumer Culture*, *11*(3), 293–318. doi:10.1177/1469540511417996

Kashyap, R., Mir, R., & Mir, A. (2011). Corporate Social Responsibility: A Call for Multidisciplinary Inquiry. *Journal of Business & Economics Research*, *2*(7), 51–58.

Khan, M. T., Khan, N. A., Ahmed, S., & Ali, M. (2012). Corporate Social Responsibility (CSR) – Definition, Concepts and Scope (A Review). *Universal Journal of Management and Social Sciences*, *2*(7), 41–52.

Khomba, J. K., Bakuwa, R. C., & Kangaude-Ulaya, E. C. (2013). Shaping Business Ethics and Corporate Governance: An Inclusive African Ubuntu Philosophy. *Global Journal of Management and Business Research Administration and Management*, *13*(5), 30–42.

Khoza, R. (2005). *Let Africa Lead*. Johannesburg: Vezubuntu Publishing Ltd.

Khumalo, R. (2001). Concern for Others: A Management attribute of Excellent Companies. *South African Journal of Business Management*, *32*(1), 57–65.

Lamberti, M. (2002, October 27). The True Gist of South African Business is Ubuntu. *Sunday Times Business Times*.

Lee, M. P. (2008, March). A Review of the Theories of Corporate Social Responsibility: Its Evolutionary Path and the Road Ahead. *International Journal of Management Reviews*, *10*(1), 53–73. doi:10.1111/j.1468-2370.2007.00226.x

Letseka, M. (2000). African philosophy and educational discourse. In P. Higgs, N. C. G. Vakalisa, T. V. Mda, & N. T. Assie-Lumumba (Eds.), *African Voices in Education*. Cape Town: Juta.

Letseka, M. (2012). In Defence of Ubuntu. *Studies in Philosophy and Education*, *31*(1), 47–60. doi:10.1007/s11217-011-9267-2

Letseka, M. (2013). Anchoring Ubuntu Morality. *Mediterranean Journal of Social Sciences*, *4*(3), 351–359.

Levitt, T. (1979). The dangers of social responsibility. In T. L. Beauchamp & N. E. Bowie (Eds.), *Ethical theory and business* (pp. 138–141). Englewood Cliffs, NJ: Prentice-Hall. (Original work published 1958)

Machobane, L. B. J. (1978). Mohlomi: Doctor, Traveller and Sage. *Mohlomi Journal of Southern African Historical Studies*, *2*, 5–27.

Mahao, L. (2006). *The power of the hegemonic theory in Southern Africa: why Lesotho cannot develop an independent foreign policy* [Unpublished master's thesis]. Rhodes University, South Africa.

Mandela, N. (2006). Foreword. In R. J. Khoza (Ed.), *Let Africa Lead - African transformational leadership for 21st century business*. Johannesburg: Vezubuntu.

Manteaw, B. (2008). From Tokenism to Social Justice: Rethinking the Bottom Line for Sustainable Community Development. *Community Development Journal: An International Forum*, *43*(4), 428–443. doi:10.1093/cdj/bsm015

Matsela, F. Z. A. (1979). *The indigenous education of the Basotho and its implications for educational development in Lesotho*. Michigan: University Microfilms International.

Mbiti, J. (1988). *African Religions and Philosophy*. Nairobi: General Printers Limited.

Metz, T. (2007). Towards an African moral theory. *Journal of Political Philosophy*, *15*(3), 321–341. doi:10.1111/j.1467-9760.2007.00280.x

Metz, T. (2013). The Ethics of Swearing: The Implications of Moral Theories for Oath-Breaking in Economic Contexts. *Review of Social Economy*, *72*(2), 228–248. doi:10.1080/00346764.2013.799968

Metz, T., & Gaie, J. B. R. (2010). The African ethic of Ubuntu/Botho: Implications for research on morality. *Journal of Moral Education*, *39*(3), 273–290. doi:10.1080/03057240.2010.497609

Minzberg, Z. (1983). The Case of Corporate Social Responsibility. *The Journal of Business Strategy*, *5*(2), 3–15. doi:10.1108/eb039015

Mohapi, M.M. (1956). *Temo ea boholo-holo Lesotho*. Morija: Morija Sesuto Book Depot.

Mohasi, M., & Turner, S. D. (1999). Land and livelihoods in southern Lesotho. Cape Town: Programme for Land and Agrarian Studies, School of Government, University of the Western Cape: Research Report 4.

Mokgoro, Y. (1998). Ubuntu and the law in South Africa. *Buffalo Human Rights Law Review*, *15*, 1–6.

Mokhehle, N. (Ed.). (1976). *Moshoeshoe 1 Profile Se-Moshoeshoe*. Maseru: Mmoho Publications.

Mokitimi, M. I. (1997). *The Voice of the People: Proverbs of the Basotho. African Proverbs Series, 4*. Pretoria: UNISA Press.

Mpeli, M. R., & Monnapula-Mapesela, M. L. E. (2009). Scraping the surface: what is the bottom line regarding ethics? Paper presented in track 8 at the 31st Annual EAIR Forum in Vilnius, Lithuania 23 to 26 August 2009.

Nussbaum, B. (2003). Ubuntu: Reflections of a South African on our common humanity. *Reflections: The SoL Journal*, *4*(4), 21–26. doi:10.1162/152417303322004175

Ofori, D. F. (2007). Corporate Social Responsibility and Corporate Financial Performance: Myth, Reality or Empty Rhetoric? *The African Finance Journal*, *9*(2), 53–68.

Owolabi, K., & Olu-Owolabi, F. E. (2009). Corporate Social Responsibility and the Crisis of Development in Africa. *Journal of Sustainable Development in Africa*, *10*(4), 218–232.

Pecoraro, M. G., & Uusitalo, O. (2014). Conflicting values of ethical consumption on diverse worlds – A cultural approach. *Journal of Consumer Culture*, *14*(1), 45–65. doi:10.1177/1469540513485273

Phillips, F. (2006). Corporate Social Responsibility in an African context. *Journal of Corporate Citizenship*, *2006*(24), 23–27. doi:10.9774/GLEAF.4700.2006.wi.00005

Ponte, S., Richey, L. A., & Baab, M. (2009). Bono's Product (RED) Initiative: Corporate Social Responsibility that solves the problems of 'distant others'. *Third World Quarterly*, *30*(2), 301–317. doi:10.1080/01436590802681074

Ramose, M. B. (2002). The philosophy of Ubuntu and Ubuntu as a philosophy. In P. H. Coetzee & A. P. J. Roux (Eds.), *Philosophy from Africa: A Text with Readings*. Cape Town: Oxford University Press.

Rossouw, G. J., & Van Vuuren, L. J. (2003). The business case for business ethics. *Journal of the South African Institute for Management Scientists*, *12*(1), 1–11.

Sanders, P. (1975). *Moshoeshoe – Chief of the Sotho*. London: Heinemann.

Sheddick, V. G. J. (1954). *Land Tenure in Basutoland*. London: Her Majesty's Stationery Office.

Shutte, A. (1994). *Philosophy for Africa*. Rondebosch: UCT Press.

Sindane, J. (1994). *Ubuntu and Nation Building*. Pretoria: Ubuntu School of Philosophy.

Sindane, J., & Liebenberg, I. (2000). Reconstruction and the Reciprocal other: The philosophy and practice of Ubuntu and democracy in African society. *Politeia*, *19*(3), 31–46.

Smith, N. C. (2008). Consumers as Drivers of Corporate Social Responsibility. In A. Crane, D. Matten, A. McWilliams, J. Moon, & D. Siegel (Eds.), *The Oxford Handbook of Corporate Social Responsibility*. New York: Oxford University Press. doi:10.1093/oxfordhb/9780199211593.003.0012

Tallontire Current Lit, A., Rentsendorj, E., & Blowfield, M. (2001). *Ethical Consumers and Ethical Trade: A Review of erature. Policy Series 12*. Chatham, UK: Natural Resources Institute.

Teffo, L. J. (1994). *The Concept of Ubuntu as a Cohesive Moral Value*. Pretoria: Ubuntu School of Philosophy.

Thomas, K. (2005, April 28). Why it pays to be socially responsible. *The Guardian*. Retrieved from http://www.theguardian.com/technology/2005/apr/28/businesssolutionssupplement5l

Tlhagale, B. (n.d). *Bringing the African Culture into the Church*. Retrieved at http://www.afrikaworld.net/afrel/tlhagale.htm

Tustin, D. H., & De Jongh, D. (2008). Ethical Consumerism as a key consideration for future brand strategy development in South Africa. *South African Business Review*, *12*(3), 24–49.

Tutu, D. (1999). *No future Without Forgiveness*. London: Rider.

Velentzas, J., & Broni, G. (2010). Ethical dimensions in the conduct of business: business ethics, corporate social responsibility and the law. *Proceedings of the International Conference On Applied Economics* ICOAE

Venter, E. (2004). The Notion of Ubuntu and Communalism in African educational Discourse Studies. *Philosophy and Education*, *23*(2/3), 149–160. doi:10.1023/B:SPED.0000024428.29295.03

Visser, W. (2005). Is South Africa World Class in Corporate Citizenship? In A. Freemantle (Ed.), *The Good Corporate Citizen*. Johannesburg: Trialogue.

Visser, W. (2006). Revisiting Carroll's CSR Pyramid: An African Perspective. In E.R. Pedersen, & M. Huniche (Eds.), Corporate Citizenship in developing countries (Ch. 1). Copenhagen Business School Press.

Visser, W., McIntosh, M., & Middleton, C. (2006). Corporate citizenship in Africa: Lessons from the past; paths to the future. In W. Visser, M. McIntosh and C. Middleton (Eds.), Corporate citizenship in Africa: Lessons from the past; paths to the future (pp. 10-17). Sheffield: Greenleaf. doi:10.9774/GLEAF.978-1-909493-63-6_2

White, A. L. (2008). *Culture Matters: The Soul of CSR in Emerging Economies. Business for Social Responsibility*. Retrieved from www.bsr. org

Yirenkyi-Boateng, S. (2011). Business Social Responsibility and the Development Process in Africa: Enlarging the Stakeholders for Sustainable Development, *Africa Institute of South Africa (AISA). Policy Brief*, *51*(June), 1–12.

Chapter 7
Universities as Drivers and Models of Corporate Social Responsibility:
An Empirical Evidence of University in Developing Country

Shahira Osama Abdel-Hameid
Emirates College of Technology, UAE

Alia Babiker Badri
Ahfad University for Women, Sudan

ABSTRACT

This study advocates that universities are prominent driving force behind corporate social responsibility. It highlights the commitment of universities in social responsibility (SR) and civic engagement with special reference to the experience of Ahfad University for Women (AUW) as a model for CSR. The main objective of this study is to develop a better understanding of the roles of universities in social responsibility (SR) and civic engagement (CE) to reveal best practices that can be useful for other universities. The unique evolution of AUW exemplified in its philosophy has created a solid foundation for SR. The study found that university social responsibility (USR) was embedded at the student, faculty and community members level supported by the values and commitment of top management.

INTRODUCTION

Universities are crucial and catalyst organizations in identifying and fulfilling the needs and demands of societies in terms of human capital. Thus the role of universities, as social institutions, extends beyond the provision of the immediate educational services. Universities are expected to play a significant role in serving their communities by being socially responsible and actively engaged in a variety of activities that help the communities to strive for development and advancement.

DOI: 10.4018/978-1-4666-9864-2.ch007

In recent years, particularly in Europe and the USA witnessed a keen interest and publication of variety of research about the concept of corporate social responsibility (CSR) particularly in profit making firms (Meiseberg & Ehrmann, 2012). However, academic institutions in general and in developing countries in particular suffer from scarcity of scientific studies in this emerging important subject.

The vast majority of existing studies on CSR (80%) were quantitative in nature (Lockett et al., 2006). This is an exploratory research based on case study methodology. The study adopts an insider, qualitative approach and non-positivistic stance. Yin (2003) illustrated that qualitative techniques offer advantages, which are not likely to be obtained from quantitative methods. The former technique provides the researcher with the opportunity to explore complex problematic phenomena that are difficult to capture having relied on quantitative methods.

From an ontological and epistemological standpoint, this research intends to give meaning to social reality through understanding and interpretation of social constructs, meanings and knowledge around the phenomena as provided by research informants and existing documents (Robnson, 2002) to minimize the likelihood of the researcher bias occurrence. In addition, the use of triangulation will also help in reducing any potential bias (Proenca and Branco, 2014)

Ahfad University for Women (AUW) has been chosen because of its unique philosophical framework that includes it both as a community-oriented private as well as a non-profit higher education institution that recognizes a wide scope of collaboration of different stakeholders including UN agencies and NGOs in Sudan. Hence it is considered as an unusual case to study (Yin, 2003).

A purposive sample using non-probability sampling techniques was utilized to target key informants with sufficient knowledge in the topic under investigation.

Semi-structured interviews were perceived to be the most appropriate method of data collection for this type of study. A number of open-ended questions were designed to guide the interviewees and invite them for in-depth discussion. The authors believe that semi-structured interviews were more likely to generate a better understanding of the CSR phenomena and identify the practices and consequences of its application by AUW.

The qualitative data was analyzed by creating concepts and categories around the different components of CSR activities, prevalence and performance outcomes.

The objectives of this chapter are two-fold: (a) to discuss the concept of CSR and outline approaches that provide an understanding of the conditions under which academic organizations may be more or less socially and ethically responsible, (b) to develop a better understanding of the CSR practices within AUW.

This chapter is an endeavor to investigate the role of universities in contributing to community development by getting involved in activities beyond the academic realm. It argues that there is an ethical dimension underpinning behaving in a socially responsible manner; in other words, academic institutions should do 'good' because it is the 'right' thing to do.

The chapter starts by exhibiting some theoretical aspects about CSR and the contextual factors within which AUW strives for both meeting its social and ethical commitment and academic excellence. Further, the chapter presents the University's contributions in CSR, followed by recommendations for future research and concluding remarks.

BACKGROUND

Corporate Social Responsibility: Concepts

CSR persists as an emerging subject and the interweaving mechanism between organizations and society still remains obscure (O'Riordan & Fairbrass, 2006), making it a vibrant subject for academics as well as a challenging issue for managers and their stakeholders.

Scholars elucidated that CSR means different things to different people. However, the common understanding and meanings associated to CSR seem to be more related to social and/or environmental accountability. Vasilescu, Barna, Epure & Baicu (2010) discoursed that CSR goes beyond the traditional concept of philanthropy. It extends to the organization's proactive role in standing up to societal and environmental and sustainable development. Within the same line, van Marrewijk (2003) and Hansen and Spitzeck (2011) advocated that CSR is the organization's voluntary activities related to protecting and improving social issues such as community development and environmental issues.

Other terms and definitions about CSR from organizations' perspectives have been reported. They have been amalgamated into popular and accepted aspects addressing financial performance and operations efficiency (Orlitzy, Schmidt & Rynes, 2003), firm's competitiveness (Porter & Kramer, 2006), moral and ethical concerns, human rights (Hansen and Spitzeck, 2011) and voluntary activities (Proenca and Branco, 2014).

The manager of any socially responsible institution should be inspired to achieve goals, obey the law, act transparently and ethically and be a good corporate citizen meeting the needed level of civic engagement. Subsequently, a social responsible behavior will reflect positively in enhancing the reputation and performance of the organization.

Some scholars highlighted the importance of integrating CSR practices into the business strategy and its operations. Others, such as Vasilescu et al. (2010) revealed that an important dimension of CSR is how organizations interact with the internal (employees) and external (customers, government, community at large) stakeholders to behave in a socially and ethically responsible manner. Vasilescu also emphasized that CSR is an endeavor to achieve a win-win situations for both the organization and society members at large in order to maintain the competitive advantage of the organization.

From the outset, one can conclude that CSR is a multidimensional and to some extent a complex concept. CSR can be summoned up to three commonly agreed standpoints. Firstly, it is associated with the economic, social and environmental universally referred to as the 'triple bottom line' facets of the business operation. Secondly, it is related to the ethical responsibility towards internal and external stakeholders. Thirdly, it is about sustaining the welfare of society where successful organizations strive to succeed. All this makes it difficult to agree on one best definition. This could imply that CSR may greatly differ based on individual perceptions of responsibility and the organization philosophy and beliefs (Woodward, et al., 2001). The next section explores some of the popular and frequently cited CSR approaches in the business literature.

Corporate Social Responsibility: Approaches

Evidence from the literature shows that there have been several approaches can be used to studying various roles and/or obligations within CSR and motivations in engaging in CSR initiatives. Among the popular and frequently cited approaches in the CSR literature are Carrol's (2008) top-bottom approach to CSR elucidating organizations obligation towards first satisfying their economic responsibility and then moving their attention to satisfying other responsibilities such as legal, ethical and philanthropic in a hierarchical order. Lockett *et al.* (2006) classified four dominant CSR themes: social, environmental, ethics, and stakeholders. The triple bottom line approach aims at achieving a balance between economic, social and environmental responsibilities. The stakeholder theory emphasizes the interests of those individuals and groups who affect and are affected by the operations of the organization. It is apparent that all these approaches have more or less shared the same characteristics.

Aguilera, Rupp, Williams & Ganapathi (2007) approach to CSR is to understand the motivations underlying organizations engagement in social responsibility (SR) activities. They have identified three motives; instrumental motives when CSR practices aimed at enhancing the competitive advantage of the firm and reputation of the firm, relational motives intending to bring about social legitimacy and moral motives instigating the values, norms and beliefs of the organizational actors to promote social good.

In this chapter, the conceptual framework of the study will be guided by the core characteristics model of CSR (Crane, Matten and Spence, 2013); emphasizing voluntary action, managing externalities, stakeholder orientation, alignment of social and economic responsibilities, practices and values, and beyond philanthropy as shown in the table below. It is noticeable that some of those CSR characteristics are captured in Carrol's and Lockett's approaches.

This CSR core characteristics model, described below, is frequently cited in the academic and/or practitioners' definitions of CSR debates (Crane, Matten and Spence, 2013). It is also believed to be more practically helpful as compared to the other models in examining how CSR is demonstrated in a university context, which the authors hope will serve in delineating the complexity of the concept (Table 1).

Table 1. Core Characteristics Model

CSR Characteristics	Description
Voluntary action	It is those actions commonly perceived to incorporate activities that are not legally bound or mandatory.
Managing externalities	Shouldering the cost of activities that could have negative consequences on the local community. A typical example of externality is pollution as community members are the ones who suffer from the business actions.
Multiple stakeholder orientation	Taking into regard the interests of all stakeholders who affect and are affected by the organizations' operations.
Alignment of social & economic responsibilities	Balancing the interests of different stakeholders.
Practices and values	Philosophies and values that underpins business practices.
Beyond philanthropy	It is about how the core functions of the business impact the society.

Source: Corporate Social Responsibility: Readings and Cases in Global Context (2008).

Universities as Socially Responsible Organizations

As mentioned earlier the fundamental concepts of CSR have been extensively discussed and debated in the business arena. This prompts one to question the applicability of those fundamental concepts over the operations of universities as an organization (Shawyun, 2011).

Universities are not only the foundation of education and learning but also the cornerstone of human development. University Social Responsibility (USR) is a rather young field and the subject of social responsibilities of universities as creators of knowledge societies was initially discussed at a global level in the 2nd Asia-Europe Education Workshop in 2011. Universities are explicitly or implicitly perceived as the star or spotlight of social responsibility and as mentioned by Shawyun (2011). They fall under the microscopic lens as transformers of society, within this understanding social responsibility is coined with university; (cannot be divorced from Universities) hence it can be termed as university social responsibility.

USR is envisioned as developing human capabilities and creativeness as potential leaders devoted towards betterment and human advancement through accessible and dissemination of knowledge and learning.

USR aims at building a better society through transforming and strengthening community potential; providing community services whether it is economic, social, cultural, peace, security and human rights that aid the government in contributing to sustainable development.

The Universidad Construye Pais (UCP, 2006) project launched in Latin America was an endeavor to raise the awareness of stakeholders to the concept of social responsibility of universities. A definition was set that USR evolves around applying and disseminating a core of ethical values such as dignity of individuals, acceptance of diversity, social equity and commitment to excellence and trans-disciplinarily representing the ethos of a university. These declared values should feed into and contribute to four fundamental functions of any university: management, teaching, research and extension activities (Jimenez, 2007).

Another definition of a USR that falls within the same line of the UCP but with different emphasis explained that USR is a policy of ethical values incorporated into university activities. These values represent the management of a university educational, cognitive and environmental responsibility developed in an interactive dialogue with society to promote a sustainable human development (Reiser, 2008).

Other definitions which evolved around putting ethics and values at the heart of universities highlighted that USR is not confined to producing graduates with academic excellence but producing graduates holding values and principles of tolerance, peace, empathy, responsiveness and commitment to community development to realize their social responsibility.

There are many challenges confronting universities' operations extending beyond steady financial resources. Some are philosophical and strategic about integrating socially responsible behavior as a core of any university's mission in a way that will contribute to the transformation of higher education (Watson, Hollister, Stroud, & Babcock, 2013). Other challenges are the emergence of private universities and commercialization of education, diversification, and technological advancement. They have not only impacted on the quality of education but rendered universities to become more competitive and corporatized with a desire to become and maintain an image of good corporate citizen by devoting its direction towards society wellbeing (Vasilescu et al., 2010, Nagy & Robb, 2008).

RESULTS AND DISCUSSION

AUW Social Responsibility: Meanings

Different meanings have emerged in relation to the meaning of USR among key informants within AUW, including top management and senior faculty members. These meanings and definitions ranged from identifying and responding to meet the needs of multiple stakeholders, particularly those disadvantaged or under-privileged segments of the society. USR is also about encouraging values of voluntarism, efficient utilization of resources necessary to engage in CSR.

The interviewees expressed the following understanding regarding USR.

USR involves sustainability in community development and civic engagement. It is about promoting and exercising the act of giving and volunteerism among the students, faculty members and administrative staff. (Top management, 30/10/2014)

USR is about engagement of the university through participatory dialogue with external stakeholders to undertake awareness raising, capacity building and advocacy activities to meet the needs of the community. (Top management, 01/10/2014)

USR indicates the university commitment, involvement in community issues in an attempt to serve the vulnerable groups via its outreach programs. (Senior faculty member, 06/10/2014)

Social responsibility is the obligation towards wellbeing of society through prevention of harm such as gender-based violence. (Senior faculty, 06/10/2014)

To be socially responsible an organization should employ all possible resources efficiently to achieve its goals and objectives while maintaining the wellbeing of the different stakeholders and the community at large. (Senior faculty member, 20/10/2014)

The above quotations show that AUW top management and senior faculty members share the Universities ethos associated with USR. Their conception typically reflects an analogy, which dictates a common understanding that the role of a socially responsible university extends beyond the provision and transformation of academic knowledge and learning. One can deduce from their responses that USR is rather a part of the AUW's commitment to its ethical values than a business practice. Furthermore, AUW's core ethical values stipulates playing a fundamental role in promoting awareness and sensitization among its various stakeholders constituting its social responsibility and good citizenship through its policies, strategies and functions should be directed towards voluntary community services by engaging internal and external stakeholders. This finding is consistent with previous studies such as Shawyun (2011).

Motives to Engage in CSR

The interviews revealed that the motives for SR date back to the unique historical story behind the establishment of AUW through fund raising from the elite, high profile and wealthy Sudanese people.

AUW was established as non- government, non-profit through people's funding, it depended on fund raising from Sudanese people rich and poor, elites and other non-Sudanese donors [contributed] in building its infrastructures and funding most of its SR activities. Hence, as it is an outcome of SR before the term is called so, it continues on this mission and also to pay back what Sudanese people offered to establish it. (Top management, 01/10/2014)

This finding suggests that AUW has been doing CSR since its inception IN 1966 and is viewed as part and parcel of the University's identity and ethos, even before being known as concepts of and named as CSR.

Another motivation for CSR was highly driven by the philosophy of the university.

By adopting the philosophy of achieving gender equity, equality and women empowerment to educate and serve members of the community will eventually contribute to the well-being of the society. Being a female university is more likely to impact on social welfare since they [students] assume the triple role due to gender ideology. (Top management, 20/10/2014)

Hence, the consequences of USR activities on AUW through close collaboration with the community has positioned the University as a close and trustworthy partner to UN agencies, specifically UNFPA, WHO, UNIFEM, UNDP, and UNHCR assisting them in identifying community needs, projects and community-based-organization to sustain those activities after the project phases out.

By being engaged in CSR, and the activities it conducts, AUW gained local and global acknowledgement and enhanced reputation supported by good academic performance. This has opened channels for external collaboration with other universities and organizations, governments and UN bodies. (Top management, 20/10/2014)

The findings indicate that unlike other firms and/or private universities who are primarily engaging in CSR to improve their financial performance (Orlitzy, Schmidt & Rynes, 2003) AUW is not targeting to enhance its financial status but driven by social improvements guided by ethical values of social justice, compassion and human rights.

Hence, the findings do not support the assumption that CSR is a matter of business or profit but rather an issue of philosophy, values and ethics. Through participation in USR activities, AUW has managed to align the different stakeholders (students, faculty members and community) interests. Both students and faculty members have the opportunity to exercise their civil rights in engaging in socially responsible activities. Community members have benefited from those voluntary actions explained in earlier sections.

Practices and Values

Universities and corporations should define their own concept that symbolizes their mission, organizational culture and CSR policy (Angelo, Amui, Caldana and Jabbour, 2012). AUW has exemplified the concept of SR in its mission and vision statements reading respectively as *to provide quality education for women to strengthen their roles in national development, and in seeking equity for themselves and other fellow women in all facets of Sudanese society.* (AUW, 2013)

AUW vision is *to be nationally prominent university and leading institution worldwide, known for gender equity, women empowerment, academic excellence, research, civic engagement and social responsibility.* (AUW, 2013)

Analysis of relevant documents (AUW, 2012) verified that USR is integrated in the strategic plan of AUW. Its strategy for SR is embodied in achieving excellence in public engagement through incorporating public engagement in the University mission, vision, objectives, programs and activities in addition to promoting stronger collaboration and partnership between the university and its stakeholders and contributing to the advancement and betterment of the cultural, economic and health dimensions of the society. Evidence is provided in the following parts.

Stakeholders Orientation

AUW has maintained to position itself as a "community-oriented" and "society-caring" academic institution. When it comes to USR, the University embraces a "three-stakeholder approach" focusing on students, faculty members, and community members.

Students

Students are key fundamental stakeholders of the University and are highly engaged in the CSR of AUW.

AUW historical role is not only restricted to fostering its role of transforming ethical values among its students through both its education mission and its production of knowledge that underlay concerns of real world but it strives to engage its students to participate in the CSR/USR activities. This exemplifies in adopting a 'community-learning approach' guided by the University philosophy of incorporating community concerns into academics. Each student gets the opportunity to practice her socially responsibility through community-oriented practical courses offered by the University.

For instance, this is witnessed in the mandatory annual extension fieldtrips (part of the rural extension curriculum) where all students in fourth year in the different academic programs are required to participate in the fieldtrips to rural areas covering diverse regions in Sudan.

Students get the opportunity to identify with the disadvantaged community by staying in targeted rural areas for an average of two weeks. These fieldtrips build their leadership skills and prepares them to become social change agents when they graduate and at the same time satisfy the interests and needs of those low-socio-economic communities with knowledge and awareness-raising in community-related problems such as gender-based violence, public health, sanitation and nutrition. (Top management, 20/09/2014)

Another academic program which engages students with the community is the Family Attachment Program, part of the medicine curriculum.

Second year students in the School of Medicine are attached to families in poor urban areas with whom they meet once a month for four years to educate families about child, maternal, and family health and to assist them with referrals and access to health services in the community. Within the same line, students in Health Sciences program provide nutritional advises to those poor families as wel.l (Top management, 30/10/2014)

Students in other specializations such as in Psychology and Preschool Education, after completing their tenure, students are assigned internships to provide counseling services in psychiatric hospitals, trauma and special needs centers located specifically in poor communities (AbdelRahman &Osama, 2009). This learning philosophy does not only allow each student a first-hand experience of practical work that is central to her academic and professional preparation but enhances her commitment to be a socially responsible citizen.

In Management Studies, students develop a deeper understanding of the complexities of CSR through their graduate research combined with engagement with the industry that are CSR-oriented to build social responsibility awareness. Management students with support from faculty have the chance to provide advice on entrepreneurship and managerial skills for those poor women wishing to apply for loans, part of the revolving fund project offered by AUW (AbdelRahman &Osama, 2009). This is discussed later in this section.

Hence, these practical academic programs expose students to get first-hand experience with community needs, raise their awareness and commitment to social responsibility. Within the same perspective, Checkoway (2001) highlighted that exposure to experiential education enables students to learn a great deal from their engagement in the community.

Students also practice their social responsibility through extra-curricula activities. This is evidenced in AUW's support extended to its students to set up different associations for good social cause. For instance, *Ana Sudan* (I am Sudan) is a national student organization involving 200,000 volunteers representing all states. Through donations from international non-governmental organizations (INGOs), the students have managed to establish 105 schools and rehabilitate 500 schools in under-privileged communities (AUW, 2012).

The Ahfad Medical Students Association receives support from World Health Organization to organize free health mobile clinics. They treat an average of 200-300 people/day for endemic diseases as indicated by the Dean of the School of Medicine (2014).

The Nuba Mountains Student Society formed by AUW is affiliated with the Nuba Mountains Students and Scholars Coalition, a national non-governmental organization (NGO) that provide disadvantaged students with scholarships on conditional terms that after they graduate have to go back and work in their villages for five years (AUW, 2012). The University helps them in finding jobs with organizations targeting women empowerment alleviation and combating gender-based violence.

Students are encouraged to document and publish their community experiences in a magazine (*The Promising Half*) funded by the University and produced by the students.

Other extra-curricula activities reflecting students' commitments to social responsibility are seen in the celebrations of important international days, such as the International Women's Day celebrated during the University annual Women's Week. The themes of the women's week correspond to those identified by the United Nations. Students develop sub-themes on which they plan and perform activities including drama, music, choral, poetry, etc. The celebrations of the population and world food days focus on raising awareness of students, government and communities of population and food security issues respectively. Similarly, students perform different activities to deliver messages tackling issues of hunger, poverty, and reproductive health. Violence against women day, cancer and heart disease awareness months are also huge events organized jointly by the faculty members and students (Abdel-Rahman and Osama, 2009).

Faculty Members

The culture of AUW faculty members shapes the beliefs and behaviours of faculty members to dedicate some of their time in civic engagement. They are believed to be the cornerstone or driving force of USR. Hence, the University strategy strives to maintain their civic involvement by developing curriculum that helps prepare students for their social-responsible roles.

Within the same line, to ensure community relevant courses, faculty members play key roles in involving different stakeholders from the community for consultation in design context-specific courses and contextualize the global into the local (Badri, 2008). This is apparent in the following quotation.

The Conflict and Population Mobility [a graduate course] is a unique course not taught in a conventional master program of peace studies. It is context-based as this issue of population mobility is escalating exceeding over five million, i.e., 1/6 of the total population is displaced in camps. (Badri, 2008)

Such involvement of stakeholders guarantees academically sound courses relevant to the Sudanese context and corresponds to international standards. Courses are regularly evaluated and updated to be responsive to current and changing community needs. Similarly Checkoway (2001) emphasized that involving communities from different professional fields, they become partners and participants rather than human subjects.

Faculty members are encouraged to engage in policy-oriented research focusing on national and community-based problems to advocate for policy makers scientific-based solutions. For instance,

Faculty research on sustainability of income generating project targeting under-privileged women conducted in collaboration with UNFPA and some local NGOs resulted in policy recommendation that led to the creation of future revolving fund projects in different parts of Sudan combined with awareness raising package. (Top management, 05/10/2014)

Another faculty research focused on communal conflicts in Sudan, its causes, resolution mechanisms and conflict transformation. As one of the research team leader mentioned

This is a joint research undertaken in collaboration with the Center of Strategic Initiative in Washington and Novib in Holland with faculty from the university of Khartoum and Juba. It covered five regions in Sudan namely Darfur, East region, River Nile State, Nuba Mountains and the Southern region. The research was considered as key case study about conflict in Sudan and was widely used by policy makers and academics. (Top management, 05/10/2014)

These researches are designed to contribute to society's welfare emphasizing the University social responsibility obligations and values towards its society.

Most importantly, faculty members are highly involved in the various CSR initiatives executed and hosted within the University through collaboration with partner organizations, such as UNFPA, UNIFEM, UNDP, WHO. These include programs of advocacy and capacity building aimed at achieving gender equity, equality and women empowerment; community outreach, awareness raising and sensitization on combating harmful traditional practices; and consultation in setting up institutional building and strengthening capacities of non-governmental organizations and community-based organizations (Badri, 2008).

Since 1999, 200 villages in ten localities of northern Sudan have been mobilized and organized into 800 community-based organizations providing services for education, health, water and sanitation and 50 adult literacy centers have been set up in conflict-zone areas. (Top management, 01/10/2014)

Faculty members dedicate their social responsibility through engaging in those partnership programs (at national, regional and international levels) implemented within a framework guided by AUW ethical principles of transparency, equality, and respect to diversity and minority.

CSR is both a proactive and reactive activity. Faculty members behave in a socially responsive manner through anticipating and responding to natural disastrous affecting poor communities.

In response to last year floods, a group of faculty members organized post disaster support by engaging students to offer medical aid and other donations to those needy people suffered from the floods in Khartoum state. (Senior faculty member, 30/10/2014)

Faculty engagement in SR activities expose them to different experiences beyond their academic circle which consequently improve their teaching and direct them towards identifying community development projects and context-specific research ideas.

Checkoway (2001) confirmed that ‘there is evidence that faculty who consult in community are more productive researchers and better teachers than those faculty who do not’ (p.136). This is contrary to the traditional belief that time consumed in community engagement might divert faculties from their professional work and jeopardize their promotion.

Voluntary Community Involvement

Community involvement is one of the primary USR activities of AUW. It is about voluntary action and a contribution to the society wellbeing that are not compelled by the law; it is also similar to Carrol’s dimension of philanthropy (2008). AUW carries out its voluntary activities through its outreach arms voluntary organizations namely: Babiker Badri Scientific Association for Women Studies (BBSAWS; 1974), Community Animator Friendly Association (CAFA; 1994) and the Sudanese American Foundation for Education (SAFE; 1980). BBSAWS and CAFA are responsible for conducting voluntary programs in the form of training and awareness raising addressing different issues related to women empowerment, human and women rights, gender-based violence and reproductive health issues, culture of peace, and eradication of harmful traditional practices. SAFE is dedicated to supplying AUW with textbooks donated from American universities. AUW distributes these books (free of charge) to other universities through an annual book exhibition. The results of the interviews and analysis of AUW documents revealed that AUW addresses its societal responsibility in its strategy with a focus on improvement of the under-privileged communities. In line with its vision and strategy, AUW has embraced the following USR activities since the early 1990s.

Since 1994, AUW with donation from UNFPA established an integrative maternal and child health care clinic (MCHC) primarily aimed at serving neighboring areas, dominated by displaced people with no access to other health care provider. The MCHC clinic also offers outreach activities in association with Family Attachment Program (FAP; 1991).

Another key contribution to marginalized communities culminates in the University teaching farm located adjacent to displaced camps. The farm has become a training avenue for internally displaced people in acquiring and developing basic livelihoods skills related to appropriate technology in farming, food production and food security. The farm also offers the community with clean drinking water a supplement to the very few existing water points (AbdelRahman & Osama, 2009).

AUW extends its social contribution to community members through its Early Childhood Development Centre since the mid-1970s, which do not only serve as a training center for AUW students but also provides free trainings and consultations in early childhood development to other kindergartens in the different poor communities inside and outside the capital.

The Early Childhood Development Center provides service to 1.5 million people living in peripheral areas of the capital. (Top management, 06/10/2014)

AUW set up the Ahfad Trauma Treatment Training Centre (ATC; 2012) to provide psychosocial support to individuals, families and communities affected by adversity and traumatic events, while also servicing the surrounding catchments. The centre also aims to provide training and internship opportunities to AUW psychology graduates in the field of mental health, counseling, and social support.

The Literacy and adult education programs offered to those illiterates in the neighborhood communities is another socially responsible contribution towards reducing illiteracy rate in poor communities (AbdelRahman & Osama, 2009).

The interviews revealed that the beliefs of the AUW leaders play a significant role in maintaining high engagement in CSR. This is evidenced in the University's contribution of the "White Nile Water Project: A Source of Food and Health" (AUW, 2012). It is a major outreach activity in providing water to rural villages. The project was carried out in collaboration with Iowa State University, USA, and an initiative of the current President of AUW as part of his visionary leadership of supporting community development.

An important voluntary initiative, which symbolizes the University's philanthropic philosophy, is the revolving fund program. It provides small loans (paid back with 0% interest) to disadvantaged women who have been reallocated to peripheral areas of the Omdurman city due to civil war. These small projects help in empowering women to become financially independent and hence impact positively on the socio-economic status of the family and ability to communicate and negotiate, as well as improved women's skills in income generating activities and boosted their self-confidence and esteem, a way towards regaining control of their own lives (Abdel-Rahman and Osama, 2009).

The current President of AUW values the principles of philanthropy which extends to offering opportunities to those marginalized students. This is evidenced in his policy of scholarships for disadvantaged students. Although the main source of income of AUW is through tuition fees, education aids are given to under-privileged students.

Over one-third (33%) of under-graduate student population receives scholarships (donation not loan). These scholarships are not offered on academic excellence-basis but on the disadvantaged status of the student, 40% of students receive reduced and/or waived fees to ensure that they are not deprived from higher education due to inability to pay full tuition fees. Few fellowships are offered for post-graduate students, usually donated by AUW counterpart projects to women coming from disadvantaged zones (Abdel-Rahman & Osama, 2009). The findings clearly indicate that philanthropy constitutes an important component of the University practices and values. CSR appeared to be value-driven supported and sustained by top management. This philanthropic commitment implies that CSR is perceived as moral obligation.

Engagement in CSR activities has been consistently emphasized as considerably benefiting the organization as whole (Pronenca and Branco, 2014; Heslin and Ochoa, 2008; Falck and Heblich, 2007). AUW's involvement in CSR activities is greatly benefiting the University instrumentally (Proenca and Branco, 2014) by maintaining a distinguished reputation as a community-oriented and socially responsible academic institution, a brand name for AUW emphasizing its competitive advantage among both private and state universities within the Sudan.

FUTURE RESEARCH DIRECTIONS

New Proposed USR Model

From the findings, this study proposes the following simple and practical model as shown in Figure 1 for implementing a sustainable strategic social responsibility within national universities, with a view for validity testing in future research.

Figure 1. Model of sustainable social responsibility of universities

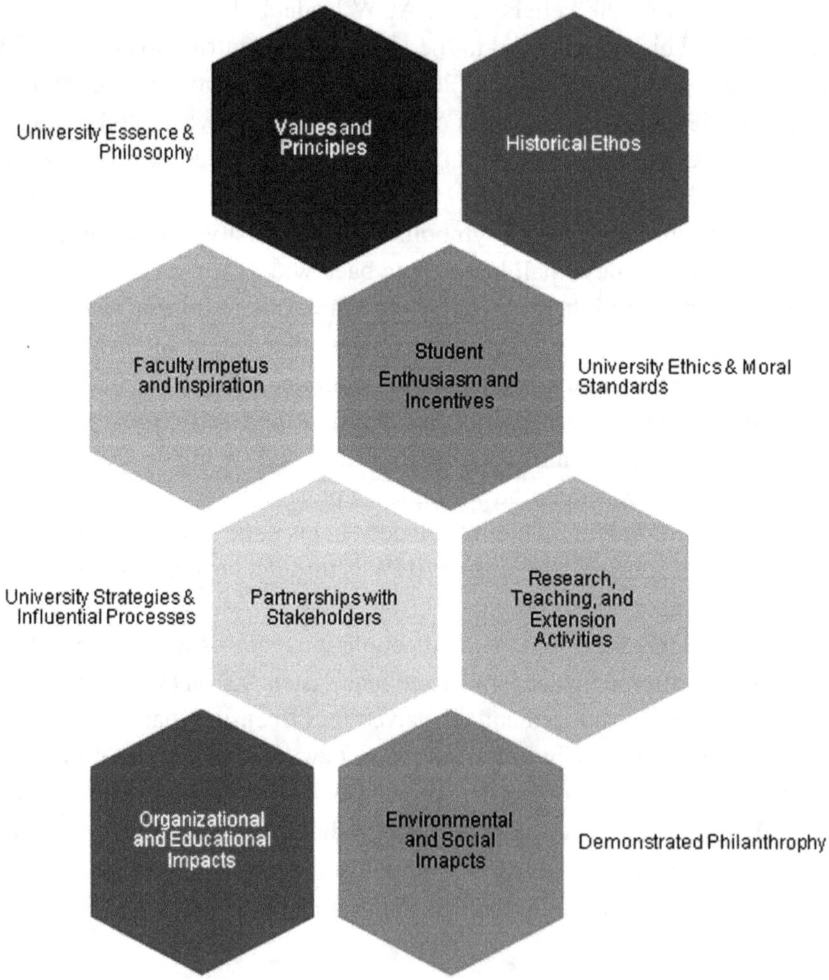

The model illustrates that despite the many challenges that may stand in the way of many universities within the Sudan in terms of operationalizing earnest social responsibility and good corporate citizenship, AUW has invested in establishing the right apparatuses to become and maintain its historical ethos devoted in its direction towards community betterment. In that, AUW has institutionalized strong partnerships with international NGOs and UN agencies, local NGOs and government organizations, has focused its curricula on community development and gender studies, has built-in research strategies that center on positively influencing community and societal behaviors and attitudes towards beneficial change. Furthermore, the model explains that by securely holding onto its non-equivocal ethical standing in which female students are given the role and responsibility of becoming change-agents within their communities both staff members and students feel empowered to support the mission and vision that AUW has held historically in improving Sudanese communities. In that light, the continuous demonstration of its philanthropic stance lends to connect and cement all other properties of USR that function as a whole within the AUW model of social responsibility, notwithstanding availing free university education by wavering tuition fees for those with low economic status. Transforming AUW into a sustainable and socially responsible institution, all four dimensions of sustainable development (environmental, economic, social and ethic), all seven principles and core subjects of social responsibility (organizational management, human rights, labour practices, environment, consumer issues, fair operating practices, community involvement and development) as well as both related terms (interdependence and holistic approach) addressed in ISO 26000 have been taken into account.

This new model (Figure 1) of a sustainable and socially responsible university will contribute to a deeper understanding of the interaction between the environmental, economic, social and ethical dimension of sustainable development.

FUTURE RESEARCH

Further research could be useful in investigating the strategic implementation of USR, use of scorecard balance for measuring implementation of USR, assessment of the impact of CSR/USR from the beneficiaries' perspectives as shown in figure 2, which are pertinent to respond to social, ethical and environmental dilemmas confronting universities.

Figure 2. Model for implementing university social responsibility

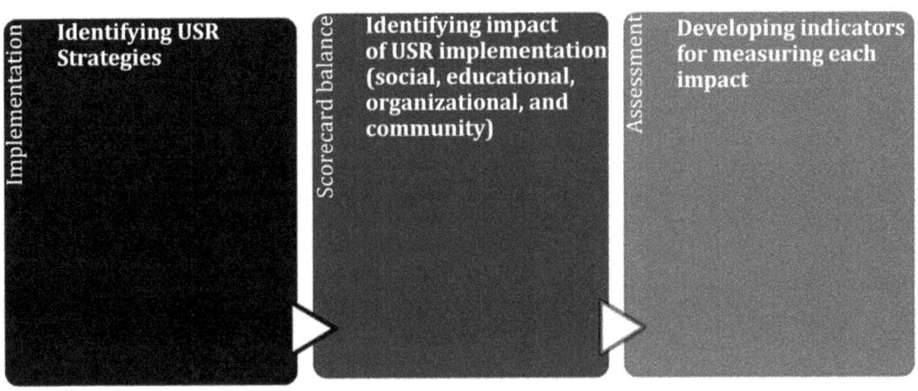

CONCLUDING REMARKS

Universities play a crucial role in educating a nation's youth. With that comes great responsibility despite challenges, successes and setbacks that may apparently face any university in a least-developed country.

The concept of USR can be understood to expound on the role of today's universities, through research and higher education for economic, ecological, technical, cultural and other advancement of societies, as well as touching on aspects relating to equality, equity, and accessibility.

This chapter has shed some positive light upon one university that may serve as a model for improving social responsibility and good corporate citizenship within the Sudan. AUW has been seen to provide innovative solutions in its ability in creating opportunities for its students and staff in their myriad contributions that have helped shaped the community from divergent perspectives such as medical, psychological, psychosocial, agricultural, and within the business community. AUW has played a key role in raising awareness of social responsibility and sustainable development through curricula reform, scientific progress, and advancement of knowledge; through research, teaching, and learning including vocational background and training, and the promotion of scientific progress; through capacity building and networking to produce critical, responsive citizens; and through the integration of handicapped and the disadvantaged.

Whilst believing that this chapter to be useful as a case study for teaching CSR in higher education institutions, it does come with some shortcomings. First, interviews were conducted with top management and senior faculty members involved in USR practices as opposed to more staff and students who may have been directly involved with the implementing processes. It is hoped that this will not undermine the study validity, but succeeded in generating valuable data on the current phenomena. Whereas the empirical material is generated from one university and thus provides no external validity with other universities because there is no national data available, the findings do contribute to the subject matter, and emphasize that much remains to be done for future similar studies.

REFERENCES

Angelo, F. et al.. (2012). Towards a strategic CSR: A Brazilian case study. *Business Strategy Series*, *13*(5), 224–238. doi:10.1108/17515631211264104

AUW. (2012). Educating Women to be Agents of Change in Sudan [Unpublished paper]. Ahfad University for Women, Sudan.

AUW. (2013). *Ahfad University Prospectus*. Sudan: Ahfad University for Women.

Badri, B. (2008). Gender studies at Ahfad University for Women: successes and challenges. Paper presented in the Government School of Dubai, United Arab Emirates.

Checkoway, B. (2001). Renewing the civic mission of the American Research University. *The Journal of Higher Education*, *72*(2), 125–147. doi:10.2307/2649319

Crane, A., Matten, D., & Spence, L. (Eds.). (2013). *Corporate Social Responsibility: Readings and Cases in Global Context*. New York, NY: Routledge.

Falck, O., & Heblich, S. (2007). Doing well by doing good. *Business Horizons*, *50*(3), 247–254. doi:10.1016/j.bushor.2006.12.002

Hansen, E. G., & Spitzeck, H. (2011). Academic paper measuring the impacts of NGO partnerships: The corporate and societal benefits of community involvement. *Corporate Governance*, *11*(4), 415–426. doi:10.1108/14720701111159253

Helsin, P. A., & Ochoa, J. D. (2008). Understanding and developing strategic corporate social responsibility. *Organizational Dynamics*, *37*(2), 125–144. doi:10.1016/j.orgdyn.2008.02.002

Meisberg, B., & Ehrmann, T. (2012). Lost in translation? The prevalence and performance Impact of Corporate Social Responsibility in Franschising. *Journal of Small Business Management*, *50*(4), 566–595. doi:10.1111/j.1540-627X.2012.00367.x

O'Riordan, L., & Fairbrass, J. (2006, September 4-5). Corporate social responsibility (CSR): Models and theories in stakeholder dialogue. Corporate Responsibility Research Conference. Trinity College Dublin, Ireland. Retrieved from http://www.academia.edu/2426506/

Orlitzy, M., Schmidt, F. L., & Rynes, S. L. (2003). Corporate social and financial performance: A meta analysis. *Organization Studies*, *24*(3), 403–441. doi:10.1177/0170840603024003910

Porter, M. E., & Kramer, M. R. (2006). Strategy and society: The link between competitive advantage and corporate social responsibility. *Harvard Business Review*, *84*(2), 4–17. PMID:17183795

Proenca, J. F., & Branco, M. C. (2014). Corporate social responsibility practices and motivations in a peripheral country: Two Portuguese illustrative cases. *Corporate Governance*, *14*(2), 252–264. doi:10.1108/CG-07-2011-0052

Rahman, W.A., & Osama, S. (2009). Ahfad University for Women Beyond academic excellence social responsibility and civic engagement. *Proceedings of the Arab Regional Conference on Higher Education, Towards an Arab Higher Education Space: International Challenges and Societal Responsibilities, Cairo* (pp.695-714). UNESCO.

Reiser (2008). University social responsibility definition cited in Vasilescu, et al. (2010). Developing university social responsibility: A model for the challenges of the new civil society. *Procedia Social and Behavioural Sciences* (Vol. 2, pp. 4177-4182).

Shawyun, T. (2011). From corporate social responsibility (CSR) to university social responsibility (USR). In Knowledge Societies: Universities and their Social Responsibilities (pp. 16-19). Singapore: Asia-Europe Foundation.

Van Marrewijk, M. (2003). Concepts and definitions of CSR and corporate sustainability: Between agency and communion. *Journal of Business Ethics*, *44*(2), 95–105. doi:10.1023/A:1023331212247

Vasilescu, , Barna, C., Epure, M., & Baicu, C. (2010). Developing university social responsibility: A model for the challenges of the new civil society. *Procedia: Social and Behavioral Sciences*, *2*(2), 4177–4182. doi:10.1016/j.sbspro.2010.03.660

Watson, D. Hollister, Stroud. S, & Babcock, E. (2013). The Engaged University: International Perspectives on Civic Engagement. New York, NY: Routledge.

Woodward, D., Edwards, P., & Birkin, F. (2001). Some evidence on executives' views of corporate social Responsibility. *The British Accounting Review*, *33*(3), 357–397. doi:10.1006/bare.2001.0165

Yin, R. (2003). *Case Study Research: Design and Methods*. London, UK: Sage Publications.

KEY TERMS AND DEFINITIONS

Ahfad University for Women: An exclusive women university established in 1966 as the first non-government and non-profit making University in Africa and Arab region. The university offers both under and graduate studies.

Aligning Social & Economic Responsibilities: Refer to balancing the different stakeholders' interests.

Civic Engagement: Is a concept that refers to institutions collective effort in an attempt to improve the quality of life of community members.

Community-Based Organizations: These are non-profit making small organizations, which operate within a single community.

Corporate Social Responsibility: This concept commonly refers to the management obligation to protect and improve society as a whole while pursuing the goals of the business. A socially responsible institution should be inspired to achieve goals, obey the law, act ethically and be a good corporate citizen.

Multiple Stakeholder Orientation: This is a concept that takes into account the interests of all stakeholders who affect and are affected by the organizations' operations.

Philanthropy: It is a term that refers to the goodwill of organizations to promote the welfare of society for humanitarian purposes.

Practices and Values: Concepts related to philosophies and values that underpin business practices.

Voluntary Action: Is a term that constitutes a common characteristic of CSR perceived to incorporate activities that are not legally bound or mandatory.

Chapter 8
Ethical Consumerism: Contextual Issues of Ethical Decision-Making Processes: An Exploratory Study

Ebtihaj A. Al A'ali
University of Bahrain, Bahrain

Abdul Redha Al-Sarraf
University of Bahrain, Bahrain

ABSTRACT

Ethical consumerism is the outcome of an ethical decision-making process. This research examines situational factors exemplified in context-related issues affecting decision-making as perceived by business students at the University of Bahrain. Reward systems, authority, bureaucracy, work role, organizational culture and national and cultural context are investigated. Qualitative research employing open-ended questions in questionnaire form is used. Two hundred and forty students participated in this research. Five questions were asked in the research. Themes involved are illustrations of reward systems, bureaucracy, organizational culture, national and cultural context and work roles. This research suggests that work roles require to be thoroughly investigated in future research. The research also shows that students are unaware of ethical consumerism. This explains reasons for not translating views of students to behavior as a reflection of ethical consumerism.

INTRODUCTION

Ethics is a weighty topic in business during the last decades. Organizations attempt to develop ethical strategies and also seek to promote ethical conduct among employees. Views of undergraduate students at the College of Business Administration of the University of Bahrain are investigated concerning ethical consumption. This research, therefore, examines awareness of ethical consumption and its related issues. The research involves three Sections. Section One discusses the Literature review concerning ethics and ethical consumptions. Section Two elaborates on research methodology. Finally a discussion and analysis of collected information is presented in Section Three.

DOI: 10.4018/978-1-4666-9864-2.ch008

Literature Review

The following section is divided into four main parts: The University of Bahrain-College of Business Administration, definition of ethics, relationships of business to ethics and finally ethical consumerism.

The University of Bahrain

The University of Bahrain is a continuation of its two components: The Gulf Polytechnic and the University of Arts, Science and Education. founded in 1986 with only two colleges: Education, Arts and Sciences which separated later into two independent colleges in 1990. *(University of Bahrain Catalogue, 1993-1994).*

To integrate past and present, the University of Bahrain has adopted a flexible joint Arabic-Islamic philosophy with high quality academic, practical and applied programs to fulfill the vast changing social and economical developments in the Kingdom of Bahrain, with a responsive system to local, regional, and global future environmental challenges. *(University of Bahrain, Undergraduate Catalogue, 2000-2001).*

Reflecting the Kingdom of Bahrain Vision 2030, the University of Bahrain vision "is to be an internationally recognized University for excellence in student learning, innovative research and community engagement that contributes to the economic vitality, sustainability, and quality of life in the Kingdom, the region and beyond". While the mission states that "the University of Bahrain is a national University dedicated to excellence in teaching and learning, innovative research; the generation and dissemination of knowledge; development of the student's personality, skills, and knowledge; and building partnerships with the public and private sectors; through distinction in its academic programs, faculty and staff, student activities, fostering innovation, cultivating a culture for quality, and reaching out to the local, regional, and global communities."

Today in 2014, the University of Bahrain is located in the Zakhir area offering 24 Diploma level courses, 34 BSc. Degree programs and 25 postgraduate academic programs (a total of 83), distributed among the following colleges: College of Arts, College of Business Administration, College of Engineering, College of Information Technology, College of Law, College of Science, College of Applied Studies, Bahrain Teachers College, College of Physical Education and Physiotherapy, and College of Health Sciences."

A total of 2,080 qualified staff serve these colleges, producing 5,500 published papers and books. The University of Bahrain offers 22 regional and internationally recognized journals, organizing up to 2014, 110 local, regional and international conferences. On the global and international settings, the University of Bahrain has been active in a variety of international bodies such as IAU, ISESCO, and UNISCO.

The drivers, nature and culture of the University of Bahrain involves international exchange student from Thailand, Turkey, USA, Japan, France, and China offering to students a variety of services for effective educational and learning process such as libraries, IT services, guidance and counselling services, language centers, transportations, medical care and many others, paying in return a relatively small amount of fees. Since its foundation, 50,000 young qualified men and women have graduated from the University of Bahrain.

Meeting future challenges, the University of Bahrain has indicated five important objectives for its strategic plan with tactical (Colleges) and operational (departments) supporting plans, including: raising the quality of teaching and learning, improving quality and increasing the amount of research, building national and international partnerships, aligning governance and administration with international best practices, and finally, sustainable infrastructure and resources.

College of Business Administration at the University of Bahrain

The roots of business education and training in Bahrain goes back to 1968 when the Gulf Technical College was established. Later, the development of the Kingdom of Bahrain as a local, regional, and international financial center brought about the establishment of the College of Business Administration at the University of Bahrain in 1986, becoming as an important source for preparing young Bahraini men and women to be leaders in the business environment. *(University of Bahrain Catalogue, 1993-1994).*

By 1987, graduate programms comprising a post-graduate Diploma (PGD), an MBA, and an MPA was officially launched, allowing students to major in Management, Finance, and Marketing. In 1992, the College of Business Administration established new specializations including: the department of Accounting, the department of Office Management, the department of Economics, and the Continuing Management Education Program. *(University of Bahrain Catalogue, 1993-1994).*

Today, in 2014, 5,413 students are enrolled in both undergraduate and postgraduate studies in the College of Business Administration at the University of Bahrain, serviced by 94 full time qualified staff.

To contribute actively to the vast developments in the Kingdom of Bahrain at all levels, the College of Business Administration has developed new academic units that are built on the best international standards and practices which include: the Department of Accounting, Department of Economics & Finance, Department of Management and Marketing, the Continuing Management Education Program (COMEP), the graduate studies program, and the Quality Assurance Office. All these units are under continuous changes, development, and revision. *(College of Business Administration, B.Sc. programs Catalogue, 1993-1994).*

Through the above academic programs, the College of Business Administration aims to develop student's abilities and skills in the various related functions of business administration and promote scientific research conducted in various business disciplines, to prepare students for challenging practical working experiences, and finally to serve the Bahraini community on the administrative, organizational, and managerial levels (College of Business Administration, B.Sc. Programs catalogue, 2013-2014).

The College of Business Administration at the University of Bahrain places emphasis on high quality teaching, continuous research studies, and community services with social responsibility. The present Dean of the College, Professor Minwir Al-Shammari reveals that "the College has sought International Accreditation for its programs and is currently in the final stages of getting accredited by the Association for the Advancement of Collegiate School of Business (AACSB) (College of Business Administration, B.Sc. programs catalogue, 2013/2014, p.7).

Teaching Ethics in the College of Business Administration at the University of Bahrain

The American Association of Colleges and Schools of Business (AACCB), the most highly rated international body in the world requires from business schools to integrate ethical education into their curriculum to meet their missions. (Floyd, Xu, Atkins & CadWell, 2013). However, the question whether ethics can be taught continues to be debated in the literature?

Many strongly believe that ethical business education is an important source of increasing student's ethical conduct and their moral obligations in business operation (SigurJonsson, Vaiman & Arnardottir, 2014, Morgan & Thiagarajan, 2008, Okafor, 2011, Davis & Welton, 1991). Further, others suggest that there is no definite evidence that ethical educational courses have positive impact on students' behaviors (Perryer & Ladd, 2014, McDonald, 2004, Tello, Swanson, Floyd & Caldwell, 2013, Bennis& O Toole, 2005).

However, there are two main models for teaching business ethics: having or offering an independent stand-alone business ethics course as part of the overall curriculum plan or distributing and integrating ethical education and topics across various courses taught in the curriculum (Altmyer, yang, Schallen-Kamp Kamp & DeBeaumont, 2014, Carlson & Burke, 1998, Sigurjonsson, Vaiman & Arnardottir, 2014, Floyd, Xu, Atkins & CaldWell, 2013). Ritter (2006) argues that there are several options for teaching ethics in business schools. One is to provide students with a single course that mainly focuses on ethical principals, issues, and topics. Second, is to incorporate all ethical topics into multiple business courses. Ritter (2006) adds a third option in which students take a core course in ethics, while related ethical topics are spread among other business classes.

In the College of Business Administration at the University of Bahrain, a stand-alone course (MGT 437) Module in business ethics is offered for students majoring in various business specializations in the College. It is a required course for both students majoring and minoring in Management Studies and an elective course of study for other business specializations. In addition, related topics of business ethics are distributed and covered across various courses in other business specializations such as Accounting, Economics and Finance and Marketing.

Definition of Ethics

"Ethics" is a Greek word meaning custom or usage (Wiley, 1995). There is no one single definition for *"ethics "* accepted among philosophers and researchers (Spark & Pan, 2009, Ferrel, Fraedrich & Ferrel, 2008). Vesilind (1988, p. 291) reveals that *"it should be clear that philosophers disagree on what ethics is. Is it a science or a concept? Is it a way of thinking or a guide to living? Is it a means of coexisting in society, or a calculation of how best to achieve ultimate happiness? Perhaps it is all of these or none".*

However, ethics is defined by many as right and wrong conduct in making various human decisions (Griffin, 1993, Pride, Hughes & Kapoor, 1996, Daft, 1997, Zgheib, 2005, Masheshwari & Ganesh, 2006, Ferrell & Fraedrich, 2014, Jones & George, 2009, Ebert & Griffin, 2011). The *"right"* and *"wrong"* values are not practically determined by comparing different alternatives to individuals' personal values only, rather it is determined also by a universal human moral-system that is based on rational reasoning's (Vitell & Hidalgo, 2006).

In a more philosophical context *"ethics"* also is seen as concerning with moral obligation, responsibility, and social justice (Wiley, 1995). It is seen as a set of rules and guidelines for proper human behaviors in a particular society. Sparks & Pan (2010, p. 409) define ethics as *"an individual's personal evaluation of the degree to which some behavior or course of action is ethical or unethical."* Despite the variation in defining *"ethics"*, there is some consensus among all these definitions (Vesilind, 1988).

In conclusion, there is no one single definition for ethics. However, there is general consensus among various definitions presented by researchers. Ethics for most of these researchers represent a set of right and wrong conducts related to individual moral philosophy.

Relationships of Business to Ethics

Business ethics is a very important subject in the business world, organizational setting, and educational institutes. Business ethics is referred to as *"principles and standards that guide behavior in the world of business"* (Ferrell & Fraedrick, 2014, P.6.). Bageac, Furrer & Reynaud (2010), also believe that business ethics is related to issues of right and wrong decisions in business situations. Others see business ethics as directing behaviors of employees ethically within organizations (Ebert & Griffin, 2011, Alayoglu, Ozturk & Babacan, 2012). A more focused definition is offered by Ahmad, Chung & Eichenseher (2003) who see ethics as a new phenomenon aiming to study values that regulate economical activities in the business environment.

The relationships between ethics and the business environment has been explored intensively by researchers (Fisscher, Frenkel, Lurie & Nijhof, 2005, Vitell & Hidalgo, 2006, Keith, Perreault, Chin & Keith, 2009, Bageac, Furrer, & Reynaud, 2010). Ethical business conduct has significant economical implications, while at the same time making an important contribution to stakeholders, managers, employees, suppliers, customers, and society in general.

Since the 1980s Hitt, Middlemist, and Maithis (1983) indicated that human economical systems are based on values of the overall society in which business organizations are operating within. Therefore, a successful business should comply with society's ethical system. During the 1990's, due to the dynamic situation of ethics in the global business environment, many organizations started to consider and integrate ethics in their corporate strategies (Saidi, 2009).

Business organizations must understand, value, and appreciate ethical business conduct. The role of the organization leaders, therefore, is to create, implement, and sustain effective ethical system within organizations (Wiley, 1995). Leaders are responsible for setting, communicating, and modeling ethical behaviors for employees, through establishing flexible organizational norms offering clear moral guidance for behaviors (Keith, Perreault, Chin & Keith 2009). Ethics are to be therefore, integrated into the corporate organizational culture (Fisscher, Frenkle, Lurie & Nijhof, 2005, Vitell & Hidalgo, 2006). Ethical conduct of both individual employees and their organizations is important for developing a positive organizational image, and essential for an organization's long term survival as well (Albert & Horowitz, 2008, Ferrell & Fraedrich, 2014).

Ethical Consumerism

Ethical consumerism is also called ethical consumption, ethical purchasing, and ethical sourcing. It professionally appeared in 1989 to produce rating tables for companies across a range of ethical and environmental issues (htti//en. Wikipedia.org, 2014). Sebastiani, Montagnini & Dalli (2013) explain that ethical consumerism emerged in 1970s with the first green consumerism movement reflecting changes in business ethical issues. Ethical consumerism is a behavioral phenomenon that combines a multi personal and a collective behavioral pattern. As a result, making the issue of consumerism very complex and difficult to investigate (Bucic, Harris & Arli, 2012, Weber, 2006, Sparks & Pan, 2009, Lau, Caracciolo, Roddenberry & Scroggins, 2012). Moreover, critics argue that researchers have neglected educational issues in relation to ethical consumerism. (weber, 2006, Carrigan & Attalla, 2001, Sebastiani, Montagnini & Dalli, 2013, Cengiz, Yazici & Erdal, 2010, Baden, 2014).

However, there has been increasing attention to the issue of ethical consumerism lately. (Cho & Krasser, 2011, Carey, Shaw, & Shiu, 2008, Szmigin, & Carrigan, 2006, Gill, 2012). Ferrell & Fraedrich (2014, p. 341) define ethical consumption as *"the conscious and deliberate choice to make certain consumption choices due to personal moral beliefs and values"*. Cho & Krasser (2011) believe that ethical consumerism involves a complex selection or decision making process in choosing goods, products, and services.

Similarly, Szmigin & Carrigan (2006) see ethical consumerism as a choosing process among various goods, products, and services, that reflect moral, ethical, and social concerns of the consumer. Carey, Shaw & Shiu (2008) expound that ethical consumerism is a decision making process reflecting consumers' social values. Gill (2012) explains that it is a concept standing for moral dimensions. Fullerton, Kerch & Dodge (1996) see ethical consumerism as a judgmental process that consumer learn from both interaction with market place and reference groups.

Consumerism is a choice made based on an ethical decision-making process. Crane and Matten (2010) state that there are two groups of factors affecting the decision-making process. The first group is related to individual influences i.e. age, gender, education, employment and psychological factors (Albert & Horowitize, 2008, Seshadri & Broekemier, 2009, Khalizani, Omar & Khalisanni, 2011, Perryer & Ladd, 2014).

The second group is situational which is divided into two categories. The first category is related to issues being looked at. This category refers to what degree the issue looked at is important to the decision maker i.e. moral intensity. It also implies that the issue looked at can be seen differently according to its related context, i.e. moral framing.

The second category of situational influences is context related. This is divided into six issues as follows:-

1. Rewards: This refers to relationship between rewards, punishment and ethical behavior. Learning by observing others is a major method to learn what is rewarded and what is punished. The majority of studies illustrate a relationship between reward and ethical behaviour.
2. Authority: This reflects influence of immediate supervisor and managers on the ethical decision making process.
3. Bureaucracy: This stands for impacts of organizational structure. Bureaucracy affects the decision-making process through four dimensions as follows:
    - Suppression of moral autonomy. Organizational rules and procedures will subjugate individuals morality. Employees will act as "moral robots"
    - Instrumental morality: decision-making will evolve around so called *"correct procedures"* to achieve a goal which may not be beneficial in itself.
    - Distancing: means supporting a person's morality by distancing the action from the consequences.
    - Denial of moral status: this refers to a Bureaucracy focused on efficiency. This focus overlooks the totality of individuals moral beings. Bureaucracy is the most investigated issue in relation to the ethical decision making processes.
4. Work-roles: This shows how work-roles can stifle individuals' values and beliefs. Work roles refer to styles of behavior expected from a person occupying a position. These roles can be functional e.g. security or hierarchical e.g. managers. A person's morality is stifled to adapt to values of a role play. However, limited research is available to measure the impact of roles on ethical decision making.

5. Organizational culture: This illustrates how organizational socialization shapes individuals, values and beliefs. Organizational culture can facilitate or impede ethical behavior. This issue has been widely examined in ethics. There is evidence that organizational culture through socialization processes has strong impacts on the ethical decision making process.
6. National and cultural context: This explains impacts of national right and wrong standards on organizational decision-making process regardless of the nationality of a decision maker. This dimension illustrates the impact of national and cultural characteristics on individual decision making processes. These impacts, according to Crane and Matten (2010), might be eroded by globalization. Besides limited research was done in relation to social and culture environment and ethics.

The relationship between ethical decision-making and reward and authority is investigated. However, the same relationship for other factors remain contested and lack empirical evidence.

Other researchers emphasize social factors as the main forces for ethical reasoning among consumers. Social motivators in the ethical judgments and decision making are higher and stronger than personal motivators (Szmigin & Carrigan, 2006, Ferrel, Fraedrich & Ferrel, 2008, Bucic, Harris & Arli, 2012). Social factors, according to Crane and Matten (2010), are parts of national and cultural context.

Ethical sensitivity and moral reasoning's could be as a result of interaction between individual and issues or factors surrounding a specific dilemma (Davis & Welton, 1991, Phau & Kea, 2006, Emerson, Conroy & Standley, 2006, Sigurjonsson, Vaiman & Arnardottir, 2014). Findings of Pulvers & Dierkhoff (1999) research confirm that the ethical behaviors of students are the results of both internal students' variables and external environmental pressures.

Basgöze and Tektäs (2012) found that the lack of information and knowledge about constituents of ethical and unethical behavior of a firm make it hard for consumers to involve in ethical consumerism. This means consumers cannot make a decision to reward or punish a given firm.

This research therefore, aims at investigating ethical consumerism and its related contextual issues. Students' views are examined in relation to three selected issues. The first issue is concerned with the University of Bahrain as a bureaucratic organization and concerned work roles. The second issue looked at faculty members' roles and authority assigned. The third issue then, looked at organizational culture exemplified in students' norms and practices.

Students' and Ethical Studies

Many researches attempt to measure relationship between consumers behaviors and their ethical awareness in business consumption in general and on college students' in particular (Fullerton, Kerch & Dodge, 1996, show, Grehan, Shuin, Hassan & Thomson, 2005: Carrigan & Attalla, 2001:Bucic, Harris & Arli 2012: Szmigin & Carrigan, 2006: Albert & Horowitz, 2008: Seshadri & Broekemier, 2009: Perryer & Ladd 2014: Gill, 2012: Khalizani, Omar, & Khalisanni, 2011: Buono, Brown, Frederick, Hall & Sultan, 2012: Ahmad, Chung & Eichenseher, 2003: Eweje & Brunton, 2009: Jones, 1990: Lau, Caracciolo, Roddenberry & Scroggins, 2012).

The majority of these researches are unable to explain to us the constitution of ethical behaviors within the consumerism process (Carrigan & Attalla, 2001: Alayoglu, Ozturk & Babacan: 2012). Many emphasize marketing elements (Ahmed, Chung & Eichenseher: 2003). Finally, there is inconsistency of results among these empirical studies (Alshaik, Elian & Tahat, 2013: Conroy & Emerson, 2004: Alayoglu, Ozturk & Babacan, 2012).

In fact, still *"Relatively little attention has been directed towards how college students actually view business ethics issues"* (Eweje & Brunton, 2010, P.97).

A positive relationship between ethical awareness of the students and their overall ethical behaviors, decisions, and reasoning's is found (Glenn, 1992: Eynon, Hill, & Stevens, 1997: Carlson & Burke, 1998, Weber & Glyptis, 2000). Results of Lau's (2009) research indicate that ethical awareness such as education in fact has significant positive impact on the students' attitudes, and sensitivity. Similar positive relationships between ethical awareness and actual behaviors is found by Comegys (2010). It is evidenced that students with educational awareness tend to behave more ethically. Jazani and Ayoobzadeh (2012) find positive correlation between completing ethical educational courses and adherence of students.

Other research studies, however show little or no significant effect of ethical education on the individuals' behaviors, decision-making process and reasoning (Davis & Welton, 1991, Peppas & Diskin, 2000, Ritte, 2006).

Conroy and Emerson (2004) argue that ethical awareness such as completing ethical courses does not affect ethical perceptions of students. Zegheib (2005) investigating the extent of application of the three principles of ethics: utility, morality, and justice on ethical decision-making and personal attitudes on undergraduate and graduate students illustrate that there is no correlation between personal attitudes toward ethical principles indicated in the study and actual behaviors of the students when facing ethical dilemmas. Similar negative relationships is also found by Davis & Welton, 1991, Phau & Kea, 2006, Khalizani, Omar & Khalisanni, 2011, Okafor, 2011, Alshaik, Elian & Tahat, 2013.

Students already have formed their own personal ethical philosophies when joining the educational institution. Therefore, no ethical education could change individual students' behavior (Cho & Krasser, 2011, Seshadri & Broekemier, 2009: Szmigin & Carrigan, 2006: Fullerton, Kerch & Dodge, 1996: Okafor, 2011: Buono, Brown, Frederick, Hall & Sultan, 2012: Gill, 2012: Lau, Caracciolo, Roddenberry & Scroggins, 2012). This fact is clearly explained by Khalizani, Omar & Khalisanni (2011 P.4) who state that *"ethics in the undergraduate and graduate curriculum is neither wise nor necessary because of the belief that college students are unlikely to change their moral outlook simply because they took an ethics course."*

Ethical consumerism is a complex process reflecting principles of morality in decision making (Okafor, 2011). The behavioral motivation within the process could be based on personal, social, and situational factors. Studies that were conducted in relation to ethical consumerism are little and very limited (Weegar, 2007).

Research Methodology

Ethical consumerism is a relatively contemporary issue. No research has been conducted earlier in Bahrain to investigate the issue of ethical consumerism. For this qualitative exploratory research is employed (Al-A'Ali (2006).

Denzin & Lincoln (2011) state that Qualitative research permits deeper understanding of different issues in organization contexts. By using participants' own words, qualitative research captures, understands and represents the perception and meanings of the issue being studied.

Open-ended question questionnaires were distributed and collected from 240 students at the College of Business Administration. Five questions were investigated. The first looked at the definition of ethics. The second examines the relationship between ethics and business leading to the third question, which enquires into the importance of business ethics to an organization. The fourth searched for a definition of ethical consumerism. The last then investigated students' perception of ethical issues in relation to their situation, i.e. university, faculty and others students.

Analysis and Discussion of Collected Information

The collected information concerning the five open-ended questions is analyzed below. Analysis of questions number one, two and three is presented in one part. This is due to the overlapping nature of the three questions.

Analysis of Collected Information for Questions One, Two and Three

The first question addressed is intended to examine students' awareness of ethics in a general context. The second question attempts to grasp students' understanding of relationship between ethics and business. The third then illustrates the importance of ethics for business.

In relation to the definition of ethics (Question No. 1) students explain ethics as *"What are accepted by society as right or wrong"* This definition is narrow in focus attributing ethics to society. A few students, however, state that ethics *"are personal values and morals guiding behavior"*. The definition can be seen as narrower in focus than the earlier definition (question No.1). regarding the definition of business ethics (QuestionNo.2) the majority define ethics as *"Organizational Standards set to differentiate between right or wrong affecting stakeholders."*.

The different definitions of ethics presented by students shed light on responses to the second and third questions concerning the relationship between ethics and business and its importance. Students assert that ethics leads to business success. However, this success can be achieved through different channels. The majority of students explain that ethics leads to success through *"... guiding employees' behavior and establishing rules for decision-making process"*.

The above stated responses by students are compatible with literature discussing the definition of ethics, the relationship between ethics and business and importance of business ethics to organization. Students' views and literature review show that ethics are organizational standards to differentiate between right and wrong (question No. 2). However, a few students equated individuals' moral philosophy to business ethics (question No. 1). Besides students explain that ethics is a necessity for organizations. This necessity is upheld by the vast interest of stakeholders in organizational contexts (response to question No. 3).

A second smaller group illustrated that business ethics will promote social responsibility. Based on this responsibility, students expound *"a positive image an organization develops. This will lead to enhanced performance"*. A few students add that ethics and social responsibility are the cornerstone for success. This can help organizations to develop accommodative strategy to stakeholders' demand. This shows the importance of business ethics (questions No. 3).

Analysis of Question Four Concerning Ethical Consumerism

This fourth question examines students' definition of ethical consumerism and its related issues.

The majority of students express their unawareness of the issue of ethical consumerism. However a few of them define ethical consumerism as *"producing products based on ethical grounds "*.

Another group of students expound that *"ethical consumerism refers to customers' desire to buy ethical products"*. A third group believed that ethical consumerism is *"to provide accurate information to customers about products purchased"*. These definitions expressed by students are compatible to some of the definitions stated by the literature review. The majority, however, stated their unawareness of the definition of ethical consumerism.

This unawareness could be attributed to the complexity of the issue as stated in the literature review. Besides this issue is a contemporary one which is still not being thoroughly investigated in relation to higher education. The unawareness upholds Basgöze and Tektäs (2012) finding that consumers are unaware of what constitute ethics and ethical behavior . This acts as a barrier for involvement in ethical consumerism.

Analysis of Question Five in Relation to Students' Situation and Ethical Consumerism

Ethical issues identified by students concerning their situation are grouped into three categories. These are university, faculty and students issues. Though the majority state their unawareness of ethical consumerism, they express dissatisfaction with some issues encountered in the university.

University Ethical Issues

Students point out many factors for experiencing unethical issues in relation to the university as an organization.

The major and recurrent themes according to students are as follows:

1. Racial and gender discrimination of the admission office with their decisions not justified.
2. A rigid bureaucratic system of registration.
3. Personnel of the security department are uncooperative and unfriendly and follow discriminatory treatment.
4. Favouritism in enrollment procedures in relation to adding additional names to full sections.
5. Student council election is unfairly manipulated based on prejudice and discrimination.

However a few students contend that they experience no unethical issues at the university as an organization.

Themes Nos. 1,4 and 5 are illustrations of denial of moral status. The themes focus on ratio of students' in terms of race or gender (theme 4), treating students as objects in terms of numbers enrolled at the university (theme 3) and granting a treat to students based on their race and gender (theme 1).

Themes 2 and 3 are reflections of instrumental morality. This morality focuses on procedures regardless of goals targeted. Theme No. 1 states that bureaucracy is rigid for it is based on procedures to follow. Theme 3 shows the overlapping nature between work roles of the security Department for being rule oriented and the goals of the Department for providing students with security on campus. This theme (No.3) as well stands for denial of moral status for this makes students describe security personnel as "Unfriendly and not co-operative". Security personnel are rule-minded based on their functional duties.

The above themes exhibit the impacts of bureaucracy and work roles on students perception of ethics. Students participating in this research do not relate the above themes to consumerism for they do not have such mental construct. The majority express their unawareness of consumerism.

Faculty Members and Ethical Practices

Ethical issues experienced by students in relation of faculty are: (listed below based on importance according to students):

1. Some faculty members do not conduct their classes in English. Students, therefore, may not develop a mental capability to tackle examination questions stated in English. Besides, non Arabic speaking students will be unable to grasp the material leading to the second problem identified by students.
2. The second unethical practice according to students, is that faculty members do not adhere to material discussed in the text book. This might lead students to not understand materials assigned for examinations.
3. Some faculty members are not punctual. Being late to class has two negative impacts. Firstly students will have less time to grasp the material assigned. Secondly faculty members who come late may stay longer to cover the materials required. This affects attendance for the class that follows.
4. Racial and gender discrimination: non Arabic speaking students feel being left behind due to language. This they attribute to racism and gender discrimination based on the sex of the faculty member.

Theme No. 1 exhibits the impact of national culture on organizational culture. Bahrain is an Arab country. Arabic is the official language used in public organization and at the University of Bahrain. The majority of students are Arabic-speaking. Therefore, faculty members allow themselves sometimes to use Arabic language in order to facilitate teaching.

The interwoven nature of national and organizational culture with denial of moral status is seen in themes 2,3 and 4. Themes 2 and 4 are reflections of granting labels to others. Therefore, actions are made toward labels i.e. sex and race. Actions, based on labels, overlook totality nature of a moral being. Themes 3 and 4 discuss faculty members' work roles as perceived by students.

These roles are shaped by national and organizational cultures. Students highlight roles of faculty members and neglect their roles in the learning process. Besides, students seem to extend their perception of school teacher roles to roles of university faculty members. This is an act of denial of moral status. The role of a faculty member is a shorthand for covering materials in the text book assigned (Theme 3).

Theme 4 related to faculty members punctuality overlaps with theme 3. Punctuality is a concern for students as it is related to covering material assigned for a given course. The holistic learning process of students is divided into parts, i.e. faculty member, text books, and students. Certain labels are attached to every part. This leads students to lose the total view of moral well being.

Themes concerning faculty members are supported by literature concerning context-related issues. National culture, organizational culture, work roles and bureaucracy are issues underpinning themes discussed. However, work roles, as stated by literature review, need to be thoroughly investigated.

Students and Ethical Practices

The common unethical practice expressed by students in relation to their fellow students are:

1. Cheating and gaining unfair high marks.
2. Some students do not participate in group work but still claim they do.

3. Some students do not respect their faculty members.
4. Students of minorities are discriminated against by other students.
5. Intolerance of individual differences in relation to race, religion and gender. This leads to harassment and bullying.

Themes emerged in relation to information collected from students in response to students and ethical practices represent reward system, bureaucracy and organizational culture as issues or context-related.

Themes 1 and 2 reflected reward system. This refers to the role of observation in learning acceptable and unacceptable behaviors. Participants in this research state that a high mark could be achieved by lying and cheating.

Themes 4 and 5 showed that traits given to individuals, situations and objects can lead to discrimination and intolerance of individual difference. This is an illustration of denial of moral status which leads to overlooking, the totality of individuals as moral beings.

Interwoven nature between organizational culture and socialization as a mechanism to learn behavior is shown in theme 3. Through socialization some students do not learn to show respect for their faculty members especially with the absence of clear regulations to monitor relationship between students and faculty members. Themes related to students viewing other students' behavior can be attributed to reward system, bureaucracy and organizational culture.

CONCLUSION

Ethical consumerism is a contemporary issue which has not been thoroughly investigated in relation to higher education. It is viewed as an outcome of an ethical decision-making process. This research examines situational factors i.e. context related issues which affect decision making. Besides, students views are investigated in relation to consumerism.

The context-related issues studied are related to three aspects of UOB. i.e. the university as an organization, faculty members and fellow students.

Themes concerning University issues revealed dimension of bureaucracy i.e. denial of moral status and instrumental morality.

Themes concerning faculty members illustrated national and cultural issues, bureaucracy exemplified in denial of moral status and work roles. The latter needs to be thoroughly investigated in future research. Themes emerged in relation to fellow students reflected a reward systems, denial of moral status (bureaucracy) and organizational culture.

Although context-related issues are present and shape views of students participating in the research, their impacts on consumers' behavior is not stated. This could be attributed to students unawareness of ethical consumerism.

Themes evolved from students' responses are compatible with literature reviewed. Bureaucracy reflected through its dimensions underpins the majority of themes. Instrumental morality emphasizing correct procedures and denial of moral status overlook the totality of the human being are the most common dimensions of bureaucracy. This upholds Crane and Metton's (2010) argument stating that bureaucracy is the most investigated contextual issue affecting the decision-making processes. The literature reviewed shows that there is limited research on impacts of work roles on ethical decision making process. This research, however, illustrates impacts of functional roles i.e. faculty members' roles and security personnel's roles on ethical decision-making processes.

Socialization as a process to perpetuating organizational culture is observed in themes related to reward system. This was illustrated by students' learning processes of rewarded behavior. This supports the literature review explaining a positive relationship between reward system, culture and ethical decision making process.

Impacts of national culture is partly reflected through the use of Arabic lecturing of a few professors. The literature review, however, stated that the effect of national culture is eroded with the introduction of globalization.

In conclusion this research argues that ethical practices at the College of Business Administration need to be reviewed and to be induced. Further studies need to be conducted to verify and investigate other contextual issues i.e. reward system and work roles affecting the decision-making processes.

LIMITATIONS AND FUTURE RESEARCH

Beside the extreme shortage of research studies in the area of ethical consumerism (Seshadri & Broekemier, 2009, Shaw, Grehan, Shiu, Hassan & Thomson. 2005, Carrigan & Attalla, 2001), ethical related studies are not only sophisticated, but also difficult to study (Gill, 2012). This study, therefore will helps Scholars to conduct additional research enhancing understanding of contextual issues affecting ethical consumerism in general and in educational institutions in particular.

This study examined the ethical perceptions of Business College students attending the University of Bahrain, for diversity purpose a larger population of students should be included in future research representing colleges of the UOB e.g. Social Sciences, Engineering, IT, Law and others. A wider range of questions including external or internal factors affecting decision-making processes concerning consumerism are suggested to investigate. It would be useful to have non-student samples for comparative purposes.

Quantitative research, it is argued, can enhance understanding of ethical consumerism and its related contextual issues concerning decision-making. This is due to the different nature of quantitative research from qualitative methods employed in this research.

REFERENCES

Ahmed, M. M., Chung, K. Y., & Eichenseher, J. W. (2003). Business students' perception of ethics and moral judgment: A cross-cultural study. *Journal of Business Ethics*, *43*(1-2), 89–102. doi:10.1023/A:1022915316112

Al-A'ali, E. (2006). Motivation of Women Leaders Between Participation and Empowerment: Self-Report. *Journal of Commerce for Scientific Research of Alexandria*, *43*(1), 265–288.

Al-shaikh, F. N., Elian, M. I., & Tahat, L. H. (2013). Business students attitudes towards business ethics: Evidence from Kuwait. *International Journal of Education and Research*, *8*(1), 59–76.

Alayoğlu, N., Öztürk, A. O., & Babacan, M. (2012). Perceptions of College Students and Attitudes of Private and Public Employees towards Business Ethics. *Turkish Journal of Business Ethics*, *5*(9), 27–35.

Albert, L. S., & Horowitz, L. M. (2009). Attachment styles and ethical behavior: Their relationship and significance in the marketplace. *Journal of Business Ethics*, *87*(3), 299–316. doi:10.1007/s10551-008-9918-6

Baden, D. (2014). Look on the bright side: A comparison of positive and negative role models in business ethics education. *Academy of Management Learning & Education*, *13*(2), 154–170. doi:10.5465/amle.2012.0251

Bageac, D., Furrer, O., & Reynaud, E. (2011). Management students' attitudes toward business ethics: A comparison between France and Romania. *Journal of Business Ethics*, *98*(3), 391–406. doi:10.1007/s10551-010-0555-5

Başgöze, P., & Tektaş, Ö. Ö. (2012). Ethical perceptions and green buying behavior of consumers: A cross-national exploratory study. *Journal of Economics and Behavioral Studies*, *4*(8), 477–488.

Bucic, T., Harris, J., & Arli, D. (2012). Ethical consumers among the millennials: A cross-national study. *Journal of Business Ethics*, *110*(1), 113–131. doi:10.1007/s10551-011-1151-z

Buono, A. F., Fletcher-Brown, D., Frederick, R., Hall, G. J., & Sultan, J. (2012). Acting Ethically: Moral reasoning and business school student behavior. *SAM Advanced Management Journal*, *77*(3), 18.

Carey, L., Shaw, D., & Shiu, E. (2008). The impact of ethical concerns on family consumer decision-making. *International Journal of Consumer Studies*, *32*(5), 553–560. doi:10.1111/j.1470-6431.2008.00687.x

Carlson, P. J., & Burke, F. (1998). Lessons learned from ethics in the classroom: Exploring student growth in flexibility, complexity and comprehension. *Journal of Business Ethics*, *17*(11), 1179–1187. doi:10.1023/A:1005740923813

Carrigan, M., & Attalla, A. (2001). The myth of the ethical consumer-do ethics matter in purchase behaviour? *Journal of Consumer Marketing*, *18*(7), 560–578. doi:10.1108/07363760110410263

Cengiz, E., Yazici, S., & Erdal, M. (2010). Ethical Perception from Students' Perspective: Understanding Instructors' Effect on Students' Ethical Sensitivity in Personal Selling. *Journal of Leadership, Accountability and Ethics*, *8*(2), 41–50.

Cho, S., & Krasser, A. H. (2011). What makes us care? The impact of cultural values, individual factors, and attention to media content on motivation for ethical consumerism. *International Social Science Review*, *86*(1/2), 3.

Comegys, C. (2010). The impact of religiously affiliated universities and courses in ethics and religious studies on students' attitude toward business ethics. *Contemporary Issues in Education Research*, *3*(6), 35–44.

Conroy, S. J., & Emerson, T. L. (2004). Business ethics and religion: Religiosity as a predictor of ethical awareness among students. *Journal of Business Ethics*, *50*(4), 383–396. doi:10.1023/B:BUSI.0000025040.41263.09

Crane, A., & Matten, D. (2004). *Business ethics: A European perspective: managing corporate citizenship and sustainability in the age of globalization*. Oxford: Oxford University Press.

Daft, R. L. (1997). Management (4th ed.). Fort Worth, TX: The Dryden Press.

Davis, J. R., & Welton, R. E. (1991). Professional ethics: Business students' perceptions. *Journal of Business Ethics*, *10*(6), 451–463. doi:10.1007/BF00382829

Denzin, N. K., & Lincoln, Y. S. (2011). *The SAGE handbook of qualitative research*. Sage.

Ebert, R. J., & Griffin, R. W. (2011). *Business essentials*. Pearson Education Canada.

Emerson, T. L., Conroy, S. J., & Stanley, C. W. (2007). Ethical attitudes of accountants: Recent evidence from a practitioners' survey. *Journal of Business Ethics*, *71*(1), 73–87. doi:10.1007/s10551-006-9125-2

Eweje, G., & Brunton, M. (2010). Ethical perceptions of business students in a New Zealand university: Do gender, age and work experience matter? *Business Ethics (Oxford, England)*, *19*(1), 95–111. doi:10.1111/j.1467-8608.2009.01581.x

Eynon, G., Hills, N. T., & Stevens, K. T. (1997). Factors that influence the moral reasoning abilities of accountants: Implications for universities and the profession. *Journal of Business Ethics*, *16*(12/13), 1297–1309. doi:10.1023/A:1005754201952

Ferrell, O. C., & Fraedrich, J. (2014). *Business ethics: Ethical decision making & cases*. Cengage learning.

Fisscher, O., Frenkel, D., Lurie, Y., & Nijhof, A. (2005). Stretching the frontiers: Exploring the relationships between entrepreneurship and ethics. *Journal of Business Ethics*, *60*(3), 207–209. doi:10.1007/s10551-005-0128-1

Fullerton, S., Kerch, K. B., & Dodge, H. R. (1996). Consumer ethics: An assessment of individual behavior in the market place. *Journal of Business Ethics*, *15*(7), 805–814. doi:10.1007/BF00381744

Gill, K. (2012). College Students Altitudes towards Ethical Consumerism – An Indian Perspective. *IOSR Journal of Business and Management*, 4(5), 01-13.

Glenn, J. R. Jr. (1992). Can a business and society course affect the ethical judgment of future managers? *Journal of Business Ethics*, *11*(3), 217–223. doi:10.1007/BF00871969

Griffin, R. (1993). *Management* (4th ed.). London: Houghton Mifflin Company.

Hitt, M., Middlemist, R., & Maith, R. (1983). *Management – Concepts and Effective Practice*. Los Angeles: West Publishing Company.

Jazani, N., & Ayoobzadeh, M. (2012). The Impact of Ethics Training Course on Ethical Behaviors of Management Students. *International Business Research*, *5*(11), 162. doi:10.5539/ibr.v5n11p162

Jones, W. A. Jr. (1990). Student views of "ethical" issues: A situational analysis. *Journal of Business Ethics*, *9*(3), 201–205. doi:10.1007/BF00382645

Keith, N. K., Perreault, H. R., Chin, M., & Keith, M. (2009). The effect of gender on the importance of business ethics and managerial decisions: A student perspective. *The Journal of Research in Business Education*, *51*(3), 125.

Khalizani, K., Omar, S. S., & Khalisanni, K. (2011). Graduate students' perceptions on business ethics and capitalism: A study in Malaysian universities. *International Journal of Education Administration and Policy Studies*, *3*(6), 85–93.

Lau, C. L. (2010). A step forward: Ethics education matters! *Journal of Business Ethics*, *92*(4), 565–584. doi:10.1007/s10551-009-0173-2

Lau, L., Caracciolo, B., Roddenberry, S., & Scroggins, A. (2012). College Students' Perception of Ethics. *Journal of Academic and Business*, *5*, 1–13.

Maheshwari, S., & Ganesh, M. (2006). Ethics In Organizations. *Vikalpa*, *31*(2), 75–86.

Okafor, G. O. (2011). The ethical behaviour of Nigerian business students (A study of undergraduate students' in business schools). *Arabian Journal of Business and Management Review*, *1*(3), 33–44.

Peppas, S. C., & Diskin, B. A. (2000). Ethical perspectives: Are future marketers any different? *Teaching Business Ethics*, *4*(2), 207–220. doi:10.1023/A:1009822500621

Perryer, C., & Scott-Ladd, B. (2014). Deceit, Misuse and Favours: Understanding and Measuring Attitudes to Ethics. *Journal of Business Ethics*, *121*(1), 123–134. doi:10.1007/s10551-012-1593-y

Pride, W., Hughes, R., & Kappor, J. (1996). *Business* (5th ed.). Boston: Houghton Mifflin Company.

Pulvers, K., & Diekhoff, G. M. (1999). The relationship between academic dishonesty and college classroom environment. *Research in Higher Education*, *40*(4), 487–498. doi:10.1023/A:1018792210076

Ritter, B. A. (2006). Can business ethics be trained? A study of the ethical decision-making process in business students. *Journal of Business Ethics*, *68*(2), 153–164. doi:10.1007/s10551-006-9062-0

Rutherford, M. A., Parks, L., Cavazos, D. E., & White, C. D. (2012). Business ethics as a required course: Investigating the factors impacting the decision to require ethics in the undergraduate business core curriculum. *Academy of Management Learning & Education*, *11*(2), 174–186. doi:10.5465/amle.2011.0039

Saidi, T. A. (2009). Relationship between ethical and Islamic banking systems and its business management implications. *South African Journal of Business Management*, *40*(1), 43–49.

Sebastiani, R., Montagnini, F., & Dalli, D. (2013). Ethical consumption and new business models in the food industry. Evidence from the Eataly case. *Journal of Business Ethics*, *114*(3), 473–488. doi:10.1007/s10551-012-1343-1

Seshadri, S., & Broekemier, G. M. (2009). Ethical decision making: Panama–United States differences in consumer and marketing contexts. *Journal of Global Marketing*, *22*(4), 299–311. doi:10.1080/08911760903022515

Shaw, D., Grehan, E., Shiu, E., Hassan, L., & Thomson, J. (2005). An exploration of values in ethical consumer decision making. *Journal of Consumer Behaviour*, *4*(3), 185–200. doi:10.1002/cb.3

Sigurjonsson, T. O., Vaiman, V., & Arnardottir, A. A. (2014). The Role of Business Schools in Ethics Education in Iceland: The Managers' Perspective. *Journal of Business Ethics*, *122*(1), 25–38. doi:10.1007/s10551-013-1755-6

Sparks, J. R., & Pan, Y. (2010). Ethical judgments in business ethics research: Definition, and research agenda. *Journal of Business Ethics*, *91*(3), 405–418. doi:10.1007/s10551-009-0092-2

Szmigin, I., & Carrigan, M. (2006). Exploring the dimensions of ethical consumption. *European Advances in Consumer Research*, *7*, 608–613.

Vesilind, P. (1988). Rules, Ethics And Morals. *English Education*, *2*(1), 289–293.

Vitell, S. J., & Hidalgo, E. R. (2006). The impact of corporate ethical values and enforcement of ethical codes on the perceived importance of ethics in business: A comparison of US and Spanish managers. *Journal of Business Ethics*, *64*(1), 31–43. doi:10.1007/s10551-005-4664-5

Weber, J. (2006). Implementing an organizational ethics program in an academic environment: The challenges and opportunities for the Duquesne University Schools of Business. *Journal of Business Ethics*, *65*(1), 23–42. doi:10.1007/s10551-005-3970-2

Weber, J., & Glyptis, S. M. (2000). Measuring the impact of a business ethics course and community service experience on students' values and opinions. *Teaching Business Ethics*, *4*(4), 341–358. doi:10.1023/A:1009862806641

Weegar, M. A. (2007). Promoting ethical practices within institutions of higher education. *Proceedings of the 2007 Association for Business Communication Annual Convention.*

Wiley, C. (1995). The ABC's of business ethics: Definitions, philosophies and implementation. *Industrial Management*, *37(1)*, 22.

Zgheib, P. W. (2005). Managerial ethics: An empirical study of business students in the American University of Beirut. *Journal of Business Ethics*, *61*(1), 69–78. doi:10.1007/s10551-004-6394-5

Chapter 9
Do Board Educational Background, Occupational Background and Ownership Structure Matter for Directors' Remuneration Disclosure?
Some Malaysian Evidence

Elinda Esa
National Energy University, Malaysia

Abdul Rahman Zahari
National Energy University, Malaysia

ABSTRACT

Following the Asian economic tumult 1997, most of the researchers in Malaysian have been focusing on the issues of disclosure, transparency and boardroom failures. The crisis had led to statements about corporate governance in times of financial crisis and the lessons that can be learnt. A lot of prior literature examined the factors influencing the aspects of disclosure without giving reference to the educational and occupational background of the board of directors and the ownership structure, which influence the decision-making regarding director remuneration disclosure. Thus, the objective of this study is to investigate how the educational and occupational background of the board of directors and ownership structure affect director remuneration disclosure in Malaysian public listed companies. Very limited research has been explored in the issue of directors' remuneration disclosure. The director remuneration checklist is used to measure the director remuneration disclosure among Malaysian public listed companies. The findings of this study revealed that ownership structure is significantly associated with the extent of directors' remuneration disclosure, while the board's educational and occupational background are found to not be associated with the extent of directors' remuneration disclosure.

DOI: 10.4018/978-1-4666-9864-2.ch009

INTRODUCTION

A number of high profile corporate collapses have arisen although their annual reports and accounts seemed salubrious. These corporate collapses have had an unpropitious effect, which were linked to the lack of efficacious corporate governance. Corporate governance is an issue that has grown very rapidly in both developed and developing countries, especially after the collapse of Enron, WorldCom and Parmalat. In Asia, extensive reforms of corporate governance practices have taken place after the ASEAN financial crisis. Additionally, most companies have been vigorously invigorating their regulatory frameworks, especially corporate governance mechanisms, particularly on boards and its composition, ethical aspects of remuneration, control and risk as well as higher accentuates on disclosure and transparency. Malaysia was one of the countries that took numerous initiatives in promoting and sustaining a vigorous culture of corporate governance through the issuance of the Malaysian Code on Corporate Governance (MCCG) in year 2000. Since then, the MCCG has perpetually stepped forward with amendment and in 2007, the code was revised to fortify the roles and responsibilities of the board of directors, audit committee and the internal audit function. Furthermore, in 2011, the Corporate Governance Blueprint was relinquished to set out the desired corporate governance landscape in moving forward. In 2012, to deliver the objectives of the Blueprint 2011, MCCG 2012 was relinquished with the focus to elucidate the role of the board in providing leadership, enhancing the board efficacy through invigorating its composition and reinforcing its independence.

Corporate governance can be defined as the process and structure used to direct and manage the business and affairs of the company towards enhancing business prosperity and corporate accountability with the ultimate objective of realizing long-term shareholders value, whilst taking into account the intrigues of other stakeholders (MCCG, 2012). In simple word, corporate governance is 'the system by which companies are directed and controlled' (Cadbury Report, 1992). Additionally, the problem in corporate governance arises from separating ownership and control (agency relationship) within business organizations. An agency theory identifies the agency relationship where one party, the principal i.e. the shareholders, delegates work to another party, the agent i.e. the directors. Generally, the self-interest of agents and information asymmetry, whereby the principal and the agent have access to different levels of information, are the consecutions of the agency relationship problem. Thus, disclosure and transparency is one of the best solutions to cure agency relation problems.

Malaysia government has initiated major corporate governance reforms to promote disclosure and transparency in MCCG (2000), (Revised, 2007). As crucial elements of good corporate governance framework, disclosure and transparency provides the basis for apprised decision-making by directors, shareholders, stakeholders and potential investors with veneration to capital allocation, financial performance and directors' emolument (Esa and Zahari, 2014). In fact, these elements are aimed to increase the confidence of investors, fortify capital market, amend the accountability and credibility of financial information provided by listed companies and additionally avails the public's meeting of minds on company's activities, policies and performance with regard to environmental and ethical standards.

Prior literatures (e.g. Esa and Mohd Ghazali, 2012; Mohd Ghazali, 2010; Akhtaruddin *et al.* 2009; Mohd Ghazali and Weetman, 2006; and Haniffa and Cooke, 2005) have examined corporate governance transparency and corporate disclosure in Malaysia. In addition, Mohd Ghazali, (2007), Tam *et al.*, (2007), Mohd Ghazali and Weetman, (2006) and Jaafar *et al.*, (2012) have also examined the association of ownership structure with the firm performance and corporate disclosure. However, none of these studies have been done between the associations of board characteristics i.e. board educational, board occupational background and ownership structure with directors' remuneration disclosure in Malaysia. In light of the above arguments, the focus of this study is twofold, first is to analyse the directors' remuneration information provided by the annual reports of Malaysian public listed companies, as revealed by the Minority Shareholder Watchdog Group (MSWG) which is only 5.6% of Malaysian directors disclosed their emolument in year 2010 in fact it being the best practice recommended under the MCCG (MSWG, 2010). Second is to analyse the impact of board educational background, board occupational background and ownership structure on directors' remuneration disclosure.

Malaysia's economy was rapidly growing in the early 1990s. A number of the listed companies in Malaysia are family owned with numerous companies having developed from conventional family-owned enterprises. Furthermore, as reported in the Social and Structural Review Update 2001, corporate ownership in Malaysia is highly concentrated (World Bank Group, 2001). A review done on East Asian corporations by Claessens *et al.* (2000) revealed that 13.4% of 238 Malaysian companies are state-owned, while 67.2% are family-owned and 19.3% are owned by widely held financial and non-financial companies. It shows that directors may not be receptive to minority shareholders' rights. Thus, better corporate governance would help to cure this and ensure the minority shareholders' rights are secured. Furthermore, transparency and disclosure should also be enhanced to restore the investors' confidence. The current study will not only be insightful but the findings also show that ownership structure has some influence on directors' remuneration disclosure.

This study is organized as follows: Section 2 discusses relevant literature to develop the research hypotheses. It is then followed by the research method outlining the sample selection and the research techniques. Results and analyses are presented in Section 4 and the conclusion is outlined in Section 5.

BACKGROUND AND HYPOTHESES DEVELOPMENT

Directors' Remuneration Disclosure

According to Abdullah (2006), the directors' remuneration issue is bounded proximately to the corporate governance issues. Directors' remuneration is the payment made for services or employment of directors on the board of the company or corporation (Talha *et al.*, 2009). This encompasses various elements including base salary or fee, bonus, stock options, stock grants, pensions, benefits in kind, and other emoluments that the directors receive during their tenure. In Malaysia, MCCG require listed company's annual reports to disclose the remuneration of each director. Additionally, all listed companies are required to promulgate and disclose the detailed emolument of directors for the financial year in the company annual report as the aggregate emolument or remuneration of directors with classification into relevant components such as directors' fees, salaries, percentages, bonuses, commission, compensation for loss of office, benefits in kind based on the estimated money value distinguishing between executive and non-executives directors as stated in the Bursa Malaysia Listing Requirement (Chapter 9, Appendix 9C, Part A). They also are required to have disclosure on the number of directors whose remuneration falls in each successive band of 50,000 RM. However, the disclosure requirement that is required by Bursa Malaysia on directors' remuneration is not mandatory.

Development of Hypotheses

Based on prior literatures, few variables were chosen to represent specific aspects of board characteristics, ownership structure and corporate characteristics for testing their association with directors' remuneration disclosure in annual reports. In each case, an expectation is formed based on prior literatures.

Board Educational and Occupational Background

Following the financial crisis, the main reason contribute to the bank failures is a shortage of board members that have a financial expertise experienced (Kirkpatrick, 2009). Given the rising importance of board, it is paramount to identify the board characteristics that make one board more effective from another. Additionally, board of directors plays an important role in overseeing the company's financial reporting process. The board responsibilities comprises of administering the management of the business, setting a strategic objective of the company, providing the leadership to put them in effect, reporting and communicating to shareholders on their stewardship (Cadbury Report, 1992). The importance of qualified members on board for conveying improved firm performance have been point up by prior literatures (see for example Haniffa & Cooke, 2002 and Smith *et al.*, 2006). Educational background and board occupational background can be important factors towards a company's performance because "different environments and backgrounds give rise to specific governance needs" (Peters et al., 2011). A director with higher education leads to better strategic decision-making (Bantel, 1993). Additionally, educated CEOs are likely to demand detailed information and extensive financial reporting (Bantel, 1993). Furthermore, Rajagopalan and Datta (1996) supported that individual's experience base is also one of the key indicators of the type of skills and cognition that the executive brings to their job. Managers with different experience backgrounds differ in their attitudes, knowledge and perspectives and thus, make different strategic choices (Guthrie and Datta, 1997). Empirical research has not been undertaken to examine the relationship between educational and occupational background and directors' remuneration disclosure. Hence, the relationship between directors' remuneration disclosures and board educational and occupational background is an empirical question and therefore a motivation for this study. For educational background, this study uses the proportion of directors who have qualification in management education (university or business school degree in business and accounting) by total directors. For board occupational background, this study uses the proportion of directors who are occupied with financial experience by total directors. Building on this argument, the hypotheses are as follows:

$H1_a$: There is a positive relationship between board educational background and the extent of directors' remuneration disclosure in annual report.

$H1_b$: There is a positive relationship between board occupational background and the extent of directors' remuneration disclosure in annual report.

Ownership Concentration

Ownership concentration is where corporate ownership is in the hands of a few individuals or relatives members. Prior studies by Haniffa and Cooke (2002) and Mohd Ghazali (2007) have examined the association between corporate disclosure and ownership concentration in Malaysia. The results revealed mix relationship. Negative relationship of ownership concentration with the extent of voluntary disclosure in the annual reports of Malaysian companies was reported in the study done by Hossain *et al.* (1994). As well as negative association in a prior study done by Mohd Ghazali (2007), while study done by Haniffa and Cooke (2002) revealed a positive relationship. Consistent with Hossain *et al.* (1994), Haniffa and Cooke (2002) and Mohd Ghazali (2007), this study uses the proportion of shares held by 10 largest shareholders to measure the ownership concentration. The hypothesis is as follows:

H2: There is a negative relationship between ownership concentration and extent of directors' remuneration disclosure in annual report.

Government Ownership

Malaysia provides a fascinating business environment with the government holding significant amount of shares in privatized organizations. It is expected that government-owned companies lead others to portray good disclosure and transparency since the activities of these companies are more in the public's consciousness (Mohd Ghazali, 2007). Additionally, prior studies (e.g. Mohd Ghazali, 2007; Amran and Devi, 2008; Said et al., 2009) revealed positive relationship between government ownership and the extent of CSR disclosure, whereas no significant association was found between ownership structure and voluntary disclosure in Malaysia in the study done by Mohd Ghazali and Weetman (2006). Government ownership in this study uses a dummy variable where 1 represents the government holding substantial amount of shares in the companies with the expectation that the government-owned companies will disclose more information pertaining to directors' remuneration in their annual reports. The hypothesis is as follows:

H3: There is a positive relationship between government ownership and the extent of directors' remuneration disclosure in annual report.

Family Members on Board

The presence of family members in the board is likely to be less disseminated of ownership (Mohd Ghazali and Weetman, 2006). These companies will have tendency to less disclose their additional information due to lower degree of conflict of interest. As well as the tendencies to report a self-interest accounting information rather than the true reflection of a firm's current financial performance. Previous studies revealed a significant negative relationship between the proportion of family members on the board and the extent of voluntary disclosure (see for example Haniffa and Cooke, 2002 and Ho and Wong, 2001). Therefore, the current study expects a negative relationship between the proportions of family members on the board and the directors' remuneration disclosure. The hypothesis is as follows:

H4: There is a negative relationship between the proportion of family members on boards and the extent of directors' remuneration disclosure in annual report.

Other Control Variables

In addition to board educational, board occupational background and ownership structure patterns, there are seven control variables in the multiple regression models for testing the main hypotheses. These are:

firm size (see for example Esa and Zahari, 2014; Esa and Mohd Ghazali, 2012; Mohd Ghazali, 2007; Haniffa and Cooke, 2005; Abdul Hamid, 2004; Belkaoui and Karpik, 1989), leverage (e.g. Esa and Zahari, 2014; Esa and Mohd Ghazali, 2012; Mohd Ghazali, 2007; Haniffa and Cooke, 2005), profitability (e.g. Esa and Zahari, 2014; Esa and Mohd Ghazali, 2012; Abdul Hamid, 2004; Balabanis *et al.*, 1998; Meek *et al.*, 1995; Patten, 1991), industry type (Esa and Zahari, 2014; Mohd Ghazali, 2007; Haniffa and Cooke, 2005), board size (e.g. Esa and Zahari, 2014; Esa and Mohd Ghazali, 2012; Cheng and Courtenay, 2006), board ethnicity (e.g. Haniffa and Cooke, 2005) and independent non-executive director (see for example Esa and Zahari, 2014; Esa and Mohd Ghazali, 2012; Huafang and Jianguo, 2007; Eng and Mak, 2003; Haniffa and Cooke, 2002).

Regression Model

Combining all these variables, the full regression model is as follows:

$$DRDI = \beta_0 + B_1 Ined + B_2 Bsize + B_3 Bedu + B_4 Boccup + B_5 Beth + B_6 ownTen + B_7 GovtOwn + B_8 FamoB + B_9 Cosize + B_{10} Lev + B_{11} Prof + B_{12} IndType + \in$$

DRDI represents director remuneration disclosure index as the dependent variable, $\beta_0, \ldots\ldots, \beta_{12}$ represent regression coefficients, independent variables are defined in Table 1 and ε represents the error term. The operationalization of independent variables and the sources of data are shown in Table 1.

RESEARCH DESIGN

Data

The data of the present study is focused on Malaysia's 100 largest listed companies that were listed on Bursa Malaysia in 2013. The annual report of the company were downloaded from the Bursa Malaysia website (www.bursamalaysia.com). The criteria of the 100 listed companies list is based on the highest in total assets and revenue size. The sample was limited to big companies due to consensus that big companies are generally good reporters. While, the financial institutions are excluded in the list of Malaysia's 100 largest listed companies due to the different regulation attached to this sector, and this approach is consistent with prior disclosure studies (e.g. Esa and Zahari, 2014; Esa and Mohd Ghazali, 2012; Mohd Ghazali and Weetman, 2006; Haniffa and Cooke, 2005). Commercial banks, finance companies, merchant banks and money brokers in Malaysia are regulated under the Banking and Financial Institution Act (BAFIA), 1989. Therefore, only 87 companies are included in the final selection and the industry representation for the sample companies is shown in Table 2.

Directors' Remuneration Disclosure Instruments

In order to gauge the extent of directors' remuneration disclosure practices in Malaysia, a disclosure checklist containing 22 items was used. The checklist was adopted from Ramli (2001) with the excep-

Table 1. Variable Definitions and Sources

Variables	Operationalization	Data Source
Independent non-executive director	[Ined] Proportion of Independent non-executive directors on the board	Company annual reports
Board Size	[Bsize] Number of directors on the board	Company annual reports
Board Educational	[Bedu] Proportion of directors who have qualification in university or business school degree in business and accounting on the board.	Company annual reports
Board occupational	[Boccu] Proportion number of directors who have occupied one of the following functions on the board: • Chief financial controller • Chief accounting officer • Management controller • External auditor • Banker • Business lawyer • Other financial functions	Company annual reports
Board ethnics	[Beth]Proportion of Malay directors on the board	Company annual reports
Ownership concentration	[OwnTen] Ratio of shares owned by 10 largest shareholders to total number of shares issued	Company annual reports
Government ownership	[GovOwn] Dummy variables, 1 = the government is a largest shareholder 0 = otherwise	Company annual reports
Family members on board	[FoB] Ratio of family members on the board to total directors	Company annual reports
Company size	[CoSize] Company size measured by total assets	Company annual reports
Leverage	[Lev] Leverage measured by total liabilities over total assets	Company annual reports
Profitability	[Prof] Profitability measured by profit before tax over total assets	Company annual reports
Industry type	[IndType] 1= properties, 2 = ind product, 3 =consumer, 4 = plantation, 5 = trade/service, 6 = technology/IPC, 7 = construction	Company annual reports

Table 2. Industry Representation of the Sample Companies.

Industry	Number of companies	%
Properties	3	3.4
Industrial products	24	27.6
Consumer products	17	19.5
Plantation	5	5.7
Trading/services	32	36.8
Technology/IPC	1	1.1
Construction	5	5.7
Total	87	100

tion of one group (i.e. the details of directors' share option scheme) which became irrelevant for most of the companies in Malaysia. The original version of checklist was used on 30 companies as a pilot. It was found that the checklist failed to capture some of the information provided in directors' remuneration disclosure specifically on the details of directors' share option schemes. Therefore, this item was excluded. The checklist was used as the study focused on measuring the extent of information pertaining to directors' affair disclosed in the annual reports of companies in an international setting. Table 3 provides the disclosure items relating to the directors' remuneration.

Table 3. Directors' Remuneration Disclosure Checklist.

Disclosure Items	
Details of directors' salary/fees.	
1.	Salary/fee of each individual director.
2.	Total directors' salary/fee for the current year.
3.	Total directors' salary/fee comparative figures.
Details of directors' bonus/performance bonus/profit sharing or other similar payments.	
4.	Bonus of each individual director.
5.	Total directors' bonus for the current year.
6.	Total directors' bonus comparative figures.
Details of directors' benefits in kind/other fringe benefits.	
7.	Value of benefits in kind of each individual director.
8.	Nature of the benefits.
9.	Total value of directors' benefits in kind for the current year.
10.	Total value of directors' benefits in kind comparative figures.
Details of directors' retirement benefit plans.	
11.	Defined contribution plan at the end at of the year of each individual director.
12.	Defined contribution plan at the beginning of the year of each individual director.
13.	Total directors' contribution plan/retirement benefits for the current year.
14.	Total directors' contribution plan/retirement benefits comparative figures.
Directors' emoluments.	
15.	Emoluments for each individual director.
16.	Emoluments for each individual director comparative figures.
17.	Total directors' emoluments for the current year.
18.	Total directors' emoluments comparative figures.
Details of directors' interest in shares or a statement stating that the directors hold no shares in the company.	
19.	Number of shares held by each individual director at the end of the year.
20.	Number of shares held by each individual director at the beginning of the year.
21.	Total number of shares held by directors at the end of the year.
22.	Total number of shares held by directors at the beginning of the year.

Scoring Method

The scoring method used in the current study was based on an unweighted index or dichotomous approach in measuring the extent of directors' remuneration disclosed information. The disclosed items are awarded as 1, and non- disclosed items are awarded as 0 which means that all information was equally valued regardless of their importance or relevance to any particular user group (Chau and Gray, 2002). The directors' remuneration disclosure index (DRDI) was used as the dependent variable in this study. DRDI was derived by computing the ratio of actual scores obtained to the maximum possible score (i.e. 22 items) by a particular company.

RESULTS AND ANALYSIS

Table 4 presents descriptive statistics of independent variables. It can be seen that the average ratio of board educational background (Bedu) to total directors on board is 0.55. It shows that 55% of board members, on average, have qualifications in business and accounting from universities or business school degrees. Furthermore, in terms of board occupational background (Boccu), it is found that 51% of board members on average are occupied with previous financial experience. Nevertheless, among the large companies in Malaysia, ownership by the 10 largest shareholders varies between 29.24% and 90.20%. The mean of 68.08% shows that on average, large companies are concentrated in the hands of the 10 largest shareholders. Furthermore, out of the sample companies, the statistic shows only 16.1% are government-owned companies. The board size ranges between 5 to 15 with an average of 8.91. This average size is slightly higher than the findings of Mohd Ghazali (2010). It might be due to the current study focus on large companies.

Table 4. Descriptive Statistics of Independent Variables.

	Minimum	Maximum	Mean	Std. Dev.
Panel A: Continuous Variables				
Ined	0.23	0.86	0.46	0.13
Bsize	5.00	15.00	8.91	2.28
Beth	0.00	1.00	0.42	0.23
Bedu	0.13	1.29	0.55	0.21
Boccu	0.18	1.14	0.51	0.18
Prof	–8.19	102.92	11.26	17.11
Lev	-209.00	114.85	47.68	34.77
CoSize	19.75	24.99	22.30	1.19
OwnTen	29.24	90.20	68.08	15.41
FoB	0.00	0.67	0.09	0.19
Panel B: Categorical Variables				
GovOwn 1 = the government is the largest shareholders 14 (16.1%) 0 = otherwise 73 (83.9%)				

Table 5 presents correlation coefficients between variables. From this table, it can be seen that company size (CoSize), government ownership (GovOwn) and family on board (FoB) were significantly correlate with the directors' remuneration disclosure at 0.01% level as well as leverage is also found to significantly correlate at 0.05% levels. However, board educational and board occupational backgrounds are found to be insignificant with directors' remuneration disclosure.

Table 6 shows the results of the regression analysis. The regression model which comprises twelve independent variables results in an adjusted R^2 of 41.7%. This indicates that the twelve variables tested were able to explain 41.7% of the variation in the extent of directors' remuneration disclosure among Malaysia's 100 largest listed companies. Family on board and government ownership was disclosed significantly more directors' remuneration disclosure. As well as company size was found significant and positively associated with the extent of directors' remuneration disclosure. However board educational and board occupational backgrounds were not statistically significant in explaining the extent of directors' remuneration disclosure.

The percentage of family members on the board with a p value of 0.001 is significant at 1% level with negative association. The negative association sign indicates that companies with more family members on the board disclose less information in their annual reports. The findings is consistent with prior studies (e.g. Esa and Zahari, 2014; Haniffa and Cooke, 2002; Ho and Wong, 2001) and thus, support Hypothesis 4. The results appear to advocate that family companies are more likely to be quiescent about their corporate activities as well as perpetuate their tradition affiliated from the past (Esa and Zahari, 2014). Additionally, the demand for information might be a main factor that contributes to the lower level of disclosure as these companies only operate with fewer outsiders and are usually smaller in size. The details of disclosure of directors' remuneration in family businesses are usually not shown (i.e. reference to directors individually) due to safety reasons. As well as the family members who sit on the boards believe that such information will not add significance to the understanding and evaluation of the company's standards of corporate governance.

Table 5. Correlation Analysis.

	CoSize	Bsize	FOB	GovOwn	Prof	Lev	Ined	Beth	OwnTen	Bedu	Boccu	DRDI
Cosize	1											
Bsize	.304**	1										
FOB	.128	.087	1									
GovOwn	.350**	.004	-.222*	1								
Prof	-.237*	-.099	-.148	-.085	1							
Lev	-.108	-.065	.108	-.152	-.008	1						
Ined	-.008	-.437**	-.071	0.135	.003	-.010	1					
Beth	.208	.490**	-.285**	0.360**	-.075	-.024	.137	1				
OwnTen	.080	-.015	-.233*	.283**	.147	.019	-.099	.207	1			
Bedu	-.125	.286**	-.058	.077	.119	.043	.145	-.036	-.031	1		
Boccu	.010	.550**	-.033	-.054	.144	.023	.106	-.004	-.101	.779*	1	
DRDI	.370**	.059	-.348**	.484**	.006	-.216*	.076	.190	-.137	.035	.055	1

* Correlation is significant at the 0.05 level (2-tailed).

** Correlation is significant at the 0.01 level (2-tailed).

Table 6. Results for the extent of directors' remuneration disclosure.

	Beta	Sig	VIF
		.175	
Cosize	.333	.005***	1.667
FOB	−.379	.001***	1.558
GovOwn	.347	.002***	1.410
Prof	.126	.646	1.152
Lev	.050	.324	1.059
Ined	.068	.590	1.380
Beth	−.403	.235	1.390
OwnTen	−.182	.634	1.247
Bedu	.080	.808	3.016
Boccu	.384	.515	2.966
Bsize	.110	.335	1.619
IndType	-.124	.209	1.226

Adjusted $R^2 = 0.417$
F statistic = 4.414
Significance = 0.000
N = 87
Note: ***, **, * are significant at 1%, 5% and 10% level, respectively.

The government ownership is statistically significant at 1% level. As hypothesized, companies in which the government is the largest shareholder, portrays a good image as they disclosed better than others. The findings prove to support Hypothesis 3 and it is consistent with prior study by Esa and Zahari (2014) and Mohd Ghazali (2007) as the studies examined the association between ownership and corporate disclosure. The findings indicate that the regulatory efforts to upgrade the effectiveness of boards and reinforce corporate governance in government-owned companies have proved to be successful (Esa and Zahari, 2014). Additionally, these companies may be necessitated to be more politically sensitive as their activities are seen more in the public eyes (Mohd Ghazali, 2007). Therefore, the clarity of directors' emolument issues are needed as this issue may signal to the public that the company is operating in accordance with the expectations of the nation.

Company size as a control variable is shown at a significant level of 1%. The result reveals that the decision to disclose directors' remuneration disclosure is also influenced by this variable. The positive association between larger companies and the extent of directors' remuneration disclosure implies that big size companies are good reporters. While, profitability, leverage, independent non-executive directors, board ethnicity, ownership concentration, and industry type are not significant. This indicates that the decision to disclose directors' remuneration information in the annual reports is not influenced by these factors.

CONCLUSION AND SUGGESTIONS FOR FUTURE RESEARCH

This study has examined directors' remuneration disclosure on the Malaysia's 100 largest listed companies. The statistical results reveals that company size, government ownership and family ownership are significant influences on directors' remuneration disclosure in annual reports. However, other variables such as board educational background, occupational background, ownership by 10 largest shareholders, board size, independent non-executive director, board ethnics, industry type, profitability and leverage are found to not be statistically significant in explaining the level of directors' remuneration disclosure in annual reports of Malaysian listed companies. Nonetheless, the present results show that company size and ownership structure are important antecedents in influencing directors' remuneration disclosure.

The generalizability of this study it's limited by its examination of the large company size, the future study might consider multiple size of companies. Future research also can include pre and post financial crisis to see whether the financial crisis had an influence on directors' remuneration disclosure. Additionally, analyzing moderating effect of corporate social responsibility disclosure towards director's remuneration disclosure also might be done for future research. As well as other methods of data collection such as interviews may help to identify other factors influencing directors' remuneration disclosure.

REFERENCES

Abdul Hamid, F. Z. (2004). Corporate social disclosure by banks and finance companies: Malaysian evidence. *Corporate Ownership and Control*, *1*(4), 118–130.

Abdullah, S. N. (2006). Directors' remuneration, firm's performance and corporate governance in Malaysia among distress companies. *Corporate Governance*, *6*(2), 162–174. doi:10.1108/14720700610655169

Akhtaruddin, M., Hossain, M. A., Hossain, M., & Yao, L. (2009). Corporate governance and voluntary disclosure in corporate annual reports of Malaysian listed firms. *Journal of Applied Management Accounting Research*, *7*(1), 1–19.

Amran, A., & Devi, S. S. (2008). The impact of government and foreign affiliate influence on corporate social reporting: The case of Malaysia. *Managerial Auditing Journal*, *23*(4), 386–404. doi:10.1108/02686900810864327

Balabanis, G., Phillips, H. C., & Lyall, J. (1998). Corporate social responsibility and economic performance in the top British companies: Are they linked? *European Business Review*, *98*(1), 25–44. doi:10.1108/09555349810195529

Bantel, K. (1993). Environment and performance effects on strategic planning formality. *Group & Organization Management*, *18*(4), 436–458. doi:10.1177/1059601193184004

Belkaoui, A. R., & Karpik, P. G. (1989). Determinants of the corporate decision to disclose social information. *Accounting, Auditing & Accountability Journal*, *2*(1), 36–51. doi:10.1108/09513578910132240

Burke, J. E. (1964). Scattering of surface waves on an infinitely deep fluid. *Journal of Mathematical Physics*, *6*(6), 805–819. doi:10.1063/1.1704182

Chau, G. K., & Gray, S. J. (2002). Ownership structure and corporate voluntary disclosure in Hong Kong and Singapore. *The International Journal of Accounting*, *37*(2), 247–265. doi:10.1016/S0020-7063(02)00153-X

Cheng, E. C. M., & Courtenay, S. M. (2006). Board composition, regulatory regime, and voluntary disclosure. *The International Journal of Accounting*, *41*(3), 262–289. doi:10.1016/j.intacc.2006.07.001

Claessens, S., Djankov, S., & Lang, L. H. P. (2000). The separation of ownership and control in East Asian corporations. *Journal of Financial Economics*, *58*(1-2), 81–112. doi:10.1016/S0304-405X(00)00067-2

Dyl, E. A. (1988). Corporate control and management compensation: Evidence on the agency problem. *Managerial and Decision Economics*, *9*(1), 21–25. doi:10.1002/mde.4090090102

Eng, L. L., & Mak, Y. T. (2003). Corporate governance and voluntary disclosure. *Journal of Accounting and Public Policy*, *22*(4), 325–345. doi:10.1016/S0278-4254(03)00037-1

Esa, E., & Mohd Ghazali, N. A. (2012). Corporate social responsibility and corporate governance in Malaysian Government linked companies. *Journal of Corporate Governance*, *12*(3), 292–305. doi:10.1108/14720701211234564

Esa, E., & Zahari, A. R. (2014). Ownership structure and directors' compensation disclosure in Malaysia, in: Sabri Boubaker and Duc.K. Nguyen (Eds.), Corporate Governance and Corporate Social Responsibility: Emerging Markets Focus (pp. 267-285). World Scientific Publishing.

Fama, E. F., & Jensen, M. C. (1983). Separation of ownership and control. *The Journal of Law & Economics*, *26*(2), 301–325. doi:10.1086/467037

James, PGuthrie Datta, D.K. (1997). Contextual influence on executive selection: Firm characteristics and experience. *Journal of Management Studies*, *34*(4), 537–560. doi:10.1111/1467-6486.00062

Haniffa, R. M., & Cooke, T. E. (2002). Culture, corporate governance and disclosure in Malaysian corporations. *Abacus*, *38*(3), 317–349. doi:10.1111/1467-6281.00112

Haniffa, R. M., & Cooke, T. E. (2005). The impact of culture and governance on corporate social reporting. *Journal of Accounting and Public Policy*, *24*(5), 391–430. doi:10.1016/j.jaccpubpol.2005.06.001

Ho, S. S. M., & Wong, K. S. (2001). A study of the relationship between corporate governance structures and the extent of voluntary disclosure. *Journal of International Accounting, Auditing & Taxation*, *10*(2), 139–156. doi:10.1016/S1061-9518(01)00041-6

Hossain, M., Tan, L. M., & Adams, M. (1994). Voluntary disclosure in an emerging capital market: Some empirical evidence from companies listed on the Kuala Lumpur Stock Exchange. *The International Journal of Accounting*, *29*, 334–351.

Huafang, X., & Jianguo, Y. (2007). Ownership structure, board composition and corporate voluntary disclosure. *Managerial Auditing Journal*, *22*(6), 604–619. doi:10.1108/02686900710759406

Jaafar, S. B., James, K., & Abdul Wahab, E. A. (2012). Remuneration committee and director remuneration in family owned companies: Evidence from Malaysia. *International Review of Business Research Papers*, *8*(7), 17–38.

Kirkpatrick, G. (2009). The corporate governance lessons from the financial crisis [OECD]. *Financial Market Trends*, *1*, 1–13.

Meek, G. K., Roberts, C. B., & Gray, S. J. (1995). Factors influencing voluntary annual report disclosures by U.S., U.K and Continental European Multinational Corporations. *Journal of International Business Studies*, *26*(3), 555–572. doi:10.1057/palgrave.jibs.8490186

Mohd Ghazali, N. A. (2007). Ownership structure and corporate social responsibility disclosure: Some Malaysian evidence. *Corporate Governance*, *7*(3), 251–266. doi:10.1108/14720700710756535

Mohd Ghazali, N. A. (2010). Ownership structure, corporate governance and corporate performance in Malaysia. *International Journal of Commerce and Management*, *20*(2), 109–119. doi:10.1108/10569211011057245

Mohd Ghazali, N. A., & Weetman, P. (2006). Perpetuating traditional influences: Voluntary disclosure in Malaysia following the economic crisis. *Journal of International Accounting, Auditing & Taxation*, *15*(2), 226–248. doi:10.1016/j.intaccaudtax.2006.08.001

Patten, D. M. (1991). Exposure, legitimacy, and social disclosure. *Journal of Accounting and Public Policy*, *10*(4), 297–308. doi:10.1016/0278-4254(91)90003-3

Peters, S., Miller, M., & Kusyk, S. (2011). How relevant is corporate governance and corporate social responsibility in emerging markets? *Corporate Governance*, *11*(4), 429–445. doi:10.1108/14720701111159262

Rajagopalan, N., & Datta, D. K. (1996). CEO characteristics: Does industry matter? *Academy of Management Journal*, *39*(1), 197–215. doi:10.2307/256636

Said, R., Yuserrie, H. Z., & Hasnah, H. (2009). The relationship between corporate social responsibility disclosure and corporate governance characteristics in Malaysian public listed companies. *Social Responsibility Journal*, *5*(2), 212–226. doi:10.1108/17471110910964496

Smith, N., Smith, V., & Verner, M. (2006). Do women in top management affect firm performance? A panel study of 2500 Danish firms. *International Journal of Productivity and Performance Management*, *55*(7), 569–593. doi:10.1108/17410400610702160

Talha, M., Sallehhuddin, A., & Masuod, M. S. (2009). Corporate governance and director remuneration in selected ASEAN countries. *The Journal of Applied Research*, *25*(2), 31–39.

Tam, O. K., & Tan, M. G. (2007). Ownership, governance and firm performance in Malaysia. *Journal Compilation Blackwell Publishing*, *15*(2).

World Bank Group. (2001). Social and structural review update: Malaysia. Retrieved from www.worldbank.org

ADDITIONAL READING

Bursa Malaysia Listing Requirement. (n. d.). *Corporate Disclosure Guide.* Retrieved from www.bursamalaysia.com

Committee on the Financial Aspects of Corporate Governance. (1992). *Report with Code of Best Practice* [Cadbury Report]. London: Gee Publishing.

Malaysia Institute of Corporate Governance. (2001). *Malaysian Code on Corporate Governance 2001.* Bhd, Kuala Lumpur: Malaysian Law Journal Sdn.

Malaysian Securities Commission. (2007). *Malaysian Code of Corporate Governance (Revised 2007).* Kuala Lumpur: Securities Commission.

Malaysian Securities Commission. (2012). *Malaysian Code of Corporate Governance 2012.* Kuala Lumpur: Securities Commission.

Minority Shareholder Watchdog Group. (2010). *Malaysian Corporate Governance Report 2010.* Kuala Lumpur: Minority Shareholder Watchdog Group.

Ramli, M. I. (2001). *Disclosure in annual reports: An agency theoretic perspective in an international setting* [Unpublished PhD Thesis]. University of Plymouth, UK.

Chapter 10
Business Ethics, Decision and Cost Relations

Mohammad Shahriari
Necmettin Erbakan University, Turkey

Ahmet Diken
Necmettin Erbakan University, Turkey

ABSTRACT

Today, all companies, local, national and international, should have a positive image as the main pre-requisite of gaining a strong position at their general social image. Creating such an image depends on adopting the work ethics principles as behavior norms. The companies whose organizational structure is based on work ethics norms have an increase in their reliability, their institutionalization comes true in short time, potential of their products being chosen increases, a large and steady customer base is created and, as a result, these companies achieve a high level competitive power. The aim of this chapter is to define ethics, business ethics and cost related to unethical decision making. At the end a case study will be analyzed based on Ethical Criteria.

1. INTRODUCTION

The companies which act with profit maximization cause a bunch of versatile problems on a global scale due to violation of ethic norms. The production of goods that negatively affect public health, pushing quality-price balance into the background, misleading ads, ignoring customer satisfaction, violation of customer rights, evasion of tax, bribery, various irregularities that lead to a strengthening in underground economy, negative propaganda of rival companies that damage prestige, exploitation of labor, ignoring the optimal work conditions and leave the employees to serious health problems, increased number of sexual harassment as a result of women taking part in work life, environmental disasters which trigger corruption of ecological balance and other irresponsible action formats that destroy the sustainable development opportunities constitute the main components of this bunch of problems. The balls-up what makes the gap existing in business ethics and seem as the source of traumatic scandal points out that the companies should be sensitive. Besides, configuring the work life on the basis of moral principles will affect not only avoiding the problems listed above, also strengthen their positions in socio-economic process in the long run.

DOI: 10.4018/978-1-4666-9864-2.ch010

Today, all companies, local, national and international, should have a positive image as the main prerequisite of gaining a strong position at their general social image. Creating such an image depends on adopting the work ethics principles as behavior norms. The companies whose organizational structure is based on work ethics norms have an increase in their reliability, their institutionalization comes true in short time, potential of their products being chosen increases, a large and steady customer base is created and, as a result, these companies achieve a high level competitive power. The businesses can be damaged materially and morally because of employees' and managers' not acting in accordance with the moral ethics. The damages can be considered in two groups "measurable" and "immeasurable". The measurable damages include the compensations and fines that are paid by the companies because of negligence or abuse of work ethics and the loss in labor force and productivity as a result of this situation. The immeasurable damages are the loss of reliability and loss of reputation as a consequence of mentioned abuses which are difficult to fix or perpetuate its effect for a long while. Thus, the sentence "trust is like a spirit, when it goes once it never comes back" sums up the situation. Due to what has been mentioned above, a strong ethical culture within any organization is important in safeguarding people, capital and the environment. Business ethics will increase productivity and teamwork among the employees. It helps in aligning the values of the business with those of the workers. It is the basic beliefs and standards that make everything run smoothly. In this chapter business ethics is discussed and analyzed to show how it is important in a workplace.

The main objectives of this chapter are:

- Describing the main concepts e.g. moral, ethics and business ethics and the differences between moral and ethic
- Discussion about business Ethics and cost relation furthermore, Decision failure due to unethical behavior
- Analysis of a case to see the effects of neglecting ethical principles.

2. METHODOLOGY

The methodology used to proceed this study is divide into two phases such as:

- A literature review to collect relevant information to fulfil the goal of the study. In order to collect information, secondary data sources are used. The data was collected from various internet sources, text books and online journals.
- A decision failure case was selected from the literature to analysis the role of business ethics in preventing the losses. The analysis of the case was conducted by brain storming and also developing a Fishbone Diagram as a tool for cause – effect analysis. The diagram named Fishbone after its Japanese inventor Kaoru Ishikawa and looks similar to a fishbone (Shahriari, 2013). This graphical tool is used in order to identify, sort, illustrate and map different causes to a problem or a condition in a structured way (Shahriari, 2013). It can be used for several purposes including planning and problem solving. When problem – solving, the diagram shows the problem, its causes, and the relations between them. On the right end of the diagram the problem to be solved is represented as a head of the fishbone. A horizontal line, like a backbone, connects it to further branches, in which the main problems for this problem are stated (Figure 1). Further levels can be added stating influential factors to the main causes (Shahriari, 2013).

Figure 1. Fishbone Diagram (Ishikawa Diagram)

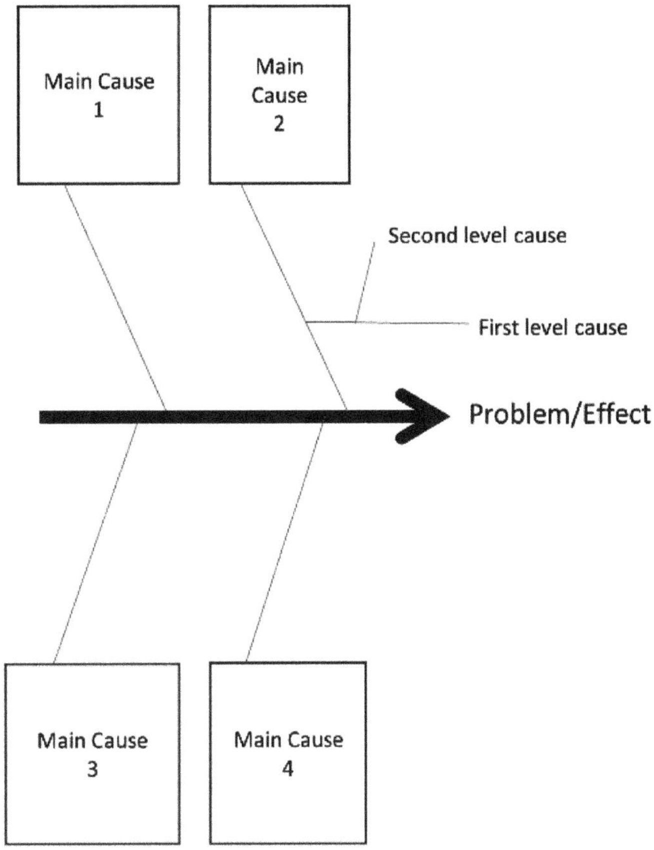

3. THE MAIN CONCEPTS OF ETHICS

3.1. Moral and Ethics

Moral relates to good and bad, right and wrong, virtue and defect conduct (Grammarist, n. d.).

The term ethics derives from the ancient Greek_word ethikos, which is derived from the word ethos (custom) (Ethics, n. d.). Moral philosophy defines the borders of moral behavior and immoral behavior (Kiliç, 1996). There is no acceptable universal moral principles and relativism and skepticism are dominant in moral field. It is too hard to determine moral behavior samples for everyone which can always be valid. But it is needed to find universal principles. This is the only way to make the peace and serenity in mankind (Kiliç, 1996).

Ethics deals with our moral judgment that lies behind our moral attitudes (Nuttal, 1993). Therefore, it is a field of philosophical study (Grammarist, n. d.).

There are differences between moral and ethics. While moral is set of rules composed by values system, ethics is the branch of philosophy subjects on moral. In other words ethics is a subject of human behaviors and the principle behind this behavior.

Ethics deals with moral in general. Ethics studies on moral's basis and essence. It works to answer what is right and what is wrong for people by using fundamental virtues and values. It works to reach non-relativistic behaviors of people. It emphasizes where human freedom is possible. Ethical behavior is an action expected by a particular group or society. Because notions such as right or wrong are instilled to us during our childhood. We are rewarded when we do something right and punished when we do something wrong. Thus, we adapt ourselves to universal behavior norms (Kiliç, 1996).

So both concept are closely related and are often interchangeable. The main difference is that moral is subjective, and often personal or religion-based, while ethics is more practical, considered as shared principles promoting fairness in social and business interactions (Grammarist, n. d.).

In sum, ethics could be a system of moral principles. They affect how people make decisions and lead their lives. Ethics is concerned with what is good for individuals and society and is also described as moral philosophy.

3.2. Ethics and Culture

According to Reason (as cited in Shahriari, 2013), culture is:

Shared values (what is important) and beliefs (how things work) that interact with an organization's structures and control systems to produce behavioral norms (the way we do things around here)

A continues success and reputation of a company or organization depends on each personnel values and his/her acting ethically, responsibly and in compliance with the law (Bryant, 2013). Values are fundamental beliefs of a person or an organization. These values are the guiding principles that help to define how the corporation would behave with the business partners and the stakeholders. Some typical values include honesty, integrity, responsibility, respect and fairness/justice. Some examples of values for a company might include being environmentally benign, commitment to provide a healthy and safe workplace.

Company values articulate those things that an organization believes in. In case these values are used effectively, they are like a cultural glue to 'connect' the team and support a social community based on shared goals. In fact the code of ethics of a company could represent the culture which company has built and the commitment has made to continue earning the trust of those who love our brands.

Since the personal values are subjective and influenced by the culture one belongs to, a frame of reference is needed to be created by the company to make the behavior predictable. This influences people's perception and decision on ethical level. This frame of reference which might be built through integrity, accountability, passion, humility, simplicity and a focus on success is called as ethical performance culture (Bryant, 2013).

Although, frame of reference in a company could help the people to do the right things, but it might happened that they face with dilemma, a situation in which one should choose between a moral and immoral act. This situation called as ethical dilemmas.

It is not easy to solve ethical dilemmas. In most cases, each available solution may have unpleasant results to be evaluated and positive benefits. The ethical issue about not sold products encountered by the producers is only one of the problems met at the workplace. Figure 2 shows the most common four

Figure 2. Common Ethical Issues (adapted from Boone & Kurtz (2013))

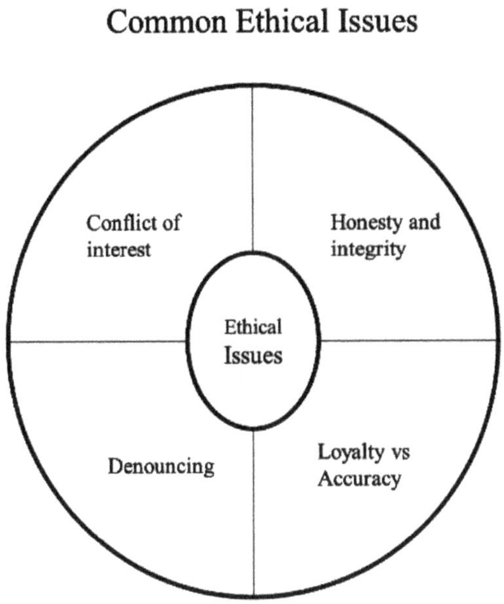

ethical issues confronted by businessmen. These are: conflict of interests, honesty and integrity, loyalty vs. accuracy and denouncing (Boone & Kurtz, 2013).

Conflict of Interests: Employee should make a decision between the welfare of the business and personal gain. Conflict of interest is the situation when the businessman encounter during giving a favor for a person or a group, he hurts others. The conflict of interest between the people or groups that have responsibilities towards each other can make ethical issues come to light.

Honesty and Integrity: evaluating the employees according to honesty and integrity has a great value. It believed that an honest employee does not lie. An employee with integrity goes further than being an honest person. Having integrity means being connected to ethical principals in situations met at the business. This include being a man of his word and accepting the responsibility of the faults. Honesty and integrity provide inspiration for trust and as a result, a long term relation with customers, employers, suppliers and public is provided. Also, the employees expect honesty and integrity from their managers and the business. Employees can check their personal emails, do shopping, play games, visit social networks, blogs, Facebook and Twitter during office hours.

Loyalty vs. Accuracy: Businessmen expect their employees be loyal and serve for the benefit of the business. When the reality about the business is not positive, ethical dilemmas may occur. Employees should decide on to be loyal or being accurate in business relations. People can find a solution to such dilemma with various ways.

Denouncing: an individual should decide how to act when he meets an unethical and illegal situation at workplace. Sometimes it is possible to solve the problem through channels in the business. If this effort fails, he should evaluate the potential faults that may affect public welfare. If the loss will be great, one should decide on denouncing. Denouncing is announcing an illegal, immoral or unethical practice through business executives, government officers or media.

Corporate culture is developed in four stages to support work ethics (Boone & Kurtz, 2013):

1. Ethical Awareness
2. Ethics Training
3. Ethical Action
4. Ethical Leadership

If one of these four factors is missing, it will weaken the ethical climate in the organization

Ethical Awareness

The basement of ethical climate is ethical awareness. As discussed before, ethical dilemmas are met at workplaces mostly. For that reason, when the ethical issue occur, the employees look for help to define the problem. Besides, the workers will need a guide for the expected reaction. One of the ways that the business provide this is developing *codes of conduct.* This is a formal declaration that has the rules for workers to be used when an ethical problem is encountered. At the most basic level, the basic rules of codes of conduct and acceptable attitudes are mentioned simply. Also, laws and regulations for the employees are included. Other companies, use codes of conduct to define basic corporate values and create a roof for the employees in solving moral and ethical dilemmas.

Ethical Training

Even though, codes of conduct are constituted in a detailed framework, it does not offer a detailed solution. Some ethical issues have white and black answers, but others do not. Businesses should offer tools to employees in order to evaluate the options in reaching the right decision.

Ethical Action

Codes of conduct and education programs help employees to define ethical issues and think on them. Apart from that, businesses should provide ethical actions and approaches in their decisions. The company, Texas Instruments, gave reference cards to their employees which will help them to make ethical decisions. Its size is like standard personal cards. It includes the following guides:

- Is this action legal?
- Does it adhere to our values?
- If you do, will you feel bad?
- How would it look in the newspapers?
- If you know that it is wrong, do not do!
- If you're not sure, ask!
- Keep asking till you get an answer.

Ethical Leadership

Senior managers should not only talk about ethical behavior, they must also show it with their action at the same time. This helps the company's employees to dedicate themselves to the core values and allows them to be willing to take action based on it. Last economic recession has shown that misconduct of senior executives damage the entire organization or almost destroy the work and the savings of people. Based on this results, two students, studying at Harvard Business School, has held talks with the respected leaders who show high moral values in India and Pakistan. Students have concluded that they are after a moral value which has three simple feature of "commands per ethics".

1. Instead of using a literary language for a corrupted behaviour, use a loud and clear language
2. Encourage the behaviour which produce ethical values and contribute its development
3. Apply the moral certainty, be insistent about doing the right thing even if it costs a lot financially.

However, ethical leaders should go a step further and give responsibility for employees at all levels to be an ethical leader. Everyone should be aware of the problem and must be willing to defend the standards of the organization.

Unfortunately, all organizations do not have a clear drafting skills for business ethics. Ethically wrong behavior will create pressure on - shareholders, customers, investors, employees and communities- to be acceptable in order to follow. But when businesses make mistake, the law is engaged to the situation to go to right direction. Laws affecting particular industries or individuals are defined in other parts of the book. Stakeholders, customers who affect the company and are affected by company, investors, employees and public.

3.3. Business Ethics

Business ethics applies moral principles of conduct that guide the way a business behaves in terms of distinguishing right and wrong to make a right choice or decision. According to McNamara (2015):

Attention to ethics in the workplace sensitizes leaders and staff to how they should act. Perhaps most important, attention to ethics in the workplaces helps ensure that when leaders and managers are struggling in times of crises and confusion, they retain a strong moral compass.

Business Ethics, states the manner, judgement and behavior of the employees as right or wrong. Its not only expresses right and wrong or trust- not to trust also reminds justice and injustice. Moral values can be perceived as soft and intangible. But being immoral can harm the tangible and measureable benefits or financial returns. Moreover, ignoring ethics may ruin our reputation and career.

Organizations may establish ethics in their workplace by implementing an ethics management program. Ethics program express corporate values, policies and guidelines to guide decisions and behavior, training, and providing guidance in Ethical dilemmas (Brian Schrag, as cited in McNamara (2015).

A corporate ethics program consists of values, policies and activities which impact the quality of manner of organization behaviors (Brenner, 1992).

As far as the ethical code is concerned, it states the ethical rules of operation. However, some business ethicists believe that codes have no value. They claim on the basis of their experiences and specify that codes themselves are not influential in managing ethics in the workplace. Many ethicists note that it's the developing and continuing dialogue around the code's values that is most important (McNamara, 2015).

As a matter of fact, in order to have a successful ethical program, it should be entirely supported by the management.

It should be noted that, business ethics is deformed at present times under hierarchical structures and bureaucratic administrative conditions in a way that emerge hazardous results in terms of ethics (UNPAN, 2004).

According to Sharon Allen, chairman of Deloitte LLP (as cited in Boone & Kurtz, 2013), "Good things start doing the right things." Her advice to the businesses owners is focusing on ethics and encouraging the employees about advanced ethical standards to provide the organization higher performance.

Unethical behavior in the workplace can cause losses in both economics and human life. The last survey by Association of Fraud Examiners professionals has revealed that US companies lose about 7% of annual earnings because of fraud (Boone & Kurtz, 2013). On the contrary, the companies in the list of Ethisphere which exhibit ethical behaviour are developing.

Employees are willing to work at a company which show corporate social responsibility, have high standards about ethical behaviour and the customers trust. In order to exhibit a good ethical behaviour to employees and customers, companies should have ethical leaders or similar politics or ethical training programs for employees.

In a study carried out by Valentine et al. (2006), a negative relationship has been found between business ethical values and business problems. The companies with a low perception level about business ethical values encounter problems such as absence of professional management mentality, lack of personal finance management and not trusting the advisory services. However, the businesses stating that they give importance to long term profitability and financial stability are known as having social responsibility and high business ethical level. The businesses stating that they give importance to customer satisfaction and social responsibility are getting more successful and rich. According to this survey again, the businesses which are known with higher social responsibility level because of having experience face less challenges inside and outside the organization. The businesses carrying out the management of customers successfully inside and outside put forth that their long term profitability increased; social responsibility activities lead investments which increase the profitability level. Social responsibility activities and organizational ethical behaviors emphasize the trust in the company in the market and this situation leads having trustable business image and continuity of long-term gains (Valentine et al., 2006).

What Can be Done about Ethical Dilemma?

Suzy Welch, a business journalist, says that because we are in tendency to get inadequate information, it is difficult to find a solution for ethical dilemmas. Welch advices to take the following steps if someone is suspicious about the unethical behaviors in workplace (Welch, as cited in Boone & Kurtz, 2013).

1. Gather all the facts. Ask questions kindly to people you trust and do not care about gossip and rumor. Give the assurance that the things mentioned will not be revealed. Talk with your company's human resources department. Be the researcher, not pushy.
2. When you get the reality ask yourself the question: Is this a real ethical dilemma? Or an office policy issue? How can an ethical violation that is hidden to gain power occur?
3. If the situation is a real ethical dilemma, tell about the issue to a trustable friend –rather than family. This person has an unbiased view and can give advice about what you can do.

The basic function of business ethics, with these dimensions of it, can be explained as providing for regulating the relationship between administrators/managers and workers/individuals, emphasizing on values belonging to social structure by fulfilling ethical needs and developing some behaviors suited to the structure.

As for the business ethics practices on public administration aim at regulating the relationship between administration and citizens, contributing to business activities, and forming behavioral standards based on ethics for civil servants.

The Ethical Principles in the Management

The ethical principles in management are listed as justice, equality, honesty and truth, neutrality, responsibility, respect for human rights, humanism, loyalty, rule of law, tolerance, respect, thriftiness, democracy, openness, resisting on illegal actions, giving somebody his labor, being a model to workers, being a polite person, hiding a secret, and being a modest person.

These principles concerning with organization are explained by Aydin Pehlivan (2002) as follows:

- **Justice:** Justice in organization, means setting a balance towards giving appropriate responses for behaviors such as giving laborers their rights in proportion to their contributions to the organization and their obeying the rules and punishing if they violate.
- **Equality:** The concept of equality is categorized in three different aspects. *Basic equality*, which means behaving individuals in equality; *partial equality,* which various applications and regulations are made to provide equality for various groups in the society; and *equality of blocks*, which provides the equality among groups and subclasses.
- **Honesty and Truth:** Truth means telling the true, and honest means being loyal to the promise and fulfilling the expectations. In fact, truth necessitates the whole life and actions to establish the realities. As for honesty is a concept including truth, but being different.
- **Neutrality:** Means that being able to see individuals or objects as it is and s/he is able to differ this image from the images that him/herself forms.
- **Responsibility**: To perform a certain duty in a desired quality and quantity.
- **Loyalty:** Organizational loyalty is that laborers carry on their organizational memberships and want to remain in the organization.
- **Thriftiness:** Means to keep the organization alive in proper for its goals and to utilize the human and material resources in a most efficient way.
- **Openness:** Is the process of mutual communication and building an atmosphere of trust between employers and employees.
- **Give Somebody His Labor:** This is concerned with returning of the value, which the laborer deserves of the value increment that he constitutes by the labor in the organization for production and service.

Bringing these principles in the organizational life will contribute to guide relations inside an organization, harmonize relations among people, and cooperation and business peace. Harmonized relations encouraging a voluntarily cooperation and will provide also the development of organizational climate at the same time.

Unethical Behaviors in Management

The behaviors having to be kept away in decisions, practices, actions and transactions in the business process are considered as "unethical behaviors". It also can be defined as any action and transaction, decision, and behavior that does not conform with the standards of conduct established by the organization (Joseph &Media, 2015).

These behaviors are included as discrimination, favoritism, bribery, terrorization, frightening, negligence, exploitation, egoism, fraud, torture, subservience, toadying, violence and aggressiveness, insult and swearing, physical and sexual harassment, bad habits, abusing of duty and authority, debiting, and fanaticism.

Under the ground of social and organizational degeneration, there is the weakening of ethical behaviors and on the other hand, the empowering of unethical behaviors.

Because ethical behaviors are not adequately encouraged and unethical behaviors are not sufficiently punished on the other side, unethical behaviors and practices develop in social atmosphere, finding fertile environments.

Understanding ethics can help economists to think productively about the moral dimensions of policy problems. Ethics can help economists and policy analyst to improve their methods of policy evaluation and to understand how peoples' economic behavior is influenced by the moral dimensions of their lives.

Expectations of business ethical behavior rising more rapidly than actual business ethics. Note that actual business ethics is assumed to be improving slightly but not as quickly as public expectations are rising. The magnitude of the current ethical problem, therefore, is seen here partially to be a function of rapidly rising societal expectations.

Business ethics has become a serious problem for the business community over the past several decades (see Figure 3). Business ethics concerns the rightness or wrongness of managerial behavior, and

Figure 3. Expected and Actual Levels of Business Ethics and Ethical problem (adapted from TOTA & Shehu (2012))

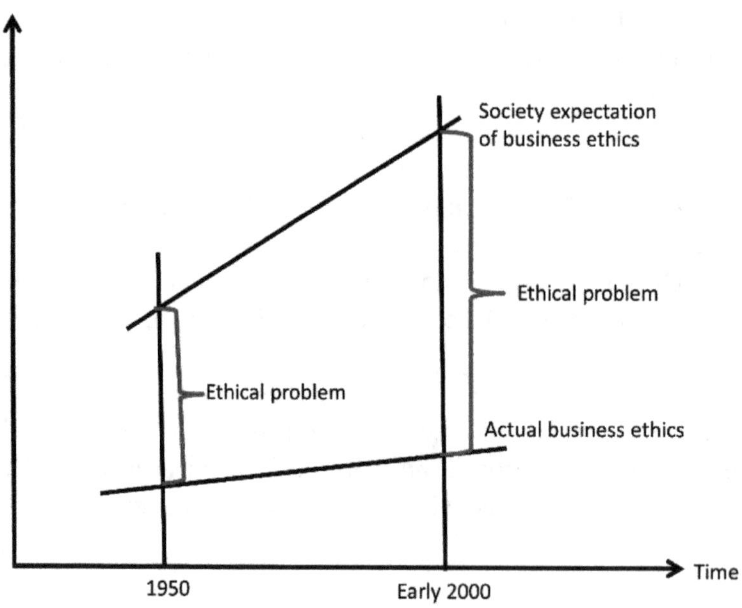

these are not easy judgments to make. Different ethical questions are more often put recently because of the pressure on financial economies, especially in emerging economies, to act unethically (TOTA & Shehu, 2012).

3.4. Ethics and Social Responsibility

Business ethics is on the agenda as it has never been before. Companies have realized that they must work much harder to gain the trust of public, and most of the companies have entered into this challenge as their business depends on this. This move extending to corporate social responsibility should provide interest for customers, environment and company itself.

The theory of social responsibility is built on a system of ethics, in which all decisions and actions must be taken to support sustainability including health and safety of the society. If this support is conducted, then social responsibility is accomplished. It is applies in both individual and group capacity. It should be incorporated into daily actions/decisions, particularly ones that will have an effect on other persons and/or the environment. Business organizations have developed a system of social responsibility that is customized to their company environment. Maintaining social responsibility within a company ensures the integrity of society and the environment are protected Pachamama Alliance (2015).

Most companies know how they can associate their ethical standards with environmental concerns. For instance, at the end of 2009, Matt Kistler, Senior Vice President of Walmart (as cited in Boone & Kurtz, 2013) have announced plans for the three sustainable objectives as follows:

1. Using only renewable energy sources
2. Ensuring the recycle of all types of waste
3. Selling products that support the existence of human and environment

But, unfortunately, social responsibility and ethics are often not practiced by many industrial companies, which result in losses including human life and the capital assets. Therefore, a strong work ethics and a compliance program is needed to provide guidance for monitoring of all areas of the business. According to Boone & Kurtz (2013) basic requirements for ethics compliance programs are:

- Compliance with standards and procedures. Preparation of standards and procedures to identify ethical rules and risk areas and to decrease the wrong behavior and crime.
- High level of staff responsibility. Board members and senior executives' lead the responsibility as a whole and observe ethical compliance programs.
- Exercising due diligence in assignments. Considering the tendency for wrong behavior and illegal activities of individuals while assigning duties.
- Communication about standards and procedures. Conveying ethical needs through applicable terms;
- Establishing a monitoring, supervision and report system. Monitoring and reviewing ethical fit and creating a report system that will help the staff convey wrong attitudes they see in the organization without being afraid of retaliation.
- Applying standards through suitable mechanisms. Performing ethical rules regularly including work discipline.

- Taking a stand according to crime. Taking reasonable steps in order to prevent further violations and catch them up.
- Private reporting. Reporting misconduct to the appropriate governing body.
- Feasible industry practices or standards. Following the laws of the state and industry standards.

4. ETHICS AND COST

Operating in an ethical way may bring additional costs to a business comparing with other companies who may not do the same Pachamama Alliance (2015).

It requires transparency and openness of mutual relationship between all stakeholders.

A study carrying out by Ghosh, et al. (2011) shows that there has been a traditional belief that profits and ethics are at conflict with each other in business. According to Ghosh et al. (2011):

"Moral codes, public interest and social values pose no threat to profit maximization of any firm. It is demonstrated with the illustration of transfer pricing and public goods-based economy that profits and ethics are quite compatible within the strait jacket of societal norms and corporate goals".

A debate was held in Paris by Good Corporation in September 2011(Good Corporation, 2015) under the title of "does run a business ethically add value or cost?" The results of the debate could be summarized as follows:

- Ethics is more preventive tool which is needed to protect the company reputation.
- Some people feel that in case ethical business could be implemented properly may cause business benefits and bring added value.
- As a matter of fact, business ethics adds cost but on the other side, it is all about the right way to do business without requiring a separate budget as it is the question of doing what is needed to run a business, but doing it ethically.
- Ethical reputation is a cost efficient marketing tool for a business.
- Some people prefer to see ethics as a way of behaving in a business rather than a form of economic model.
- In the debate the impact of ethics on customers and employees was investigated. It was supposed that customers prefer to deal with an ethical business, even if a little more should be paid. As far as the employees are concerned, the ethical behavior of an organization is seen as an important factor for new workforces, particularly younger employees who would prefer to work in an organization which respect ethical principles as was noted by those were involved in human resources.
- Many organizations consider ethics to be vital to the way they do business. But, there still remain plenty whose principle aim is to generate revenue and profits.
- Some suggestions were that building an ethical reputation for a business can be a highly effective and in fact, cost efficient marketing tool.
- It was suggested that ethical conduct should be at the heart of an organisation, and should derive from the top managers to all stakeholders and business partners.
- Customers prefer to deal with an ethical business, even if that means paying a little more. As for employees, those in human resources noted that the ethical conduct of an organisation is a key motivating factor for new workforce, particularly younger employees who want to feel proud of, rather than embarrassed by, the organisations for which they work.

Ethics exhibits difference between different areas across the world due to different cultures and economic situation. Global organizations which have facilities in some countries may do not respect business ethics principles and as a result, environmental or safety disasters could be occurred. Disaster occurred in 1984 in one of the United Carbide India Limited (UCIL) factories located in Bhopal, India could be a good example in this regard. Since India is a developing country, the pesticide company originated from U.S. may have focused only on the profit and might have been thinking that they could ignore the ethical principles such as human health and safety and environmental issues in Bhopal plant in India (Andersson, Appelberg, Johansson, Lindqvist, & Mohd Nasir, 2012). The economic oriented goals of the company had been supported by the loose regulations in India as they also need some economic development in their country in order to promote job opportunities to the citizens. This could be seen as a win-win situation for both parties from an economic aspect.However, they put safety and health of the people as collateral. Indeed, such unethical behavior which is associated with taking too high risks tends in the long terms to be very costly.

5. ETHICS AND DECISION MAKING

Decision making, as one of the central activities of management, could be influenced by interfaces between different factors such as business goal/company benefits, manager decision maker culture and value and the company ethics. In fact the role of managers when making a decision is very critical. For instance, when a manager makes a decision about health and safety in his/her organization, one must realize that an organization that does not place health and safety as the top priority of the business attitude is an unethical organization. In other words, if health and safety for the workers and the surrounding society is not the highest priority in manager decision making, it entails that in events of conflicting interests (e.g. profit), the company may be faced with unwanted losses. Ethical decisions in business involve judgment of right and wrong and respect to the rights of the society including stakeholders. Reviewing the historical decision cases in the literature shows that many decisions have been taken in companies failed due to overlooking of ethics. Therefore, ethics in our society is very necessary because it has a large influence on today, as well as our future life. We need to learn about and integrate good ethics in our life and business because they could effect on making right decisions. An example of the importance of ethical reasoning in decision-making can be illustrated by a company and their chemical plant in Stenungsund, Sweden. When the economic recession swept across the globe during the late 2000's there were calls for downsizing. However, when operating a large chemical plant, downsizing is not only a question of pure costs. If a large share of the company's workforce is relieved there may not be sufficient manpower at place when a situation that may lead to an accident arises. In addition, the managers must take into account that it takes approximately three years to fully train an operator, making frequent changes in the workforce a poor managerial alternative. Not having fully trained operators may be potentially harmful for third parties – in this case the 10'000 inhabitants in the adjacent town of Stenungsund. Clearly, it would not be morally acceptable to expose the employees as well as the other citizens to a risk in an attempt to minimize the economic losses for the company. This example highlights the importance of looking at the greater picture and considering the potential losses (both economical and publicity related) before making organizational changes that may jeopardize safety.

Unfortunately, today's business is associated with irresponsibility and dishonesty. Disregarding the ethics in business could effect on health and safety not only on the people who are working there but on the society as well. In addition, climate changes and environmental damages are another consequence of lack of ethics in business. Due to that ethics should be considered very seriously in any business. A strong ethical culture within any organization is important in safeguarding people, capital and the environment. Business ethics will increase productivity and teamwork among the employees. It helps in aligning the values of the business with those of the workers. Itis the basic beliefs and standards that make everything run smoothly. According to Robbins & Judge (2012), there might be three ways to reach to ethical decisions. These are described as follows:

The first criterion is ethical utilitarianism. Utilitarianism is the method which aims to do the best for the majority while decision making, considering the objectives such as efficiency, effectiveness and higher profits.

The second ethical criterion is to make decisions based on fundamental human rights and freedoms enumerated in the Universal Declaration of Human Rights.

The third criterion is implementation of justice fairly or at least a certain percentage or fair distribution of gain and costs. This opinion is often adopted by union members. This view confirms the equal wage distribution regardless of the performance and dismissal decision depending on seniority.

Each criterion has its own advantages and commitments. Focusing on utilitarianism brings efficiency and effectiveness; but it may cause violation of individual rights of some minor groups. Focusing on rights is consistent with freedom and privacy and protects people; however efficiency can create an environment of rule which cause a decrease in productivity.

Focusing on justice protect the rights of minorities and powerless ones; however this may create a negative effect on taking risk, innovation and productivity. Decision makers at profit making organizations generally enjoys using the utilitarianism opinion. 'the best' term for organization and shareholders may justify questionable acts such as big layoffs. But most of the critics believe that this point of view should be changed. The public view about human rights and social justice is that executives should develop ethical standards which do not include utilitarianism. This is a though process, because providing individual rights and social justice will cause more unanswerable situations than productivity and utilitarianism effects create. This situation may help to understand why the executives are being criticized about their acts. Increasing prices, selling harmful products for people, closing inefficient factories, dismissing lots of workers, moving the factories to overseas in order to decrease production costs and similar activities can be explained by utilitarian view. But this criteria is not the only whether it is a good decision or not.

6. CASE STUDY: SHELL BRENT SPAR

Every decision making situation in any organisation or company involves some degree of uncertainty which may result some kinds of risk in terms of either benefits or losses. On the other side, decision making could be influenced by interfaces between other factors such as business goal/company benefits, risk perception of manager as the decision maker including his/her culture and value, and the company ethics. In fact the role of managers when making a decision about risk on others is very critical. When making decisions about risk and safety one must realize that an organization that does not place health and safety as the top priority of the business attitude is an unethical organization. If health and safety for the workers and the surrounding society is not the highest priority in manager decision making, it entails that in events of conflicting interests (e.g. profit), the company may be faced with unwanted losses. Ethical decisions involve judgment of right and wrong and respect to the rights of the society including stakeholders. Reviewing the historical decision cases in the literature shows that many decisions have been taken in companies during the last two decades failed due to that decision makers do not pay enough attention to some important factors including ethics. It may happen that a decision which seems to be right might face considerable risk (Probability of Losses) due to its sensitivity to some other factors including *ETHICS*.

6.1. Aim of the Study

The aim of the study is to analyse the Brent Spar case and assess interactions of different actors which have been involved in by means of a *hazard identification tool* and, to identify the main influencing factors including *ETHICS* affecting the failure of the decision.

6.2. The Case History

The Brent Spar was a tanker loading station owned by Royal Dutch Shell and Esso. In 1995 it became obsolete and Shell sought for a way to dismantle it. After some research the company decided that it would be best to sink the structure into the deep sea. The other option, dismantling on land, was thought to be more dangerous, more expensive and more harmful for the environment. When Shell revealed its plans, it raised the fury of Greenpeace. Greenpeace claimed that sinking the structure would cause tremendous environmental problems as they were convinced that the platform still contained large amounts of heavy metals and crude oil. Greenpeace summoned Shell to dismantle the station on land but Shell refused initially. Greenpeace then used the public opinion to enforce Shell and eventually Shell admitted to the pressure and dismantled the Brent Spar on land in Norway. The decision procedure is shown in Figure 4.

Figure 4. Shows decision procedure concerning with Bren Spar Project

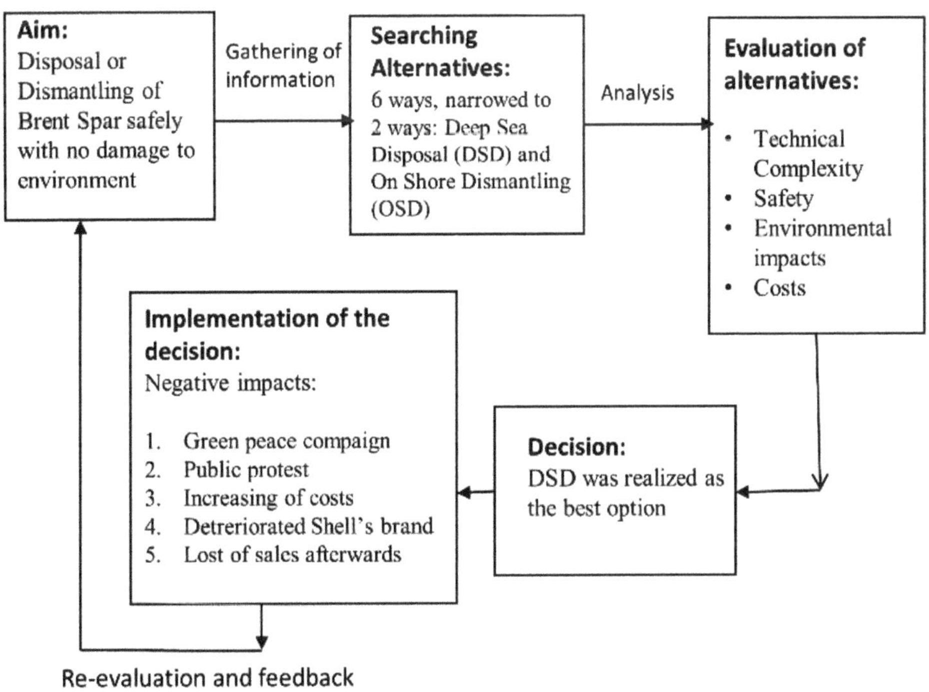

6.3. Methodology

The data needed for the analysis and evaluation were collected from available sources e.g., the literature and reviewing the Shell (2007a, 2007b, 2007c), Wikipedia (2007), and Greenpeace (2007) websites. Then the case was analyzed to see what went wrong causing the decision failure? In this study the scenarios leading to decision failure are identified using brain storming procedure. In addition the effects of the final decision conducted by using Fishbone Diagram. The paper is partly based on earlier studies carried out at Chalmers University of Technology (Koster et al., 2007) and (Shahriari et al., 2008).

6.4. Description of the Final Options

Out of different alternatives, and based on the unique characteristics of the Spar and its surrounding waters Shell proposed two first hand choices for further evaluation: Deep Sea Disposal (DSD) and On-Shore Dismantling (OSD). General description of this two options are given as:

- Deep Sea Disposal (DSD)
    - Tow the Brent Spar to the North Atlantic.
    - Use explosives to sink the platform.
    - Allow the structure to settle on the sea bed.

  This was assumed technically the easiest option and the cost estimated to £17-20 million.

- On-shore Dismantling (OSD)
    - Tow the Brent Spar into a deep harbour.
    - Decontaminate the structure and reuse the materials.
    - Dispose of the waste on land.

This was assumed technically more complex than DSD and with a greater hazard to the workforce. The cost was estimated to £41 million.

With the constraints described above in view detailed studies by several independent companies established that deep sea disposal of the Spar at a site in the deep Northern Atlantic was the Best Practicable Environmental Option (BPEO). The UK Government publicly approved this original plan in February 1995, and it became Shell's choice.

Analysis of the Decision Making Procedure

A brain storming study of all the operational steps concerning both options was conducted. Seven scenarios were recognized concerning the operation of the both options. Analysis of outcomes and impacts concerning with different scenarios on the basis of safety and ethical safety, in terms of providing a safe workplace by a deep sense of commitment to ethical principles such as for instance value for human life, justice, integrity, shows that Shell's initial proposal was in fact done with not enough consideration.

Shell's initial evaluation should have been more careful and their communication towards the society should have been way better. In fact:

- No environmental impacts have been properly assessed (Lack of Business Ethics- *Dishonesty*)
- There was not enough understanding of the deep sea environment and ecosystem *(Uncertainty in deep sea ecosystem –Lack of Engineering/Business Ethics)*
- The documents, which supported Shell's decision, contain numerous unconfirmed assumptions, minimal data and extrapolations from unnamed studies *(Uncertainties –Lack of Business Ethics - Irresponsibility)*
- Dumping the Brent Spar would create a pattern for dumping other contaminated structures in the sea and would undermine current international agreements (Irresponsibility – Lack of Business Ethics)

Detail causes of DSD decision failure are illustrated in Figure 5.

6.5. Discussion and the Results

Analysis carried out in this study showed that neither "deep sea disposal" nor "on shore dismantling" of the Brent Spar would have any big environmental impact. However, the environmental impact of the on

Figure 5. Causes of DSD decision failure

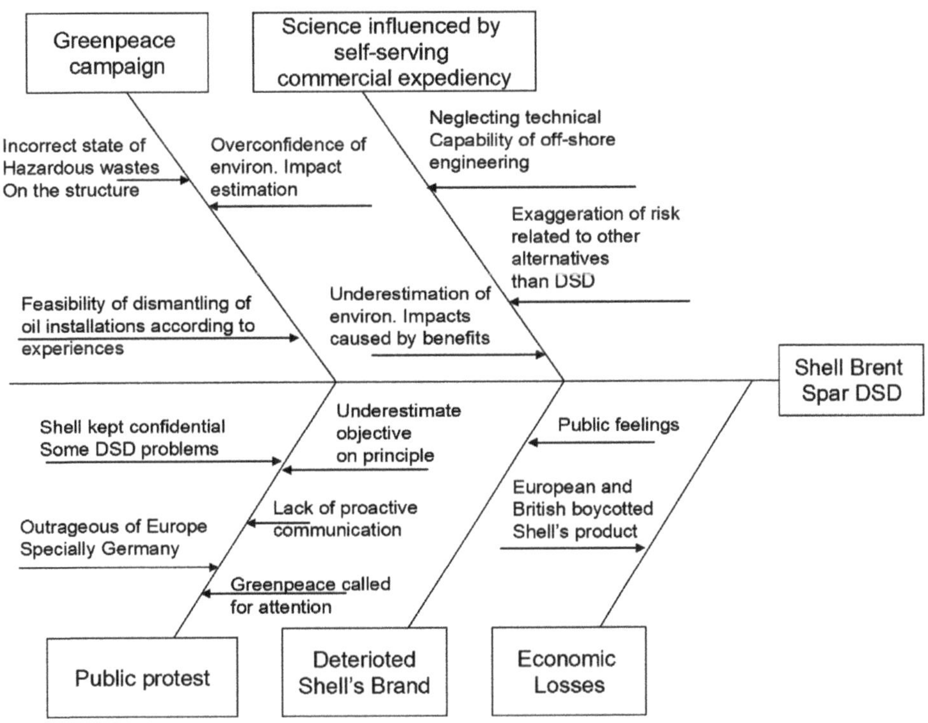

shore scrapping is less than the deep sea disposal. On the other hand the costs for on shore dismantling are much higher than for deep sea disposal, and more uncertainties play role in the case of deep sea disposal. It seems that neither Greenpeace nor Shell was completely right or wrong, they just had different views on ethical grounds and the economic and environmental consequences which they based their "best option" decision on. The most interesting point of discussion is the controversy between Greenpeace and Shell. The most important force in this controversy seems to be the public. Shell admitted that they had totally underestimated the public reaction that their plans might induce. Greenpeace actions mobilized the public and this tactic seemed to be very efficient. Greenpeace sparked an international moral outrage which caused some attacks on Shell stations in Germany.

Such an outrage is possible in a society with already existing beliefs about good and bad parties. Greenpeace is generally seen as the good guy (although the Brent Spar controversy was not good altogether for their image). Shell, on the other hand (and other oil companies as well) is generally seen to be the bad guy conducting questionable and environmentally harming business. It would be in the interest of oil companies to conduct their business in a transparent way. The public needs to be aware of the actual facts surrounding controversies like the Brent Spar disposal, and this might prevent them from willingly absorb an NGO's standpoint without further consideration. However, we know that the general public is normally not involved to actively shape their attitudes towards a company. Therefore it is necessary not only to inform people on the actual state of affairs but to always conduct business based on principles of ethics and in a transparent and way and actively enforce people to develop a rightful attitude.

In conclusion we think that Shell's initial evaluation should have been more careful and their communication towards the society should have been way better. There will always be controversies in society as people just have opposite opinions. We cannot expect parties like Greenpeace and Shell to always agree on each other's position. Great care should however be taken to find an efficient and relatively harmless solution (based on principles of business ethics), with a reasonable cost.

Although UK Government and regional authorities approved the selected option, the project never started because Greenpeace reacted fiercely, claiming that the project would have severe impact on the environment. This reaction was strongly supported by the public. Shell realized that the power of the angry society and its economic consequences had been underestimated when the choice was made and were likely to cause a crisis. Shell was forced to find a solution to get rid of the crises.

The final decision was to use the Spars' hull to build a quay extension at Mekjarvik near Stavanger in Norway. The project was approved by UK Government. The project was effectively completed in July 1999 when cut and cleaned ring sections of the buoy's hull were placed on the seabed to form the base of a new quay. The results of analysis show that poor business and engineering ethics consideration by Shell (being distracted by economic benefits), poor communication of Shell with the society as an important stakeholder, were the most important influencing factors affecting the decision.

The consequences of the decision failure were about four years delay, expenses of £60 millions instead of the original estimation of £21.5 million for the dismantling project, and losing millions of dollars due to the public reactions in UK and the other parts of the region.

7. CONCLUSION

Decision is the core transaction of an organization and has a profound influence on organizations achievement. Despite the importance it happens that decision makers do not pay enough attention to some important factors. A decision which seems to be right might face unwanted consequences due to its sensitivity to other factors such as ethics. In fact, The companies which act with profit maximization cause a bunch of problems on a global scale due to making decisions associated with violation of ethics principles.

A study was conducted on the basis of a literature survey to see how respecting business ethics is important in a workplace. The aim of the study was to discuss business ethics and cost relations. Furthermore, to analyze decision failures due to unethical behavior. This was done through analysis of a case; Shell Brent Spar. Four main errors were found in the alternative evaluation. These are: Uncertainty, lack of business ethics, dishonesty and irresponsibility. These errors all resulted in the failure to achieve the original objectives, either directly or indirectly. Ignorance might be also caused by overconfidence where the decision makers have had high feelings of trust about something that has been supported by their experiences or personal values. This could be an important parameter that makes the decision makers fail to see some hidden factors e.g., respecting stakeholders. Beside these errors, human thought about right or wrong also needs to be taken into account, because of the differences for every person thought about this. The judgment influenced by these factors makes it possible to begin some blunders which point decision makers towards a situation that bring about failure. Analysis showed that different views on ethical grounds and the economical and environmental consequences which Shell based their "best option" decision on. The chain of events that leads to failure begins with one or some of the blunders such as; overlooking peoples interest and feelings, ignoring ethical questions, and failing to see hide factors.

The project was effectively completed in July 1999 when cut and cleaned ring sections of the buoy's hull were placed on the seabed to form the base of a new quay. The consequences of the decision failure were about four years delay, expenses of £60 millions instead of the original estimation of £21.5 million for the dismantling project, and losing millions of dollars due to the public reactions in UK and the other parts of the region.

Analysis of the case shows that, a strong ethical culture within any organization is important in safeguarding people, capital and the environment. In fact, business ethics will increase productivity and helps in aligning the values of the business and neglecting of ethical principles will cause unwanted loses.

REFERENCES

Andersson, J., Appelberg, I., Johansson, E., Lindqvist, Y. & MohdNasir N. H. (2012). *Analysis of Bhopal Disaster applying Swiss Cheese Model and Fishbone Diagram*. Department of Production and Product Development, Chalmers University of Technology, Gothenburg, Sweden.

Aydin Pehlivan, I. (2002). *Yönetsel, Mesleki ve Örgütsel Etik. Pegema Yayıncılık, 3* (pp. 62–241). İstanbul: Baskı.

Boone Louis E. & Kurtz David L.(2013). *Contemporary Business* (2013 ed.). South Western: Cengage Learning.

Brenner, S. N. (1992). Ethics Programs and Their Dimensions. *Journal of Business Ethics, 11*(5-6), 391–399. doi:10.1007/BF00870551

Brent Spar. (n. d.). *Wikipedia*. Retrieved from http://en.wikipedia.org/wiki/Brent_spar

Bryant, J. (2013, July 17). *Living our values, Kellogg Company's global code of ethics*. Retrieved from http://www.kelloggcompany.com/content/dam/kelloggcompanyus/corporate_responsibility/pdf/2012CR_Reports/EN_COE_Final1.pdf

Providing consumers with ethically sourced garments. (2015, July, 17). *Primark case study.*

Ethics. (n. d.). *Wikipedia.* Retrieved from https://en.wikipedia.org/wiki/Ethics

Ghosh, D., Ghosh, D. K., & Abdel Zaher, A. (2011). Business, ethics, and profit: Are they compatible under corporate governance in our global economy? *Global Finance Journal*, *22*(1), 72–79. doi:10.1016/j.gfj.2011.05.006

Good Corporation. (2015, July, 17). Does run a business ethically add value or cost? Retrieved from http://goodcorporation.com/business-ethics-debates/does-running-a-business-ethically-add-value-or-cost/#sthash.qWZxjPl2.dpuf

Grammarist. (n. d.). Ethics vs Morals. Retrieved from http://grammarist.com/usage/ethics-morals/

Greenpeace (2007, July, 22). Greenpeace Tours North Sea Oil Rigs on Brent Spar Anniversary. [Web log comment]. Retrieve from http://archive.greenpeace.org/comms/toxics/dumping/jun20.html

Joseph, C., & Media, D. (2015, July 17). Examples of Unethical Behavior in an Organization. Retrieved from http://smallbusiness.chron.com/examples-unethical-behavior-organization-13629.html

Kiliç, R. (1996). Ahlakın Dini temeli, Ankara. *Türkiye diyanet vakfi yay*, 85.

Koster, F., Van Oort, S., & Snoep, L. (2007). *The Brent Spar controversy - An illustrating case of risk assessment and communication*. Göteborg, Sweden: Department of Product and Production Development, Chalmers University of Technology.

McNamara, C. (2015, July 17). Business ethics and social responsibility. Retrieved from http://managementhelp.org/businessethics/(2015, July 17)

Nuttal, J. (1993). *Moral questions: An introduction to ethics*. Cambridge, UK: Polity Press.

Social Responsibility and Ethics. (2015, July, 17). *Pachamama Alliance*. Retrieved from http://www.pachamama.org/social-justice/social-responsibility-and-ethics

Robbins, S. P., & Judge, T. A. (2012). Organizational Behavior (15th ed.). Pearson Education, Inc., USA. Retrieved from https://jahanzaibyousaf.files.wordpress.com/2014/02/organizational-behavior-15e-stephen-p-robbins-timothy-a-judge-pdf-qwerty.pdf

Shahriari, M. (Ed.), (2013). Loss Prevention & Safety - A Practical Risk Management Handbook (2nd ed.). Göteborg, Sweden: Chalmers University of Technology.

Shahriari, M., Örtengren, R., Aliandrina, D., & Feng, Y. (2008). Human Errors in Decision Making-Analysis of two historical cases. *Journal of Ergonomia*, *30*(1), 47–62.

Shell. (2007a). Brent Spar Dossier, Biological Effects. Retrieved from http://www.shell.com/home/Framework?siteId=uk-en&FC2=/uk-en/html/iwgen/about_shell/brentspardossier/impacthypothesis/zzz_lhn.html&FC3=/uk-en/html/iwgen/about_shell/brentspardossier/impacthypothesis/biologicaleffects_09121440.html

Shell. (2007b). Brent Spar Dossier, BPEO. Retrieved from http://www.shell.com/home/Framework?siteId=uk-en&FC2=/uken/html/iwgen/about_shell/brentspardossier/bpeoassessment/zzz_lhn.html&FC3=/uk-en/html/iwgen/about_shell/brentspardossier/bpeoassessment/synopsis_09121530.html

Shell. (2007c). Brent Spar Dossier, Brent Spar. Retrieved from http://www.shell.com/home/Framework?siteId=uk-en&FC2=/uk-en/html/iwgen/zzz_lhn.html&FC3=/uken/html/iwgen/about_shell/brentspardossier/dir_brent_spar.html

Tota, I., & Shehu, H. (2012). The Dilemma of Business Ethics. *Sciance and Direct Procedia Economics and Finance*, *3*, 556.

UNPAN. (2004). Administrative Ethics: Sociological Aspects. *UNPAN Documents.* Retrieved from http://unpan1.un.org/intradoc/groups/public/documents/NISPAcee/UNPAN004661.pdf

Valentine, S., Greller, M. M., & Richtermeyer, S. (2006). Employee job response as a function of ethical context and perceived organization support. *Journal of Business Research*, *59*(5), 582–588. doi:10.1016/j.jbusres.2005.06.004

Chapter 11
Impact of Islamic and Conventional Corporate Governance Mechanisms on Financial Performance of Islamic Banks:
Evidence from Malaysia

Jamel Eddine Mkadmi
University of Gafsa, Tunisia

Khamoussi Halioui
Imam Mohammad Ibn Saud Islamic University, Saudi Arabia

ABSTRACT

This study aims to analyze the effects of Islamic and conventional corporate governance mechanisms on financial performance. Six hypotheses have been developed and tested on 17 Malaysian Islamic banks observed over 7 years from 2005 to 2011. The measures used for financial performance were ROA; ROE and Operating Ratio (COSR). Using an econometric panel data, the results show that two among three conventional corporate governance mechanisms have significant effects on financial performance: the size of the board of director (SBD) and the degree of independence of the Board (INDEP); Whereas concerning the impact of the three other Islamic corporate governance mechanisms; our results show that only the visibility of supervisors is negatively as well as significantly related to financial performance. Regarding the relevance of control variables, two among three are relevant and positively related to financial performance (the age and the debt of the bank ratio.

1. INTRODUCTION

Most studies (Ahmed and Chapra, 2002; Claessens, 2006; Ghayad, 2008; Nathan and Ribiere, 2008) have neglected the governance problems in Islamic Banks mainly in emerging countries. Indeed, many

DOI: 10.4018/978-1-4666-9864-2.ch011

think that Islamic bank transactions are not different from conventional banks and that they have the same products that go through the same investment channels[1].

However, this topic is important for several reasons. Today, Islamic banks occupy an important role in the economies. They play a crucial role in any economy as they are in close contact with several partners. Then, the change in the international environment following the recent financial crisis affects deeply the functioning of banks.

The recent financial crisis and its dramatically consequences on the real economy raise the fundamental question of ethics. Newspapers, academic and professional press reported numerous scandals related to executive compensation and other misbehavior of managers, which arouse a feeling and a need for more regulation. Some went until blaming the capitalistic system because it is built on opportunism and selfish behavior.

Meanwhile, more and more people are interested in Islamic finance and started to focus on Islamic Banks, which are supposed to pursue the ethics of Islam in their transactions. Indeed, Islamic banks seem to resist better the financial crisis and reported better performance (Moody's, 2008; Karyotis et al., 2009)[2].

Malaysia is one of the countries where the Islamic banking sector is the core of the financial system. In 1979, the first Islamic bank was established in Malaysia. From this date, other Islamic banks and Islamic financial institutions settled down in the realm, making of this island the country for most large concentration of the Islamic banks operating side by side with the conventional banks. In recent years, Malaysia has quickly become a global leader in Islamic finance, playing host to the largest concentration of Islamic financial institutions in the south East Asia. In 2014, there are 25 Islamic banks operating in the country.

It is therefore important to scrutinize the governance of Malaysian Islamic banks, particularly their Board of Directors (BD) and the Supervisory Board of the Sharia (SBS) and their effects on performance. Many researchers declare that the Sharia Supervisory Board, as an intellectual capital, adds values to the Board of Director and influence and impacts the Islamic banks performance (Siagh et al., 2004; Nathan and Ribiere, 2008).

Our work is based on a research relating to corporate governance and proposing several control mechanisms to mitigate agency conflicts within financial institutions and improve their performance (Levine, 2004). More specifically, our goal is to determine the impact of internal governance mechanisms on the financial performance of Malaysian Islamic banks.

Since performance is a complex concept and embraces several dimensions, we have to make a choice to measure this variable. Shall we use the same measures as in conventional finance? Muslims scholars define an ethical performance as the one which permit the compliance with sharia. In fact, the evaluation of Islamic financial institutions performance and the conventional ones should not be measured in the same way because of the divergence of their objectives (Ghayad, 2008). Indeed, the roles and responsibilities of Islamic financial institutions are not only limited to the financial wishes of different stakeholders, but more important are how they conduct their business and what are the measures they use to ensure that all the activities of the Islamic bank are in accordance with Islamic law (Shahul et al., 2006). Hence, we can say that the performance of Islamic financial institution is a compound performance that admits two aspects: the financial aspect and the ethical aspect.

Although, the SBS is advanced as the corner stone of Islamic banking governance system and the driver of its performance, little research has focused on the effect of the corporate governance structure on Islamic banks performance.

This research aims to fill in this gap by analyzing a sample of Islamic and conventional banks from Malaysia. We focus on the case of Malaysia because, despite its small size it has rapidly became a global leader in Islamic Finance, playing host to the largest concentration of financial institution in the Asian countries.

This study is organized as follows. The first section presents the theoretical framework and research hypotheses. The second section discusses the methodological aspects. The analysis and discussion of our results are presented in the third section. The conclusion summarizes the main results, points out the contribution, the limits and the openings of this research.

2. THEORETICAL FRAMEWORK AND HYPOTHESES DEVELOPMENT

Talking about corporate governance of the bank requires firstly to take into consideration particular features of corporate governance of this financial sector (Adams and Mehran, 2003). The Islamic Banks are not similar to other firms and that's why they should be treated differently. The Islamic Bank is characterized by general banks' specificities (the liquidity production function; the deposit assurance fund; the assets structure and the greater opaqueness…) and other special corporate governance features. In fact, the risk of incompliance to sharia law can create financial problems. Moreover, Islamic banks operate in special environment characterized by less transparency, weaker market forces.

This study seeks to examine the impact of internal corporate governance mechanisms on financial performance in Islamic banks in Malaysia. In particular, this study provides a comprehensive investigation about the particularities of the corporate governance mechanisms of Islamic Banks and their impact on their performance with reference to agency theory.

The literature review gives supports to develop six hypotheses: three of them are related to the impact of the board of director characteristics and the three others are related to the impact of the Supervisory Board of the Sharia.

2.1 The Impact of the Characteristics of Board of Directors on the Performance of Islamic Banks

The effectiveness of the BD to perform its role largely depends on its characteristics. It is the size of the board, its composition, including the presence of outside directors, and finally combine the functions of Chairman of the Board and the chief executive officer (CEO).

In what follows, we cite the main studies dealing with the relationship between internal governance mechanisms and performance, explains their results and we deduce hypotheses to be tested empirically.

2.1.1 The Impact of the Size of the Board of Directors

The literature on the impact of the size of the board of directors on bank's performance is plentiful. The results of these studies are generally inconclusive and conflicting.

Some studies do not have any significant relationship: Simpson and Gleason (1999) found that the number of members of BD doesn't have any significant impact on the probability of bank failure. Adams and Mehran (2003, 2005) advocated that banks with larger BD are not less efficient than their peers in terms of performance measured by Tobin's Q. Zulkafli and Samad (2007) who have also studied a sample of 107 banks operating in nine countries in Asian emerging markets (Malaysia, Thailand, Philippines, Indonesia, Korea, Singapore, Hong Kong, Taiwan, India) in the year 2004. Their results indicate that there is no significant relationship between performance indicators such as ROA, Tobin's Q, and the size of the BD. This result was confirmed by Praptiningsih (2009) and Samad, A., Hassan, K, (2000).

Other studies have supported the negative relationship between the bank's performance and the size of the BD. Staikouras et al., (2007) have tested this relationship on a sample of 58 major European banks over the period 2002-2004. Their results show that banks' profitability, measured in terms of the ROA, the ROE and Tobin's Q is negatively and significantly linked to the size of the BD. In Malaysian context; Adnan et al., (2011) have examined the impact of governance variables on the efficiency of twelve listed banks during the period 1996 to 2005. Their results showed that the performance increases with a smaller board.

According to this reasoning, the size of the board should have negative impact on bank's performance. Thus, the first hypothesis could be formulated as follow:

H1: There is a negative relationship between the Islamic Bank's performance and the size of the board of directors.

2.1.2 The Impact of Independent Directors

Studies dealing with the impact of the degree of independence of the Board on bank's financial performance are not abundant and found conflicting results.

Some studies indicate that there is no statistically significant relationship between the proportion of inside and outside directors and bank's performance, measured in terms of Tobin's Q, the ROA and the ROE (Pi and Timme, 1993; Adams and Mehran, 2005 and 2008; Belkhir, 2006; Staikouras et al., 2007; Praptiningsih, 2009). In the same way, Spong et al., (2001) found that the number of outside directors, their average age and the CEO tenure do not affect the bank's performance.

Few researches tend to support a negative perspective (eg, Hermalin and Weisbach, 1991; Agrawal and Knoeber 1996; Yermack, 1996, Bhagat and Black, 1999; Kiel and Nicholson, 2003).They found a negative and statistically significant relationship between Tobin's Q and the number of outside directors

Others support a positive perspective. Skully (2002) found that the presence of independent outside directors increases the efficiency in monitoring and controlling the management, and therefore the performance of banking firms. Sierra et al., (2006) also found that the percentage of outside directors is positively associated with the bank performance measured in terms of ROA. Hence, we deduce the second hypothesis as follows:

H2: There is a positive relationship between board independence and Islamic Bank performance.

2.1.3 The Impact of CEO Duality

Banking literature shows that studies have addressed the effect of duality on performance which are not numerous and have separate opinions. Indeed, Stoeberl and Sherony (1985), Anderson and Anthony (1986) argue that the separation of CEO and chairman of the board, results in superior performance. Based on a sample of U.S. banks during the period 1987-1990, Pi and Timme (1993) found that the return on assets (ROA) is higher in firms that have separated the functions of the President of BD and CEO versus those that combine both functions. Other researchers (Fogelberg and Griffith; 2000) examined 100 bank holding companies in 1996, and did not notice any impact of the dual function of leader and Chairman of the Board on the performance of banks (as measured by Economic Value Added). Conversely, in an empirical validation on 10 Tunisian commercial banks observed from 1990 to 2004, Louizi (2007) showed that the dual leadership influences positively the accounting or market performance of these banks. Thus we formulate the following hypothesis:

H3: The CEO duality has no effect on the Islamic Bank performance.

2.2 The Impact of the Supervisory Board of the Sharia on the Performance of Islamic Banks

Similarly to the impact of the characteristics of the BD, the effectiveness of SBS depends on several characteristics such as the size of SBS, the competence of SBS, and the visibility of supervisors. The literature review gives some supports to formulate hypotheses related to them.

2.2.1 The Impact of the Size of SBS

Although the ability to control, the SBS increases with the number of advisor and a large council has the advantage of being more rich experience and expertise, these benefits can be wiped out by the difficulty of coordinating the individual contributions, conflicts during decision-making, the difficulty of maintaining good relations between members and the high cost of communication. This lack of harmony between the ideas of board members increases the scope and influence of the leader and bank performance (Quttainah et al., 2011). Hence the following hypothesis could be developed:

H4: There is a negative relationship between the size of SBS and Islamic Bank performance.

2.2.2 The Impact of the Competence of SBS

Some authors believe that the presence of members, with particular competence in finance and / or accounting within the SBS is so important, because they help to improve the performance of Islamic banks. These members can assist the Board to have a solid understanding of what is happening in the operations of the bank daily. In addition, the presence of qualified members can get the exact decision problem (Khan, 2004).

Such a dynamic interaction between the positive financial and Islamic scholars will undoubtedly benefit both the process of innovation and continuous improvement of products and services Islamic banking and performance (Ghayad, 2008). Hence the following hypothesis may be formulated:

H5: There is a positive relationship between the supervisor having financial and / or the accounting skill and the Islamic Bank performance.

2.2.3 The Impact of the Visibility of *SBS*

Some studies show that being a member of the SBS in other Islamic banks, provide access to several operations and transactions, and thus gain more knowledge in business. Moreover, when you are solicited by many banks, this is a sign of good competency and a sense of responsibility, and certainly can provide, indirectly, greater uniformity in the decisions of the various Islamic committees (Lezoul, 2009). In addition, the ban on members of SBS who examine several banks at the same time, could lead to other problems such as reducing the number of experts in Sharia (Grais and Pellegrini, 2006), which may decrease the economic attractiveness of the profession, and therefore the performance of the sector. The following hypothesis can be deduced:

H6: There is a positive relationship between the percentage of supervisors of the SBS who are member in other religious board of other Islamic Bank and Islamic Bank performance.

3 THE METHODOLOGY

3.1 Sample and Data Collection

Let's recall that the objective of this study is to determine the impact of governance mechanisms on the performance of Malaysian Islamic banks. We choose the case of Malaysia for two reasons: first because this country has become in few years a global leader in Islamic finance (Bank Negara, Malaysia); and second because to overcome the challenge with the established conventional banking sector, Islamic banks have to be competitive and innovative.

This study applies panel data study for seven continuous years from 2005 to 2011. A static panel is adopted over seven years for 17 Islamic banks in Malaysia (119 observations). This represents the total number of Islamic banks in Malaysia.

We collected information from their annuals reports. Our data base covers information about financial data collected from financial statements and governance data collected from annual reports available at (http://www.bnm.gov.my).

In what follows, we present the variables used to measure both the corporate governance mechanisms and financial performance of Islamic banks.

3.2 Definitions and Measurement of Variables

3.2.1 The Dependent Variable: The Financial Performance

Three types of performance measures were included in this study, namely: The Return on Assets (ROA), the Return on Equity (ROE) and the operating ratio (OR).

- The return on assets (ROA) represents the return on invested capital and expresses the ability of capital to create a certain level of operational profits. It shows the ability of management to acquire deposits at a reasonable cost and invest in profitable investments (Simpson and Kohers, 2002).

- The return on equity (ROE): This variable expresses the ability of capital invested by shareholders to reach a certain level of net profit. Hopkins et al., (1997: 642) argues that the ultimate measure of the strength of any financial institution is the ROE.
- The operating ratio or "cost to income ratio" (COSR): This variable is considered one of the best indicators to measure economic efficiency and bank performance. The higher the ratio is, the lower the performance of a bank increases. Ghosh et al., (2003), Francis and Hess (2004) and Mathuva (2009) observe that there is an inverse relationship between the ratio COSR and profitability of the bank.

3.2.2 The Independent Variables

The independent variables are the governance mechanisms which are divided into two groups. Those related to the Supervisory Board of the Sharia and those to Board of Directors of Islamic Banks.

Concerning the characteristics of the Supervisory Board of the Sharia, we will consider: the size of the Supervisory Board of the Sharia (SSBS), the competence in accounting and / or finance of the Supervisory Board of the Sharia (CSBS) and the visibility of the Supervisory Board of the Sharia (VSBS).

- The size of the Supervisory Board of the Sharia (SSBS) is measured by the number of members who serve.
- The competence in accounting and / or finance of the Supervisory Board of the Sharia (CSBS) is measured by the proportion of the number of members with expertise and / or financial accounting relative to the total number of members of the Supervisory Board the Sharia.
- The visibility of the Supervisory Board of the Sharia (VSBS): This variable is measured by the ratio between the number of members serving on the supervisory boards of other banks Sharia and the total number of members of the Supervisory Board Sharia.
- While, for the characteristics of the director's board, we will use: the size of the board (SBD), the independence of outside directors (INDEP) and the dual roles of CEO and Chairman (DUAL).
- The size of the board of directors (SBD) is measured by the number of directors that comprise the board of directors. This measure was also used by Simpson and Gleason (1999); Adams and Mehran (2005) and Belkhir (2006).
- The independence of outside directors (INDEP) is measured by the proportion of the number of independent outside directors and the total number of directors on the board. This measure was adopted by Griffith and Fogelberg, (2000); Bhagat and Black (2001) and Adam and Mehran (2003).
- The dual roles of the CEO and the Chairman of the Board (DUAL) is measured by a dummy variable that takes the value 1 when the two positions are occupied by the same person and 0 otherwise. This measure has been used by Pi and Timme (1993); Fogelberg and Griffith (2000); Belkhir (2005) and Mamoghli and Dhouibi, (2009).

3.2.3 The Control Variables

The control variables are the variables that have a significant effect on performance. We retain: the Size of the bank (SB), the Age of the bank (AB) and the Debt Ratio of the bank (END).

- The size of the bank (SB): The size of the bank is measured by the natural logarithm of the book value of total assets at the end of the accounting year. This measure is used in several studies such as Mak and Ong (1999); Godard (2001) and Fernandez and Arrondo (2005).
- The age of the bank (AB): Generally, the variable age of the firm is expressed by the logarithm of the number of years in practice (Brown and Caylor, 2006; Ben Cheikh and Zarai, 2008).
- The debt ratio of the bank (END) is measure by the ratio of the book value of debt and total assets. This measure has been used by most authors that integrate business debt as a variable in their models (Agrawal and Knoeber, 1996; Mak and Ong, 1999; Fernandez and Arrondo, 2002).

4. ANALYSIS AND DISCUSSION OF RESULTS

Before testing our basic model, further analysis should be conducted to ensure the adequacy of the variables used.

4.1 Descriptive Statistics

Table 1. presents the descriptive statistics of the variables used in our study. The average of Sharia Supervisory Board Size (SSBS) is 3.79381. Its minimum value is 3 and the maximum is seven. The proportion of the members with knowledge in accounting and finance (CSBS) is 0.00188, with the minimum of .001491 and maximum of .0034. Frequency of Sharia Supervisory Board visibility (VSBS) is about .54722. It has the minimum value of 0 and the maximum value of one. These results reveal the scarceness of qualified scholars to satisfy the demand of Islamic banks, which can be a bad sign of competence, but is also a good sign for fulfillment because they will have time to accomplish their responsibility. We can see also that the totality of scholars qualified in sharia don't background in accounting and finance. The percentage size of the board of directors (SBD) estimated is given as 7.29896. The minimum and maximum value of this size is estimated to be 4, 11 respectively. This size is less than the average size usually observed in corporations. Vafeas (1999) documents a bank board size of 12, Shivdasani and Yermack (1999) report a size of 11 and Adams and Mehran (2005) report a size of 18. This can be explained by the existence of another board (SSB). The presence of independence of outside directors in the Board of Directors (INDEP) varies from 25% to 80%, with a mean of 47,814%. This proportion is lower that what is reported by others studies (Vafeas (1999) which find that on average 55.6% of banks boards of directors is represented by outside directors; Shivdasani and Yermack (1999) found that 46% of banks board of directors is outsiders. This proportion was 69% in Adams and Mehran, 2005). Finally, the Malaysian Islamic banks seem separate between the roles of the CEO and the Chairman of the Board while the DUAL ratio, on average, is .15463. For the performance measures, the minimum and maximum values of ROA are respectively estimated to be -2.17450 and .1425 while its average value is -.0817. Another measure of performance, ROE has an average value of -.3528, with the minimum of -8.77993 and maximum of 1.0439. The mean value for the third measure of performance (COSR) is estimated at 105.803 while its minimum and maximum values are -1514.27 and 1232.1 respectively. The maximum AGE of the banks is 4 years while its minimum value is zero years. The mean of the age estimated is 2. The mean value for Debt Ratio of the bank (END) is .87503. It has the minimum of .000539 and the maximum of 1.0190. The average of bank size is 9.07511 with minimum of 4.879189 and maximum of 10.460.

Table 1. Descriptive Statistic

Variables	Mean *Statistic*	Maximum *Statistic*	Minimum *Statistic*	Median *Statistic*	Nbr of obs
SSBS	3.79381	7	3	3	80
CSBS	0.00188	0.0034	0.001491	0.001496	80
VSBS	0.54722	1	0	0.666666	80
SBD	7.29896	11	4	7	80
INDEP	0.47814	0.8	0.25	0.444444	80
DUAL	0.15463	1	0	0	80
SB	9.07511	10.460	4.879189	9.145224	80
AB	1.92368	3.5263	0	1.94591	80
END	0.87503	1.0190	0.000539	0.916778	80
ROA	-0.0817	0.1425	-2.17450	0.004932	80
ROE	-0.3528	1.0439	-8.77993	0.066888	80
COSR	105.803	1232.1	-1514.27	94.35957	80

Source: Author's estimates using STATA 9.0.

4.2 Examination of Multicollinearity

To verify the presence or absence of multicollinearity between the independent variables, we calculated the Pearson correlation coefficients. The test results confirm the absence of a collinearity problem. Indeed, from Table 2, all the coefficients of Pearson correlation between the independent variables are less than 0.6, limit from which the phenomenon of collinearity becomes more pronounced.

Table 2. Pearson correlation matrix

	SSBS	CSBS	VSBS	SBD	INDEP	DUAL	SB	AB	END	ROA	ROE	COSR
SSBS	1											
CSBS	0.0043	1										
VSBS	0.0550	0.0546	1									
SBD	0.2658	0.2657	0.0492	1								
INDEP	-0.021	-0.022	-0.054	-0.244	1							
DUAL	-0.091	-0.092	0.0852	-0.018	-0.03	1						
SB	0.1922	0.1916	0.1543	0.3907	0.040	0.1163	1					
AB	0.3477	0.3473	0.5293	-0.010	-0.08	0.0721	0.0263	1				
END	0.1570	0.1566	-0.224	0.2101	0.088	-0.055	0.5062	-0.171	1			
ROA	0.1403	0.1403	-0.264	-0.158	0.198	-0.158	-0.052	0.0256	0.3115	1		
ROE	0.0296	0.0294	-0.201	-0.198	0.227	-0.135	-0.110	-0.037	0.1201	0.8892	1	
COSR	-0.015	-0.015	-0.190	-0.167	0.000	0.0976	0.1055	-0.248	0.1084	0.1034	0.1157	1

Source: Author's estimates using STATA 9.0.

Specification Tests

The static estimate of the linear function that connects the financial performance for a sample of 17 Malaysian Islamic Banks during a study period from 2005 to 2011, annual data, requires as a first step to check the specification homogeneous or heterogeneous data generating process. The specification tests is back to determine if it is reasonable to assume that financial performance is exactly the same for the 17 Islamic banks, or on the contrary, there are specific to each bank.

Our theoretical model can be written as follows:

$$FP_{it} = \alpha_i + \beta_i SSBS_{it} + \chi_i CSBS_{it} + \delta_i VSBS_{it} + \varphi_i SBD_{it} + \eta_i INDEP_{it} + \theta_i DUAL_{it} + \gamma_i SB_{it} + \lambda_i AB_{it} + \phi_i END_{it} + \varepsilon_{it}$$

Where;

FP: The dependent variable measuring the financial performance of bank i at time t, measured by ROA_{it}, ROE_{it} and $COSR_{it}$; with i = 1...........N, t = 1.........T;

$SSBS_{it}$, $CSBS_{it}$, $VSBS_{it}$, SBD_{it}, $INDEP_{it}$, $DUAL_{it}$, SB_{it}, AB_{it}, END_{it}: are the explanatory variables;

$\beta_i, \chi_i, \delta_i, ..., \eta_i, \theta_i, \gamma_i, \lambda_i, \phi_i$: Are the constant coefficients;

α_i: The intercept of the regression;

ε_{it}: The error term.

This model has several possible configurations (Hurlin, 2006). To discriminate between these different configurations and to ensure the validity of the panel structure of the theoretical model, it is necessary to adopt a procedure for testing homogeneities. The general procedure of the test is presented in Hsiao (1986). Table 3 gives the results of the homogeneity tests of Malaysian Islamic banks during the period 2005 - 2011 annual data.

Table 3. shows that all the coefficients of the model describe the financial performance of Islamic banks from the three endogenous variables namely: the return on assets (ROA), the return on equity (ROE) and the coefficient operating (COSR) which are homogeneous. In contrast, the constants are heterogeneous in base model for the three dependent variables. To achieve this, we specify the theoreti-

Table 3. Homogeneity tests

	Homogeneity constants	Homogeneity of coefficients
ROA_{it}	0.26 (0.9825)	3.66 (0.0002)
ROE_{it}	0.61 (0.7839)	3.40 (0.0004)
$COSR_i$	0.32 (0.9635)	10.98 (0.0000)

Source: Author's estimates using STATA 9.0.

cal model by a panel with individual effects and we use the methods within and GLS to estimate the financial performance of the Malaysian Islamic banks.

4.4 Static Estimate of Financial Performance

The specification tests show that our theoretical model can be generated as a panel with individual effects. To estimate the financial performance for the seventeen Malaysian Islamic banks during the period 2005 to 2011 annual data, we use techniques within and GLS. Table 4 summarizes these two estimation procedures in compliance with the static relationship that describes the financial performance from three equations. The results show that the estimation of the three static relations, the techniques within and GLS give expected results and insignificant. Then, we need additional tests leading to the choice of appropriate estimator. We will choose between the two estimation techniques by arbitration Hausman test (1978).

Table 5. summarizes the Hausman test (1978) for the three endogenous variables that describe the financial performance of Islamic Banks. From the Hausman statistic we find that the individual effects are random for the three variables explained: The return on assets (ROA), the return on equity (ROE) and the operating ratio (COSR).

To correct the problems of heteroscedasticity and auto-correlation errors, we re-estimate the three models by reference to an econometric technique that eliminates appropriately both statistical problems. Table 6 shows the result of this technique to estimate the three measures of financial performance of the seventeen Malaysian Islamic banks.

Table 4. Estimate of financial performance

	ROA		ROE		COSR	
	Within	GLS	Within	GLS	Within	GLS
SSBS	-2.474 (0.88)	-2.30 (0.801)	27.7 (0.803)	38.545 (0.520)	9464.9(0.658)	1150.985 (0.902)
CSBS	4987.91 (0.8)	4665.1(0.800)	-55741.8 (0.8)	-77240.1 (0.52)	-1.9e+07(0.6)	-2237822 (0.905)
VSBS	0.1537(0.658)	-0.152(0.262)	2.112 (0.355)	-0.664(0.418)	-138.8(0.751)	-73.64358(0.454)
SBD	-0.020(0.604)	-0.025(0.278)	-0.002 (0.992)	-0.143 (0.331)	-3.604(0.942)	-48.49055(0.016)
INDEP	0.110 (0.718)	0.224 (0.383)	0.497 (0.805)	1.524(0.363)	-200.3(0.604)	-214.705 (0.393)
DUAL	-0.042(0.542)	-0.026(0.713)	-0.360 (0.432)	-0.211(0.664)	19.89 (0.821)	72.16859 (0.392)
SB	0.0355 (0.57)	-0.022(0.637)	0.391(0.349)	-0.1353354 (0.6)	63.0043 (0.4)	65.3949 (0.124)
AB	-0.062(0.513)	0.022 (0.634)	-0.739 (0.243)	-0.0026 (0.992)	-134.7(0.267)	-69.8092 (0.051)
END	-0.011(0.971)	0.349 (0.208)	-2.482 (0.234)	0.502(0.783)	-156.2(0.695)	-78.59894(0.778)

Source: Author's estimates using STATA 9.0.

Table 5. Hausman test (1978)

	ROA	ROE	COSR
Hausman statistic	0.00 (0.9909)	0.01 (0.9083)	0.19 (0.6608)
The individual effects are	Random	Random	Random

Source: Author's estimates using STATA 9.0.

Table 6. Estimate with correcting problems of heteroscedasticity and autocorrelation

	ROA		ROE		COSR	
	Coefficient	**Significance**	**Coefficient**	**Significance**	**Coefficient**	**Significance**
SSBS	-8.634886	0.330	3.47586	0.951	1150.985	0.896
CSBS	17427.1	0.327	-6568.441	0.954	-2237822	0.899
VSBS	-0.23350**	0.012	-1.0730***	0.073	-73.64358	0.424
SBD	-0.0229504	0.226	-0.1525095	0.211	-48.49055*	0.010
INDEP	0.43542***	0.067	2.65901***	0.082	-214.705	0.362
DUAL	0.004124	0.959	-0.0521637	0.919	72.16859	0.360
SB	-0.0563738	0.160	-0.3115155	0.228	65.3949	0.100
AB	0.05805***	0.086	0.169618	0.436	-69.8092**	0.037
END	0.7253012*	0.006	2.448866	0.148	-78.59894	0.763

*, ** And ***: Significance respectively at 1%, 5% and 10%. Source: Author's estimates using STATA 9.0.

The results indicate that two out of three conventional corporate governance mechanisms; only one out of three Islamic corporate governance mechanisms and two out of three control variables have significant effects on Malaysian Islamic Bank's financial performance.

The size of board of directors (SBD) affects negatively the financial performance measured by cost operation ratio (COSR) confirming the first hypothesis.

The second hypothesis is also confirmed when we found a significant positive effect of the board independence (INDEP) on ROA and ROE. However, the CEO duality is not statistically significant; hence the third hypothesis is rejected.

Concerning the impact of the three Islamic corporate governance mechanisms on financial performance; our results indicate that only the visibility of Supervisory Board of the Sharia (VSBS) has a negative and significant impact on financial performance measured by the ROA and ROE, confirming our hypothesis 6. The competence (CSBS) and the size of SBS or of the BD do not have significant effect on any financial performance measurement, rejecting the fourth and the fifth hypothesis. These results might be explained by the fact that the accumulation of other mandates of supervisors affects negatively the effectiveness of supervisors in carrying out their tasks and hence, might adversely affect the performance of Islamic banks.

Regarding the impact of control variables, the Age (AB) and the Debt ratio of banks (END) affect positively the ROA but negatively the Operating Ratio (COSR), while the size of the bank has no impact on any measurement of financial performance.

CONCLUSION

The objective of this study is to investigate the impact of internal conventional and Islamic corporate governance mechanisms and control variables on Malaysian Islamic Bank's financial performance.

Six hypotheses have been developed and tested applying an econometric modeling panel data for 17 Malaysian Islamic Banks over the period 2005 to 2011.

The results suggest that the effect of conventional corporate governance mechanisms on financial performance of Malysian Islamic banks is more important than the Islamic ones. The controversy effect of Visibility of Supervisory Board of the Sharia is surprising. In fact; hypothesis 6 expects a positive effect while the result indicates a negative effect on financial performance. To support this result; we join the argument of Ghayad (2008, 207) when she claims that "the members of Sharia board were a serious obstacle for the directors of the Islamic banks. Directors and members of Sharia board did not use the same language. The members of the Sharia board were not specialized in the fields other than Sharia". The scarcity of scholars and their lack of knowledge in accounting and finance is a real problem. Instead of putting an SBS for each bank, it would be better to harmonize the Sharia compliance rules by creating an internal Sharia Board that gives guidelines or "standards". The bank has to find a way to cope with guidelines without an SBS, who constrains the management action. The International SBS could give notation for good compliance and sanctions for bad compliance with sharia principles.

This study highlights the impact of conventional and Islamic corporate governance mechanisms on financial performance of Islamic banks in a specific context (Malysia). It shows that these two types of mechanisms play a significant role in explaining financial performance. Hence, the conventional corporate governance mechanisms has with the Islamic ones a substitution and / or complementarily relationship in the framework of their respective influences on financial performance. Thus, Islamic banks are forced to choose the most efficient combination of both mechanisms to align the interests of directors with those of shareholders. Moreover, the divergence of the results between Islamic banks reveals that the better performance of Islamic banks is associated with better compliance with Sharia principles, enabling the standardization and the uniformity of the operating rules, and facilitating any kind of comparison between Islamic banks around the world.

However, the limits of this research might be the inadequacy of traditional financial indicators to express the Islamic Bank's performance (Ghayad, 2008; Badreldin, 2010). In fact there are other indicators more suitable to Islamic Finance, taking into accounts the principles of Sharia; called Islamic or ethical indicators provided by Shahul et al., (2006), such as: the profit sharing ratio (the rapport Mudaraba and Musharaka on total financing); the Zakat performance ratio (the total Zakat over net assets) and the Islamic income versus non-Islamic income ratio (the ratio of Islamic income over total income).

Future extension of this study may examine mainly the relationship between these internal mechanisms of governance and the ethical performance of Malaysian Islamic Banks.

REFERENCES

Adams, R., & Mehran, H. (2003). Is corporate governance different for bank holding companies? *Economic Policy Review*, *4*, 123–142.

Adams, R., & Mehran, H. (2008). *Corporate performance, board structure and their determinants in the banking Industry.* Federal Reserve Bank of New York Staff Report N° 330.

Adnan, M. A., Ab Rashid, H. M., Meera, A. K. M., & Htay, S. N. N. (2011, February 21-22). A Panel Data Analysis on the Relationship between Corporate Governance and Bank Efficiency. *Proceedings of the Asia-Pacific Business Research Conference*, Hotel Istana-Jalan Raja Chulan, Kuala Lumpur. Retrieved from http://ebookbrowse.com/606-adnan-pdf-d71737492

Agoraki, M.-E. K., & Delis, M. D. Staikouras, P. (2008, December 26).The Effect of Board Size and Composition on Bank Efficiency. Retrieved from http://ssrn.com/abstract=1320671

Agrawal, A., & Knoeber, C. (1996). Firm performance and mechanisms to control agency problems between managers and shareholders. *Journal of Financial and Quantitative Analysis*, *31*(3), 377–397. doi:10.2307/2331397

Ahmed, H., & Chapra, U. (2002). *Corporate governance in Islamic financial institution, periodical document N°6, Islamic research and training institute Sector Network*. The Islamic Financial Services Board.

Claessens, S. (2006). *Corporate Governance of Islamic Banks: Why is Important, How is it Special and What does this Imply? The World Bank Financial Sector Network*. The Islamic Financial Services Board.

Fama, E., & Jensen, M. (1983). Separation of ownership and control. *The Journal of Law & Economics*, *26*(2), 301–325. doi:10.1086/467037

Fernandez C, Arrondo R(2005).Alternative internal controls as substitute of the board of directors. *Corporate governance: an international review*, 13(6), 856-866.

Finance Committee on Corporate Governance. (2001). *Malaysian Code on Corporate Governance*. Securities Commission.

Ghayad, R. (2008). Corporate governance and the global performance of Islamic banks. *Humanomics*, *24*(3), 207–216. doi:10.1108/08288660810899368

Ghosh, S., Nachane, D. M., Narain, A., & Sahoo, S. (2003). Capital requirements and bank behaviour: An empirical analysis of Indian public sector banks. *Journal of International Development*, *15*(2), 145–156. doi:10.1002/jid.947

Godard L (2001). *La taille du conseil d'administration: déterminants et impact sur la performance*. Cahier du FARGO n° 1010702.

Godard, L., & Schatt, A. (2000). *Faut-il séparer les fonctions de décision et de contrôle? Papier de recherche présenté aux journaux internationaux de l'AFFI*. ESC Paris. Juin.

Graham, J. R., & Harvey, C. R. (2001). The theory and practices of corporate finance: Evidence from the field. *Journal of Financial Economics*, *60*(2-3), 187–243. doi:10.1016/S0304-405X(01)00044-7

Griffith, J. M., & Fogelberg, L. (2000). Control and bank performance. *Journal of Financial and Strategic Decisions*, *13*(3), 63–69.

Guru, B.K., Staunton, J., Shanmugam, B. (2002). *Determinants of commercial banks profitability in Malaysia*. University Multimedia working papers.

Hausman, J. A. (1978). Specification Tests in Econometrics. *Econometrica*, *46*(6), 1251–1271. doi:10.2307/1913827

Hermalin, B. E., & Weisbach, M. S. (1991). The effects of board composition and direct incentives on firm Performance. *Financial Management*, *20*(4), 101–112. doi:10.2307/3665716

Hess, K., & Francis, G. (2004). Cost income ratio benchmarking in banking. *International Journal (Toronto, Ont.)*, *3*, 303–319.

Hsiao C (1986). *Analysis of Panel data. Econometric Society Monographs* (2nd ed.).

Hurlin, C. (2006). *L'Econométrie des Données de Panel: Modèles Linéaires Simples*. Séminaire Méthodologique, Ecole Doctorale Edocif.

Karyotis, C., Bouslama, G., Bouteiller, C., Le Guirriec-Milner, G., & Vernier, E. (2009). *La crise financière en 40 concepts clés*. Revue Banque Edition.

Kaymak, T., & Bektas, E. (2008). East meets west? Board characteristics in an emerging market: Evidence from Turkish Banks. *Corporate Governance*, *16*(6), 550–561. doi:10.1111/j.1467-8683.2008.00713.x

Kiel, G. C., & Nicholson, G. J. (2003). Board composition and corporate performance: How the Australian experience informs contrasting theories of corporate governance. *Corporate Governance: An International Review*, *11*(3), 189–205. doi:10.1111/1467-8683.00318

Kwan, S. (2003). Risk and Return of Publicly Held versus Privately Owned Banks. Federal Reserve Bank of New York. *Economic Policy Review*.

Lipton, M., & Lorsch, J. (1992). A modest proposal for improved corporate governance. *Business Lawyer*, *48*, 59–77.

Louizi G (2007). Role of the board in banks' governance and impact on performance; Case of Tunisian banks. *Euro-Mediterranean Economics and Finance Review*, 1(6).

Mathuva DM (2009).Capital adequacy, cost income ratio and the performance of commercial banks: The Kenyan scenario. *The international journal of applied economics and finance*, 3(2), 35-47.

Montandrau, S. (2006). *Activisme des investisseurs institutionnels et performance boursière: les caractéristiques du conseil d'administration qui permettent la confiance*. CEROG –IAE d'Aix en Provence Université d'Aix- Marseille III.

Moody's Investors Services. (2008). Gulf Islamic Banks Resilient Amid Global Credit Woes, Special Comment.

Nathan S, Ribiere V (2008). From knowledge to the wisdom: the case of corporate governance in Islamic bank. *The journal of information and knowledge management systems*, 4(37), 471-483.

Pathan, S., Skully, M., & Wickramanayake, J. (2007). Board size, independence and performance: An analysis of Thai banks. *Asia-Pacific Financial Markets*, *14*(3), 211–227. doi:10.1007/s10690-007-9060-y

Pi, L., & Timme, S. G. (1993). Corporate control and bank efficiency. *Journal of Banking & Finance*, *17*(2-3), 515–530. doi:10.1016/0378-4266(93)90050-N

Rammal, H. (2006). The importance of Shariah supervision in Islamic financial institutions. *Corporate Ownership and Control*, *3*(3), 204–208.

Samad, A. (2005). Performance of Interest-free Islamic banks vis-à-vis Interest-based Conventional Banks of Bahrain. *IIUM Journal of Economics and Management*, *12*(2), 1–15.

Samad, A., & Hassan, K. (2000). The Performance of Malaysian Islamic Bank during 1984-1997: An Exploratory Study. *Thoughts on Economics*, *10*(1 & 2), 7–26.

Shahul, H., Ade, W., Bakhtiar, A., Mohd, N., & Sigit, P. (2006, April 19-21). Alternative disclosure and performance measures for Islamic banks. *Proceedings of the Conference on Administrative Sciences*. King Fahd University of Petroleum & Minerals, Saudi Arabia.

Shivdasani, A., & Yermack, D. (1999). CEO involvement in the selection of new board members: An empirical analysis. *The Journal of Finance*, *54*(5), 1829–1853. doi:10.1111/0022-1082.00168

Siagh, L. (2001). Le fonctionnement des organisations dans les milieux de culture intense, le cas des Banques Islamiques [Thèse du Doctorat]. Ecole des Hautes Etudes Commerciales, Montréal.

Siagh, L., Diallo, O. A., & Hafsi, T. (2004).Environnement intense et choix stratégique: le cas des banques islamiques. Cahier de recherche N°20-46, ISSN 1711-6309 HEC Montréal.

Sierra, G., Talmor, E., & Wallace, J. (2006). An examination of multiple governance forces within banking holding companies. *Journal of Financial Services Research*, *29*(2), 105–123. doi:10.1007/s10693-006-5921-1

Simpson, W., G., , & Gleason, A.E. (1999). Board structure, ownership and financial distress in banking firms. *International Review of Economics & Finance*, *8*(3), 281–292. doi:10.1016/S1059-0560(99)00026-X

Simpson, W. G., & Gleason, A. E. (1999). Board structure, ownership and financial distress in banking firms. *International Review of Economics & Finance*, *8*(3), 281–292. doi:10.1016/S1059-0560(99)00026-X

Simpson, W. G., & Kohers, T. (2002). The Link between Corporate Social and Financial Performance: Evidence from the Banking Industry. *Journal of Business Ethics*, *35*(2), 97–109. doi:10.1023/A:1013082525900

Skully, M. T. (2002, August 9–11). Banking and corporate governance: some prudential issues. *Presented in Second International Conference on Banking and Finance*, Greece.

Spong, K., DeYoung, R., & Sullivan, R. J. (2001). Who's minding the store? Motivating and monitoring hired managers at small, closely held commercial banks. *Journal of Banking & Finance*, *25*(7), 1209–1243. doi:10.1016/S0378-4266(00)00127-8

Sridharan, U., & Marsinko, A. (1997). CEO duality in the paper and forest products industry. *Journal of Financial and Strategic Decisions*, *10*(1).

St-Onge S, Magnan, M, Calloc H Y (2001).Conseil d'administration et rémunération des dirigeants d'entreprise au Canada: une perspective politique. *Revue canadienne des sciences de l'administration*, 18(2), 57-76.

Staikouras, P. K., Staikouras, C. K., & Agoraki, M. E. K. (2007). The effect of board size and composition on European bank performance. *European Journal of Law and Economics*, *23*(1), 1–27. doi:10.1007/s10657-007-9001-2

Vafeas, N. (1999). Board meeting frequency and firm performance. *Journal of Financial Economics*, *53*(1), 113–142. doi:10.1016/S0304-405X(99)00018-5

Worrel, D. L., Nemec, C., & Davidson, W. N., III (1997). One hat too many: Key executive plurality and shareholder wealth. *Strategic Management Journal*, *18*(6), 499–507. doi:10.1002/(SICI)1097-0266(199706)18:6<499::AID-SMJ898>3.0.CO;2-F

Yan, Y. (1998).The FDICIA and bank CEO's pay-performance relationship: An empirical investigation (Working Papers N° 9805). Federal Reserve Bank of Cleveland.

Yermack, D. (1996). Higher market valuation of companies with a small board of directors. *Journal of Financial Economics*, *40*(2), 185–211. doi:10.1016/0304-405X(95)00844-5

Zulkafli, A. H., & Samad, F. A. (2007). Corporate governance and performance of banking firms: Evidence from Asian emerging markets. *Advances in Financial Economics*, *12*, 49–74. doi:10.1016/S1569-3732(07)12003-X

ENDNOTES

[1] Mahmoud El Gamal, Chair of Islamic Economics, Finance and Management at Rice University in Houston affirmed: "Islamic banks did not provide true Islamic banking products. Instead, they gave an Islamic name to products of the commercial banks to attract clients who did not want to deal in interest" (Khaleej Times, 06 March 2009).

[2] According to Anouar Hassoune, a Moody's Vice-President/Senior Credit Officer, Islamic bank displayed strong resilience amid the global financial crisis not only thanks to their typically conservative approach, but also because the core principles of Islamic banking have protected them from elements of the crisis (Al Bawaba, November 27, 2008).

APPENDIX

Table 7. Nomenclature

Variable definition	Variable code	Variable measurement
Size of the Board of Directors.	**SBD**	Number dialing the Board of Directors.
Independence of Directors External.	**INDEP**	Percentage of independent outside directors on the board of directors.
Dual roles of director General and Chairman.	**DUAL**	Dichotomous variable equal to 1 if aggregate functions, 0 otherwise.
Size of the supervisory board of supervisors Sharia.	**SSBS**	Number of members in the SBS of the bank.
Competence of the supervisory board of Sharia.	**CSBS**	Number of members having accounting and financial skills / Total number of the SBS.
Visibility of the supervisory board of Sharia.	**VSBS**	Number of SBS members sitting in SBS of other banks / Total number of SSB members.
The size of the bank.	**SB**	Log (total assets)
The age of the bank.	**AB**	Log (age of the bank).
The debt ratio of the bank.	**END**	Total debt / total assets.

Chapter 12
Toward Responsive Corporate Governance:
Engaging Stakeholders from Beyond

Paul van Seters
Tilburg University, The Netherlands

Rob Maessen
Province of Noord-Brabant, The Netherlands

ABSTRACT

Since the early 1980s, globalisation has deeply affected the way in which corporations typically conduct their affairs. This is true not only for business organisations that are active in the OECD countries but also for those operating in the emerging markets of the less affluent parts of the world. New social and ethical perspectives have become relevant for management strategy and have highlighted the need to acknowledge the existence of stakeholders—old and new—in a way that may benefit the interests of firms as well as those of local communities and society at large. In this chapter we argue that of all possible stakeholders the ones beyond the present periphery of the firm have the most potential for its long-term survival. Responsive corporate governance, therefore, will seek to engage with stakeholders from beyond.

PARADIGM SHIFT IN MANAGEMENT STRATEGY

Economic globalisation seriously took off after the fall of the Berlin Wall in November 1989, when the number of participants in the global market grew almost overnight from one billion and a half to six billion people—thus tremendously expanding the possibilities for trade and consumption. The globalising economy has come with the discovery of new management territories to be explored for companies operating from multiple nations, including the so-called emerging economies of the BRICS countries: Brazil, Russia, India, China, and South Africa (Guest, 2011). New social and ethical perspectives, sometimes embodied in new codes of conduct, have become relevant and have prioritized the need to deal with stakeholders in a way that may benefit the interests of firms in the long run as well as those of local communities and society at large (Van Tulder & Van der Zwart, 2006; Crane & Matten, 2010; Griseri & Seppala, 2010; Chandler & Werther, 2013). This shift in perspective is a trend in management strategy that we refer to as a move toward responsive corporate governance.

DOI: 10.4018/978-1-4666-9864-2.ch012

The story of the role of stakeholders in management strategy starts, of course, with the work of Edward Freeman and with the huge impact of this prominent American business school professor. In 1984 Freeman published his seminal book, *Strategic management: A stakeholder approach.* Freeman explicitly addressed a corporate audience, for which he defined the concept of "stakeholder" as "any group or individual who can affect or is affected by the achievement of the organization's objectives" (Freeman, 1984, p. 46). Freeman's own objective was pragmatic: to provide corporate managers with an instrument for dealing with the important, unexpected changes that were taking place in society at the time. From the 1960s onwards, corporations had been confronted with new groups, events, and issues that until then were not part of standard corporate affairs and which the traditional managerial view of the firm was not able to address. For Freeman, the stakeholder approach was a way to make managers more responsive to these changes in the world outside. This new approach intended to make not only traditional interest groups (owners, customers, employees, and suppliers) but also these newly emerging groups (governments, competitors, consumer advocates, environmentalists, special interest groups, and the media) relevant for management strategy development. Freeman's main message was that every single one of these groups of stakeholders could play an equally vital role in the success of the business enterprise (Freeman, 1984, p. 25).

A few years later, Freeman's stakeholder approach took off in a slightly new direction to become the hallmark of corporate social responsibility or CSR. It was increasingly used to describe and clarify the responsibilities of corporations towards society with a growing concern for social, ethical, and environmental issues. Subsequently the concepts of "stakeholder management" and "multi-stakeholder dialogue" have come to play a central role in discussions concerning CSR (Clarkson, 1995; Jones & Wicks, 1999; Kakabadse, Rozuel, & Lee-Davies, 2005; Waddell, 2005, 2011; Kakabadse & Morsing, 2006; Visser, 2011; Blowfield & Murray, 2011; Crane, Matten, & Spence, 2013; Beal, 2014).

A CHANGING GLOBAL ENVIRONMENT TO DEAL WITH

Since the publication of Freeman's book, the environment for doing business has again changed dramatically. We now live in the era of globalisation (Barber, 1995; Friedman, 1999, 2005; Van Seters, De Gaay Fortman, & De Ruijter, 2003), in which the combined effect of a demographic explosion and a fundamental makeover of the world economy is becoming more and more visible (Rischard, 2002). Following World War II, the reconstruction of infrastructure and industrial production in Europe and Japan paved the way for the reestablishment of an integrated global trade system. Initially, during the Cold War period, there were three different worlds. They were divided in political terms and mirrored the struggle between two economic systems—capitalism and communism. The first world of capitalist countries was based on private enterprise and a free market; the second world of communist countries was based on state ownership and central planning of production; while the third world referred to the rapidly rising number of postcolonial countries that economically belonged to neither capitalism nor communism, but were wooed by either side. Both the second and the third world had its own reason, seemingly valid at the time, for not joining the economic system of the first world (Sachs, 2005, 2009). However, after the end of the Cold War, the global economy experienced a sharp upturn. Because now only one economic system, i.e., capitalism, was left, it became possible to think of the world as a whole. Hundreds of millions of people in Eastern Europe, but also in Africa, Asia, and South America, had to orient themselves to this one remaining economic system.

In general, globalisation refers simultaneously to the "distanciation" of time and space as well as to the growth of interconnectedness and interdependency (Giddens, 1990, 2003; Castells, 1996; Beck, 2000). Globalisation was enabled by the revolutionary changes in transport and telecommunications and took off with the expansion of businesses and the growth of multinational enterprises. In fact, the creation of the global fibre-optic network during the craze of the dot-com bubble and the exponential growth of digitized information and application software to handle it set the stage for what Thomas Friedman (2005) identified as "the next phase" of globalisation. Its unique character is the newly found power for individuals—rather than for nation-states or multinational corporations, which were so characteristic for earlier phases of globalisation—to collaborate and compete globally. By the start of the 21st century, the world for doing business had become flat, a level playing field for corporations and individuals alike, connecting knowledge-pools and resources. Moreover, this flattening and shrinking of the world was not restricted to or even primarily taking place in the countries belonging to the OECD. "Clearly, it is now possible for more people than ever to collaborate and compete in real time with more other people on different kinds of work from more different corners of the planet and on more equal footing than at any previous time in the history of the world—using computers, e-mail, networks, teleconferencing and dynamic new software" (Friedman, 2005, p. 8).

More and more non-Western individuals and groups of individuals are driving this development as it moves forward. A good example of this comes from Bangalore, India's Silicon Valley, where an IT revolution has taken place that was able to provide a growing number of valuable goods and services to all countries around the world where business is conducted in English. The growth of the Internet, a young, English-speaking work force with high-tech skills, and a new openness to foreign investment all make India a top choice for foreign companies looking to outsource work that used to be done at their home territory. Business is thriving and moving from data transcription and financial-record keeping, to consulting and advising, to full-fledged back-office processing and call-centre operations. Distance is of no importance and can even become an advantage. For instance, radiologists of many small and some medium-size hospitals in the US are now outsourcing the analysis and interpretation of CAT and MRI scans overnight to doctors in India and Australia. Diagnosis of medical data can now be provided around the clock, often at lower salary costs. Shipping these images, which are already available in digital format on a network with a standardized protocol across the globe, and viewing them is no problem whatsoever (Friedman, 2005, pp. 11-16; Sachs, 2005, pp. 15-16).

It may be useful to think of globalisation in terms of three levels: firstly the primary process of economic expansion and the dominance of free-market neoliberalism; secondly the political, societal, and ecological deficits that become apparent as the consequences of the process of primary globalisation; and thirdly the human response that is evoked by those secondary consequences and is aimed at achieving a more sustainable global development (Van Seters, 2012). Not surprisingly, globalisation on all three levels is creating new and significantly more complex challenges for businesses and their interactions with society.

Corporations are now increasingly conducting their operations at locations around the world. As a consequence, their interdependence has grown enormously and a complex web of production chains and relationships is more and more connecting them. At the same time they have lost their original social embeddedness and are thus also contributing to the distanciating effect of globalisation (Granovetter, 1985). Furthermore, when global entities operate in local communities, corporate management is typically confronted with unfamiliar issues. Decision-makers live far away from the societies on which they have an impact (Googins & Rochlin, 2000). As the social context of their operations changes, so do the expectations of society toward corporations; this profoundly affects the social responsibilities of doing business. Smoking chimneys and employment opportunities were once welcomed as part of modern life as the industrial revolution swept over Europe and North America in the 19th and early 20th century. When some of the true costs became apparent, the expectations of society changed, first on social issues and later on, in the 1970s and 1980s, also with regard to the environment. The subsequent national legislation that was drawn up in the Western world to deal with these externalities has left the door wide open for over-exploitation of social and ecological resources in other parts of the world. Meanwhile nation-states went on trying to attract the establishment of international corporate headquarters by offering highly competitive tax rebate schemes, a race to the bottom where taxes no longer need to be paid. Multinationals clearly learned to benefit from operating on different continents. Since they often failed to address the over-exploitation of resources, they also met with a new kind of opposition. Corporations discovered that their nationally and internationally known brands were not just marketing investments. Their reputation is also a liability that makes them vulnerable to the critical eye of outsiders. A growing number of social groups and individuals, campaigning on specific issues and social concerns, are challenging corporations and dispute their license to operate. These critics are often well-organised, innovative, and powerful (Doh & Teegen, 2003) and their influence is needed and noticeable, even today (SOMO, 2014).

The intended disposal of the Brent Spar by Shell in 1995 is still considered a milestone in the development of antagonistic relationships between business and NGOs. "Industry was considered the 'bad guy' by the environmental movement, while business had regularly condemned the utopianism, radicalism and amateurism of environmental organisations" (Arts, 2002, p. 26). Even though Shell UK had done its homework with the government's tacit approval and the technical reports to back up their proposed solution of dumping the platform in the deep-water of the Atlantic Ocean, they underestimated the political implications and were caught off-guard by a consumer boycott, organised by Greenpeace, in Germany and elsewhere in continental Europe (Winsemius & Guntram, 2002, p. 108).

In the eyes of many critics it would be better, of course, to keep a long distance away from the green wash of the modern corporate world at all times. Firms simply cannot be trusted because, by definition, they only have the short-term interests of shareholders in mind (Vogel, 2005; Reich, 2007). And even if their moral intentions are sincere, they still cannot be trusted. The concept of "moral licensing" explains that CEOs are inclined to corporate social irresponsibility (CSiR)—consciously or not—as soon as they feel pleased about the moral credits they have achieved through CSR (Ormiston & Wong, 2013). This is illustrated by BP's CEO, Tony Hayward. Prior to the Deepwater Horizon disaster, BP's safety record was promoted as one of the best in the industry. "However, in 2010, the Deepwater Horizon explosion shattered BP's positive safety record when managers missed key safety warning signs (…) Moreover, Hayward's reaction to the spill was seen as cold and perceived as minimizing BP's responsibility for the spill as well as the environmental damage to the Gulf of Mexico" (Ormiston & Wong, 2013, pp. 861-862). The more outspoken a CEO is about his or her social reputation, the more likely subsequent less ethical stakeholder treatment is to occur. They are only human.

THE CHANGING RELATIONSHIP BETWEEN BUSINESS AND SOCIETY

The struggle of how to deal with these ever-changing corporate social responsibilities is taking place not only in practice at the level of individual firms, but also in the academic literature. The relationship between business and society has been studied for decades. The idea that business has duties toward society is widely acknowledged, but what these duties entail has changed radically over time. This is reflected, for instance, in the multitude of definitions of CSR academic writers have proposed over the years. The subject has been addressed in different ways and covered by an interesting array of banners, ranging from Corporate Social Responsibility to Sustainable Development, from Business Ethics to Corporate Social Contract, from Corporate Accountability to Business in Society, and from Corporate Citizenship to Corporate Governance (Kakabadse et al., 2005, p. 280). This certainly indicates the richness of the concept and its susceptibility for being studied from many different viewpoints: the relationship between business and society is multifaceted, complex, and constantly changing. It may also account for the many discussions and misunderstandings each time the concept is being implemented or studied within a specific context (Blowfield & Murray, 2011; Crane, et al. 2013; Beal, 2014).

Historically, Freeman's stakeholder approach is said to have emerged in opposition to the prevailing neoclassical economic theory of the firm, creating a dichotomy between a stakeholder's perspective and a shareholder's perspective. The neoclassical economic position is often expressed by Milton Friedman's well-known statement that profitability is the ultimate social responsibility of corporations. Free to pursue profits—following Adam Smith's 1776 argument—business will eventually benefit the common good. In contrast, it is argued following Edward Freeman—and with the endorsement of an elaborate set of moral and legal obligations in view of a variety of stakeholders—that business could and should serve society in a way that goes far beyond its primary responsibility of making profits (Kakabadse et al., 2005; Kakabadse & Morsing, 2006). However, this dichotomy between a stakeholder's perspective and a shareholder's perspective is somewhat misleading because it appears to imply that some of business's profits are sacrificed when stakeholders are taken into account. It is as if some of the benefits are used to please others rather than the company's shareholders. It is crucial to note that Freeman's stakeholder approach does not reject profitability as a corporate purpose. On the contrary, it rather widens the shareholder model to the ultimate benefit of all, shareholders included. In order to be able to go on making profits in the future, organisations must try to achieve their own objectives while satisfying the legitimate claims of their stakeholders at the same time.

Of course, it is also very unlikely that Adam Smith back in 1776 had the modern, multinational corporation in mind when he was writing about the invisible hand that harmonizes the activities of individuals pursuing their own entrepreneurial ends. It is, furthermore, often overlooked that corporations were originally invented to serve a specific public purpose for a restricted period of time, for example to build a road or a bridge. In 1776, when the USA was founded, there were no more than six corporations in the whole country (Moore Lappé, 2011). The original corporate charters of these early enterprises used to spell out an obligation to serve the public as a condition for the privilege of operating in the corporate form and for the generous grants of money and land they received from the government to deliver the agreed services. Serving the public was their reason for being. "In fact, the first corporations in the Anglo-American tradition had nothing to do with profits (…) [but] were actually regulatory agencies, such as guilds, or local governments such as townships (…) Later, the British Crown adapted the corporate form to what we would call today a *public-private partnership*. The Queen wanted to lay claim to the New World, but such ventures required huge amounts of capital, and were risky in the extreme. To amass the capital, there was a need to insulate investors from responsibility for the undertaking, beyond the amount of their investment. Thus the *joint stock company* was born" (Rowe, 1995, p. 31). This legal tradition carried over to the American colonies. By the middle of the 19th century the prerequisite of providing a public service became less prominent, while the public resentment of being granted special privileges grew. In view of the explosive growth of commerce at the time, however, privileges of incorporation were not curtailed or abolished but rather extended to everyone. No longer were corporations limited to specific activities that served the public: anyone could form one to do whatever they wished. Hence, the invisible hand of the market grew more significant as a token to safeguard serving the public good. The history of the relationship between business and society is thus much more revealing than a simple choice between favouring shareholders or stakeholders.

Making profit as the driving force of doing business remains a necessity, but cannot be accepted at any price. Rather than trying to replace profitability with human decency or blaming the corporate sector for all evil, it is important to understand better what doing business entails and how the objectives of individual benefits and common goods can complement each other and be achieved simultaneously. The ultimate purpose of engaging stakeholders is not to manipulate them in order to avoid being manipulated by them, as is often suggested. Contrary to popular belief, there is a genuine business interest in improving the social environment in which business operates and in becoming more knowledgeable about the global context (Winsemius & Guntram, 2002; Prahalad, 2005; Hart, 2005; Esty & Winston, 2006). Against this background, some authors therefore claim that doing business in the 21st century requires a new type of business enterprise, the "civil corporation" (Zadek, 2007), or even an entirely new economy, the "sustainable enterprise economy" (McIntosh, 2013).

THE RISE OF PARTNERSHIPS

People have always joined forces and collaborated to improve their living conditions and achieve social change in view of existing circumstances. The term "civil society" is used to cover this kind of social activity by individuals, groups, and social movements and refers to society as a community of citizens, linked by common interests and collective action. The early development of social movements was connected, for instance, to the broad economic and political changes that were taking place in England in the middle of the 18th century. According to James and Van Seters (2014) a social movement should thus be defined as a form of political association between persons who have at least a minimal sense of themselves as connected to others in a common purpose and who come together across an extended period of time to effect social change in the name of that purpose.

Civil society is often called the third sector of society, distinct from both the state and the market. Associations that are referred to as nongovernmental organisations or NGOs are part of civil society and may focus on social change via advocacy and political influence, on providing social and humanitarian services—often in cross-national contexts—or on a combination of both (Boli & Thomas, 1999; Doh & Teegen, 2003). As part of an organised group, individuals are better informed at lower costs. The effective gathering and dissemination of information can, therefore, be seen as a core business of NGOs. Furthermore, organised groups of individuals addressing the authorities are also able to play an important role in influencing public policy (Keim, 2003). However, NGOs are hard to define unambiguously and the term "NGO" is rarely used consistently. Even so, three types of organisations are clearly excluded from consideration: political parties, criminal groups, and profit-making organisations (Willetts, 2002). Increasingly, "civil society organizations" or CSOs is also used as a more general term to describe this wide range of organizations, networks, and associations.

NGOs have a new and vital role to play in today's volatile world and have demonstrated an increased influence and ability to shape global public policy during the past couple of decades. They have, for instance, mobilized successfully a large support around the world on issues such as climate change, fair trade, and poverty reduction. The considerable authority and influence of NGOs is also more and more contributing to new corporate practices (Winsemius & Guntram, 2002; Prahalad, 2005). NGOs have a significant impact on the way business is conducted: either directly through blaming and shaming, or indirectly via the changing of ideas and attitudes of particular stakeholder groups like employees, shareholders, and customers. Lately, a more intimate relationship is becoming popular, indicated by a spectacular rise of so-called partnerships (Glasbergen, Biermann, & Moll, 2007; Van Huijstee, 2010; Pattberg, Biermann, Chan, & Mert, 2012).

The term "nongovernmental organisation" was first used when the United Nations was created in 1945 (Willetts, 2002). When drafting the UN Charter, the need arose to differentiate between participation rights for specialized agencies established by *inter*governmental agreement of the member-states, and participation rights for internationally operating private organisations, commonly denominated as *non*governmental in nature. The UN, itself an intergovernmental organisation, made it possible for certain approved specialized international non-state agencies—i.e., nongovernmental organizations—to be awarded observer status at its assemblies and some of its meetings. From the early 1970s onward, the term "NGO" also received a growing popular meaning outside UN circles, and NGOs can now best be understood as organised components of social movements and civil society.

Since the UN's creation in 1945, roughly three generations of NGOs can be distinguished (Hill, 2004). The first generation lasted up till the end of the Cold War. By and large, the relationship between the UN and this first generation of NGOs was formal and ceremonial rather than political. It consisted mostly of professional and business associations, and similar kinds of internationally established NGOs. Examples of this first generation are the International Chamber of Commerce, the International Confederation of Trade Unions, and the International Committee of the Red Cross.

In the 1990s a second generation of NGOs appeared on stage. This generation is characterised by a rapid increase in the numbers of NGOs, primarily operating at a national level, and by a much greater variety of issues that is addressed. However, at the same time many new forms of global collaboration and transnational NGO networks were initiated This in turn has contributed significantly to the operational capacity and growing political influence of individual, nationally operating organisations as well as to the size, role, and visibility of civil society in general (Keck & Sikkink, 1998; Florini, 2000). A rough estimate by the Union of International Associations in Brussels indicates that some 47,000 international NGOs and 20,000 transnational NGO networks are active in the world at the turn of the century, 90 per cent of which have been formed since 1970 (Edwards, 2004, p. 23). Examples are the Third World Network, the Coalition for the International Criminal Court, and Oxfam International. Taken together, these quantitative and qualitative changes have been identified as the emergence of a global civil society (James & Van Seters, 2014). It is one of the most momentous developments taking place in the world today, according to Anthony Giddens: "Taking globalisation seriously means emphasising that democratisation cannot be confined to the level of the nation-state. A global public sphere outside the state and the market is needed: an arena for public life created by citizens" (as cited in Anheier, Glasius, & Kaldor, 2001, p. iii).

In marked contrast with the first generation, the second generation NGOs intended to engage directly in intergovernmental deliberations and to influence the outcomes of the major UN Conferences and Summits (Hill, 2004). They were politically motivated and wanted to become part of the institutional architecture of global governance. Second generation NGOs did also become significant players in global development assistance. It accounts for the important role civil society plays today in humanitarian relief, social development, and improved governance. The Organization for Economic Cooperation and Development (OECD) estimated, for instance, that in 2011 $19.3 billion in official development assistance was channeled through NGOs, signifying a substantial increase in operational cooperation of NGOs with UN agencies. Since the middle of the1990s the breadth and quality of relations between the World Bank and civil society intensified while NGO involvement in Bank-funded projects has risen steadily over the past decade from 21 percent of the total number of projects in1990 to an estimated 81 percent in 2009. And for good reasons. By engaging with civil society the World Bank was able to improve the development outcomes of its investments by making good use of the technical expertise and institutional support of NGOs on the ground within local contexts. In particular, NGOs could help to ensure that governments heard the voices of poor and marginalized communities, that social services were provided, also in fragile governance and post-conflict settings, and that public sector accountability and transparency in such contexts improved (World Bank, 2015). Establishing operational relationships with this second generation of NGOs has thus stimulated an intensive information exchange between the UN agencies concerned and local civil society. This capacity of NGOs to organise themselves on a global scale, while remaining deeply rooted within local activities, also accounts for the attractiveness of NGOs to the corporate sector. It might be considered a key element for understanding the next generation.

Toward the end of the 20th century, with the power shifting from national governments to international government organisations and multinational corporations, NGOs once again started to reorient themselves (Kaldor, 2003; Kaldor, Anheier, & Glasius; Kaldor, Moore, & Selchow, 2012). A few years later, the emergence of a third generation of NGOs can be observed, characterized predominantly by the involvement of various types of networks and partnerships and by its engagement in multistakeholder processes (Hemmati, 2002; Wadell, 2005, 2011; Glasbergen et al., 2007; Pattberg et al., 2012). Some of these third generation initiatives are closely related to the UN, e.g., the Global Compact and the World Summit on Sustainable Development with its more than 200 "Track II" partnerships (Hill, 2004). Other developments, like the World Social Forum that started up in Porto Alegre, Brasil, in 2001 and its manifold regional counterparts, have taken their inspiration from elsewhere, are in fact opposing the neoliberal Washington Consensus, and largely ignore the UN (Glasius, 2003).

The state, the corporate world, and the civil society are gradually recognizing the need for concerted efforts in the pursuit of global peace, economic stability, and human dignity. In an increasingly complex political, social, and economic environment, like-minded representatives of all three sectors are teaming up to work together, ensuring a new kind of governance in which traditional roles and interventions become redefined. This third generation of NGOs is hybrid in character, for even though such partnerships are not intended for making a profit, they certainly contribute to improving the conditions for doing so. And even though such partnerships are not initiated to rule the world, they certainly help to generate the commitment that makes global governance possible (Stern & Seligman, 2004). Partnerships between the private, the public, and the civil sector are learning to become more and more effective indeed. There is a growing awareness that traditional, sector-specific, or national solutions are not sufficient to address today's most urgent issues such as economic development, health care, poverty alleviation, social justice, and environmental sustainability. Public or private sector solutions, therefore, must be enhanced by learning and borrowing from organisations in other sectors (Reinicke & Deng, 2000; Rischard, 2002; Selsky & Parker, 2005).

TOWARD A COMMON FRAMEWORK FOR BUSINESS AND SOCIETY

In studies of the relationship between business and society, two basic strands can be distinguished: one predominantly ethically oriented and normative to what the corporation ought to do or not; the other more practical oriented and instrumental to achieving desired outcomes (Scholl, 2001; Kakabadse et al., 2005). While some of the earlier models of CSR focused on clarifying its moral content, Max Clarkson (1995) took a practical approach and argued that a firm's social responsibilities are best understood by the way in which its relationships are actually managed: "It became clear that all the corporations being studied had relationships with various groups or constituencies, which could be defined as stakeholder groups, and that these relationships were either managed, or not being managed, for better or worse (…) Obligations and responsibilities to customers, shareholders, employees, and other important constituencies are defined by most companies, together with corresponding accountabilities. Consequently, there are data concerning the management of corporate relationships with these constituencies or stakeholder groups" (Clarkson, 1995, pp. 98-99).The change of perspective from motives and moral content to stakeholder relationships and to the management of these relationships, therefore, helped to remedy the lack of empirical accessibility for Clarkson. His data from more than fifty case studies were better explained by the concepts and models of stakeholder management, based on the work of Freeman (1984), than by the slightly earlier models based on normative notions (Preston, 1975; Carroll, 1979).

Ann Svendsen and her colleagues at the Centre for Innovation in Management in Vancouver have also reported about the quality of stakeholder relationships. They collected substantial evidence that links the quality of stakeholder relationships to competitive advantage and business success (Svendsen, 1998; Svendsen, Boutilier, Abbott, & Wheeler, 2002). Such evidence demonstrates that strategic management of private sector firms could become more effective and efficient, if managerial efforts would regard various stakeholders' concerns and invest in the development of good relationships. Shareholders will benefit long-term if other legitimate interests in the firm do not fall by the wayside (Scholl, 2001). Business has to deal with other constituencies than its owners for its prosperity, if not for its survival.

Taking a look at the relationships of a corporation will help to better understand the policies and practices of its social responsibilities. This focus on relationships becomes much more significant when the modern-day version of a socially responsible corporation is considered. According to the Dutch Social and Economic Council (SER, 2000), a socially responsible corporation is defined by two key elements:

- Maintaining a relationship with the various stakeholders. This relationship is based on transparency and dialogue and responds to legitimate demands from society.
- Consciously targeting business activities at value creation in three dimensions—Profit, People, Planet—and hence at contributing to society's prosperity in the longer term (SER, 2000, p. 86).

It is interesting to note that both key elements, taken separately, represent earlier paradigm shifts in the recent history of CSR. Just like the "stakeholder approach" was triggered by Edward Freeman's *Strategic management* (1984), the "triple bottom line" is associated with John Elkington's landmark study, *Cannibals with forks* (1997). The crux to a proper understanding of CSR, we argued elsewhere (Maessen, Van Seters, & Van Rijckevorsel, 2007), lies not in the distinction between these two elements, nor in merely combining them, but rather in the recognition of their intrinsic relationship: a comprehensive approach to value creation crucially depends on effective relationships with stakeholders—and vice versa. This idea of the interconnectedness of value creation and stakeholder relationships underlies what we proposed to call a relational approach to CSR (ibid.). The focus of a relational approach to CSR is not primarily on the company, but rather on the relationships between a company and its stakeholders, a practical representation of society. It thus regards the organisation as part of a larger network, and the quality of the network relationships will benefit the corporation as well as its stakeholders.

CIRCLES OF STAKEHOLDERS

Let us have a closer look at these stakeholders and the relationships they have with a particular corporation. Clarkson (1995, p. 106), for instance, closely follows Freeman and defines stakeholders as "persons or groups that have, or claim, ownership, rights, or interests in a corporation and its activities, past, present, or future." Next, he makes the distinction between primary and secondary stakeholders. Primary stakeholders are defined as "a group, without whose continuing participation the corporation cannot survive as a going concern." The other or secondary stakeholders are subsequently distinguished from these primary stakeholder groups because they are "not involved in transactions with the corporation, but have the capacity to mobilize public opinion in favour of, or in opposition to, a corporation's performance" (ibid.). It can thus be empirically established by the number of contacts and the institutionalised character of such contacts that not all stakeholders are involved with the company to the same degree. Some relationships are clearly more important for a particular firm than others. In fact, the institutionalised character of these relationships—e.g., contracts or other legal obligations, regular meetings, client panels, responsible issue managers, financial commitment, or the exchange of money—can be seen as a good indicator of the present status of a particular relationship and of the amount of corporate attention it should receive.

Allowing, in principal, for more than a binary distinction between primary and secondary stakeholders, we have suggested "the level of involvement" or "the relative distance" of a stakeholder group to a particular firm as a label for describing the underlying dimension; we also have suggested the representation of a number of concentric circles around the corporation to depict different categories of stakeholders and their relative distance to the firm (Maessen et al., 2007). Building on the original theory of Freeman (1984), the idea of circles of stakeholders visualises that the various groups of stakeholders are not related in the same way to a corporation, but have different levels of involvement.

Of course, such a circle representation for the level of involvement of stakeholders will be different for different corporations, or at different moments in time. Extra circles may be added if and when needed to give an adequate representation of a specific situation. Moreover, circle representations should not be applied exclusively to corporations. Other entities may be placed in the middle of the concentric circles in order to illustrate that any particular organisation is always under the influence of a number of other organisations: every organisation can indeed be construed as part of a larger network. Additionally, it is important to note that other relational aspects could be relevant in a particular context. For instance, more closely related stakeholders, like customers, employees, or shareholders, might be under the influence of stakeholders at a larger distance, like consumer interest groups, trade unions, or social responsible investment agencies. Finally, it can be pointed out that a representation of stakeholders by concentric circles is a useful model to express the dynamics of the relationship between a company and its stakeholders by envisaging how a stakeholder may move from one circle to the next when the level of involvement is increasing or decreasing.

Based on earlier investigations, we proposed a generic classification model for the level of involvement using three circles to represent three major categories of stakeholders (Maessen et al., 2007). The involvement of a first category of stakeholders—the company's primary interest groups—is based on structured, economic relationships and long-term commitment based on formal contracts. Both sides have a stake in the continuity and prosperity of the company and violating these relationships may thus have important implications for both sides. Shareholders and employees are likely candidates for this first category. The involvement of a second category of stakeholders is based on relationships that may have been established by means of temporary agreements, but also by branding or advertising. In contrast to the company's primary interest groups, the continuity of these relationships has to be reestablished time and again. While the first category of stakeholders will be investing in the firm, it is the firm that will need to invest in the second category. Clients, business partners, and suppliers are likely candidates for this second category.

Finally, the third category of stakeholders at an even greater distance is assumed to have much more ambivalent feelings toward the continuity of the company, or may have no feelings yet about the company whatsoever. Any third party with a potential interest in the company's operations or products might be placed in that group: neighbours, government agencies, and nongovernmental organisations are the most likely candidates for this third category. Under conditions of globalisation, however, with corporations operating on a global scale, more and more people will affect or will be affected and one may even wonder if any groups can be excluded from this third category—groups that could be called non-stakeholders. In a rapidly changing environment this third category of stakeholders, therefore, is by far the most interesting category; it allows most for making strategic choices. For instance, a company may decide to establish a regular contact with a representational group of people from the local community, maybe even based on formal agreements, with the aim to settle a potential conflict or avoid expensive legal battles. As soon as both parties start investing in this relationship, the mutual benefits are likely to become larger—as was illustrated earlier with the emerging relationship between the World Bank and civil society (World Bank, 2015). That particular group of stakeholders could be visually represented as involved in an inward movement, starting from one of the outer circles.

THE DYNAMICS OF STAKEHOLDER RELATIONSHIPS

Traditionally, within the corporate sector NGOs were seen as entities exclusively focused on social reform—as businesses were seen as entities exclusively focused on making money. NGOs and businesses seemed to live on different planets, conducting their respective affairs in completely different ways. Also, the corporate sector saw NGOs predominantly as a nuisance, best to be kept at a safe distance. In recent years, that stereotype image is gradually changing. Today, NGOs are recognized by corporations, at least in parts of the corporate world, as a vital source of knowledge and strategic information. They may help to find new pathways in the open and unsettled situations in which corporations find themselves all the time. It was stipulated above that companies seek to strengthen the ties with NGOs more and more by developing strategic partnerships. Within the corporate sector indeed it has been recognized now that

NGOs are no longer seen as of only peripheral interest for business. Many corporations these days are interested to draw at least some of these NGOs into their inner circle (Beloe, Elkington, Fry Hester, & Newell, 2003).

Hart and Sharma (2004) take this line of argument one step further when they point out that the work on stakeholder management until recently has focused almost exclusively on investors, employees, customers, suppliers, the government regulators, and NGOs. Only groups that are salient, presently known to be in a position to affect the firm, and ready to do so, have been able to draw the manager's attention. In other words—following the terminology introduced by Mitchell, Agle, and Wood (1997)—only groups whose claims are considered powerful, urgent, and legitimate have been the subject of the work on business–stakeholder relations. "Current approaches to stakeholder engagement are based on either resource dependence or on moral arguments for managing stakeholders to achieve cost reduction, differentiation, or legitimacy in *existing* businesses" (Hart & Sharma, 2004, p. 9, emphasis added). Such strategies may indeed have helped to gain the firm competitive advantages in the form of customer loyalty, supplier relationships, lower employee turnover, and improved reputation. But they also indicate that Freeman's urge to be ready for the *un*expected has not been actively pursued yet.

With irony, Hart and Sharma (2004) observe that Freeman's strategic management model will only become sensitive to *future* developments by paying attention to those stakeholders who are affected or may be affected in due course, but are *presently* not in a position to influence the firm and therefore do not get the management's attention. It is by gaining access to those stakeholders that are considered extreme or *on the fringe* of the firm's current operations that the firm will better understand future change and learn to deal with the uncertainty of constantly evolving knowledge. Hart and Sharma (2004, p. 10) distinguish fringe or peripheral stakeholders from the visible and well-known core-stakeholders, which, incidentally, is a class that also includes the well-established NGOs in their opinion. Fringe stakeholders are typically invisible to the firm and are placed, therefore, in the outer ring of the three-circle model outlined above. They are disconnected because they are remote, weak, poor, disinterested, isolated, non-legitimate, or even non-human. Engaging in a two-way dialogue with some of these fringe stakeholder groups extends the firm outside its present boundaries. The learning processes involved offer the possibility to understand the complex and evolving issues that may potentially affect the firm's future competitive advantage. The creation of the Grameen Bank in Bangladesh more than twenty years ago by Muhammad Yunus is cited by Hart and Sharma (2004) as an excellent example of the kind of learning processes that are taking place when engaging in such a two-way dialogue. This business concept was developed as a direct result of Yunus' personal experiences with poor people in rural villages in Bangladesh. Much to his surprise, and contrary to the predominant stereotype of most bankers regarding the laziness and lack of competence of the poor, by travelling through their villages Yunus experienced that these poor people knew exactly how they wanted to move forward. However, they badly needed access to modest amounts of credit to launch or expand their small enterprises. The Grameen Bank was set up to serve these needs and has been very successful in doing so (Bornstein, 1997).

Exploring these uncharted territories populated by the firm's fringe stakeholders can be very promising. The world's most exciting, and fastest growing market is to be found with the billions of poor people at the bottom of the pyramid, even though the mainstream consumer industry is still predominantly targeted at the top (Prahalad, 2005; Hart, 2005). The corporate sector could be the catalyst for a truly sustainable force of global development and for improving health and safety of the poor—in theory at least—if only more attention would be given to the question of *who* to produce for and *what*. There is no principled or inherent conflict between making the world a better place for the underprivileged and achieving economic prosperity for all, within the constraints of our natural resources. It will take a lot of well-organised support from locally active actors and many unusual partners to turn these promises into a feasible business model. Paradoxically, without the business community the prospect for sustainable development might be bleaker (Kandachar & Halme, 2008).

ENGAGING STAKEHOLDERS FROM BEYOND

Some commentators still maintain that social responsibility programmes are bad for both business and society; CSR, they argue, is no more than a fig leaf (Salls, 2004, quoting Matthew Bishop, American business editor of *The Economist*). That does not necessarily imply that companies not taking an ethical stand will act socially irresponsibly. CSR might even morally licence CSiR, as was pointed out above following Ormiston and Wong (2013). Moreover, pressures put on businesses by NGOs may simply have the opposite effect of what is intended. Companies may decide to pull their factories out of poor countries rather than operate below standards acceptable in the Western world. Alternatively, CSR programmes may not even be initiated in the best interest of the company or shareholders, but only as a strategy to pacify NGOs—even though there is no guarantee that cooperating with NGOs buys a company any long-term reputation protection (Salls, 2004). This point of view nicely echoes one of the more popular themes within the NGO community: all this CSR is no more than green wash, confirming the stereotypical antagonism between business and NGOs. However, while this may provide a clear, normative beacon, it is not a very accurate image of what is actually happening in the world today.

Therefore, it is not surprising that other commentators, illuminating a more practical perspective, are pointing in the opposite direction. In January 1999, UN Secretary-General Kofi Annan warned his audience at the World Economic Forum in Davos, Switzerland, that globalisation would be only as sustainable as the social pillars on which it rests. Annan explicitly called upon companies to widen their social responsibilities and enter into a Global Compact with the UN for the endorsement of universally accepted principles (Annan, 1999). In January 2004, again addressing the World Economic Forum in Davos, Annan pointed to the deterioration of the global security climate because of international terrorism and the reaction of international politics: "In just a few short years, the prevailing atmosphere has shifted from a belief in the near-inevitability of globalisation to deep uncertainty about the very survival of our global order. This is a challenge for the UN. But it obliges the business community, too, to ask how it can help put things right" (Annan, 2004).

At the time of Kofi Annan's invitation, more and more companies recognized the need to collaborate and partner with governments and with civil society and labour organisations. More than ever before they felt that business was affected by various social, political, and economic challenges. Now, about fifteen years after its inception, the UN Global Compact has become the largest voluntary corporate responsibility initiative in the world with over 12,000 corporate participants and other stakeholders from over 145 countries. The UN Global Compact is a strategic policy initiative for businesses that are committed to aligning their operations and strategies with ten principles in the areas of human rights, labour, environment, and anti-corruption. It has grown to become a critical platform for the UN to engage effectively with enlightened global business. The UN Global Compact is committed to voluntarism, as a complement to regulation. By drawing on partnership, learning, and dialogue the initiative has been shaped to provide collaborative solutions to the most fundamental challenges facing both business and society. Business, as a primary driver of globalisation, thus helps to ensure that markets, commerce, technology, and finance advance in ways that benefit economies and societies everywhere (The Global Compact, 2015).

We are living in what some have termed a VUCA world: Volatile, Uncertain, Complex, and Ambiguous (Bennett & Lemoine, 2014). Never before have we seen such a rapid increase of the global population, radical shifts in power, and pressures on our natural resources. Since the role of national governments has been gradually scaled back around the turn of the 21st century, they experience difficulties or appear to lack the ability to cooperate in addressing even the most urgent global challenges. Multilateralism is in decline, just when the world needs it most. Meanwhile, expectations of corporate responsibility have increased, requiring firms to organise a more responsive way of corporate governance to get by in this VUCA world. Learning to deal with social and environmental problems is now crucial for continuing to do business. The corporate sector is as much in need of resolving global problems and maintaining our global order as anyone else. Since the role of national governments was scaled back, expectations of corporate responsibility have increased, requiring firms to organise a more responsive way of corporate governance. Learning to deal with social and environmental problems is crucial for continuing to do business.

As the progressive development of globalisation is forcing companies to face the challenges of a changing social environment, these companies increasingly realize that CSR is not just an extra burden but can be of direct economic value too. For major tracts of industry and commerce, the sustainable development agenda is already becoming a competitive and strategic issue (Elkington, 1997; Beloe, Elkington, Prakash-Mani, Thorpe, & Zollinger, 2004). Even though the prime responsibility of a company is to generate profits, companies can at the same time contribute to social and environmental objectives through integrating CSR as a strategic investment into their core business strategy, their management instruments, and their operations. There is a growing body of literature exploring these new territories (Demirag, 2005; Churie-Kallhauge, Sjöstedt, & Corell, 2005; Petschow, Rosenau, & Von Weizsäcker, 2005; Waddell, 2005, 2011). It pictures a new image of corporations serving their customer base while dealing effectively with some of those global challenges at the same time. This vision was strongly expressed recently by Unilever's CEO Paul Polman, when he explained his motives for the 2010 Unilever Sustainable Living Plan to an audience of politicians, business people, and civil society representatives: "Capitalism has lifted many people out of poverty, but we have not yet figured out how to do this without incurring enormous levels of public and private debt, over-consumerism, and leaving too many behind. We need to develop a more equitable and sustainable form of capitalism in which business sees itself, first, as part of society not separate from it; second, the focus is on the long term, not on quarterly earnings; and, third, the needs of citizens and communities carry the same weight as shareholders" (Polman, 2013, p. 6).

We may conclude that it will benefit both the firm and its stakeholders to look after stakeholders' relationships and the legitimate interests these relationships represent. In a world where everyone can be seen as a potential stakeholder, the firm's long-term survival is limited most severely by lack of knowledge about those stakeholders that are not actually visible yet. Of all possible stakeholders, the ones beyond the present periphery of the firm—the ones not *en vogue*—are the most valuable for future developments. As the world is flattening and the newly found power for individuals to collaborate globally is discovered, making contact with those stakeholders and learning about their worlds, wishes, and needs has become a reality. That is why truly responsive corporate governance will seek to engage with those stakeholders from beyond.

REFERENCES

Anheier, H., Glasius, M., & Kaldor, M. (Eds.). (2001). *Global civil society 2001*. Oxford, UK: Oxford University Press.

Annan, K. (1999). *Secretary-General proposes Global Compact on Human Rights, Labour, Environment, in address to World Economic Forum in Davos* (Press Release SG/SM/6881). Retrieved from http://www.un.org/News/Press/docs/1999/19990201.sgsm6881.html

Annan, K. (2004). *Special Address by Kofi Annan*. Quoted in B.S. Raghavan, *The call of the 21st century and other essays* (p. 69). Hyderabad, India: ICFAI University Press, 2006.

Arts, B. (2002). 'Green alliances' of business and NGOs: New styles of self-regulation or 'dead-end roads'? *Corporate Social Responsibility and Environmental Management*, *9*(1), 26–36. doi:10.1002/csr.3

Barber, B. R. (1995). *Jihad vs McWorld: Terrorism's challenge to democracy*. New York, NY: Ballantine Books.

Beal, B. D. (2014). *Corporate social responsibility: Definition, core issues, and recent developments*. London, UK: Sage.

Beck, U. (2000). *What is globalization?* Cambridge, UK: Polity Press.

Beloe, S., Elkington, J., Fry Hester, K., & Newell, S. (2003). *The 21st century NGO: In the market for change*. London, UK: SustainAbility.

Beloe, S., Elkington, J., Prakash-Mani, K., Thorpe, J., & Zollinger, P. (2004). *Gearing up: From corporate responsibility to good governance and scalable solutions*. London, UK: SustainAbility.

Bennett, N., & Lemoine, J. (2014). What VUCA really means for you. *Harvard Business Review*, *92*(1/2), 27.

Blowfield, M., & Murray, A. (2011). *Corporate responsibility*. Oxford, UK: Oxford University Press.

Boli, J., & Thomas, G. M. (Eds.). (1999). *Constructing world culture: International nongovernmental organizations since 1875*. Palo Alto, CA: Stanford University Press.

Bornstein, D. (1997). *The price of a dream: The story of the Grameen Bank*. Chicago, IL: University of Chicago Press.

Carroll, A. B. (1979). A three-dimensional conceptual model of corporate performance. *Academy of Management Review*, *4*(4), 497–505.

Castells, M. (1996). *The rise of the network society*. Oxford, UK: Blackwell.

Chandler, D. B., & Werther, W. B. (2013). *Strategic corporate social responsibility: Stakeholders, globalization, and sustainable value creation*. London, UK: Sage.

Churie-Kallhauge, A., Sjöstedt, G., & Corell, E. (Eds.). (2005). *Global challenges: Furthering the multilateral process for sustainable development*. Sheffield, UK: Greenleaf.

Clarkson, M. B. E. (1995). A stakeholder framework for analyzing and evaluating corporate social performance. *Academy of Management Review*, *20*(1), 92–117.

Crane, A., & Matten, D. (2010). *Business ethics: Managing corporate citizenship and sustainability in the age of globalization*. Oxford, UK: Oxford University Press.

Crane, A., Matten, D., & Spence, L. J. (Eds.). (2013). *Corporate social responsibility: Readings and cases in a global context*. London, UK: Routledge.

Demirag, I. (Ed.). (2005). *Corporate social responsibility, accountability and governance: Global perspectives*. Sheffield, UK: Greenleaf.

Doh, J. P., & Teegen, H. (Eds.). (2003). *Globalisation and NGOs: Transforming business, government, and society*. Westport, CT: Praeger.

Edwards, M. (2004). *Civil society*. Cambridge, UK: Polity Press.

Elkington, J. (1997). *Cannibals with forks: The triple bottom line of 21st century business*. Oxford, UK: Capstone.

Esty, D. C., & Winston, A. S. (2006). *Green to gold: How smart companies use environmental strategy to innovate, create value, and build competitive advantage*. New Haven, CT: Yale University Press.

Florini, A. M. (Ed.). (2000). *The third force: The rise of transnational civil society*. Tokyo, Japan: Japan Centre for International Exchange.

Freeman, R. E. (1984). *Strategic management: A stakeholder approach*. Marshfield, MA: Pitman.

Friedman, T. L. (1999). *The Lexus and the olive tree: Understanding globalization*. New York, NY: Farrar, Straus, and Giroux.

Friedman, T. L. (2005). *The world is flat: A brief history of the globalized world in the 21st century*. New York, NY: Farrar, Straus, and Giroux.

Giddens, A. (1990). *The consequences of modernity*. Cambridge, UK: Polity Press.

Giddens, A. (2003). *Runaway world: How globalisation is reshaping our world*. New York, NY: Routledge.

Glasbergen, P., Biermann, F., & Mol, A. P. J. (Eds.). (2007). *Partnerships, governance and sustainable development: Reflections on theory and practice*. Cheltenham, UK: Edward Elgar. doi:10.4337/9781847208668

Glasius, M. (2003). Global civil society: Theories and practices. In P. van Seters, B. de Gaay Fortman, & A. de Ruijter (Eds.), *Globalisation and its new divides: Malcontents, recipes, and reform* (pp. 193–207). Amsterdam, The Netherlands: Dutch University Press.

Googins, B., & Rochlin, S. (2000). Creating the partnership society: Understanding the rhetoric and reality of cross-sectoral partnerships. *Business and Society Review*, *105*(1), 127–144. doi:10.1111/0045-3609.00068

Granovetter, M. (1985). Economic action and social structure: The problem of embeddedness. *American Journal of Sociology*, *91*(3), 481–510. doi:10.1086/228311

Griseri, P., & Seppala, N. (2010). *Business ethics and corporate social responsibility*. Andover, Hampshire, UK: South-Western Cengage Learning.

Guest, R. (2001). *Borderless economics: Chinese sea turtles, Indian fridges and the new fruits of global capitalism*. New York, NY: Palgrave Macmillan.

Hart, S. L. (2005). *Capitalism at the crossroads: The unlimited business opportunities in solving the world's most difficult problems*. Upper Saddle River, NJ: Wharton School Publishing.

Hart, S. L., & Sharma, S. (2004). Engaging fringe stakeholders for competitive imagination. *The Academy of Management Executive*, *18*(1), 7–18. doi:10.5465/AME.2004.12691227

Hemmati, M. (2002). *Multi-stakeholder processes for governance and sustainability: Beyond deadlock and conflict*. London, UK: Earthscan.

Hill, T. (2004). *Three generations of UN-civil society relations: A quick sketch*. Global Policy Forum. Retrieved from https://www.globalpolicy.org/component/content/article/177-un/31824-three-generations-of-un-civil-society-relations.html

James, P., & Van Seters, P. (Eds.). (2014). *Global social movements and global civil society*. London, UK: Sage.

Jones, T., & Wicks, A. (1999). Convergent stakeholder theory. *Academy of Management Review*, *24*(2), 206–221.

Kakabadse, A., & Morsing, M. (Eds.). (2006). *Corporate social responsibility: Reconciling aspiration with application*. New York, NY: Palgrave Macmillan. doi:10.1057/9780230599574

Kakabadse, N. K., Rozuel, C., & Lee-Davies, L. (2005). Corporate social responsibility and stakeholder approach: A conceptual review. *International Journal of Business Governance and Ethics*, *1*(4), 277–302. doi:10.1504/IJBGE.2005.006733

Kaldor, M. (2003). *Global civil society: An answer to war*. Cambridge, UK: Polity Press.

Kaldor, M., Anheier, H., & Glasius, M. (Eds.). (2003). *Global civil society 2003*. Oxford, UK: Oxford University Press.

Kaldor, M., Moore, H. L., & Selchow, S. (Eds.). (2012). *Global civil society 2012: Ten years of critical reflection*. New York, NY: Palgrave Macmillan.

Kandachar, P., & Halme, M. (Eds.). (2008). *Sustainability challenges and solutions at the base of the pyramid: Business, technology and the poor*. Sheffield, UK: Greenleaf.

Keck, M. E., & Sikkink, K. (1998). *Activists beyond borders: Advocacy networks in international politics*. Ithaca, NY: Cornell University Press.

Keim, G. (2003). Nongovernmental organizations and business–government relations: The importance of institutions. In J. P. Doh & H. Teegen (Eds.), *Globalization and NGOs: Transforming business, government, and society* (pp. 19–34). Westport, CT: Praeger.

Maessen, R., Van Seters, P., & Van Rijckevorsel, E. (2007). Circles of stakeholders: Towards a relational theory of corporate social responsibility. *International Journal of Business Governance and Ethics*, *3*(1), 77–94. doi:10.1504/IJBGE.2007.011935

McIntosh, M. (Ed.). (2013). *The necessary transition: The journey towards the sustainable enterprise economy*. Sheffield, UK: Greenleaf.

Mitchell, R. K., Agle, B. R., & Wood, D. J. (1997). Towards a theory of shareholder identification and salience: Defining the principles of who and what really counts. *Academy of Management Review*, *22*(4), 853–886.

Moore Lappé, F. (2011). *Eco mind: Changing the way we think to create the world we want*. New York, NY: Nation Books.

Ormiston, M. E., & Wong, E. M. (2013). License to ill: The effects of corporate social responsibility and CEO moral identity on corporate irresponsibility. *Personnel Psychology*, *66*(4), 861–893. doi:10.1111/peps.12029

Pattberg, P., Biermann, F., Chan, S., & Mert, A. (Eds.). (2012). *Public–private partnerships for sustainable development: Emergence, influence and legitimacy*. Cheltenham, UK: Edward Elgar. doi:10.4337/9781849809313

Petschow, U., Rosenau, J., & Von Weizsäcker, E. U. (Eds.). (2005). *Governance and sustainability: New challenges for states, companies, and civil society*. Sheffield, UK: Greenleaf.

Polman, P. (2013, March 6). *From license to operate to license to lead.* Ernst & Young Hofstad Lecture, The Hague, The Netherlands. Retrieved from http://www.unilever.nl/Images/2013-03-06-Hofstadlezing-Paul-Polman_tcm164-348071.pdf

Prahalad, C. K. (2005). *The fortune at the bottom of the pyramid: Eradicating poverty through profits*. Upper Saddle River, CT: Wharton School Publishing.

Preston, L. E. (1975). Corporations and society: The search for a paradigm. *Journal of Economic Literature*, *13*(2), 434–453.

Reich, R. B. (2007). *Supercapitalism: The transformation of business, democracy, and everyday life*. New York, NY: Vintage Books.

Reinicke, W. H., & Deng, F. (2000). *Critical choices: The United Nations, networks, and the future of global governance*. Ottawa, Canada: International Development Research Centre.

Rischard, J.-F. (2002). *High noon: Twenty global problems, twenty years to solve them*. New York, NY: Basic Books.

Rowe, J. (1995). Corporations and the public interest: A look at how the original purpose behind corporate charters has been lost. *In Context*, 41, 26-35.

Sachs, J. D. (2005). *The end of poverty: How we can make it happen in our lifetime*. New York, NY: Penguin Books.

Sachs, J. D. (2009). *Common wealth: Economics for a crowded planet*. New York, NY: Penguin Books.

Salls, M. (2004). *An opposing view of corporate social responsibility*. Harvard Business School Working Knowledge. Retrieved from http://hbswk.hbs.edu/archive/4008.html

Scholl, H. J. (2001). Applying stakeholder theory to e-government: Benefits and limits. In B. Schmid, K. Stanoevska-Slabeva, & V. Tschammer (Eds.), *Towards the e-society: E-commerce, e-business, and e-government* (pp. 735–747). Boston, MA: Kluwer Academic Publishers.

Selsky, J. W., & Parker, B. (2005). Cross-sector partnerships to address social issues: Challenges to theory and practice. *Journal of Management*, *31*(6), 849–873. doi:10.1177/0149206305279601

SER, Social and Economic Council of the Netherlands. (2000). *De winst van waarden*. The Hague, The Netherlands: SER (English abstract: *Advisory Report on Corporate Social Responsibility: Summary of Conclusions*). Retrieved from https://www.ser.nl/nl/publicaties/adviezen/2000-2007/2000/b19054.aspx

SOMO, Center for Research on Multinational Corporations. (2014). *Flawed fabric: The abuse of girls and women workers in the South Indian textile industry*. Amsterdam, The Netherlands: SOMO.

Stern, S., & Seligman, E. (2004). *The partnership principle: New forms of governance in the 21st century*. London, UK: Archetype Publishers.

Svendsen, A. C. (1998). *The stakeholder strategy*. San Francisco, CA: Berrett-Koehler.

Svendsen, A. C., Boutilier, R. G., Abbott, R. M., & Wheeler, D. (2002). *Measuring the business value of stakeholder relationships: Part one*. Vancouver, Canada: Centre for Innovation in Management. Retrieved from http://www.cim.sfu.ca/folders/research/1%20-%20Measuring%20social%20capital%20-%201.pdf

The Global Compact. (2015). *What is the UN Global Compact?* Retrieved from https://www.unglobal-compact.org/

Van Huijstee, M. (2010). *Business and NGOs in interaction: A quest for corporate social responsibility* (Doctoral dissertation). Utrecht, The Netherlands: Faculty of Geosciences, Utrecht University.

Van Seters, P. (2012). The sustainability movement. In K. Zoeteman (Ed.), *Sustainable development drivers: The role of leadership in government, business and NGO performance* (pp. 249–256). Cheltenham, UK: Edward Elgar. doi:10.4337/9781781009130.00021

Van Seters, P., De Gaay Fortman, B., & De Ruijter, A. (Eds.). (2003). *Globalisation and its new divides: Malcontents, recipes, and reform*. Amsterdam, The Netherlands: Dutch University Press.

Van Tulder, R., & Van der Zwart, A. (2006). *International business–society management: Linking corporate responsibility and globalization*. London, UK: Routledge.

Visser, W. (2011). *The age of responsibility: CSR 2.0 and the new DNA of business*. London, UK: Wiley.

Vogel, D. (2005). *The market for virtue: The potential and limits of corporate social responsibility*. Washington, DC: Brookings.

Waddell, S. (2005). *Societal learning and change: How governments, business and civil society are creating solutions to complex multi-stakeholder problems*. Sheffield, UK: Greenleaf.

Waddell, S. (2011). *Global action networks: Creating our future together*. New York, NY: Palgrave Macmillan.

Willetts, P. (2002). *What is a non-governmental organization?* Retrieved from http://www.staff.city.ac.uk/p.willetts/CS-NTWKS/NGO-ART.HTM

Winsemius, P., & Guntram, U. (2002). *A thousand shades of green: Sustainable strategies for competitive advantage*. London, UK: Earthscan.

World Bank. (2015). Information on website. Retrieved from http://web.worldbank.org/WBSITE/EXTERNAL/TOPICS/CSO/0,contentMDK:20092185~menuPK:220422~pagePK:220503~piPK:220476~theSitePK:228717,00.html

Zadek, S. (2007). *The civil corporation: The new economy of corporate citizenship*. London, UK: Earthscan.

Chapter 13
Does Trust Matter for Foreign Direct Investment Decisions?

Sibel Bali Eryigit
Uludag University, Turkey

ABSTRACT

Factors affecting the investment decisions of multinational companies are heavily researched in the literature. However, the number of studies dealing with the socio-cultural characteristics of host countries among these factors is quite limited. Among the cultural characteristics affecting location decisions, one of the primary cultural characteristics is the general level of trust between individuals. In this scope, this chapter intends to research whether the general level of trust in a society has an effect on the location decisions of foreign investors. In line with this objective, an analysis will be conducted by employing the panel data method for 39 emerging market countries for the period between 1998 and 2011. According to the results of the study, a low general level of trust in the host country represents a significant disadvantage for the attraction of foreign direct investments.

1. INTRODUCTION

The impact of foreign direct investments (FDIs) on economic development is intensively researched in the literature. The relevant literature has proven many times that FDI promotes economic growth in the host country by providing the transfer of new knowledge and technologies, creating employment opportunities and increasing capital accumulation. Thus, FDIs are particularly important for emerging markets, as they do not have sufficient capital accumulation for industrialization. Due to the importance of FDIs, the literature has heavily researched the factors affecting FDI decisions. The studies underline that there are many factors that influence multinational firms' decisions about FDIs, such as the host country's market size the distance to other markets, openness, and incentives given to foreign investors, macroeconomic stability, tax advantages, human capital, and infrastructure quality. However, there are quite a few studies on the impacts of the socio-cultural dynamics of host countries on FDI decisions in the relevant literature.

DOI: 10.4018/978-1-4666-9864-2.ch013

Among the socio-cultural characteristics of host countries that affect location decisions, one of the primary cultural characteristics is the general level of trust between individuals. So, the primary objective of this study is to assess the impact of the general level of trust in the host country on the FDI decisions in that country. As there are quite few studies conducted in this sphere, it is thought that this study will contribute significantly to the literature. In line with this objective, an analysis will be conducted by employing the panel data method for 39 emerging market countries for the period between 1998 and 2011.

The plan of this study is as follows: The introduction section will present the subject and aim of the study, as well as its contributions to the literature. The theoretical background and related literature section will deal with the place and importance of trust in economics, and it will also address the impact of the level of trust on investment relations by discussing the impact mechanisms. The third section will deal with the empirical methodology employed in the study. The fourth section presents the model and data. The fifth section will present the empirical findings. Lastly, the empirical results obtained under the title conclusions are discussed.

2. THEORETICAL BACKGROUND AND RELATED LITERATURE

According to Fukuyama (1995), a nation's well-being, as well as its ability to compete, is conditioned by a single pervasive cultural characteristic, which is the level of trust inherent in the society. As communities rely on association based on trust, and *trust is determined by culture*, it may be said that the general level of trust differs in distinct cultures. In fact, there are many studies in the literature advocating that trust and, particularly, the level of social trust are important determinants of the performance of economies.

The first study known to comprehensively address the effects of mutual trust on the economy is "The Moral Basis of Backward Society", conducted by Banfield and published in 1958. Banfield (1958) attributes the economic backwardness of Southern Italy, in comparison with Northern Italy, to the low general level of trust in the south. Family ties in Southern Italy are very strong, but the other individuals of the society beyond the family exhibit a low level of mutual trust. According to Banfield (1958), the poor general level of trust hampers the communication, cooperation, and interaction between individuals. This prevents the creation of large organizations that would promote economic development. Similarly, La Porta et al. (1997) stated that in large organizations and social structures in which the members interact with each other infrequently, trust was needed to support cooperation. In fact, La Porta et al. (1997) supported this claim by detailing empirical evidence as well.

According to Arrow (1972), the lack of trust plays a significant role in economic backwardness and underdevelopment. Arrow (1972) emphasizes that each commercial transaction relies, in itself, on trust, and that each transaction will definitely come to an end within a given period. Simply, the level of mutual trust is important for the formation of a market. This is because the future involves uncertainty and risk, and economic activities require that economic units trust the future behaviors of others. The linking of supply and demand implies that there has been an explicit or implicit mutual agreement in the background. Economic units that comply with their contracts and thus have gained trust in the market are forced to resort to legal action when the other party fails to comply with the conditions set, which causes significant losses for the complying party in terms of time and money. In other words, the low level of general trust in a society is expected to increase the cost of transactions due to asymmetric information and associated market distortions.

The relationship between the level of trust and FDIs is based on cooperative behavior, market distortions, and the costs arising from them. In the location decisions of multinational companies for the FDI, the perception of risk regarding the host country and the ensuing costs have an important role to play. As is the case with all economic exchanges, each party in a given FDI possesses special information, resulting in information asymmetry. However, this information asymmetry is greater due to the differences in social-cultural, economic, and legal structures of countries involved, especially with respect to foreign investments. Accordingly, it is possible to say that multinational companies may encounter greater uncertainty and risks when they make investments in another country in comparison to the ones they make at home. Contracts, which bind multiple parties in legal agreement over the transaction period, represent an attempt to mitigate the problem of asymmetric information and uncertainty. However, all of these contracts result in significant incremental costs that may eventually impact the location decisions of multinational companies (Bhadwarj et al. 2007; Kukharsky, 2012).

The general level of trust in a society is the result of the mutual experiences of its members. High interpersonal trust is expected to be created in an orderly, honest, and cooperative society, relying on norms mutually shared by its members. In other words, in order to attain a high level of interpersonal trust in a society, the relationships must be based on cooperation, and they should avoid opportunistic behavior (Fukuyama, 1995; Bhadwarj et al., 2007). In other words, each and every transaction has intrinsic information asymmetry; however, the societies with high generalized trust have a lower tendency to take advantage of this information for their own advantage. Accordingly, the monitoring and transaction costs are expected to be lower in societies with a high level of trust than in those societies with a low level of trust (Butter and Mosh, 2003).

People who do not trust each other in societies with a low level of trust will conduct their business relations within a system of formal rules, which ultimately pushes them to negotiate, come to terms with, and bring actions against others. This process considerably increases the transaction costs. This also indicates that the quality of functioning of the formal institutions becomes even more important in communities with a low level of trust. Nevertheless, a high level of trust is expected to substantially eliminate the adverse effects of an underdeveloped institutional environment on the location decisions made by the FDI's decision makers (Delios and Henizs, 2003; Kolstad and Villanger, 2004). For instance, despite the fact that the formal institutions of China are not sufficiently developed, its economy has grown so rapidly and has attracted FDI based on its high level of social trust. Given the fact that law and enforcement in developing countries in general are relatively weak, it is possible to say that the high level of general trust in the host country may reduce the perception of risk among foreign investors (Ang et al., 2009).

In conclusion, the steps that must be taken in order to consider and prevent any problems that could arise from a low level of trust do not only increase transaction costs, but they also result in significant opportunity costs for multinational companies in an environment where global competition is on the rise. The perception that opportunistic behavior is rarer in societies with a high level of trust and therefore the transaction costs will be lower and information sharing will be higher thanks to cooperative behavior, is expected to affect the location decisions of multinational companies. This high level of trust not only reduces the contractual costs, but it also decreases litigiousness, thus cutting legal transaction costs (Bhadwarj et al., 2007; Dearmon and Grier, 2009; Durlauf and Fafchamps, 2005)

However, the number of studies on this subject in the relevant literature is quite limited. The first known study to empirically research the effect of trust on bilateral trade was conducted by Butter and Mosch (2003). They determined that increasing trust by one standard deviation can encourage changes of up to 90-150% in bilateral trade. Guiso et al. (2004) found that the level of trade, portfolio investments, and direct investments are at a lower level in countries where the level of mutual trust is low. As far as known, this is the first study investigating the effects of trust on FDIs. Moreover, Bhardwarj et al. (2007), Bottazzi et al. (2007) and Zhao (2011) noted that a high level of trust in the host country is an important determinant for the location decisions in relation to FDI. Additionally, Botazzi et al. (2007) stated that education and work experience reduce the effect of trust but do not eliminate it. Finally, Kukharsky (2012) found that a 1% increase in a country's level of trust leads to a more than 3% increase of the US FDI in this country.

3. EMPIRICAL METHODOLOGY

This study employs the dynamic panel approach. Many economic behaviors substantially involve a dynamic structure. As such, panel data may be extended in such way where economic behaviors can be adjusted dynamically at the individual level. At this point, with the inclusion of the lagged values of the dependent variable into the model as regressors, dynamic relationships are distinguished from the static panel data approach:

$$Y_{it} = \delta Y_{i,t-1} + X_{it}^{'}\beta + \mu_{it},\ i \in \{1,2,....,N\},\ \text{and}\ t \in \{1,2,....,T\} \tag{1}$$

Here, *i* denotes the units such as individuals, countries, regions, etc. – in other words, the cross-section dimension of the panel data. Further, *t* denotes the time and is the time-series dimension of the panel data, Y_{it} denotes the dependent variable vector, X_{it} denotes the explanatory variables matrix, β denotes the parameter vector, μ_i denotes the unobservable unit specific impact, and μ_{it} denotes the error term. δ is a constant and denotes the dynamic adjustment. The error term is as follows:

$$\mu_{it} = \mu_i + \varepsilon_t + \nu_{it}. \tag{2}$$

Here, $\mu_i \sim iid\left(0,\sigma_\mu^2\right)$, $\varepsilon_i \sim iid\left(0,\sigma_\varepsilon^2\right)$ and $\nu_i \sim iid\left(0,\sigma_\nu^2\right)$ apply and are independent from each other.

In dynamic models, there may be a correlation between $Y_{i,t-1}$ and $\mu_{i,t-1}$ due to the impact of past shocks. Additionally, as Y_{it} is a function of μ_i in panel data models, $Y_{i,t-1}$ is also a function of μ_i. Therefore, for the model given in (1), $Y_{i,t-1}$ is correlated with the error term containing μ_i. So, the assumption of strict exogeneity, which implies uncorrelatedness between the regressors and the error term, is invalid. Therefore, the estimators are not unbiased and consistent.

Arellano and Bond (1991) suggested the use of the generalized moments method (GMM) for dynamic panel data. This approach is also known as "two-stage instrumental variables" approach. The first-differenced model with the general instrumental variable can be written as:

$$Z'\Delta Y = \Delta Y_{-1}\delta + Z'\Delta X\beta + Z'\Delta u_{it} \tag{3}$$

or

$$Z'\Delta Y = \Delta Y_{-1}\delta + Z'\Delta X\beta + Z'\Delta u_{it} \tag{4}$$

again, where $\Delta X = \left[\left(Y_{i,t-1} - Y_{i,t-2}\right);\left(X'_{it} - X'_{i,t-1}\right)\right]$. Accordingly, the GMM estimator can be obtained as:

$$\tilde{\Theta} = \left[\Delta X'Z\left(Z'\Omega Z\right)^{-1} Z'\Delta X\right]^{-1} \Delta X'Z\left(Z'Z\right)^{-1} Z'\Delta Y, \tag{5}$$

where Ω is the variance–covariance matrix.

To test the validity of the set of instruments, the Sargan (1958) test can be applied for GMM estimation. Additionally, the use of GMM requires the assumption that the first difference of the error term does not have a second-order serial correlation. The invalidity of this assumption implies that the lagged instrumental variables have not been set correctly. It is natural for the model to have first-order autocorrelation when the model includes the one lagged value of the dependent variable; this does not imply the presence of a specification error. Thus, it is important to test the presence of a second-order autocorrelation. For this purpose, the Arrelano-Bond (1991) *m*2 autocorrelation test is widely used.

4. MODEL AND DATA

For the objective of this study, this section delves into the effects of trust in emerging-market countries on FDI within the framework of a dynamic panel data model. The dynamic panel data model that was set up in line with this objective is as follows:

$$\begin{aligned} fdi_{it} &= \beta_0 + \delta fd_{i,t-1} + \beta_1 trst_{it} + \beta_2 \inf_{it} + \beta_3 \ln gdp_{it} + \beta_4 gfc_{it} \\ &\quad + \beta_5 invpr_{it} + \beta_6 enr_{it} + \beta_7 tax_{it} + \beta_8 opn_{it} + u_{it} \end{aligned}, \tag{6}$$

where fdi_{it} represents the percentage of inward FDI to GDP, δ is the coefficient indicating the dynamic adjustment for FDI, and $\beta_k \ (k = 0,1,....,8)$ is the coefficient vector of the explanatory variables. Furthermore, $u_{it} = \mu_i + \varepsilon_t + v_{it}$ denotes the error term involving country- and time-specific effects.

This approach inevitably includes the control variables in the model for the accurate estimation of the effect of the level of trust in emerging market countries on FDI. Based on this, information regarding the effects of the control variables on the attraction of FDI and the dataset used is given below.[1]

- ***Trust*** $\left(trst_{it}\right)$ represents the general level of trust in a given society, and the present study uses the Gallup World Poll's measure of trust as data. The dataset from 2011 was used, as it is the most comprehensive dataset for the countries within the scope of this research. Interpersonal trust is measured using the question, "*Generally speaking, would you say that most people can be trusted or that you can't be too careful in dealing with people*?" Trust is the percentage of respondents in each country replying, "*most people can be trusted*".

- ***Inflation*** (inf_{it}) was added into the model to represent macro-economic stability. Kairuki (2015) notes that high inflation may increase the foreign companies' costs of doing business. A high inflation rate in the host country may also deter foreign investment, as the real local currency value of capital is already invested, and future returns may become smaller due to high inflation (Hayakawa et al., 2013). Additionally, inflation causes the prices to lose their signaling function. This makes it more difficult for foreign investors to make cost/profit predictions and long-term plans (Lewandowski, 1997). Gedik (2013) claims that policies aiming at reducing inflation have demand-restricting effects, and that this may adversely affect the decisions of foreign investors.
- ***Real per capita GDP*** (gdp_{it}) is widely used as a proxy for market size in host countries. Market size represents the domestic demand, and therefore the volume of sales. It is an important determinant, especially when the reason underlying the FDI decision of multinational companies is the market-seeking strategy. In other words, when multinational companies intend to carry out production for domestic demand, the market size and growth potential of the host country become more important (Busse and Hefeker, 2007). In this context, FDI becomes economically sensible, only when the volume exceeds a level at which the average cost of serving the market through exports exceeds the average cost of production within the market (Davidson, 1980). However, there are also views holding that market size does not affect or adversely affect investment decisions. Loree and Guisinger (1995) assert that factors affecting location decisions vary de pending on the FDI strategy used, and that location decisions of export-oriented FDIs are affected by costs rather than the market size. According to Asiedu (2004), who holds a different viewpoint, foreign investors tend toward economies where the return on capital is high. Since capital is scarce in countries in which the income per capita is relatively low, the return on capital is higher. In conclusion, when it comes to export-oriented foreign investments, a high GDP per capita is expected to negatively affect the FDI decisions.
- ***Gross fixed capital formation*** (gfc_{it}) is used as a proxy for infrastructure in the host country. Insufficient infrastructure causes disruption at each stage of production, thus increasing costs. On the other hand, with good infrastructure, it becomes more efficient to transport goods from one place to another, communicate with people involved in business operations through the use of technology, have buildings that are well set up and have uninterrupted power, and have ample water supplies (Kariuki, 2015). Therefore, it is thought that the high level of infrastructure in the host country positively affects the location decisions of foreign investors.
- ***Investment profile*** $(invpr_{it})$ includes the factors related to the risk of investment that are not covered by other financial and economic risk components. The investment profile index was derived from the dataset of the International Country Risk Guide (ICRG), provided by the PRS Group. The investment profile rating assigned is the sum of three subcomponents (Contract Viability / Expropriation, Profits Repatriation, and Payment Delays), each with a maximum score of 4 points and a minimum score of 0 points. A score of 4 points equates to Very Low Risk and a score of 0 points to Very High Risk. As high values of the investor profile imply low risk, high index values are expected to positively affect FDI decisions.

- ***Secondary school enrolment rate*** (enr_{it}) is used to represent the level of human capital in the country. High skills and trained labor are expected to reduce the transaction costs, as they minimize the duration of training required for the use of new production techniques and new technologies. Furthermore, the level of human capital is determinative of management skills, communication in business relationships, and the effectiveness of decision-making processes. In conclusion, a low level of human capital is expected to adversely affect location decisions since it reduces the efficiency and profitability of investments.
- ***Taxes*** (tax_{it}) are one of the basic factors taken into account by foreign investors in their assessments, which are based on costs. The model uses the corporate tax rate of the host country to represent the taxes. High tax rates are expected to adversely affect location decisions.
- ***Openness*** (opn_{it}) refers to the trade openness of the host country. The ratio of the sum of imports and exports to GDP was used to represent openness. In the case of export-oriented FDI (called vertical FDI), foreign investors prefer more open economies, as trade restrictions substantially increase transaction costs. However, according to the tariff-jumping hypothesis, in horizontal FDIs, foreign investors tend to prefer less open economies to protect against the competition brought about by imports. In line with these explanations, it may be said that the effect of openness on the decisions of foreign investors varies depending on the country in question.

5. EMPIRICAL RESULTS

The model given in equation (11) in the study is estimated to take into account the annual panel data for 39 emerging market countries for the period between 1998 and 2011.[2] Table 1 gives the descriptive statistics for the variables.

Examining Table 1, it is evident that the null hypothesis that all variables in the model are normally distributed is rejected. The estimation results of the dynamic model given in Equation (6) are shown in Table 2.

Paying close attention, one can see that the model is estimated by adding the one-period lagged values of all variables, excluding trust. This is related to the purpose of eliminating the potential problem of endogeneity among the variables, and to the expectation that investment decisions will be taken with a delay (see Asiedu and Lien, 2004; Naude and Krugell, 2007; Majocchi and Presutti, 2009; Anyanwu, 2011).

Examining the estimation results, it can be seen that the general level of trust in the host country is a significant determinant of the FDIs flowing into the country. In other words, economies with a low level of trust have a significant disadvantage in attracting FDIs. This finding is consistent with the findings of Guiso, Sapienza, and Zingales (2004), Botazzi et al. (2006), Bhardwarj et al. (2007), Ang et al. (2009), Zhao (2011), and Kukharsky (2012). As stated in Ang et al. (2009), high general levels of trust in a society facilitates social exchange by reducing the need for time-consuming and costly monitoring, and therefore makes it possible for more efficient economic exchanges in a more favorable business environment that attracts foreign investors. Besides, level of generalized trust in host country for foreign investors determines perception of their risk of dealing with strangers in host country. Additionally, it was observed that the high general level of trust in emerging markets was better able to attract FDIs than macroeconomic stability, trade openness and human capital. As stated above, since institutional

Table 1. Descriptive statistics

	Mean	Median	Max.	Min.	Std. Dev.	Skewness	Kurtosis	Jarque-Bera	p-value
fdi_{it}	28.15	24.01	101.35	1.02	18.87	1.07	3.92	122.92	0.00
$trst_{it}$	21.03	20.00	58.00	8.00	10.38	2.10	8.13	998.54	0.00
$invpr_{it}$	8.63	9.00	12.00	2.42	2.19	-0.57	2.73	31.22	0.00
gdp_{it}	8204.03	4942.45	57558.72	326.68	10397.85	2.70	10.89	2077.84	0.00
gfc_{it}	24.21	23.01	48.27	5.47	6.99	0.54	3.71	37.99	0.00
$\inf_{it}$	7.45	4.88	85.74	-11.37	9.54	4.07	26.32	13880.64	0.00
enr_{it}	81.48	85.92	110.03	23.25	19.09	-1.15	3.75	132.93	0.00
tax_{it}	26.48	28.00	55.00	0.00	9.10	-0.01	4.95	86.47	0.00
opn_{it}	83.27	69.88	220.41	15.87	43.06	0.95	3.20	82.49	0.00

and legal environments of emerging economies are not sufficiently development, this finding indicates that general level of trust in host country has a greater effect on location decisions of foreign investor.

Assessing the control variables in the model, it can be seen that all variables, excluding inflation, are individually significant and generally fit the expectations. However, the parameter concerning the inflation rates variable is significant only at a significance level of 10%, but it may be said to fit the expectations. The finding that inflation adversely affects the location decisions of a given FDI is consistent with the findings of Kolstad and Villanger (2004). Furthermore, Naude and Krugel (2007) and Demirhan and Masca (2008) estimated that the sign of inflation is negative at a level of significance of 10%, which is similar to the findings of our study. Kok and Acikgoz Ersoy (2009) found that the effect of inflation was negative, although very minor. Finally, Schneider and Frey (1985), Vijaakumar et al. (2010), and Mhlanga et al. (2010) could not find a statistically significant relationship.

The sign of real GDP per capita, which represents the market size, is negative according to the model estimation. Asiedu (2002) states that foreign investors prefer those countries where the return on capital is high. Since the capital is scarce in the countries where the GDP per capita is low, the return on capital in these countries is higher. In other words, since the return on capital is lower in the countries where the GDP per capita is high, there is an inverse relationship between real GDP per capita and FDI. On the other hand, according to Asiedu (2004), in order for the real GDP per capita to positively affect FDI decisions, it must exceed a certain threshold. The findings of this study are consistent with the findings of Edwards (1992), Jaspersen et al. (2000), and Asiedu (2002; 2004) in that real GDP per capita is inversely related to FDI/GDP.

It is clear from the model findings that gross fixed capital formation, which represents the infrastructure of the host country, is a crucial determinant of location decisions. According to the model results,

Table 2. Dynamic panel GMM estimation results

Dependent Variable: fdi_{it}	*Coefficient*	*t-Statistics*	*p-Values*
constant	7.7020	2.2397	0.0256
fdi_{it-1}	0.7066	8.2928	0.0000
$trst_{it}$	0.1047	3.0786	0.0022
inf_{it-1}	-0.0160	-1.8177	0.0697
$\ln gdp_{it-1}$	-0.6652	-2.0820	0.0379
gfc_{it-1}	0.1963	3.2902	0.0011
$invpr_{it-1}$	0.5173	3.5408	0.0004
enr_{it-1}	0.0526	2.5458	0.0113
tax_{it-1}	-0.1519	-2.6387	0.0086
opn_{it-1}	0.0502	2.9954	0.0029
Adjusted R-squared	0.9235		
Observations	546		
Wald test	3274.147 (*p-value*=0.000)		
Sargan test	0.3227 (*p-value*=0.57)		
$m2$ *serial corelation test*	1.0795 (*p-value*=0.281)		

the infrastructure of the host country has a greater effect on location decisions than all other explanatory variables, excluding the investor profile. This finding indicates that the transportation, communication, and technological facilities of the host country substantially contribute to the attraction of FDI. This finding is consistent with the findings of Habib and Zurawick (2002), Kariku (2015), Kok and Acikgöz Esoy (2009), Awan et al. (2011), and Gichamo (2012).

With respect to the investor profile index, it can be seen that its sign is positive and that it is the factor with the greatest effect on investment decisions within the framework of the model.[3] High values of the investor profile index, consisting of three subcomponents – namely, contract viability, profit repatriation, and payment delays – represent low investment risk. As the host country's risk decreases in terms of these three subcomponents, it has greater advantages for attracting FDIs. Since the effect of the investor profile index is positive, and given that this effect is relatively high, the findings of this study are consistent with those of Busse and Hefeker (2007), and Baek and Qian (2011).

According to the results of the model, human capital has a positive effect on FDIs. This finding verifies the opinions of Lucas (1990) and Dunning (1988), in that a low level of human capital increases transaction costs and decreases efficiency, thereby detracting from the return on FDI. This finding is also consistent with the findings of Noorbakhsh, et al. (2001), Asiedu (2006), Bhadwarj et al. (2007), Dutta and Osei-Yeboah (2010), and Kim and Park (2013).

With respect to taxes, it is seen that environments where high taxes are imposed adversely affect the location decisions of foreign investors, which is in accordance with expectations. This finding is consistent with those of Demirhan and Masca (2008), Tang (2012), and Gedik (2013). Additionally, tax policies have a greater effect on location decisions than human capital, macroeconomic stability, and even trade openness.

It can be seen that trade openness has a positive effect on FDI. It was previously noted that there are different views in the literature regarding the effect of trade openness on location decisions, and that the results vary depending on the countries and FDI strategies. In the model that was formulated, trade openness positively affects location decisions. This finding verifies the view that foreign companies intending to make export-oriented FDIs prefer countries that have higher trade openness, which is based on the idea that trade restrictions increase transaction costs. The finding that trade openness contributes to the attraction of FDIs is consistent with the findings of Asiedu (2006), Kariuki (2015), and Janicki and Wunnava (2004).

Finally, the high adjusted determination coefficient in the model implies that the changes in the explanatory variables substantially account for the changes in the dependent variable, and that the null hypothesis where the coefficients for the Wald test are simultaneously equal to zero is rejected in favor of the alternative hypothesis that the model is generally significant. Additionally, the Sargan test statistic calculated for the model fails to provide sufficient evidence for the rejection of the null hypothesis, which implies the suitability of the instrumental variables used to estimate the dynamic model. That is, the instrumental variables used for the dynamic panel GMM estimations are suitable. Moreover, when the *m*2 serial correlation test statistic proposed by Arellano and Bond (1991) – as required by the use of second lags as instrumental variables for GMM estimations – is examined, the null hypothesis implying that none of the models have serial correlations cannot be rejected. Accordingly, this means that there is no second-order serial correlation problem in the model.

6. CONCLUSION

In addition to its contribution to capital accumulation and employment, FDI also provides important advantages for emerging economies, such as the transfer of technology, management, and organization applications. In their location decisions, foreign companies tend to gravitate toward countries that would provide them with various advantages. The factors that have an effect on FDI decisions are widely researched in the literature. Characteristics of host countries, such as the presence of domestic demand, proximity to markets, and costs, are heavily researched. However, the number of studies on the cultural identities of countries is quite limited.

The primary characteristic among the cultural characteristics that affect location decisions is the general level of trust between the individuals in the host country. Each commercial transaction is based on the mutual trust between parties. The lack of trust between parties requires that various measures be taken for the accomplishment of the commercial transaction. Each measure taken will increase the transaction costs. In FDIs, it is difficult for the home country to know and assess to the full extent of all legislations and procedures in the host countries. In addition to the knowledge of legal processes, it is necessary to assess the quality of functioning of the legal processes as well. In other words, the presence of laws does not necessarily mean that the enforcement of law is satisfactory.

At this point, the importance of interpersonal trust for commercial relationships becomes more obvious. The level of interpersonal trust results from the mutual experiences of individuals in the society. A high general level of trust in a given society indicates that the parties are unlikely to act contrary to expectations. In societies where the general level of trust is low, the problems arising out of the information asymmetry between parties are more serious. Information asymmetry exists in any society, irrespective of whether they have low or high levels of trust. However, societies with a low level of trust are more likely to suffer from problems arising from information asymmetry. Such an environment increases transaction costs, and it also makes it more difficult to carry out management/organization activities and to make predictions and long-term plans. Consequently, a low general level of trust in a society puts that country at a disadvantage in relation to the location decisions for FDI. The model that was set up for 39 emerging economies also shows that a low level of interpersonal trust poses a serious disadvantage in attracting FDIs.

REFERENCES

Ang, J., Cheng, Y., & Wu, C. (2009). Social capital, cultural biases, and foreign investment in innovation: Evidence from China. Florida State University, Working Paper.

Anyanwu, J. C. (2012). Why Does Foreign Direct Investment Go Where It Goes?: New Evidence From African Countries. *Annals of Economics and Finance*, *13*(2), 425–462.

Arellano, M., & Bond, S. (1991). Some tests of specification for panel data: Monte Carlo evidence and an application to employment equations. *The Review of Economic Studies*, *58*(2), 277–297. doi:10.2307/2297968

Arrow, K. J. (1972). Gifts and exchanges. *Philosophy & Public Affairs*, 1(4), 343–362.

Asiedu, E. (2002). On the determinants of foreign direct investment to developing countries: Is Africa different? *World Development*, *30*(1), 107–119. doi:10.1016/S0305-750X(01)00100-0

Asiedu, E. (2004). The determinants of employment of affiliates of US multinational enterprises in Africa. *Development Policy Review*, *22*(4), 371–379. doi:10.1111/j.1467-7679.2004.00255.x

Asiedu, E. (2006). Foreign direct investment in Africa: The role of natural resources, market size, government policy, institutions and political instability. *World Economy*, *29*(1), 63–77. doi:10.1111/j.1467-9701.2006.00758.x

Asiedu, E., & Lien, D. (2004). Capital controls and foreign direct investment. *World Development*, *32*(3), 479–490. doi:10.1016/j.worlddev.2003.06.016

Awan, M. Z., Khan, B., & Uz Zaman, K. (2011). Economic determinants of foreign direct investment (FDI) in commodity producing sector: A case study of Pakistan. *African Journal of Business Management*, *5*(2), 537–545.

Baek, K., & Qian, X. (2011). An analysis on political risks and the flow of foreign direct investment in developing and industrialized economies. *Economics, management, and financial markets, 6*(4), 60-91.

Banfield, E. C. (1958). The moral basis of a backward society. *New York. Glencol, 3*, 4.

Bhardwaj, A., Dietz, J., & Beamish, P. W. (2007). Host country cultural influences on foreign direct investment. *Management International Review, 47*(1), 29–50. doi:10.1007/s11575-007-0003-7

Bottazzi, L., Da Rin, M., Hellmann, T., & Advantage, R. R. C. (2007). The Importance of Trust for Investment: Evidence from Venture Capital (Working Papers 325). IGIER (Innocenzo Gasparini Institute for Economic Research), Bocconi University.

Busse, M., & Hefeker, C. (2007). Political risk, institutions and foreign direct investment. *European Journal of Political Economy, 23*(2), 397–415. doi:10.1016/j.ejpoleco.2006.02.003

Butter, F. A., & Mosch, R. H. (2003). Trade, Trust and Transaction Cost (No. 03-082/3). Tinbergen Institute Discussion Paper.

Davidson, W. H. (1980). The location of foreign direct investment activity: Country characteristics and experience effects. *Journal of International Business Studies, 11*(2), 9–22. doi:10.1057/palgrave.jibs.8490602

Dearmon, J., & Grier, K. (2009). Trust and development. *Journal of Economic Behavior & Organization, 71*(2), 210–220. doi:10.1016/j.jebo.2009.02.011

Delios, A., & Henisz, W. J. (2003). Political hazards, experience, and sequential entry strategies: The international expansion of Japanese firms, 1980–1998. *Strategic Management Journal, 24*(11), 1153–1164. doi:10.1002/smj.355

Demirhan, E., & Masca, M. (2008). Determinants of foreign direct investment flows to developing countries: a cross-sectional analysis. *Prague economic papers, 4*(2008), 356-369.

Durlauf, S., & Fafchamps, M. (2005). Social capital. In P. Aghion & S. Durlauf (Eds.), *Handbook of Economic Growth* (1st ed., Vol. 1, pp. 1639–1699). Elsevier.

Dutta, N., & Osei-Yeboah, K. (2013). A new dimension to the relationship between foreign direct investment and human capital: The role of political and civil rights. *Journal of International Development, 25*(2), 160–179. doi:10.1002/jid.1739

Edwards, S. (1992). *Capital flows, foreign direct investment, and debt-equity swaps in developing countries (No. w3497).* National Bureau of Economic Research.

Fukuyama, F. (1995). *Trust: The social virtues and the creation of prosperity (No. D10 301 c. 1/c. 2).* New York: Free press.

Gedik, M. A. (2013). Determinants of Foreign Direct Investment for OECD Countries: Evidence from Dynamic Panel Data Analysis. *British Journal of Economics, Finance and Management Sciences, 7*(2), 119–140.

Gichamo, T. Z. (2012). Determinants of Foreign Direct Investment Inflows to Sub-Saharan Africa: a panel data analysis.

Guiso, L., Sapienza, P., & Zingales, L. (2004). *Cultural biases in economic exchange (No. w11005)*. National Bureau of Economic Research. doi:10.3386/w11005

Habib, M., & Zurawicki, L. (2002). Corruption and foreign direct investment. *Journal of International Business Studies*, *33*(2), 291–307. doi:10.1057/palgrave.jibs.8491017

Hayakawa, K., Kimura, F., & Lee, H. H. (2013). How does country risk matter for foreign direct investment? *The Developing Economies*, *51*(1), 60–78. doi:10.1111/deve.12002

Janicki, H. P., & Wunnava, P. V. (2004). Determinants of foreign direct investment: Empirical evidence from EU accession candidates. *Applied Economics*, *36*(5), 505–509. doi:10.1080/0003684041000l682214

Jaspersen, F. Z., Aylward, A. H., & Knox, A. D. (2000). The effects of risk on private investment: Africa compared with other developing areas. *Investment and risk in Africa*, 71-95.

Kariuki, C. (2015)... *The Determinants of Foreign Direct Investment in the African Union*, *3*(3), 346–351.

Kim, J., & Park, J. (2013). Foreign Direct Investment and Country-Specific Human Capital. *Economic Inquiry*, *51*(1), 198–210. doi:10.1111/j.1465-7295.2012.00478.x

Kok, R., & Ersoy, B. A. (2009). Analyses of FDI determinants in developing countries. *International Journal of Social Economics*, *36*(1/2), 105–123. doi:10.1108/03068290910921226

Kolstad, I., & Villanger, E. (2004). *How does social development affect FDI and domestic investment? Chr.* Michelsen Institute.

Kukharsky, B. (2012). *Trust and Foreign Direct Investment: An Empirical Analysis* (No. 127). BGPE Discussion Paper.

La Porta, R. (1997). Trust in Large Organizations. *The American Economic Review*, *87*(2), 333–338.

Lewandowski, J. P. (1997). Risk and foreign direct investment in emerging economies: Lessons from the former Soviet Union. *Middle States Geographer*, *30*, 97–104.

Loree, D. W., & Guisinger, S. E. (1995). Policy and non-policy determinants of US equity foreign direct investment. *Journal of International Business Studies*, *26*(2), 281–299. doi:10.1057/palgrave.jibs.8490174

Majocchi, A., & Presutti, M. (2009). Industrial clusters, entrepreneurial culture and the social environment: The effects on FDI distribution. *International Business Review*, *18*(1), 76–88. doi:10.1016/j.ibusrev.2008.12.001

Mhlanga, N., Blalock, G., & Christy, R. (2010). Understanding foreign direct investment in the southern African development community: An analysis based on project-level data. *Agricultural Economics*, *41*(3-4), 337–347. doi:10.1111/j.1574-0862.2010.00440.x

Naudé, W. A., & Krugell, W. F. (2007). Investigating geography and institutions as determinants of foreign direct investment in Africa using panel data. *Applied Economics*, *39*(10), 1223–1233. doi:10.1080/00036840600567686

Noorbakhsh, F., Paloni, A., & Youssef, A. (2001). Human capital and FDI inflows to developing countries: New empirical evidence. *World Development*, *29*(9), 1593–1610. doi:10.1016/S0305-750X(01)00054-7

Pedersen, K., Svendsen, G. L., & Svendsen, G. T. (2013). Multinational Enterprises and Social Capital as Location Factor: A Review. *Business and Management Research*, *2*(3), 81–89. doi:10.5430/bmr.v2n3p81

Sargan, J. D. (1958). The estimation of economic relationships using instrumental variables. *Econometrica*, *26*(3), 393–415. doi:10.2307/1907619

Schneider, F., & Frey, B. S. (1985). Economic and political determinants of foreign direct investment. *World Development*, *13*(2), 161–175. doi:10.1016/0305-750X(85)90002-6

Tang, L. (2012). The direction of cultural distance on FDI: Attractiveness or incongruity? *Cross Cultural Management: An International Journal*, *19*(2), 233–256. doi:10.1108/13527601211219919

Vijayakumar, N., Perumal, S., & Rao, K. C. (2010). Determinants of FDI in BRICS Countries: A panel analysis. *International Journal of Business Science and Applied Management*, *5*(3), 1–13.

Zhao, H., & Kim, S. H. (2011). An exploratory examination of the social capital and FDI linkage and the moderating role of regulatory quality: A cross-country study. *Thunderbird International Business Review*, *53*(5), 629–646. doi:10.1002/tie.20439

ENDNOTES

1 The definitions and sources of the variables are listed in the appendix, Table 3.

2 The list of 39 emerging market countries is given in the appendix, Table 4.

3 Note that real per capita GDP is used in logarithmic form.

APPENDIX

Table 3. Emerging Market Countries

Code	Country	Code	Country
ARE	United Arab Emirates	LVA	Latvia
ARG	Argentina	MAR	Morocco
BGD	Bangladesh	MEX	Mexico
BGR	Bulgaria	MYS	Malaysia
BHR	Bahrain	NGA	Nigeria
BRA	Brazil	PAK	Pakistan
CHL	Chile	PER	Peru
CHN	China	PHL	Philippines
COL	Colombia	POL	Poland
CZE	Czech Republic	QAT	Qatar
EGY	Egypt, Arab Republic	ROU	Romania
EST	Estonia	RUS	Russia
GRC	Greece	SVN	Slovenia
HUN	Hungary	THA	Thailand
IDN	Indonesia	TUR	Turkey
IND	India	UKR	Ukraine
IRN	Iran, Islamic Republic	VEN	Venezuela
ISR	Israel	VNM	Vietnam
KOR	Korea, Republic	ZAF	Republic of South Africa
LTU	Lithuania		

Table 4. Emerging Market Countries

Variables	Definition	Source
Definition of the Variables		
FDI	Percentage of Inward FDI to GDP	The United Nations Conference on Trade and Development (UNCTAD)
Explanatory Variable		
Trust	Percentage of respondents answering "can be trusted" to the Gallup World Poll question, "Generally speaking, would you say that most people can be trusted or that you have to be careful in dealing with people?	Galup World Poll
Control Variables		
Inflation	Inflation rates of consumer prices (2005=100)	International Financial Statistics CD-Rom
GDP per capita	Real GDP per capita in US Dollar (2005=100)	International Financial Statistics CD-Rom
Gross fixed capital formation	Percentage of Gross fixed capital formation to GDP	International Financial Statistics CD-Rom
Investment profile	Investment profile index	International Country Risk Guide
Enrolment rates	Secondary school enrolment rates	UNESCO
Taxes	Corporate tax rates	World Tax Database
Openness	Percentage of import and export to GDP	International Financial Statistics CD-Rom

Chapter 14
An Integrated Model of Perceived Risk and Risk-Reducing Strategies in the Tunisian Stock Market:
Risk-Behavior Model

Azza Béjaoui
University of Sousse, Tunisia

Adel Karaa
College of Business Administration, University of Hail, Saudi Arabia

ABSTRACT

This chapter examines the antecedents and consequences of the perceived risk of investors towards the Tunisian stock market. A questionnaire was developed and distributed to 411 individual investors chosen by 24 brokerage firms. Using the structural equation model, we operationalize the risk following the psychometric paradigm according to subjective variables (i.e. familiarity and controllability). Results prove that controllability is a significant factor in the formation of perceived risk. We also show that several factors related to the investor, the listed companies and to the stock market can influence the perceived risk by the investor towards the Tunisian stock market. Similarly, we find that perceived risk leads to intensive information search, good performance and a strong reinvestment intention. These results attest the importance of the risk perception in the decision-making process.

INTRODUCTION

Risk is a very important topic of investing since apprehending what it is and how it is measured is crucial for developing an investing strategy (Ricciardi, 2004). For this end, many researchers continue to look for a more thorough understanding of what constitutes risk and how it should be measured and priced in financial markets. In spite of previous and subsequent researchers, there is no widely accepted definition in the extent literature. Earlier studies such as Lopes (1981) and March and Shapira (1987) consider risk as the product of the consequences of an event and it probability of occurrence whereas other studies

DOI: 10.4018/978-1-4666-9864-2.ch014

like Kaplan and Garrich (1981) define risk as the sum of danger and opportunity. By emphasizing on a 'negative connotation', some researchers prefer to define risk as virtually expected loss after a decision making (Loppe, 1988), or everything that leads to involuntarily harm (Cuny and Gaillard, 2003), or the possibility of harm, loss, destruction or an undesirable event (Ricciardi, 2004). The lack of consensus about straightforward definition of risk is not without impact at the empirical level. Indeed, academic research in finance distinguishes two different approaches of risk namely: traditional and behavioral approaches. The traditional approach of risk is based on the Efficient Markets Hypothesis and the rationality of investors. Under these assumptions, investors process information instantaneously and the prices entirely reflect all existing information (Fama, 1965a and 1965b). Besides, investors make financial decisions based on their own approach toward risk and to the actual degree of risk (Ricciardi, 2004). In this regard, Garland (2002) pinpoints that persons focus on objective risk "they have in minds that have been confirmed scientifically utilizing the obtainable knowledge and data". Indeed, objective risk is quantitative which relies on past occurrences of an event and incorporates into numerical assessments to estimate risk. So, the traditional approach of risk is based on quantitative (or objectives) measures (e.g. beta, standard deviation, semivariance, skewness, and kurtosis) which rely on a number of observations (i.e. long-term data over a specific time period) and are generally computed from sophistically statistical methods.

On the other hand, the behavioral approach of risk is based on the behavioral finance theory which is "an interdisciplinary field, developing theoretical basis, know-how, and research from the diverse making sciences of psychology and behavioral economics" (Ricciardi, 2008). Individuals make irrational decisions due to their limitations of capacity to process the information (Simon, 1986) and are influenced by heuristics, cognitive factors and affective issues. Moreover, behavioral finance scholars claim that the objective aspect of risk within decision-making and an individual's understanding of it, known as subjective (or perceived risk), are not necessarily the same (Ricciardi, 2004). So, the behavioral approach of risk attempts to pay more attention to a person and explore risk, not at the aggregate or market level, but at the individual level. In this respect, McDonald and Stehle (1975) pinpoint that "perceived risk is an exante measure which may be based on past returns, fundamental analysis, present hunches and all other information that portfolio managers and analysts believe to be germane". So, the behavioral approach of risk develops subjective measures of risk based on methods of experimental, exploratory, or survey research or psychometric paradigm.

Interestingly, the present research attempts to contribute to this line of research through an investigation of the risk perception of individual investors in the Tunisian stock market. In this respect, we study the risk perceived by investors toward the stock market by proposing a risk-behavior model which includes the antecedents and consequences of perceived risk. In the marketing literature, the perceived risk consists of two distinct components, namely: uncertainty and importance (or significance) of consequences (Mallet, 2000; Dandouau, 2000; Verhage et al., 1990; Mitchell and Greatorex, 1989) causing the information search and reduction of the amount at stake (risk-reducing strategies) in order to decrease risk (Cho and Lee 2006; Taylor, 1974; Cox, 1967a). For instance, Taylor (1974) claims that "uncertainty about the outcome can be reduced by acquiring and "handling" information. Uncertainty about the consequences can be dealt with by reducing the consequences through reducing the amount at stake or putting off the choice". So, we examine the information search and reduction of amount at stake as two different modes of behavioral responses to attenuate the perceived risk of individual investors. Also, we investigate the effect of risk perception on the investment behavior through the investment performance and the reinvestment intention.

Aside from consequences, we examine factors related to listed companies (the perceived quality of disclosed information and the satisfaction with yield reallocation), the investor (investor's individual profile) and the stock market (the information asymmetry and social influences) as key antecedents of the perceived risk.

From empirical standpoint, sets of questions were identified as items in questionnaire (distributed to individual investors). In particular, we use the two-dimension psychometric model of Slovic (1987) (i.e. familiarity and controllability) as a measure of risk perceptions for Tunisian individual investors.

The outline of the paper is as follows. Section 1 exhibits the model development as well as the empirical literature of risk perception. In section 2, we expose the data set used in this research. The different estimation results are provided in section 3. Discussion is reported in section 4.

SECTION 1. RISK-BEHAVIOR MODEL DEVELOPMENT

The following section reports the empirical literature of risk perception in the investment context and discusses conceptual grounds for the different constructs and relationships described in our model.

1.1. Risk Perception in the Investment Context: Some Empirical Evidence

The risk perception can be defined as an assessment of risk in an uncertain investment environment (Mahmood et al., 2011) which may or may not actually prove because of many factors (Douglas and Wildavstry, 1982). Traditionally, Gooding (1975) attempted to study the risk perception in the investment context. By testing if investors perceive difference among nine stocks in terms of risk and return. To do this, a survey was mailed to randomly selected participants (professors, portfolio managers and individual investors) based on their investment related to experience and education. Results show that "while investor groups' average stock perceptions are highly related to relevant risk and return measures, significant differences may exist between portfolio managers and nonprofessional investors' average multidimensional perceptions". Subsequently, many studies attempt to examine and explain the differences of risk perception between investors (e.g. Yates and Firer, 1997 ; Gendron and Genest, 1993 ; Capstaff, 1989 ; Mear and Firth, 1988 ; Farrelly et al., 1984, 1985, 1987 ; Firer et al., 1986). For example, Farrelly et al. (1985) investigate the relationship between perceived risk and the accounting based proxies for risk identified by Beaver et al. (1970). Results prove that leverage, variability in earnings and current ratio explained 79% of the variation in average perceived risk. Farrelly et al. (1987) try to identify the accounting variables which predict risk classes as defined by investors' risk ratings. Results display that the debt ratio has a positive relationship with risk ratings whereas profit margin, return on equity, times interest earned, book value and current ratio have a negative relationship with risk perceptions.

Firer et al. (1986) attempt to study the risk perception of individual and institutional investors in the Johannesbourg stock exchange. By means of questionnaires, they show no significant differences in the risk perception between the two sets of investors. Firer et al. (1986) also display that individual's risk perceptions are correlated with other measures of risk. Moreover, Mear and Firth (1988) show that six accounting variables (e.g. liquidity ratio, industry concentration, profitability) explain approximately 93% of the variation in the mean risk perceptions by developing a regression model. Results show that earning variability, total risk, four year price performance and familiarity with the firm explain the risk perceptions of financial analysts. In particular, knowledge and familiarity with stocks are factors that influence the risk perception. This finding was confirmed by Yates and Firer (1997). Besides, Gendron and Genest (1993) examine the impact of socioeconomic and institutional factors on the risk perception of portfolio managers. They display the importance of some factors (e.g. management quality) in the risk perception. Recently, Veld and Veld-Mercoulova (2008) study the risk perceptions of individual investors by asking experimental questions to 2226 members of a consumer panel. Results prove that most investors implicitly use more than one risk measure to assess the market risk. Vlaev et al. (2009) pinpoint the influence of some factors on the risk perception of investors.

Another studies point out the importance of psychological factors in the formation of the risk perception and investment decisions (e.g. MacGregor et al., 2000 ; MacGregor and Slovic, 1999 ; Olsen, 1997 ; Slovic, 1983). For example, MacGregor et al. (2000) attest that imagery and affect influence the risk perception of investors. Olsen (1997) show that four risk features which investors assign to their perceptions of risk are the concern for a large loss, the feeling of control, the potential for a below-target return and a perceived degree of knowledge. Other contextual factors can influence the risk perception of investors (MacGregor et Slovic, 1999).

Mahmood et al. (2011), Cho and Lee (2006) and Wang et al. (2006), among others, prefer to study the risk perception of investors by proposing a conceptual model in order to highlight this "complex psychological process" (Yates and Firer, 1997). Indeed, Mahmood et al. (2011) develop a psychological based investment model which includes past investment experience of investors, variations in regulatory policies, information asymmetry, sensational attitude, marital status and gender. These antecedents affect the reinvestment intentions of investors and their return propensity and risk perception. Moreover, Wang et al. (2006) develop a risk perception centered model for psychological mechanism of investment behavior. The proposed model encompasses factors (variations in policies related to stock market, information asymmetry, satisfaction with information dissemination by listed company and satisfaction with yield reallocation by listed company) which influence the investment behavior of Chinese individual investors (investment performance, reinvestment intention and investment satisfaction) via the risk perception toward the stock market. To measure the risk perception of investors, Wang et al. (2006) use the two-dimension psychometric model of Slovic (1987). By using a 42-item questionnaire distributed to 1547 investors, results display a speculative orientation and a low level of risk perception among investors. On the other hand, Cho and Lee (2006) investigate the role of perceived risk in consumers' adoption of risk-reducing strategies in the context of household investment decisions. Results display that higher self-efficacy, greater wealth position and risk-taking propensity lower an individual's perceived risk for investing in the stock market. Cho and Lee (2006) also find that perceived risk increases the amount of information search and transaction frequency whereas it reduces the proportion of assets invested in the stock market.

1.2. Conceptual Framework

The model investigated in this study is depicted in figure 1. The proposed model encompasses the antecedents and consequences of the perceived risk when investing in the stock market.

The model (figure 1) is based on the following propositions: (1) The investor's individual profile (factor related to investor), the perceived quality of disclosed information and satisfaction with yield reallocation by listed company (two factors related to company) and the information asymmetry (factor related to stock market) influence the investor's risk perception; (2) The risk perception affects the

Figure 1. Conceptual Model of Antecedents and Consequences of Perceived Risk

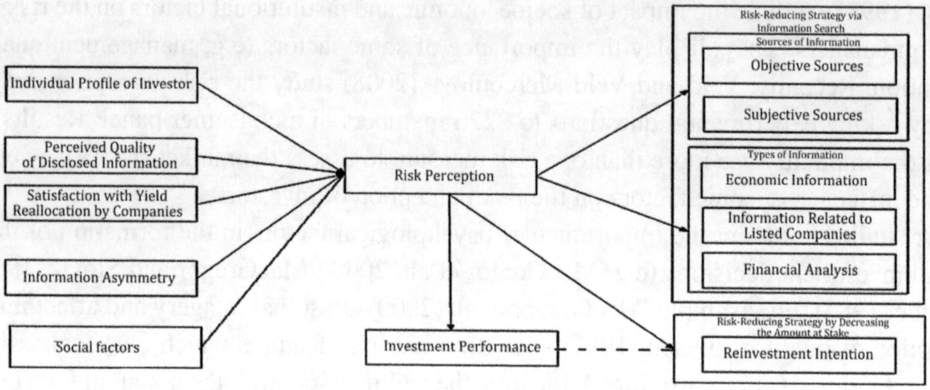

behavior intended to manage uncertainty and significance of consequences; (3) The risk perceived by the investor has an impact on his investment performance.

As reported in figure 1, the proposed model rests on the following propositions: (1) The investor's individual profile (factor related to investor), the perceived quality of disclosed information and satisfaction with yield reallocation by listed companies (two factors related to company) and the information asymmetry and social influences (factors related to stock market) influence the investor's risk perception; (2) The risk perception affects the behavior intended to manage uncertainty and significance of consequences; (3) The investment performance plays a mediating role in affecting risk perception's impact on reinvestment intention.

1.2.1. Definitions of Perceived Risk

Despite of the abundance of research studies on risk perception, it is still difficult to pinpoint a straightforward definition of perceived risk. To illustrate this, Mallet (2001) reveals that "*the vagueness which characterizes the concept of perceived risk stands out as well at the level of the proposed definitions as at the level of its various facets*". Besides, Brunel (2002) reports that "*if there is no agreement around the definition of the perceived risk, there does not exist either of consensus relating to nature even contents of the latter*". Nevertheless, some attempts to define the perceived risk exist in the literature. Indeed, Bauer (1960) introduces the perceived risk by indicating that "consumer behavior involves risk in the sense that any action of a consumer will produce consequences which he cannot anticipate with anything approximating certainty, and some of which at the least are likely to be unpleasant". So, the perceived risk involves two components: the uncertainty and the negative consequences (losses). As matter of fact, Cox and Rich (1964) assert that perceived risk is "a function of two main factors, namely the amount at stake in the purchase decision, and the individual's feeling of subjective certainty that he/she will "win" or "lose" all or some of the amount at stake". As reported by Kogan and Wallach (1964), the perceived risk includes "[…] two somewhat different facets: a "chance" aspect where the focus is on probability: and a "danger" aspect where the emphasis is on severity of negative consequences". By emphasizing on the first component, Yates and Stone (1992) point out that there is no risk if there is no uncertainty. More explicitly, a decision situation is so-called risky when a person is uncertain about consequences of his choices (Cox, 1967a). Such a situation is likely on the one hand when possible outcomes generated by a decision vary considerably (Libby and Fishburn, 1977) and on the other hand, obtaining the desired results is strongly affected by chance. The degree of such uncertainty is judged differently from one person to another (i.e. perceived risk) (Cho and Lee, 2006). So, if the immanent uncertainty of a decision situation corresponds to objective risk, then perceived risk would be a subjective and biased evaluation of this objective risk encouraging afterward a decision-maker to choose a particular behavior (Dowling and Staelin, 1994).

Perceived risk also has a second component: significance of consequences. According to Dandouau (2000), uncertainty is *"a necessary but not sufficient condition, in order to have risk perception. Perceive uncertainty without buyer having to bear any consequences does not lead to represent his choice problem in terms of perceived risk*". The consequences relate to how the financial losses related to negative consequences are harmful (Mitchell, 1999). Cox (1967a) indicates that potential losses include the unachieved goals, loss incurred in the purchase (e.g. money and time), the penalties imposed on the person by his environment and other hazards associated with the purchase. In particular, if this loss affects significantly their financial situations, then people will tend to perceive such a risky decision situation.

Sitkin and Pablo (1992) define risk perception as a decision maker's assessment of the risk inherent in a situation. In this regard, Sitkin and Weingart (1995) refer perceived risk to "an individual's assessment of how risky a situation is in terms of probabilistic estimates of the degree of situational uncertainty, how controllable that uncertainty is, and confidence in those estimates". According to Ricciardi (2004), perceived risk is a person's opinion of the likelihood of risk related to engaging in as specific activity. Perceived risk seems to be an individual's biased assessment of a risky situation and its assessment is dependent on one's psychological and situational features.

1.2.2. Antecedents of Perceived Risk

Slovic (1988) reports that many factors that may influence the person's risk perception. Indeed, "several factors influence it, but some of the models suggested for risk perception have failed to explain more than a small fraction of it" (Sjöberg, 2000). In marketing research, these factors can be classified according to belonging to the characteristics of the individual, the product and the situation (e.g. Mallet, 2004; Volle, 1995). We attempt to identify factors influencing risk perception in the investment context as belonging to the investor, the listed company and the stock market.

1.2.2.1. Antecedent Related to Investor

Among factors that influence risk perceived by investor is his individual profile. This profile can be defined in terms of two personality traits namely: self-confidence and optimism. According to Ricciardi and Simon (2000), the self-confidence can be depicted as "the belief in oneself and one's abilities with full conviction". Wright (1975) considers self-confidence as the individual's ability to think after observations over time, in order to understand several problems of everyday life. Self-confident individuals perceive themselves as able to manage and cope with inherent risk of investing in the stock market. So, the self-confidence can influence the way the investors perceive risk towards the stock market. Optimism is defined as "the overestimation of one's chances or one's ability" (Page, 2009). According to Weinstein (1980), individuals have unrealistic views of their own abilities. Many studies attest its existence in students' behavior (Grimes, 2002), professionals' behavior (Olsen, 1997), managers' behavior (Malmendier and Tate, 2005, Cooper et al., 1988; Larwood and Whittaker, 1977) and investors' behavior

(Barber and Odean, 2001, Gervais and Odean, 2001; Bernatzi and al., 1999). This personality trait may affect the risk perceived by a person. This was confirmed by Roy and Tvszka (2005) who argue that "a robust finding on risk perception is that most people tend to be optimistic in evaluating their own future. That is, comparing to objective criteria, people assign too high probabilities to their attainments of desired outcomes". Kouabenan et al. (2006) report that optimism is an obstacle to assessing risk in the extent where people feel they are less exposed to risk than others. Moreover, Kouabenan et al. (2006) point out that "this perception is underpinned; it seems, by some overestimation of his personal ability to cope with risks involved and to perception rather poor capabilities of others to manage them". Thus, optimistic people tend to perceive risk level lower than pessimists in the investment context. Therefore, we posit the following hypothesis:

H1: The higher the optimism and self-confidence of investor the lower the perceived level of risk toward the stock market

1.2.2.2. Antecedents Related to Listed Company

A. Perceived Quality of Disclosed Information by Listed Company

The quality of information transmitted to the stock market play crucial role in the financial theory. Indeed, Rogers (2008) indicates that "well-functioning capital markets rely on high quality disclosure". According to Djongoue (2007), it is deemed relevant when it offers the opportunity to its users to evaluate all events in a correct manner (past, present and future). In this regard, Boisselier and Mekaoui (2005) reveal that the choice of disclosure strategy is an important constraint which a company has to deal with in the response of the stock market's expectations. Therefore, the quality of information delivered to stock market is the only guarantee to satisfy investors. Moreover, Declerck and Martinez (2004) indicate that "the information disclosure aims to better developing company by improving perception of investors and other market participants". Gao (2008) asserts that information disclosure influences the investor's perception. As a matter of fact, he reports that "while disclosure reduces the risk of per unit investment, it could increase the total investment."

Unlike the previous studies which explore the quantitative aspect of the information reporting, we focus on the impact of the disclosed information's perceived quality on the investor's risk perception. The perceived quality of disclosed information can be defined as the individual judgment experienced by the investor toward the information communicated by the listed company. In other words, it could indicate the level of information's quality as it was perceived, in a subjective way, by investor. Perceiving good quality of disclosed information leads to a lower level of risk perceived toward the stock market. Moreover, Wang et al. (2006) specify that "good quality of information disclosure (e.g. transparency, timely release, integration and authenticity) could reduce investors' risk perception". We thus formulate the following hypothesis:

H2.1: The higher the perceived quality of disclosed information by listed companies the lower the perceived level of risk toward the stock market.

B. Satisfaction with Yield Reallocation by Listed Companies

Satisfaction with yield reallocation by listed company is an antecedent of perceived risk related the features of listed companies. Investors can be concerned with the manner in which listed companies reallocate the profits from their activities. Thus, the choice of particular strategy in terms of reallocation of profits inevitably determines the relationship between the company and the investor. In fact, we can define satisfaction with yield reallocation as judgment experienced by an investor with respect to the choice of company's reallocation of profits. Given the importance of this element for market participants, satisfaction with yield reallocation by listed companies could exert significant influence on their risk perception. People satisfied with yield reallocation by listed companies perceive lower level of investment risk compared to persons who are less satisfied, as stated in the following hypothesis:

H2.2: The higher the satisfaction with yield reallocation by listed companies the lower is the perceived level of risk toward the stock market.

1.2.2.3. Antecedents Related to the Investment Context

In marketing research, many studies show that antecedents related to purchase situation may affect individual's risk perception (Mallet, 2004; Dowling and Staelin, 1994; Lumpkin and Dunn, 1990; Dash et al., 1976). For example, Mallet (2004) reveals that "*purchase situation in which is consumer influences on risk he perceives*". Besides, many psychological studies display that risk perception can be highly influenced by the context in which individuals find themselves when making their decisions (e.g. Cohen et al., 2007).

A. Information Asymmetry

The stock market (i.e. investment situation) can influence the risk perceived by the investor. Specially, information asymmetry is retained as an explanatory factor of risk perception. The information asymmetry refers to a situation where investors in stock market do not all have the same information; some investors are more informed than others. Liao et al. (2010) argue that information asymmetry refers to a situation where financial market participants have a set of unequal information. More explicitly, Chan et al. (2008) indicate that it exists when groups of investors hold different information; i.e. informed investors have private information while the uninformed investors have only publicly available information. Sveral studies investigated the information asymmetry between investors has been studied (e.g. Brown and Hillegeist, 2007; Chen, 2003; Admati and Pfleiderer, 1988, Kyle, 1985; Grossman, 1976). For example, Cheng (2003) reveals that information asymmetry is a salient feature of information on China's stock markets. Okpara (2010) indicates that "the level of information asymmetry can be characterized by the risk of trading with a privately informed investor". Thus, the less the investors share the same information, the more they perceive a high level of risk toward the stock market. Therefore, we posit the following hypothesis:

H3.1: The greater the information asymmetry in the stock market, the lower the perceived level of risk toward the stock market.

B. Social Influences

The interpersonal relationships play generally an important role in a decision-making situation. Indeed, many researchers report that several social factors influence the risk perception of customers in the purchase situation (e.g. Poumadère, 2000). In the making-decision situation, people often rely on information which they collect from others. Leaders, family, reference groups, among others, can be one source of such influence since, through their knowledge; they can attenuate their risk perception. In the investment context characterized by high uncertainty, persons can reduce the risk perception of investors. Thus, we expect that social factors can influence negatively the perceived risk of investors toward the stock market, as stated in the following hypothesis:

H3.2: The social factors reduce the perceived level of risk toward the stock market.

1.2.3. Consequences of Perceived Risk

According to Ingene and Hughes (1985), the risk perception leads to risk-reduction activities. The perceived risk can be handled by using two different risk-reducing strategies. The first strategy is to diminish uncertainty through information search and the second strategy is to attenuate vulnerability by decreasing the amount at stake.

Besides, a person who invests in the stock market will inevitably seek to make gains. Cognizant of this fact, we attempt to investigate the impact of risk perception on investment behavior.

1.2.3.1. Information Search

The relationship between perceived risk and information search activity was studied by several researchers in marketing (Cho and Lee, 2006; Murray, 1991; Lutz and Reilly, 1973; Sheth and Venkatesan, 1968; Cox, 1967a). For example, Murray (1991) indicates that "in the purchase decision process, search information behavior is motivated in part by perceived risk and consumer's ability to acquire relevant information which purchase uncertainty can be addressed". By attempting to explain this link, Cho and Lee (2006) note that high perceived risk drives individuals into a distressed and anxious state which thereafter incites them to pursue problem solving activities. Thus, they use information search as a problem-resolving strategy in order to mitigate perceived risk (Dowling and Staelin, 1994). Nevertheless, other researchers reject the existence of this link. In particular, Volle (1995) indicates that high risk perception causing more information search is questionable. Gemunden (1985) points out that the half of empirical studies in the risk perception literature rejects positive relationship between perceived risk and information search. Some proposals for explanation were provided by Simon (2000) such as the existence of information costs, a degree of risk perception below a minimum threshold, potential dissonance generated by additional information. According to Cho and Lee (2006), the absence of the relationship between the risk perception and information search is due to decision situations examined in previous studies which characterized by relatively low levels of risk (e.g. products that were bought routinely). That is why the consumer does not seek the information. In contrast, in another decision contexts where the level of risk is relatively high (e.g. investment in stock market), risk perception leads necessarily to important search information.

A. Information Sources

Each investor must bear the risk associated with fluctuating securities prices. So, searching for information is an essential activity in order to make the investment decisions (Lin and Lee, 2004). In this regard, Loibl and Hira (2009) pinpoint that risk of financial loss and high costs caused by the revision of a bad investment decision motivate investors to seek information. More precisely, Engel et al. (1993) and Locander and Hermann (1979), among others, indicate that information search would be equivalent to consult information sources. Several typologies of sources exist in the information search literature. For instance, Engel et al. (1993) classify information sources as either an internal source or external source. Internal information search is applied when individuals use information already stored in memory while external search involves gathering information from the environment.

In this study, external information can be categorized as objectives and subjective sources. In the investment context, the objective sources comprise the periodic reports, the websites specializing in information as well as the ratings agencies. The subjective sources include investor's entourage (friends, colleagues ...) and word of mouth. To cope with a high perceived risk, an investor who seeks information prefers to consult not only a particular source but different information sources. As matter of fact, Murray (1991) indicates that "consumers use various amounts and types of information sources to reduce perceived risk, depending on the amount and type of risk". Individuals seek information from a variety of sources when they perceive risk (Cox, 1967a). We thus predict the following hypothesis in our context:

H4: The higher the perceived level of risk toward the stock market the higher the number of information sources consulted.

B. Information Types

Perceived risk determines not only the number of information sources consulted but also the type of information used by the investor. By attempting to reduce uncertainty surrounding the decision situation, consumers will use more diverse types of information (Murray, 1991). The same behavior could be observed as well in the stock market given that information allows to limit uncertainty surrounding the investment situation. So, when facing high perceived risk, investor tends to use more different types of information. The information used by the investor is classified in three categories. The first category includes economic information (e.g. fluctuation of interest rate ...). The second category contains information related to listed companies (e.g. publication of financial statements...). Finally, the last category encompasses the financial analysis provided by engineering consulting firms and brokerage firms. So, we formulate the following hypothesis:

H5: The higher the perceived level of risk toward the stock market the greater the different types of information.

1.2.3.2. Decrease in the Amount at Stake

Risk perception could be reduced by diminishing the amount at stake or vulnerability associated with adverse outcomes. Such behavior is intended to decrease the impact of negative consequences which result from a decision-making. In this study, the key behavior would be to revise the intention of reinvestment on the stock market. In social psychology, the intention is the best predictor of an individual's behavior since person can incorporate independently relevant factors which may influence current behavior (Fishbein and Ajzen, 1975). Among these factors, we could retain risk perception. Individuals perceiving a high level of risk would tend to change their intention to reinvest in the stock market. Like Lehu (2004), we could define reinvestment intention as the disposition of an investor to renew the next time his investment's experience in the stock market. So, we posit the following hypothesis:

H6: The higher the perceived level of risk toward the stock market the lower the perceived level the reinvestment intention in the stock market.

1.2.3.3. Investment Performance

By opting for investment in stock market, each investor tries to make profitable his financial placements. Thayer (2008) indicates that "[…] one universal factor in making an investment decision is the desire to realize a positive return". Swanson and Lin (2005) point out that investment performance is the result of the investor's behavior in stock market. Although the research is limited, performance achieved by an investor in the stock market (i.e. investment performance) can be affected by risk perception. By investigating the psychological mechanisms of risky investment behavior of 1547 individual investors in Chinese stock markets, Wang et al. (2006) show a positive relationship between risk perception and investment performance. Thus, higher risk perception can engender higher investment performance. Perceiving a high level of risk toward stock market leads the investor to carry out a good investment performance. In this study, we attempt to examine if the investment performance play a mediating role in the relationship between risk perception and reinvestment intention, as stated in the following hypothesis:

H7: The investment performance plays a mediating role between the risk perception and the reinvestment intention.

SECTION 2. QUESTIONNAIRE, DATA AND OPERATIONALIZATION OF CONSTRUCTS

2.1. Questionnaire

Questionnaire is the most commonly used tool in survey research. In this study, the questionnaire is distributed to individual investors via the brokers in the Tunisian stock market. The Tunisian stock market was founded in 1969 and was privatized in 1994. It has been an electronic pure order driven market. Orders are placed by investors via 24 brokers. The Tunisian stock market is a pure order driven market without market makers and operates as continuous market for the more actively traded stocks and a call auction (fixing) for the less liquid stocks. In 2015, the Tunis stock exchange lists 78 stocks.

The trading system used by the Tunisian stock market provides a good transparency; in that the five best quotes on the sell and buy sides of the book with the corresponding cumulated volumes are available to investors in real time via computer screens. However, the limit order book is entirely visible to regulatory authorities and brokers. In 1969, the stock market represents 23% of Tunisia GDP and the share of foreigners in stock market capitalization represents 21.92%. To encourage many companies to access on the stock market, a law was promulgated by reducing the rate tax to 20% during 5 years for companies that issues more than 30% of their capital. Finally, the questionnaire was structured around seven themes as follows:

Theme 1: Knowledge about the stock market ;
Theme 2: The individual's behavior when making an investment decision ;
Theme 3: Factors that may change the investor's behavior ;
Theme 4: Information (information search, perceived quality of disclosed information, satisfaction the yield by companies, asymmetric information) ;
Theme 5: Risk perception ;
Theme 6: Investment behavior (performance, satisfaction investment, reinvestment intention) ;
Theme 7: Sociodemographic characteristics.

2.2. Description of Data

The data set used to examine the proposed conceptual framework was collected by using a self-administered questionnaire to the individual investors in the Tunis Stock Exchange. Surveyed individuals were chosen by twenty-four brokers in the Tunisian stock market. About 600 questionnaires were distributed among which 487 were recovered, showing a response rate of 81%. Nevertheless, after counting, seventy questionnaires were removed because of a high number of non-responses. Finally, only 411 questionnaires were considered to be exploitable.

2.2.1. Typology of Respondents

Table 1 reports the key sociodemographic features of individual investors including gender, age, status, employment and income.

Table 1. summarizes the main social sociodemographic characteristics of individual investors. The majority of investors are men who generally are between 40 and 49 years old. Most of investors are married with children and earn between 1000 and 1500 TND.

80.3% of investors were men while women represented only 19.7%. The most important age group in the sample is that of 30-39 years (37%), followed by the 40-49 years (27.5%) and then those aged 20 to 29 (20.2%). Finally, the least important age group is that of more than 60 years (4.1%). Moreover, the majority of respondents are married and has children (54.4%). Besides, the sample includes senior officials (40.1%), middle managers (28.6%), employees (12.1%), freelancers (12.1%), retirees (4.7%), students (2.2%) and unemployed persons (0.2%). Finally, 26.5% of respondents earn between 1500TND and 2000TND while only 5.3% have incomes below 500TND.

2.2.2. Characteristics of Investment Behavior in Stock Market

Table 2. reports the features related to knowledge of investors about the Tunisian stock market and their investment behavior.

Table 2. summarizes the main characteristics of individual investors in terms of investment behavior. In general, the majority of respondents think that have professional knowledge and lost money by investing in a financial asset. Besides, 40.3% of respondents are quite satisfied with their investments and they are quite satisfied with the Tunis Stock Exchange.

Table 1. Description of Sociodemographic Profile of Respondents

Characteristics		Frequency (%)
Gender	Man Woman	80.3 19.7
Age	20-29 years 30-39 years 40-49 years 50-59 years More than 60 years	20.2 37 27.5 11.2 4.1
Statuts	Unmarried Widowed or Divorced Married without Children Married with Children	31 1.2 13.4 54.4
Employment	Employee Freelancer Middle Manager Senior Official Student Unemployed Retiree	12.1 12.1 28.6 40.1 2.2 0.2 4.7
Income	Less than 500 TND Between 500 TND and 750 TND Between 750 TND and 1000 TND Between 1000 TND and 1500 TND Between 1500 TND and 2000 TND Plus de 2000 TND	5.3 8.5 20.8 26.5 16.5 22.5

2.7% of respondents admit that they do not have any knowledge on the investment in stock market, whereas only 37.8% feel they have professional knowledge, although the majority of investors (94.4%) believe that a better knowledge of the investment in the stock market makes the investment more profitable. Also, most respondents (98.8%) indicate that they already invested in the stock market via one or more investment channels (internet, banks, private manager or others) while less than 2% of investors (1.2%) are inexperienced. Moreover, 29% of respondents have experience ranging between 2 and 5 years followed successively by those with more than 10 years (25.8%) and between 5 and 10 years (20.9%) while those having only experience of 1 and 2 years and less than one year are respectively about 14.4% and 10%.

Only 79% of respondents lost money by investing in a financial asset. Besides, the majority of respondents (76.6%) choose one broker, whereas 21% opt to two or several financial institutions when investing in the Tunis Stock Exchange. Meanwhile, 38.8% of the individual investors spend less than 25% of their savings to invest in a financial asset. 31.7% and 15.1% of respondents devote between 25% and 50%, 50% and 75% respectively for investment.

Results also show that almost half of respondents (49.4%) invest in the medium term. 32.3% and 9.5% of people invest respectively in the short and long term. Moreover, we find that 30% of investors keep, on average, a stock between 3 and 6 months, while 26.6% hold it from 6 months to one year. However, 21.2% of respondents hold it less than 3 months while 17.1% preserve it between one year and 3 years.

We also note that 40.3% of respondents are quite satisfied with their investments last year while only 7.5% are not satisfied at all. In addition, 6.8% of respondents are completely satisfied with the investment

Table 2. Description of Sample in terms of Investment Behavior

Characteristics		Frequency (%)
Self-assessment of investment knowledge	No knowledge	2.7
	Basic knowledge	28.3
	Good knowledge	31.2
	Professional knowledge	37.8
Judgment on the impact of knowledge on the profitability of stock market investment	No	5.6
	Yes	94.4
Previous investment	No	1.2
	Yes	98.8
Pecuniary loss by investing in financial asset	No	21
	Yes	79
Number of brokerage firms	None	2.4
	One	76.6
	Two or more	21
Proportion of saving for investment	Less than 25%	38.8
	Between 25% and 50%	31.7
	Between 50% and75%	15.1
	More than 75%	14.4
Investment horizon	No idea	8.8
	Short term	32.3
	Medium term	49.4
	Long term	9.5
Average holding period of a security	Less than 3 months	21.2
	Between 3 months and 6 months	30
	Between 6 months et one year	26.6
	Between one year et 3 years	17.1
	More than 3 years	5.1

Investment experience				
Less than one year	Between 1 and 2 years	Between 2 and 5 years	Between 5 and 10 years	More than 10 years
10%	14.4%	29%	20.9%	25.8%

Investment Satisfaction					
	Not at all satisfied	Unsatisfied	Somewhat satisfied	Satisfied	Quite satisfied
Investment satisfaction last year	7.6%	21.4%	40.3%	24.8%	5.9%
Satisfaction about the Tunisian stock market	5.1%	18.8%	38.6%	30.6%	6.8%

on the Tunis Stock Exchange whereas 5.1% are unsatisfied. The majority of the individuals are quite satisfied with the Tunis Stock Exchange (38.6%).

2.3. Operationalization of Constructs

First, the exploratory factor analysis (or principal component analysis) is used to purify and test the homogeneity of the constructs. Specifically, the principal component analysis is useful because it allows us to identify the dimensions (Churchill, 1979). Evrard et al. (2003) report that the principal component analysis allow "from a theoretical point of view [...] to pass measures to theoretical concepts that can be measured directly; variables are considered to be combinations of a number of unobservable common underlying factors (latent variables)". Then, the confirmatory factor analysis enables us to verify the factor structure extracted from the exploratory phase. In this regard, Roussel et al. (2002) reveal that unlike the exploratory factor analysis with "a posteriori factor structure" confirmatory factor analysis defines "a priori factor structure that we are trying to confirm". According to Gerbing and Hamilton (1996), the confirmatory factor analysis offers the opportunity to test "strictly a model that must be specified a priori". In this study, confirmatory factor analysis was conducted using the structural equation modeling[1].

Exploratory and confirmatory factor analyzes of the different constructs were performed on the data set (N = 411) through SPSS version 17 and AMOS version 18 respectively. The following section reports results of exploratory and confirmatory factor analyzes.

2.3.1. Measures of Perceived Risk's Antecedents

As previously indicated, the antecedents of perceived risk are:

- Individual Profile of Investor
- Perceived Quality of Disclosed Information
- Satisfaction with Yield Reallocation by Companies
- Information Asymmetry
- Social Factors

2.3.1.1. Measure of Individual Profile of Investor's Construct

To operationalize the individual investor profile, we ask each respondent to self-assess personality traits (Table 3). In this respect, we use the semantic differential (i.e. the Osgood scale) which takes the form of a 5-point bipolar scale. The scale is thus encoded from (-2) to (+2) where the neutral point is zero. The two antonyms adjectival words are placed on the two extreme points (e.g. cautious - go-getter).

Table 3. reports the different personality traits. In this table, two antonyms adjectival words are placed on the two extreme points.

Following a first principal component analysis on data (N = 411), the item TRAIT_PERS1 (Cautious /Go-Getter) and the item TRAIT_PERS2 (Intuitive/Cartesian) should be removed given their very poor communalities (0.442 and 0.10 respectively). A second factor analysis with varimax rotation shows that items are related and are therefore factorizable (KMO = 0.500 and Bartlett's sphericity test is significant). Results show hence that the investor's individual profile is a one-dimensional structure. Factor explains

Table 3. List of Items of the Individual Investor Profile's Measure

Items	Investor's Individual Profile
TRAIT_PERS1	Cautious Person/Go-Getter Person
TRAIT_PERS2	Intuitive Person/ Cartesian person
TRAIT_PERS3	Pessimistic Person/ Optimistic Person
TRAIT_PERS4	Skeptical Person / Confident Person

76.971% of the variance of the concept. Reliability of the construct is satisfactory (> 0.5 and Jöreskog's rhô is close to 0.7). Table 4 below summarizes all the results obtained from the exploratory factor analysis.

By performing a principal component analysis of the data (Table 4), we find one-dimensional structure of the concept of Investor's individual profile.

Table 5 reports results of confirmatory factor analysis which allows us to confirm one-dimensional structure of the concept.

By performing a confirmatory component analysis of the data (Table 5), we show the one-dimensional structure of the concept of Investor's individual profile.

Table above includes the standardized (i.e. column 5) and non-standardized (i.e. column 3) loadings related to the items (i.e. column 2) of the factor (i.e. column 1). Results show that the factor loadings are significantly different from zero since all values of t-statistics (or CR) are greater than 1.96 for a significance level of 0.001. These results are then satisfying in order to confirm the factor structure extracted from the exploratory phase.

By checking that all loadings are significantly different from zero, we can a priori ensure the convergent construct validity. The coefficient of convergent validity ($rhô_{vc}$=0.531) shows hence that the average variance extracted for this factor is acceptable.

Table 4. Results of Exploratory Factor Analysis on the Individual Profile's Investor

Investor's Individual Profile					
Items	**Loading**	**Communality**	**MSA**	**Cronbach's Alpha**	**Jöreskog's Rhô**
TRAIT_ PERS3	0.877	0.770	0.500	0.701	0.694
TRAIT_ PERS4	0.877	0.770	0.500		
Eigenvalue	1.539				**KMO = 0.500**
Bartlett's Sphericity Test	$\chi^2 = 135.659 \;\; d.f = 1 \;\; p = 0.000$				
Explained Variance	76.971%				N = 411

Note: *d.f*: degree of freedom.

Table 5: Results of Confirmatory Factor Analysis and Test of Convergent Validity related to the Individual Profile's Investor

Factor	Items	Non Standardized	CR	Standardized	
Investor's Individual Profile	TRAIT_PERS3	0.957	3.521***	0.727	**0.531**
	TRAIT_PERS4	1.000		0.731	

Notes: - *** Signification Level: 0.001 ; - CR: CRITICAL RATIO.

Table 6. List of Items of Perceived Quality of Disclosed Information's Measure

Items	Perceived Quality of Disclosed Information
QUAL_PERC_INF1	Complete information
QUAL_PERC_INF2	Transparent information
QUAL_PERC_INF3	Authentic information
QUAL_PERC_INF4	Real-time information
QUAL_PERC_INF5	Relevant information
QUAL_PERC_INF6	Timely information
QUAL_PERC_INF7	Regular information

2.3.1.2. Measure of Perceived Quality of Disclosed Information's Construct

The perceived quality of disclosed information's construct is created using seven items (Table 6). Investors are asked to assess the degree of (dis)agreement according to a 5-point Likert scale to the following question: "Do you think that the information disclosed by listed companies is…"

Table 6 reports the different items used to measure the concept of the perceived quality of disclosed information.

After conducting an exploratory factor analysis, the item QUAL_PERC_INF7 (i.e. regular information) is removed due to the communality (i.e. 0.466) is less than 0.5. A new factor analysis on the remaining 6 items converges to a one-dimensional structure of the perceived quality of the disclosed information. This structure explains 61.299% of the concept (Table 7). Furthermore, the perceived quality of the disclosed information's construct is deemed reliable (i.e. = 0.872) since the exclusion of any item does not improve the coefficient of internal consistency. The Jöreskog's rhô coefficient exceeds 0.7 confirming consequently the good reliability.

All results in Table 7 allow us to retain the one-dimensional structure of the concept of perceived quality of disclosed information.

Table 7. Results of Exploratory Factor Analysis on Perceived Quality of Disclosed Information

Perceived Quality of Disclosed Information					
Items	**Loading**	**Communality**	**MSA**	**Cronbach's Alpha**	**Jöreskog's Rhô**
QUAL_PERC_INF1	0.794	0.630	0.872	**0.872**	**0.866**
QUAL_PERC_INF2	0.843	0.711	0.834		
QUAL_PERC_INF3	0.802	0.643	0.853		
QUAL_PERC_INF4	0.737	0.543	0.920		
QUAL_PERC_INF5	0.791	0.625	0.855		
QUAL_PERC_INF6	0.725	0.526	0.844		
Eigenvalue	3.678			**KMO = 0.860**	
Bartlett's Sphericity Test					
Explained Variance	**61.299%**			N = 411	

Note: *d.f.* degree of freedom.

Table 8. reports results of confirmatory factor analysis which allows us to confirm one-dimensional structure of the concept.

Results in Table 8 show the one-dimensional structure of the concept of the perceived quality of disclosed information.

All factor loadings are significantly different from zero (i.e. t > 1.96). In addition, the convergent construct validity is good (= 0.522). These results lead us to validate the one-dimensional structure extracted from the principal component factor analysis.

2.3.1.3. Measure of Satisfaction with Yield Reallocation's Construct

Satisfaction with Yield Reallocation was measured by considering five items simultaneously. The satisfaction's degree of investors with reallocated yield (ranging from 'not at all satisfied' to 'very satisfied') was assessed via a 5-point Likert scale. Respondents were asked to answer the question "Are you satisfied with the yield reallocation of listed companies?". Table 9 reports the five items which measure the concept of satisfaction with yield reallocation of listed companies.

Table 9. reports the different items used to measure the concept of the yield reallocation of listed companies.

After the first principal component factor analysis, there was a deletion of two items REAL_YIELD4 (i.e. the yield reallocation as split) and REAL_ YIELD 5 (i.e. the yield reallocation as reinvestment in future projects), since the communality is less than 0.5 (respectively about 0.446 and 0.4). Results from a new factor analysis (Table 10) display that three items are factorisable (KMO = 0.662 and Bartlett's sphericity test is significant). So, we show the one-dimensional structure of satisfaction with yield re-

Table 8. Results of Confirmatory Factor Analysis and Test of Convergent Validity related to the Perceived Quality of Disclosed Information

Factor	Items	Non Standardized	CR	Standardized	
Perceived Quality of Disclosed Information	QUAL_PERC_INF1	1.201	11.123***	0.753	**0.522**
	QUAL_PERC_INF2	1.299	10.496***	0.833	
	QUAL_PERC_INF3	1.277	12.091***	0.780	
	QUAL_PERC_INF4	1.086	12.647***	0.638	
	QUAL_PERC_INF5	1.044	11.860***	0.689	
	QUAL_PERC_INF6	1.000		0.615	

Notes: - *** Signification Level: 0.001 ; - CR: CRITICAL RATIO.

Table 9. List of Items of Satisfaction with Yield Reallocation of Listed Companies' Measure

Items	Satisfaction with Yield Reallocation of Listed Companies
REAL_ YIELD1	Yield Reallocation as Dividend
REAL_ YIELD2	Yield Reallocation as Allocation of Shares
REAL_ YIELD3	Yield Reallocation as Cash Capital Increase
REAL_ YIELD4	Yield Reallocation as Split
REAL_ YIELD5	Yield Reallocation as Reinvestment in Future Projects.

allocation. Furthermore, this factor explains 72.752% of the concept with satisfying reliability (i.e. = 0.810 and = 0.824).

Results in Table 10 display the one-dimensional structure of the concept of satisfaction with yield reallocation by companies.

The confirmatory factor analysis enables us to confirm the one-dimensional structure extracted from the exploratory factor analysis. Results are reported in Table 11.

All results in Table 11 permit us to confirm the one-dimensional structure of the concept of the satisfaction with yield reallocation by companies.

Results show that coefficients are significantly different from zero (i.e. t > 1.96). This reassures us a priori the convergent validity. By computing the coefficient of convergent validity (), we find that the extracted average validity for this factor is good since rhô_{vc} is equal to 0.615. Hence, we can validate the factor structure obtained from the exploratory phase.

2.3.1.4. Measure of Information Asymmetry

Asymmetric information plays critical role in the finance theory. However, Hautcoeur (1994) reports that there is a paucity of attempts to directly measure it. This is attributed to the degree of information asymmetry which is not directly observable (Liao et al., 2010). Therefore, researchers most often use variable proxies (Clarcke and Shastri, 2000).

There are three main categories of information asymmetry's measures, namely: measures based on analysts' forecasts (Brennan and Subrahmanyam, 1995; Elton et al., 1984; Blackwell and Dubins, 1962),

Table 10. Results of Exploratory Factor Analysis on Satisfaction with Yield Reallocation

Satisfaction with Yield Reallocation by Companies					
Items	**Loading**	**Communality**	**MSA**	**Cronbach's Alpha**	**Jöreskog's Rhô**
REAL_ YIELD1	0.846	0.715	0.671	**0.810**	**0.824**
REAL_ YIELD2	0.908	0.824	0.612		
REAL_ YIELD3	0.802	0.644	0.738		
Eigenvalue	2.183			**KMO = 0.662**	
Bartlett's Sphericity Test					
Explained Variance	**72.752%**			N = 411	

Note: *d.f.* degree of freedom.

Table 11. Results of Confirmatory Factor Analysis and Test of Convergent Validity related to Satisfaction with Yield Reallocation

Factor	**Items**	**Non Standardized**	**CR**	**Standardized**	
Satisfaction with Yield Reallocation by Companies	REAL_YIELD1	1.157	12.649***	0.734	**0.615**
	REAL_ YIELD2	1.398	12.262***	0.940	
	REAL_ YIELD3	1.000		0.651	

Notes: - *** Signification Level: 0.001 ; - CR: CRITICAL RATIO.

measures of investment opportunities (Chung and Charoenwong, 1998; Collins and Kothari, 1989) and measures of market microstructure (Huang and Stoll, 1997; Lin et al., 1995; Choi et al., 1988). In this study, information asymmetry is measured by asking investors to answer the following closed question: "Do you think that the Tunisian stock market is characterized by asymmetric information?" ('no idea'; 'the asymmetry does not exist in the Tunisian stock market'; 'we hear of information asymmetry but it was not supported by evidence'; others). In order to ensure that the question is understood by respondents, information asymmetry is defined in our questionnaire as follows: "The information asymmetry corresponds to the idea that the same information is not shared equally by all agents".

2.3.1.5. Measure of Social Factors

We measure social factors by using six items simultaneously. Social factors were measured by considering five items simultaneously. Each item was assessed via a 5-point Likert scale ('never', 'not at all', 'quite frequently', 'often', 'always'). Table 12 shows the six items measuring social factors.

Table 12. reports the different items used to measure the concept of social factors.

After the first principal component factor analysis, there was a deletion of three items SOCIAL_FACT4 (i.e. a variation of your fortune) and SOCIAL_ FACT3 (i.e. your mood) and SOCIAL_FACT5 (i.e. weather) since the communality is less than 0.5. Results (Table 13) from a new factor analysis prove that three items are factorisable (KMO = 0.662 and Bartlett's sphericity test is significant). So, we show the one-dimensional structure of social factors. Besides, factor explains only 72.752% of the concept with acceptable reliability (i.e. = 0.500 and = 0.500).

Results in Table 13 indicate that we can retain one dimension for the concept of social factors.

The confirmatory factor analysis allows us to confirm the one-dimensional structure obtained from the exploratory factor analysis. Results are reported in Table 14.

Results in Table 14 clearly show the one-dimensional structure of the concept of social factors.

Results show that coefficients are significantly different from zero (i.e. $t > 1.96$), which reassures us a priori the convergent validity. By calculating the coefficient of convergent validity (), we conclude that the extracted average validity for this factor is acceptable since $\hat{rho}_{vc}$ is equal to 0.505. Hence, we can validate the factor structure obtained from the exploratory phase.

Table 12. List of Items of Social Factors' Measure

Items	Social Factors
SOCIAL_ FACT1	Your relatives (children, parents, spouses)
SOCIAL_ FACT2	Your friends and knoweledge
SOCIAL_ FACT3	Your mood
SOCIAL_ FACT4	Avariation of your fortune
SOCIAL_ FACT5	Weather
SOCIAL_ FACT6	An investment advisor

Table 13. Results of Exploratory Factor Analysis on Social Factors

Social Factors					
Items	**Loading**	**Communality**	**MSA**	**Cronbach's Alpha**	**Jöreskog's Rhô**
SOCIAL_FACT1	0.722	0.521	0.571	**0.500**	**0.500**
SOCIAL_FACT2	0.692	0.500	0.582		
SOCIAL_FACT6	0.693	0.500	0.611		
Eigenvalue	1.409			**KMO = 0.585**	
Bartlett's Sphericity Test					
Explained Variance	**46.977%**			N = 411	

Note: *d.f.* degree of freedom.

Table 14. Results of Confirmatory Factor Analysis and Test of Convergent Validity related to Social Factors

Factor	Items	Non Standardized λ	CR	Standardized λ	
Social Factors	SOCIAL_FACT1	1.086	11.349***	0.638	**0.505**
	SOCIAL_FACT2	1.034	11.062***	0.509	
	SOCIAL_FACT6	1.000		0.595	

Notes: - *** Signification Level: 0.001 ; - CR: CRITICAL RATIO.

2.3.2. Measures of Perceived Risk's Consequences

As previously reported, the consequences of perceived risk are:

- The sources of information ;
- The types of information ;
- The reinvestment intention ;
- The investment performance.

2.3.2.1. Measure of Information Sources' Construct

Information sources are measured by using items reported in Table 15. Respondents must assess, using a scale ranging from "not at all important" to "very important", the degree of importance it attaches to the question "Before your investment decisions, you consult ...".

Table 15. reports the different items in order to measure the concept of the information sources.

By performing a principal component factor analysis on the data, no item has been deleted since they all have a high communality. All items are factorisable (KMO = 0.648 and Bartlett's sphericity test is significant). Besides, there are two distinct dimensions namely: Objectives Sources (SOURC_OBJ) and Subjective Sources (SOURC_SUB). This bidimensional structure is used to explain 64.030% of the variance of the concept.

Table 15. List of Items of Information Sources' Measure

Dimensions	Items	Information Sources
OBJECTIVE SOURCES	SOURC_OBJ1	Specialized financial information websites (Tustex ...)
	SOURC_OBJ2	The daily media such as newspapers, television ...
	SOURC_OBJ3	Periodic reporting
	SOURC_OBJ4	Rating agencies
SUBJECTIVE SOURCES	SOURC_SUB1	Word of mouth
	SOURC_SUB2	The environment (circle of friends, colleagues ...)

The reliability of construct's information sources is considered relatively good since the values taken by the Cronbach's alpha and Jöreskog's rhô coefficients exceed 0.7. Table 16 shows all the results already mentioned.

By performing the principal component analysis of the data (Table 16), we show the bidimensional structure of the concept of information sources.

Next, we attempt to confirm the bidimensional structure of information sources' construct obtained from exploratory factor analysis. To do this, we conduct a confirmatory factor analysis on all the data (N=411). Table 17 summarizes all the results.

Results in Table 17 allow us to retain two dimensions in order to measure the concept of information sources.

From Table 17, results indicate that the loadings are all significantly different from zero since all values of t-statistics (or CR) are strictly greater than 1.96. Moreover, the converging construct validity of information sources is acceptable since rhô$_{vc}$ for each dimension is greater than or equal to 0.5 (0.646 and 0.5 respectively for the subjective and objective sources). So, we can confirm the two-dimensional structure for information sources' construct.

Table 16. Results of Exploratory Factor Analysis on Information Sources

Information Sources						
Items	Loading		Communality	MSA	Cronbach's Alpha	Jöreskog's Rhô
	F1	F2				
SOURC_OBJ1	0.760		0.591	0.725	**0.722**	**0.707**
SOURC_OBJ2	0.690		0.502	0.733		
SOURC_OBJ3	0.721		0.543	0.738		
SOURC_OBJ4	0.759		0.580	0.701		
SOURC_SUB1		0.897	0.822	0.540	**0.779**	**0.784**
SOURC_SUB2		0.893	0.804	0.527		
Eigenvalue	2.439	1.402	**KMO = 0.648**			
Bartlett's Sphericity Test						
Explained Variance (%)	40.655	23.375	N = 411			
	64.030%					

Note: *d.f.* degree of freedom.

Table 17. Results of Confirmatory Factor Analysis and Test of Convergent Validity related to Information Sources

Factor	Items	Non Standardized	CR	Standardized	
Objective Sources	SOURC_OBJ1	1.000		0.635	**0.500**
	SOURC_OBJ2	0.775	8.577***	0.535	
	SOURC_OBJ3	0.842	9.832***	0.640	
	SOURC_OBJ4	0.984	9.834***	0.641	
Subjective Sources	SOURC_SUB1	1.000		0.728	**0.646**
	SOURC_SUB2	1.192	5.046***	0.873	

Notes: - *** Signification Level: 0.001 ; - CR: CRITICAL RATIO.

2.3.2.2. Measure of Information Types' Construct

The information types are measured using a set of items which are shown in Table 18. Investors are invited to assess the degree of importance that they attach to the question "When making your investment decisions, you use the following information ...".

Table 18. reports the different items used to quantify the concept of information types.

After purification items, three independent dimensions are found: Economic Information (INF_ECQ), Information related to Listed Companies (INF_COMP) and Financial Analysis (ANAL_FIN). Results also show that items are factorisable (KMO = 0.790 and Bartlett's sphericity test is significant). Items

Table 18. List of Items of Information Types' Measure

Dimensions	Items	Information Types
ECONOMIC INFORMATIONS	**INF_ECQ1**	The information about the fluctuation of policy interest rate
	INF_ECQ2	The information about the fluctuation of inflation rate
	INF_ECQ3	The information about the fluctuation of rates of economic growth
	INF_ECQ4	The macro-economic information
	INF_ECQ5	The micro-economic information
	INF_ECQ6	International information (economic, political ...)
	INF_ECQ7	The information related to public persons, parallel information
INFORMATIONS RELATED TO LISTED COMPANIES	**INF_COMP1**	Provisional statements
	INF_COMP2	Information about future investment of the company
	INF_COMP3	Information about top management
	INF_COMP4	Consultation of financial statement
	INF_COMP5	Information about capital transactions
	INF_COMP6	Monitoring the price evolution
	INF_COMP7	Rumors on the stock market
FINANCIAL ANALYSIS	**ANAL_FIN1**	Analysis communicated by engineering office
	ANAL_FIN2	Analysis communicated by brokerage firms
	ANAL_FIN3	Echoes

INF_ECQ6 (international information) INF_ECQ7 (information related to public persons, parallel information) INF_COMP5 (Information about capital transactions) INF_COMP7 (rumors on the stock market) and ANAL_FIN3 (echoes) are deleted because their communality is less than 0.5. Item INF_COMP6 (monitoring the price evolution) is removed due to its communality is less than 0.5 (i.e. 0.435). Furthermore, the three factors alone are enough to explain 67.956% of the variance of the concept. Table 19 summarizes these results.

Results in Table 19 related to loading, communality, Cronbach's alpha as well as the Jöreskog's rhô indicate that three factors can measure the concept of information types.

The reliability of the information types' construct is satisfying since the values taken by the Cronbach's alpha and Jöreskog's rhô coefficients exceed 0.7.

Results in Table 20 show the three factors can measure the concept of information types.

Table 20. shows that loadings are all significantly different from zero. Besides, the convergent validity's rho of each dimension is greater than or equal to 0.5. Hence, we can validate the tridimensional structure of the information types' construct retained from the exploratory analysis.

2.3.2.3. Measure of Reinvestment Intention

In order to operationalize the reinvestment intention, we adopt the measure proposed by Wang et al. (2006), we measure the reinvestment intention. Indeed, each respondent must answer to the question "What is your investment plan in the stock market next year? while choosing one of the answers: Invest more; Keep the same setting; Reduce investment and ultimately Withdraw from the stock market.

Table 19. Results of Exploratory Factor Analysis on Information Types

Information Types							
Items	**Loading**			**Communality**	**MSA**	**Cronbach's Alpha**	**Jöreskog's Rhô**
	F1	**F2**	**F3**				
INF_ECQ1	0.811			0.701	0.772	**0.851**	**0.845**
INF_ECQ2	0.834			0.776	0.765		
INF_ECQ3	0.761			0.660	0.927		
INF_ECQ4	0.744			0.709	0.751		
INF_ECQ5	0.676			0.671	0.736		
INF_COMP1		0.747		0.602	0.828	**0.776**	**0.780**
INF_COMP2		0.780		0.676	0.836		
INF_COMP3		0.689		0.516	0.866		
INF_COMP4		0.712		0.594	0.881		
ANAL_FIN1			0.807	0.764	0.719	**0.838**	**0.834**
ANAL_FIN2			0.860	0.806	0.688		
Eigenvalue	4.415	1.783	1.278	**KMO = 0.790**			
Bartlett's Sphericity Test							
Explained Variance (%)	40.134	16.205	11.618	N = 411			
	67.956%						

Note: *d.f.* degree of freedom.

Table 20. Results of Confirmatory Factor Analysis and Test of Convergent Validity related to Information Types

Factor	Items	Non Standardized	CR	Standardized	
ECONOMIC INFORMATIONS	INF_ECQ1	1.000		0.800	**0.526**
	INF_ECQ2	1.036	17.443***	0.846	
	INF_ECQ3	0.987	15.315***	0.746	
	INF_ECQ4	0.811	12.759***	0.639	
	INF_ECQ5	0.722	10.940***	0.557	
INFORMATIONS RELATED TO LISTED COMPANIES	INF_COMP1	1.000		0.699	**0.500**
	INF_COMP2	0.980	12.377***	0.751	
	INF_COMP3	1.003	10.783***	0.631	
	INF_COMP4	0.865	11.249***	0.660	
FINANCIAL ANALYSIS	ANAL_FIN1	1.000		0.862	**0.716**
	ANAL_FIN2	0.917	10.142***	0.830	

Notes: - *** Signification Level: 0.001 ; - CR: CRITICAL RATIO.

2.3.2.4. Measure of Investment Performance

Following again Wang et al. (2006), the investment performance is measured using a closed question. Indeed, each investor is asked to answer the following question: "What was your investment performance of the previous year?" (Gain; Neither gain nor loss; Loss).

2.3.3. Measures of Perceived Risk

Slovic (1987) indicates that people have "intuitive judgments of risk typically named perceptions of risk". Risk Perception seems to be "*more complex than that depicted by the most common conceptions*" (Cadet and Kouabénan, 2005). Renn (1992) suggests that individuals perceive risk as a multidimensional phenomenon. Hence, risk perception cannot define as the product of probability and consequences. Slovic (1992) reveals that risk is subjective and does not exist independently of cultures and minds of human beings.

Many psychology studies attempt to understand and assess people's perceptions towards risks by developing the psychometric paradigm (Fischhoff et al., 1987; Lichtenstein et al., 1978; Slovic et al., 1979, 1980, 1985). According to Slovic (1987), the psychometric paradigm uses "psychometric scaling and multivariate analysis techniques to produce quantitative representations or 'cognitive maps' of risk attitudes and perceptions". Results show that there are major differences between lay people and experts in terms of risk perception. In particular, lay persons assess any risk event from two dimensions namely familiarity and controllability.

According to Gigerenzer and Todd (1999), familiarity is "a degree of knowledge or experience a person has respect to a task or object". In this regard, Ricciardi (2004) reveals that familiarity is "an inclination or prejudice that alters individual's perception of risk". Other than familiarity, controllability is broadly defined as "the ability to foresee and navigate potential hazards, thus erasing risk in a material way" (Natalier, 2001). Slovic (1987) affirms that controllability is the most important factor in risk perception. Indeed, people tend to perceive less risk for situations where they feel they can control them. Thus, we use these two factors in order to quantify the risk perceived by investors. In operational terms, familiarity and controllability were measured by a set of items representing the instruments necessary for investment (e.g. financial ratios, fluctuation of interest rates...) but as the two dimensions of perceived risk can be distinguished from each other. Once measured, we believe that the degree of familiarity and controllability of tools used for investment in stock market determine risk perceived by investors. In other words, these two dimensions are not manifestations of perceived risk but conversely are constructive (or formative) of this construct. Thus, we assume that the perceived risk is a second-order formative construct.

2.3.3.1. Measure of Familiarity's Construct

The concept of familiarity is measured using seven items reported in Table 21 below. For each item, the degree of familiarity of investors has been assessed based on a 5-point Likert scale (ranging from 'not at all familiar' to 'very familiar'). In order to ensure the understanding of the term by investors, we define the familiarity in the questionnaire as "the feeling of the individual about situations that he has personal knowledge".

Table 21. reports the different items used to quantify the concept of familiarity.

By conducting an exploratory factor analysis, item FAM7 (excessive speculation) should be removed, since the communality was low (0.251). Results related to a second exploratory factor analysis are reported in Table 22 below. Ensuring that the items are factorisable (KMO = 0.886 and Bartlett's test is significant), one-dimensional structure explain 62.088% of the variance of the concept of familiarity.

Results in Table 22 related to loading, communality, Cronbach's alpha as well as the Jöreskog's rhô indicate that one factor can measure the concept of familiarity.

The Reliability of construct is satisfying since Cronbach's alpha is equal to 0.876. This is confirmed by the Jöreskog's rhô which exceeds 0.7 (i.e. 0.863).

2.3.3.2. Measure of Controllability's Construct

The construct of controllability is measured by using seven items listed in Table 23. These items are assessed on a 5-point Likert scale (ranging from 'not controlled' to 'very controlled').

Table 21 reports the different items used to quantify the concept of controllability.

Table 21. List of Items of Familiarity' Measure

Items	Familiarity
FAM1	Fluctuation of Interest Rate
FAM2	Knowledge of the Stock Market
FAM3	The Bond Market
FAM4	The Management of Listed Companies
FAM5	The Intervention of the Authorities in the Financial Market
FAM6	Financial Ratios
FAM7	Excessive Speculation

Table 22. Results of Exploratory Factor Analysis on Familiarity

Familiarity					
Items	**Loading**	**Communality**	**MSA**	**Cronbach's Alpha**	**Jöreskog's Rhô**
FAM1	0.786	0.619	0.884	**0.876**	**0.863**
FAM2	0.756	0.572	0.907		
FAM3	0.821	0.674	0.872		
FAM4	0.800	0.640	0.882		
FAM5	0.820	0.673	0.873		
FAM6	0.740	0.548	0.905		
Eigenvalue	3.725			**KMO = 0.886**	
Bartlett's Sphericity Test	X^2=1076.627. .p=0.000				
Explained Variance	**62.088%**			N = 411	

Note: *d.f.* degree of freedom.

Table 23. List of Items of Controllability

Items	Controllability
CONT1	Fluctuation of Interest Rate
CONT2	Knowledge of the Stock Market
CONT3	The Bond Market
CONT4	The Management of Listed Companies
CONT5	The Intervention of the Authorities in the Financial Market
CONT6	Financial Ratios
CONT7	Excessive Speculation

A first principal component factor analysis allows us to exclude the item MAT7 (excessive speculation) due to its low communality (0.356 <0.5). A second factor analysis leads to one-dimensional structure which can explain 61.614% of the concept.

The reliability of the concept is satisfying since the value of the Cronbach's alpha is acceptable (i.e. 0.874). The Jöreskog's rhô is greater than 0.7 (i.e. 0.863) which allows us to further confirm the good reliability of the construct. Table 24 below summarizes results related to the exploratory factor analysis.

By performing the principal component analysis of the data (Table 24), we show the one-dimensional structure of the concept of controllability.

2.3.3.3. Specification of Perceived Risk's Measurement Model

Many researchers define the formative measurement model compared to reflective model (e.g. Diamantopoulos et al., 2008; Lacroux 2008; Crié, 2005). For example, Crié (2005) reveals that the formative

Table 24. Results of Exploratory Factor Analysis on Controllability

Controllability					
Items	**Loading**	**Communality**	**MSA**	**Cronbach's Alpha**	**Jöreskog's Rhô**
CONT1	0.763	0.582	0.888	**0.874**	**0.863**
CONT2	0.776	0.602	0.895		
CONT3	0.803	0.645	0.881		
CONT4	0.809	0.655	0.879		
CONT5	0.801	0.641	0.879		
CONT6	0.756	0.571	0.898		
Eigenvalue	3.697			**KMO = 0.886**	
Bartlett's Sphericity Test					
Explained Variance	**61.614%**			N = 411	

Note: *d.f.* degree of freedom.

measurement model specifies that "the observed variables are multiple causes of the concept which they determine by minimizing the residue of the structural equation" whereas the reflective indicator is "a reflection of the construct that accounts for their observed variance and covariance". As reported by Lacroux (2008), in reflective construct, "indicators are assumed o represent the influence of latent underlying construct, the causal relationship is supposed to operate from construct to its indicators". However, a formative construct is "a combination of indicators, not necessarily correlated, contributing to 'shape' the latent construct. The causal relationship to these 'formative' constructs is reversed: It proceeds from indicators to latent construct".

As previously indicated, we assume that the measurement model of perceived risk is a formative model. This construct is as a combination of two factors, namely familiarity and controllability. These two variables are not manifestations of the perceived risk. They are constitutive (or formative) of the perceived risk.

Results of the confirmatory factor analysis are reported in Table 26. Thc first part of Table reports the results of the reflective first-order model. The second part indicates results of formative second-order model.

Table 26. comprises two parts. The first part reports the results of the reflective first-order model. Our results show two different constructs of familiarity and controllability. The second part displays results of formative second-order model.

From the first part of Table 26, all factor loading relating the items FAM_i and $CONT_i$ ($i = 1,..., 6$) to the two respective factors Familiarity and Controllability are significantly different from zero ($t > 1.96$). Besides, the convergent validity of each construct is acceptable since are just above 0.5 (0.514 and 0.513 for the familiarity and controllability, respectively). Hence, we can retain the two measures used in the measurement model of perceived risk.

From formative perspective, the second part of Table 26 contains standardized (i.e. column 4) and non-standardized (i.e. column 2) coefficients (structural parameters) that capture the effect of both latent variables (Familiarity and Controllability) on the perceived risk (i.e. column 1). We note that the relationship between familiarity and perceived risk is positive and significant (= 0.784). However, the

Table 25. Reflective Construct versus Formative Construct

	Reflective Measurement Model	*Formative Measurement Model*
GRAPHICALLY	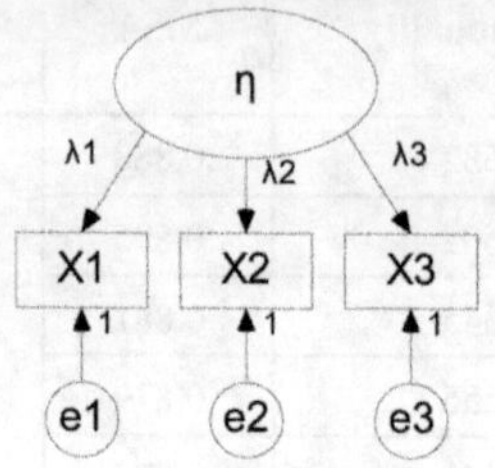	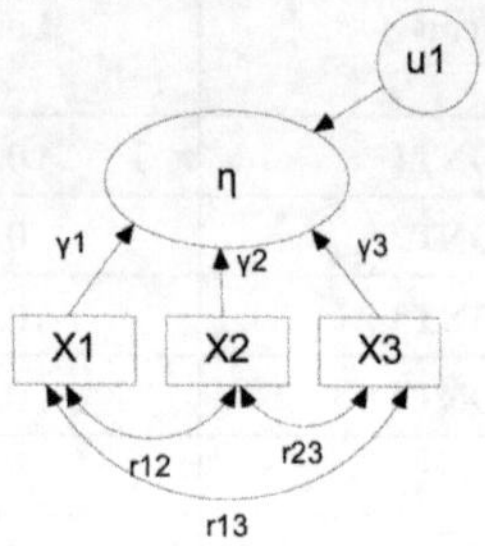
Mathematically	where: *The construct ; *:The ith indicator of the latent variable η which affects it ; *:The random measurement error ; *:The factor *loading* depicting the magnitude of the effect of on the.	where: * Latent variable ; *: The measures ; *:The structural parameters depicting the magnitude of the effects of the () on ; *: The disturbance term representing the part of the construct that is not explained by the measures.
	The direct reflective model specifies direct effects from a construct to its measures. (*Edward and Bagozzi, 2000*)	**The direct formative model specifies measures as correlated causes of a construct.** (*Edward and Bagozzi, 2000*)

Table 26. Results related to Perceived Risk's Measurement Model

Reflective First-Order					
Factor	**Items**	**Non Standardized**	**CR**	**Standardized**	
Familiarity	FAM1	1.000		0.704	**0.514**
	FAM2	0.828	12.351***	0.675	
	FAM3	1.148	13.805***	0.765	
	FAM4	0.973	13.459***	0.742	
	FAM5	1.098	13.672***	0.757	
	FAM6	0.974	11.917***	0.651	
Controllability	CONT1	1.000		0.691	**0.513**
	CONT2	0.904	12.541***	0.710	
	CONT3	1.062	13.080***	0.745	
	CONT4	1.002	1.084***	0.746	
	CONT5	1.084	12.838***	0.730	
	CONT6	1.031	11.966***	0.673	
Formative Second-Order					
		Non Standardized	**CR**	**Standardized**	
Familiarity Risque Perçu		1.000		0.784	
Controllability Risque Perçu		-0.251	-5.121***	-0.249	

Notes: - *** Signification Level: 0.001 ; - CR: CRITICAL RATIO.

effect of controllability on perceived risk is negative and significant (= -0.249, t = -5.121, p = 0.001). On the one hand, an increase in the degree of familiarity of investors with investment tools does not cause inevitably a corresponding increase in the level of controllability of these instruments. On the other hand, the more the investor knows and does not control the necessary instruments for investment, the higher the perceived risk is towards the stock market. Clearly, the perception of risk is high when investor knows but does not control the tools necessary for investment by an investor. This finding is not surprising since Wang and al. (2006) argue, from a mapping of risk perceptions, that Chinese investors have a low perceived risk when they feel familiar and control some sources of risk existing in the stock market. In contrast, their risk perception is high when they are familiar and do not control other sources of risk. So, we can conclude that both latent variables, Familiarity and Controllability, are formatives of the construct 'Perceived Risk'.

SECTION. 3: RISK-BEHAVIOR MODEL

Since the measurement model of perceived risk is a formative model, factors influencing risk perception will be subsequently considered as antecedents of familiarity and controllability. More explicitly, as depicted in figure 2, the investor's individual profile, perceived characteristics of listed companies and information asymmetry will affect risk perception through familiarity and controllability of tools necessary to investment.

Figure 2. reports the risk-behavior model which illustrates the relationships between different constructs.

Before explaining results of model estimation, it is necessary to first introduce the structural equation method.

3.1. Overview of Structural Equation Method

Since Jöreskog (1969), Keesling (1972) and Wiley (1973) first developed the statistical model of structural equations, it has become a fairly sophisticated statistical method. It is frequently used by many researchers in various fields such as psychology, marketing. The structural equation method attempts to examine

Figure 2. Integrated Model of Antecedents & Consequences of Perceived Risk

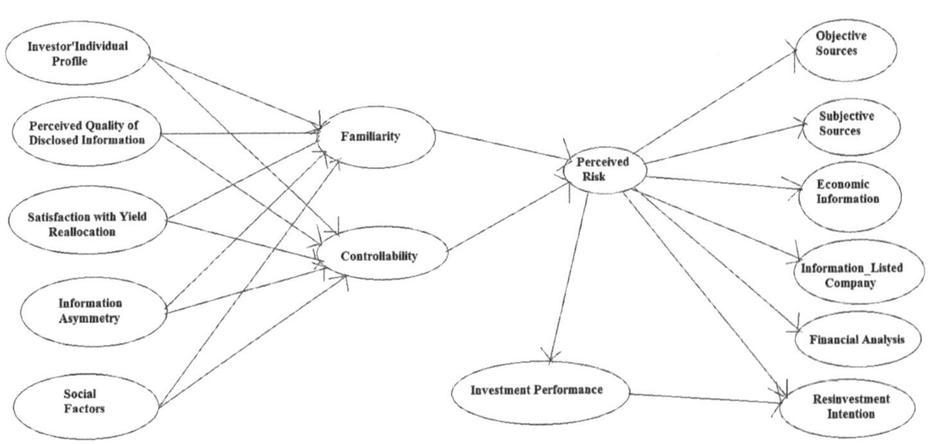

the causal relationships in a complex theoretical model (Hoyle, 1985). According to Kaplan (2000), the structural equation models are a class of methodologies trying to represent certain assumptions about the average, variance and covariance of observed data in terms of a smaller number of structural parameters defined by an underlying theoretical model.

Raykov and Marcoulides (2006) pinpoint that the structural equation modeling which attempts to examine and quantify the substantive theories. Byrne (2006) reports that the structural equation modeling conveys two important aspects of the procedure: (a) « that the causal processes under study are represented by a series of structural (i.e. regression) equations » and (b) « that these structural relations can be modeled pictorially to enable a clearer conceptualization of the theory under study ».

Researchers propose several appellations to depict this method such as "structural equation models with latent variables" (Jöreskog and Sorbom, 1989), "model analysis of covariance structures" (Valette-Florence, 1988) or "structural equation models" (Pedhazur and Schmelkin, 1991).

Due to its ability to treat concomitantly a set of dependence relations, structural equation models are the most appropriate to be used in the current study. Unlike other conventional approaches (i.e. regression), this method allows to simultaneously estimate the multiple interrelated dependence relations and incorporate the measurement errors directly in the estimation process (Roussel et al., 2002).Also, Hair et al. (1998) indicate that taking into account measurement errors permits to estimate more accurately regression coefficients in comparison to classical methods. The structural equation method enables us to assess the model fit.

3.2. Evaluation of Model Fit

Assessing the quality of a model's fit to the observed data requires the use of the adjustment indices. Measures of goodness of fit typically summarize the discrepancy between observed values and the values expected under the model in question. To this end, researchers use three types of indices namely the absolute, incremental and parsimony indices. Table 27 reports the main results.

Table 27. reports results of calculation of different indices (absolute, incremental and parcimony indices) to assess the model fit.

Results prove that RMSEA is less than 0.08 (equal to 0.070) and GFI is greater than 0.9 (equal to 0.951). So, our conceptual model can reproduce accurately the data. Besides, the value of CFI (equal to 0.930) is acceptable since it is above the key value. This shows therefore the good fit of the model tested against the restrictive model (or basic model) in which all the observed variables are not correlated

Table 27. Model Fit

Type of Index	*Index*	*Observed Value*	*Key Value*
Absolute Indices	***d.f (prob)***	**128.405** **43 (0.000)**	***None***
	RMSEA	**0.070**	***<0.08***
	GFI	**0.951**	***>0.9***
Incremental INDICES	**CFI**	**0.957**	***>0.9***
PARCIMONY INDICES		**2.986**	***Entre 1 et 5***
	PNFI	**0.611**	***>0.5***

(Roussel et al., 2002). These results are confirmed by the values of the parsimony indices. Indeed, the less than 5 (equal to 2.986) and PNFI greater than 0.5 (about 0.611) indicate that the model is parsimonious. In other words, the selected model shows a good fit for each estimated coefficient. Thus, the model is acceptable and fits satisfactorily with empirical data.

3.3. Estimation Results and Interpretation

Table 28. reports results of the non-standardized and standardized coefficient estimates as well as the value of t statistics (CR).

Table 28. reports results of the estimation of the conceptual model. All coefficients are statistically significant.

First, results indicate that the investor's individual profile has a significant and positive effect on familiarity ($\beta = 0.165$, $t = 2.632$, $p = 0.01$) and controllability ($\beta = 0.168$, $t = 2.601$, $p = 0.01$) which leads us to keep R2.1 and R2.2. Thus, we can support H1. Second, we find that the perceived quality of information disclosed by listed companies has a positive and significant influence not only on familiarity ($\beta = 0.363$, $t = 6.113$, $p = 0.001$) but also controllability ($\beta = 0.275$, $t = 4.836$, $p = 0.001$), retaining R3.1 and R3.2. Consequently, we can support H2.1. Third, the effect of satisfaction with yield reallocation by listed companies on familiarity and controllability is positive and significant (respectively $\beta = 0.205$, $t = 3.892$, $p = 0.001$, $\beta = 0.259$, $t = 4.038$, $p = 0.001$). Thus, we support H2.2. Fourth, we report

Table 28. Structural Relationships in the ModelLire phonétiquementLire phonétiquement

Path	**Regression Coefficients**	**Standardized Regression Coefficients**	**CR**
R1.1: Individual Profile Familiarity	0.135	0.165	2.632**
R1.1: Individual Profile Controllability	0.175	0.168	2.601**
R2.1: Perceived Quality of disclosed Information Familiarity	0.356	0.363	6.113***
R2.2: Perceived Quality of disclosed Information Controllability	0.342	0.275	4.836***
R3.1: Satisfaction with yield Reallocation Familiarity	0.19	0.205	3.892***
R3.2: Satisfaction with yield Reallocation Controllability	0.259	0.22	4.038***
R4.1: Information Asymmetry Familiarity	0.16	0.273	5.495***
R4.2: Information Asymmetry Controllability	0.194	0.26	5.130***
R4.3: Social Factors Familiarity	-21.603	-0.611	-1.101
R4.4: Social Factors Controllability	-42.237	-1.26	-0.917
R5.1: Perceived Risk Objective Sources	1.005	0.901	11.199***
R5.2: Perceived Risk Subjective Sources	1	0.628	10.197***
R6.1: Perceived Risk Economic Information	0.823	0.656	11.567***
R6.2: Perceived Risk Information related to Listed Companies	0.884	0.866	10.415***
R6.3: Perceived Risk Financial Analysis	0.896	0.671	3.321***
R7 : Perceived Risk Reinvestment Intention	0.208	0.178	3.560***
R8 : Perceived Risk Investment Performance	0.196	0.192	

Notes: -***Significance level: 0.001 ; -**Significance level: 0.01; -CR: *CRITICAL RATIO*.

that information asymmetry has a positive and significant impact on familiarity ($\beta = 0.273$, $t = 5.495$, $p = 0.001$). In addition, the effect of information asymmetry on controllability is significant and positive, instead of being negative ($\beta = 0.260$, $t = 5.130$, $p = 0.001$). Therefore, we reject H3.1. Results show that social factors do not affect both familiarity and controllability, rejecting R4.3 and R4.4. Therefore, we do not support H3.1.

Results also suggest to retain R5.1indicating that perceived risk has a positive and significant effect on the number of objective sources ($\beta = 0.901$, $t = 11.199$, $p = 0.001$). We also find that risk perception increases the number of subjective sources ($\beta = 0.628$), retaining R5.2. Therefore, we support H4. Results show that the higher the perceived risk of investor is, the more he will try to use simultaneously the economic information ($\beta = 0.656$, $t = 10.197$, $p = 0.001$), information related to listed companies ($\beta = 0.866$, $t = 11.567$, $p = 0.001$) and financial analysis ($\beta = 0.671$, $t = 10.415$, $p = 0.001$). We retain R6.1, R6.2 and R6.3. The hypothesis H5 is supported. We also find that risk perception has a significant and positive, instead of being negative, effect on the reinvestment intention ($\beta = 0.178$, $t = 3.321$, $p = 0.001$). This result leads us to reject H6. Results also display the risk perception influences positively investment performance ($\beta = 0.192$, $t = 3.650$, $p = 0.001$), retaining R8.2. Thus, we support H7.

Lastly, we check the possibility that investment performance plays a mediating role between risk perception and intention to reinvest. According to Baron and Kenny (1986), a mediator variable is defined as "the generative mechanism through which the focal independent variable is able to influence the dependent variable of interest". A mediator variable sheds light on the relationship between the independent variable and the dependent variable.

Mathematically, we estimate two different models. In the first model (constrained model), we impose two simultaneous constraints on the regression coefficients, and, whereas at the second model (complete model) no constraint has been imposed. Results obtained from estimating two models are reported in Table 29.

Results of the estimation of different coefficients (Table 29) indicate the partial mediator between risk perception and reinvestment intention.

Table 29. Results of Both Models' Estimation

		Constrained Model	Complete Model
Perceived Risk Reinvestment Intention		0.214	0.178
		0.249	0.208
	CR	3.959***	3.321***
Perceived Risk Investment Performance		0.000	0.192
		0.000	0.196
	CR	-	3.560***
Investment Performance Reinvestment Intention		0.000	0.193
		0.000	0.222
	CR	-	3.931***

Notes: -***Significance level: 0.001 ; -CR: *CRITICAL RATIO* ; β^{st}: Standardized Regression Coefficients ; -β: Regression Coefficients.

The relationship between investment performance and reinvestment intention is significant and positive ($\beta = 0.193$, $t = 3.931$, $p = 0.001$). Besides, perceived risk has always significant and positive effect on intention to reinvest. Nevertheless, while passing from constrained to complete model (i.e. when investment performance is taken into account), we find that the influence of risk perception on intention reinvestment becomes weaker ($\beta = 0.178 < 0.214$) but remains significant ($\beta = 0.178$, $t = 3.321$, $p = 0.001$). So, we support that investment performance plays role of a partial mediator between risk perception and reinvestment intention.

SECTION. 4: LESSONS FROM RISK-BEHAVIOR MODEL

This research investigates the interactions between antecedents of risk perception, perceived risk and behavioral responses induced by risk in the investment context. Results of this study leads to the following implications.

4.1. Antecedents of Perceived Risk

Results show that when the investor is familiar and does not control the tools necessary for investment in stock market his risk perception is high. Conversely, when investor is familiar and controls these instruments he perceives a low level of risk towards the stock market. We explicitly recognize that the controllability is a significant factor in the formation of perceived risk. This finding is confirmed by Slovic (1987) which highlights its importance in the risk perception.

Results also indicate that individual profile of investor is positively related to familiarity and controllability of investment tools. These findings confirm that a self-confident and optimistic investor believes he knows and controls instruments necessary for investment. So, he will perceive a low level of risk towards the stock market. We explicitly recognize that these two personality traits (self-confidence and optimism) play a crucial role in risk perception through the two psychometric variables (familiarity and controllability).

Besides, the perceived quality of disclosed information and the satisfaction with the yield reallocation by listed companies display a positive relationship with familiarity and controllability. The more the investor perceives that listed companies transmit to the stock market good quality information (e.g., relevant, complete) the more he feels familiar and controls the tools of investment. Similarly, a great satisfaction with yield reallocation encourages better understanding and controlling of the tools of investment. Hence, the perceived quality of disclosed information and satisfaction with yield reallocation by listed companies both strengthen the familiarity and controllability of investment instruments. Henceforth, the investor's risk perception toward the market will be even lower.

Lastly, results do not support that the more the market participants do not share the same information the higher the degree of familiarity and controllability of investor. This could be explained by the fact that an investor who feels more informed than others tends to feel more familiar with and controls the tools of investment. Therefore, he will perceive a lower level of risk toward the stock market. AS argued by Wang et al. (2006) "investors' risk perception was not increased by asymmetric information although they knew that information asymmetry would greatly influence their decision". Besides, the social factors do not affect the familiarity and controllability of investment tools. That is, the existence of investment advisor, family, among others, do not reduce the perceived level of risk toward the stock market.

Contrary to many studies which prove the impact of social factors in the purchase situation, the current study do not support the relationship between the social influences and the perceived risk of investors.

4.2. Behavioral Responses to Perceived Risk

The proposed model suggests that risk perception influences the activity of information search and investment behavior.

The activity of information search is measured through the information sources and types. Results indicate that the higher the perceived risk of investor the higher the investor will consult various information sources. Thus, we show that as perceived risk increases, a greater number of information sources are consulted. The current study was not limited only to information sources but it was interested in the type of information. Indeed, results suggest that by facing a high perceived level of risk toward the stock market the investor will tend to use different types of information (economic information, financial analysis, information relative to listed companies). In other words, investor uses various types of information in order to decrease his perceived risk. We conclude that the link between risk perception and information search can be established within the investment context. This finding is confirmed by Cho and Lee (2006) who argue that "the link between perceived risk and the extent of information search (a link that has often been rejected in the extant literature) can be established within the context of investment".

Results also indicate that a higher perception of risk has simultaneously created a strong intention to reinvest in the stock market and higher investment performance. Facing a high level of perceived risk, investors reinforce (rather they decrease) their intention to reinvest. This behavioral response clearly shows that investors do not seek to reduce the vulnerability associated with negative outcomes. Although they perceive a high risk toward the stock market, investors do not adopt the second risk-reducing strategy (i.e. decrease in the amount at stake) in the investment context. However, persons with higher perceived risk toward the stock market have a higher investment performance. According to Wang and al. (2006), these results can explain the frequent stock exchange behaviors prevailing on the stock markets. Moreover, we find that investment performance can play the role of partial mediator between risk perception and intention to reinvest. Although the perceived risk towards the stock market is high the investor seeks to reinvest more by making frequent stock trading under the attraction and reinforcement of returns generated from the invested funds.

CONCLUSION

In this study, the proposed model examines the antecedents and consequences of perceived risk in the investment context. Results show that controllability plays a crucial role in the formation of perceived risk. Moreover, we find that the individual profile of investor, the factors related to the listed company and the stock market have an impact on perceived risk. A future study could examine the effect of other variables on risk perception such as investment experience and sociodemographic characteristics of investors (age, gender, income ...). Besides, we conclude that investors seek to mitigate the perceived risk toward the stock market through information search. The attraction of returns generated from the invested funds strengthens the reinvestment intention of investors in spite of the fact that they perceive risk toward the stock market. Thus, the specific context (i.e. the stock market investment) leads the investor not to adopt the second risk-reducing strategy namely the decrease in the amount at stake.

Our research could be extended by including the concept of the ethic in the investment context. In marketing research, many researchers consider the ethics is a very important. Unfortunately, the questionnaire of this study does not comprise items related to ethical attributes perceived by the individual investors. A future study would examine the relationship between the perceived ethics toward the stock market and the risk-reducing strategies.

REFERENCES

Admati, A. R., & Pfleiderer, P. (1988). A Theory of Intraday Trading Patterns: Volume and Price Variability. *Review of Financial Studies*, *43*(1), 3–40. doi:10.1093/rfs/1.1.3

Barber, B., & Odean, T. (2001). Boys will be Boys: Gender, Overconfidence, and Common Stock Investment. *The Quarterly Journal of Economics*, *14*(1), 261–292. doi:10.1162/003355301556400

Baron, R. M., & Kenny, D. A. (1986). The Moderator-Mediator Variable Distinction in Social and Psychological Research: Conceptual, Strategic and Statistical Considerations. *Journal of Personality and Social Psychology*, *51*(6), 1173–1182. doi:10.1037/0022-3514.51.6.1173 PMID:3806354

Bauer, R. A. (1960). Consumer Behavior as Risk Taking. In R. S. Hancock (Ed.), *Dynamic marketing for a changing world* (pp. 389–398). Chicago: American Marketing Association.

Beaver, B., Kettler, P., & Scholes, M. (1970). The Association Between Market Determined and Accounting Determined Risk Measures. *Accounting Review*, *45*, 654–682.

Blackwell, D., & Dubins, L. (1962). Merging of Opinions with Increasing Information. *Annals of Mathematical Statistics*, *38*(3), 882–886. doi:10.1214/aoms/1177704456

Boisselier, P., & Mekaoui, S. (2005, May 11-13). Qualité de l'Information Financière et Introduction des Sociétés sur le Nouveau Marché: Enjeux et Proposition d'un Cadre d'Analyse. *Proceedings of the XXVième Congrès Annuel de l'Association Francophone de Comptabilité*, Lille.

Brennan, M. J., & Subrahmanyam, A. (1995). Investment Analysis and Price Formation in Securities Markets. *Journal of Financial Economics*, *38*(3), 361–381. doi:10.1016/0304-405X(94)00811-E

Brown, S., & Hillegeist, S. A. (2007). How Disclosure Quality Affects the Level of Information Asymmetry. *Review of Accounting Studies*, *12*(2-3), 443–477. doi:10.1007/s11142-007-9032-5

Brucks, M. (1985). The Effects of Product Class Knowledge on information Search Behavior. *The Journal of Consumer Research*, *12*(1), 1–16. doi:10.1086/209031

Brunel, O. (2002). *Les Stratégies d'Ajustement au Risque Alimentaire: Modèle Théorique et Test Empirique* [Thèse de Doctorat en Sciences de Gestion]. IAE, Université Lyon 3.

Byrne, B. M. (2006). Structural Equation Modeling with EQS: Basic Concepts, Applications, and Programming (2nd ed.). London: Lawrence Erlbraum associates Publishers.

Cadet, B., & Kouabenan, D. (2005). Evaluer et Modéliser les Risques: Apports et Limites de Différents Paradigmes dans le Diagnostic de Sécurité. *Le Travail Humain*, *68*(1), 7–35. doi:10.3917/th.681.0007

Capstaff, J. (1989). The Risk Perceptions of Investment Analysts. *The Investments Analysts*, *91*, 2–15.

Chang, M., D'Anna, G., Watson, I., & Wee, M. (2008). Does Disclosure Quality via Investor Relations Affect Information Asymmetry? *Australian Journal of Management*, *33*(2), 2. doi:10.1177/031289620803300208

Cheng, S. W. (2003). *Diagnosis and Treatment Revealing the Chinese Stock Markets*. China: Economic Sciences Publication.

Cho, J., & Lee, J. (2006). An Integrated Model of Risk and Risk-Reducing Strategies. *Journal of Business Research*, *59*(1), 112–120. doi:10.1016/j.jbusres.2005.03.006

Choi, J., Salandro, D., & Shastri, K. (1988). On the Estimation of Bid-Ask Spreads: Theory and Evidence. *Journal of Financial and Quantitative Analysis*, *23*(2), 219–230. doi:10.2307/2330882

Chung, K. H., & Charoenwong, C. (1998). Insider Trading and the Bid-Ask Spread. *Financial Review*, *33*(3), 1–20. doi:10.1111/j.1540-6288.1998.tb01379.x

Churchill, G. A. (1979). A Paradigm for Developing Better Measures of Marketing Constructs. *JMR, Journal of Marketing Research*, *16*(1), 64–73. doi:10.2307/3150876

Cohen, M., Etner, J., & Jeleva, M. (2008). Dynamic Decision Making When Risk Perception Depends on Past Experience. *Theory and Decision*, *64*(2-3), 173–192. doi:10.1007/s11238-007-9061-3

Collins, D., & Kothari, C. (1989). An Analysis of the Cross-Sectional and Intertemporal Determinants of Earnings Response Coefficients. *Journal of Accounting and Economics*, *11*, 143–181. doi:10.1016/0165-4101(89)90004-9

Cooper, A. C., Woo, C. Y., & Dunkelberg, W. C. (1988). Entrepreneurs' Perceived Chances for Success. *Journal of Business Venturing*, *3*(2), 97–108. doi:10.1016/0883-9026(88)90020-1

Cox, D. F. (1967a). *Risk Taking and Information Handling in Consumer Behavior*. Cambridge, MA: Harvard University Press.

Cox, D. F., & Rich, S. U. (1964). Perceived Risk and Consumer decision Making-The Case of Telephone Shopping. *JMR, Journal of Marketing Research*, *1*(4), 32–39. doi:10.2307/3150375

Crié, D. (2005). De l'Usage des Modèles de Mesure Réflectifs ou Formatifs dans les Modèles d'Equations Structurelles. *Recherche et Applications en Marketing*, *20*(2), 5–27. doi:10.1177/076737010502000201

Cuny, X., & Gaillard, I. (2003). Les Risques Professionnels Aujourd'hui: Problèmes Actuels, Perspectives et Orientations Méthodologiques. In D. R. Kouabénan & M. Dubois (Eds.), *Les risques professionnels: nouvelles approches, perspectives actuelles* (pp. 25–36). Toulouse: Octarès.

Dandouau, J. C. (2000). *Le Comportement de Recherche d'Informations des Différents Profils de Risque Perçu selon la Nature de l'Achat. In les Actes des liers ateliers de recherche de l'AFM, Percevoir, identifier et gérer le risque en marketing* (pp. 133–151). Paris: La Sorbonne.

Declerck, F., and Martinez, I. (2004). Informations Volontaires et Microstructure des Marchés Financiers: Quel Impact sur le Marché des Titres NextEconomy et NextPrime? *Cahier de recherche*, 161.

Diamantopoulos, A., Riefler, P., & Roth, K. P. (2008). Advancing Formative Measurement Models. *Journal of Business Research*, *61*(12), 1203–1218. doi:10.1016/j.jbusres.2008.01.009

Djongoue, G. (2007). *Fiabilité de l'Information Comptable et Gouvernance d'Entreprise: Une Analyse de l'Audit Légal dans les Entreprises Camerounaises*. Colloque International le Gouvernance: Quelles Pratiques pour Promouvoir le Développement de l'Afrique. Université Catholique de Lille – France.

Douglas, M., & Wildavsky, A. B. (1982). *Risk and Culture: An Essay on the Selection of Technical and Environmental Dangers. Berkley*, University of California Press.

Dowling, G. R., & Staelin, R. (1994). A Model of Perceived Risk and Intended Risk Handling Activity. *The Journal of Consumer Research*, *21*(1), 119–134. doi:10.1086/209386

Edwards, J. R., & Bagozzi, R. P. (2000). On the Nature and Direction of Relationships Between Constructs and Measures. *Psychological Methods*, *5*(2), 155–174. doi:10.1037/1082-989X.5.2.155 PMID:10937327

El Akremi, A., and Roussel, P. (2003). *Analyse des Variables Modératrices et Médiatrices par les Méthodes d'équations Structurelles: Application à une Etude en GRH*. Communication présentée au Congrès Annuel de l'AGRH.

Elton, E., Gruber, M., & Gultekin, M. (1984). Professional Expectations: Accuracy and Diagnosis of Errors. *Journal of Financial and Quantitative Analysis*, *19*(4), 351–363. doi:10.2307/2330778

Engel, J. F., Blackwell, R. D., & Miniard, P. W. (1993). *Consumer Behavior*. New York: The Dryden Press.

Evrard, Y., Pras, B., & Roux, E. (2003). *Market – Etudes et Recherches en Marketing, Connaître et Pratiquer la Gestion* (2nd ed.). Nathan.

Fama, E. F. (1965a). Random Walks in Stock Market Prices. *Financial Analysts Journal*, *21*(5), 55–59. doi:10.2469/faj.v21.n5.55

Fama, E. F. (1965b). The Behavior of Stock Market Prices. *The Journal of Business*, *38*(1), 34–105. doi:10.1086/294743

Farrelly, G., Levine, P., & Reichenstein, W. (1984). Risk Perceptions of Institutional Investors. *Journal of Portfolio Management*, *10*(4), 5–12. doi:10.3905/jpm.1984.408966

Farrelly, G., Levine, P., & Reichenstein, W. (1987). Perceptions of Risk Classes: A Discriminant Analysis Using Financial Ratios. *Akron Business and Economic Review*, *18*(2), 78–91.

Farrelly, G. E., Ferris, K. R., & Reichenstein, W. R. (1985). Perceived Risk, Market Risk, and Accounting Determined Risk Measures. *Accounting Review*, *60*(2), 278–288.

Firer, C., Oliver, M. C., & Farrelly, G. E. (1986). Risk Perceptions of Individual vs. Institutional Investors: A Comparaison Based on the Johannesburg Stock Exchange. *Journal of Applied Business Research*, *5*(4), 5–14.

Fischhoff, B., Slovic, P., Lichtenstein, S., Reed, S., & Combs, B. (1978). How Safe is Safe Enough? A Psychometric Study of Attitudes Toward Technological Risks and Benefits. *Policy Sciences*, *9*(2), 127–152. doi:10.1007/BF00143739

Fishbein, M., & Ajzen, I. (1975). *Belief, Attitude, Intention and Behavior: An Introduction to Theory and Research Reading*. Boston, MA: Addison-Wesley.

Gao, P. (2008). Disclosure Quality, Cost of Capital, and Investors' Welfare. Retrieved from http://mpra.ub.uni muenchen.de/9478/2/MPRA_paper_9478.pdf

Garland, D. (2002). The Rise of Risk. In R. Ericson (Ed.), *Risk and Mortality*. University of Toronto Press.

Gemunden, H. G. (1985). Perceived Risk and Information Search, A Systematic Meta-Analysis of the Empirical Evidence. *International Journal of Research in Marketing*, *2*(2), 79–100. doi:10.1016/0167-8116(85)90026-6

Gendron, M., & Genest, C. (1993). La Perception du Risque de Titres Financiers: L'Importance Relative et l'Influence de Certains Facteurs de Risque. *L'Actualite Economique*, *69*(1), 142–170. doi:10.7202/602100ar

Gerbing, D. W., & Hamilton, J. G. (1996). Viability of Exploratory Factor and a Precursor to Confirmatory Factor Analysis. *Structural Equation Modeling*, *3*(1), 62–72. doi:10.1080/10705519609540030

Gervais, S., & Odean, T. (2001). Learning to be Overconfident. *Review of Financial Studies*, *14*(1), 1–27. doi:10.1093/rfs/14.1.1

Gigerenzer, G., Todd, P. M., & Group, A. B. C. (Eds.). (1999). *Simple Heuristics That Make Us Smart*. New York: Oxford University Press.

Gooding, A. E. (1975). Quantification of Investors' Perceptions of Common Stocks: Risk and Return Dimensions. *The Journal of Finance*, *30*(5), 1301–1316. doi:10.1111/j.1540-6261.1975.tb01057.x

Grimes, P. (2002). The Overconfident Principles of Economics Student: An Examination of a Metacognitive Skill. *The Journal of Economic Education*, *33*(1), 15–30. doi:10.1080/00220480209596121

Grossman, S. (1976). On the Efficiency of Competitive Stock Markets When Traders Have Diverse Information. *The Journal of Finance*, *31*(2), 573–585. doi:10.1111/j.1540-6261.1976.tb01907.x

Guo, C. (2001). A Review on Consumer External Search: Amount and Determinants, 15(3). *Journal of Business and Psychology*, *15*(3), 505–519. doi:10.1023/A:1007830919114

Hair, J. F., Anderson, R. E., Tatham, R. L., & Black, W. C. (1988). *Multivariate Data Analysis with Reading* (5th ed.). Upper Slade River, N.J.: Prentice Hall.

Hoyle, R. H. (1985). *Structural Equation Modeling: Concepts, Issues and Applications*. Thousand Oaks, CA: Sage Publications.

Huang, R. D., & Stoll, H. R. (1997). The Components of the Bid-Ask Spread: A General Approach. *Review of Financial Studies*, *10*(4), 995–1034. doi:10.1093/rfs/10.4.995

Jöreskog, K. G. (1973). Analysis of Covariance Structures. In P. R. Krishnaiah (Ed.), *Multivariate Analysis-III* (pp. 263–285). New York: Academic Press.

Kaplan, D. (2000). *Structural Equation Modeling: Foundations and Extensions*. Thousand Oaks, CA: Sage.

Kaplan, S., & Garrick, J. B. (1981). On the Quantitative Definition of Risk. *Risk Analysis*, *1*(1), 11–27. doi:10.1111/j.1539-6924.1981.tb01350.x PMID:11798118

Keesling, J. W. (1972). *Maximum Likelihood Approach to Causal Analysis* [Thèse de Doctorat]. University of Chicago, Chicago, IL, USA.

Kogan, N., & Wallach, M. A. (1964). *Risk Taking: A Study in Cognition and Personality. Holt, New-York.* Rinehart & Winston.

Kouabenan, D. R., Cadet, B., Hermand, D., & Munoz Sastre, M. T. (Eds.). (2006). *Psychologie du Risque: Identifier, Evaluer, Prévenir les Risques*. Bruxelles: De Boeck Université.

Kyle, A. (1989). Continuous Auctions and Insider Trading. *Econometrica*, *53*(6), 1315–1335. doi:10.2307/1913210

Lacroux, A. (2008), L'Analyse des Modèles de Relations Structurelles par la Méthode PLS: Une Approche Emergente dans la Recherche Quantitative en GRH. Retrieved from http://www.reims-ms.fr/agrh/docs/actes-agrh/pdf-des-actes/2009lacroux073.pdf

Larwood, L., & Whittaker, W. (1977). Managerial Myopia: Self-Serving Biases in Organizational Planning. *The Journal of Applied Psychology*, *62*(2), 194–198. doi:10.1037/0021-9010.62.2.194

Lehu, J.-M. (2004). L'Encyclopédie du Marketing (1st ed.). Editions d'Organisation, Paris.

Libby, R., & Fishburn, P. C. (1977). Behavioral Models of Risk Taking Business Decisions: A Survey and Evaluation. *Journal of Accounting Research*, *15*(2), 272–292. doi:10.2307/2490353

Lin, J.-C., Sanger, G. C., & Booth, G. G. (1995). Trade Size and Components of the Bid-Ask Spread. *Review of Financial Studies*, *8*(4), 1153–1183. doi:10.1093/rfs/8.4.1153

Lin, Q., & Lee, J. (2004). Consumer Information Search When Making Investment Decisions. *Financial Services Review*, *13*, 319–332.

Locander, W. B., & Hermann, P. W. (1979). The Effect of Self-Confidence and Anxiety on Information Seeking in Consumer Risk Reduction. *JMR, Journal of Marketing Research*, *16*(2), 268–274. doi:10.2307/3150690

Loibl, C., & Hira, T. K. (2009). Investor Information Search. *Journal of Economic Psychology*, *30*(1), 24–41. doi:10.1016/j.joep.2008.07.009

Lopes, L. L. (1987). In L. Berkowitz (Ed.), *Between Hope and Fear: The Psychology of Risk* (pp. 255–295). Advances in Experimental Social Psychology San Diego, CA: Academic Press.

Lu, C.-W., Chen, T.-K., & Liao, H.-H. (2010). Information Uncertainty, Information Asymmetry and Corporate Bond Yield Spreads. *Journal of Banking & Finance*, *34*(9), 2265–2279. doi:10.1016/j.jbankfin.2010.02.013

Lumpkin, J. R., & Dunn, M. G. (1990). Perceived Risk as a Factor in Store Choice: An Examination of Inherent Versus Handled Risk. *Journal of Applied Business Research*, *6*(2), 104–118.

Lutz, R. J., & Reilly, P. J. (1973). *An Exploration of the Effect of Perceived Social and Performance Risk on Consumer Information Acquisition.* In S. Ward, & P. Wright (Eds.), *Advances in Consumer Research, Proceedings of the 4th Annual Convention of the Association for Consumer Research* (pp. 393-405).

MacGregor, D. G., & Slovic, P. (1999). Perception of Financial Risk: A Survey Study of Advisors and Planners. *Journal of Financial Planning*, *12*, 68–79.

MacGregor, G. G., Slovic, P., Dreman, D., & Berry, M. (2000). Imagery, Affect and Financial Judgment. *The Journal of Psychology and Financial Markets*, 1(2), 104-110.

Mahmood, I., Ahmad, H., Khan, A. Z., & Anjum, M. (2011). Behavioral Implications of Investors for Investments in the Stock Market. *European Journal of Soil Science*, *20*(2), 240–247.

Mallet, S. (2000). *Le Concept de Risque Perçu: Composantes, Antécédents et Proposition de Recherche. in les Actes des liers ateliers de recherche de l'AFM, « Percevoir, identifier et gérer le risque en marketing* (pp. 46–62). Paris: La Sorbonne.

Mallet, S. (2001). *Pour une Classification de la Mesure du Risque Perçu. Proceedings of the 17ème congrès International de l'Association Française du Marketing*, Deauville.

Mallet, S. (2004). Vers une Clarification des Déterminants du Risque Perçu à l'Egard de l'Achat d'un Produit. *Proceedings of the 20ème Congrès de l'AFM, Actes sur CD-Rom*, Saint-Malo.

Malmendier, U., & Tate, G. (2005). CEO Overconfidence and Corporate Investment. *The Journal of Finance*, *60*(6), 2661–2700. doi:10.1111/j.1540-6261.2005.00813.x

March, J. G., & Shapira, Z. (1987). Managerial Perspectives on Risk and Risk Taking. *Management Science*, *33*(11), 1404–1418. doi:10.1287/mnsc.33.11.1404

McDonald, J. G., & Stehle, R. E. (1975). How do institutional investors perceive risk? *Journal of Portfolio Management*, *2*(1), 11–16. doi:10.3905/jpm.1975.11

Mear, R., & Firth, M. (1988). Risk Perceptions of Financial Analysts and the Use of Market and Accounting Data. *Accounting and Business Review*, *18*(72), 335–339. doi:10.1080/00014788.1988.9729380

Mezghani, A., & Ellouze, A. (2007). *Gouvernance de l'Entreprise et Qualité de l'Information Financière, 28ème Congrés de l'AFC- 'Comptabilité et Environnement'*. Retrieved from http://halshs.archives-ouvertes.fr/docs/00/54/49/34/PDF/p185.pdf

Mitchell, V.-W. (1999). Consumer Perceived Risk: Conceptualizations and Models. *European Journal of Marketing*, *33*(1/2), 163–195. doi:10.1108/03090569910249229

Mitchell, V.-W., & Greatorex, M. (1989). Risk Reducing Strategies Used in the Purchase of Wine in the UK. *European Journal of Marketing*, *23*(9), 31–46. doi:10.1108/EUM0000000000589

Murray, K. B. (1991). A Test of Services Marketing Theory: Consumer Information Acquisition Activities. *Journal of Marketing*, *55*(1), 10–25. doi:10.2307/1252200

Okpara, G. C. (2010). Information Asymmetric and Dividend Policy in Emerging Markets: Empirical Evidence from Nigeria. *International Journal of Economics and Finance*, *2*(4). doi:10.5539/ijef.v2n4p212

Olsen, R. (1997). Desirability Bias among Professional Investment Managers: Some Evidence from Experts. *Journal of Behavioral Decision Making*, *10*(1), 65–72. doi:10.1002/(SICI)1099-0771(199703)10:1<65::AID-BDM246>3.0.CO;2-S

Oppe, S. (1988). The Concept of Risk: A Theoretical Approach. *Ergonomics*, *31*(4), 435–440. doi:10.1080/00140138808966690

Page, L. (2009). Is there an Optimistic Bias on Betting Markets? *Economics Letters*, *102*(2), 70–72. doi:10.1016/j.econlet.2008.10.006

Pedhazur, E. J., & Schmelkin, L. P. (1991). *Measurement, Design, and Analysis: An Integrated Approach*. Hillsdale, N.J.: Lawrence Erlbaum Associates.

Raykov, T., & Marcoulides, G. A. (2006). *A First Course in Structural Equation Modeling* (2nd ed.). Lawrence Erlbaum Associates, Inc. Publishers.

Renn, O. (1992). Concepts of Risk: A Classification. In S. Krimsky & D. Golding (Eds.), *Social Theories of Risk. Westport, CT* (pp. 83–116). London: Praeger.

Ricciardi, V. (2004). A risk Perception Primer: A Narrative Research Review of The Risk Perception Literature in Behavioral Accounting and Behavioral Finance, *Working Paper*.

Ricciardi, V. (2008). Risk: Traditional Finance versus Behavioral Finance. In F.J. Fabozzi (Ed.), Handbook of Finance (Vol. 3, pp. 11-38). John Wiley & Sons. doi:10.1002/9780470404324.hof003002

Rogers, J. L. (2008). *Disclosure Quality and Management Trading Incentives*. Chicago GSB Working Paper N°. 08-18.

Roussel, P., Durrieu, F., Campoy, Y., & El Akremi, A. (2002). Méthodes d'Equations Structurelles: Recherche et Applications en Gestion. *Economica*.

Simon, H. A. (1986). Rationality in Psychology and Economics. *The Journal of Business*, *59*(S4), 209–224. doi:10.1086/296363

Sitkin, S. B., & Pablo, A. L. (1992). Reconceptualizing the Determinants of Risk Behavior. *Review of Academic Management*, *17*, 9–38.

Sitkin, S. B., & Weingart, L. R. (1995). Determinants of Risky-Making Behavior: A Test of Mediatic Role of Risk Perceptions and Propensity. *Academy of Management Journal*, *38*(6), 1573–1592. doi:10.2307/256844

Sjöberg, L. (2000). Factors of Risk Perception. *Risk Analysis*, *20*(1), 1–11. doi:10.1111/0272-4332.00001

Slovic, P. (1987). Perception of Risk. *Science*, *236*(4799), 280–285. doi:10.1126/science.3563507 PMID:3563507

Slovic, P. (1988). Risk Perception. In C. C. Travis (Ed.), Contemporary issues in risk analysis (Vol. 3,pp. 171-181). New York: Plenum. doi:10.1007/978-1-4684-5484-0_13

Slovic, P., Fischhoff, B., & Lichtenstein, S. (1979). Risk Assessment: Technical and Behavioral Issues. In Risk/Benefit analysis in the legislative process (Joint Hearings before the Committee on Science and Technology, U.S. House of Representatives and the Committee on Commerce, Science and Transportation, U.S. Senate) (pp. 133-188). Washington, DC: Government Printing Office.

Slovic, P., Fischhoff, B., & Lichtenstein, S. (1980). Facts and Fears: Understanding Perceived Risk. In R. Schwing & W.A. Albers, Jr. (Eds.), Societal risk assessment: How safe is safe enough? (pp. 181-214). New York: Plenum. (Revision in D. Kahneman, P. Slovic, & A. Tversky (Eds.), Judgment under uncertainty: Heuristics and biases. New York: Cambridge University, 1982; in F. Farley & C. H. Null (Eds.), Using psychological science: Making the public case. Washington, DC: Federation of Behavioral, Psychological and Cognitive Sciences, 1987. doi:10.1007/978-1-4899-0445-4_9

Slovic, P., Fischhoff, B., & Lichtenstein, S. (1982). Why Study Risk Perception? *Risk Analysis*, *2*(2), 83–93. doi:10.1111/j.1539-6924.1982.tb01369.x

Slovic, P., Fischhoff, B., & Lichtenstein, S. (1985). Regulation of Risk: A Psychological Perspective. In R. G. Noll (Ed.), *Regulatory policy and the social sciences* (pp. 241–278). Berkeley: University of California.

Swanson, P. E., & Lin, A. Y. (2005). Trading behavior and Investment Performance of U.S. Investors in Global Equity Markets. *Journal of Multinational Financial Management*, *15*(2), 99–115. doi:10.1016/j.mulfin.2004.03.006

Taylor, J. (1974). The Role of Risk in Consumer Behavior. *Journal of Marketing*, *38*(2), 54–60. doi:10.2307/1250198

Thayer, J. (2008). Determinants of Shareholders' Information Search: Credibility versus Confirmation. *Unpublished working Paper,* Emory University.

Valette-Florence, P. (1988). Spécificités et Apports des Méthodes d'Analyse Multivariée de la Deuxième Génération. *Recherche et Applications en Marketing*, *3*(4), 23–56. doi:10.1177/076737018800300402

van Raaij, W. F. (1977). *Consumer Choice Behavior: An Information Processing Approach* [Doctoral Dissertation]. Univeristé de Tilburg.

Veld, C., & Veld-Merkoulova, Y. V. (2008). The Risk Perceptions of Individual Investors. *Journal of Economic Psychology*, *29*(2), 226–252. doi:10.1016/j.joep.2007.07.001

Verhage, B. J., Yavas, U., & Green, R. T. (1990). Perceived Risk: A Cross-Cultural Phenomenon. *International Journal of Research in Marketing*, *7*(4), 297–303. doi:10.1016/0167-8116(90)90007-A

Vlaev, I., Chater, N., & Stewart, N. (2009). Dimensionality of Risk Perception: Factors Affecting Consumer Understanding and Evaluation of Financial Risk. *Journal of Behavioral Finance*, *10*(3), 158–181. doi:10.1080/15427560903167720

Volle, P. (1995). Le Concept du Risque en Psychologie du Consommateur: Antécédents et Statuts Théoriques. *Recherche et Applications en Marketing*, *10*(1), 39–56. doi:10.1177/076737019501000103

Wang, X. L., Shi, K., & Fan, H. X. (2006). Psychological Mechanisms of Investors in Chinese Stock Markets. *Journal of Economic Psychology*, *27*(6), 762–780. doi:10.1016/j.joep.2006.06.007

Weber, E. U., & Hsee, C. K. (1998). Cross-Cultural Differences in Risk Perception but Cross-Cultural Similarities in Attitudes toward Perceived Risk. *Management Science*, *44*(9), 1205–1217. doi:10.1287/mnsc.44.9.1205

Weber, E. U., & Hsee, C. K. (1999). Cross-National Differences in Risk Preferences and Lay Predictions for the Differences. *Journal of Behavioral Decision Making*, *12*(2), 165–179. doi:10.1002/(SICI)1099-0771(199906)12:2<165::AID-BDM316>3.0.CO;2-N

Weinstein, N. D. (1980). Unrealistic Optimism about Future Life Events. *Journal of Personality and Social Psychology*, *39*(5), 806–820. doi:10.1037/0022-3514.39.5.806

Wiley, D. E. (1973). The Identification Problem for Structural Equation Models in Unmeasured Variables. In A. S. Goldberger & O. D. Duncan (Eds.), *Structural Equation Models in the Social Sciences.* New York: Seminar Press/Harcourt Brace.

Wright, P. (1975). Factors Affecting Cognitive Resistance to Advertising. *The Journal of Consumer Research*, *2*(1), 1–9. doi:10.1086/208610

Yates, A., & Firer, C. (1997). The Determinants of Investor Risk Perceptions. *Investment Analysis Journal*, *44*, 61–70.

Yates, J. F., & Stone, E. R. (1992). The Risk Construct. In J. F. Yates (Ed.), *Risk-Taking Behavior* (pp. 1–25). Chichester: Wiley.

KEY TERMS AND DEFINITIONS

Controllability: The ability to foresee and navigate potential hazards, thus erasing risk in a material way.

Decrease in the Amount at Stake: The decrease of vulnerability associated with adverse outcomes.

Familiarity: A degree of knowledge or experience a person has respect to a task or object.

Formative Construct: A combination of indicators contributing to form the latent construct. The causal relationship proceeds from indicators to latent construct.

Information Search: The activity that each investor must do to make the investment decisions. Search for information is to consult information sources.

Risk Perception: A person's assessment of the risk inherent in a situation.

Risk-Reducing Strategies: Two different modes of behavioral responses to decrease the risk perception of decision's maker.

Structural Equation Method: The method that attempts to examine the causal relationships in a model.

ENDNOTES

1 The structural equation method will be presented in the following section.

Chapter 15
Rise of Experiential Marketing in Emerging Markets:
An Analysis of Advertising in Experiential Markets

Mervat Medhat Youssef
Art and Design Academy, Higher Institute of Applied Arts, Egypt

Hanan Atef Abdallah
Emirates College of Technology, UAE

ABSTRACT

This chapter aims to contribute towards the improvement of using Experiential Marketing as a business model in Emerging Markets. This chapter also clarifies how experiential marketing fits within the Emerging marketing climate, and how to go about planning and evaluating it for best results. It provides examples focused on Emerging Markets ethics, market mix strategies, customer brand consumption experience and consumer word of mouth. The finding suggests how Experiential Marketing strategies can best utilize marketing communication channels to achieve Emerging Markets objectives. This chapter will encourage companies and brands in Emerging Markets to look into using experiential advertising in their marketing strategies. The chapter will focus on highlighting the connection between Emerging Markets and Experiential Marketing in different aspects, which then will be analyzed in order to determine how functional and successful Experiential Marketing can be. It concludes with analysis of demonstrating views from the public and experiential specialists.

INTRODUCTION

In the twenty-first century of virtual connections, the use of Experiential marketing as a communication tool is highly used by brands and companies that believe, when it comes to connecting with consumers, there is nothing like a real experience. Experiential Marketing is about providing a live brand experience that gives consumers the opportunity to interact with the brand. While most traditional marketers

DOI: 10.4018/978-1-4666-9864-2.ch015

continue to bombard consumers with thousands of messages per day, Experiential marketing has the power to reach consumers in a more direct and personal level.

The strategy of Emerging Markets (EMs) focuses on the central pillars of marketing segmentation, the key ingredients of product price, distribution and communication. It is characterized by non-traditional user behavior and the rise of new user groups. It means that, economic conditions and technology movement have reached a high stage where the wide majority of consumers have significantly greater replaceable income. As a result of growing industrialization and the increase in employment, the high-speed growth of EMs gives millions of consumers' a new spending power as they tend to consider smaller sets of brands initially. Compared with other consumers in developed countries, they are less likely to change later to a brand that was not in their initial set. This issue increases the importance of adopting new advertising strategies in EMs to include new brands in the initial consumers consideration set. By achieving recognition through advertising and real communication, experience is the essential first step. The data introduced in this chapter reveal that word of mouth is more important in EMs, consumers will respond to products and brands that were able to establish an interaction that gives people an unexpected experience, and makes them not only remember it, but also talk about it.

This chapter has an exploratory approach and involved investigation of the existing literature reviews. The main chapter objective is to understand the role of experiential marketing and Word of Mouth marketing and how they create meaningful relationships between the customers and the brand. In order to prove how experiential marketing could be a future to EMs strategies and fits within its current marketing climate. The chapter is organized as follows:

- The first section introduces both EMs and Experiential Marketing definition, tool and characteristics.
- The second section introduces the connection between EMs and experiential marketing through five generic market aspects: 1) Market mix component, 2) Brand consumption experience, 3) The impact of word of mouth in consumer behavior, 4) EMs consumer segment and 5) Experiential market best practices. This through looking at what published statistical and survey data say about the EMs consumer segment, experiential market case studies.
- The third section contains first an analysis of experiential advertising case studies in EMs using the five market aspects, then the conclusion and the model approach presentation, and finally the recommendation for the use of experiential advertising in EMs.

BACKGROUND

The big rise of competition in the twenty-first century of virtual connections has made companies design new strategies focusing on customers in order to develop a competitive advantage to survive. To differentiate products by only using the traditional elements such as price, product and quality is no longer a competitive advantage. The use of experiential marketing as a communication tool is growing with smart brands and companies that believe in real customer experience. The Customer Experience is the next competitive field of battle (Gentile, 2007). Besides, the consumers have changed their demands nowadays; they are looking for consuming that stimulates emotions and sensations to satisfy not only their needs but also it has to be meaningful to them as an individual (Schmitt, 1999). A survey done by Morton (2009) bring out that the majority of marketers believed "experiential marketing builds customer relationships for the long term and it generates sales and leads in the short term, increases awareness of the product, drives word of mouth and can align internal audiences with business goals".

Ethics is the difference between knowing what you have the right to do and what is right to do (Potter, 2004). According to PWC.com, the comparative average of GDP growth rate for emerging countries such as China, Brazil, Vietnam, India, Turkey, and others has been about twice more than advanced nations over the past 15 years; this direction is expected to continue in the foreseeable future.

Experiential marketing can be executed through a number of activities such as roadshows, ambient & in-store advertising, free product sampling, exhibitions, retail brands and fast-moving consumer goods. It gives the customers the chance to engage and interact with the brand, products and services face-to-face in an emotional and sensible way. There is a big difference between telling people about the products or service features and allow them to experience the benefits so they can take more informed purchasing decisions. Today the customers have more power to force the global brand managers to turn their attention to the fast-growing countries in Africa, Asia and Latin America, with their huge population and a growing number of middle class consumers that have high purchasing power. They deal with them as partners, sharing information and sometimes letting them participate in the decision making and join the competences in a profitable and beneficial way (Bagozzi & Dholakia, 2006). Now the challenge of building strong brands is to gain consumer's emotional support and commitment (Boyle & Ponsonby, 2006). The more important is to create word of mouth, to concentrate on a new set of building blocks such as in-depth communication with customers, transparency and freedom to exchange information to compete with local players in EMs (Tsai, 2005).

Develop an Understanding of (EMs): Definition and Characteristics

The term EMs was created by economists at the International Finance Corporation (IFC) in 1981 when the group was promoting the first mutual fund investments in developing countries. Since then, EMs have become everywhere in the media, foreign policy, trade debates, investment fund prospectuses and multinationals' annual reports (Khanna & Palepu, 2010). Miller (1998) showed in his previous work that all EMs are similar in their potential for future growth. According to the US government estimates, only 10 of the most attractive EMs- called by Clinton's administration big EMs will double their share of global GDP in the next 20 years, from 10.2% to 20.7% (Garten, 1996). Dr. Vladimir Kvint (2009), the president of the international Academy of EMs, describe an EMs country as a society change from a dictatorship to a free market-oriented economy, with increasing the freedom of the economic, gradual combination within the global marketplace, an expanding middle class, improving standards of living and social stability, and an increase in cooperation with multilateral institutions. Amadeo (2013), the US Economy Expert in Ems, defined the emerging economies or developing countries as countries that are investing in more productive capacity. Leaders of developing countries intend to design a better quality of life for their people. Therefore, they are hastily industrializing, and adopting a free market or mixed economy. According to the business dictionary (2014), EMs is new structures of market that arising from deregulation, digitalization, globalization, and open-standards that are devious the balance of economic power from the vendor to the purchaser. The authors agreed that EMs is a term that investors use to describe a developing country, in which investment would be expected to achieve higher returns but be accompanied by greater risk.

EMs such as Brazil, China, India and Russia, are emerging by excellence of their modern fast economic growth, the opening of these large economies to global capital, technology and talent through the past

Table 1. The twenty-one countries classified as emerging markets

Emerging Markets		
Brazil	India	Poland
Chile	Indonesia	Russia
China	Korea	South Africa
Colombia	Malaysia	South Korea
Czech republic	Morocco	Taiwan
Egypt	Peru	Thailand
Hungary	Philippines	Turkey

two decades has actually changed their business environments and economic (Khanna & Palepu, 2010). As a result of this change, the GDP growth rates of these countries have dramatically raised more than those of developed economies, lifting millions out of need, creating new middle classes and creating a big new markets for consumer products and services. Large, low-cost and increasingly educated laborers give these markets enormous competitive advantage in production; also information technology is enabling companies to contribute laborers in these markets in a very unique ways (Khanna & Palepu, 2010). The twenty-one countries listed in Table 1 are classified as EMs.

Miller (1998) defined the characteristics of EMs. In his study he includes three characteristics: 1) Physical characteristics, in terms of an inappropriate commercial infrastructure as well as inefficiency of all other aspects of physical infrastructure such as communication, transport and power generation. 2) Socio-political characteristics which include: unsuitable legal framework, political instability, weak social discipline and reduced technological levels, besides cultural characteristics. 3) Economic characteristics in terms of limited individual income, centrally guided currencies with an effective role of government in economic life, expressed, among others, in managing the process of transition to market economy. We can study these characteristics through main EMs countries like China and India. These two countries are home to 40% of the world's labor force and population. Their economic output which is $15.9 trillion in 2011 is greater than that of either the EU ($15.6 trillion) or the U.S. ($15.3 trillion). Consequently, any discussion of EMs must keep in mind the powerful influence of these two giants (CIA World Facebook, 2011).

According to the study of Amadeo (2014), the EMs characteristics are divided into five categories:

1. Lower than average per person income: The World Bank defines developing countries as "those with either low or lower middle per capita income, basically less than $4,034".
2. The rapid growth: for example the economic increase of most developed countries, such as Germany, the U.S., the U.K. and Japan, was between 1-2% in 2011. But in Russia, Turkey, Mexico and South Africa, it was between 3-4% in the same year, while Brazil's economy increases 4.5%. China and India both saw their economies grow more than big to increase 8% (NASDAQ, 2012).
3. High volatility: occurs from three factors, External price shocks, Natural disasters, and Instability in local policy.
4. The capital markets are less mature: it means they don't have a strong track record of foreign direct investment. And it's very difficult to have information on companies listed in their stock markets.
5. Higher than average return for investors: This happened because many of these countries focus on an export driven strategy so they don't have the demand at home, so they manufacture lower cost consumer goods and commodities for developed markets.

Ethical Challenges in Emerging Markets

The biggest ethical challenge that many companies will face is gaining an understanding of differences in various cultural. Some companies take a "one size fits all" process to ethics, and trying to apply their normal corporate standards in new markets. However, this often affect in a policy that fails to meet the needs of the market or is met with opposition (Ann. E, 1997). These companies realized that, when it comes to ethics in EMs, the rules for doing business aren't necessarily the same as at home.

In order to avoid ethical problems in EMs, companies must perform to some extent delicate balancing act. They must find a way to balance between standards, the rapidly developed global values; norms with the needs, cultures and business practices of those markets that they wish to do business with (Andrew, 2014).

It may be the situation in some EMs countries that corruption is taking as a prerequisite for doing business or as a provenance of profit and competitive advantage. But empirical evidence suggests that corruption poses a cost on economic growth in EMs. In addition to this international guidance statement, specific areas of emphasis for investors in EMs can include (George. D, 2013):

1. Detection on ethics management: Investors in EMs should request more transparency on standards of behavior and policies on corruption and how these standards are enforced in the company.
2. Audit quality: The auditors of the company are on the frontline of assessing the preciseness of its financial statements and controls. For auditors it is better positioned to detect abnormalities or corrupt practice than investors.
3. Foreign first-hand investment: While most institutional investors have portfolio holdings in EMs through investment in registered equities, the influence of foreign direct (first-hand) investment can be even greater in terms of providing fresh capital and sources of employment in EMS.
4. Creditors: The main role of creditors is sometimes unnoted in terms of potential effect on EMs companies especially for closely held companies. They do not wish to dilute their control on shareholders through external equity offerings. Debt capital can represent an important source of funding for EM firms. They should power this influence through demanding high ethical standards of companies they provide credit to, whether in the form of loans or bonds.
5. Public policy engagement: In EMs the Governments tend to welcome both portfolio and direct investment flows to provide capital for the growth and development of the economic. Investor's mast communicates their concerns to governments about the negative economic effect of corruption on valuations, economic development, and the cost of capital and the latest access to capital.

Experiential Marketing: Definition, Tools and Objectives

Economic value at a societal level has developed through three stages (Pine & Gilmore, 1998): The earliest stage was the economy that was concerned with the extraction of various substances from the world around us. The second stage started with the Industrial revolution in the 19th century, followed by the manufacturing economy where the primary economic display was the making of products. The fourth stage started in the twenty-first century, the experience economy where the highest value economic offerings are experiences. This shift toward experiential marketing occurred as a result of three simultaneous developments in the broader business environment (Schmitt, 1999, 2011): 1) The Digital Revolution, where information and transformation are some of the fastest growing marketing channels.

2) The Supremacy of the Brand, where everything will soon be a brand. 3) The Advancement in Information Technology, which makes everything become a form of communication and entertainment.

Experiential Marketing is defined as a promotional system used to increase awareness and improve brand image and loyalty. According to Jobber & Fahy (2009) Experiential Marketing does not appear to be limited to the realm of exclusively promotional activity. It is the experience that customers face every day to deal with an organization and how an organization's delivery of the marketing mix can boost the customer's experience. This in return, will increase loyalty, sales and profit (Smith & Wheeler, 2002). Schmitt (1999) views Experiential Markets consumers as intellectual and emotional human who are interested in achieving pleasurable experiences. Kotler (2002) believes experiential marketing occurrences are created to communicate special messages to target audiences. According to Augustine (2003) Experiential Marketing goes well beyond simply delivering consumption experiences to consumers as a way to give them the information they need to make a purchase decision. According to the authors, Experiential Marketing is the variation between telling people about features or benefits within the limit of the thirty-second TV commercial and letting them experience it and get their own "a-ha!" event. Experiential Marketing is a communication messages through media or other exists marketing channels to communicate with different consumers or business sectors (Smilansky, 2009). It will create higher connection between brands and target audiences through actions and engagements that aim to achieve marketing communication objectives, and add value to consumers' lives.

Experiential Marketing explores motivation more than any other channel of communication and provokes word-of-mouth. Brands that engage people have more power in the subconscious level of the mind because it stimulates the neural region that makes decisions (Moré, 2011). Zena and Hadisumarto (2012) view Experiential Marketing tries to submerge the consumers with the product by fascinating as many human senses as possible. This fact refers to the big change in nowadays consumers, they look not only for product/service quality, functionality, and benefits, but also look for products communications that touch them and suit their lifestyle. According to the authors, Experiential Marketing gives an especial framework to merge elements of experience and entertainment into the product or service.

During the twenty-first century the focus has changed from product to experiences. Marketers started to use experiential marketing tools to be directed to a target audience and they try to emphasize on technologies that can deliver highly interactive brand experiences. Experiential Marketing develops tools that enable the customers to share their feelings, opinions, researching, identifying and reaching out to influential individuals or communities, tracking online chats and motivating the talkers to promote. Some of the most familiar tools used to provide experiences are: Product demonstrations, Online reviews, Point-of-purchase displays, Sponsorship and Brand community's samples. These are the basic examples of Experiential Marketing tools that have existed in the marketing mix for a while. When these tools are double with targeted messages they can achieve key components for success in any campaign. In today's world Experiential Marketing has changed, for example: the publicity of social media among customers has opened up new ways for marketers to provide them with holistic brand experience. Social networks, the Internet, a demand for transparency and shortened consumer attention tools have contributed to a big shift in Experiential Marketing strategies (Duncan, 2006).This shift has achieved a much wider approach between marketing and business that is heavily fixed in consumer opinion and dependent on target audience feedback.

There is a common fact that stems from the most essential belief in psychology that "we learn from experience". The same principle applies to Experiential Marketing objectives, therefore there are many causes for the obvious need of Experiential Marketing: 1) Current Trends in Advertising: a live brand experience is the two-way interaction that allows the consumer to interact and develop a relationship with the brand to raise brand loyalty and advocacy. They offers not only communicating messages like that traditional marketing could do, but they are also creating something unique called a personal recommendation or word of mouth (Smilansky, 2009). 2) Consumers Need: consumers are now keener on marketing communications that are closely connected for them as an individual and can recognize their need for modernity. The customers need to be entertained, stimulated, challenged and educated by the brands which are expected to become a part of their lives (Aronne & de Vasconcelos, 2009). 3) From Consumer to Participant Behavior: Consumers want personalized interaction and customization. In other words marketing has to be about a consumer dialogue rather than a brand monologue. There is a growing need amongst consumers to be a part of the experiential aspects of consumption (Holbrook & Hirschman 1981). 4) Big Data vs. Real Data: Experiential Markets do not think only about product; they think in terms of consumption real experience, what products fit into this consuming situation and how these products external features and their advertising can enhance the consumption experience (Schmitt, 1999).

Experiential Marketing Four Keys Characteristics

"Experiential Marketing theories and practices are rapidly changing and becoming less relevant," this writes by Erik Hauser, Director of the International Experiential Marketing Association (IXMA). He also added that "Experiential Marketing is leading the way into the new marketing paradigm." The Traditional marketing characteristics are now shifting to following characteristics of experiential marketing. Schmitt's (1999) differentiates between traditional and experiential marketing in four main keys: 1) focus on customer experience: Experiential Marketing is defined as any form of focused customer marketing activity that creates a good connection to customers. Based on this view, experiences may be evoked by packaging, products, in-store interactions, communications, sales relationships and events or they may occur as a result of online or offline activities (Schmitt, 2011). As Brakus, Schmitt and Zarantonello (2009) discussed it; the experience construct differs from evaluative, affective, and associative constructs such as attitudes, involvement, attachment, and brand associations. This experience engage the consumer at different levels (sensorial, emotional, cognitive, physical lifestyle and relational) that can be explored by marketer (Gentile, Spiller & Noci, 2007). 2) Focus on holistic consumption experience: In facts, nowadays consumers have changed their demands, now they have more interest in social context than on maximizing their benefits. The customers are looking for consumption that stimulates emotions and sensations to satisfy their needs (CARÙ & COVA2008). Usually the most experience after consumption of a particular goods or services are revealed, but in Experiential Marketing, what goods or services have been used is not a case of concern but what matters is the ultimate experience. 3) Customers are rationalistic and emotional: this is the case In Experiential Marketing while selecting a particular brand (goods or services), this happens because consumption experiences are often directed toward the chase of fantasies feelings and fun (Holbrook and Hirschman, 1982). The results from Gentile et al. (2007) survey showed that the sensorial component was the most important one across several experiential brands (Swatch, Pringles, Harley-Davidson, Smart, iPod, Nike, HC Brands Bar, PlayStation, Gatorade, McDonald's, Ikea, and Swarovski). Nowadays recognizing both the rational and emotional drivers of consumption is the most challenge faced by marketers to provide effective interaction with customers and engage them to share their experiences with others. Building a bonding relation between the consumer and brands is called brand loyalty, which consists of four indicators: repurchase determination, recommend a brand or company, price tolerance and preparedness to do cross purchase (Gronholdt, Martensen & Kristensen, 2000). 4) Experiential Marketing methods and tools are eclectic: The methodology that used in Experiential Marketing research is diverse in compare to the traditional one.

One of the strongest reasons that make Experiential Marketing a key trend for upcoming years is because the need of brand ambassadors to collect a real data in the midst of an existing experiential campaign is a valuable add, and in comparison with traditional research methods it is incredibly affordable. So in the one to one interaction people are more than willing to answer, they feel normal and natural, and it is easy to get honest feedback and information about both the brand and its programs. After this introduction to present the main definitions in the subject the authors in the next section will start introduces the connection between EMs and experiential marketing through five generic market aspects, In order to prove how experiential marketing could be a future to EMs strategies and fits within its current marketing climate.

EMs AND EXPERIENTIAL VALUE IN MARKETING MIX

EMs had enjoyed exponential growth. In 1990 Ems represented 21% of the global GDP; by 2008 this had grown to 34% and by 2010 to 38%. It is also expected by 2015 to account for 50% of the world's GDP. (Deloittee Development LLC, 2012) However, it is likely that EMs can provide essential opportunities for companies or investors in the expected future. So in order to understand and work with Ems, companies must not just focus on what customer's need but also to focus on what they want. Corporates will likely do better in mega-markets such as (Brazil, Russia, India, and China). To take advantage of the opportunities in EMs, the marketer needs to get back to the basics of what marketing is supposed to bring to people. EMs countries are usually characterized by political uncertainty, and direct foreign investment can be very risky. Besides that, EMs countries are not all the same and do not even necessarily move in tandem. Table 2 demonstrates the 4Ps market components (place, product, price and promotion) in the biggest EMs countries including (Russia- China- India) (Johansson, 2009).

Table 2. The 4Ps in the biggest EMs countries

	Russia	China	India
Product	Customers initially feel hesitant about their domestic products.	Quality gap between foreign & local products still large. High tariffs make it hard for foreign brands to compete with lower quality domestic brands.	With increasing maturity, the market can support a full line of products from foreign firms.
Price	Entering global brands will be able to command a price premium over existing local brands	Entering global brands will be risky; Chinese are very price-sensitive consumers (due to low income and due to habit).	Middle-income group of consumers are price sensitive. Price level is especially important when brand name is less known.
Place	The market Suffers from Weak infrastructure, weak Marketing education and Service training	Most of the market channels are government run and most department stores are state-owned, so personal contacts play an important role in transactions	Market Infrastructure is still weak in a vast country. Entering companies are assisting with structural improvements. Urban distribution channels are becoming more efficient.
Promotion	Advertising communications often have to be revised. Also common advertising media may not be available or may have only limited reach. Also lack of advertising claims credibility is a problem.	Advertising still strictly controlled by government away from counterfeit, also Media penetration is weak. Print, outdoor ads and in-store promotions play a large role.	Global advertising campaigns are adapted to meet local Indian tastes and localized to India's many dialects. TV advertising very is popular, but print and outdoor are more cost-effective.

Lauterborn (1990) research shows that 4Ps represented a narrative particularly focused on the marketing organization to some extent than on the customer. He suggests greater emphasis on the customer 4Cs (customer value and benefits, customer cost convenience and customer communication). The common between these models is that they represent a combination of influencing instruments designed and specific marketing demand to achieve desired restraint from target customers. With reference to the 4Ps or 4Cs and the different definitions of Experiential Marketing, it appears that Experiential Marketing is simply one of the tools of the promotional mix or customer communication. Experience is perceived both emotionally and rationally; it is highly subjective. Now it includes feelings fantasies, and fun or rich in emotion and symbolic meaning. According to Schmitt (1999), the five strategic modules *(SEMs)* are: think, sense, act, feel, and relate. These modules act as experience providers. The think appeals to problem solving experiences that involve the customers creatively, the sense experience includes sensory qualities and aesthetics that appeals to consumers' senses (sound, sight, touch, taste, and smell). The act refers to actions and behavioral experiences of the target customers. The Relate point to a social experiences or consumer desires to be part of a social context.

Poulsson and Kale (2004) presumed that the Experience oriented marketing mix consists of the elements of 4Cs. 4Cs for Experiential Marketing must be viewed not as an alternative to the 4Ps mix (EMs) but as a way of encouraging companies to consider the customer experience and to understand how the traditional mix is capable of being used to stimulate rational and emotional demand. Table 3 summarizes the relation of 4Cs, 4Ps with Experiential Marketing and EMs to understand what is the marketing activities in any organizations that focus on the customer's experience.

Table 3. The opportunities of applying 4PS, 4Cs in experiential marketing and EMs

Experiential Marketing / 4Cs			
Customer Value And Benefits	**Customer Cost**	**Convenience**	**Customer Communication**
Experiential Provides customers with some form of rational solution. The benefit becomes the sense in which the customer's life has been modified	In Experiential cost being both tangible and psychological to create meaningful value. Consider not just the price of the product or the total cost price to the customer, but Balance between what must be given to the customer and the range to which they receive as a life enhancing benefits. Experiential uses low cost campaign with high impact.	Experiential considers often the easiest channels and ways of allocation work best for today customer choice. Makes balance between organization's values and individual customer's values.	Experiential is personally relevant (media, message, tone, color, language and so on). It needs to align with customers' expectations. Complements customers' lifestyles. Experiential helps create meaning and has trusty stories that are in keeping with customers' needs, and aligns with their values.
EMs / 4Ps			
Product	**Pricing**	**Place**	**Promotion**
EMs Initial offers are usually standardized simpler selections from existing lines. Limited features make it possible to sell through low-service outlets	EMs policies are dominated by governments. Pricing fluctuates between a skimming price and a lower penetration price	Weak logistics systems in EMs make it difficult for marketing organization and control. Cheap domestic, labor offers, alternative routes for marketing distribution	Initially limited in EMs due to lack of broadcast media. Literacy levels differ from more developed nations, promotions must be more visual versus verbal

BRAND CONSUMPTION EXPERIENCE IN BOTH EXPERIENTIAL AND EMs

Brands have become such an integral part of the cultural and economic landscape because the growth of EMs gives millions of consumer's new spending power. Those consumers are facing a marketing environment. Every part seen as complex and swiftly evolves the same as their counterparts in developed countries (Kalinowski, J. D. 2012). Lately brand experience has attracted a lot of attention in marketing practices, product choices and communication channels. In market strategies live brand experiences are becoming a two way branded experiences, and can be equally successful across many platforms and interactive technologies that simplify the communication between consumers and brands in real time. Creating brand experience is the most obvious challenge of executing Experiential Marketing on how to get someone involved in the experience. Brand experience is conceptualized as feelings, cognitions, sensations, and behavioral responses evoked by brand stimulations that are part of a brand's design / identity, packaging, communications and environments (May edition of Journal of Marketing, 2009).

The Experiential aspects of consumption are: Consumer Feelings, Fantasies and Fun, including playful leisure activities, sensual pleasures, Aesthetic, Daydreams, Enjoyment and Emotional Responses (Leigh, 2006). However, the main values of a product cannot be forgotten, these values are still part of the main factors of customer's evaluation and perception of a good brand. So these should be explored in order to enable factors for great experiences when possible" (Gentile, Spiller & Noci, 2007). Hirschman and Holbrook (1985) created a model that describe the consumption experience called (TEAV), this model suggest that the Thoughts, Emotions, Activities, and Evaluations that occur during an experience are clearly connected and feed into one another as a good experience. It makes the consumer understand what the brand's identity is. Chernatony, in his research (2006), found that brand experience affects consumer loyalty and satisfaction in a direct way and indirect way through the brand personality associations.

Experiences in Experimental Marketing occur when consumers are looking for products, they examine and evaluate them (Hoch, 2002). Schmitt (2011) suggests that "experience provides more guidance in order to add value to the customer than satisfaction". According to literature review of consumer and marketing research which examines how experiential occurs and its types of experience in marketing approaches by Schmitt (1999), there are five types of experience marketing approaches called "Strategic Expericntial Modules" (SEMs) includes feel, sense, think, act and relate. These attributes act as Experience providers. Dub´e and LeBel (2003) have featured four similar approaches called "Pleasure Dimensions", which include intellectual, emotional, physical, and social pleasures.

Gentile, Spiller, and Noci (2007) defined (CEM) Customer Experience Management as a procedure of managing a product or company with all the experiences that the customer might have in a strategic way; they also add six experiential components include: Emotional, Sensorial, Cognitive, Pragmatic (practical act of doing experience and usability), Lifestyle, and Relational. Brakus, Zarantonello and Schmitt (2009) built their work in brand experiences on the five components featured by Schmitt (1999). They viewed these components, as internal and behavioral outcomes. This study defined brand experiences as subjective and internal responses from consumers (feelings, sensations, and knowledge) as well as behavioral responses evoked by brand's design identity, packaging, environments and communications. Experiential Marketing allows consumers to be in a completely experience the brand using all five senses; it is useful to conceptualize experiences through multiple experience dimensions. These experience dimensions include sensory-affective, cognitive intellectual, behavior and action-oriented components, besides the word of mouth (figure 1).

Figure 1. Experiential Modules Elements (adapted from [Experiential Marketing. Journal of Marketing Management, 15(1), 53-67])

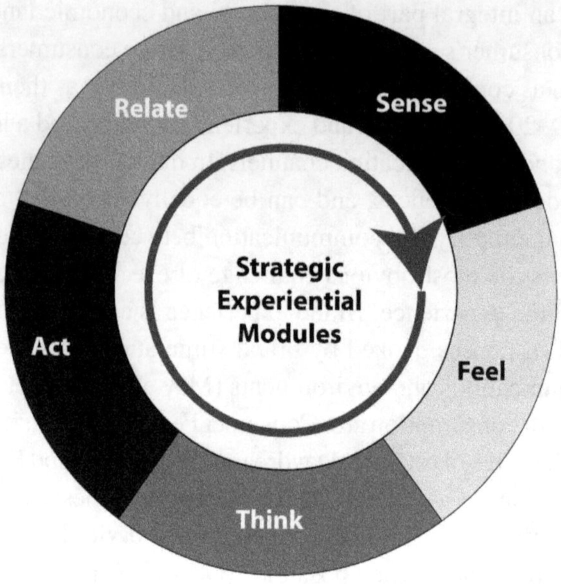

On the other hand, EMs consumers may behave slightly differently in brand consumption experience, which generally doesn't have the equal level of experience with product and brands categories in compared with what developed market counterparts do. EMs consumers are still looking to buy first television, their first car or first package of diapers. From the author's points of view, there is a need to identify the underlying dimensions of experiential brand during the consumption process with the EMs consumer and develop a scale that helps to find the relation between them. The study by Carú and Cova (2008) proposed a new approach to understand consumer behavior. They designed a framework which they called (consumer decision journey), the consuming experiences are spread over a period of time and have four major stages that influence on the consumer's decisions and define future actions. Table 4 shows how the four factors in the brand consumption experience take a great importance in experiential and EMs (Atsmon, Kuentz & Seong, 2012).

The role of Experiential Marketing is closed connected to promoting a product in a dynamic manner. Essentially, we are discussing marketing strategy, increasing brand experience, raising the experience of the customers and word of mouth in order to reach a higher brand loyalty. Therefore, customer's experiences will not occur only after consumption or after use and post purchase activities. They occur whenever a direct or indirect interaction with the brand. Moreover, a brand experience may be expected or unexpected and does not have to be surprising all the time. The idea is to make the customers go through positive memorable experiences through all those steps (Brakus et al., 2009). It will be an effective way of advertising in EMs consumers, for example IKEA tried to engage their consumers in real experience in their experiential campaign for IKEA Hotels - IKEA choose to furnish some hotels with their products and these hotels get a complete makeover including tables, beds, sofas, chairs and kitchenware. This experience gave people the opportunity to live with IKEA and really experience their brand for a few days rather than just examine the products briefly at an IKEA store.

Table 4. Shows the brand consumption experience factors in experiential and EMs

Brand Consumption Experience	Consumer Behavior in Experiential Markets	Consumer Behavior in EMs
1. Pre-consumption	• Consumer experience is related to their expectation, the planning and search, predict of the experience. Experiential Marketing is very effective at driving that all important purchase. • Word of mouth occurs on daily basis through Experiential Marketing. • The inside event experience influence a huge portion of consumers final decision.	• Consumer experience is related to initial brand consecration, consumers are not in common to switch to a brand that was not in their initial set. • Word of mouth is playing a big role, because of a shorter history of familiarity with brands culture, the higher amount mix of first time buyers, and a fragmented media landscape. • The inside store experience influences a higher portion of consumers final decision.
2. Active evaluation	• Consumers are affected by the payment, selection, and packaging of a product as well as the interaction with environment, service and experience activities, such as social media and word of mouth suggestions from friends (This affects consumer choices). • Customers can truly understand the brand values and benefits	• When the consumer researches potential purchases, the particular number of brands under sight during the active evaluation stage may now expand as consumers seek information and shop a category. • Two of the touch points during the active evaluation stage that involves consumer in marketing activities, such as Internet reviews and word of mouth suggestions from friends and family.
3. Closure (Buy)	• Happens when Core consumption consumer experience take place involves sensations, satisfaction levels and transformation. • Pleasure principle is very important selling factor, pleasant sensations, immediate pleasure, Response or gratification is a primary process.	• Happens when the consumer choose a brand at the purchase moment. • Most consumers hold off their final purchase decision until they're in a store. Merchandising design and packaging have then become very important selling factors or a fact that is not widely understood.
4. Post purchase	• The consumer will remember consuming experience and the interesting experience: classification of these memories used to relive and remember the past experiences • Poste production affected by consumer word of mouth, Stories and arguments with friends.	• When consumers at the moment of purchase reach a decision, the marketer's work has just started: the post purchase experience shapes their opinion for every following decision in the future, so the journey is like an ongoing cycle. • Post production affected by the consumer experiences of the product or after service selected.

THE IMPACT OF WORD OF MOUTH IN EMs AND EXPERIENTIAL ON CONSUMER BEHAVIOR

Millions of dollars may spend on advertising campaigns, but making up a consumer's mind by using a word of mouth recommendation or suggestions from a trusted source is not only simple but also free. Word of mouth can cut through the noise quickly and effectively. In fact, "word of mouth is the primary factor behind 20% to 50% of all purchasing decisions" (Bughin, Doogan & Vetvik, 2010). It has a greatest influence when consumers are buying a product for the first time or when products are relatively expensive, seek more opinions, and deliberate longer than they otherwise would. Because of the digital revolution, reviews of the product are posted online and opinions are distributed through social networks. Some customers even create Web sites or blogs to praise or punish brands (Chatterjee, 2001; Dholakia & Soltysinski, 2001; Lee, & Talukdar, 2003). A lot of researches have shown the impact of the Internet as a communication medium on consumer behavior and feedback. All these studies tend to look at the marketer-led aspects of communication via the Internet. The term "word of mouth" means a communication between consumer to consumer with no financial incentives. It is the act of consumers providing online or offline by sending honest information to other consumers. Word of mouth has different degrees of influence on consumers at each stage of consumption journey. Figure 2 shows the impact of word of mouth in both matured and developing markets.

While word of mouth is undeniably complex and has a great number of potential origins and motivations, there are three forms of word of mouth that marketers should understand: "consequential, experiential and intentional" (Bughin, 2010). Consequential happen when consumers are exposed directly to traditional marketing campaigns that transfer on publicized messages about the brands. Experiential Marketing is the most powerful and common form, typically accounting for 50% to 80% of word of mouth activity in any given product category. Experiential Marketing uses developing tools and strategies that enable people to share their opinions by creating the chance to responding well to concerns and criticisms.

Word-of-mouth is another means of amplifying the reach of an experiential campaign. When a consumer examines a memorable brand experience, they will tell 17 other people about the activity (Smilansky, 2009). Those people will tell other people what they know, so increasing exponentially the reach of the campaign. Also as online communities increase in number/size and character, marketers have come to observe the importance of word of mouth. Most of marketing company's aim to engage it is target group through social networking websites such as Facebook and YouTube. It aims to use the social media platform optimally to listen to, encourage, engage and support customers in new innovative channels. Experiential Marketing with it is five strategic modules "sense, feel, think, act and relate", and with its pleasure dimensions (emotional, intellectual, physical, and social pleasure) gives people a reason to talk about product or stuff to make it easier for that real experience to take place. People can forget

Figure 2. Top 3 factors that influence whether a product is considered at each stage of the consumer decision journey for mobile phone (adapted from [Quarterly, 2010, a new way to measure word-of-mouth marketing, Insights & Publications])

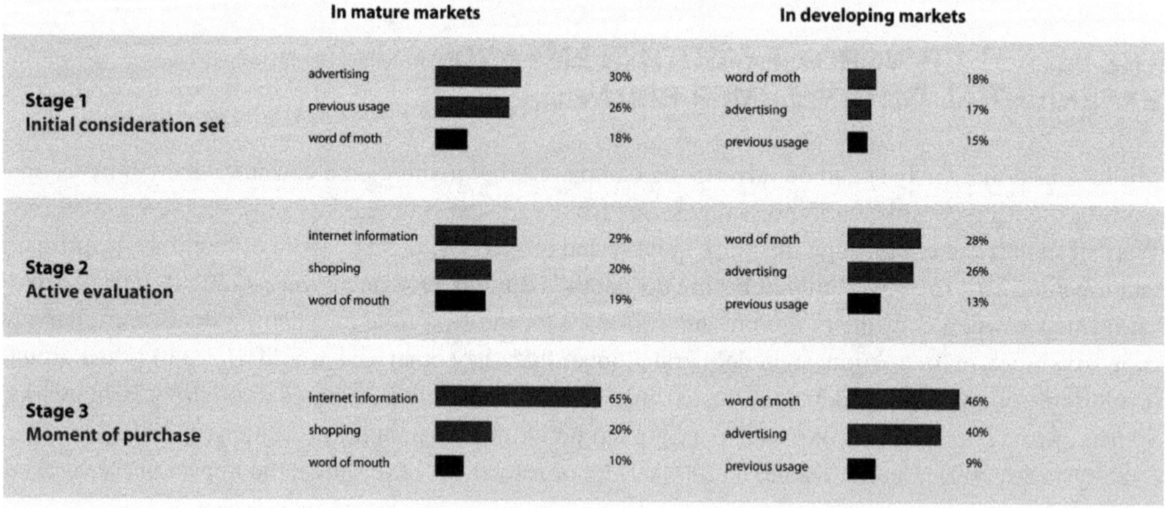

what they hear or what they could see but no one can forget what makes him feel. For example, Adidas on July 10th 2013 organized the "D Rose Jump Store" in London to promote "Derrick Rose's signature",

The concept aim to use "Derrick Rose's" presence to create buzz among fans, Adidas took the experience to another level by adding depth to their activation. In addition to meeting the Chicago Bulls famous point guard, fans had the opportunity to win a free pair of the signature sneaker if they could jump 10 feet to reach them. By having participants jump the same distance needed to reach a normal basketball hoop, gives each consumer a real perspective into the basketball player's life. Whether participants walked away with empty handed or with $100 set of shoes, they all had an experience that they will always remember and tell others about. "Experiential word of mouth" is the most powerful and common form of advertising. The most successful Experiential Marketing campaigns get people buzzing about the brand.

The extreme goal of any campaign is to influence positive reaction in-person and creates online conversations about the experience. There are three factors that affect word-of-mouth impact: 1) The message content must address important features of the product or service to influence consumer's decisions. 2) The identity of the person who sends a message because the word-of-mouth receiver must trust the sender and believe that he or she really knows the product or service. 3) The context of the environment where word of mouth spreads is important to the power of messages. So if the messages passed through tight and trusted networks, they may have less reach but they will have greater impact than those spread through traditional media (Jaques, 2010).

Word of Mouth in Consumer Decision-Making

In the decision journeys of EMs consumer's word of mouth plays a more central role than for those in developed markets. The study of Atsmon, Kuentz, and Seong (2012) surveyed food and beverage consumers in a range of developed markets and EMs. It shows roughly "30% to 40%of the respondents in the United Kingdom and the United States said they received recommendations from friends or family members before making purchases". In Africa and Asia Consumers reported higher figures, "more than 70% in China and 90% in Egypt". Similarly, "64% of the Chinese respondents said they would consider recommendations from friends and family for moisturizers, compared with less than 40% of respondents in the United States and the United Kingdom". Word of mouth can push a consumer to think about a brand or product in a way that incremental advertising spending simply cannot. The good messages will expand through an interested network affecting purchase rates, brand perceptions, and market share (Bughin, Doogan, Vetvik, 2010). In spite of the increase in online communities, communication has increased dramatically the possibility for significant and far-reaching activity effects.

Word of mouth is a native phenomenon in EMs because the EMs consumers mostly live close to friends and family. Especially, digital forms of word of mouth which exceed geography and are growing rapidly in EMs still have limited reach and credibility than in developed ones. According to the study of Atsmon, Kuentz and Seong (2012), the survey results of Chinese consumers showed that 93% trusted in recommendations from friends and family. The same survey showed that only 23% of Chinese consumers obtained information from the Internet about products they bought. However, in India, the same approach worked for "P&G Company", with its "Whisper brand of sanitary napkins", which introduced by the company in targeted local communities by offering free samples and training to in schools juvenile girls. After the success of creating word of mouth in those communities, "P&G gradually expanded the campaign to reach two million girls at 150,000 schools". The result was a robust reduction in the use of cloth based protection to "6%, from 66%, among the targeted group", according to the assessment of the company. For the organizations, the challenge of sustaining and building strong brands is connected to the ability to win consumer's cognitive and emotional commitment and support (Aronne & de Vasconcelos, 2009).

According to Gen Y survey in 2011 "psychographic in the Event Marketing Institute and leading Experiential Marketing agency in USA" the results found that 93.5% of respondents said "they told others about a brand experience they participated in". So, there's a real opportunity to increase the reach by using the maximum advantage from word of mouth as not only an objective, but also as a metric. The results when they asked their participants found that "43% told between one and five people about the event, 27% told between six and 10 people, 8% told between 11 and 15 people and 22% told more than 15 people". And when they asked them how they spread the word, they found that almost "34% told others in person, 18.8% emailed their friends about the event, 18.2% used social media, 17.8% called their friends and 11.6% used text messaging" (Event Marketing Institute/MKTG INC consumer survey, 2011). Stewart Easterbrook, "CEO at Starcom MediaVest Group UK", talks about new study which aims to confirm just how much word of mouth influences consumer decision making and brand loyalty. He said: "Talk Track is a crucial new study for brands in the UK, given its unrivaled ability to track brand advocacy via word of mouth". We have long time since we know how much word of mouth can affect brand success, but Talk Track allows us to track who, what, when and where brand conversations are taking place(Jaques, 2010).

EMs CONSUMER SEGMENTS: HOW IT AFFECTS EXPERIENTIAL MARKETING ACTIVITY

Knowing the customers' needs and wants is a basic tool for successful marketing strategy. Consumer segmentation can be identified through different variables like demographics, geographies and behavioral aspects (Gentile, Spiller & Noci, 2007). With the consumer segments data gathering and declining effectiveness of traditional media, mapping the consumer journey is a great way to enable marketer to understand their consumers' behavior and how they connect with the brand. What makes your brand stand out from the crowed is presenting your product or service within the right groups, and finding an ideal balance between consumers satisfaction and achieving increased consumer value through performing organizational functions more effectively (Bughin, et al, 2010). Selling to EMs is a big challenge for major Traders and manufacturers, to force their penetration of these markets, and to keep sustainable profits over time. These companies must offer Ems consumers with different beneficial offers to modify their distribution and marketing strategies for achieving global scale and local focus. The company's growth will be limited until they can better understand the needs of EMs consumers and adapt new business models that can serve them more efficiently and effectively.

EMs consumers spend from 50% to 75% of their disposable income on products (David J. Teece, 2010). So to understand the EMs consumers the authors explored the study of D'Andrea, Stengel and Krstelj (2014). This study covered EMs in Argentina, Colombia, Costa Rica, Brazil, Chile, and Mexico. The study classifies EMs consumers according to four socioeconomic layers (SES): "upper-class", "upper- to middle-class"; "lower-class" and "lower- to middle-class". SES ratings are typically based on a number of variables including education, occupation, and asset ownership. The total number of the participants in the focus group in each country amounted to 208 participants. Target participants were EMs consumers and women who shop regularly in at least one type of small-scale trade outlet and typically make the big share of their household purchases in the food, beverage, personal care, cleaning products categories. From the previous study we can identify six EMs consumer segments: 1) the spending of Low-income consumers is little on material goods. 2) The needs of Low-income and subsistence-level consumers' are simple. 3) EMs consumers are attracted to the lowest shelf prices, if they did not face budgetary constraints. 4) Modern supermarkets are preferred by EMs consumers. 5) EMs consumers are highly dependent on credit. 6) EMs consumers all belong to one segment "the popular class".

According to another study of EMs consumer segments in India in 2014, there are seven buying behaviors of EMs consumer:

1. First-time User: Three key factors drive first-time consumer's purchasing decisions: word of mouth publicity, the high aspirational value and significant input from influencers and, the strong payer to explore and discover new products (Nielsen Insights, 2013).
2. Bottom of Pyramid (BOP) Consumer: The study noticed that media spread increasing and brand exposure had led to a noticeable change in the Bottom of the Pyramid segment's buying behavior. The business model itself has to be renewed, create livelihoods and consumer surplus and save time (Mint, November 2013). "The (BOP) consumer segment in India continues to move up the consumption ladder. This movement is also marked by drastic changes in their consumption habits. The growth in incomes is modest as compared to other segments which imply that value consciousness would continue to significantly influence their purchasing decisions" (Nielsen Insights, 2013).
3. Time-starved Consumer: "Rapid urbanization and lifestyle changes have increased Time-starved Consumers exponentially; they derive value from the quality of service. For example the time-starved working consumer in India is in no mood to spend an hour in the kitchen preparing breakfast, so she is adopting this new eating habit to suit her lifestyle." (Times of India, July 2011).
4. EMs Affluent Consumer: EMs Affluent Consumer can be characterized by their need for different treatment than the crowd. "According to market estimates, around 35–40% individuals within EMs affluent are entrepreneurs. Customers within this segment in India are highly digitized and adapt to new technologies more quickly as compared to other global markets."(Anand Selvakesari, May 2012). They can almost share digitally on Facebook what they like and dislike, their opinion of the products when they get them, and even they may share other people's opinions. CEO Mark Zuckerberg says: "People have really gotten comfortable not only sharing more information in different kinds, but more openly with more people." (Mark Zuckerbergquotes, 2012).
5. Value Conscious Consumer: This consumer is typically less brand conscious, actively looks for deals, which demonstrate his/her high promotion sensitivity and may impact brand loyalty. "Deal seeking is now combined with growing preference for bulk packs acting as an important strategy to neutralize the impact of rising prices" (Nielsen, 2012). "Even though the average size of the family has shrunk over the years, along with decreasing sizes of houses, the new generation customer is still willing to pick up goods in wholesale if convinced of quality and value" (Singhal, 2013).
6. Online Consumer: The online consumer increasingly comes from newer regions; small markets consumers observe fashion trends closely and are now at par with the fashion sense in different EMs cities like Delhi and Mumbai (Manu Jain, February 2013). So we can say that EMs have more online shoppers: "just 2% of Chinese and Brazilians have no interest in buying online, compared with 8% of Americans and 7% of Australians. This pattern reflects the high internet and mobile penetration of the EMs, as they leapfrog technology: India has almost one billion cell phones, 15

million subscribers and with 100 million internet users. Also web services are also less advanced in some mature economies than in emerging markets" (Nielsen, 2012).

7. Urban consumer: consumption in Urban is characterized by high brand recognition and strong local tastes and preferences

EXPERIENTIAL MARKETING CONCEPTS OF BEST PRACTICES

This part will highlight what published statistical and survey data say about the, experiential market best practices in EMs. Gen Y psychographic, the Event Marketing Institute and leading experiential marketing agency MKTG INC 2011 asked its survey participants about the things that make them want to participate in a company's event or promotion. the events consumers calcify Free stuff as 20.1%, Product demo as 13.5%, something takes place at an event or location they like as 11.9%, Exclusive things they can buy as 8.6%, Visually engaging (looked cool) 13.2%, Games and activities as 9.1%, Cool brand ambassadors as 8.8%, if they like the company/product being promoted as 13.8%, and Other as 1.0%. And when they had been asked how they'd like to continue the conversation after a live event ends, almost 22.1% request email correspondence, 21% of survey respondents said they'd like to be driven to a web site, 20.6% asked for promotions and 16.9% wanted invites to future events. Interestingly, only 0.6% said they didn't want to continue communicating with a brand.

Experiential marketing campaigns can be incorporated with different components such as microsites, street teams and product promotions. Engagement Experiential marketing, focusing on particular touch points, that give users the opportunity to truly experience the product or service which is good chanced for Bottom of pyramid, sophisticated and the first time emerging shopper. However, for organizations those with a smaller budget, experiential marketing can be as simple as creating an opportunity for influencers to sample the product. On the other hand online consumer from newer regions is a large and growing in EMs; they are most of the participant in the event marketing. Consumers' primary digital devices moved to laptop or mobile. Most of consumers said they use their mobile phones to connect with brands and post comments to social media, rather than a computer. "About 75% consumer would be more likely to communicate digitally with a company using Facebook and other social media sites as a result of a good experience with that company event or promotion, 5.4% less and 19.6% not sure. Three-quarters of consumers in events said they would be more likely to communicate with a company using social media as a result of a good experience with that company's" (Event Marketing Institute/ MKTG INC consumer survey, 2011).

The realm of social media consumer is becoming a powerful element in the event marketer's toolbox. For example one of the social media experiential marketing campaign recently activated by Milka (2001). The chocolate brand manufacture 10 million bars that were missing one piece. Puzzled chocolate eaters informed that the one piece had been set aside for them to choose whether they would want it mailed back to them or mailed with a personalized message to a friend or loved one. This campaign helps the brand not only form an emotional connection with its consumer, but also to connect with whomever the consumers decides to send the single piece of chocolate to. According to Event Marketing Institute/ MKTG INC consumer survey "Almost 45% said that posted a consumer to initiate social media connections is easier than maintaining them. Another 36.7% of consumers said they eventually "unfriended" or unsubscribed from a brand's on Facebook page or web site, and when they had been asked why, almost 50% of them said they received too many communications, other 30.2% said there was nothing relevant on the site and the rest 10.9% felt they were being marketed to". (Event Marketing Institute/MKTG INC consumer survey, 2011).

According to Masterman & Wood (2008) study, Companies seeking to employ successful experiential marketing must provide seven event attributes which enhance the event experience: 1) Involvement like an emotional involvement with the brand in the event through experience or Interaction with brand ambassadors and other attendees. 2) Immersion for all senses, isolated from other messages. 3) Intensity by making the experience memorable with high impact. 4) Individuality in one-to-one unique. 5) Customization opportunities, each experience should be different. 6) Innovation experience should be creative in content, location, timing, and audience etc., to surprise the consumer. 7) Integrity experience should be seen as genuine and authentic and providing real benefits and value to the consumer. For example Events and sponsorships are effective tools focus on consumer experiences, they use a promotional activity designed to communicate with attendees and provides an opportunity to engage with a company. Through it is brands, industry community creates a business/ social setting for attendees. Attendees are likely to be more receptive to marketing visual messages associated with the event than they are to those presented via other methods. According to Gen Y survey "94% of consumers say they would be more likely to buy a product as a result of a good experience at an event, and 47.8% said they'd prefer to buy that company's products in a store, 29.3% said online and 22.9% of respondents want to purchase products on-site at an event". (Event Marketing Institute/MKTG INC consumer survey, 2011).

For organizations there are main keys that make the concept of Experiential marketing more powerful and easier to be memorized in any experiential campaign:

- Targeting the right segmentation.
- Live brand experiences focusing on particular touch points that will create value for both brand and consumer.
- Giving consumers ability to have the control and the opportunity to truly experience the product or service.
- Creating ongoing dialogues with consumers. 99.4% of Gen Y consumers say they may have ongoing communication with a brand after an event.
- Finding success in today's evolving marketplace. The adaptation to the local market process, which is influenced by cultural aspects, lifestyles, mentality, and even by politics.
- Generating word of mouth turn brand engagements. Give the users something to talk about.
- Activating social media as a communication channels. This allows Spreading of positive feedback and personal experiences to live in publicly accessible areas, and become a trusted referral source.

To summarize the authors findings after studying these five market aspects to examine adaptation of Experiential marketing in EMs, The most of Experiential specialists should understand what the real market supposed to bring to consumers, how to use the brand consumption steps effectively in their marketing strategy and the effective ways to use the realm word of mouth in EMs. This will be after prioritizing the importance of EMs consumer needs within a live environment and along with well-trained brand ambassadors they can make consumers understand the brand and the product better by spending time with them. Then combine their campaigns with social media to raise the impact and applying the experiential best practices. By the end these guidelines will allow them to focus on higher yielding processes that consumers love and value.

EXPERIENTIAL ADVERTISING IN EMs CASE STUDIES:

Many big brands are involved with Experiential marketing, some of the best 'big-brand' marketing campaigns are conducted by specialist Experiential Marketing Companies. Coca-Cola, IMRB, McKinsey, Jack Morton these Brands utilize a variety of marketing strategies in order to achieve this emotional connection with their consumers. Brands are taking opportunities to a great movement in advertising that matters to the world. Indian, Brazil, South Africa and China as the biggest EMs have already experimented with this experiential concept. In this section authors will analyze experiential advertising in EMs case studies using the previous five market aspects to examine how experiential advertising could work in EMs. Here are the notable ones as described in table 5, 6 and 7

Table 5. Analyze experiential advertising in EMs case studies using the previous five market aspects

Case study 1	Coca-Cola-Small World Machines, IN India and Pakistan by Leo Burnett Sydney and Chicago. Coca-Cola India created experiential marketing unity between India and Pakistan Coca-Cola placed 'Small World Machines' across various malls in New Delhi and Lahore using two interactive vending machines. Each machines placed in a local mall for the period of a three-day event, were decked out with special touchscreens and streaming video capabilities that allowed users to stand face-to-face and interact through shared gestures such as drawing a peace sign.
Experiential activity	The experiential campaign used the technical innovation, beside its putting emotional communication into the world through brands and making that brand stand for something in a way that it hadn't before. Brands that matter are the ones that succeed. Consumers in both countries were given a chance to interact with each other in real time through 3D touch-screens. At the end the machine dispensed a can of Coca-Cola to each one with the brand message 'Open Happiness'.
Examine The activity through the fifth market aspects	
Market mix	• The sensory Solution that add happiness to the customer's life. • The participants get free sample and the product cost being related with both tangible and psychological to create meaningful value. • Choosing local mall event was easy way of distribution the machines, it works best for today customers types and their Choice. • The idea made balance between organization's values and individual customer's values. Experiential uses low cost campaign with high impact.
Brand consumption	• Experiential idea related the brand with values and benefits. • this was extremely effective to driving the later purchase and to put the brand in their initial set • Word of mouth happens and the real time experience influences the final decision of a higher portion of consumers. • Poste production affected by the consumer event memories and affected by consumer word of mouth, Stories and arguments with friends
Word of mouth	• The story was the most widespread in the history of coca-cola.com, 55% of total reach came from India and Pakistan, the 10,000 attendees to real live event created 700 connections across social media, the effort reached more than 18 million Facebook and Twitter users, the video garnered 2 million YouTube views and counting, More than 58 million earned media impressions were gained.
EMs consumers	• The idea relates the drink with the lower income consumer in sensational experience attracted them through the lower price and the free sample. • The exposure percentage was high; the Ad visited them in place they like to shop in. • The idea reached the online shopper.
Experiential best practices	• The idea used sensory elements added feeling and emotion and physical action • The results show how brand marketers can coordinate their social and digital marketing for maximum effect • Coca-Cola Company achieved success and high expectations of what a brand can do with interactive technology. A three-minute social media video of the event helped Coca-Cola to expand its impact beyond these two countries, out to the entire world.

Table 6. Analyze experiential advertising in EMs case studies using the previous five market aspects

Case study 2	China Environmental Protection Foundation: More Walking, Less Driving by Cannes Creative Lions, Creative Effectiveness Lions, 2011. The China Environmental Protection Foundation created its "walks more drive less" campaign to encourage people to consider the effects car usage is having on the environment. China is the world's largest car market with over 500 million vehicles on the road, creating 40% of all of the nation's carbon monoxide emissions. The aims of the campaign were by using an interactive campaign; the general public would be dissuaded from overly using their cars.
Experiential activity	The outdoor advertisement saw people walking over a giant canvas, covering pedestrian crossings with a large leafless tree. Underneath traffic lights was sponge cushions painted in green, environmentally friendly, quick-dry paint. This simulated the positive effect they have on the environment by walking -as they stepped onto the green sponge the soles of their foot imprints would create the tree on the ground. Each green footprint added to the canvas like leaves growing on a bare tree.
Examine The activity through the fifth market aspects	
Market mix	• The sensory and benefit behavior in which the customer life has been enhanced. • The participants get thinking and active experience. • Choosing the Underneath traffic light in streets was very creative, easy and low cost channel to target walkers and cares drivers. • The idea made balance between organization's values and individual customer's values. Experiential uses low cost campaign with high impact.
Brand consumption	• Experiential idea related the brand with values and enhancing life concept. • This was extremely effective to driving the positive thinking and to put protecting environment in their initial behaviors. • Word of mouth happens and the in event experience influences final decision of consumers. • Poste production affected by the consumer event memories, consumer word of mouth, Stories and arguments through the online and offline media.
Word of mouth	A total number of walkers that participated exceeded 3,920,000 people. Key media both online and offline rapidly wrote about the campaign. Without any investment, the campaign generated RMB 62 million worth of free publicity. According to China Environmental Protection Foundation research, the overall awareness of environmental protection had increased 86%. After the campaign, the print was exhibited at the Shanghai Zheng Da Art museum.
EMs consumers	• The idea create connection to persons culture relates the idea with participant in sensational experience. • The experience engage consumers physically and stimulate their curiosity in the situation • The idea reached the online and offline viewer to fit the new trend consumers.
Experiential best practices	• The Green Pedestrian Crossing was carried out in 7 main streets of Shanghai and later expanded to 132 roads in 15 cities across China. Making people feel that by walking they could create a greener environment. • Experiential idea used low cost scenario campaign to engage thinking and create the high impact.• Using offline and online media. • The idea touched the participant imagination and mental stimulation

FUTUER RESERCH DIRECTIONS

To this end, we hope that more future research can derive some insights and inspirations to make companies better understand the needs of EMs consumers and adapt their business models to serve them more efficiently and effectively. Although the case studies used limited brands ads from different but not all EMs countries, which was not enough to investigate further differences among different EMs countries consumer consumption. Future research should deepen in understanding of the different EMs consumers persuasion strategies by investigating the same brand experiential among different EMs market regions (for example, between the Middle East, India, china and Latin America). A second limitation concerns the advertising medium involved investigation. To develop a new marketing strategies experiential Ads can be used to utilize traditional advertising channels to their full possibility in order to engage their target audiences on a deeper level that create brand loyalty. And investigate whether the same processing

Table 7. Analyze experiential advertising in EMs case studies using the previous five market aspects

Case study 3	Huawei mobile, create a 3D fighting game on a big screen the same size of two basketball courts. By Saachi/ China, September 2012. The unexpected super-large outdoor 3D game was played at the world-renowned Suntec City - Fountain of Wealth in Singapore.
Experiential activity	The creative video show of the Huawei MediaPad 10 FHD and Huawei Ascend D1 Quad-Core XL mobile phone new features. The show was demonstrated from all dimensions by projectors from a plaza building to a larger than 950m 2 huge screen, the excellent performance of the Huawei China-made core, made people very excited about trying the mobile and encouraged them to take part in this huge interactive game.
	Examine The activity through the fifth market aspects
Market mix	• The benefit Solution becomes the sense, feelings and action in which adds joys to the customer's life. • The participants get exciting experience, tried the product discovered its feature so the product being related with both tangible and psychological to create meaningful value. • The event take place in street to ensure high exposure also used high technology which it works best for today customer Choice. • The idea made balance between organization's values and individual customer's values. The experiential Ads use low cost campaign with high impact.
Brand consumption	• Experiential idea related the brand with values and benefits. • Experience was extremely effective to driving the later purchase and to put the brand in their initial set. • Word of mouth happens and the in event experience influences the final decision of consumers. • Poste production affected by the consumer event memories and affected by consumer word of mouth, Stories and arguments with friends
Word of mouth	This experiential campaign Build a brand engagement with participants this video was on Facebook and YouTube The campaign has generated more than 1 million online views and web site visitors could also viewed the unprecedented super-large outdoor 3D game fighting on the homepage of Huawei Device Weibo at Sina Weibo.
EMs consumers	• The product fits the consumer life style by its modern appeal. • The idea relates the Huawei mobile with the lower income consumer in sensational experience attracted them through the game, music, joy and exciting. • The exposure percentage was high 2 huge screen demonstrated. • Short video about the event reached the online shopper on social media
Experiential best practices	• The results show how brand marketers can coordinate their social and digital marketing for maximum effect. • The related to consumers through imagination and mental stimulation • All the action is captured in two-and-a-half-minute videos that can be found on the Facebook created by local Huawei mobile teams.

differences between EMs markets and developing markets, but the growing of experimental marketing is based on the quality and function of products or the service, not all products are fit to carry out experimental marketing.

CONCLUSION

This chapter stands a new angle to look insight into EMs market future strategies; investigating the call of experiential marketing is the next big future in EMs. In fact Economic growth across EMs countries is still projected to grow at a steady rate through the next decade. Also there is a desire to raise the standard of living in EMs by goods and services to high levels comparable to those of developed markets. Thus, lead necessarily to changes in the way investors worldwide allocate their available funds and value their investments in EMs countries. Experiential marketing, as stated clearly in the chapter, is the result of the social development that consumer's consumption demands transmit from the practical level to the experience level. Even EMs consumer are characterized by non-traditional user behavior according to the differences in demographics, geographies, politics and behavioral aspects, the experiential marketing consider a powerful marketing tool to enhance the consumer experience (interaction, involvement, immersion, intensity, innovation, individuality and integrity). Bring the Brand personality to life, creating a memorable experience, gaining credibility with specific target audiences after they try the product and creating consumer conversations about a product. Experiential marketing create brand advocates who will further spread the brand messages through word of mouth advertising to become a loyal customer. Most experiential advertising case studies chapter presents, took place in EMs countries. They were analyzed through the five aspects the authors discussed in the beginning of the chapter: Market mix component, Brand consumption experience, the impact of word of mouth in consumer behavior, EMs consumer segment and Experiential market best practices. The findings showed that the experiential was successful in changing the attendees' perception of the brand's essence and create a positive change of consumption behavior which might lead to loyalty. Specially the impact of word of mouth on purchase behavior as previously explained, create competitive advantage and an effective influence on changing people's opinions as compared to traditional advertisement. Authors believes word of mouth will fit in EMs countries much more in the devolved counties marketing structure, word of mouth is a local phenomenon in EMs which gives it an immediate and huge advantage over print and media advertising. The Authors present a model illustrated in figure 3 to summarize their finding and how they find the relation that can affectively apply Experiential Marketing in EMs.

In conclusion authors believe that the Experiential Marketing route drives word of mouth, which in fact has a great impact on the EMs countries consumer behavior led to brand loyalty and increase return on marketing investment in long term. In EMs word of mouth is creating value, marketer can derive positive consumption behavior from it so development of experiential model and create ideas is a key to success in EMs, which allows a company to reach the unreachable customers with collaboration with

Figure 3. Applying Experiential Marketing in Ems model

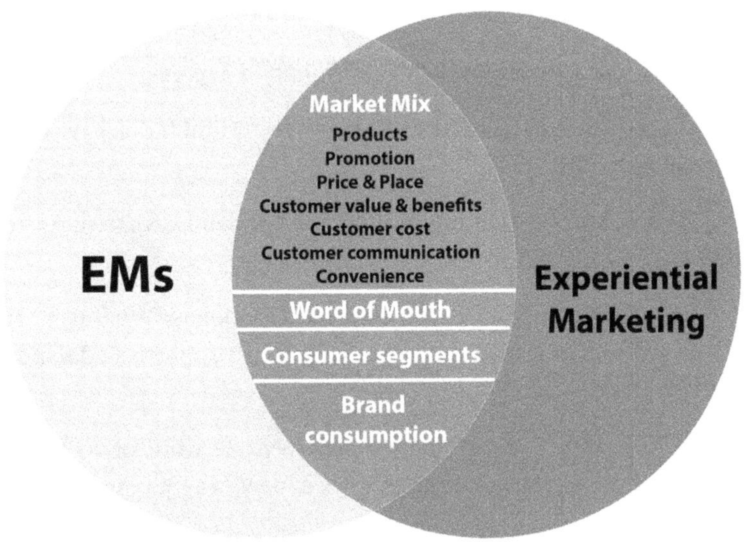

local firms and suppliers. For a successful experiential marketing concept to be born, company should study and target the right consumer segment, plan for experiential experience that Engages all 5 senses of consumer, to be more concern about creating of positive consequential word of mouth by using interactivity and creativity.

REFERENCES:

ADDIS, M. (2005). New Technologies and Cultural Consumption - Edutainment is born. *European Journal of Marketing*, *39*, 7–8.

Albanese, S. (2013). What Customers Want: The Brand Experience. Retrieved from http://www.slideshare.net/sonjaalbanese/what-customers-want-the-brand-experience

Amadeo, K. (2014). What are Emerging Markets? How to Pick the Real. *About News,* Retrieved from http://useconomy.about.com/od/glossary/g/emerging_market.htm

Andrew. (2014), Emerging markets and their ethical challenge, Retrieved from http://www.ethicalleadership.co.uk/emerging-markets/

Arnold, J. D., & Quelch, A. J. (1998). New Strategies in Emerging Markets. *Sloan Management Review*, *40*(1), 7–20.

Aronne, C. V., & Vasconcelos, M. (2009). The Impact of Experiential Marketing on the Customer's Perception of a Brand's Essence, *Encontro da ANPAD*, xxxIII,1-16.

Atsmon, Y., Kuentz, J., & Seong, J. (2012).Building brands in emerging markets, *article in Insights & Publications*, pp1.

Bagozzi, R., & Dholakia, U. (2006). Antecedents and Purchase Consequences of Customers Participating in Small Group Communities. *International Journal of Research in Marketing*, *23*(1), 45–61. doi:10.1016/j.ijresmar.2006.01.005

Banga, K., & Mahajan, V. (2005). The Lands of Opportunity. FT press.

Bhattacharya, P., & Deshpande, A. (2013). The changing face of rural India. Live mint website, Retrieved from http://www.livemint.com/Politics/

Boyle, E., & McCabe, S. (2006). Understanding Brands as Experiential Spaces: Axiological Implications for Marketing Strategists. *Journal of Strategic Marketing*, *14*(2).

Brakus, J., Schmitt, B., & Zarantonello, L. (2009). Brand Experience: What is it? How do We Measure It? And Does It Affect Loyalty? Retrieved from http://www8.gsb.columbia.edu/sites/globalbrands/files/Brand_Experience.pdf

Bughin, J., Doogan, J., & Vetvik, O. (2010).A new way to measure word-of-mouth marketing, Retrieved from http://www.mckinsey.com/insights/marketing_sales/a_new_way_to_measure_word-of-mouth_marketing

Building Effective Business Models in Emerging Markets. (2012). *Deloittee Development LLC.* New Delhi, India.

Cadbury's drumming gorilla spawns Facebook group. (2007). Brand Republic, p11, Retrieved from repository.upenn.edu/cgi/viewcontent.cgi?article=1054&context

Cao, M. (2012). International Expansion of Emerging Market Multinationals: An Integrated Perspective. *Proceedings of the International Conference on Innovation and Information Management (ICIIM)*

Cavusgil, S. T. (1985). Guidelines for Export Market Research. *Business Horizons*, *28*(6), 27–33. doi:10.1016/0007-6813(85)90082-5

Chatterjee, P. (2001). Online reviews: Do consumers use them? *Advances in Consumer Research. Association for Consumer Research (U. S.)*, *28*(1), 129–133.

Chaudhuri, A., & Holbrook, M. B. (2001). The Chain of Effects from Brand Trust and Brand Affect to Brand Performance: The Role of Brand Loyalty. *Journal of Marketing*, *65*(2), 81–93. doi:10.1509/jmkg.65.2.81.18255

Chernatony, L. (2006). From Brand Vision to Brand Evaluation: the strategic process of growing. Oxford: Butterworth-Heinemann, 3,369.

Consumer segmentation: How it affects your Experiential Marketing activity. (2012). Retrieved from http://www.hotcow.co.uk/Buzz-Blog/consumer-segmentation-how-it-affects-your-experiential-marketing-activity.htm#sthash.KEdyprbE.dpuf

Court, D., Elzinga, D., Mulder, S., & Vetvik, O. (2009). The consumer decision journey. Insights & Publications. Retrieved from mckinseyquarterly.com.

Cullers, R. (2013). Adidas Lets Fans Jump for Derrick Rose Sneakers in London Retrieved from http://www.adweek.com/adfreak/adidas-lets-fans-jump-derrick-rose-sneakers-london-pop-store-151483

D'andrea, G., Stengel, E., & Krstelj, A. (2014). 6 Truths about Emerging-market consumers. *Strategy and business*, 34. Retrieved from http://www.strategy-business.com/article

Dallas, G. (2013), Business Ethics in Emerging Markets and Investors' Expectations Standards, Retrieved from http://corpgov.law.harvard.edu/2013/01/19/business-ethics-in-emerging-markets-and-investors-expectations-standards/

David, J. T. (2010). Business Models, Business Strategy and Innovation. *Long Range Planning*. Retrieved from http://www.businessmodelcommunity.com/fs/Root/8jig8-businessmodelsbusinessstrategy.pdf

Dholakia, U. M., & Soltysinski, K. (2001). Coveted or overlooked. The psychology of bidding for comparable listings in digital actions. *Marketing Letters*, *12*(3), 225–237. doi:10.1023/A:1011164710951

Diaz, A., Magni, M., & Poh, F. (2012). From oxcart to Wal-Mart: Four keys to reaching emerging-market consumers. *Insights & Publications*. Retrieved from http://www.mckinsey.com

Duncan-Durst, L. (2006). Customer Relationships - What are the Difference between Customer Experience Management and Experiential Marketing? *MarketingProfs*. Retrieved from http://www.marketingprofs.com/articles/2006/1717/whats-the-difference-between-customer-experience-management-and-experiential-marketing

Fou, A. (2003). Experiential Marketing. *VISION an executive brief*. Retrieved from http://www.mktsci.com/experiential-marketing.htm

Freedman, L., & Schooley, S. (2011). Closing the cross-channel gap. *The e-tailing group/MyBuys*. Retrieved from http://www.e-tailing.com/content/wp-content/uploads/2011/06/MyBuys_etailing-group_webinar_6-28-2011

Garten, J. E. (1997). Troubles ahead in emerging markets. *Harvard Business Review*, *75*(3). Retrieved from www.opf.slu.cz/vvr/akce/turecko/pdf/Sunje.pdf

Gentile, C., Spiller, N., & Noci, G. (2007). How to Sustain the Customer Experience: An Overview of Experience Components that Co-create Value With the Customer. *European Management Journal*, *25*(5).

Global Investable Market Indices Methodology. (2010). MSCI Emerging Markets Indices. Retrieved from http://www.msci.com/products/indices

Gronholdt, L., Martensen, A., & Kristensen, K. (2000). The relationship between Customer Satisfaction and Loyalty: Cross-Industry differences. *Total Quality Management*, *11*(4-6), 509–514. doi:10.1080/09544120050007823

Growth spike brings, India closer to one billion subscribers. (2011). mobiSights *website*. Retrieved from www.mobisights.com/2011/08/30/

Hoch & Stephen, J. (2002). Product Experience Is Seductive. *The Journal of Consumer Research*, *2*, 448–454.

Holbrook, M. B., & Hirschman, E. C. (1981). The experiential aspects of consumption: Consumer fantasy, feelings and fun. *The Journal of Consumer Research*, *9*(2), 132–140. doi:10.1086/208906

Jacques, B., Jonathan, D., & Ole, J. V. (2010). A new way to measure word-of-mouth marketing. Retrieved from http://www.mckinsey.com/insights/marketing_sales/a_new_way_to_measure_word-of-mouth_marketing

Jaques, L. (2010). How much does word of mouth really affect brand success? Newline, Retrieved from http://mediatel.co.uk/newsline/2010/09/23/how-much-does-word-of-mouth-really-affect-brand-success/

Jobber, D., & Fahy, J. (2009). Foundations of Marketing. Maidenhead: McGraw-Hill. 4, 214-226.

Johansson, J. (2009). *Global Marketing*. McGraw-Hill Higher Education. Retrieved from http://highered.mheducation.com/sites/

Joseph, P., & Gilmore, J. H. (1998). Welcome to the Experience Economy. *Harvard Business Review*, 76(4), 97–105. PMID:10181589

Kalinowski, J. D. (2012). Positioning for Growth in Emerging Markets. Proactive Worldwide, 15(3), 1-11.

Khanna, T., & Palepu, K. (2010). *A Road Map for Strategy and Execution*. Harvard Business Press. Retrieved from www.forbes.com/2010/05/27/winning-in-emerging-markets-opinions-book-excerpts-khanna-palepu.html

Kvint, V. (2009). *The Global Emerging Market: Strategic Management and Economics*. New York, London: Routledge.

Lauterborn, R. (1990, October 1). New Marketing Litany: 4Ps Passé; 4Cs Take Over. *Advertising Age*.

Leigh, D. (2006). Customer Relationships - What's the Difference between Customer Experience Management and Experiential Marketing? Retrieved from http://www.marketingprofs.com/6/duncan4.asp

Lin, J. Y. (2003). International Expansion of Emerging Market. *Economic Development and Cultural Change*, *51*, 277. doi:10.1086/367535

Lum, R. (2013). Milka Chocolate Bars Now Missing Square In New Campaign. *Creative Guerilla Marketing*. Retrieved from http://www.creativeguerrillamarketing.com/guerrilla-marketing/milka-chocolate-bars-now-missing-square-new-campaign

Luo, Y., & Tung, R. (2007). International Expansion of Emerging Market. *Journal of International Business Studies*, *38*(4), 481–498. doi:10.1057/palgrave.jibs.8400275

Masterman, G., & Wood, E. (2008). Event Marketing: Measuring an Experience? *Proceedings of the 7th International Marketing Trends Congress*, Venice. Retrieved from http://escp-eap.net/conferences/marketing/2008_cp/Materiali/Paper/Fr/Wood_Masterman

Mayer, A. (1997). Symposium on Law and Ethics in Emerging Markets: Introduction. *Journal of International Law,* 18(4).

McGuigan, C. (2013). 2014 Experiential Marketing Trends. *Creative Guerrilla Marketing*, Retrieved from http://www.creativeguerrillamarketing.com/guerrilla-marketing/2014-experiential-marketing-trends/

Miller, R. R. (1998). *Selling to Newly Emerging Markets. New York.* Westport, CT: Quorum Books.

Moré, M. E. (2011). building Brands through Experiential Marketing: Retrieved from http://morethanbranding.com/2011/11/28/building-brands-through-experiential-marketing-11-awesome-examples

NASDAQ. (2012. May 11). The difference Between Developed, Emerging and Frontier Markets. Retrieved from http://www.nasdaq.com/article/what-is-the-difference-between-a-developed-emerging-and-frontier-market-cm140649

Palepu. (2010). *Winning In Emerging Markets: A Roadmap for Strategy and Execution for Emerging Markets*. Harvard Business School Press.

Poulsson, S. H. G., & Kale, S. H. (2004). The Experience Economy and Commercial Experiences. *The Marketing Review*, *4*(3), 267–277. doi:10.1362/1469347042223445

Ratchford, B. T., Lee, M. S., & Talukdar, D. (2003). The impact of the Internet on information search for Automobiles. *JMR, Journal of Marketing Research*, *40*(2), 193–209. doi:10.1509/jmkr.40.2.193.19221

World Investment Report. (2008). United Nations. Retrieved from unctad.org/en/Docs/wir2008_en.pdf

Schmitt, B. (1999a). Experiential marketing: How to get customers to sense, feel, think, act and relate to your company and brands. The Free Press, New York, USA.

Schmitt, B. (1999b). Experiential Marketing. *Journal of marketing management New York: The Free Press*, 1(6), 57–69.

Schmitt, B. (2003). Customer Experience Management. *Journal of Consumer Psychology*, *22*, 7–17. doi:10.1016/j.jcps.2011.09.005

Schmitt, B. (2011a). *Experiential Marketing: How to Get Customers to Sense, Feel, Think, Act (Updated Edition by B. Joseph Pine)*. Free Press.

Schmitt, B. (2011b). Experience Marketing: Concepts. *Frameworks and Consumer Insights Foundations and Trends in Marketing*, *5*(2), 55–112. doi:10.1561/1700000027

Smilansky, S. (2009). Experiential Marketing: A Practical Guide to Interactive Brand Experiences (Google eBook). Kogan Page Publishers.

Smith, S., & Wheeler, J. (2002). *Managing the Customer Experience: Turning Customers into Advocates*. Harlow: Prentice-Hall.

Sunjeand, A., & Civi, E. (2008). Emerging markets: a review of conceptual, frameworks. *Proceedings of 1st International Joint Symposium on Business Administrator*: Challenges for Business Administrators in the New Millennium. Retrieved from http://www.opf.slu.cz/vvr/akce/turecko/pdf/sunje.pdf

Terron, A., & Kulkarni, M. (2013). *Uncovering the Billion $ Shopper unity: The First Time Modern Trade Shopper* (pp. 1–4). Nielsen Featured Insights.

Tsai, S. (2005). Integrated Marketing as Management of Holistic Consumer Experience. *Business Horizons*, *48*(5), 431–441. doi:10.1016/j.bushor.2005.02.005

Weisberg, R. (2009), Ethical Challenges in Developing Markets Markkula Center for Applied Ethics, Retrieved from http://www.scu.edu/ethics/practicing/focusareas/business/Ethical%20business%20Markkula.pdf

Zena, P. A., & Hadisumarto, A. D. (2012). The Study of Relationship among Experiential Marketing, Service Quality, Customer Satisfaction, and Customer Loyalty. *Asean Marketing Journal*, 4(1).

Zuckerberg, M. (2012). Great Quotes. *Powerful Minds website*. Retrieved from www.great-quotespowerfulminds.com/markzuckerberg-quotes

ADDITIONAL READING

Drucker, P. (2000, November-December). "Meeting of the Minds." Across the Board (The Conference Board).

Finn, G. (2009, January 19). A Dimensional View of Experiential Marketing.

Gardner, S., & Jardin, X. (2005). *Buzz Marketing with Blogs for Dummies*. Chichester: Wiley.

Kahn, G., Bilefsky, D., & Lawton, C. (2004, March 10). Burned Once, Brewers Return to China—with Pint-Size Goals. *The Wall Street Journal*, p. A1.

Khanna, T., Palepu, K. G., & Sinha, J. (2005, June). Strategies that fit emerging markets. *Harvard Business Review*.

McConnell, B., & Huba, J. (2002). *Creating Customer Evangelists: How loyal customers become a volunteer sales force*. Wokingham: Kaplan.

O'Leary, S., & Sheehan, K. (2008). *Building Buzz to Beat the Big Boys: Word of mouth marketing for small businesses*. Westport, CT: Greenwood.

Schmitt, B. H. (2003). *Customer Experience Management: A revolutionary approach to connecting with your customers*. Chichester: Wiley.

Wilson, D., & Purushothaman, R. (2003, October 1). *Dreaming with BRICs: The Path to 2050.* Goldman Sachs, Global Economics Paper No. 99.

KEY WORDS AND DEFINITIONS

4Cs: The "4 Cs" marketing mix definition seeks to turn traditional marketing thinking on its head by looking sales and marketing in a customer-centric way. Instead of looking at how each aspect of marketing is seen by the business, you look at these from the customer's perspective. The "4Cs" changes marketing mix definition from Product, Price, Place and Promotion to Customer Value, Cost, Convenience and Communication.

4Ps: The categories that can be controlled in the marketing of a good or service: product, price, place and promotion. The four Ps, often referred to as the marketing mix, are all constrained by internal and external factors in the overall environment. Designs made in the "product" component determine the name, design and packaging of the good. "Price" involves the cost of the good and if volume or seasonal discounts will be offered. "Place" decisions outline where the product will be sold and how it will be delivered to the market. "Promotion" involves advertising, public relations and promotional strategy.

Brand Loyalty: Considered to be one of the ultimate goals of marketing: a consumer's commitment to consistent repurchasing of a brand.

Consumer Behavior: According to Smriti Chand Consumer behavior is the study of how individual customers, groups or organizations select, buy, use, and dispose ideas, goods, and services to satisfy their needs and wants. It refers to the actions of the consumers in the marketplace and the underlying motives for those actions.

Consumer Experience: According to Vangie Beal consumer experience is the phrase used to describe the relationship a customer has with a business. Customer experience refers to the total of all experiences the customer has with the business, based on all interactions and thoughts about the business. Customer experience is an integral part of customer relationship management (CRM), and it is important to businesses because customers who have a positive experience are more likely to become repeat customers and loyal customers of the business.

Consumptions: according According to the business dictionary consumption is the process in which the substance of a thing is completely destroyed, used up, or incorporated or transformed into something else. Consumption of goods and services is the amount of them used in a particular time period. Consumption is a major concept in economics and is also studied by many other social sciences. Economists are particularly interested in the relationship between consumption and income, and therefore in economics the consumption function plays a major role.

Developing Countries: According to the world bank, A developing country is one in which the majority lives on far less money—with far fewer basic public services—than the population in highly industrialized countries. Five million of the world's 6 billion people live in developing countries where incomes are usually under $2 per day and a significant portion of the population lives in extreme poverty (under $1.25 per day).

Word of Mouth: Means consumer-to-consumer communication with no economic incentives When a consumer engages in a memorable brand experience, It is the act of consumers providing online or offline honest information to other consumers. Word of mouth has different degrees of influence on consumers at each stage of consumption journey.

Compilation of References

Abdul Hamid, F. Z. (2004). Corporate social disclosure by banks and finance companies: Malaysian evidence. *Corporate Ownership and Control*, *1*(4), 118–130.

Abdullah, S. N. (2006). Directors' remuneration, firm's performance and corporate governance in Malaysia among distress companies. *Corporate Governance*, *6*(2), 162–174. doi:10.1108/14720700610655169

Abuznaid, S. (2009) Business Ethics in Islam: The Glaring Gap in Practice, International *Journal of Islamic and Middle Eastern Finance and Management*, 2(4), 279.

Ackerman, R., & Bauer, R. (1976), Corporate Social Responsiveness: The Modern Dilemma, VA, Reston.

Acquier, A., & Gond, J. P. (2007). Aux sources de la responsabilité sociale de l'entreprise: À la (re) découverte d'un ouvrage fondateur, Social Responsabilities of the Businessman d'Howard Bowen. *Finance Contrôle Stratégie*, *10*(2), 5–35.

Adam, L., Valérie, S., & Johnston, W. J. (2009). Corporate Social Responsibility: An Empirical Investigation of U.S. Organizations. *Journal of Business Ethics*, *85*(2), 303–323.

Adams, R., & Mehran, H. (2008). *Corporate performance, board structure and their determinants in the banking Industry*. Federal Reserve Bank of New York Staff Report N° 330.

Adams, R., & Mehran, H. (2003). Is corporate governance different for bank holding companies? *Economic Policy Review*, *4*, 123–142.

ADDIS, M. (2005). New Technologies and Cultural Consumption - Edutainment is born. *European Journal of Marketing*, *39*, 7–8.

Admati, A. R., & Pfleiderer, P. (1988). A Theory of Intraday Trading Patterns: Volume and Price Variability. *Review of Financial Studies*, *43*(1), 3–40. doi:10.1093/rfs/1.1.3

Adnan, M. A., Ab Rashid, H. M., Meera, A. K. M., & Htay, S. N. N. (2011, February 21-22). A Panel Data Analysis on the Relationship between Corporate Governance and Bank Efficiency. *Proceedings of the Asia-Pacific Business Research Conference*, Hotel Istana-Jalan Raja Chulan, Kuala Lumpur. Retrieved from http://ebookbrowse.com/606-adnan-pdf-d71737492

Agoraki, M.-E. K., & Delis, M. D. Staikouras, P. (2008, December 26).The Effect of Board Size and Composition on Bank Efficiency. Retrieved from http://ssrn.com/abstract=1320671

Agrawal, A., & Knoeber, C. (1996). Firm performance and mechanisms to control agency problems between managers and shareholders. *Journal of Financial and Quantitative Analysis*, *31*(3), 377–397. doi:10.2307/2331397

Ahmed, H., & Chapra, U. (2002). *Corporate governance in Islamic financial institution, periodical document N°6, Islamic research and training institute Sector Network.* The Islamic Financial Services Board.

Ahmed, M. M., Chung, K. Y., & Eichenseher, J. W. (2003). Business students' perception of ethics and moral judgment: A cross-cultural study. *Journal of Business Ethics*, *43*(1-2), 89–102. doi:10.1023/A:1022915316112

Akhtaruddin, M., Hossain, M. A., Hossain, M., & Yao, L. (2009). Corporate governance and voluntary disclosure in corporate annual reports of Malaysian listed firms. *Journal of Applied Management Accounting Research*, *7*(1), 1–19.

Al Amri, A., & Haynes, J. (2014). ICT and Organizations: A Model for the Management of Errors in Organizations with Reference to SMEs in Oman. *Proceedings of the 2nd International Conference on Applied Information and Communication Technologies, ICAICT.* Muscat.

Al-A'ali, E. (2006). Motivation of Women Leaders Between Participation and Empowerment: Self-Report. *Journal of Commerce for Scientific Research of Alexandria*, *43*(1), 265–288.

Alayoğlu, N., Öztürk, A. O., & Babacan, M. (2012). Perceptions of College Students and Attitudes of Private and Public Employees towards Business Ethics. *Turkish Journal of Business Ethics*, *5*(9), 27–35.

Albanese, S. (2013). What Customers Want: The Brand Experience. Retrieved from http://www.slideshare.net/sonjaalbanese/what-customers-want-the-brand-experience

Albert, L. S., & Horowitz, L. M. (2009). Attachment styles and ethical behavior: Their relationship and significance in the marketplace. *Journal of Business Ethics*, *87*(3), 299–316. doi:10.1007/s10551-008-9918-6

Al-Rodhan, N. R., & Stoudmann, G. (2006). Definitions of globalization: A comprehensive overview and a proposed definition. *Geneva Centre for Security Policy*. Retrieved from http://s3.amazonaws.com/academia.edu.documents/30929642/

Al-shaikh, F. N., Elian, M. I., & Tahat, L. H. (2013). Business students attitudes towards business ethics: Evidence from Kuwait. *International Journal of Education and Research*, *8*(1), 59–76.

Amadeo, K. (2014). What are Emerging Markets? How to Pick the Real. *About News,* Retrieved from http://useconomy.about.com/od/glossary/g/emerging_market.htm

Amaeshi, K., Adi, B., Ogbechie, C., & Amao, O. (2006). *Corporate Social Responsibility in Nigeria: Western Mimicry or Indigenous Influences?* ICCSR Research Paper Series, The University of Nottingham, Nottingham.

Amaeshi, K. B., Ogbechie, A. C., & Amao, O. (2006). Corporate Social Responsibility in Nigeria: Western Mimicry or Indigenous Influences. *Journal of Corporate Citizenship*, *24*(Winter), 83–99.

Amaeshi, K. M., Adi, B., Ogbechie, C., & Amao, O. O. (2006). Corporate Social Responsibility in Nigeria: Western Mimicry or Indigenous Influence? *Journal of Corporate Citizenship*, *2006*(24), 83–99. doi:10.9774/GLEAF.4700.2006.wi.00009

Amran, A., & Devi, S. S. (2008). The impact of government and foreign affiliate influence on corporate social reporting: The case of Malaysia. *Managerial Auditing Journal*, *23*(4), 386–404. doi:10.1108/02686900810864327

Andag, R. A. (2010). Corporate social responsibility and the mining industry. Ingraining people's participation in mining communities through CSR (pp. 25–27). Human Rights Forum. Retrieved from http://smallbusiness.chron.com/corporate-social-responsibility-construction-industry-72475.html

Andersson, J., Appelberg, I., Johansson, E., Lindqvist, Y. & MohdNasir N. H. (2012). *Analysis of Bhopal Disaster applying Swiss Cheese Model and Fishbone Diagram.* Department of Production and Product Development, Chalmers University of Technology, Gothenburg, Sweden.

Andrew. (2014), Emerging markets and their ethical challenge, Retrieved from http://www.ethical-leadership.co.uk/emerging-markets/

Ang, J., Cheng, Y., & Wu, C. (2009). Social capital, cultural biases, and foreign investment in innovation: Evidence from China. Florida State University, Working Paper.

Angelo, F. et al.. (2012). Towards a strategic CSR: A Brazilian case study. *Business Strategy Series*, *13*(5), 224–238. doi:10.1108/17515631211264104

Anheier, H., Glasius, M., & Kaldor, M. (Eds.). (2001). *Global civil society 2001.* Oxford, UK: Oxford University Press.

Annan, K. (1999). *Secretary-General proposes Global Compact on Human Rights, Labour, Environment, in address to World Economic Forum in Davos* (Press Release SG/SM/6881). Retrieved from http://www.un.org/News/Press/docs/1999/19990201.sgsm6881.html

Annan, K. (2004). Special Address by Kofi Annan. Quoted in B.S. Raghavan, The call of the 21st century and other essays (p. 69). Hyderabad, India: ICFAI University Press, 2006.

Anyanwu, J. C. (2012). Why Does Foreign Direct Investment Go Where It Goes?: New Evidence From African Countries. *Annals of Economics and Finance*, *13*(2), 425–462.

Arellano, M., & Bond, S. (1991). Some tests of specification for panel data: Monte Carlo evidence and an application to employment equations. *The Review of Economic Studies*, *58*(2), 277–297. doi:10.2307/2297968

Argandoña, A. (2012). The "Management Case" for Corporate Social Responsibility. In R. J. E. Costa, & J. M. R. Marti (Eds.), *Towards a New Theory of the Firm.* Bilbao: Fundacion BBVA.

Arnold, J. D., & Quelch, A. J. (1998). New Strategies in Emerging Markets. *Sloan Management Review*, *40*(1), 7–20.

Arockiasamy, S., Haynes, J., & Al Rashdi, M. (2012). Strategic Planning to Protect Information Resources in the Event of Disasters and Suggestions for Recovery (with Importance for Oman). *Proceedings of the International Conference on Psychological Sciences and Behaviors ICPSB '12*, Hong Kong, China (Vol. 40, pp. 101-104). IPEDR. Retrieved from http://www.ipedr.com/vol40/021 ICPSB2012-P10012.pdf

Aronne, C. V., & Vasconcelos, M. (2009). The Impact of Experiential Marketing on the Customer's Perception of a Brand's Essence, *Encontro da ANPAD*, xxxIII,1-16.

Arrow, K. J. (1972). Gifts and exchanges. *Philosophy & Public Affairs*, 1(4), 343–362.

Arts, B. (2002). 'Green alliances' of business and NGOs: New styles of self-regulation or 'dead-end roads'? *Corporate Social Responsibility and Environmental Management*, *9*(1), 26–36. doi:10.1002/csr.3

Ashton, H. (1967). *The Basuto: A Social Study of Traditional and Modern Lesotho* (2nd ed.). London, UK: Oxford University Press.

Asiedu, E. (2002). On the determinants of foreign direct investment to developing countries: Is Africa different? *World Development*, *30*(1), 107–119. doi:10.1016/S0305-750X(01)00100-0

Asiedu, E. (2004). The determinants of employment of affiliates of US multinational enterprises in Africa. *Development Policy Review*, *22*(4), 371–379. doi:10.1111/j.1467-7679.2004.00255.x

Asiedu, E. (2006). Foreign direct investment in Africa: The role of natural resources, market size, government policy, institutions and political instability. *World Economy*, *29*(1), 63–77. doi:10.1111/j.1467-9701.2006.00758.x

Asiedu, E., & Lien, D. (2004). Capital controls and foreign direct investment. *World Development*, *32*(3), 479–490. doi:10.1016/j.worlddev.2003.06.016

Atsmon, Y., Kuentz, J., & Seong, J. (2012).Building brands in emerging markets, *article in Insights & Publications*, pp1.

Attarca, M., & Jacquot, T. (2005). La représentation de la Responsabilité Sociale des Entreprises: une confrontation entre les approches théoriques et les visions managériales. Paper presented at *Journée Développement Durable de l'Association Internationale de Management Stratégique, Aix en Provence*.

AUW. (2012). Educating Women to be Agents of Change in Sudan [Unpublished paper]. Ahfad University for Women, Sudan.

AUW. (2013). *Ahfad University Prospectus*. Sudan: Ahfad University for Women.

Avi-Yonah, R. S. (2005). The Cyclical Transformations of the Corporate Form: A Historical Perspective on Corporate Social Responsibility, *Delaware. The Journal of Corporation Law*, *30*(3), 767–818.

Awan, M. Z., Khan, B., & Uz Zaman, K. (2011). Economic determinants of foreign direct investment (FDI) in commodity producing sector: A case study of Pakistan. *African Journal of Business Management*, *5*(2), 537–545.

Aydin Pehlivan, I. (2002). *Yönetsel, Mesleki ve Örgütsel Etik. Pegema Yayıncılık, 3* (pp. 62–241). İstanbul: Baskı.

Badaracoo, J.L., Jr., Webb, A.P. (1995). Business Ethics: A view from the Trenches. *California Management Review*, *37*(2), 8–28. doi:10.2307/41165786

Baden, D. (2014). Look on the bright side: A comparison of positive and negative role models in business ethics education. *Academy of Management Learning & Education*, *13*(2), 154–170. doi:10.5465/amle.2012.0251

Badri, B. (2008). Gender studies at Ahfad University for Women: successes and challenges. Paper presented in the Government School of Dubai, United Arab Emirates.

Baek, K., & Qian, X. (2011). An analysis on political risks and the flow of foreign direct investment in developing and industrialized economies. *Economics, management, and financial markets, 6*(4), 60-91.

Bageac, D., Furrer, O., & Reynaud, E. (2011). Management students' attitudes toward business ethics: A comparison between France and Romania. *Journal of Business Ethics*, *98*(3), 391–406. doi:10.1007/s10551-010-0555-5

Bagozzi, R., & Dholakia, U. (2006). Antecedents and Purchase Consequences of Customers Participating in Small Group Communities. *International Journal of Research in Marketing*, *23*(1), 45–61. doi:10.1016/j.ijresmar.2006.01.005

Bailey, W., & Spicer, A. (2007, December). When Does National Identity Matter? Convergence and Divergence in International Business Ethics. *Academy of Management Journal*, *50*(6), 1462–1480. doi:10.5465/AMJ.2007.28225989

Bakr, A., & Homewood, B. (2013). Alarming exploitation of workers in Qatar. *Reuters*. Retrieved from http://www.reuters.com/article/2013/11/18/us-soccer-world-qatar-amnesty-idUSBRE9AH0HH20131118

Balabanis, G., Phillips, H. C., & Lyall, J. (1998). Corporate social responsibility and economic performance in the top British companies: Are they linked? *European Business Review*, *98*(1), 25–44. doi:10.1108/09555349810195529

Banfield, E. C. (1958). The moral basis of a backward society. *New York. Glencol*, *3*, 4.

Banga, K., & Mahajan, V. (2005). The Lands of Opportunity. FT press.

Banque Misr website. (n. d.). *About us, CSR*. Retrieved fromhttp://www.banquemisr.com/sites/engbm/Pages/csr1.aspx

Banque Misr website. (n. d.). *Mohamed Talaat Pasha Harb*. Retrieved fromhttp://www.banquemisr.com/sites/engbm/Pages/TalaatHarb.aspx

Banque Misr website. (n. d.). Retrieved from http://www.banquemisr.com

Bantel, K. (1993). Environment and performance effects on strategic planning formality. *Group & Organization Management*, *18*(4), 436–458. doi:10.1177/1059601193184004

Barabasi, A. L., & Frangos, J. (2002). *Linked: The New Science of Networks*. Perseus Publishing.

Barber, B. R. (1995). *Jihad vs McWorld: Terrorism's challenge to democracy*. New York, NY: Ballantine Books.

Barber, B., & Odean, T. (2001). Boys will be Boys: Gender, Overconfidence, and Common Stock Investment. *The Quarterly Journal of Economics*, *14*(1), 261–292. doi:10.1162/003355301556400

Barnett, M. L. (2007). Stakeholder Influence Capacity and Variability of Financial Return to Corporate Social Responsibility. *Academy of Management Review*, *32*(3), 794–816. doi:10.5465/AMR.2007.25275520

Barney, J. B., & Clark, D. N. (2007). *Resource-based theory: Creating and sustaining competitive advantage*. Oxford: Oxford University Press.

Barney, J., Wright, M., & Ketchen, D. J. (2001). The resource-based view of the firm: Ten years after 1991. *Journal of Management*, *27*(6), 625–641. doi:10.1177/014920630102700601

Baron, R. M., & Kenny, D. A. (1986). The Moderator-Mediator Variable Distinction in Social and Psychological Research: Conceptual, Strategic and Statistical Considerations. *Journal of Personality and Social Psychology*, *51*(6), 1173–1182. doi:10.1037/0022-3514.51.6.1173 PMID:3806354

Barrier, , M et al. (1998). Doing the Right Thing. *Nation's Business*, March, 33–38.

Başgöze, P., & Tektaş, Ö. Ö. (2012). Ethical perceptions and green buying behavior of consumers: A cross-national exploratory study. *Journal of Economics and Behavioral Studies*, *4*(8), 477–488.

Baskin, J. (2006). Corporate responsibility in emerging markets. *Journal of Corporate Citizenship*, *2006*(24), 29–47. doi:10.9774/GLEAF.4700.2006.wi.00006

Battat, J., & Aykut, D. (2005). Southern Multinationals–A Growing Phenomenon. *Note prepared for the conference Southern Multinationals: A Rising Force in the World Economy* (Vol. 9).

Battle, M. (1996). The Ubuntu Theology of Desmond Tutu. In L. Huley et al. (Eds.), *Archbishop Tutu: Prophetic witness in South Africa*. Cape Town: Human & Rousseau.

Battle, M. (2009). *Ubuntu: I in You and You in Me*. New York: Seabury Books.

Bauer, R. A. (1960). Consumer Behavior as Risk Taking. In R. S. Hancock (Ed.), *Dynamic marketing for a changing world* (pp. 389–398). Chicago: American Marketing Association.

Beal, B. D. (2014). *Corporate social responsibility: Definition, core issues, and recent developments*. London, UK: Sage.

Beaver, B., Kettler, P., & Scholes, M. (1970). The Association Between Market Determined and Accounting Determined Risk Measures. *Accounting Review*, *45*, 654–682.

Beck, U. (2000). *What is globalization?* Cambridge, UK: Polity Press.

Beets, P., & Le Grange, L. (2005). 'Africanising' Assessment Practices: Does the Notion of Ubuntu Hold Any Promise? *SAJHE* (Special Issue), 19, 1197-1207.

Belkaoui, A. R., & Karpik, P. G. (1989). Determinants of the corporate decision to disclose social information. *Accounting, Auditing & Accountability Journal*, *2*(1), 36–51. doi:10.1108/09513578910132240

Beloe, S., Elkington, J., Fry Hester, K., & Newell, S. (2003). *The 21st century NGO: In the market for change*. London, UK: SustainAbility.

Beloe, S., Elkington, J., Prakash-Mani, K., Thorpe, J., & Zollinger, P. (2004). *Gearing up: From corporate responsibility to good governance and scalable solutions*. London, UK: SustainAbility.

Bennett, N., & Lemoine, J. (2014). What VUCA really means for you. *Harvard Business Review*, *92*(1/2), 27.

Berens, C. (2004). Green Grossers. *Financial Management*, September, 20.

Bergh, K., Lefkovitch, J., Scotti, S., & Warner, B. (2009). *General Motors Corporation Case One – Internal Analysis.*

Bessler, J. D. (2008). In the Spirit of Ubuntu: Enforcing the Rights of Orphans and Vulnerable Children Affected by HIV/AIDS in South Africa. *Hastings International and Comparative Law Review*, *31*(1), 33–113.

Bhardwaj, A., Dietz, J., & Beamish, P. W. (2007). Host country cultural influences on foreign direct investment. *Management International Review*, *47*(1), 29–50. doi:10.1007/s11575-007-0003-7

Bhattacharya, P., & Deshpande, A. (2013). The changing face of rural India. Live mint website, Retrieved from http://www.livemint.com/Politics/

Bio-Tchné, & Christensen B. (2006). Right Time for Africa. *Finance & Development*, *43*(4), 8–13.

Birkin, F., Polesie, T., & Lewis, L. (2009). A new business model for sustainable development: An exploratory study using the theory of constraints in Nordic organizations. *Business Strategy and the Environment*, *18*(5), 277–290. doi:10.1002/bse.581

Blackwell, D., & Dubins, L. (1962). Merging of Opinions with Increasing Information. *Annals of Mathematical Statistics*, *38*(3), 882–886. doi:10.1214/aoms/1177704456

Blowfield, M. E., & Dolan, C. S. (2008). Stewards of Virtue? The Dilemma of CSR in African Agriculture. *Development and Change*, *39*(1), 1–23. doi:10.1111/j.1467-7660.2008.00465.x

Blowfield, M., & Murray, A. (2008). *Corporate Responsibility: A critical introduction*. Oxford: Oxford University press.

Blowfield, M., & Murray, A. (2011). *Corporate Responsibility*. Oxford University Press.

Blowfield, M., & Murray, A. (2011). *Corporate responsibility*. Oxford, UK: Oxford University Press.

Boisselier, P., & Mekaoui, S. (2005, May 11-13). Qualité de l'Information Financière et Introduction des Sociétés sur le Nouveau Marché: Enjeux et Proposition d'un Cadre d'Analyse. *Proceedings of theXXV[ième] Congrès Annuel de l'Association Francophone de Comptabilité*, Lille.

Boli, J., & Thomas, G. M. (Eds.). (1999). *Constructing world culture: International nongovernmental organizations since 1875*. Palo Alto, CA: Stanford University Press.

Boluk, K. A. (2011). Fair Trade Tourism South Africa: Consumer virtue or moral selving? *Journal of Ecotourism*, *10*(3), 235–249. doi:10.1080/14724049.2011.617451

Boone Louis E. & Kurtz David L.(2013). *Contemporary Business* (2013 ed.). South Western: Cengage Learning.

Bornstein, D. (1997). *The price of a dream: The story of the Grameen Bank*. Chicago, IL: University of Chicago Press.

Boschma, R., & Martin, R. (2007). Editorial: Constructing an evolutionary economic geography. *Journal of Economic Geography*, (June): 18.

Bottazzi, L., Da Rin, M., Hellmann, T., & Advantage, R. R. C. (2007). The Importance of Trust for Investment: Evidence from Venture Capital (Working Papers 325). IGIER (Innocenzo Gasparini Institute for Economic Research), Bocconi University.

Bowen, H. R. (1978). Social responsibilities of the businessman: Twenty years later. In E. Epstein, & E.D. Votaw (Eds.), Rationality, Legitimacy, Responsibility: Search for New Directions in Business and Society (pp. 116-130). Santa Monica, CA: Goodyear Publishing Co.

Bowen, H. R. (1953). *Social Responsibility of the Businessman* (1st ed.). New York: Harper & Brothers.

Bowen, H.-R. (1953). *Social Responsibilities of the Businessman* (p. 6). Brothers, New York: Harper.

Boyle, E., & McCabe, S. (2006). Understanding Brands as Experiential Spaces: Axiological Implications for Marketing Strategists. *Journal of Strategic Marketing*, *14*(2).

Brakus, J., Schmitt, B., & Zarantonello, L. (2009). Brand Experience: What is it? How do We Measure It? And Does It Affect Loyalty? Retrieved from http://www8.gsb.columbia.edu/sites/globalbrands/files/Brand_Experience.pdf

Brandenburger, A., & Nalebuff, B. (1997). *Coopetition*. New York: Doubleday.

Brennan, M. J., & Subrahmanyam, A. (1995). Investment Analysis and Price Formation in Securities Markets. *Journal of Financial Economics*, *38*(3), 361–381. doi:10.1016/0304-405X(94)00811-E

Brenner, S. N. (1992). Ethics Programs and Their Dimensions. *Journal of Business Ethics*, *11*(5-6), 391–399. doi:10.1007/BF00870551

Brent Spar. (n. d.). *Wikipedia*. Retrieved from http://en.wikipedia.org/wiki/Brent_spar

British Consulate. (2015, May 11). *Doing Business with the Palestinian Territories, the Palestinian Economy and Britain*.

Broodryk, J. (2002). *Ubuntu: Life lessons from Africa*. Pretoria: Ubuntu School of Philosophy.

Brown, S., & Hillegeist, S. A. (2007). How Disclosure Quality Affects the Level of Information Asymmetry. *Review of Accounting Studies*, *12*(2-3), 443–477. doi:10.1007/s11142-007-9032-5

Brucks, M. (1985). The Effects of Product Class Knowledge on information Search Behavior. *The Journal of Consumer Research*, *12*(1), 1–16. doi:10.1086/209031

Brunel, O. (2002). *Les Stratégies d'Ajustement au Risque Alimentaire: Modèle Théorique et Test Empirique* [Thèse de Doctorat en Sciences de Gestion]. IAE, Université Lyon 3.

Bryant, J. (2013, July 17). *Living our values, Kellogg Company's global code of ethics.* Retrieved from http://www.kelloggcompany.com/content/dam/kelloggcompanyus/corporate_responsibility/pdf/2012CR_Reports/EN_COE_Final1.pdf

Buccholz, R. A. (2009). *Essentials of Public Policy for Management* (2nd ed.). Upper Saddle River, NJ: Prentice Hall.

Bucic, T., Harris, J., & Arli, D. (2012). Ethical consumers among the millennials: A cross-national study. *Journal of Business Ethics, 110*(1), 113–131. doi:10.1007/s10551-011-1151-z

Bughin, J., Doogan, J., & Vetvik, O. (2010).A new way to measure word-of-mouth marketing, Retrieved from http://www.mckinsey.com/insights/marketing_sales/a_new_way_to_measure_word-of-mouth_marketing

Building Effective Business Models in Emerging Markets. (2012). *Deloittee Development LLC.* New Delhi, India.

Buono, A. F., Fletcher-Brown, D., Frederick, R., Hall, G. J., & Sultan, J. (2012). Acting Ethically: Moral reasoning and business school student behavior. *SAM Advanced Management Journal, 77*(3), 18.

Burke, J. E. (1964). Scattering of surface waves on an infinitely deep fluid. *Journal of Mathematical Physics, 6*(6), 805–819. doi:10.1063/1.1704182

Burke, L., & Logsdon, J. M. (1996). How corporate social responsibility pays off. *Long Range Planning, 29*(4), 495–502. doi:10.1016/0024-6301(96)00041-6

Busch, L. (2014). Individual Choice and Social Values: Choice in the Agrifood Sector. *Journal of Consumer Culture, 26*(May). doi:10.1177/1469540514536190

Business Roundtable Institute for Corporate Ethics. (1988, February).

Busse, M., & Hefeker, C. (2007). Political risk, institutions and foreign direct investment. *European Journal of Political Economy, 23*(2), 397–415. doi:10.1016/j.ejpoleco.2006.02.003

Butter, F. A., & Mosch, R. H. (2003). Trade, Trust and Transaction Cost (No. 03-082/3). Tinbergen Institute Discussion Paper.

Byrne, B. M. (2006). Structural Equation Modeling with EQS: Basic Concepts, Applications, and Programming (2nd ed.). London: Lawrence Erlbraum associates Publishers.

Cadbury's drumming gorilla spawns Facebook group. (2007). Brand Republic, p11, Retrieved from repository.upenn.edu/cgi/viewcontent.cgi?article=1054&context

Cadet, B., & Kouabenan, D. (2005). Evaluer et Modéliser les Risques: Apports et Limites de Différents Paradigmes dans le Diagnostic de Sécurité. *Le Travail Humain, 68*(1), 7–35. doi:10.3917/th.681.0007

Campbell, J. L. (2007). Why would corporations behave in socially responsible ways? An institutional theory of corporate social responsibility. *Academy of Management Review, 32*(3), 946–967. doi:10.5465/AMR.2007.25275684

Cao, M. (2012). International Expansion of Emerging Market Multinationals: An Integrated Perspective. *Proceedings of theInternational Conference on Innovation and Information Management (ICIIM)*

Capron, M., & Quairel-Lanoizelée, F. (2007). La responsabilité sociale d'entreprise. Coll. Repères, éd. La Découverte.

Capstaff, J. (1989). The Risk Perceptions of Investment Analysts. *The Investments Analysts, 91*, 2–15.

Carey, L., Shaw, D., & Shiu, E. (2008). The impact of ethical concerns on family consumer decision-making. *International Journal of Consumer Studies, 32*(5), 553–560. doi:10.1111/j.1470-6431.2008.00687.x

Carlson, P. J., & Burke, F. (1998). Lessons learned from ethics in the classroom: Exploring student growth in flexibility, complexity and comprehension. *Journal of Business Ethics*, *17*(11), 1179–1187. doi:10.1023/A:1005740923813

Carrigan, M., & Attalla, A. (2001). The myth of the ethical consumer-do ethics matter in purchase behaviour? *Journal of Consumer Marketing*, *18*(7), 560–578. doi:10.1108/07363760110410263

Carroll, A. B. (2008). A History of Corporate Social Responsibility: Concepts and Practices. In A. Crane, D. Matten, A. McWilliams, J. Moon, & D.S. Siegel. (Eds.), Oxford Handbook of Corporate Social Responsibility (pp. 19-46). USA: Oxford University Press.

Carroll, A. B. October (1979). A three –Dimensional Conceptual Model of Corporate Performance. Academy of Management Review, 4(4), 497-505.

Carroll, A.B. & Buchholtz, A. (2014). *Business and Society: Ethics, Sustainability, and Stakeholder Management* (9th ed.). USA: Cengage Learning.

Carroll, A. (1979). A Three Dimensional Conceptual Model of Corporate Performance. *Academy of Management Review*, *4*(4), 497–505.

Carroll, A. (2000). A Commentary and Overview of Key Questions on Corporate Social Performance Measurement. *Business & Society*, *39*(4), 466–478. doi:10.1177/000765030003900406

Carroll, A. B. (1979). A Three-Dimensional Conceptual Model of Corporate Performance. *Academy of Management Review*, *4*, 497–505.

Carroll, A. B. (1979). A three-dimensional conceptual model of corporate performance. *Academy of Management Review*, *4*(4), 497–505.

Carroll, A. B. (1979). A Three-Dimensional Model of Corporate Performance. *Academy of Management Review*, *4*(4), 497–505.

Carroll, A. B. (1983). Corporate social responsibility: Will industry respond to cut-backs in social program funding? *Vital Speeches of the Day*, *49*, 604–608.

Carroll, A. B. (1991). The pyramid of corporate social responsibility: Toward the moral management of organizational stakeholders. *Business Horizons*, *34*(4), 39–48. doi:10.1016/0007-6813(91)90005-G

Carroll, A. B. (1994). Social issues in management research: Experts' views, analysis and commentary. *Business & Society*, *33*(1), 5–29. doi:10.1177/000765039403300102

Carroll, A. B. (1998). The Four Faces of Corporate Citizenship. *Business and Society Review*, *100*(1), 1–7. doi:10.1111/0045-3609.00008

Carroll, A. B. (1999). Corporate Social Responsibility: Evolution of a Definitional Construct. *Business & Society*, *38*(3), 268–295. doi:10.1177/000765039903800303

Carroll, A. B. (2000). Ethical Challenges for Business in the New Millennium: Corporate Social Responsibility and Models of Management Morality. *Business Ethics Quarterly*, *10*(1), 33–42. doi:10.2307/3857692

Carroll, A. B. (2004). Managing ethically with global stakeholders: A present and future challenge. *The Academy of Management Executive*, *18*(2), 114–120. doi:10.5465/AME.2004.13836269

Carroll, A. B., & Buchholtz, A. K. (2003). *Business and Society: Ethics and Stakeholder Management* (5th ed.). Australia: Thomson South-Western.

Carroll, A. B., & Shabana, K. M. (2010). The business case for corporate social responsibility: A review of concepts, research and practice. *International Journal of Management Reviews*, *12*(1), 85–105. doi:10.1111/j.1468-2370.2009.00275.x

Casanova, L. (2009). *Global Latinas: Latin America's Emerging Multinationals*. Palgrave Macmillan. doi:10.1057/9780230235021

Castells, M. (1996). *The rise of the network society*. Oxford, UK: Blackwell.

Cavusgil, S. T. (1985). Guidelines for Export Market Research. *Business Horizons*, *28*(6), 27–33. doi:10.1016/0007-6813(85)90082-5

Cavusgil, S. T., Ghauri, P. N., & Akcal, A. A. (2012). Doing business in emerging markets. *Sage (Atlanta, Ga.)*.

Cengiz, E., Yazici, S., & Erdal, M. (2010). Ethical Perception from Students' Perspective: Understanding Instructors' Effect on Students' Ethical Sensitivity in Personal Selling. *Journal of Leadership, Accountability and Ethics*, *8*(2), 41–50.

Cerff, K. (2004). *Exploring Ubuntu and the African Renaissance: A Conceptual Study of Servant Leadership from an African Perspective*. Regent University: the School of Leadership Studies.

Chahal, H., Mishra, S., Raina, S., & Soni, T. (2014). A comprehensive model of business social responsibility (BSR) for small scale enterprises in Indian context. *Journal of Small Business and Enterprise Development*, *21*(4), 716–739. doi:10.1108/JSBED-05-2014-0091

Chambers, R. (1983). *Rural Development: Putting the Last First*. Harlow, London: Pearson Education.

Chambers, R. (2007). *Whose Really Counts? Putting the First Last*. London: Intermediate Technology.

Chandler, D. B., & Werther, W. B. (2013). *Strategic corporate social responsibility: Stakeholders, globalization, and sustainable value creation*. London, UK: Sage.

Chang, M., D'Anna, G., Watson, I., & Wee, M. (2008). Does Disclosure Quality via Investor Relations Affect Information Asymmetry? *Australian Journal of Management*, *33*(2), 2. doi:10.1177/031289620803300208

Chatterjee, P. (2001). Online reviews: Do consumers use them? *Advances in Consumer Research. Association for Consumer Research (U. S.)*, *28*(1), 129–133.

Chaudhuri, A., & Holbrook, M. B. (2001). The Chain of Effects from Brand Trust and Brand Affect to Brand Performance: The Role of Brand Loyalty. *Journal of Marketing*, *65*(2), 81–93. doi:10.1509/jmkg.65.2.81.18255

Chau, G. K., & Gray, S. J. (2002). Ownership structure and corporate voluntary disclosure in Hong Kong and Singapore. *The International Journal of Accounting*, *37*(2), 247–265. doi:10.1016/S0020-7063(02)00153-X

Chauveau, A., & Rosé, J.-J. (2003). *L'entreprise responsable: responsabilité sociale-éthique*. Editions d'Organisation.

Checkoway, B. (2001). Renewing the civic mission of the American Research University. *The Journal of Higher Education*, *72*(2), 125–147. doi:10.2307/2649319

Cheng, E. C. M., & Courtenay, S. M. (2006). Board composition, regulatory regime, and voluntary disclosure. *The International Journal of Accounting*, *41*(3), 262–289. doi:10.1016/j.intacc.2006.07.001

Cheng, S. W. (2003). *Diagnosis and Treatment Revealing the Chinese Stock Markets*. China: Economic Sciences Publication.

Chernatony, L. (2006). From Brand Vision to Brand Evaluation: the strategic process of growing. Oxford: Butterworth-Heinemann, 3,369.

Cherrington, J. O., & Cherrington, D. J. (1995). *Ethical Decision Making*. Englewood, CO: Micro Mash.

Choi, J., Salandro, D., & Shastri, K. (1988). On the Estimation of Bid-Ask Spreads: Theory and Evidence. *Journal of Financial and Quantitative Analysis*, *23*(2), 219–230. doi:10.2307/2330882

Cho, J., & Lee, J. (2006). An Integrated Model of Risk and Risk-Reducing Strategies. *Journal of Business Research*, *59*(1), 112–120. doi:10.1016/j.jbusres.2005.03.006

Cho, S., & Krasser, A. H. (2011). What makes us care? The impact of cultural values, individual factors, and attention to media content on motivation for ethical consumerism. *International Social Science Review*, *86*(1/2), 3.

Chung, K. H., & Charoenwong, C. (1998). Insider Trading and the Bid-Ask Spread. *Financial Review*, *33*(3), 1–20. doi:10.1111/j.1540-6288.1998.tb01379.x

Churchill, G. A. (1979). A Paradigm for Developing Better Measures of Marketing Constructs. *JMR, Journal of Marketing Research*, *16*(1), 64–73. doi:10.2307/3150876

Churie-Kallhauge, A., Sjöstedt, G., & Corell, E. (Eds.). (2005). *Global challenges: Furthering the multilateral process for sustainable development*. Sheffield, UK: Greenleaf.

Ciravegna, L., Fitzgerald, R., & Kundu, S. (2013). *Operating in emerging markets: a guide to management and strategy in the new international economy*. FT Press.

Claessens, S. (2006). *Corporate Governance of Islamic Banks: Why is Important, How is it Special and What does this Imply? The World Bank Financial Sector Network*. The Islamic Financial Services Board.

Claessens, S., Djankov, S., & Lang, L. H. P. (2000). The separation of ownership and control in East Asian corporations. *Journal of Financial Economics*, *58*(1-2), 81–112. doi:10.1016/S0304-405X(00)00067-2

Clapp, J., & Rowlands, I. H. (2014). Corporate Social Responsibility. In J. F. Morin & A. Orsini (Eds.), *The Essential Guide to Global Environmental Governance*. Routledge.

Clarkson, M. B. E. (1995). A stakeholder framework for analyzing and evaluating corporate social performance. *Academy of Management Review*, *20*(1), 92–117.

Clark, T. S., & Grantham, K. N. (2012). What CSR is not: Corporate social irresponsibility. *Critical Studies on Corporate Responsibility. Governance and Sustainability*, *4*, 23–41.

Cohen, M., Etner, J., & Jeleva, M. (2008). Dynamic Decision Making When Risk Perception Depends on Past Experience. *Theory and Decision*, *64*(2-3), 173–192. doi:10.1007/s11238-007-9061-3

Colley, J., Doyle, J., Logan, G., & Stettinius, W. (2004). *What is Corporate Governance?* London: McGraw-Hill.

Collins, D. (2009). *Essentials of Business Ethics: Creating an Organization of High Integrity and Superior Performance*. John Wiley & Sons Inc. doi:10.1002/9781118386163

Collins, D., & Kothari, C. (1989). An Analysis of the Cross-Sectional and Intertemporal Determinants of Earnings Response Coefficients. *Journal of Accounting and Economics*, *11*, 143–181. doi:10.1016/0165-4101(89)90004-9

Comegys, C. (2010). The impact of religiously affiliated universities and courses in ethics and religious studies on students' attitude toward business ethics. *Contemporary Issues in Education Research*, *3*(6), 35–44.

Commission of the European Communities. (2009). Green Paper, Promoting a European Framework for Corporate Social responsibility.

Connolly, J., & Prothero, A. (2008). Green Consumption: Life-politics, risk and contradictions. *Journal of Consumer Culture*, *8*(1), 117–145. doi:10.1177/1469540507086422

Conroy, S. J., & Emerson, T. L. (2004). Business ethics and religion: Religiosity as a predictor of ethical awareness among students. *Journal of Business Ethics*, *50*(4), 383–396. doi:10.1023/B:BUSI.0000025040.41263.09

Consumer segmentation: How it affects your Experiential Marketing activity. (2012). Retrieved from http://www.hotcow.co.uk/Buzz-Blog/consumer-segmentation-how-it-affects-your-experiential-marketing-activity.htm#sthash.KEdyprbE.dpuf

Cooper, A. C., Woo, C. Y., & Dunkelberg, W. C. (1988). Entrepreneurs' Perceived Chances for Success. *Journal of Business Venturing*, *3*(2), 97–108. doi:10.1016/0883-9026(88)90020-1

Corporate Social Responsibility Picks up in Kuwait. CSR Middle East, AME Info online. Retrieved from www.ameinfo.com/145699.html

Court, D., Elzinga, D., Mulder, S., & Vetvik, O. (2009). The consumer decision journey. Insights & Publications. Retrieved from mckinseyquarterly.com.

Coveney, P., & Highfield, R. (1995). *Frontiers of complexity: The search for order in a chaotic world*. New York: Ballantine.

Cox, D. F. (1967a). *Risk Taking and Information Handling in Consumer Behavior*. Cambridge, MA: Harvard University Press.

Cox, D. F., & Rich, S. U. (1964). Perceived Risk and Consumer decision Making-The Case of Telephone Shopping. *JMR, Journal of Marketing Research*, *1*(4), 32–39. doi:10.2307/3150375

Crane, A., & Matten, D., McWilliams, A., Moon, J., & Siegel, D.S. (Eds.), (2008). Oxford Handbook of Corporate Social Responsibility. USA: Oxford University Press.

Crane, A., & Matten, D. (2004). *Business Ethics*. Oxford University Press.

Crane, A., & Matten, D. (2004). *Business ethics: A European perspective: managing corporate citizenship and sustainability in the age of globalization*. Oxford: Oxford University Press.

Crane, A., & Matten, D. (2010). *Business ethics: Managing corporate citizenship and sustainability in the age of globalization*. Oxford University Press.

Crane, A., Matten, D., & Spence, L. (Eds.). (2013). *Corporate Social Responsibility: Readings and Cases in Global Context*. New York, NY: Routledge.

Crane, A., Matten, D., & Spence, L. J. (Eds.). (2013). *Corporate social responsibility: Readings and cases in a global context*. London, UK: Routledge.

Crié, D. (2005). De l'Usage des Modèles de Mesure Réflectifs ou Formatifs dans les Modèles d'Equations Structurelles. *Recherche et Applications en Marketing*, *20*(2), 5–27. doi:10.1177/076737010502000201

Cubeddu, M. L. M., Culiuc, M. A., Fayad, M. G., Gao, Y., Kochhar, M. K., Kyobe, A., . . . Zhang, Z. (2014). Emerging Markets in Transition: Growth Prospects and Challenges (No. 14-16). International Monetary Fund.

Cullers, R. (2013). Adidas Lets Fans Jump for Derrick Rose Sneakers in London Retrieved from http://www.adweek.com/adfreak/adidas-lets-fans-jump-derrick-rose-sneakers-london-pop-store-151483

Cuny, X., & Gaillard, I. (2003). Les Risques Professionnels Aujourd'hui: Problèmes Actuels, Perspectives et Orientations Méthodologiques. In D. R. Kouabénan & M. Dubois (Eds.), *Les risques professionnels: nouvelles approches, perspectives actuelles* (pp. 25–36). Toulouse: Octarès.

Daft, R. L. (1997). Management (4th ed.). Fort Worth, TX: The Dryden Press.

Daft, R. L. (2006). *The New Era of Management* (International ed.). South-Western.

Dahlsrud, A. (2008). How corporate social responsibility is defined: An analysis of 37 definitions. *Corporate Social Responsibility and Environmental Management*, *15*(1), 1–13. doi:10.1002/csr.132

Dallas, G. (2013), Business Ethics in Emerging Markets and Investors' Expectations Standards, Retrieved from http://corpgov.law.harvard.edu/2013/01/19/business-ethics-in-emerging-markets-and-investors-expectations-standards/

Dandouau, J. C. (2000). *Le Comportement de Recherche d'Informations des Différents Profils de Risque Perçu selon la Nature de l'Achat. In les Actes des liers ateliers de recherche de l'AFM, Percevoir, identifier et gérer le risque en marketing* (pp. 133–151). Paris: La Sorbonne.

D'andrea, G., Stengel, E., & Krstelj, A. (2014). 6 Truths about Emerging-market consumers. *Strategy and business*, 34. Retrieved fromhttp://www.strategy-business.com/article

Darkwa, S. (2014). Knowledge of nutrition fact on food labels and their impact on food choices on consumers in Koforidua, Ghana: A case study. *South African Journal of Clinical Nutrition*, *27*(1), 13–17.

Dartey-Baah, K., & Amponsah-Tawiah, K. (2011). Exploring the limits of Western Corporate Social Responsibility Theories in Africa. *International Journal of Business and Social Science*, *2*(18), 126–137.

David, J. T. (2010). Business Models, Business Strategy and Innovation. *Long Range Planning*. Retrieved from http://www.businessmodelcommunity.com/fs/Root/8jig8-businessmodelsbusinessstrategy.pdf

David, F. R. (2011). *Strategic management: Concepts and cases*. Pearson Education, Inc.

Davidson, P., Wood, S., & Griffin, R. W. (2009). *Management*. John Wiley and Sons Australia.

Davidson, W. H. (1980). The location of foreign direct investment activity: Country characteristics and experience effects. *Journal of International Business Studies*, *11*(2), 9–22. doi:10.1057/palgrave.jibs.8490602

Davis, J. R., & Welton, R. E. (1991). Professional ethics: Business students' perceptions. *Journal of Business Ethics*, *10*(6), 451–463. doi:10.1007/BF00382829

Davis, K. (1973). The case for and against business assumption of social responsibilities. *Academy of Management Journal*, *16*(2), 312–322. doi:10.2307/255331

Davis, K., & Fredrick, W. C. (1996). *Business and Society: Corporate Strategy, Public policy, Ethics* (8th ed.). New York: McGraw Hill.

De Bakker, G. A., Groenwegen, P., & Den Hond, F. (2005). A Bibliometric Analysis of 30 years of Research and Theory on Corporate Social Responsibility and Corporate Social Performance. *Business & Society*, *44*(3), 283–317. doi:10.1177/0007650305278086

De George, R. T. (2008). An American perspective on corporate social responsibility and the tenuous relevance of Jacques Derrida. *Business Ethics (Oxford, England)*, *17*(1), 74–86. doi:10.1111/j.1467-8608.2008.00522.x

De Jager, P. (2010). *Ubuntu, Zimbabwe and the Ethics of Intervention* [Unpublished masters dissertation]. University of the Witwatersrand, Johannesburg, South Africa.

Dearmon, J., & Grier, K. (2009). Trust and development. *Journal of Economic Behavior & Organization*, *71*(2), 210–220. doi:10.1016/j.jebo.2009.02.011

Declerck, F., and Martinez, I. (2004). Informations Volontaires et Microstructure des Marchés Financiers: Quel Impact sur le Marché des Titres NextEconomy et NextPrime? *Cahier de recherche*, 161.

Delios, A., & Henisz, W. J. (2003). Political hazards, experience, and sequential entry strategies: The international expansion of Japanese firms, 1980–1998. *Strategic Management Journal*, *24*(11), 1153–1164. doi:10.1002/smj.355

Demirag, I. (Ed.). (2005). *Corporate social responsibility, accountability and governance: Global perspectives*. Sheffield, UK: Greenleaf.

Demirhan, E., & Masca, M. (2008). Determinants of foreign direct investment flows to developing countries: a cross-sectional analysis. *Prague economic papers*, *4*(2008), 356-369.

Denzin, N. K., & Lincoln, Y. S. (2011). *The SAGE handbook of qualitative research*. Sage.

Dessler, G. (2011). *Human Resource Management* (12th ed.). Pearson Education Inco.

Deutsche Gesellschaft für Internationale Zusammenarbeit (GIZ) GmbH. (2011). *Fast Growth and Big Impacts: How Emerging Market Multinationals are Advancing Sustainable Development*. Retrieved from http://www.giz.de/Wirtschaft/de/downloads/giz2011-de-fastgrowth-incl-impacts.pdf

Dholakia, U. M., & Soltysinski, K. (2001). Coveted or overlooked. The psychology of bidding for comparable listings in digital actions. *Marketing Letters*, *12*(3), 225–237. doi:10.1023/A:1011164710951

Diamantopoulos, A., Riefler, P., & Roth, K. P. (2008). Advancing Formative Measurement Models. *Journal of Business Research*, *61*(12), 1203–1218. doi:10.1016/j.jbusres.2008.01.009

Diaz, A., Magni, M., & Poh, F. (2012). From oxcart to Wal-Mart: Four keys to reaching emerging-market consumers. *Insights & Publications*. Retrieved from http://www.mckinsey.com

Dicken, P. (2003). Global shift: Reshaping the global economic map in the 21st century. *Sage (Atlanta, Ga.)*.

Dicken, P. (2007). *Global shift: Mapping the changing contours of the world economy*. Sage Publications Ltd.

Djongoue, G. (2007). *Fiabilité de l'Information Comptable et Gouvernance d'Entreprise: Une Analyse de l'Audit Légal dans les Entreprises Camerounaises*. Colloque International le Gouvernance: Quelles Pratiques pour Promouvoir le Développement de l'Afrique. Université Catholique de Lille – France.

Doh, J. P., & Teegen, H. (Eds.). (2003). *Globalisation and NGOs: Transforming business, government, and society*. Westport, CT: Praeger.

Dolan, C. S. (2005). Fields of Obligation Rooting ethical sourcing in Kenya horticulture. *Journal of Consumer Culture*, *5*(3), 365–389. doi:10.1177/1469540505056796

Dolan, C. S. (2010). Virtual moralities: The mainstreaming of Fairtrade in Kenya tea fields. *Geoforum*, *41*(1), 33–43. doi:10.1016/j.geoforum.2009.01.002

Donaldson, T., & Preston, L. E. (1995). The stakeholder theory of the corporation: Concepts, evidence, and implications. *Academy of Management Review*, *20*(1), 65–91.

Douglas, M., & Wildavsky, A. B. (1982). *Risk and Culture: An Essay on the Selection of Technical and Environmental Dangers. Berkley*, University of California Press.

Dowling, G. R., & Staelin, R. (1994). A Model of Perceived Risk and Intended Risk Handling Activity. *The Journal of Consumer Research*, *21*(1), 119–134. doi:10.1086/209386

Drucker, P. F. (1984). The New Meaning of Corporate Social Responsibility. *California Management Review*, *26*(2), 53–63. doi:10.2307/41165066

Duncan-Durst, L. (2006). Customer Relationships - What are the Difference between Customer Experience Management and Experiential Marketing? *MarketingProfs*. Retrieved from http://www.marketingprofs.com/articles/2006/1717/whats-the-difference-between-customer-experience-management-and-experiential-marketing

Durlauf, S., & Fafchamps, M. (2005). Social capital. In P. Aghion & S. Durlauf (Eds.), *Handbook of Economic Growth* (1st ed., Vol. 1, pp. 1639–1699). Elsevier.

Dutta, N., & Osei-Yeboah, K. (2013). A new dimension to the relationship between foreign direct investment and human capital: The role of political and civil rights. *Journal of International Development*, *25*(2), 160–179. doi:10.1002/jid.1739

Dyl, E. A. (1988). Corporate control and management compensation: Evidence on the agency problem. *Managerial and Decision Economics*, *9*(1), 21–25. doi:10.1002/mde.4090090102

Ebert, R. J., & Griffin, R. W. (2011). *Business essentials*. Pearson Education Canada.

Edwards, J. R., & Bagozzi, R. P. (2000). On the Nature and Direction of Relationships Between Constructs and Measures. *Psychological Methods*, *5*(2), 155–174. doi:10.1037/1082-989X.5.2.155 PMID:10937327

Edwards, M. (2004). *Civil society*. Cambridge, UK: Polity Press.

Edwards, S. (1992). *Capital flows, foreign direct investment, and debt-equity swaps in developing countries (No. w3497)*. National Bureau of Economic Research.

El Akremi, A., and Roussel, P. (2003). *Analyse des Variables Modératrices et Médiatrices par les Méthodes d'équations Structurelles: Application à une Etude en GRH*. Communication présentée au Congrès Annuel de l'AGRH.

Elkington, J. (2004). Enter the triple bottom line. *The triple bottom line: Does it all add up*, 1-16.

Elkington, J. (1997). *Cannibals with forks: The triple bottom line of 21st century business*. Oxford, UK: Capstone.

Elkington, J. (1998). Partnership from cannibals with forks: The triple bottom line of 21st century business. *Environmental Quality Management*, *8*(1), 37–51. doi:10.1002/tqem.3310080106

Elliott, G., Rundle-Thiele, S., & Waller, D. (2014). Marketing (3rd ed.). John Wiley &Sons Australia, Ltd.

Elton, E., Gruber, M., & Gultekin, M. (1984). Professional Expectations: Accuracy and Diagnosis of Errors. *Journal of Financial and Quantitative Analysis*, *19*(4), 351–363. doi:10.2307/2330778

Emerson, T. L., Conroy, S. J., & Stanley, C. W. (2007). Ethical attitudes of accountants: Recent evidence from a practitioners' survey. *Journal of Business Ethics*, *71*(1), 73–87. doi:10.1007/s10551-006-9125-2

Engel, J. F., Blackwell, R. D., & Miniard, P. W. (1993). *Consumer Behavior*. New York: The Dryden Press.

Eng, L. L., & Mak, Y. T. (2003). Corporate governance and voluntary disclosure. *Journal of Accounting and Public Policy*, *22*(4), 325–345. doi:10.1016/S0278-4254(03)00037-1

Epstein, M., & Buhovac, A.R. (2014). Making Sustainability Work: Best Practices in Managing and Measuring Corporate Social, Environmental, and Economic Impacts (2nd revised updated vers.). San Francisco, California: Berrett-Koehler Publishers.

Epstein, M. J., & Buhovac, A. R. (2014). *Making sustainability work: Best practices in managing and measuring corporate social, environmental, and economic impacts*. Berrett-Koehler Publishers.

Esa, E., & Zahari, A. R. (2014). Ownership structure and directors' compensation disclosure in Malaysia, in: Sabri Boubaker and Duc.K. Nguyen (Eds.), Corporate Governance and Corporate Social Responsibility: Emerging Markets Focus (pp. 267-285). World Scientific Publishing.

Esa, E., & Mohd Ghazali, N. A. (2012). Corporate social responsibility and corporate governance in Malaysian Government linked companies. *Journal of Corporate Governance*, *12*(3), 292–305. doi:10.1108/14720701211234564

Esty, D. C., & Winston, A. S. (2006). *Green to gold: How smart companies use environmental strategy to innovate, create value, and build competitive advantage*. New Haven, CT: Yale University Press.

Ethics. (n. d.). *Wikipedia*. Retrieved from https://en.wikipedia.org/wiki/Ethics

Evrard, Y., Pras, B., & Roux, E. (2003). *Market – Etudes et Recherches en Marketing, Connaître et Pratiquer la Gestion* (2nd ed.). Nathan.

Eweje, G. (Ed.), (2014). Corporate Social Responsibility and Sustainability: Emerging Trends in Developing Economies. Book Series: Critical Studies on Corporate Responsibility, Governance and Sustainability (Vol.8). Emerald Group Publishing Limited.

Eweje, G. (2006). Environmental costs and responsibilities resulting from oil exploitation in developing countries: The case of the Niger Delta of Nigeria. *Journal of Business Ethics*, *69*(1), 27–56. doi:10.1007/s10551-006-9067-8

Eweje, G., & Brunton, M. (2010). Ethical perceptions of business students in a New Zealand university: Do gender, age and work experience matter? *Business Ethics (Oxford, England)*, *19*(1), 95–111. doi:10.1111/j.1467-8608.2009.01581.x

Eynon, G., Hills, N. T., & Stevens, K. T. (1997). Factors that influence the moral reasoning abilities of accountants: Implications for universities and the profession. *Journal of Business Ethics*, *16*(12/13), 1297–1309. doi:10.1023/A:1005754201952

Falck, O., & Heblich, S. (2007). Doing well by doing good. *Business Horizons*, *50*(3), 247–254. doi:10.1016/j.bushor.2006.12.002

Falk, S. (2009). "Shift of power" or multipolarity? *Zeitschrift für Politikberatung*, *2*(4), 577–589. doi:10.1007/s12392-010-0223-2

Fama, E. F. (1965a). Random Walks in Stock Market Prices. *Financial Analysts Journal*, *21*(5), 55–59. doi:10.2469/faj.v21.n5.55

Fama, E. F. (1965b). The Behavior of Stock Market Prices. *The Journal of Business*, *38*(1), 34–105. doi:10.1086/294743

Fama, E. F., & Jensen, M. C. (1983). Separation of ownership and control. *The Journal of Law & Economics*, *26*(2), 301–325. doi:10.1086/467037

Farrelly, G. E., Ferris, K. R., & Reichenstein, W. R. (1985). Perceived Risk, Market Risk, and Accounting Determined Risk Measures. *Accounting Review*, *60*(2), 278–288.

Farrelly, G., Levine, P., & Reichenstein, W. (1984). Risk Perceptions of Institutional Investors. *Journal of Portfolio Management*, *10*(4), 5–12. doi:10.3905/jpm.1984.408966

Farrelly, G., Levine, P., & Reichenstein, W. (1987). Perceptions of Risk Classes: A Discriminant Analysis Using Financial Ratios. *Akron Business and Economic Review*, *18*(2), 78–91.

Fathy, N. (2011). Corporate social responsibility approaches and practices in developing countries: Lessons to be learned from Egypt. *International Journal of Arts and Science*, *4*(7), 123–135.

Fayyad, S. (2005). *Conference in Support of the Palestinian Economy for the Construction of Gaza*. Egypt: Sharm El Shiekh.

Feagin, J., Orum, A., & Sjoberg, J. (Eds.). (1991). *A case for the case study*. Chapel Hill, London: The University of North California Press.

Fernandez C, Arrondo R(2005).Alternative internal controls as substitute of the board of directors. *Corporate governance: an international review*, 13(6), 856-866.

Fernández-Feijóo Souto, B. (2009). Crisis and corporate social responsibility: threat or opportunity? *International Journal of Economic Sciences and Applied Research*, 2(1), 36-50.

Ferrell, O. C., & Fraedrich, J. (2014). *Business ethics: Ethical decision making & cases*. Cengage learning.

Filippov, S. (2012). Emerging Russian Multinational Companies: Managerial and corporate challenges. *European Journal of International Management*, *6*(3), 323–341. doi:10.1504/EJIM.2012.047027

Finance Committee on Corporate Governance. (2001). *Malaysian Code on Corporate Governance*. Securities Commission.

Firer, C., Oliver, M. C., & Farrelly, G. E. (1986). Risk Perceptions of Individual vs. Institutional Investors: A Comparaison Based on the Johannesburg Stock Exchange. *Journal of Applied Business Research*, *5*(4), 5–14.

Fischhoff, B., Slovic, P., Lichtenstein, S., Reed, S., & Combs, B. (1978). How Safe is Safe Enough? A Psychometric Study of Attitudes Toward Technological Risks and Benefits. *Policy Sciences*, *9*(2), 127–152. doi:10.1007/BF00143739

Fishbein, M., & Ajzen, I. (1975). *Belief, Attitude, Intention and Behavior: An Introduction to Theory and Research Reading*. Boston, MA: Addison-Wesley.

Fisscher, O., Frenkel, D., Lurie, Y., & Nijhof, A. (2005). Stretching the frontiers: Exploring the relationships between entrepreneurship and ethics. *Journal of Business Ethics*, *60*(3), 207–209. doi:10.1007/s10551-005-0128-1

Florini, A. M. (Ed.). (2000). *The third force: The rise of transnational civil society*. Tokyo, Japan: Japan Centre for International Exchange.

Fontaine, M. (2013). Corporate Social Responsibility and Sustainability: The New Bottom Line? *International Journal of Business & Social Science*, *4*(4), 110–119.

Fou, A. (2003). Experiential Marketing. *VISION an executive brief*. Retrieved from http://www.mktsci.com/experiential-marketing.htm

Frederick, W. C. (1987). Theories of Corporate Social Performance. In S. Prakash Sethi, & C.M. Falbe (Ed.), Business and Society: Dimensions of Conflict and Cooperation (pp. 142-61). MA: Lexington Books.

Frederick, W. C. (1986). Towards CSR3: Why Ethical Analysis is Indispensable and Unavoidable in Corporate Affairs. *California Management Review*, *28*(2), 126–141. doi:10.2307/41165190

Frederick, W. C. (1994). From CSR1 to CSR2: The Maturing of Business-and-Society Thought. *Business & Society*, *33*(2), 150–164. doi:10.1177/000765039403300202

Freedman, L., & Schooley, S. (2011). Closing the cross-channel gap. *The e-tailing group/MyBuys*. Retrieved from http://www.e-tailing.com/content/wp-content/uploads/2011/06/MyBuys_etailing-group_webinar_6-28-2011

Freeman, R. E. (2010). *Strategic management: A stakeholder approach*. Cambridge University Press. doi:10.1017/CBO9781139192675

Freeman, R. E., Wicks, A. C., & Parmar, B. (2004). Stakeholder Theory and the "Corporate Objective Revisited". *Organization Science*, *15*(3), 364–369. doi:10.1287/orsc.1040.0066

French, P. A. (1979). The Corporation as a Moral Person. *American Philosophical Quarterly*, *16*(3), 207–215.

French, P. A. (1995). *Corporate Ethics. Harcourt Brace*. Florida: ICSA Publishing.

Friedman, M. (1970) The Social Responsibility of Business is to Increase its Profits. *New York Times Magazine*, 33, 122-26.

Friedman, M. (2002). The social responsibility of business is to increase its profits. In L. P. Hartman (Ed.), *Perspectives in business ethics* (2nd ed., pp. 260–264). New York: The McGraw-Hill Companies. (Original work published 1970).

Friedman, M. (2007). *The social responsibility of business is to increase its profits* (pp. 173–178). Springer Berlin Heidelberg. doi:10.1007/978-3-540-70818-6_14

Friedman, T. L. (1999). *The Lexus and the olive tree: Understanding globalization*. New York, NY: Farrar, Straus, and Giroux.

Friedman, T. L. (2003). *The world is flat*. New York: Farrar, Straus and Giroux.

Friedman, T. L. (2005). *The world is flat: A brief history of the globalized world in the 21st century*. New York, NY: Farrar, Straus, and Giroux.

Fukuyama, F. (1995). *Trust: The social virtues and the creation of prosperity (No. D10 301 c. 1/c. 2)*. New York: Free press.

Fullerton, S., Kerch, K. B., & Dodge, H. R. (1996). Consumer ethics: An assessment of individual behavior in the market place. *Journal of Business Ethics*, *15*(7), 805–814. doi:10.1007/BF00381744

Galbreath, J. (2009). Building corporate social responsibility into strategy. *European Business Review*, *21*(2), 109–127. doi:10.1108/09555340910940123

Gao, P. (2008). Disclosure Quality, Cost of Capital, and Investors' Welfare. Retrieved from http://mpra.ub.unimuenchen.de/9478/2/MPRA_paper_9478.pdf

Garland, D. (2002). The Rise of Risk. In R. Ericson (Ed.), *Risk and Mortality*. University of Toronto Press.

Garriga, E., & Melé, D. (2004). Corporate social responsibility theories: Mapping the territory. *Journal of Business Ethics*, *53*(1-2), 51–71. doi:10.1023/B:BUSI.0000039399.90587.34

Garten, J. E. (1997). Troubles ahead in emerging markets. *Harvard Business Review*, *75*(3). Retrieved from www.opf.slu.cz/vvr/akce/turecko/pdf/Sunje.pdf

Gedik, M. A. (2013). Determinants of Foreign Direct Investment for OECD Countries: Evidence from Dynamic Panel Data Analysis. *British Journal of Economics, Finance and Management Sciences*, *7*(2), 119–140.

Geetanee, N. (2013). Incorporating CSR and sustainability in business strategy. *Proceedings of theAnnual International Conference on Enterprise Marketing & Global* (p. 189).

Gemunden, H. G. (1985). Perceived Risk and Information Search, A Systematic Meta-Analysis of the Empirical Evidence. *International Journal of Research in Marketing*, *2*(2), 79–100. doi:10.1016/0167-8116(85)90026-6

Gendron, M., & Genest, C. (1993). La Perception du Risque de Titres Financiers: L'Importance Relative et l'Influence de Certains Facteurs de Risque. *L'Actualite Economique*, *69*(1), 142–170. doi:10.7202/602100ar

Gentile, C., Spiller, N., & Noci, G. (2007). How to Sustain the Customer Experience: An Overview of Experience Components that Co-create Value With the Customer. *European Management Journal*, *25*(5).

Gerbing, D. W., & Hamilton, J. G. (1996). Viability of Exploratory Factor and a Precursor to Confirmatory Factor Analysis. *Structural Equation Modeling*, *3*(1), 62–72. doi:10.1080/10705519609540030

Gervais, S., & Odean, T. (2001). Learning to be Overconfident. *Review of Financial Studies*, *14*(1), 1–27. doi:10.1093/rfs/14.1.1

Ghayad, R. (2008). Corporate governance and the global performance of Islamic banks. *Humanomics*, *24*(3), 207–216. doi:10.1108/08288660810899368

Ghemawat, P., & Hout, T. (2008). Tomorrow's Global Giants. Not the usual suspects. *Harvard Business Review*, *86*(11), 80–88.

Ghosh, D., Ghosh, D. K., & Abdel Zaher, A. (2011). Business, ethics, and profit: Are they compatible under corporate governance in our global economy? *Global Finance Journal*, *22*(1), 72–79. doi:10.1016/j.gfj.2011.05.006

Ghosh, S., Nachane, D. M., Narain, A., & Sahoo, S. (2003). Capital requirements and bank behaviour: An empirical analysis of Indian public sector banks. *Journal of International Development*, *15*(2), 145–156. doi:10.1002/jid.947

Gichamo, T. Z. (2012). Determinants of Foreign Direct Investment Inflows to Sub-Saharan Africa: a panel data analysis.

Giddens, A. (1990). *The consequences of modernity*. Cambridge, UK: Polity Press.

Giddens, A. (2003). *Runaway world: How globalisation is reshaping our world*. New York, NY: Routledge.

Gigerenzer, G., Todd, P. M., & Group, A. B. C. (Eds.). (1999). *Simple Heuristics That Make Us Smart*. New York: Oxford University Press.

Gill, K. (2012). College Students Altitudes towards Ethical Consumerism – An Indian Perspective. *IOSR Journal of Business and Management*, 4(5), 01-13.

Glasbergen, P., Biermann, F., & Mol, A. P. J. (Eds.), (2007). *Partnerships, governance and sustainable development: Reflections on theory and practice*. Cheltenham, UK: Edward Elgar. doi:10.4337/9781847208668

Glasius, M. (2003). Global civil society: Theories and practices. In P. van Seters, B. de Gaay Fortman, & A. de Ruijter (Eds.). *Globalisation and its new divides: Malcontents, recipes, and reform* (pp. 193–207). Amsterdam, The Netherlands: Dutch University Press.

Glenn, J. R. Jr. (1992). Can a business and society course affect the ethical judgment of future managers? *Journal of Business Ethics*, *11*(3), 217–223. doi:10.1007/BF00871969

Global Investable Market Indices Methodology. (2010). MSCI Emerging Markets Indices. Retrieved from http://www.msci.com/products/indices

Godard L (2001). *La taille du conseil d'administration: déterminants et impact sur la performance.* Cahier du FARGO n° 1010702.

Godard, L., & Schatt, A. (2000). *Faut-il séparer les fonctions de décision et de contrôle? Papier de recherche présenté aux journaux internationaux de l'AFFI.* ESC Paris. Juin.

Goldstein, A. (2009). Multinational Companies from Emerging Economies Composition, Conceptualization & Direction in the Global Economy. *Indian Journal of Industrial Relations*, 45(1), 137–147.

Good Corporation. (2015, July, 17). Does run a business ethically add value or cost? Retrieved from http://goodcorporation.com/business-ethics-debates/does-running-a-business-ethically-add-value-or-cost/#sthash.qWZxjPl2.dpuf

Gooding, A. E. (1975). Quantification of Investors' Perceptions of Common Stocks: Risk and Return Dimensions. *The Journal of Finance*, *30*(5), 1301–1316. doi:10.1111/j.1540-6261.1975.tb01057.x

Googins, B., & Rochlin, S. (2000). Creating the partnership society: Understanding the rhetoric and reality of cross-sectoral partnerships. *Business and Society Review*, *105*(1), 127–144. doi:10.1111/0045-3609.00068

Gossett, W. T. (1957). *Corporate Citizenship*. Lexington, VA: Washington and Lee University Press.

Graham, J. R., & Harvey, C. R. (2001). The theory and practices of corporate finance: Evidence from the field. *Journal of Financial Economics*, *60*(2-3), 187–243. doi:10.1016/S0304-405X(01)00044-7

Grammarist. (n. d.). Ethics vs Morals. Retrieved from http://grammarist.com/usage/ethics-morals/

Granovetter, M. (1985). Economic action and social structure: The problem of embeddedness. *American Journal of Sociology*, *91*(3), 481–510. doi:10.1086/228311

Grauel, J. (2014, July7). Being authentic or being responsible? Food consumption, morality and the presentation of self. *Journal of Consumer Culture*, *2014*. doi:10.1177/1469540514541880

Greenpeace (2007, July, 22). Greenpeace Tours North Sea Oil Rigs on Brent Spar Anniversary. [Web log comment]. Retrieve from http://archive.greenpeace.org/comms/toxics/dumping/jun20.html

Green, S. (2008). The evolution of corporate social responsibility in construction: defining the parameters. In A. Murray & M. Dainty (Eds.), *Corporate Social Responsibility in the Construction Industry* (pp. 24–53). Abingdon: Taylor & Francis.

Green, S. (2009). The evolution of corporate social responsibility in construction: defining the parameters. In M. Murray & A. Dainty (Eds.), *Corporate social responsibility in the construction industry* (pp. 24–53). Oxon: Taylor & Francis.

Griffith, J. M., & Fogelberg, L. (2000). Control and bank performance. *Journal of Financial and Strategic Decisions*, *13*(3), 63–69.

Grimes, P. (2002). The Overconfident Principles of Economics Student: An Examination of a Metacognitive Skill. *The Journal of Economic Education*, *33*(1), 15–30. doi:10.1080/00220480209596121

Griseri, P., & Seppala, N. (2010). *Business ethics and corporate social responsibility*. Andover, Hampshire, UK: South-Western Cengage Learning.

Gronholdt, L., Martensen, A., & Kristensen, K. (2000). The relationship between Customer Satisfaction and Loyalty: Cross-Industry differences. *Total Quality Management*, *11*(4-6), 509–514. doi:10.1080/09544120050007823

Grossman, S. (1976). On the Efficiency of Competitive Stock Markets When Traders Have Diverse Information. *The Journal of Finance*, *31*(2), 573–585. doi:10.1111/j.1540-6261.1976.tb01907.x

Growth spike brings, India closer to one billion subscribers. (2011). mobiSights *website*. Retrieved from www.mobisights.com/2011/08/30/

Guest, R. (2001). *Borderless economics: Chinese sea turtles, Indian fridges and the new fruits of global capitalism*. New York, NY: Palgrave Macmillan.

Guiso, L., Sapienza, P., & Zingales, L. (2004). *Cultural biases in economic exchange (No. w11005)*. National Bureau of Economic Research. doi:10.3386/w11005

Guo, C. (2001). A Review on Consumer External Search: Amount and Determinants, 15(3). *Journal of Business and Psychology*, *15*(3), 505–519. doi:10.1023/A:1007830919114

Guru, B.K., Staunton, J., Shanmugam, B. (2002). *Determinants of commercial banks profitability in Malaysia*. University Multimedia working papers.

Habib, M., & Zurawicki, L. (2002). Corruption and foreign direct investment. *Journal of International Business Studies*, *33*(2), 291–307. doi:10.1057/palgrave.jibs.8491017

Hair, J. F., Anderson, R. E., Tatham, R. L., & Black, W. C. (1988). *Multivariate Data Analysis with Reading* (5th ed.). Upper Slade River, N.J.: Prentice Hall.

Halme, M., Roome, N., & Dobers, P. (2009). Corporate responsibility: Reflections on context and consequences. *Scandinavian Journal of Management*, *25*(1), 1–9. doi:10.1016/j.scaman.2008.12.001

Handy, C. (1997). The Citizen Corporation. *Harvard Business Review*, *75*(5), 26–28.

Handy, C. (2002). What is a Business for? *Harvard Business Review*, 80(12), 49–55. PMID:12510537

Haniffa, R. M., & Cooke, T. E. (2002). Culture, corporate governance and disclosure in Malaysian corporations. *Abacus*, *38*(3), 317–349. doi:10.1111/1467-6281.00112

Haniffa, R. M., & Cooke, T. E. (2005). The impact of culture and governance on corporate social reporting. *Journal of Accounting and Public Policy*, *24*(5), 391–430. doi:10.1016/j.jaccpubpol.2005.06.001

Hansen, E. G., & Spitzeck, H. (2011). Academic paper measuring the impacts of NGO partnerships: The corporate and societal benefits of community involvement. *Corporate Governance*, *11*(4), 415–426. doi:10.1108/14720701111159253

Hart, S. L. (2005). *Capitalism at the crossroads: The unlimited business opportunities in solving the world's most difficult problems*. Upper Saddle River, NJ: Wharton School Publishing.

Hart, S. L., & Sharma, S. (2004). Engaging fringe stakeholders for competitive imagination. *The Academy of Management Executive*, *18*(1), 7–18. doi:10.5465/AME.2004.12691227

Hatch, M. J., & Schultz, M. (2008). *Taking Brand Initiative: How Companies Can Align Strategy, Culture and Identity Through Corporate Branding*. San Francisco: Jossey–Bass.

Hausman, J. A. (1978). Specification Tests in Econometrics. *Econometrica*, *46*(6), 1251–1271. doi:10.2307/1913827

Hayakawa, K., Kimura, F., & Lee, H. H. (2013). How does country risk matter for foreign direct investment? *The Developing Economies*, *51*(1), 60–78. doi:10.1111/deve.12002

Haynes, J. (2003). *Perspectival Thinking: A Phenomenological Approach to Knowledge Management*. Retrieved from http://www.dfki.uni-kl.de/~klein/wm2003-pre-proceedings/pdf/haynes.pdf

Haynes, J. (2003). The Management of Intuition. *AJIS*, *11*(1), 12–18. doi:10.3127/ajis.v11i1.135

Haynes, J. (2007). *Perspectival Thinking: For Inquiring Organizations*. California: Information Science Press.

Haynes, J. (2008). *Technique and Technology: Ethical Guidelines for the Role of Technology for Medical Science in Arab Countries. Journal of the Arab Society For Medical Research, 3(2), 185 – 191*. Retrieved from.

Haynes, J. (2013). Why 'Ethics and Social Responsibility' is Important for Knowledge Management. Muscat: *International Conference on Knowledge and Resource Sharing*.

Held, D., & McGrew, A. G. (Eds.). (2007). *Globalization theory: Approaches and controversies* (Vol. 4). Cambridge: Polity.

Helsin, P. A., & Ochoa, J. D. (2008). Understanding and developing strategic corporate social responsibility. *Organizational Dynamics*, *37*(2), 125–144. doi:10.1016/j.orgdyn.2008.02.002

Hemmati, M. (2002). *Multi-stakeholder processes for governance and sustainability: Beyond deadlock and conflict*. London, UK: Earthscan.

Hendy, N. (2014). Co-opetition: the new business buzzword. *The Age*. Retrieved from http://www.theage.com.au/small-business/franchising/coopetition-the-new-business-buzzword-20140304-341lc.html

Hermalin, B. E., & Weisbach, M. S. (1991). The effects of board composition and direct incentives on firm Performance. *Financial Management*, *20*(4), 101–112. doi:10.2307/3665716

Hess, K., & Francis, G. (2004). Cost income ratio benchmarking in banking. *International Journal (Toronto, Ont.)*, *3*, 303–319.

Hill, T. (2004). *Three generations of UN-civil society relations: A quick sketch*. Global Policy Forum. Retrieved from https://www.globalpolicy.org/component/content/article/177-un/31824-three-generations-of-un-civil-society-relations.html

Hillman, A. J., & Keim, G. D. (2001). Shareholder value, stakeholder management, and social issues: What's the bottom line? *Strategic Management Journal*, *22*(2), 125–139. doi:10.1002/1097-0266(200101)22:2<125::AID-SMJ150>3.0.CO;2-H

Hitt, M., Middlemist, R., & Maith, R. (1983). *Management – Concepts and Effective Practice*. Los Angeles: West Publishing Company.

Hobdari, B., Sinani, E., Papanastassiou, M., & Pearce, R. (2010). The determinants of global integration strategies of Chinese multinationals - Some empirical evidence. *Review of Market Integration*, *2*(1), 61–86. doi:10.1177/097492921000200105

Hoch & Stephen, J. (2002). Product Experience Is Seductive. *The Journal of Consumer Research*, *2*, 448–454.

Holbrook, M. B., & Hirschman, E. C. (1981). The experiential aspects of consumption: Consumer fantasy, feelings and fun. *The Journal of Consumer Research*, *9*(2), 132–140. doi:10.1086/208906

Homer-Dixon, T. (2011) Complexity Science. Oxford Leadership Journal, 2(1).

Hopkins, M. (2011). A Planetary Bargain: Corporate Social Responsibility Comes of Age.

Hopwood, B., Mellor, M., & O'Brien, G. (2005). Sustainable development: Mapping different approaches. *Sustainable Development, 13*(1), 38–52. doi:10.1002/sd.244

Ho, S. S. M., & Wong, K. S. (2001). A study of the relationship between corporate governance structures and the extent of voluntary disclosure. *Journal of International Accounting, Auditing & Taxation, 10*(2), 139–156. doi:10.1016/S1061-9518(01)00041-6

Hoskisson, R. E., Eden, L., Lau, C. M., & Wright, M. (2000). Strategy in emerging economies. *Academy of Management Journal, 43*(3), 249–267. doi:10.2307/1556394

Hossain, M., Tan, L. M., & Adams, M. (1994). Voluntary disclosure in an emerging capital market: Some empirical evidence from companies listed on the Kuala Lumpur Stock Exchange. *The International Journal of Accounting, 29*, 334–351.

Hoyle, R. H. (1985). *Structural Equation Modeling: Concepts, Issues and Applications*. Thousand Oaks, CA: Sage Publications.

Hsiao C (1986). *Analysis of Panel data. Econometric Society Monographs* (2nd ed.).

Huafang, X., & Jianguo, Y. (2007). Ownership structure, board composition and corporate voluntary disclosure. *Managerial Auditing Journal, 22*(6), 604–619. doi:10.1108/02686900710759406

Huang, R. D., & Stoll, H. R. (1997). The Components of the Bid-Ask Spread: A General Approach. *Review of Financial Studies, 10*(4), 995–1034. doi:10.1093/rfs/10.4.995

Huberman, M., & Miles, M. (1994). Data management and analysis methods. In N.K Denzin, & Y.S Lincoln (Eds.), Handbook of Qualitative Research (pp. 428-444). London/New Delhi: SAGE Publications.

Huberman, M., & Miles, M. (1991). *Analyse des données qualitatives: recueil de nouvelles méthodes*. Bruxelles: De Boeck Université.

Hughes, A., McEwan, C., & Bek, D. (2013). Retailers, Supply Networks and Changing Articulations of Ethicality: Lessons from Flower Valley in South Africa. *Journal of Economic Geography, 13*(2), 211–230. doi:10.1093/jeg/lbs049

Hurlin, C. (2006). *L'Econométrie des Données de Panel: Modèles Linéaires Simples*. Séminaire Méthodologique, Ecole Doctorale Edocif.

Husted, B. W. (2000). A contingency theory of corporate social performance. *Business & Journal of Corporate Citizenship, 17*, 33–50.

Husted, B. W., & Allen, D. B. (2006). Corporate social responsibility in the multinational enterprise: Strategic and institutional approaches. *Journal of International Business Studies, 37*(6), 838–849. doi:10.1057/palgrave.jibs.8400227

Hvidt, M. (2013). *Kuwait programme on development, governance and globalization in the gulf states. Economic diversification in GCC countries: Past record and Future trends*. The London School of Economics and Political Science.

Idowu, S., Schmidpeter, R., & Fifka, M. S. (Eds.). (2015). *Corporate Social Responsibility in Europe: United in Sustainable Diversity*. Switzerland: Springer International Publishing. doi:10.1007/978-3-319-13566-3

International Labor Office. (2009). Geneva: ILO.

International Monetary Fund. (2014, April). *Global Financial Stability Report. Moving from Liquidity-to Growth-Driven Markets*. Retrieved from http://www.imf.org/

Jaafar, S. B., James, K., & Abdul Wahab, E. A. (2012). Remuneration committee and director remuneration in family owned companies: Evidence from Malaysia. *International Review of Business Research Papers*, *8*(7), 17–38.

Jackson, G., Brammer, S., Karpoff, J. M., Lange, D., Zavyalova, A., Harrington, B., & Deephouse, D. L. et al. (2014). Grey areas: Irresponsible corporations and reputational dynamics. *Socio-economic Review*, *12*(1), 153–218. doi:10.1093/ser/mwt021

Jacques, B., Jonathan, D., & Ole, J. V. (2010). A new way to measure word-of-mouth marketing. Retrieved from http://www.mckinsey.com/insights/marketing_sales/a_new_way_to_measure_word-of-mouth_marketing

Jamali, D. (2008). A stakeholder approach to corporate social responsibility: A fresh perspective into theory and practice. *Journal of Business Ethics*, *82*(1), 213–231. doi:10.1007/s10551-007-9572-4

James, PGuthrie Datta, D.K. (1997). Contextual influence on executive selection: Firm characteristics and experience. *Journal of Management Studies*, *34*(4), 537–560. doi:10.1111/1467-6486.00062

James, P., & Van Seters, P. (Eds.). (2014). *Global social movements and global civil society*. London, UK: Sage.

Janicki, H. P., & Wunnava, P. V. (2004). Determinants of foreign direct investment: Empirical evidence from EU accession candidates. *Applied Economics*, *36*(5), 505–509. doi:10.1080/00036840410001682214

Jaques, L. (2010). How much does word of mouth really affect brand success? Newline, Retrieved from http://mediatel.co.uk/newsline/2010/09/23/how-much-does-word-of-mouth-really-affect-brand-success/

Jaspersen, F. Z., Aylward, A. H., & Knox, A. D. (2000). The effects of risk on private investment: Africa compared with other developing areas. *Investment and risk in Africa*, 71-95.

Jazani, N., & Ayoobzadeh, M. (2012). The Impact of Ethics Training Course on Ethical Behaviors of Management Students. *International Business Research*, *5*(11), 162. doi:10.5539/ibr.v5n11p162

Jenkins, R. (2005). Globalization, Corporate Social Responsibility and Poverty. *International Affairs*, *81*(3), 525–540. doi:10.1111/j.1468-2346.2005.00467.x

Jensen, M. C. (2001). Value Maximization, Stakeholder Theory, and the Corporate Objective Function. *European Financial Management*, *7*(3), 297–317. doi:10.1111/1468-036X.00158

Jensen, M. C., & Meckling, W. (1976). The Theory of the Firm: Managerial Behavior, Agency Costs, and Ownership Structure. *Journal of Financial Economics*, *3*(4), 305–360. doi:10.1016/0304-405X(76)90026-X

Jobber, D., & Fahy, J. (2009). Foundations of Marketing. Maidenhead: McGraw-Hill. 4, 214-226.

Johansson, J. (2009). *Global Marketing*. McGraw-Hill Higher Education. Retrieved from http://highered.mheducation.com/sites/

Johnson, C. (2012). *Organizational Ethics. A Practical Approach*. SAGE Publications.

Johnston, J., Szabo, M., & Rodney, A. (2011). Good food, good people: Understanding the cultural repertoire of ethical eating. *Journal of Consumer Culture*, *11*(3), 293–318. doi:10.1177/1469540511417996

Jonas, W. (2005). *Mosby's dictionary of complementary & alternative medicine*. St. Louis, Mo.: Elsevier Mosby.

Jones, A. (2010). *Globalization: key thinkers* (Vol. 1). Polity.

Jones, R. (2004). Construction sector in Qatar in 3.35% growth. *Arabian Business*. Retrieved from http://www.arabianbusiness.com/construction-sector-in-qatar-in-3-35-growth-134074.html

Jones, P., Comfort, D., & Hillier, D. (2006). Corporate social responsibility and the UK construction industry. *Journal of Corporate Real Estate*, *8*(3), 134–150. doi:10.1108/14630010610711757

Jones, T., & Wicks, A. (1999). Convergent stakeholder theory. *Academy of Management Review*, *24*(2), 206–221.

Jones, W. A. Jr. (1990). Student views of "ethical" issues: A situational analysis. *Journal of Business Ethics*, *9*(3), 201–205. doi:10.1007/BF00382645

Jöreskog, K. G. (1973). Analysis of Covariance Structures. In P. R. Krishnaiah (Ed.), *Multivariate Analysis-III* (pp. 263–285). New York: Academic Press.

Joseph, C., & Media, D. (2015, July 17). Examples of Unethical Behavior in an Organization. Retrieved from http://smallbusiness.chron.com/examples-unethical-behavior-organization-13629.html

Joseph, P., & Gilmore, J. H. (1998). Welcome to the Experience Economy. *Harvard Business Review*, 76(4), 97–105. PMID:10181589

Jothi, M., & Mathiraj, S. P. (2013). An Embedded Corporate Social Responsibility Matrix: A Way Ahead for Sustainable and Equitable Benefit for the Firm and the Society. *International Journal of Research in Computer Application & Management*, *3*(6), 62–68.

Kakabadse, A., & Morsing, M. (Eds.). (2006). *Corporate social responsibility: Reconciling aspiration with application*. New York, NY: Palgrave Macmillan. doi:10.1057/9780230599574

Kakabadse, N. K., Rozuel, C., & Lee-Davies, L. (2005). Corporate social responsibility and stakeholder approach: A conceptual review. *International Journal of Business Governance and Ethics*, *1*(4), 277–302. doi:10.1504/IJBGE.2005.006733

Kaldor, M., Moore, H. L., & Selchow, S. (Eds.). (2012). Global civil society 2012: Ten years of critical reflection. New York, NY: Palgrave Macmillan.

Kaldor, M. (2003). *Global civil society: An answer to war*. Cambridge, UK: Polity Press.

Kaldor, M., Anheier, H., & Glasius, M. (Eds.). (2003). *Global civil society 2003*. Oxford, UK: Oxford University Press.

Kalinowski, J. D. (2012).Positioning for Growth in Emerging Markets.Proactive Worldwide, 15(3), 1-11.

Kandachar, P., & Halme, M. (Eds.). (2008). *Sustainability challenges and solutions at the base of the pyramid: Business, technology and the poor*. Sheffield, UK: Greenleaf.

Kaplan, D. (2000). *Structural Equation Modeling: Foundations and Extensions*. Thousand Oaks, CA: Sage.

Kaplan, S., & Garrick, J. B. (1981). On the Quantitative Definition of Risk. *Risk Analysis*, *1*(1), 11–27. doi:10.1111/j.1539-6924.1981.tb01350.x PMID:11798118

Kaplinsky, R. (2000). Globalisation and unequalisation: What can be learned from value chain analysis? *The Journal of Development Studies*, *37*(2), 117–146. doi:10.1080/713600071

Kaptein, S. P., & Kolthof, E. (2003). Six principles for ethical leadership. *PA Times*, *26*(4), 8–9.

Kariuki, C. (2015).. . *The Determinants of Foreign Direct Investment in the African Union*, *3*(3), 346–351.

Karyotis, C., Bouslama, G., Bouteiller, C., Le Guirriec-Milner, G., & Vernier, E. (2009). *La crise financière en 40 concepts clés*. Revue Banque Edition.

Kashyap, R., Mir, R., & Mir, A. (2011). Corporate Social Responsibility: A Call for Multidisciplinary Inquiry. *Journal of Business & Economics Research*, *2*(7), 51–58.

Katamba, D., Katamba, D., Zipfel, C., Haag, D., & Tushabomwe-Kazooba, C. (2012). *Principles of Corporate Social Responsibility (Csr): A Companion for Students and Practicing Managers in Developing and Emerging Markets*. Strategic Book Publishing.

Kaymak, T., & Bektas, E. (2008). East meets west? Board characteristics in an emerging market: Evidence from Turkish Banks. *Corporate Governance*, *16*(6), 550–561. doi:10.1111/j.1467-8683.2008.00713.x

Kearney, C. (2012). Emerging markets research: Trends, issues and future directions. *Emerging Markets Review*, *13*(2), 159–183. doi:10.1016/j.ememar.2012.01.003

Keck, M. E., & Sikkink, K. (1998). *Activists beyond borders: Advocacy networks in international politics*. Ithaca, NY: Cornell University Press.

Keesling, J. W. (1972). *Maximum Likelihood Approach to Causal Analysis* [Thèse de Doctorat]. University of Chicago, Chicago, IL, USA.

Keim, G. (2003). Nongovernmental organizations and business–government relations: The importance of institutions. In J. P. Doh & H. Teegen (Eds.), *Globalization and NGOs: Transforming business, government, and society* (pp. 19–34). Westport, CT: Praeger.

Keith, N. K., Perreault, H. R., Chin, M., & Keith, M. (2009). The effect of gender on the importance of business ethics and managerial decisions: A student perspective. *The Journal of Research in Business Education*, *51*(3), 125.

Kelly, K. (2006). Speculations on the Future of Science. *Edge*. Retrieved from www.edge.org/3rd_culture/kelly06/kelly06_index/htmal

Kelly, K. (2014). Speculations On The Future Of Science. Retrieved from http:edge.org/3rd_culture/kelly06/kelly06_index/htm

Khalizani, K., Omar, S. S., & Khalisanni, K. (2011). Graduate students' perceptions on business ethics and capitalism: A study in Malaysian universities. *International Journal of Education Administration and Policy Studies*, *3*(6), 85–93.

Khan, M. T., Khan, N. A., Ahmed, S., & Ali, M. (2012). Corporate Social Responsibility (CSR) – Definition, Concepts and Scope (A Review). *Universal Journal of Management and Social Sciences*, *2*(7), 41–52.

Khanna, T., & Palepu, K. (2010). *A Road Map for Strategy and Execution*. Harvard Business Press. Retrieved from www.forbes.com/2010/05/27/winning-in-emerging-markets-opinions-book-excerpts-khanna-palepu.html

Khanna, T., & Palepu, K. (2013). *Winning in emerging markets: A road map for strategy and execution*. Harvard Business Press.

Khomba, J. K., Bakuwa, R. C., & Kangaude-Ulaya, E. C. (2013). Shaping Business Ethics and Corporate Governance: An Inclusive African Ubuntu Philosophy. *Global Journal of Management and Business Research Administration and Management*, *13*(5), 30–42.

Khoza, R. (2005). *Let Africa Lead*. Johannesburg: Vezubuntu Publishing Ltd.

Khumalo, R. (2001). Concern for Others: A Management attribute of Excellent Companies. *South African Journal of Business Management*, *32*(1), 57–65.

Kiel, G. C., & Nicholson, G. J. (2003). Board composition and corporate performance: How the Australian experience informs contrasting theories of corporate governance. *Corporate Governance: An International Review*, *11*(3), 189–205. doi:10.1111/1467-8683.00318

Kiliç, R. (1996). Ahlakın Dini temeli, Ankara. *Türkiye diyanet vakfı yay*, 85.

Kim, J., & Park, J. (2013). Foreign Direct Investment and Country-Specific Human Capital. *Economic Inquiry*, *51*(1), 198–210. doi:10.1111/j.1465-7295.2012.00478.x

Kirkpatrick, G. (2009). The corporate governance lessons from the financial crisis[OECD]. *Financial Market Trends*, *1*, 1–13.

Knez-Riedl, J., & Mulej, M. (2008). Developing a sustainable/holistic firm. In E. A. Stuhler & S. Misra (Eds.), *Across disciplinary boundaries towards a sustainable life: psychodynamic reflection on human behaviour; dedicated with eternal gratitude and in high esteem to Prof. Dr. Rainer Fuchs* (pp. 217–226). Munchen: Hampp.

Kogan, N., & Wallach, M. A. (1964). *Risk Taking: A Study in Cognition and Personality. Holt, New-York*. Rinehart & Winston.

Kok, R., & Ersoy, B. A. (2009). Analyses of FDI determinants in developing countries. *International Journal of Social Economics*, *36*(1/2), 105–123. doi:10.1108/03068290910921226

Kolstad, I., & Villanger, E. (2004). *How does social development affect FDI and domestic investment? Chr.* Michelsen Institute.

Koster, F., Van Oort, S., & Snoep, L. (2007). *The Brent Spar controversy - An illustrating case of risk assessment and communication*. Göteborg, Sweden: Department of Product and Production Development, Chalmers University of Technology.

Kotler, P., & Armstrong, G. (2010). Principles of Marketing (13th ed.). Pearson education Incorporation, New Jersey.

Kotler, P., & Keller, K. L. (2012). *Marketing Management, 12e* (p. 706). Upper Saddle River, New Jersey: Pearson Education, Inc.

Kotler, P., & Keller, K. L. (2012). *Marketing Management, Global edition* (14th ed.). Pearson.

Kouabenan, D. R., Cadet, B., Hermand, D., & Munoz Sastre, M. T. (Eds.). (2006). *Psychologie du Risque: Identifier, Evaluer, Prévenir les Risques*. Bruxelles: De Boeck Université.

Kraus, P., & Bernd, B. (2012). A literature review on corporate social responsibility: definitions, theories and recent empirical research. *International Journal of Management Cases* (Special Issue: *Papers from the 9th International CIRCLE Conference)*, 14(4), 282-296.

Kraut, R. (2001). *Aristotle's Ethics. Plato.stanford.edu*. Retrieved from http://plato.stanford.edu/entries/aristotle-ethics/

Krugman, P. (2011). The new economic geography, now middle-aged. *Regional Studies*, *45*(1), 1–7. doi:10.1080/00343404.2011.537127

Kukharsky, B. (2012). *Trust and Foreign Direct Investment: An Empirical Analysis* (No. 127). BGPE Discussion Paper.

Kvint, V. (2009). *The Global Emerging Market: Strategic Management and Economics*. New York, London: Routledge.

Kvint, V. (2010). *The global emerging market: strategic management and economics*. Routledge.

Kwan, S. (2003). Risk and Return of Publicly Held versus Privately Owned Banks. Federal Reserve Bank of New York. *Economic Policy Review*.

Kyle, A. (1989). Continuous Auctions and Insider Trading. *Econometrica*, *53*(6), 1315–1335. doi:10.2307/1913210

La Porta, R. (1997). Trust in Large Organizations. *The American Economic Review*, *87*(2), 333–338.

Lacroux, A. (2008), L'Analyse des Modèles de Relations Structurelles par la Méthode PLS: Une Approche Emergente dans la Recherche Quantitative en GRH. Retrieved from http://www.reims-ms.fr/agrh/docs/actes-agrh/pdf-des-actes/2009lacroux073.pdf

Lamberti, M. (2002, October 27). The True Gist of South African Business is Ubuntu. *Sunday Times Business Times*.

Langtry, B. (1994). Stakeholders and the moral responsibilities of business. *Business Ethics Quarterly*, *4*(4), 431–443. doi:10.2307/3857342

Larwood, L., & Whittaker, W. (1977). Managerial Myopia: Self-Serving Biases in Organizational Planning. *The Journal of Applied Psychology*, *62*(2), 194–198. doi:10.1037/0021-9010.62.2.194

Lau, C. L. (2010). A step forward: Ethics education matters! *Journal of Business Ethics*, *92*(4), 565–584. doi:10.1007/s10551-009-0173-2

Lau, L., Caracciolo, B., Roddenberry, S., & Scroggins, A. (2012). College Students' Perception of Ethics. *Journal of Academic and Business*, *5*, 1–13.

Lauterborn, R. (1990, October 1). New Marketing Litany: 4Ps Passé; 4Cs Take Over. *Advertising Age*.

Layne, C. (2012). This time it's real: The end of unipolarity and the Pax Americana. *International Studies Quarterly*, *56*(1), 203–213. doi:10.1111/j.1468-2478.2011.00704.x

Lee, M. D. P. (2008). A review of the theories of corporate social responsibility: Its evolutionary path and the road ahead. *International Journal of Management Reviews*, *10*(1), 53–73. doi:10.1111/j.1468-2370.2007.00226.x

Lehu, J.-M. (2004). L'Encyclopédie du Marketing (1st ed.). Editions d'Organisation, Paris.

Leigh, D. (2006). Customer Relationships - What's the Difference between Customer Experience Management and Experiential Marketing? Retrieved from http://www.marketingprofs.com/6/duncan4.asp

Letseka, M. (2000). African philosophy and educational discourse. In P. Higgs, N. C. G. Vakalisa, T. V. Mda, & N. T. Assie-Lumumba (Eds.), *African Voices in Education*. Cape Town: Juta.

Letseka, M. (2012). In Defence of Ubuntu. *Studies in Philosophy and Education*, *31*(1), 47–60. doi:10.1007/s11217-011-9267-2

Letseka, M. (2013). Anchoring Ubuntu Morality. *Mediterranean Journal of Social Sciences*, *4*(3), 351–359.

Levitt, T. (1979). The dangers of social responsibility. In T. L. Beauchamp & N. E. Bowie (Eds.), *Ethical theory and business* (pp. 138–141). Englewood Cliffs, NJ: Prentice-Hall. (Original work published 1958)

Lévy, B. (2007). The interface between globalization, trade and development: Theoretical issues for international business studies. *International Business Review*, *16*(5), 594–612. doi:10.1016/j.ibusrev.2007.06.004

Lewandowski, J. P. (1997). Risk and foreign direct investment in emerging economies: Lessons from the former Soviet Union. *Middle States Geographer*, *30*, 97–104.

Lewin, R. (2000). *Complexity*. University of Chicago Press Economics Books.

Libby, R., & Fishburn, P. C. (1977). Behavioral Models of Risk Taking Business Decisions: A Survey and Evaluation. *Journal of Accounting Research*, *15*(2), 272–292. doi:10.2307/2490353

Lindgreen, A., Córdoba, J.-R., Maon, F., & Mendoza, J. M. (2010). Corporate Social Responsibility in Colombia: Making Sense of Social Strategies. *Journal of Business Ethics*, *91*(2), 229–242. doi:10.1007/s10551-010-0616-9

Lindgreen, A., & Swaen, V. (2010). Corporate Social Responsibility. *International Journal of Management Reviews*, *12*(1), 1–7. doi:10.1111/j.1468-2370.2009.00277.x

Lindgreen, A., Valérie, S., & Campbell, T. T. (2009). Corporate Social Responsibility Practices in Developing and Transitional Countries: Botswana and Malawi. *Journal of Business Ethics*, *90*(S3), 429–440. doi:10.1007/s10551-010-0415-3

Lin, J. Y. (2003). International Expansion of Emerging Market. *Economic Development and Cultural Change*, *51*, 277. doi:10.1086/367535

Lin, J.-C., Sanger, G. C., & Booth, G. G. (1995). Trade Size and Components of the Bid-Ask Spread. *Review of Financial Studies*, *8*(4), 1153–1183. doi:10.1093/rfs/8.4.1153

Lin, Q., & Lee, J. (2004). Consumer Information Search When Making Investment Decisions. *Financial Services Review*, *13*, 319–332.

Lipton, M., & Lorsch, J. (1992). A modest proposal for improved corporate governance. *Business Lawyer*, *48*, 59–77.

Li, S., Fetscherin, M., Alon, I., Lattemann, C., & Yeh, K. (2010). Corporate social responsibility in emerging markets. *Management International Review*, *50*(5), 635–654. doi:10.1007/s11575-010-0049-9

Locander, W. B., & Hermann, P. W. (1979). The Effect of Self-Confidence and Anxiety on Information Seeking in Consumer Risk Reduction. *JMR, Journal of Marketing Research*, *16*(2), 268–274. doi:10.2307/3150690

Lockett, A., Moon, J., & Visser, W. (2006). Corporate Social Responsibility in Management Research: Focus, Nature, Salience and Sources of Influences. *Journal of Management Studies*, *43*(1), 115–136. doi:10.1111/j.1467-6486.2006.00585.x

Loibl, C., & Hira, T. K. (2009). Investor Information Search. *Journal of Economic Psychology*, *30*(1), 24–41. doi:10.1016/j.joep.2008.07.009

Lopes, L. L. (1987). In L. Berkowitz (Ed.), *Between Hope and Fear: The Psychology of Risk* (pp. 255–295). Advances in Experimental Social PsychologySan Diego, CA: Academic Press.

Loree, D. W., & Guisinger, S. E. (1995). Policy and non-policy determinants of US equity foreign direct investment. *Journal of International Business Studies*, *26*(2), 281–299. doi:10.1057/palgrave.jibs.8490174

Louizi G (2007). Role of the board in banks' governance and impact on performance; Case of Tunisian banks. *Euro-Mediterranean Economics and Finance Review*, 1(6).

Low Kim Cheng, P., & Ang Sik, L. (2012). Confucian leadership and corporate social responsibility (CSR), the way forward. *Asian Journal of Business Research*, *2*(1), 92–116.

Lu, C.-W., Chen, T.-K., & Liao, H.-H. (2010). Information Uncertainty, Information Asymmetry and Corporate Bond Yield Spreads. *Journal of Banking & Finance*, *34*(9), 2265–2279. doi:10.1016/j.jbankfin.2010.02.013

Luetkenhorst, W. (2004). Corporate social responsibility and the development agenda. *Inter Economics*, *39*(3), 157–166. doi:10.1007/BF02933583

Lum, R. (2013). Milka Chocolate Bars Now Missing Square In New Campaign. *Creative Guerilla Marketing*. Retrieved from http://www.creativeguerrillamarketing.com/guerrilla-marketing/milka-chocolate-bars-now-missing-square-new-campaign

Lumpkin, J. R., & Dunn, M. G. (1990). Perceived Risk as a Factor in Store Choice: An Examination of Inherent Versus Handled Risk. *Journal of Applied Business Research*, *6*(2), 104–118.

Luo, Y. (2002). *Multinational enterprises in emerging markets*. Copenhagen Business School Press DK.

Luo, Y., & Tung, R. (2007). International Expansion of Emerging Market. *Journal of International Business Studies*, *38*(4), 481–498. doi:10.1057/palgrave.jibs.8400275

Lutz, R. J., & Reilly, P. J. (1973). *An Exploration of the Effect of Perceived Social and Performance Risk on Consumer Information Acquisition*. In S. Ward, & P. Wright (Eds.), *Advances in Consumer Research,Proceedings of the 4th Annual Convention of the Association for Consumer Research* (pp. 393-405).

MacDonald, A. (2015). GCC construction sector may face skills shortage. Retrieved from http://www.gulf-dailynews.com/NewsDetails.aspx?storyid=347321

MacGregor, D. G., & Slovic, P. (1999). Perception of Financial Risk: A Survey Study of Advisors and Planners. *Journal of Financial Planning*, *12*, 68–79.

MacGregor, G. G., Slovic, P., Dreman, D., & Berry, M. (2000). Imagery, Affect and Financial Judgment. *The Journal of Psychology and Financial Markets*, 1(2), 104-110.

Machobane, L. B. J. (1978). Mohlomi: Doctor, Traveller and Sage. *Mohlomi Journal of Southern African Historical Studies*, *2*, 5–27.

Mackey, A., & Barney, J. B. (2007, July). Corporate Social Responsibility and Firm Performance: Investor Preference s and Corporate Strategies. *Academy of Management Review*, *32*(3), 817–835. doi:10.5465/AMR.2007.25275676

Madsen, H., & Ulhoi, J. P. (2001). Integrating Environmental and Stakeholder Management. *Business Strategy and the Environment*, *10*(2), 77–88. doi:10.1002/bse.279

Maessen, R., Van Seters, P., & Van Rijckevorsel, E. (2007). Circles of stakeholders: Towards a relational theory of corporate social responsibility. *International Journal of Business Governance and Ethics*, *3*(1), 77–94. doi:10.1504/IJBGE.2007.011935

Mahajan, V., & Banga, K. (2005). *The 86 percent solution: How to succeed in the biggest market opportunity of the next 50 years*. Pearson Education.

Mahao, L. (2006). *The power of the hegemonic theory in Southern Africa: why Lesotho cannot develop an independent foreign policy* [Unpublished master's thesis]. Rhodes University, South Africa.

Maheshwari, S., & Ganesh, M. (2006). Ethics In Organizations. *Vikalpa*, *31*(2), 75–86.

Mahmood, I., Ahmad, H., Khan, A. Z., & Anjum, M. (2011). Behavioral Implications of Investors for Investments in the Stock Market. *European Journal of Soil Science*, *20*(2), 240–247.

Majocchi, A., & Presutti, M. (2009). Industrial clusters, entrepreneurial culture and the social environment: The effects on FDI distribution. *International Business Review*, *18*(1), 76–88. doi:10.1016/j.ibusrev.2008.12.001

Malayan Banking Berhad website. (n. d.). Retrieved from http://www.baybank.com

Mallet, S. (2001). *Pour une Classification de la Mesure du Risque Perçu. Proceedings of the17ème congrès International de l'Association Française du Marketing*, Deauville.

Mallet, S. (2004). Vers une Clarification des Déterminants du Risque Perçu à l'Egard de l'Achat d'un Produit. *Proceedings of the 20ème Congrès de l'AFM, Actes sur CD-Rom*, Saint-Malo.

Mallet, S. (2000). *Le Concept de Risque Perçu: Composantes, Antécédents et Proposition de Recherche. in les Actes des liers ateliers de recherche de l'AFM, « Percevoir, identifier et gérer le risque en marketing* (pp. 46–62). Paris: La Sorbonne.

Malmendier, U., & Tate, G. (2005). CEO Overconfidence and Corporate Investment. *The Journal of Finance*, *60*(6), 2661–2700. doi:10.1111/j.1540-6261.2005.00813.x

Mandela, N. (2006). Foreword. In R. J. Khoza (Ed.), *Let Africa Lead - African transformational leadership for 21st century business*. Johannesburg: Vezubuntu.

Mankin, D. (2009). *Human resource development*. Oxford University Press.

Manteaw, B. (2008). From Tokenism to Social Justice: Rethinking the Bottom Line for Sustainable Community Development. *Community Development Journal: An International Forum*, *43*(4), 428–443. doi:10.1093/cdj/bsm015

March, J. G., & Shapira, Z. (1987). Managerial Perspectives on Risk and Risk Taking. *Management Science*, *33*(11), 1404–1418. doi:10.1287/mnsc.33.11.1404

Marrewijk, M. V. (2003). Concepts and Definitions of CSR and Corporate Sustainability: Between Agency and Communion. *Journal of Business Ethics*, *44*(2), 95–105. doi:10.1023/A:1023331212247

Masterman, G., & Wood, E. (2008). Event Marketing: Measuring an Experience? *Proceedings of the 7th International Marketing Trends Congress*, Venice. Retrieved from http://escp-eap.net/conferences/marketing/2008_cp/Materiali/Paper/Fr/Wood_Masterman

Mathuva DM (2009).Capital adequacy, cost income ratio and the performance of commercial banks: The Kenyan scenario. *The international journal of applied economics and finance*, 3(2), 35-47.

Matsela, F. Z. A. (1979). *The indigenous education of the Basotho and its implications for educational development in Lesotho*. Michigan: University Microfilms International.

Matten, D., & Moon, J. (2008). Implicit and Explicit CSR: A Conceptual Framework for a Comparative Understanding of Corporate Social Responsibility. *Academy of Management Review*, *33*(2), 404–424. doi:10.5465/AMR.2008.31193458

MayBank Foundation website. (n. d.). *Corporate Governance*. Retrieved from http://www.maybankFoundation.com/corporate_governance.html

Maybank Foundation website. (n. d.). *Corporate Responsibility Committee*. Retrieved from http://www.maybankFoundation.com/corporate_responsibility.html

Maybank Foundation website. (n. d.). *History*. Retrieved from http://www.maybankFoundation.com/history.html

Maybank Foundation website. (n. d.). *Mission*. Retrieved fromhttp://www.maybankFoundation.com/mission.html

Mayer, A. (1997). Symposium on Law and Ethics in Emerging Markets: Introduction. *Journal of International Law*, 18(4).

Maznevski, M., Steger, U., & Amann, W. (2007) *Managing complexity in global organizations*. IMD. No. 141, February.

Mbiti, J. (1988). *African Religions and Philosophy*. Nairobi: General Printers Limited.

McDonald, J. G., & Stehle, R. E. (1975). How do institutional investors perceive risk? *Journal of Portfolio Management*, *2*(1), 11–16. doi:10.3905/jpm.1975.11

McElhaney, K. (2007). Strategic CSR. *Sustainable Enterprise Quarterly*, *4*(1), 1–7.

McGuigan, C. (2013). 2014 Experiential Marketing Trends. *Creative Guerrilla Marketing*, Retrieved from http://www.creativeguerrillamarketing.com/guerrilla-marketing/2014-experiential-marketing-trends/

McGuire, J. B., Sundgren, A., & Schneeweis, T. (1988). Corporate Social Responsibility and Firm Financial Performance. *Academy of Management Journal*, *31*(4), 854–872. doi:10.2307/256342

McIntosh, M. (Ed.). (2013). *The necessary transition: The journey towards the sustainable enterprise economy*. Sheffield, UK: Greenleaf.

McNamara, C. (2015, July 17). Business ethics and social responsibility. Retrieved from http://managementhelp.org/businessethics/(2015, July 17)

McWilliams, A., & Siegel, D. (2001). Corporate social responsibility: A theory of the firm perspective. *Academy of Management Review*, *26*(1), 117–127.

McWilliams, A., Siegel, D. S., & Wright, P. M. (2006). Corporate Social Responsibility: Strategic Implications. *Journal of Management Studies*, *43*(1), 1–18. doi:10.1111/j.1467-6486.2006.00580.x

Mear, R., & Firth, M. (1988). Risk Perceptions of Financial Analysts and the Use of Market and Accounting Data. *Accounting and Business Review*, *18*(72), 335–339. doi:10.1080/00014788.1988.9729380

Meek, G. K., Roberts, C. B., & Gray, S. J. (1995). Factors influencing voluntary annual report disclosures by U.S., U.K and Continental European Multinational Corporations. *Journal of International Business Studies*, *26*(3), 555–572. doi:10.1057/palgrave.jibs.8490186

Meisberg, B., & Ehrmann, T. (2012). Lost in translation? The prevalence and performance Impact of Corporate Social Responsibility in Franschising. *Journal of Small Business Management*, *50*(4), 566–595. doi:10.1111/j.1540-627X.2012.00367.x

Mendoza, K., & Irmak, I. (2008). K. P. Sauvant (Ed.), *The rise of transnational corporations from emerging markets: threat or opportunity?* Edward Elgar Publishing.

Metz, T. (2007). Towards an African moral theory. *Journal of Political Philosophy*, *15*(3), 321–341. doi:10.1111/j.1467-9760.2007.00280.x

Metz, T. (2013). The Ethics of Swearing: The Implications of Moral Theories for Oath-Breaking in Economic Contexts. *Review of Social Economy*, *72*(2), 228–248. doi:10.1080/00346764.2013.799968

Metz, T., & Gaie, J. B. R. (2010). The African ethic of Ubuntu/Botho: Implications for research on morality. *Journal of Moral Education*, *39*(3), 273–290. doi:10.1080/03057240.2010.497609

Mezghani, A., & Ellouze, A. (2007). *Gouvernance de l'Entreprise et Qualité de l'Information Financière, 28ème Congrés de l'AFC- 'Comptabilité et Environnement'*. Retrieved from http://halshs.archives-ouvertes.fr/docs/00/54/49/34/PDF/p185.pdf

Mhlanga, N., Blalock, G., & Christy, R. (2010). Understanding foreign direct investment in the southern African development community: An analysis based on project-level data. *Agricultural Economics*, *41*(3-4), 337–347. doi:10.1111/j.1574-0862.2010.00440.x

Michelini, L., & Fiorentino, D. (2012). New business models for creating shared value. *Social Responsibility Journal*, *8*(4), 561–577. doi:10.1108/17471111211272129

Middle East-peace process. (n. d.). *Wikipedia.* Retrieved from http://en.wikipedia.org/wiki/MiddleEast-peaceprocess

Miller, R. R. (1998). *Selling to Newly Emerging Markets. New York.* Westport, CT: Quorum Books.

Ministry of foreign Affairs of Netherland, Policy and Operations Evaluation Department Study (IOB). (2013). *Corporate Social Responsibility: the role of public policy - A systematic literature review of the effects of government supported interventions on the corporate social responsibility (CSR) behavior of enterprises in developing countries.* The Hague: The Netherlands.

Minzberg, Z. (1983). The Case of Corporate Social Responsibility. *The Journal of Business Strategy*, *5*(2), 3–15. doi:10.1108/eb039015

Mitchell, R. K., Agle, B. R., & Wood, D. J. (1997). Towards a theory of shareholder identification and salience: Defining the principles of who and what really counts. *Academy of Management Review*, *22*(4), 853–886.

Mitchell, V.-W. (1999). Consumer Perceived Risk: Conceptualizations and Models. *European Journal of Marketing*, *33*(1/2), 163–195. doi:10.1108/03090569910249229

Mitchell, V.-W., & Greatorex, M. (1989). Risk Reducing Strategies Used in the Purchase of Wine in the UK. *European Journal of Marketing*, *23*(9), 31–46. doi:10.1108/EUM0000000000589

Mohapi, M.M. (1956). *Temo ea boholo-holo Lesotho.* Morija: Morija Sesuto Book Depot.

Moharana, S. (2013, November-December). Corporate Social Responsibility: A Study of Selected Public Sector Banks in India. *Journal of Business and Management*, *15*(4), 1–9.

Mohasi, M., & Turner, S. D. (1999). Land and livelihoods in southern Lesotho. Cape Town: Programme for Land and Agrarian Studies, School of Government, University of the Western Cape: Research Report 4.

Mohd Ghazali, N. A. (2007). Ownership structure and corporate social responsibility disclosure: Some Malaysian evidence. *Corporate Governance*, *7*(3), 251–266. doi:10.1108/14720700710756535

Mohd Ghazali, N. A. (2010). Ownership structure, corporate governance and corporate performance in Malaysia. *International Journal of Commerce and Management*, *20*(2), 109–119. doi:10.1108/10569211011057245

Mohd Ghazali, N. A., & Weetman, P. (2006). Perpetuating traditional influences: Voluntary disclosure in Malaysia following the economic crisis. *Journal of International Accounting, Auditing & Taxation*, *15*(2), 226–248. doi:10.1016/j.intaccaudtax.2006.08.001

Mokgoro, Y. (1998). Ubuntu and the law in South Africa. *Buffalo Human Rights Law Review*, *15*, 1–6.

Mokhehle, N. (Ed.). (1976). *Moshoeshoe 1 Profile Se-Moshoeshoe.* Maseru: Mmoho Publications.

Mokitimi, M. I. (1997). *The Voice of the People: Proverbs of the Basotho. African Proverbs Series, 4.* Pretoria: UNISA Press.

Montandrau, S. (2006). *Activisme des investisseurs institutionnels et performance boursière: les caractéristiques du conseil d'administration qui permettent la confiance.* CEROG –IAE d'Aix en Provence Université d'Aix- Marseille III.

Montiel, I. (2008). Corporate Social Responsibility and Corporate Sustainability: Separate Pasts, Common Futures. *Organization & Environment*, *21*(3), 245–269. doi:10.1177/1086026608321329

Moody's Investors Services. (2008). Gulf Islamic Banks Resilient Amid Global Credit Woes, Special Comment.

Moon, J. (2002). Corporate Social Responsibility: An Overview. In C. Hartley (Ed.), The International Directory of Corporate Philanthropy (1st ed., pp. 3-14). London and New York: Europa Publications.

Moore Lappé, F. (2011). *Eco mind: Changing the way we think to create the world we want.* New York, NY: Nation Books.

Moré, M. E. (2011). building Brands through Experiential Marketing: Retrieved from http://morethanbranding.com/2011/11/28/building-brands-through-experiential-marketing-11-awesome-examples

Morris, S., Rehbein, K. A., Hosselni, J. C., & Armacost, R. L. (1995). A test of Environmental, Situational, and Personal Influences on the Ethical Intentions of CEOs. *Business & Society*, *34*(2), 119–147. doi:10.1177/000765039503400202

Mpeli, M. R., & Monnapula-Mapesela, M. L. E. (2009). Scraping the surface: what is the bottom line regarding ethics? Paper presented in track 8 at the 31st Annual EAIR Forum in Vilnius, Lithuania 23 to 26 August 2009.

Muel, K. (2003). The Dimond of Managerial Integrity. *European Management Journal*, *21*(1), 99–108. doi:10.1016/S0263-2373(02)00157-3

Mullerat, R. (2010). *International corporate social responsibility: The role of corporations in the economic order of the 21st century*. Kluwer Law International.

Murray, K. B. (1991). A Test of Services Marketing Theory: Consumer Information Acquisition Activities. *Journal of Marketing*, *55*(1), 10–25. doi:10.2307/1252200

Murray, M., & Dainty, A. (2009). Corporate social responsibility: challenging the construction industry. In M. Murray & A. Dainty (Eds.), *Corporate social responsibility in the construction industry* (pp. 3–23). Oxon: Taylor & Francis.

Nalebuff, B. (1996). Co-opetition. Presentation. Yale School of Management, New Haven, CT, USA

NASDAQ. (2012. May 11). The difference Between Developed, Emerging and Frontier Markets. Retrieved from http://www.nasdaq.com/article/what-is-the-difference-between-a-developed-emerging-and-frontier-market-cm140649

Nathan S, Ribiere V (2008). From knowledge to the wisdom: the case of corporate governance in Islamic bank. *The journal of information and knowledge management systems*, 4(37), 471-483.

Naudé, W. A., & Krugell, W. F. (2007). Investigating geography and institutions as determinants of foreign direct investment in Africa using panel data. *Applied Economics*, *39*(10), 1223–1233. doi:10.1080/00036840600567686

Nölke, A., & Taylor, H. (2010). Non-triad multinationals and global governance. In M. Ougaard, & A. Leander (Eds.), *Business and Global Governance* (pp. 156–178). Oxon: Routledge.

Noorbakhsh, F., Paloni, A., & Youssef, A. (2001). Human capital and FDI inflows to developing countries: New empirical evidence. *World Development*, *29*(9), 1593–1610. doi:10.1016/S0305-750X(01)00054-7

Nussbaum, B. (2003). Ubuntu: Reflections of a South African on our common humanity. *Reflections: The SoL Journal*, *4*(4), 21–26. doi:10.1162/152417303322004175

Nuttal, J. (1993). *Moral questions: An introduction to ethics*. Cambridge, UK: Polity Press.

O'Riordan, L., & Fairbrass, J. (2006, September 4-5). Corporate social responsibility (CSR): Models and theories in stakeholder dialogue. Corporate Responsibility Research Conference. Trinity College Dublin, Ireland. Retrieved from http://www.academia.edu/2426506/

Odonnat, I., & Rahmouni, I. (2006). Do emerging market economies still constitute a homogenous asset class? *Banque de France, Financial Stability Review*, (9), 39-48.

Ofori, D. F. (2007). Corporate Social Responsibility and Corporate Financial Performance: Myth, Reality or Empty Rhetoric? *The African Finance Journal*, *9*(2), 53–68.

Okafor, G. O. (2011). The ethical behaviour of Nigerian business students (A study of undergraduate students' in business schools). *Arabian Journal of Business and Management Review*, *1*(3), 33–44.

Okpara, G. C. (2010). Information Asymmetric and Dividend Policy in Emerging Markets: Empirical Evidence from Nigeria. *International Journal of Economics and Finance*, *2*(4). doi:10.5539/ijef.v2n4p212

Oliveira, J. A. (2012). Rio+ 20: what we can learn from the process and what is missing. *Cadernos EBAPE. BR, 10*(3), 492-507.

Olsen, R. (1997). Desirability Bias among Professional Investment Managers: Some Evidence from Experts. *Journal of Behavioral Decision Making*, *10*(1), 65–72. doi:10.1002/(SICI)1099-0771(199703)10:1<65::AID-BDM246>3.0.CO;2-S

Oppe, S. (1988). The Concept of Risk: A Theoretical Approach. *Ergonomics*, *31*(4), 435–440. doi:10.1080/00140138808966690

Orlitzky, M., Siegel, D. S., & Waldman, D. A. (2011). Strategic corporate social responsibility and environmental sustainability. *Business & Society*, *50*(1), 6–27. doi:10.1177/0007650310394323

Orlitzy, M., Schmidt, F. L., & Rynes, S. L. (2003). Corporate social and financial performance: A meta analysis. *Organization Studies*, *24*(3), 403–441. doi:10.1177/0170840603024003910

Ormiston, M. E., & Wong, E. M. (2013). License to ill: The effects of corporate social responsibility and CEO moral identity on corporate irresponsibility. *Personnel Psychology*, *66*(4), 861–893. doi:10.1111/peps.12029

Osterwalder, A., & Pigneur, Y. (2011). Aligning profit and purpose through business model innovation. *Responsible management practices for the 21st century. Pearson International*, 61-75.

Owolabi, K., & Olu-Owolabi, F. E. (2009). Corporate Social Responsibility and the Crisis of Development in Africa. *Journal of Sustainable Development in Africa*, *10*(4), 218–232.

Page, L. (2009). Is there an Optimistic Bias on Betting Markets? *Economics Letters*, *102*(2), 70–72. doi:10.1016/j.econlct.2008.10.006

Palepu. (2010). *Winning In Emerging Markets: A Roadmap for Strategy and Execution for Emerging Markets*. Harvard Business School Press.

Palestine Human Resource Development Report (PHRDR). (2004). Birzeit University.

Palestinian Business Women's Association. (2010). Women's Economic Empowerment in the West Bank. Palestine.

Pathan, S., Skully, M., & Wickramanayake, J. (2007). Board size, independence and performance: An analysis of Thai banks. *Asia-Pacific Financial Markets*, *14*(3), 211–227. doi:10.1007/s10690-007-9060-y

Pattberg, P., Biermann, F., Chan, S., & Mert, A. (Eds.). (2012). *Public–private partnerships for sustainable development: Emergence, influence and legitimacy*. Cheltenham, UK: Edward Elgar. doi:10.4337/9781849809313

Patten, D. M. (1991). Exposure, legitimacy, and social disclosure. *Journal of Accounting and Public Policy*, *10*(4), 297–308. doi:10.1016/0278-4254(91)90003-3

Pecoraro, M. G., & Uusitalo, O. (2014). Conflicting values of ethical consumption on diverse worlds – A cultural approach. *Journal of Consumer Culture*, *14*(1), 45–65. doi:10.1177/1469540513485273

Pedersen, E. R. (2006). Making corporate responsibility (CSR) operable: How companies translate stakeholder dialogue into practice. *Business and Society Review*, *111*(2), 137–163. doi:10.1111/j.1467-8594.2006.00265.x

Pedersen, K., Svendsen, G. L., & Svendsen, G. T. (2013). Multinational Enterprises and Social Capital as Location Factor: A Review. *Business and Management Research*, *2*(3), 81–89. doi:10.5430/bmr.v2n3p81

Pedhazur, E. J., & Schmelkin, L. P. (1991). *Measurement, Design, and Analysis: An Integrated Approach*. Hillsdale, N.J.: Lawrence Erlbaum Associates.

Pelle, S. (2007). Understanding emerging markets: Building business BRIC by brick. *Sage (Atlanta, Ga.)*.

Peloza, J., & Shang, J. (2011). How can corporate social responsibility activities create value for stakeholders? A systematic review. *Journal of the Academy of Marketing Science*, *39*(1), 117–135. doi:10.1007/s11747-010-0213-6

Peppas, S. C., & Diskin, B. A. (2000). Ethical perspectives: Are future marketers any different? *Teaching Business Ethics*, *4*(2), 207–220. doi:10.1023/A:1009822500621

Perryer, C., & Scott-Ladd, B. (2014). Deceit, Misuse and Favours: Understanding and Measuring Attitudes to Ethics. *Journal of Business Ethics*, *121*(1), 123–134. doi:10.1007/s10551-012-1593-y

Peters, S., Miller, M., & Kusyk, S. (2011). How relevant is corporate governance and corporate social responsibility in emerging markets? *Corporate Governance*, *11*(4), 429–445. doi:10.1108/14720701111159262

Petkoski, D., & Twose, N. (Eds.), (2003). *Public Policy for Corporate Social Responsibility*. World Bank Institute Series on Corporate Responsibility, Accountability and Sustainable Competitiveness.

Petschow, U., Rosenau, J., & Von Weizsäcker, E. U. (Eds.). (2005). *Governance and sustainability: New challenges for states, companies, and civil society*. Sheffield, UK: Greenleaf.

Pfitzer, M., Bockstette, V., & Stamp, M. (2013). Innovating for shared value. *Harvard Business Review*,*September*, 100–107.

Phillips, F. (2006). Corporate Social Responsibility in an African context. *Journal of Corporate Citizenship*, *2006*(24), 23–27. doi:10.9774/GLEAF.4700.2006.wi.00005

Pi, L., & Timme, S. G. (1993). Corporate control and bank efficiency. *Journal of Banking & Finance*, *17*(2-3), 515–530. doi:10.1016/0378-4266(93)90050-N

Pillania, R. K. (2009). Multinationals and emerging markets. *Business Strategy Series*, *10*(2), 100–103. doi:10.1108/17515630910942232

Polman, P. (2013, March 6). *From license to operate to license to lead.* Ernst & Young Hofstad Lecture, The Hague, The Netherlands. Retrieved from http://www.unilever.nl/Images/2013-03-06-Hofstadlezing-Paul-Polman_tcm164-348071.pdf

Ponte, S., Richey, L. A., & Baab, M. (2009). Bono's Product (RED) Initiative: Corporate Social Responsibility that solves the problems of 'distant others'. *Third World Quarterly*, *30*(2), 301–317. doi:10.1080/01436590802681074

Porter, M. E., & Kramer, M. R. (2006). Strategy and society: The link between competitive advantage and corporate social responsibility. *Harvard Business Review*, *84*(2), 4–17. PMID:17183795

Porter, M. E., & Kramer, M. R. (2006). The link between competitive advantage and corporate social responsibility. *Harvard Business Review*, *84*(12), 78–92. PMID:17183795

Porter, M. E., & Kramer, M. R. (2011). Creating shared value. *Harvard Business Review*, *89*(1/2), 62–77.

Porter, M.-E., & Kramer, M.-R. (2006). Strategy and society: The link between competitive advantage and corporate social responsibility. *Harvard Business Review*, *84*(12), 78–92. PMID:17183795

Porter, T., & Derry, R. (2012). Sustainability and business in a complex world. *Business and Society Review*, *117*(1), 33–53. doi:10.1111/j.1467-8594.2012.00398.x

Poulsson, S. H. G., & Kale, S. H. (2004). The Experience Economy and Commercial Experiences. *The Marketing Review*, *4*(3), 267–277. doi:10.1362/1469347042223445

Pour, B. S., Kamran, N., & Mostafa, E. (2014). Corporate social responsibility: A literature review. *African Journal of Business Management*, *8*(7), 228–234. doi:10.5897/AJBM12.106

Prahalad, C. K. (2004). *The Fortune at the Bottom of the Pyramid: Eradicating Poverty Through Profits*. London: FT Prentice Hall.

Prahalad, C. K. (2005). *The fortune at the bottom of the pyramid: Eradicating poverty through profits*. Upper Saddle River, CT: Wharton School Publishing.

Prahalad, C. K. (2006). *The Fortune at the Bottom of the Pyramid*. Pearson Education India.

Preston, L. E. (1975). Corporations and society: The search for a paradigm. *Journal of Economic Literature*, *13*(2), 434–453.

Pride, W., Hughes, R., & Kappor, J. (1996). *Business* (5th ed.). Boston: Houghton Mifflin Company.

Proenca, J. F., & Branco, M. C. (2014). Corporate social responsibility practices and motivations in a peripheral country: Two Portuguese illustrative cases. *Corporate Governance*, *14*(2), 252–264. doi:10.1108/CG-07-2011-0052

Providing consumers with ethically sourced garments. (2015, July, 17). *Primark case study.*

Przychodzeń, W., & Justyna, P. (2014). Corporate Social Responsibility for Sustainability. *Management and Business Administration Central Europe*, *2*(125), 80–97. doi:10.7206/mba.ce.2084-3356.100

Pulvers, K., & Diekhoff, G. M. (1999). The relationship between academic dishonesty and college classroom environment. *Research in Higher Education*, *40*(4), 487–498. doi:10.1023/A:1018792210076

Qatar Admits Deaths in Migrant Workers. (2014, May 14). *The Guardian.* Retrieved from http://www.theguardian.com/world/2014/may/14/qatar-admits-deaths-in-migrant-workers

Rahman, W.A., & Osama, S. (2009). Ahfad University for Women Beyond academic excellence social responsibility and civic engagement.*Proceedings of the Arab Regional Conference on Higher Education, Towards an Arab Higher Education Space: International Challenges and Societal Responsibilities, Cairo* (pp.695-714). UNESCO.

Rajagopalan, N., & Datta, D. K. (1996). CEO characteristics: Does industry matter? *Academy of Management Journal*, *39*(1), 197–215. doi:10.2307/256636

Ramalingam, B., Jones, H., Reba, T., & Young, J. (2008). *Exploring the science of complexity: Ideas and implications for development and humanitarian efforts* (Vol. 285). London: Overseas Development Institute.

Rammal, H. (2006). The importance of Shariah supervision in Islamic financial institutions. *Corporate Ownership and Control*, *3*(3), 204–208.

Ramose, M. B. (2002). The philosophy of Ubuntu and Ubuntu as a philosophy. In P. H. Coetzee & A. P. J. Roux (Eds.), *Philosophy from Africa: A Text with Readings*. Cape Town: Oxford University Press.

Rani, G., & Kalpana, H. (2013). Corporate Social Responsibility: Review of Literature. *International Journal of Social Science & Interdisciplinary Research, 2*(6), 38–44.

Rapoza, K. (2011). *Forbes Welcome. Forbes.com.*

Ratchford, B. T., Lee, M. S., & Talukdar, D. (2003). The impact of the Internet on information search for Automobiles. *JMR, Journal of Marketing Research, 40*(2), 193–209. doi:10.1509/jmkr.40.2.193.19221

Raval, K., & Himanshu, R. (2014). Corporate social responsibility and sustainable development study of most valuable companies. *Indian Streams Research Journal, IV*(II), 1–11.

Ravenhill, J. (Ed.). (2014). *Global political economy*. Oxford University Press.

Raykov, T., & Marcoulides, G. A. (2006). *A First Course in Structural Equation Modeling* (2nd ed.). Lawrence Erlbaum Associates, Inc. Publishers.

Redclift, M. (2005). Sustainable development (1987–2005): An oxymoron comes of age. *Sustainable Development, 13*(4), 212–227. doi:10.1002/sd.281

Reich, R. B. (2007). *Supercapitalism: The transformation of business, democracy, and everyday life*. New York, NY: Vintage Books.

Reimann, F., Ehrgott, M., Kaufmann, L., & Carter, C. R. (2012). Local stakeholders and local legitimacy: MNEs' social strategies in emerging economies. *Journal of International Management, 18*(1), 1–17. doi:10.1016/j.intman.2011.06.002

Reinicke, W. H., & Deng, F. (2000). *Critical choices: The United Nations, networks, and the future of global governance*. Ottawa, Canada: International Development Research Centre.

Reiser (2008). University social responsibility definition cited in Vasilescu, et al. (2010). Developing university social responsibility: A model for the challenges of the new civil society. *Procedia Social and Behavioural Sciences* (Vol. 2, pp. 4177-4182).

Renn, O. (1992). Concepts of Risk: A Classification. In S. Krimsky & D. Golding (Eds.), *Social Theories of Risk. Westport, CT* (pp. 83–116). London: Praeger.

Report Qatar Construction Industry. (2011, February). Ventures Middle East ID 1574166.

Report, S. (2002, December). Corporate Social Responsibility. *The Economist*, 62-63.

Rettab, B., Brik, A. B., & Mellahi, K. (2009). A study of management perceptions of the impact of corporate social responsibility on organisational performance in emerging economies: The case of Dubai. *Journal of Business Ethics, 89*(3), 371–390. doi:10.1007/s10551-008-0005-9

Ricciardi, V. (2004). A risk Perception Primer: A Narrative Research Review of The Risk Perception Literature in Behavioral Accounting and Behavioral Finance, *Working Paper.*

Ricciardi, V. (2008). Risk: Traditional Finance versus Behavioral Finance. In F.J. Fabozzi (Ed.), Handbook of Finance (Vol. 3, pp. 11-38). John Wiley & Sons. doi:10.1002/9780470404324.hof003002

Richardson, S., Courtney, J., & Haynes, J. (2006). Theoretical principles for knowledge management system design: Application to pediatric bipolar disorder. *Decision Support Systems, 42*(3), 1321–1337. doi:10.1016/j.dss.2005.11.001

Rigg, J., Bebbington, A., Gough, K. V., Bryceson, D. F., Agergaard, J., Fold, N., & Tacoli, C. (2009). The World Development Report 2009 'reshapes economic geography': Geographical reflections. *Transactions of the Institute of British Geographers*, *34*(2), 128–136. doi:10.1111/j.1475-5661.2009.00340.x

Rischard, J.-F. (2002). *High noon: Twenty global problems, twenty years to solve them.* New York, NY: Basic Books.

Ritter, B. A. (2006). Can business ethics be trained? A study of the ethical decision-making process in business students. *Journal of Business Ethics*, *68*(2), 153–164. doi:10.1007/s10551-006-9062-0

Rivera, I. M. (2010). What drives indigenous corporations in the developing world to engage in CSR as a management strategy? Case study of the sugarcane and ethanol industry in the Cauca Valley, Colombia. Retrieved from http://www.banrepcultural.org/sites/default/files/Isabella-Marino-rivera-Dissertation-280810-what-drives-indigenous-corporations.pdf

Robbins, S. P., & Judge, T. A. (2012). Organizational Behavior (15th ed.). Pearson Education, Inc., USA. Retrieved from https://jahanzaibyousaf.files.wordpress.com/2014/02/organizational-behavior-15e-stephen-p-robbins-timothy-a-judge-pdf-qwerty.pdf

Robbins, S., & Coulter, M. (2009). Management (10th ed.). Pearson Education Incorporation, 118.

Robbins, S., Coulter, M., Sidani, Y., & Jamali, D. (2011). *Management (Arab World Edition).* Pearson Education Limited.

Robbins, S., & Judge, T. (2015). *Organizational Behavior* (16th ed.). Pearson.

Roberts, R. W. (1992). Determinants of corporate social responsibility disclosure: An application of stakeholder theory. *Accounting, Organizations and Society*, *17*(6), 595–612. doi:10.1016/0361-3682(92)90015-K

Robins, F. (2005). The future of corporate social responsibility. *Asian Business & Management*, *4*(2), 95–115. doi:10.1057/palgrave.abm.9200125

Rodriguez, P., Siegel, D. S., Hillman, A., & Eden, L. (2006). Three lenses on the multinational enterprise: Politics, corruption, and corporate social responsibility. *Journal of International Business Studies*, *37*(6), 733–746. doi:10.1057/palgrave.jibs.8400229

Rogers, J. L. (2008). *Disclosure Quality and Management Trading Incentives.* Chicago GSB Working Paper N°. 08-18.

Rossouw, G. J., & Van Vuuren, L. J. (2003). The business case for business ethics. *Journal of the South African Institute for Management Scientists*, *12*(1), 1–11.

Roussel, P., Durrieu, F., Campoy, Y., & El Akremi, A. (2002). Méthodes d'Equations Structurelles: Recherche et Applications en Gestion. *Economica.*

Rowe, J. (1995). Corporations and the public interest: A look at how the original purpose behind corporate charters has been lost. *In Context*, 41, 26-35.

Rutherford, M. A., Parks, L., Cavazos, D. E., & White, C. D. (2012). Business ethics as a required course: Investigating the factors impacting the decision to require ethics in the undergraduate business core curriculum. *Academy of Management Learning & Education*, *11*(2), 174–186. doi:10.5465/amle.2011.0039

Sachs, J. D. (2005). *The end of poverty: How we can make it happen in our lifetime.* New York, NY: Penguin Books.

Sachs, J. D. (2009). *Common wealth: Economics for a crowded planet.* New York, NY: Penguin Books.

Sahlin-Andersson, K. (2006). Corporate Social Responsibility: A Trend and a Movement, but of What and For What? *Corporate Governance*, *6*(5), 595–608. doi:10.1108/14720700610706081

Saidi, T. A. (2009). Relationship between ethical and Islamic banking systems and its business management implications. *South African Journal of Business Management*, *40*(1), 43–49.

Said, R., Yuserrie, H. Z., & Hasnah, H. (2009). The relationship between corporate social responsibility disclosure and corporate governance characteristics in Malaysian public listed companies. *Social Responsibility Journal*, *5*(2), 212–226. doi:10.1108/17471110910964496

Salehizadeh, M. (2007). Emerging economies' multinationals: Current status and future prospects. *Third World Quarterly*, *28*(6), 1151–1166. doi:10.1080/01436590701507586

Salls, M. (2004). *An opposing view of corporate social responsibility*. Harvard Business School Working Knowledge. Retrieved from http://hbswk.hbs.edu/archive/4008.html

Samad, A. (2005). Performance of Interest-free Islamic banks vis-à-vis Interest-based Conventional Banks of Bahrain. *IIUM Journal of Economics and Management*, *12*(2), 1–15.

Samad, A., & Hassan, K. (2000). The Performance of Malaysian Islamic Bank during 1984-1997: An Exploratory Study. *Thoughts on Economics*, *10*(1 & 2), 7–26.

Sanders, P. (1975). *Moshoeshoe – Chief of the Sotho*. London: Heinemann.

Saran, C. (2015). *Interview: Ralph Szygenda, group vice-president and CIO at General Motors. ComputerWeekly*.

Sargan, J. D. (1958). The estimation of economic relationships using instrumental variables. *Econometrica*, *26*(3), 393–415. doi:10.2307/1907619

Schmidheiny, S. (1992). *Changing course: A global business perspective on development and the environment* (Vol. 1). MIT Press.

Schmidheiny, S. (2006). A View of Corporate Citizenships in Latin America. *Journal of Corporate Citizenship*, *21*(Spring), 21–24. doi:10.9774/GLEAF.4700.2006.sp.00004

Schmitt, B. (1999a). Experiential marketing: How to get customers to sense, feel, think, act and relate to your company and brands. The Free Press, New York, USA.

Schmitt, B. (1999b). Experiential Marketing. *Journal of marketing management New York: The Free Press*, 1(6), 57–69.

Schmitt, B. (2003). Customer Experience Management. *Journal of Consumer Psychology*, *22*, 7–17. doi:10.1016/j.jcps.2011.09.005

Schmitt, B. (2011a). *Experiential Marketing: How to Get Customers to Sense, Feel, Think, Act (Updated Edition by B. Joseph Pine)*. Free Press.

Schmitt, B. (2011b). Experience Marketing: Concepts. *Frameworks and Consumer Insights Foundations and Trends in Marketing*, *5*(2), 55–112. doi:10.1561/1700000027

Schneider, F., & Frey, B. S. (1985). Economic and political determinants of foreign direct investment. *World Development*, *13*(2), 161–175. doi:10.1016/0305-750X(85)90002-6

Scholl, H. J. (2001). Applying stakeholder theory to e-government: Benefits and limits. In B. Schmid, K. Stanoevska-Slabeva, & V. Tschammer (Eds.), *Towards the e-society: E-commerce, e-business, and e-government* (pp. 735–747). Boston, MA: Kluwer Academic Publishers.

Sebastiani, R., Montagnini, F., & Dalli, D. (2013). Ethical consumption and new business models in the food industry. Evidence from the Eataly case. *Journal of Business Ethics*, *114*(3), 473–488. doi:10.1007/s10551-012-1343-1

Secchi, D. (2007). Utilitarian, managerial and relational theories of corporate social responsibility. *International Journal of Management Reviews*, *9*(4), 347–373. doi:10.1111/j.1468-2370.2007.00215.x

Seifert, B., Morris, S. A., & Bartkus, B. R. (2004). Having, Giving, and Getting: Slack Resources, Corporate Philanthropy, and Firm Financial Resources. Business and Society (pp. 135-161).

Selsky, J. W., & Parker, B. (2005). Cross-sector partnerships to address social issues: Challenges to theory and practice. *Journal of Management*, *31*(6), 849–873. doi:10.1177/0149206305279601

SER, Social and Economic Council of the Netherlands. (2000). *De winst van waarden*. The Hague, The Netherlands: SER (English abstract: *Advisory Report on Corporate Social Responsibility: Summary of Conclusions*). Retrieved from https://www.ser.nl/nl/publicaties/adviezen/2000-2007/2000/b19054.aspx

Seshadri, S., & Broekemier, G. M. (2009). Ethical decision making: Panama–United States differences in consumer and marketing contexts. *Journal of Global Marketing*, *22*(4), 299–311. doi:10.1080/08911760903022515

Shahriari, M. (Ed.), (2013). Loss Prevention & Safety - A Practical Risk Management Handbook (2nd ed.). Göteborg, Sweden: Chalmers University of Technology.

Shahriari, M., Örtengren, R., Aliandrina, D., & Feng, Y. (2008). Human Errors in Decision Making- Analysis of two historical cases. *Journal of Ergonomia*, *30*(1), 47–62.

Shahul, H., Ade, W., Bakhtiar, A., Mohd, N., & Sigit, P. (2006, April 19-21). Alternative disclosure and performance measures for Islamic banks. *Proceedings of theConference on Administrative Sciences*. King Fahd University of Petroleum & Minerals, Saudi Arabia.

Shangquan, G. (2000). Economic globalization: Trends, risks and risk prevention. *Economic & Social Affairs, CDP Backround Paper* 1.

Shaw, D., Grehan, E., Shiu, E., Hassan, L., & Thomson, J. (2005). An exploration of values in ethical consumer decision making. *Journal of Consumer Behaviour*, *4*(3), 185–200. doi:10.1002/cb.3

Shawyun, T. (2011). From corporate social responsibility (CSR) to university social responsibility (USR). In Knowledge Societies: Universities and their Social Responsibilities (pp. 16-19). Singapore: Asia-Europe Foundation.

Shea, G. F. (1988). Practical Ethics, New York: American Management Association.

Sheddick, V. G. J. (1954). *Land Tenure in Basutoland*. London: Her Majesty's Stationery Office.

Shell. (2007a). Brent Spar Dossier, Biological Effects. Retrieved from http://www.shell.com/home/Framework?siteId=uk-en&FC2=/uk-en/html/iwgen/about_shell/brentspardossier/impacthypothesis/zzz_lhn.html&FC3=/uk-en/html/iwgen/about_shell/brentspardossier/impacthypothesis/biologicaleffects_09121440.html

Shell. (2007b). Brent Spar Dossier, BPEO. Retrieved from http://www.shell.com/home/Framework?siteId=uk-en&FC2=/uken/html/iwgen/about_shell/brentspardossier/bpeoassessment/zzz_lhn.html&FC3=/uk-en/html/iwgen/about_shell/brentspardossier/bpeoassessment/synopsis_09121530.html

Shell. (2007c). Brent Spar Dossier, Brent Spar. Retrieved from http://www.shell.com/home/Framework?siteId=uk-en&FC2=/uk-en/html/iwgen/zzz_lhn.html&FC3=/uken/html/iwgen/about_shell/brentspardossier/dir_brent_spar.html

Shivdasani, A., & Yermack, D. (1999). CEO involvement in the selection of new board members: An empirical analysis. *The Journal of Finance*, *54*(5), 1829–1853. doi:10.1111/0022-1082.00168

Shutte, A. (1994). *Philosophy for Africa*. Rondebosch: UCT Press.

Siagh, L. (2001). Le fonctionnement des organisations dans les milieux de culture intense, le cas des Banques Islamiques [Thèse du Doctorat]. Ecole des Hautes Etudes Commerciales, Montréal.

Siagh, L., Diallo, O. A., & Hafsi, T. (2004).Environnement intense et choix stratégique: le cas des banques islamiques. Cahier de recherche N°20-46, ISSN 1711-6309 HEC Montréal.

Sierra, G., Talmor, E., & Wallace, J. (2006). An examination of multiple governance forces within banking holding companies. *Journal of Financial Services Research*, *29*(2), 105–123. doi:10.1007/s10693-006-5921-1

Sigurjonsson, T. O., Vaiman, V., & Arnardottir, A. A. (2014). The Role of Business Schools in Ethics Education in Iceland: The Managers' Perspective. *Journal of Business Ethics*, *122*(1), 25–38. doi:10.1007/s10551-013-1755-6

Simon, H. A. (1986). Rationality in Psychology and Economics. *The Journal of Business*, *59*(S4), 209–224. doi:10.1086/296363

Simpson, W., G., , & Gleason, A.E. (1999). Board structure, ownership and financial distress in banking firms. *International Review of Economics & Finance*, *8*(3), 281–292. doi:10.1016/S1059-0560(99)00026-X

Simpson, W. G., & Kohers, T. (2002). The Link between Corporate Social and Financial Performance: Evidence from the Banking Industry. *Journal of Business Ethics*, *35*(2), 97–109. doi:10.1023/A:1013082525900

Sims, R. L. (2006). Comparing Ethical Attitudes across Cultures. *Cross Cultural Management: An International Journal*, *13*(2), 101–113. doi:10.1108/13527600610662294

Sindane, J. (1994). *Ubuntu and Nation Building*. Pretoria: Ubuntu School of Philosophy.

Sindane, J., & Liebenberg, I. (2000). Reconstruction and the Reciprocal other: The philosophy and practice of Ubuntu and democracy in African society. *Politeia*, *19*(3), 31–46.

Sirkin, H., Hemerling, J., & Bhattacharya, A. (2008). *Globality: Competing with everyone from everywhere for everything*. Hachette Digital, Inc.

Sitkin, S. B., & Pablo, A. L. (1992). Reconceptualizing the Determinants of Risk Behavior. *Review of Academic Management*, *17*, 9–38.

Sitkin, S. B., & Weingart, L. R. (1995). Determinants of Risky-Making Behavior: A Test of Mediatic Role of Risk Perceptions and Propensity. *Academy of Management Journal*, *38*(6), 1573–1592. doi:10.2307/256844

Sjöberg, L. (2000). Factors of Risk Perception. *Risk Analysis*, *20*(1), 1–11. doi:10.1111/0272-4332.00001

Skully, M. T. (2002, August 9–11). Banking and corporate governance: some prudential issues. *Presented in Second International Conference on Banking and Finance*, Greece.

Slovic, P. (1988). Risk Perception. In C. C. Travis (Ed.), Contemporary issues in risk analysis (Vol. 3,pp. 171-181). New York: Plenum. doi:10.1007/978-1-4684-5484-0_13

Slovic, P., Fischhoff, B., & Lichtenstein, S. (1979). Risk Assessment: Technical and Behavioral Issues. In Risk/Benefit analysis in the legislative process (Joint Hearings before the Committee on Science and Technology, U.S. House of Representatives and the Committee on Commerce, Science and Transportation, U.S. Senate) (pp. 133-188). Washington, DC: Government Printing Office.

Slovic, P., Fischhoff, B., & Lichtenstein, S. (1980). Facts and Fears: Understanding Perceived Risk. In R. Schwing & W.A. Albers, Jr. (Eds.), Societal risk assessment: How safe is safe enough? (pp. 181-214). New York: Plenum. (Revision in D. Kahneman, P. Slovic, & A. Tversky (Eds.), Judgment under uncertainty: Heuristics and biases. New York: Cambridge University, 1982; in F. Farley & C. H. Null (Eds.), Using psychological science: Making the public case. Washington, DC: Federation of Behavioral, Psychological and Cognitive Sciences, 1987. doi:10.1007/978-1-4899-0445-4_9

Slovic, P. (1987). Perception of Risk. *Science*, *236*(4799), 280–285. doi:10.1126/science.3563507 PMID:3563507

Slovic, P., Fischhoff, B., & Lichtenstein, S. (1982). Why Study Risk Perception? *Risk Analysis*, *2*(2), 83–93. doi:10.1111/j.1539-6924.1982.tb01369.x

Slovic, P., Fischhoff, B., & Lichtenstein, S. (1985). Regulation of Risk: A Psychological Perspective. In R. G. Noll (Ed.), *Regulatory policy and the social sciences* (pp. 241–278). Berkeley: University of California.

Slywotzky, A., & Wise, R. (2003). Demand innovation: GM's OnStar case. *Strategy and Leadership*, *31*(4), 17–22. doi:10.1108/10878570310483942

Smick, D. M. (2008). *The world is curved: Hidden dangers to the global economy*. Penguin.

Smilansky, S. (2009). Experiential Marketing: A Practical Guide to Interactive Brand Experiences (Google eBook). Kogan Page Publishers.

Smith, N. C. (2008). Consumers as Drivers of Corporate Social Responsibility. In A. Crane, D. Matten, A. McWilliams, J. Moon, & D. Siegel (Eds.), *The Oxford Handbook of Corporate Social Responsibility*. New York: Oxford University Press. doi:10.1093/oxfordhb/9780199211593.003.0012

Smith, N. C., Bhattacharya, C. B., Vogel, D., & Levine, D. I. (Eds.). (2010). *Global challenges in responsible business*. Cambridge University Press. doi:10.1017/CBO9780511777660

Smith, N., Smith, V., & Verner, M. (2006). Do women in top management affect firm performance? A panel study of 2500 Danish firms. *International Journal of Productivity and Performance Management*, *55*(7), 569–593. doi:10.1108/17410400610702160

Smith, S., & Wheeler, J. (2002). *Managing the Customer Experience: Turning Customers into Advocates*. Harlow: Prentice-Hall.

Social Responsibility and Ethics. (2015, July, 17). *Pachamama Alliance*. Retrieved from http://www.pachamama.org/social-justice/social-responsibility-and-ethics

SOMO, Center for Research on Multinational Corporations. (2014). *Flawed fabric: The abuse of girls and women workers in the South Indian textile industry*. Amsterdam, The Netherlands: SOMO.

Sousa Filho, J. M. D., Wanderley, L. S. O., Gómez, C. P., & Farache, F. (2010). Strategic corporate social responsibility management for competitive advantage. *BAR-Brazilian Administration Review*, *7*(3), 294–309. doi:10.1590/S1807-76922010000300006

Sparks, J. R., & Pan, Y. (2010). Ethical judgments in business ethics research: Definition, and research agenda. *Journal of Business Ethics*, *91*(3), 405–418. doi:10.1007/s10551-009-0092-2

Spong, K., DeYoung, R., & Sullivan, R. J. (2001). Who's minding the store? Motivating and monitoring hired managers at small, closely held commercial banks. *Journal of Banking & Finance*, *25*(7), 1209–1243. doi:10.1016/S0378-4266(00)00127-8

Sridharan, U., & Marsinko, A. (1997). CEO duality in the paper and forest products industry. *Journal of Financial and Strategic Decisions*, *10*(1).

Staikouras, P. K., Staikouras, C. K., & Agoraki, M. E. K. (2007). The effect of board size and composition on European bank performance. *European Journal of Law and Economics*, *23*(1), 1–27. doi:10.1007/s10657-007-9001-2

Stake, R. (2000). Case studies. In N.K. Denzin, & Y.S. Lincoln (Eds.). Handbook of qualitative research (2nd ed., pp. 435-454). Thousand Oaks, California: Sage.

Stake, R. (1995). *The Art of Case Study Research*. Thousand Oaks, CA: Sage.

Steger, M. (2013). *Globalization: A Very Short Introduction*. Oxford University Press. doi:10.1093/actrade/9780199662661.001.0001

Stern, S., & Seligman, E. (2004). *The partnership principle: New forms of governance in the 21st century*. London, UK: Archetype Publishers.

Steurer, R., Langer, M. E., Konrad, A., & Martinuzzi, A. (2005). Corporations, stakeholders and sustainable development I: A theoretical exploration of business–society relations. *Journal of Business Ethics*, *61*(3), 263–281. doi:10.1007/s10551-005-7054-0

St-Onge S, Magnan, M, Calloc H Y (2001).Conseil d'administration et rémunération des dirigeants d'entreprise au Canada: une perspective politique. *Revue canadienne des sciences de l'administration*, 18(2), 57-76.

Stubbs, W., & Cocklin, C. (2008). Conceptualizing a "sustainability business model". *Organization & Environment*, *21*(2), 103–127. doi:10.1177/1086026608318042

Su, R.-J., & Jie, X.-W. (2015). Literature Review on Corporate Social Responsibility. *Proceedings of the International Conference on Management Engineering and Management Innovation.*

Sunjeand, A., & Civi, E. (2008). Emerging markets: a review of conceptual, frameworks. *Proceedings of 1st International Joint Symposium on Business Administrator*: Challenges for Business Administrators in the New Millennium. Retrieved from http://www.opf.slu.cz/vvr/akce/turecko/pdf/sunje.pdf

Su, W., Peng, M. W., Tan, W., & Cheung, Y. L. (2014). The Signaling Effect of Corporate Social Responsibility in Emerging Economies. *Journal of Business Ethics*.

Svendsen, A. C., Boutilier, R. G., Abbott, R. M., & Wheeler, D. (2002). Measuring the business value of stakeholder relationships: Part one. Vancouver, Canada: Centre for Innovation in Management. Retrieved from http://www.cim.sfu.ca/folders/research/1%20-%20Measuring%20social%20capital%20-%201.pdf

Svendsen, A. C. (1998). *The stakeholder strategy*. San Francisco, CA: Berrett-Koehler.

Swanson, D. L. (1995). Addressing a Theoretical Problem by Reorienting the Corporate Social Performance Model. *Academy of Management Review*, *20*(1), 43–64.

Swanson, P. E., & Lin, A. Y. (2005). Trading behavior and Investment Performance of U.S. Investors in Global Equity Markets. *Journal of Multinational Financial Management*, *15*(2), 99–115. doi:10.1016/j.mulfin.2004.03.006

Szmigin, I., & Carrigan, M. (2006). Exploring the dimensions of ethical consumption. *European Advances in Consumer Research*, *7*, 608–613.

Talha, M., Sallehhuddin, A., & Masuod, M. S. (2009). Corporate governance and director remuneration in selected ASEAN countries. *The Journal of Applied Research*, *25*(2), 31–39.

Tallontire Current Lit, A., Rentsendorj, E., & Blowfield, M. (2001). *Ethical Consumers and Ethical Trade: A Review of erature. Policy Series 12*. Chatham, UK: Natural Resources Institute.

Tam, O. K., & Tan, M. G. (2007). Ownership, governance and firm performance in Malaysia. *Journal Compilation Blackwell Publishing*, *15*(2).

Tang, L. (2012). The direction of cultural distance on FDI: Attractiveness or incongruity? *Cross Cultural Management: An International Journal*, *19*(2), 233–256. doi:10.1108/13527601211219919

Taylor, H., & Nölke, A. (2010). Global Players from India: A Political Economy Perspective. In K. P. Sauvant, G. McAllister, & W. A. Maschek (Eds.), *Foreign Direct Investments from Emerging Markets: The Challenges Ahead* (pp. 145–172). New York: Palgrave MacMillan.

Taylor, J. (1974). The Role of Risk in Consumer Behavior. *Journal of Marketing*, *38*(2), 54–60. doi:10.2307/1250198

Tchaman, J.-P., & Estay, Ch. (2004). La pratique de la responsabilité sociale et ses implications dans l'entreprise. *Gestion*, *2000*(July-August), 31–47.

Teffo, L. J. (1994). *The Concept of Ubuntu as a Cohesive Moral Value*. Pretoria: Ubuntu School of Philosophy.

Terron, A., & Kulkarni, M. (2013). *Uncovering the Billion $ Shopper unity: The First Time Modern Trade Shopper* (pp. 1–4). Nielsen Featured Insights.

Thayer, J. (2008). Determinants of Shareholders' Information Search: Credibility versus Confirmation. *Unpublished working Paper,* Emory University.

The Global Compact. (2015). *What is the UN Global Compact?* Retrieved from https://www.unglobalcompact.org/

Thomas, K. (2005, April 28). Why it pays to be socially responsible. *The Guardian*. Retrieved from http://www.theguardian.com/technology/2005/apr/28/businesssolutionssupplement5l

Tlhagale, B. (n.d). *Bringing the African Culture into the Church*. Retrieved at http://www.afrikaworld.net/afrel/tlhagale.htm

Torres-Baumgarten, G., & Yucetepe, V. (2009). Multinational firms' leadership role in corporate social responsibility in Latin America. *Journal of Business Ethics*, *85*(1), 217–224. doi:10.1007/s10551-008-9940-8

Tota, I., & Shehu, H. (2012). The Dilemma of Business Ethics. *Sciance and Direct Procedia Economics and Finance*, *3*, 556.

Trevino, L. K. (1986). Ethical Decision Making in Organizations: A Person Situation Integrationist Model. *Academy of Management Review*, *11*, 601–617.

Treviño, L. K., Weaver, G. R., Gibson, D. G., & Toffler, B. L. (1999). Managing Ethics and Local Compliance: What Works and What Hurts? *California Management Review*, *41*(2), 131–151. doi:10.2307/41165990

Tsai, S. (2005). Integrated Marketing as Management of Holistic Consumer Experience. *Business Horizons*, *48*(5), 431–441. doi:10.1016/j.bushor.2005.02.005

Tustin, D. H., & De Jongh, D. (2008). Ethical Consumerism as a key consideration for future brand strategy development in South Africa. *South African Business Review*, *12*(3), 24–49.

Tutu, D. (1999). *No future Without Forgiveness*. London: Rider.

Tyagi, R. K., & Vasiljeviene, N. (2013). The case of CSR and irresponsible management practices. *Competitiveness Review: An International Business Journal incorporating Journal of Global Competitiveness, 23*(4/5), 372-383.

UNCTAD. (1986). Recent Economic Development in the Occupied Territories, UNCTAD/TD/B/1102.

United Nations Office for the Coordination of Humanitarian Affairs (OCHA). (2009). *Humanitarian Overview*. Presentation.

United Nations. (1987). *Report of the World Commission on Environment and Development: Our Common Future*. Retrieved from http://www.un-documents.net/our-common-future.pdf

United Nations. (2013). *Global Sustainable Development Report – Executive Summary: Building the Common Future We Want*. New York: United Nations Department of Economic and Social Affairs, Division for Sustainable Development. Retrieved from http://sustainabledevelopment.un.org/

United Nations. (2013). *World Economic and Social Survey 2013. Sustainable Development Challenges*. Retrieved from http://sustainabledevelopment.un.org/content/documents/2843WESS2013.pdf

UNPAN. (2004). Administrative Ethics: Sociological Aspects. *UNPAN Documents*. Retrieved from http://unpan1.un.org/intradoc/groups/public/documents/NISPAcee/UNPAN004661.pdf

Urip, S. (2010). *CSR strategies: corporate social responsibility for a competitive edge in emerging markets*. John Wiley & Sons.

Utting, P. (2000). Business responsibility for sustainable development (Vol. 2). Geneva: United Nations Research Institute for Social Development. Retrieved from http://www.unrisd.org/

Vafeas, N. (1999). Board meeting frequency and firm performance. *Journal of Financial Economics*, *53*(1), 113–142. doi:10.1016/S0304-405X(99)00018-5

Valentine, S., Greller, M. M., & Richtermeyer, S. (2006). Employee job response as a function of ethical context and perceived organization support. *Journal of Business Research*, *59*(5), 582–588. doi:10.1016/j.jbusres.2005.06.004

Valette-Florence, P. (1988). Spécificités et Apports des Méthodes d'Analyse Multivariée de la Deuxième Génération. *Recherche et Applications en Marketing*, *3*(4), 23–56. doi:10.1177/076737018800300402

Van Huijstee, M. (2010). *Business and NGOs in interaction: A quest for corporate social responsibility* (Doctoral dissertation). Utrecht, The Netherlands: Faculty of Geosciences, Utrecht University.

van Raaij, W. F. (1977). *Consumer Choice Behavior: An Information Processing Approach* [Doctoral Dissertation]. Univeristé de Tilburg.

Van Seters, P. (2012). The sustainability movement. In K. Zoeteman (Ed.), *Sustainable development drivers: The role of leadership in government, business and NGO performance* (pp. 249–256). Cheltenham, UK: Edward Elgar. doi:10.4337/9781781009130.00021

Van Seters, P., De Gaay Fortman, B., & De Ruijter, A. (Eds.). (2003). *Globalisation and its new divides: Malcontents, recipes, and reform*. Amsterdam, The Netherlands: Dutch University Press.

Van Tulder, R., & Van der Zwart, A. (2006). *International business–society management: Linking corporate responsibility and globalization*. London, UK: Routledge.

Varey, R. J., & Storbacka, K. (2011). *Business model design for sustainable society: Therapy for the consumerist mindset*. ANZMAC.

Vasilescu, , Barna, C., Epure, M., & Baicu, C. (2010). Developing university social responsibility: A model for the challenges of the new civil society. *Procedia: Social and Behavioral Sciences*, *2*(2), 4177–4182. doi:10.1016/j.sbspro.2010.03.660

Velasquez, M. (1992). *Business Ethics: Concepts and Cases*. Upper Saddle River, NJ: Prentice Hall.

Veld, C., & Veld-Merkoulova, Y. V. (2008). The Risk Perceptions of Individual Investors. *Journal of Economic Psychology*, *29*(2), 226–252. doi:10.1016/j.joep.2007.07.001

Velentzas, J., & Broni, G. (2010). Ethical dimensions in the conduct of business: business ethics, corporate social responsibility and the law. *Proceedings of the International Conference On Applied Economics* ICOAE

Venter, E. (2004). The Notion of Ubuntu and Communalism in African educational Discourse Studies. *Philosophy and Education*, *23*(2/3), 149–160. doi:10.1023/B:SPED.0000024428.29295.03

Verhage, B. J., Yavas, U., & Green, R. T. (1990). Perceived Risk: A Cross-Cultural Phenomenon. *International Journal of Research in Marketing*, *7*(4), 297–303. doi:10.1016/0167-8116(90)90007-A

Vesilind, P. (1988). Rules, Ethics And Morals. *English Education*, *2*(1), 289–293.

Vijayakumar, N., Perumal, S., & Rao, K. C. (2010). Determinants of FDI in BRICS Countries: A panel analysis. *International Journal of Business Science and Applied Management*, *5*(3), 1–13.

Visser, W. (2006). Revisiting Carroll's CSR Pyramid: An African Perspective. In E.R. Pedersen, & M. Huniche (Eds.), Corporate Citizenship in developing countries (Ch. 1). Copenhagen Business School Press.

Visser, W. (2006a). Revising Carroll's CSR Pyramid: An African Perspective. In E.R. Pedersen, & M. Huniche (Eds.), Corporate Citizenship in Developing Countries (pp. 29–56). Copenhagen: Copenhagen Business School Press.

Visser, W. (2006b). Research on Corporate Social Responsibility in Africa: a Ten-Year Review (1995-2005). In W. Visser, M. McIntosh, & C. Middleton (Eds.), Corporate citizenship in Africa: Lessons from the past; paths to the future (pp. 18-28). Sheffield: Greenleaf.

Visser, W. (2008). Corporate social responsibility in developing countries, In A. Crane, A. McWilliams, D. Matten, J. Moon & D. Siegel (Eds.), The Oxford Handbook of Corporate Social Responsibility (pp. 473-479). Oxford: Oxford University Press.

Visser, W., McIntosh, M., & Middleton, C. (2006). Corporate citizenship in Africa: Lessons from the past; paths to the future. In W. Visser, M. McIntosh and C. Middleton (Eds.), Corporate citizenship in Africa: Lessons from the past; paths to the future (pp. 10-17). Sheffield: Greenleaf. doi:10.9774/GLEAF.978-1-909493-63-6_2

Visser, W. (2005). Is South Africa World Class in Corporate Citizenship? In A. Freemantle (Ed.), *The Good Corporate Citizen*. Johannesburg: Trialogue.

Visser, W. (2011). *The age of responsibility: CSR 2.0 and the new DNA of business*. John Wiley & Sons.

Visser, W., Matten, D., Pohl, M., & Tolhurst, N. (Eds.), (2007). *The A to Z of Corporate Social Responsibility: a Complete Reference Guide to Concepts, Codes and Organizations*. London: Wiley.

Vitell, S. J., & Hidalgo, E. R. (2006). The impact of corporate ethical values and enforcement of ethical codes on the perceived importance of ethics in business: A comparison of US and Spanish managers. *Journal of Business Ethics*, *64*(1), 31–43. doi:10.1007/s10551-005-4664-5

Vives, A. (2006). Social and environmental responsibility in small and medium enterprises in Latin America. *Journal of Corporate Citizenship*, *2006*(21), 39–50. doi:10.9774/GLEAF.4700.2006.sp.00006

Vlaev, I., Chater, N., & Stewart, N. (2009). Dimensionality of Risk Perception: Factors Affecting Consumer Understanding and Evaluation of Financial Risk. *Journal of Behavioral Finance*, *10*(3), 158–181. doi:10.1080/15427560903167720

Vogel, D. (2005). The market for virtue: The potential and limits of corporate social responsibility. Washington, DC: Brookings.

Volle, P. (1995). Le Concept du Risque en Psychologie du Consommateur: Antécédents et Statuts Théoriques. *Recherche et Applications en Marketing*, *10*(1), 39–56. doi:10.1177/076737019501000103

Waddell, S. (2005). *Societal learning and change: How governments, business and civil society are creating solutions to complex multi-stakeholder problems*. Sheffield, UK: Greenleaf.

Waddell, S. (2011). *Global action networks: Creating our future together*. New York, NY: Palgrave Macmillan.

Waddock, S. (2004). Parallel universes: Companies, academics and the progress of corporate citizenship. *Business and Society Review*, *109*(1), 5–42. doi:10.1111/j.0045-3609.2004.00002.x

Waddock, S. A., Bodwell, C., & Graves, S. B. (2002). Responsibility: The new business imperative. *The Academy of Management Executive*, *16*(2), 132–148. doi:10.5465/AME.2002.7173581

Wang, S. (2015). Literature Review of Corporate Social Responsibility. In S. Wang, (Ed.), Chinese Strategic Decision making on CSR (pp. 7-19). Springer. doi:10.1007/978-3-662-44997-4_2

Wang, X. L., Shi, K., & Fan, H. X. (2006). Psychological Mechanisms of Investors in Chinese Stock Markets. *Journal of Economic Psychology*, *27*(6), 762–780. doi:10.1016/j.joep.2006.06.007

Wataniya Report. (n. d.). Retrieved from http://www.wataniya.ps/en/corporate/about

Watson, D. Hollister, Stroud. S, & Babcock, E. (2013). The Engaged University: International Perspectives on Civic Engagement. New York, NY: Routledge.

Weber, E. U., & Hsee, C. K. (1998). Cross-Cultural Differences in Risk Perception but Cross-Cultural Similarities in Attitudes toward Perceived Risk. *Management Science*, *44*(9), 1205–1217. doi:10.1287/mnsc.44.9.1205

Weber, E. U., & Hsee, C. K. (1999). Cross-National Differences in Risk Preferences and Lay Predictions for the Differences. *Journal of Behavioral Decision Making*, *12*(2), 165–179. doi:10.1002/(SICI)1099-0771(199906)12:2<165::AID-BDM316>3.0.CO;2-N

Weber, J. (2006). Implementing an organizational ethics program in an academic environment: The challenges and opportunities for the Duquesne University Schools of Business. *Journal of Business Ethics*, *65*(1), 23–42. doi:10.1007/s10551-005-3970-2

Weber, J., & Glyptis, S. M. (2000). Measuring the impact of a business ethics course and community service experience on students' values and opinions. *Teaching Business Ethics*, *4*(4), 341–358. doi:10.1023/A:1009862806641

Weegar, M. A. (2007). Promoting ethical practices within institutions of higher education.*Proceedings of the 2007 Association for Business Communication Annual Convention*.

Weinstein, N. D. (1980). Unrealistic Optimism about Future Life Events. *Journal of Personality and Social Psychology, 39*(5), 806–820. doi:10.1037/0022-3514.39.5.806

Weisberg, R. (2009), Ethical Challenges in Developing Markets Markkula Center for Applied Ethics, Retrieved from http://www.scu.edu/ethics/practicing/focusareas/business/Ethical%20business%20Markkula.pdf

Welford, R. (2004). Corporate Social Responsibility in Europe and Asia: Critical Elements and Best Practice. *Journal of Corporate Citizenship, 2004*(13), 31–47. doi:10.9774/GLEAF.4700.2004.sp.00007

Werther, W. B. Jr, & Chandler, D. (2010). *Strategic corporate social responsibility: Stakeholders in a global environment.* Sage Publications.

Wheeler, D., Colbert, B., & Freeman, R. E. (2003). Focusing on value: Corporate social responsibility, sustainability and a stakeholder approach in a network world. *Journal of General Management, 28*(3), 1–28.

Whetten, D. A., Rands, G., & Godfrey, P. (2002). What are the responsibilities of business to society. Handbook of Strategy and Management, 373-408.

White, A. L. (2008). *Culture Matters: The Soul of CSR in Emerging Economies. Business for Social Responsibility.* Retrieved from www.bsr. org

Wiley, C. (1995). The ABC's of business ethics: Definitions, philosophies and implementation. *Industrial Management, 37(1)*, 22.

Wiley, D. E. (1973). The Identification Problem for Structural Equation Models in Unmeasured Variables. In A. S. Goldberger & O. D. Duncan (Eds.), *Structural Equation Models in the Social Sciences.* New York: Seminar Press/Harcourt Brace.

Wilkie, W. L., & Moore, E. S. (2002). Marketing's Relationship to Society. In B. A. Weitz & R. Wensley (Eds.), *Handbook of Marketing* (pp. 1–38). London: Sage Publications. doi:10.4135/9781848608283.n2

Willetts, P. (2002). *What is a non-governmental organization?* Retrieved from http://www.staff.city.ac.uk/p.willetts/CS-NTWKS/NGO-ART.HTM

Windsor, D. (2001). The future of corporate social responsibility. *The International Journal of Organizational Analysis, 9*(3), 225–256. doi:10.1108/eb028934

Winsemius, P., & Guntram, U. (2002). *A thousand shades of green: Sustainable strategies for competitive advantage.* London, UK: Earthscan.

Wood, D. (1991). Corporate Social Performance Revisited. *Academy of Management Review, 16*(4), 691–718.

Woodward, D., Edwards, P., & Birkin, F. (2001). Some evidence on executives' views of corporate social Responsibility. *The British Accounting Review, 33*(3), 357–397. doi:10.1006/bare.2001.0165

World Bank Group. (2001). Social and structural review update: Malaysia. Retrieved from www.worldbank.org

World Bank. (2015). Information on website. Retrieved from http://web.worldbank.org/WBSITE/EXTERNAL/TOPICS/CSO/0,contentMDK:20092185~menuPK:220422~pagePK:220503~piPK:220476~theSitePK:228717,00.html

World Investment Report. (2008). United Nations. Retrieved from unctad.org/en/Docs/wir2008_en.pdf

Worrel, D. L., Nemec, C., & Davidson, W. N., III (1997). One hat too many: Key executive plurality and shareholder wealth. *Strategic Management Journal, 18*(6), 499–507. doi:10.1002/(SICI)1097-0266(199706)18:6<499::AID-SMJ898>3.0.CO;2-F

Wright, P. (1975). Factors Affecting Cognitive Resistance to Advertising. *The Journal of Consumer Research*, *2*(1), 1–9. doi:10.1086/208610

Yakovleva, N., & Diego, V.-B. (2012). Stakeholder Perspectives on CSR of Mining MNCs in Argentina. *Journal of Business Ethics*, *106*(2), 191–211. doi:10.1007/s10551-011-0989-4

Yan, Y. (1998).The FDICIA and bank CEO's pay-performance relationship: An empirical investigation (Working Papers N° 9805). Federal Reserve Bank of Cleveland.

Yates, A., & Firer, C. (1997). The Determinants of Investor Risk Perceptions. *Investment Analysis Journal*, *44*, 61–70.

Yates, J. F., & Stone, E. R. (1992). The Risk Construct. In J. F. Yates (Ed.), *Risk-Taking Behavior* (pp. 1–25). Chichester: Wiley.

Yermack, D. (1996). Higher market valuation of companies with a small board of directors. *Journal of Financial Economics*, *40*(2), 185–211. doi:10.1016/0304-405X(95)00844-5

Yin, R. (2003). *Case Study Research: Design and Methods*. London, UK: Sage Publications.

Yin, R. K. (2003). *Case Study Research Design and Methods*. Thousand Oaks, California: Sage Publications.

Yirenkyi-Boateng, S. (2011). Business Social Responsibility and the Development Process in Africa: Enlarging the Stakeholders for Sustainable Development, *Africa Institute of South Africa (AISA). Policy Brief*, *51*(June), 1–12.

Young, S. (2003). *Moral capitalism: reconciling private interest with the public good*. Berrett-Koehler Publishers.

Young, S. L., & Makhija, M. V. (2014). Firms' corporate social responsibility behavior: An integration of institutional and profit maximization approaches. *Journal of International Business Studies*, *45*(6), 670–698. doi:10.1057/jibs.2014.29

Yunus, M. (2007). *Creating a world without poverty: Social business and the future of capitalism*. Public Affairs.

Zadek, S. (2007). *The civil corporation: The new economy of corporate citizenship*. London, UK: Earthscan.

Zena, P. A., & Hadisumarto, A. D. (2012). The Study of Relationship among Experiential Marketing, Service Quality, Customer Satisfaction, and Customer Loyalty. *Asean Marketing Journal*, 4(1).

Zgheib, P. W. (2005). Managerial ethics: An empirical study of business students in the American University of Beirut. *Journal of Business Ethics*, *61*(1), 69–78. doi:10.1007/s10551-004-6394-5

Zhang, F. (2008). Corporate Social Responsibility in Emerging Markets: The Role of Multinational Corporations. *The Foreign Policy Centre.* Retrieved from http://fpc.org.uk/fsblob/920.pdf

Zhao, H., & Kim, S. H. (2011). An exploratory examination of the social capital and FDI linkage and the moderating role of regulatory quality: A cross-country study. *Thunderbird International Business Review*, *53*(5), 629–646. doi:10.1002/tie.20439

Zuckerberg, M. (2012). Great Quotes. *Powerful Minds website*. Retrieved from www.great-quotespowerful-minds.com/markzuckerberg-quotes

Zu, L. (2009). *Corporate Social Responsibility, Corporate Restructuring and Firm's Performance: Empirical Evidence from Chinese Enterprises* (1st ed.). Springer.

Zulkafli, A. H., & Samad, F. A. (2007). Corporate governance and performance of banking firms: Evidence from Asian emerging markets. *Advances in Financial Economics*, *12*, 49–74. doi:10.1016/S1569-3732(07)12003-X

About the Contributors

Minwir Al-Shammari is Dean and Professor of Management at the University of Bahrain, College of Business Administration. He holds a PhD in Business Administration (Industrial Management) from University of Glasgow (UK, 1990) and M.S in Industrial Management from Central Missouri State University (USA, 1986). He has been involved for about 25 years in teaching, research, training, and/or consultancy in the areas of operations management, knowledge management, supply chain management, management information systems, business process re-engineering, organization theory, organizational change and development, project management, spreadsheet modeling, management science, and business research methodology. He is the author of the premier reference source: *Customer Knowledge Management: People, Processes, and Technology*, IGI-Global Publishing, U.S.A. He is the editor of the book: *Knowledge Management in Emerging Economies: Social, Organizational, and Cultural Implementation*, and the book: *Customer-Centric Knowledge Management: Concepts and Applications*, IGI Global, USA. Prof Al-Shammari has published more than 30 research papers that have appeared in international refereed journals.

Hatem Masri is an Associate Professor and Director of the Quality Assurance and Accreditation office at the College of Business Administration, in the University of Bahrain, Kingdom of Bahrain. He received his PhD in Management in 2004 and Master in Operations Research in 1999 from the University of Tunis, Tunisia. His research interests include multiple objective stochastic programming, supply chain management, financial engineering, and vehicle routing problems. His research has been published in more than 15 international journals (EJOR, ANOR, FSS, IJAR, ...) and funded by the University of Tunis, the University of Nizwa and the University of Bahrain. He is a member of the International Society on Multiple Criteria Decision Making, IEEE and the Tunisian Decision Aid Society.

***

Ebtihaj Al A'li is an associate professor with more than 30 years of teaching experience at University of Bahrain. She graduated from University of Lancaster in England with Ph.D. in Industrial psychology and Industrial Sociology. Her research interest focuses on woman in management, Business ethics, Strategic management and H/R.

Hanan Atef Abdallah Master's degree from Helwan University, Cairo, Egypt 2005. Graphic design (artistic considerations on advertising design and its influence on the increasing of the effect of the electronic commerce throw the internet). Working in the ECT since 2009 as lecturer. Research interests are in e-learning and design education.

Samir Ahmad Abuznaid Professor and Dean, School of Finance and Management, Hebron University, Prior to this, Dr. Abuznaid was President of State Audit and Administrative Control Bureau, Cabinet rank, Ramallah, for two years. He was the Acting Governor of Hebron Governorate for three years and later served as President of Hebron University. He is Associate Professor of Management and Marketing where, since he established the School of Finance and Management in 1994, he has served as a Professor and Dean at that school and later served as Vice President for Academic Affairs. Prior to this, Samir taught business and marketing at An-Najah National University in Nablus, West Bank, for eleven years. He has given lectures in the USA, UK, France, Spain, Italy, Jordan and Germany. He is the recipient of several awards and honors. More recently, he was selected as a Fulbright Scholar and was asked to teach cross-cultural management courses at Portland Community College, Oregon, USA .Dr. Abuznaid is a senior trainer and expert in management, marketing and strategic management. He has developed training material and conducted almost one thousand workshops in Arabic and English. He is a key founder and member of several institutions in the West Bank, such as Palestine for Credit and Development (Faten), Palestine Development Fund (PDF), Palestinian Banking Corporation (PBC). His current research interests include cross-cultural management, intercultural management, business ethics, business ethics in Islam, Islamic management, Islamic marketing, global marketing, SMEs and entrepreneurship and poetry management.

Said Mohammed Ali Alrashdi, Master of Science in Information Systems, is an Information Technology Teacher at the Ministry of Education, and a Visiting Lecturer in the Department of Economics, Management and Information Systems, University of Nizwa, Sultanate of Oman. Mr Said specializes in the Management of Information Systems and Programming and Database Management with Internet Technology. He has published 4 papers related to his research major, with other papers as work in progress. Recently he was awarded the Outstanding Master's Thesis Award on research day, March 2015, at the University of Nizwa.

S. Arockiasamy, is an Assistant Dean for Training and also a Head of the Department of Information systems, University of Nizwa. He received M.Sc, M.Phil and Ph.d in Computer Science. He is specialized in applications of Image processing. He has published over 25 research papers and articles in various leading International journals and Conferences. He was a Co-investigator for a TRC approved research project in Oman. He has been a chief editor of two IT related in-house magazines in India. He was also a leading column writer in a daily newspaper in India. Recently, he was awarded Best Professor in Information Technology by Asian Education Council in 2012.

Alia Babiker Badri obtained her PhD in promotion of mental health from the School for Public Health and Primary Care: CAPHRI, Department of Health Promotion, Maastricht University, The Netherlands in 2013 and MS in Psychology from the University of Warwick, UK in 1992. She initiated the Counselling and Health Psychology sub-specialization in the School of Psychology, Ahfad University for Women (AUW) in 1994. In the early-mid 2000s, she held up lecturing positions in the Arab Open

University in Kuwait, and Abu Dhabi University in the UAE, as well as becoming an affiliate employee counsellor with the UK-based Personal Performance Consultants International. In 2013, Alia gave public talks on Sudanese war-related trauma at the University of Western and worked as a counsellor in the Muslim Resource Center for Social Support and Integration in London Ontario. In 2014, she took up the position of vice-dean for academic affairs in the School of Psychology and Pre-school Education as well as lecturer and trainer in the Ahfad Trauma Treatment Training Center. Alia has publications in peer-reviewed journals such as the International Journal of Psychology.

Azza Bejaoui is an Assistant Professor in Accounting and Finance at the Faculty of Economic Sciences and Management of Sousse, Tunisia.

Naglaa Fathy El Dessouky, Ph.D., is an Associate Professor of Public Administration and Public Policy Analysis and has a Post-Doctoral Fellow Environmental Policy Institute Memorial University of Newfoundland Canada, Post-Doctoral Fellow Public Administration Program University of Ottawa Canada, Post-Doctoral Fellow Department of Political Sciences, Université du Québéc à Montréal (UQAM), Philosophiae Doctor (Ph.D.) in Public Administration and Public Policy Analysis École Nationale d'Administration Publique (ENAP) Université du Québéc, Canada, M.Sc. degree in Public Administration Faculty of Economics & Political Sciences Cairo University Egypt. Dr. El Dessouky is an Associate Professor in Sadat Academy for Management Sciences, Faculty of Management Sciences, Public Administration Department, Egypt. Currently, she is affiliated with University of Bahrain, Bahrain. She have a vast sixteen years of experience working in different international programs as professor and researcher, as Adjunct and Visiting Professor University of Ottawa Canada, Researcher Faculty of Political Sciences McGill University, Canada, Adjunct Professor Environmental Policy Institute Memorial University of Newfoundland Canada, Visiting Professor Senghor University, Egypt and currently affiliated with University of Bahrain, Bahrain In Addition, she has other academic activities as Professional Lecturer in UNICEF QUEBEC (United Nations children's fund) Canada, The Institute for Diplomatic Studies Ministry of Foreign Affairs Egypt, The Canadian Chamber of Commerce Egypt, the Leadership and Management Development Center the Cabinet of Ministries Egypt, Management Center-The American University in Cairo (AUC) and Faculty Leadership Development Center (FLDC) Cairo University and Ain Shams University, Egypt. She held several administrative positions in SAMS Egypt as Deputy Director of the Consultancy Research and Development Center-CRDC, Director of the Quality Assurance Unit, General Program coordinator of the American program SAMS and University of Toledo (UT) College of Business Administration (COBA) USA, and General Coordinator of the English program - SAMS. In addition, she held the position of executive Director of the Egyptian Women Economic Empowerment Initiative funded by UN Women in collaboration with the ministry of Manpower and Emigration in Egypt. In Canada she held different administrative position as Development coordinator of the project of: la Fondation de l'Université du Québec à Montréal, Chair of the Academic and Professional Commission of the African Network for the Environment (Réseau Africain en Environnement (RAE) Université du Québéc à Montréal (UQAM). She also expended her career further into consultancy and training activities. Moreover, she is an academic reviewer in different international peer-reviewed journals and she has been a chair for different programs and sessions of several national and international conferences. Dr. El Dessouky is a supervisor of a good number of national and international theses for the Masters and Ph.D. degrees. In University of Bahrain, Bahrain, she is member in different committees, as Student Advising and Examination Committee, Events Committee, and, Peer-Review of Courses Portfolio Materials Committee for Quality Assurance and Accreditation. She has a number of international publications and book reviews and her work covers a wide range of topics related to Environmental and Energy Policy, International and local Environmental Governance, Public Administration, Public Policy Analysis and Evaluation and different topics related to Management Sciences and Soft Skills. She is a holder of distinguished international scholarships, fellowships and awards related to her academic and research work.

Ahmet Diken is working as Professor at Social and Humanity Sciences Faculty, Business department, and Manager of Applied Sciences School at the University of Necmettin Erbakan, Konya, Turkey. He received his PhD in Total Quality Management and is Professor in Business Administration. He has been involved in academic world for more than 25 years. Since 1995, he has offered some courses such as Organizational Behavior and Management, Human Resources Management, Introduction to Business, and Total Quality Management at Selcuk University, and Necmettin Erbakan University in Konya, Turkey. In addition, from 1999 to 2005, he has worked as General Manager at three private firms in the food, steel, and education sectors. He also has worked as a consultant of mayor of Konya municipality from 2004 to 2012. His two books; Total Quality Management, and Structural Problems related to SMEs published in Turkish Language. He has a lot of articles and presentations which are published by national and international organizations. In addition he has been involved as supervisor for a lot of master and doctoral thesis and managed some projects in different universities.

Sibel Bali Eryigit, PhD (Füssen, 1978) She graduated from the Uludag University, Faculty of Economics and Administrative Sciences, Department of Business Administration in 2000. She received her PhD from the Uludag University, Institute of Social Sciences and the topic of her thesis was "The Institutional of Determinants of Financial Development: A Cross-Country Analysis". Bali Eryigit works at Uludag University, Department of Economics as a Dr. Assistant. The research interests of Bali Eryigit research interests are institutional economics, financial development, economic growth, monetary economics, defense economics and demographic economics, and her presentations, projects and published works cover these areas as well.

Elinda Esa is a lecturer in the College of Business Management and Accounting, National Energy University (NEU), Malaysia. She holds a Master Science in Accounting from International Islamic University, Malaysia (IIUM). She has more than 15 years teaching experiences. Her research interests include corporate social responsibility and sustainability, corporate governance, financial reporting, accounting education & ethics, brand equity and renewable energy. She is one of the author that contributes in the book chapter title, *Corporate Governance and Corporate Social Responsibility: Emerging Market Focus,* WSP Publishing. She also involved in consultancy projects with Malaysia Electric Utility Company (TNB).

Khamoussi Halioui received his Ph.D. degree in Management Accounting from Reims University (France) in 2005, and served as Lecturer and Assistant Professor at Sfax University in Tunisia, Faculty of Economics and Management from 1984 to 2008, afterwards, Dr. Khamoussi joined the Higher Business Institute at Gafsa University as Associate Professor of Accounting and Finance. From 2011 to 2013, he served as associate professor of accounting at College of Economics and Information Systems at University of Nizwa (Sultanate of Oman). From 2013 till now, he is full professor of accounting at College of Economics and Administrative Science at Al-Imam Muhammed Ibn Saud Islamic University at Riyadh (KSA). His research interest are around auditing, management accounting and financial accounting issues. He published many papers in referees journals, particularly in the following issues: Budgetary control and effectiveness of control systems; Ethical dimension and slack budgetary; Determinants of fraudulent financial reporting; Audit quality and earnings management in the Tunisian context; Effective audit committee, audit quality and earnings management: Evidence From Tunisia; Environmental and social policy and earning persistence in French context; Accounting treatment of R&D expenditures and earnings management in French context; Fair value and financial instability: comparative study between Islamic and conventional bank.

Shahira O. Abdel-Hameid obtained her Ph.D. in Human Resource Management from the University of Manchester, UK in 2003 and MA in Labour and Employment studies from the Institute for Social Studies, The Netherlands in 1995. She is currently the HRM program coordinator at the Emirates College of Technology, United Arab Emirates. Other positions held as coordinator of the MBA Program at Ahfad University for Women, Sudan. Shahira has published papers in conference proceedings and peer reviewed journals, such as Ahfad Journal: Women & Change. In conjunction with academics, she was a national project director for UNFPA supported project on women empowerment and gender mainstreaming; part of the Population Development Strategy Sub-program. Shahira has conducted consulting and training activities in the area of women empowerment and gender mainstreaming. Areas of research interests include strategic human resource management with special focus on the differing worldviews of human resources and the relation between strategic planning and performance improvement, corporate social responsibility and work-life balance.

John D Haynes, is Professor and Assistant Dean of Graduate Studies, Deanship of Graduate Studies, Office of the Vice Chancellor for Graduate Studies and Research, University of Nizwa, Oman. He has held prior University positions as Professorial Visiting Fellow at The University of NSW Australia, and Professor and Head of School of IT at Charles Darwin University Australia; Visiting full Professor in MIS at the University of Central Florida and Personal Chaired Professor (and Dean) at UCOL New Zealand and formerly, Head of Artificial Intelligence at Bond University Australia. Dr John D Haynes has completed research grants totaling more than US$250,000. Professor John D Haynes has over 70 publications in Journals, Chapters in books and conference papers, including 4 books, 2 of which are personally authored and the remaining 2 in an editorial capacity, one as single editor and the other as joint editor. Professor John D Haynes was awarded "Best Professor in ICT Management for 2013" by the World Education Congress in June, 2013.

Mihaela Herciu is a Professor in the Department of Finance and Accounting at the "Lucian Blaga" University of Sibiu. She received the PhD in Management in 2002, from the same university, with a thesis on The financial management of the firm of the future; she graduated the post-doctoral studies in 2013 – at the Romanian Academy, with a thesis on National Competitiveness. Her interests are in Competitiveness, Knowledge Society, International Management, Comparative Management, and Financial Management.

Adel Karaa is a Professor of Quantitative Methods at College of Business Administration, University of Hail, Saudi Arabia.

Rob Maessen is a senior policy advisor for sustainable development and environmental issues at the Province of Noord-Brabant in The Netherlands. Over the years, he has been involved with a great variety of topics: the development of waste management policies; scenario studies for agriculture; environmental management strategies for SME; corporate social responsibility; and civic engagement. He has a special interest in the interplay at the regional level between public administrations, the corporate sector and civil society with regard to the realization of a more sustainable society. Recent topics of interest include the culture of local food—in particular its values for shaping our urbanized society in prosperity and good health—and the role of the next generation in delivering sustainable development. He has a master's degree in psychology and was trained in experimental and cognitive psychology and the philosophy of science. He has several years of experience in social welfare projects and voluntary work in The Netherlands as well as abroad.

Khali Mofuoa is currently a long-distance PhD Student at the Centre for Applied Philosophy and Public Ethics, Charles Sturt University, Australia. His PhD thesis is on the topic of corporate social responsibility in the light of an African moral theory. His areas of research interest include professional and business ethics, applied ethics, leadership, public administration and management. He is a former Assistant lecturer/Research Assistant in applied ethics at St. Augustine College of South Africa, and a former Lecturer in Political and Administrative Studies at National University of Lesotho. Khali holds a MPhil in Applied Ethics from University of Stellenbosch (South Africa); a Master's degree in Public Sector Management from University of the West Indies (Jamaica); a Post-Graduate Diploma in Law from Universities of Cape Town (South Africa), Namibia and Lesotho; and a Bachelor of Arts in Political Science and Public Administration from the National University of Lesotho.

Claudia Ogrean is a Professor of Management in the Department of Management-Marketing-Business Administration at the "Lucian Blaga" University of Sibiu. She received the PhD in Management in 2002, from the same university, with a thesis on Coordinates of firm management within the context of globalization; she graduated the post-doctoral studies in 2012 – at the Romanian Academy, with a thesis on Multinationals and Development. Her interests are in Strategic Management, Organizational Behavior, Business Ethics and Corporate Social Responsibility.

Abdual R. AL - Sarraf earned his Ph.D. from Strathclyde University in Scotland – UK. Since 1991 he has been working at The University of Bahrain – College Of Business Administration as an Assistant Professor for Management Studies. His research interests centers around Management Field in general; including: Human Resource Management, Ethics, Strategic Management, Total Quality Management, and Globalization in Business.

Paul van Seters studied law at Utrecht University and sociology at the University of California, Berkeley. Currently he is Director of Globus and Professor of Globalization and Sustainable Development at Tias School for Business and Society at Tilburg University, The Netherlands. Previously he was Professor of Legal Sociology in the Faculty of Law at Tilburg University. He has published widely on socio-legal theory, public administration, and cultural sociology. His current research interests include law and communitarianism, corporate social responsibility, and the global civil society. Recent books he (co-)edited are *Globalization and its new divides* (Dutch University Press, 2003), *Communitarianism in law and society* (Rowman and Littlefield, 2006), *Bedrijfsleven en civil society* (Stichting Synthesis, 2008), *Handbook of globalisation and environmental policy, second edition* (Edward Elgar, 2012), and *Global social movements and global civil society* (Sage, 2014). He also regularly writes for the *OMFIF Bulletin*, *NRC Handelsblad*, *de Volkskrant*, *Het Financieele Dagblad*, *Trouw*, and *Brabants Dagblad*. Since 2011 he has been writing blogs for *Trouw Groen*.

Mohammad Shahriari is working as Professor (chair) and Director of Competence Center for HSE &Ethics, at the Faculty of Engineering, Department of Industrial Engineering at the University of Necmettin Erbakan, Konya, Turkey. He has cooperation with different universities including Chalmers University of Technology, Gothenburg, Sweden, University of Savoie, France and University of Minho, portugal. He received his PhD in logistics & transportation and Docent degree in human factors Engineering from Chalmers University of Technology, Gothenburg/Sweden. He has been involved for more than 25 years in risk assessment and environmental issues at Chalmers University of Technology. Since 1998, he has had intensive/short training courses, in risk assessment and hazardous waste minimization, in different countries including France, UK, Spain, Portugal, Italy, Turkey, Poland, and Indonesia. In addition he has been involved with several training workshops in Risk Assessment, Waste Minimization, and Productivity in different countries e.g., Iran, Indonesia, Singapore, Poland, Spain, Portugal, UK and USA. After gaining MSc degree in mining from the University of Tehran, he worked for 18 years in Iran with National Iranian Steel Corporation (in coal mines), IDRO (Industrial Development Renovation Organization of Iran) (in alumina/aluminum projects), and Ministry of Mines and Metals (as the project manager for preparation of aluminum raw materials). He is principal author for 2 books (in English), 2 books (in Persian), and more than 50 research papers (in English) in the field of risk assessment, human factors, man-machine interaction (alarm systems in refineries and process industries), complexity, environmental risk assessment, inherent safety. In addition, he has been supervisor for more than 20 master thesis and 300 industrial projects concerning risk assessment carried out by master's students at Chalmers University of Technology. Shahriari has been involved as supervisor in several PhD thesis in different universities. As reviewer and member of the editorial committee he has been collaborating with more than 6 international peer-reviewed scientific journals.

Mervat Medhat Ali Youssef is an assistant professor in computer Graphic and Animation in Emirates college of Technology, UAE. She hold PHD degree in graphic Design from the University of Applied Arts, Cairo, Egypt in 2010. Her main research interest is ambient environmental advertising, interactive branding in e-marketing and creativity in teaching methodology.

Abdul Rahman Zahari is a senior lecturer in College of Business Management and Accounting, National Energy University (NEU), Malaysia. He obtained MBA in Marketing from the Graduate School of Business, National University of Malaysia (UKM). He has more than 16 years teaching experiences in strategic management, principles of marketing, organizational behavior, human resource management, operations management, engineering management, business ethics, integrated marketing communication, internet marketing, sales management, international business, marketing research, entrepreneurship research and entrepreneurship. His research interests include brand management, brand equity, corporate social responsibility, corporate governance, renewable energy and entrepreneurship education. He is one of the author that contributes in the book chapter title, *Corporate Governance and Corporate Social Responsibility: Emerging Market Focus,* WSP Publishing. He also holds a trainer certificate from PSMB and has been involved in consultancy projects with Malaysia Electric Utility Company (TNB).

Index

www.ingramcontent.com/pod-product-compliance
Lightning Source LLC
LaVergne TN
LVHW060409300926
849162LV00006B/1385

* 9 7 8 1 4 6 6 6 9 8 6 4 2 *